FINANCIAL MANAGEMENT FOR NONPROFIT ORGANIZATIONS

FINANCIAL MANAGEMENT FOR NONPROFIT ORGANIZATIONS

POLICIES AND PRACTICES

JOHN ZIETLOW

JO ANN HANKIN

ALAN SEIDNER

BICENTENNIAL
1807
WILEY
2007
BICENTENNIAL

Copyright © 2007 by John Wiley & Sons, Inc. All rights reserved.

Published by John Wiley & Sons, Inc., Hoboken, New Jersey.
Published simultaneously in Canada.

For general information on our other products and services please contact our Customer Care Department within the U.S. at 877-762-2974, outside the U.S. at 317-572-3993, or fax 317-572-4002.

Wiley also publishes its books in a variety of electronic formats. Some content that appears in print, however, may not be available in electronic format.

For more information about Wiley products, visit our Web site at http://www.wiley.com.

Library of Congress Cataloging-in-Publication Data:

Zietlow, John T.
   Financial management for nonprofit organizations: policies and procedures
/ John Zietlow, Jo Ann Hankin, and Alan Seidner.
       p. cm.
   Rev. of: Financial management for nonprofit organizations / Jo Ann Hankin, Alan G. Seidner, John T. Zietlow. c1998.
   Includes index.
   ISBN-13: 978–0–471–74166–4 (cloth)
   ISBN-10: 0–471–74166–3 (cloth)
 1. Nonprofit organizations—Finance—Management. I. Hankin, Jo Ann. II. Seidner, Alan G. III. Hankin, Jo Ann. Financial management for nonprofit organizations. IV. Title.
   HG4027.65.Z54 2007
   658.15—DC22

                                             2006031245

Printed in the United States of America.

10 9 8 7 6 5

CONTENTS

13 Information Technology and Knowledge Management 465

ABOUT THE AUTHORS

JOHN T. ZIETLOW, D.B.A., CTP, is a professor of finance at Malone College in Canton, Ohio, where he teaches corporate finance, investments, short-term financial management, personal finance, and macroeconomics. He previously taught at Lee University (Cleveland, TN) and Mount Vernon Nazarene University (Mount Vernon, OH). He is certified through the Association for Financial Professionals as a Certified Treasury Professional (CTP). Dr. Zietlow also serves as associate faculty member at Indiana University-Purdue University at Indianapolis (IUPUI), where he teaches graduate nonprofit financial management, and as an adjunct instructor for the University of Maryland University College, where he teaches graduate short-term financial management. He has done corporate training and consulting in the areas of cash management, treasury management, and investment management and portfolio performance evaluation. He holds membership in the Financial Management Association, Association for Financial Professionals, Association for Research on Nonprofit Organizations and Voluntary Action (ARNOVA), and the Financial Education Association. He may be reached via e-mail at: jzietlow@hotmail.com, and maintains a web site at: www.johnzietlow.com.

JO ANN HANKIN is a nationally recognized consultant in the field of fundraising, and financial/administrative mangement for nonprofits. She has served as Vice President of Finance of The UCLA Foundation, Vice President of Advancement for California State Unversity, San Bernardino and has held various fundraising/financial positions with liberal arts colleges. In addition, she worked in the for profit world with several Fortune 500 companies.

Jo Ann also continues to be actively involved with her own community and does volunteer work for organizations promoting music and education.

ALAN G. SEIDNER was the founder of Seidner & Company of Pasadena, California, an investment management and consulting firm whose roster included high-net-worth investors, healthcare organizations, major corporations, nonprofit institutions, and municipalities. Mr. Seidner has written many financial reference works and is a frequent speaker on investment techniques and strategies. He has also provided testimony before federal government agencies on the performance of pension fund investments.

ACKNOWLEDGMENTS

John Zietlow acknowledges and is deeply grateful for the contributions of the following individuals who lent their expertise to specific areas of the book: Gregg Capin, Dan Busby, Nick Wallace, Bill Hopkins, Steve Dawson, Carolyn King, Wayne Kissinger, Georgette Cipolla, William Michels, John Webb, Darryl Smith, Darryl Deardorff, Jerry Trecek, Bob Reynhout, Dave McFee, Phillip Purcell, Rob Licht, David Holt, and Eric Lane. He also thanks Anna Ellis, student assistant at Lee University, and Gretchen Sudar, administrative assistant at Malone College, for their clerical and research assistance.

A special thanks goes to Lilly Endowment, Inc., for initiating the study of the financial management of faith-based organizations by providing grant money to Indiana State University. The individuals responsible for evaluating and guiding the grant process were Fred Hofheinz and Jim Hudnut-Beumler. Members of the advisory panel assembled as part of that grant project were invaluable in shaping the research project that underlies some of the significant findings presented in this book. They believed, as we do, that proficient financial management can greatly aid in the accomplishment of charitable missions. A particular thanks goes to the 288 financial managers who took part in the exhaustive survey covering financial management practices employed by their organizations. Thanks also for research input and critiques provided by Dr. Raj Aggarwal and Dr. Kathleen Eisenhardt.

We are particularly grateful to Susan McDermott, senior editor at John Wiley, who was instrumental in directing the project from inception to publication.

Graduate students at Indiana University-Purdue University at Indianapolis (IUPUI) have enriched and helped shaped this book as they learned from and commented on content in the previous edition of this guide as part of the graduate nonprofit financial management class taught each summer there since 1999.

Finally, we thank our families for bearing with us in the arduous process of putting this guide together. My contribution is dedicated to my parents, Harold and Miriam Zietlow, for their continual encouragement, support, and prayers.

Jo Ann Hankin thanks Clariza Mullins, currently Treasurer, Pepperdine University, for her important contribution to Chapter 11 on Cash Management and Banking Relations. Clariza's technical expertise, hands-on experience, and communication style are part of what make this chapter an extremely useful one.

Alan Seidner wishes to thank former professional staff members of Seidner & Company, Investment Management, for their help in researching and completing some of the material in this publication. Specifically, special thanks go to Joan West, Leah Romero, Sandee Glickman, Joe Flores, and Lina Macias.

PREFACE

Financial Management for Nonprofits is written for use by those responsible for financial management in the nonprofit organization. There are many titles used to identify persons assigned these responsibilities including, but not limited to, director of finance, chief financial officer, treasurer, controller, chief accountant, director of operations, business administrator, and financial secretary. In small organizations, the chief executive officer (executive director) may carry out these responsibilities. Actually, the title of the position is not important; the *responsibility* is extremely important.

Our book is written from a managerial decision-making perspective for those in leadership and day-to-day management positions who have oversight responsibility for financial functions or are members of the Board. These leaders and managers may, or may not, be experienced financial managers. Most of the subjects and issues that confront those responsible for financial management and related functions in the small- to medium-size nonprofit organization are not determined by size but rather by the mix of assets and strategies employed to accomplish the organization's mission.

Another important focus of this book is to demonstrate that financial management functions are expanding, and when done well, these strategies will make a real difference in the organization's ability to achieve its mission. Effective and responsible financial management contributes toward accomplishing the mission in a number of significant ways, including:

- Financial policy setting
- Financial reporting and accountability
- Establishing liquidity policy and guiding decisions to maintain that liquidity or rebuild it when depleted
- Strategic planning
- Evaluation of existing and new programs
- Marketing planning
- Fundraising evaluating
- Budgeting and long-run financial planning
- Debt and other liability management
- Operational expertise and strategic internal business consulting
- Empowerment through the sharing of information and harnessing of technology
- Catalyst for cultural change in the organization
- Increase in investment income
- Preservation of investment assets

Depending on your nonprofit organization's size and scope of activities, the nature and complexity of its financial functions will range from simple to highly sophisticated and complex. In any case, the financial systems used must be designed to provide the information necessary to meet management, fiduciary, and legal requirements. This book is unique among those available on nonprofit accounting and finance in that it develops a basis for liquidity targeting as the primary financial objective of the nonprofit—especially noncommercial nonprofit organizations. It then ties other financial decision areas to this liquidity target throughout the book. We include coverage of five major topical categories in order to emphasize the positive contributions of the financial and business functions to the organization and its mission:

- Managing your organization's financial resources
- Establishing and revising financial policies
- Accounting, budgets, and financial reports
- Investing for the short and long term
- Controlling and managing risk

Working for a nonprofit organization is an exciting and meaningful opportunity. There are many similarities and differences between nonprofit and for-profit organizations, and it is important to recognize and understand how they are similar as well as dissimilar. By virtue of their mission, nonprofit organizations benefit society by improving the public good.

Hundreds of thousands of nonprofit organizations of all sizes exist today, employing many people. Each nonprofit organization has a responsibility to its mission, its constituents, its employees, and its volunteers. The effective financial management of the organization's resources will enable it to succeed in fulfilling its mission and goals.

As you can see from the material covered in this book, those involved in managing the finances of the organization have a great deal of responsibility. In the process of carrying out these responsibilities, some members of the organization may feel disliked or undervalued by those they serve on a regular basis. Under these circumstances, it is critical for the responsible financial manager to be fair, to understand the interplay between facts and people, and to understand that accountability is not always popular with those being held accountable.

This book is intended to provide financial personnel with a clear sense of the technical expertise and skills needed to manage this function well for their organization. It will also reinforce the fact that you are part of a larger group in the nonprofit community who fulfill the same set of major responsibilities and uphold the same ethics and values. We hope that the information contained in this book will enable readers to better manage the financial resources of the nonprofit organizations they serve and enhance their overall financial health and viability.

Finally, this book serves as a textbook for certificate programs, undergraduate courses, and graduate courses in nonprofit financial management. We believe that the private nonprofit sector is sufficiently dissimilar to business and public sector organizations to merit special focus for students in this fascinating arena. We help the student gain an appreciation and understanding of financial decision making in educational, healthcare, and charitable organizations. There is a dedicated course support Web site for students and faculty members at www.wiley.com/go/zietlow..

CHAPTER 1

UNDERSTANDING NONPROFIT ORGANIZATION FINANCES

Almost 1.7 million nonprofits are registered in the United States today, not including churches and small nonprofit organizations that are not required to register with the Internal Revenue Service (IRS). The number of registered charitable organizations has exploded from roughly 300,000 in 1970 to 1,680,000 today. One-half of the nonprofit sector's revenue goes to the largest 15 percent of these organizations, some of which are large hospitals and universities. Faced with growing missions and shrinking resources, many organizations have turned to for-profit activities, such as issuing credit cards with their logos and selling their mailing lists to advertising firms, in order to augment their revenues. Most of these same organizations have overlooked the potential of better financial management to enhance revenues (from better investment management and faster cash collections) or reduce costs (from better negotiations with banks and process reengineering).

Our framework is intended to be of immediate value to nonprofit financial professionals. This handbook caters to the treasurer with little or no formal training, business-only training, or too little time (perhaps due to a multitude of responsibilities) or support staff to do the job the way he or she knows it can be done. Our other target audiences are the chief executive officer (or executive director) and board members. This handbook specifically includes material for small and resource-constrained organizations, as well as large ones. Material is presented in an easy-to-use format, including forms or checklists where helpful. The discussion goes beyond the buzzwords to provide reasonable steps toward more proficient treasury management. We incorporate a number of concepts:

- Donor accountability and stewardship
- Learning organization, reengineering, and benchmarking
- Balanced scorecard
- Program selection and cost-benefit evaluation
- Social entrepreneurship
- Strategic alliances and collaborations
- Financial statements and ratio analysis
- Budgeting techniques, including cash budgeting
- Financial forecasting
- Liquidity measurement and analysis
- Fundraising evaluation
- Fraud prevention and detection
- Advanced cash flow management
- Investment and other financial policies
- E-business
- Executive performance incentives

1.1 DEFINITION OF NONPROFIT ORGANIZATIONS

In the broadest terms, *nonprofit* is a designation given by the IRS to describe organizations that are allowed to make a profit but that are prohibited from distributing their profits or earnings to those in control of the organizations. If these organizations apply for and receive tax-exempt status from the IRS, they are not required to pay federal income taxes or state business income taxes except in specific cases, which are discussed later in this book. This classification makes them distinctly different from for-profit corporations, which distribute profits to their owners or shareholders and must pay corporate income taxes on their earnings. Furthermore, tax-exempt organizations *may* also be exempt from paying property tax, sales tax, and use tax—not all states exempt nonprofits from all of these taxes. As a Section 501(c)(3) organization, the entity does not have to pay federal unemployment taxes. In addition, contributions to some nonprofit organizations are tax deductible for donors. After receiving federal tax exemption, refer to the Web site of the National Association of State Charity Officials (www.nasconet.org) to see whether your organization is required to register with a state to solicit for contributions or be exempt from state taxes in that state. Further details regarding nonprofit organizations can be found in Sections 501 through 521 of the IRS code.

The approximately 2 million nonprofit organizations in the United States include almost 1.7 million tax-exempt organizations registered with the IRS as well as the 400,000 churches that are not registered with the IRS. The number of nonprofit organizations in the United States must be estimated because many churches and very small nonprofits are not included in the IRS statistics. Churches, integrated auxiliaries of churches, and associations or conventions of churches, as well as any organization normally having gross receipts each year that are $5,000 or less may be considered tax exempt under Section 501(c)(3) even without filing the IRS Form 1023. Some of these may file this form to obtain recognition from exemption from federal income tax anyway, simply to receive a determination letter from the IRS that both recognizes their 501(c)(3) status and indicates whether contributions to them are tax deductible for federal income tax purposes.[1]

The significance of the nonprofit sector in the U.S. economy—the Johns Hopkins Institute for Policy Studies estimates that it accounts for 7.5 percent of gross domestic product—is further underscored by these estimates compiled by the Independent Sector and the Urban Institute:[2]

- Over 9 percent of all paid employees in the United States are employed in the nonprofit sector. (Johns Hopkins state-level studies indicate that a high percentage of these are employed in health services, with social services being a distant second.)

- About 6 percent of all organizations in the United States are nonprofit organizations, and more nonprofit organizations are formed each year than businesses.

- Total nonprofit revenues in 1997 were estimated to be $665 billion, with 38 percent coming from private dues and services, 31 percent flowing from government grants and contracts, 20 percent arising from private contributions, and the remaining 11 percent from other sources, such as investments, interest, and dividends.

- Healthcare and education garnered about 67 percent of total nonprofit sector revenues in 1997.

- Private contributions go largely to religious organizations: In 2005, $93 billion of the estimated $260 billion in private contributions were received by congregations and other religious entities, according to the Indiana University Center on Philanthropy's Giving USA report. Education ranked a distant second, gathering $39 billion in private gifts.[3]

(a) 501 (c)(3) CORPORATIONS.   Most organizations are qualified for tax-exempt status under Section 501(c)(3) of the IRS code. These organizations are usually termed "charitable" nonprofits. Included here are religious, educational, scientific, literary, social welfare, private foundations, and other charities. Their 501(c)(3) status gives them tax-exempt status *and* enables donors to give tax-deductible donations to them. Other 501(c) organizations are tax-exempt, but donors may not deduct donations to these organizations from their federal income taxes.

The management implications of tax-exempt status are fourfold:

1. Organizations are responsible for putting the mission first. Programs and activities must support that mission, which is to be of benefit to society and serves as the foundation for the organization's founding and ongoing existence. This stipulation implies that income-earning activities may be taxed if not closely linked to the organization's primary programs and services.

2. The organization does not issue stock and may not pay out excess revenues (those over and above expenses) to employees, board members, clients, or donors. This

stipulation *does not* imply that the organization may not make a "profit," or net revenue, however. It does imply that the capital structure of the nonprofit is limited to debt financing, which many nonprofits limit or shun entirely, and equity, which may be obtained only by taking in revenues over and above period expenses. In the for-profit world those accumulated profits are labeled "retained earnings." One advantage for nonprofit financial managers is that they need not concern themselves with issues of when and how much in cash dividends and share repurchases to initiate.

3. Nonprofits are not owned by their permanent capital providers, unlike the shareholder-owned for-profit organization. This stipulation implies that outside parties such as donors may not exercise direct control over the organization's affairs, particularly its financial policies.

4. Without shareholders as the stewardship focus of the nonprofit, the primary financial objective is not maximizing profits or shareholder wealth. This stipulation implies that the organization must determine and implement in its operations a different primary financial objective.

We shall see the significance for managers and board members of items 2 and 4 later in this chapter and then more fully in Chapter 2.

The 501(c)(3) category includes about 60 percent of all tax exempt organizations registered with the IRS in 2004. Exhibit 1.1 profiles the various categories of tax-exempt organizations in the United States and Exhibit 1.2 provides a numerical breakdown of 501(c)(3) and other categories of 501(c) organizations. Faith-based organizations are the largest single category within the 501(c)(3) world, and they will receive correspondingly greater attention in this volume. We also highlight managerial applications for healthcare and education in most chapters due to the disproportionate size of many of these entities. Many of these are also faith-based organizations since they are affiliated with religious organizations.

(b) BYLAWS AND ARTICLES OF INCORPORATION.   The articles of incorporation (or charter) and bylaws are the initial documents that spell out the rules, regulations, and procedures for nonprofit corporations and form the basis for subsequent policy setting.

Nonprofit charitable organizations are exempt under Section 501(c)(3) of the Internal Revenue Code. Other tax-exempt organizations covered in this section include those exempt under Sections 501(c) (4) through 501(c)(9). Descriptions of these organizations are below:

501(c)(3)	Religious, educational, charitable, scientific, or literary organizations; testing for public safety organizations. Also, organizations preventing cruelty to children or animals, or fostering national or international amateur sports competition
501(c)(4)	Civic leagues, social welfare organizations, and local associations of employees
501(c)(5)	Labor, agriculture, and horticultural organizations
501(c)(6)	Business leagues, chambers of commerce, and real estate boards
501(c)(7)	Social and recreational clubs
501(c)(8)	Fraternal beneficiary societies and associations
501(c)(9)	Voluntary employee beneficiary associations

Source: US Internal Revenue Service.

EXHIBIT 1.1   TAX-EXEMPT CATEGORIES—IRS

Type of Organization, Internal Revenue Code Section	2001 (1)	2002 (2)	2003 (3)	2004 (4)
Tax-exempt organizations and other entities, total	1,567,580	1,580,767	1,640,949	1,680,061
Section 501(c) by subsection	1,399,558	1,444,905	1,501,772	1,540,554
(1) Corporations organized under act of Congress	48	88	103	116
(2) Title-holding corporations	6,984	6,998	7,078	7,144
(3) Religious, charitable, and similar organizations	865,096	909,574	964,418	1,010,365
(4) Social welfare organizations	136,882	137,526	137,831	138,193
(5) Labor and agriculture organizations	62,944	62,246	62,641	62,561
(6) Business leagues	82,706	83,712	84,838	86,054
(7) Social and recreation clubs	67,289	68,175	69,522	70,422
(8) Fraternal beneficiary societies	81,112	80,193	79,390	69,798

Tax-exempt organizations and other entities listed on the exempt organization business master file, by type of organization and Internal Revenue Code section, fiscal years 2001–2004.
Source: U.S. Internal Revenue Service.
EXHIBIT 1.2 BREAKDOWN OF TAX-EXEMPT ORGANIZATIONS IN THE UNITED STATES

The trustees are responsible for preparing, periodically reviewing, and amending these documents to keep pace with the mission and support structure of the organization.

The articles of incorporation are prepared and submitted when the organization first applies for state corporate status, and they are maintained in the state office responsible for corporate records (i.e., secretary of state's office).

The board of trustees (or board of directors) is also responsible for drafting the bylaws, which serve as the organization's operating rules. Bylaws are more detailed than the charter and include information such as the number and tenure of trustees, how and when meetings are to be called, when reports are to be presented, how board vacancies are to be filled, and other details needed to ensure the consistent and efficient operation of the organization.

The trustees are legally responsible for periodically reviewing the nonprofit organization's bylaws and articles of incorporation to ensure that they accurately reflect what is happening in the organization. It is also the trustees' responsibility to ensure that those provisions of the governing documents are followed.

Once these two documents are in place, the trustees should develop policy manuals covering their own service, personnel, finances, equipment, and other areas. These policies should address issues related to the operational and financial means of implementing the organizational mission, such as conflict of interest, human resource management, cash controls, cash management, investment guidelines, debt and liability guidelines, risk management, property, and facility use.

1.2 CHARACTERISTICS OF NONPROFIT ORGANIZATIONS

A nonprofit organization has most or all of these characteristics:

- Public service mission
- Organizational structure of a not-for-profit or charitable corporation
- Governance structures that preclude self-interest and personal financial gain
- Exemption from paying federal taxes
- Special legal status stipulating that gifts made to the organization are tax-deductible

We shall introduce the mission and the organizational structure in this chapter. We detail these items as well as governance structures and tax and legal provisions in subsequent chapters.

(a) ORGANIZATIONAL MISSION.   One essential difference between a nonprofit and for-profit corporation centers on its mission. The ultimate mission of for-profit organizations is to make money for the owners/shareholders, ranging from an individual, as sole proprietor, to corporate ownership through the purchase of shares.

A nonprofit organization does not include the concept of ownership and, therefore, has a completely different thrust. Its mission is to serve a broad public purpose, which is clearly incompatible with ownership and personal gain. This prohibition of "private inurement" does not prevent nonprofit organizations from paying salaries to their employees, including the chief executive officer or chief financial officer. The board members typically donate their time as a public service and receive no compensation.

These requirements also do not prevent nonprofit organizations from making money. Nonprofit organizations can and do make money in the same way as for-profit organizations. The difference is that the monies earned must be directed to the public purpose for which the nonprofit organization was established, held in reserve, or turned over to another organization with a public purpose. Thus, a key element of all nonprofit organizations is the use of earnings from the endeavor to promote the organizational goals, not to enrich the owners or stockholders.

The customers of nonprofit organizations are as diverse as their missions. Constituencies may include not only people, but also historic buildings, forests, endangered animals, and sports teams, individually or collectively. In addition, the people who have given their time, money, and other types of assets to further the cause are as much customers of the nonprofit as the actual recipients of the service being provided. They ask the most difficult questions of the nonprofit, have the greatest knowledge of the asset base, and are able to measure it against the activity performed on behalf of the organization. The organization acts as a steward both for its clients and its donors.

A for-profit organization has a clear mission (to make a profit) and a clear decision-making path for achieving it. However, the public service nature of a nonprofit poses a major challenge in terms of identifying and articulating its mission and developing criteria for measuring its success. The mission statement must not only define what the organization is and does; it must also state these concepts in a way that enables its achievements to be measured and evaluated. As we shall see a bit later in this chapter, many nonprofits are unclear even as to the primary financial objective(s) that they are or should be pursuing.

After developing its mission statement, a nonprofit organization faces two additional major challenges: identifying its client population and identifying its donor constituency and level of involvement. After clearly identifying the group it intends to serve, a nonprofit must design an organizational structure that reinforces its commitment to the target group. It must then establish an image in the community, provide direction to potential fund sources, and either attract or repel the people to be served by the nonprofit organization.

(b) ORGANIZATIONAL STRUCTURE.   The structure of an organization defines the roles and responsibilities of those charged with pursuing its mission—the board of directors/trustees, committees, staff, officers, outside contractors, and volunteers. A nonprofit organization must be structured to meet its goals. Water reclamation projects will require a structure involving engineers and construction experts, while feeding the homeless requires a completely different set of skills and hard assets to meet that goal. Although both operate as nonprofits, one may need to retain a huge amount of capital-intensive equipment, while the other may require only a portable cooking facility.

The type of nonprofit determines the organizational structure and complexity of its membership. Medical research, conducted in conjunction with commercial medical development, requires a strict accounting for the input of each member or contributor and an equally strict accounting for any profit or gain realized from the joint venture. The organizational structure for financial management, including treasury and controller duties, will be addressed in greater detail in Chapter 4. We shall document how control and reporting duties, due to chief financial officer (CFO) education and training as well as time and staffing concerns, have unfortunately taken precedence over treasury duties.

1.3 UNDERSTANDING THE LANGUAGE OF THE NONPROFIT ORGANIZATION

Some of the terms most commonly used by nonprofits with working definitions follow:

Articles of incorporation Legal document used to create a nonprofit organization; sometimes termed a "charter."

Board of directors Two or more individuals who serve as the governing body of an organization.

Board of trustees Governing board of the nonprofit corporation (trust or charity); see *board of directors.*

Bylaws Set of rules that govern a nonprofit organization's internal affairs.

Chair of board Person selected by board to be its leader.

Chief financial officer Staff member most responsible for financial analysis and decision-making; in smaller organizations without finance staff this role may be jointly assumed by the CEO and the bookkeeper or board treasurer.

Conflict of interest State of affairs that looks suspicious and raises questions of appearances.

Deferred giving A charitable gift made before one's death.

Endowment An accumulation of contributions that is held for investment; earnings, if any, can be distributed to programs.

Fiduciary One who is legally bound to oversee the affairs of another using the same standards as one would employ to look after his or her own assets.

501(c)(3) Section of the IRS Internal Revenue Code that defines charities as a special type of tax-exempt, nonprofit corporation; other than testing for public safety organizations, all 501(c)(3) organizations are eligible to receive tax-deductible donations.

Fund Separate accounting records for a part of the organization, such as permanent endowment, board-designated investment amounts, or restricted for a specific purpose by donors.

Fund accounting Technical accounting term that refers to a system of accounting for funds by project, so that assets and liabilities are grouped by the purpose for which they will be used; use of fund accounting is inconsistent with newer accounting standards' emphasis on showing the financial position of the organization as a whole, but many organizations continue to use fund accounting for internal bookkeeping and stewardship purposes.

Nonprofit Corporation that is not allowed to distribute profits or surpluses to its board or those in control of the organization.

Officer of corporation Legal representative of the board of nonprofit corporation: president, vice president, secretary.

Permanent fund A fund in which the principal is never spent.

Philanthropy Goodwill; active effort to promote human welfare.

Restricted fund A fund that has been contributed to a nonprofit organization for a specific, designated purpose and cannot be used for general operations.

Secretary Officer of nonprofit board responsible for preparing board agendas, minutes, and other documentation of business of the nonprofit board.

Stewardship Holding something in trust for another.

Tax-exempt Not subject to income taxes.

Treasurer Traditionally, the chief financial officer of nonprofit organization; now used in more restricted sense as board member having the primary responsibility for the board's oversight of financial policy and financial issues such as budget approval.

Unrestricted fund A fund contributed to a nonprofit organization whose use is determined by the board of directors.

Volunteer One who does meaningful, but unpaid, work for the nonprofit organization.

1.4 FINANCIAL POLICIES

We cannot emphasize this strongly enough: The most important aspects of proficient financial management in the nonprofit sector are the primary financial objective and the financial policies the organization uses. Second in importance are the tools and practices used, but these are primarily means of implementing the objective and policies. Throughout this book, we emphasize how the various financial management areas link up to the primary financial objective, and we provide guidance on appropriate financial policies in those areas.

Policy is the rule of law for an organization in a particular decision area. We often hear of an organization's investment policy or internal cash control policy. Policies should be viewed as a set of guidelines (laws, rules) or principles for how day-to-day business should be performed. Some policies are determined internally; others are prescribed for the organization by outside organizations and are necessary in order to accept funds from those organizations or to work within applicable laws and regulations. Even if policies are not written down, all organizations have some financial policies that comprise the guiding principles regarding how they do certain things. Were it not for policies, a method or plan would have to be established each time someone needed to do something.

To help us distinguish between policy and procedure, let's consider two general definitions for policy and procedure, one authoritative and the other practical:

	Authoritative	Practical
Policy	A definite course of action adopted as expedient or from another managerial consideration	A set of guidelines or principles defining an organization's philosophy about how business should be conducted
Procedure	The act or manner of proceeding in any action or process; conduct	Steps and/or actions to be taken to comply with a specific policy

Throughout this book, we illustrate financial policies and some financial procedures. In addition, for those wishing to further investigate policies and procedures, Chapter 5 provides guidance on how to go about setting policies in many areas, for organizations that have never before formalized their policies and for those organizations that wish to revisit their policies periodically to modify and update them. In today's donor, grantor, and regulatory environments, it is extremely important to be able to document policy.

1.5 FINANCIAL PRACTICES

A special focus in this book is the "state of the art" regarding practices in nonprofit financial management. We develop this profile in three ways:

1. We provide survey evidence from studies we have done as well as others on the degree to which organizations use tools and techniques in carrying out the finance function.

2. We profile business-sector practices that nonprofit sectors may adapt for their charitable missions and for earned income ventures.

3. We present brief case studies or single-organization illustrations of "best practice" implementation, including anecdotal observations we have made and illustrations gathered from consulting firms and financial service providers.

Practices covered include the following:

- Primary financial objectives
- Organizing the finance function
- Accountability structure
- Use of technology in treasury
- Conforming to external watchdog standards
- Cash and liquidity management
- Banking selection and relationship management
- Budgeting
- Cash forecasting
- Financial ratio analysis

- Long-range financial planning
- Capital project evaluation
- Investment policies and management, short-term and long-term
- Relative use of different forms of debt
- Bank borrowing and how banks view nonprofit organizations
- Tax-exempt bond issuance
- How bond raters view nonprofit organizations
- Earned income ventures
- Evaluating mergers and acquisitions
- Risk management
- Foreign exchange and interest rate risk exposure
- Board duties and how they are viewed
- Internal controls
- Financial accountability

In the companion book, *Cash & Investment Management for Nonprofit Organizations* (scheduled for publication in May 2007), we provide in-depth guidance on:

- How and why cash management and investments provide financial strength for the nonprofit
- Cash and liquidity management
- Appropriate size for cash and operating reserves
- Using reserves to self-fund new program and program expansion capital expenditures and maintenance
- Short-term investment policies and practices
- Long-term investment policies and practices
- Endowment
- Pensions

All of these decision areas steer the organization toward accomplishment of its primary financial objective.

1.6 PRIMARY FINANCIAL OBJECTIVE

Board members and financial executives who come to nonprofit organizations from the business sector are often frustrated and confused by the different environment. Consider the two polar extremes in Exhibit 1.3. At one extreme are organizations that are able to gain all of their revenue from product or service sales. These "commercial" organizations look much like businesses and are sometimes labeled "businesses in disguise." But most nonprofits are religious organizations or charities, which find themselves at or near the opposite pole, with their revenues coming from grants and gifts. These are termed "donative" or donation-dependent nonprofits. They provide "public goods" free of charge to their clients. Before directly addressing the most appropriate financial objective for a nonprofit, let us discuss why this is important.

Exhibit 1.3 Spectrum of Nonprofit Organizations

(a) DIFFERENCES BETWEEN BUSINESSES AND DONATIVE NONPROFITS.

(i) Businesses Have a Numerical, Specific Objective: Maximize Stock Price. This specific objective typically translates into maximizing long-run risk-adjusted profits. Intermediate targets that foster increased profits and stock price are also pursued. These targets include increasing market share (a company's percent of total industry sales), increasing quality, increasing share of mind (identified by company's target audience), and increasing short-run revenues or reducing short-run costs (or both). Nonprofits that are businesslike in nature, such as hospitals and private schools or colleges, can adopt many of these same intermediate targets. However, donative nonprofits generally do not see their revenues automatically increase when they provide more services. This fact is significant for two reasons.

1. The donative organization is forced to do additional fundraising just to cover the added costs of providing more of the same or new services, instead of simply collecting higher revenues from additional sales, as a business would.

2. The nonprofit that does not understand this linkage will find itself in an ever-worsening financial shortfall each period that transpires without new donations.

For both of these reasons, financial management is more challenging for the donative nonprofit. Soon we shall point to a more appropriate primary financial objective.

(ii) Businesses Can Price Their Services and Then Use Revenues to Gauge Their Marketing Success. "Businesslike" nonprofit entities, such as hospitals and educational organizations, can and do gauge marketing success from revenues for some of their programs and services, insofar as they do not violate their exempt status and societal role. Donatives and dues-based nonprofits may also apply this standard to certain of their earned income ventures. Revenues do not clearly reflect the quality and quantity of all services provided, however.

(iii) Businesses Typically Know Who Their Customers and Owners Are. Knowing who customers and owners are may be difficult for nonprofit organizations, particularly donative ones. Are the donors the customers, the owners, both, or neither? Or is the organization tied permanently to the activities specified in the charter and/or articles of incorporation, in a sense owned by society? Determining this is important because in order to assess trade-offs correctly when making major programmatic decisions, especially

when finances are tight, managers must make the assessment based on the proper criteria. Some organizations have gone overboard with this, defunding or mothballing key programs due to declining financial support, even though those programs were central to their missions.

(iv) The Typical Pattern of Cash Flows Often Differs, Particularly for the Donative Nonprofit.   In donative nonprofits, the fiscal year often begins with a stockpile of financial resources that must cover the shortfall of donations experienced prior to the major inflow around Thanksgiving and Christmas. The stockpile may include one or more of: cash on hand, short-term securities, bank loans, soon-due pledges receivable, or salable merchandise. The service effort is typically constant or almost so during the year, and the payroll and supplies expenditures continue on a fairly steady basis. Donations tend to cluster around Easter and the period from Thanksgiving to Christmas. The organization lives off its stockpile, to a large degree, until the heavy inflows materialize, at which time it replenishes its stockpile. When face-to-face fundraising is done, and wills and bequests are received periodically as a matter of course—as with Father Flanagan's Boys Home—the organization may use an income stream generated by endowments to partly offset the dry periods. The restricted nature of many of the large gifts, wills, and bequests may preclude interest or principal from being used for operational needs. Consequently, many nonprofits may experience a short-term need for funds during their operating cycles. The need for funds may have resulted from a downward trend in donations, a predictable seasonality in the receipt and disbursement of cash, or an unexpected event affecting costs, such as a strike. The worst case may occur when demand suddenly accelerates: When a business experiences higher sales, the sales revenues typically offset the higher costs, but a nonprofit has no assurance that donations will increase quickly when more services are provided.

Taken together, these operating characteristics of organizations that depend on donations for a significant percentage of their annual revenues drive their financial focus to a different objective. We now turn to some survey evidence to find out what that is.

(b) SURVEY EVIDENCE ON THE PRIMARY FINANCIAL OBJECTIVE.   In our 1992 to 1994 Lilly study of 288 chief financial officers of faith-based organizations, "financial break-even" (revenue equals expenses) was the dominant financial objective (111 respondents), followed by "maximize net revenue" (59 respondents).[4] As secondary objective, respondents indicated a concern for cost minimization (34 respondents), avoiding financial risk (25 respondents), and maximizing net donations (20 respondents). One observation we make here is that financial risk avoidance is justifiably gaining attention from nonprofit organizations. Yet we believe that break-even and cost minimization are inadequate as primary financial objectives. It would be much better to focus on net revenue, financial risk, net donations, or cash flow—all of which represent more focused attention to the positive contribution the finance function can make to mission achievement. Maximizing cash flow or net revenue, or attempting to break even, will force attention on cost control. Accordingly, cash flow or net revenue may retain the best of each of the other two related objectives while adding to them. This in no way negates the importance of program outreach and quality attainment, but indicates ways in which resources will be allocated to carry out the mission. (See Exhibit 1A.1 for more on this study and its results.)

More recently, the Lilly survey instrument was revised to include more objectives from which to choose as the organization's primary financial objective. A fax-back survey was administered in late 2002 to member organizations of the Evangelical Fellowship of Mission Agencie (EFMA). The results are fascinating. Respondents were asked first to select their organization's primary financial objective. The results are shown below:

Percent of Respondents	Primary Financial Objective
35.7%	Break even financially
21.4%	Maintain a targeted level of cash reserves and financial flexibility
14.3%	Maximize cash flow
7.1%	Minimize costs
7.1%	Maximize net revenue
7.1%	Maximize net donations
7.1%	Make a small surplus
0.0%	Avoid financial risk

The key point to note is that ten years after the original survey 35.7 percent (21.4% + 14.3%) of nonprofit organizations are focusing much more on cash flow and cash position—or "liquidity management" (just as many as are following the "received wisdom" that has been recommended by various sources to nonprofits: of not making a profit but covering costs).

Cash flow refers to the difference between cash inflows and cash outflows in a given period. **Cash position** is the amount of amount of cash and near-cash investments held by the organization. **Liquidity management** includes forecasting, and managing cash flow and the cash position, and ideally should include setting and managing toward a preferred cash position, or liquidity target. A **liquidity target** includes the elements of the cash position, along with unused short-term borrowing capacity. Your organization may have a pre-approved line of credit with a bank, some of which has not been borrowed or "taken down" at present.

Also important to note here is that the majority of respondents, 64.3 percent, chose an objective *other than financial break-even* as best describing their organization's primary financial objective. Apparently an increasing number of CFOs have concluded that striving for financial break-even cannot suffice as a nonprofit's primary financial objective. We elaborate on liquidity targeting below.

(c) FINANCIAL OBJECTIVE FOR PURELY FINANCIAL DECISIONS. Richard Wacht, an academic who has written on nonprofits, proposes that a nonprofit's financial objective be limited to "purely financial decisions" and is best stated as "cost minimization, subject to the absolute constraint of maintaining organizational liquidity and solvency over time."[5] He arrives at this objective by assuming that the financial objective must be largely divorced from the programmatic, mission-related objectives. While this is true up to a point, we believe that the program and financial objectives are more closely linked in most organizations and in most major spending and service-level decisions.

(d) RECOMMENDED PRIMARY FINANCIAL OBJECTIVE: APPROXIMATE LIQUIDITY TARGET. Our view, based on field evidence we have gathered and on the environmental and management constraints nonprofits face, is that the primary financial objective of organizations is to *strive to meet an "approximate liquidity target" over time*. Managing cash flow and the cash position are the keys to accomplishing this. We develop the basis for this conclusion in Appendix 1A and in Chapter 2.

For those uncomfortable with a single objective, consider the financial objectives articulated by William Hopkins, the treasurer of the Christian Children's Fund, in a presentation at the 2002 annual conference of the Association for Financial Professionals:[6]

- Cost effectiveness
- Financial accountability
- Maximization and protection of cash flows
- Maintaining liquidity that ensures the future of the organization

Were we to adopt these objectives, we would order them in terms of importance:

- Maintaining liquidity that ensures the future of the organization
- Maximization and protection of cash flows
- Cost effectiveness
- Financial accountability

No doubt some readers will express surprise that we placed financial accountability last. We do so for two reasons:

1. Managers tend to focus on one or at most two primary objectives, and we believe the first two in our ordering of Hopkins's list are the most important objectives.

2. Environmental factors and the accounting training of the CFO of many organizations ensure that much attention will be paid to financial accountability.[7] We have seen a small number of organizations that are not as careful in being accountable as we would hope.

1.7 CONCLUSION

The nonprofit environment is a challenging one for financial managers. Multiple stakeholders, confusion about what financial objective to pursue, limited staff, funding, and technology resources, and inattention to treasury management are all factors contributing to the difficulty of the nonprofit financial management.

We have presented the main structural components, the key policy areas, and the primary financial objective in this chapter. We profiled the survey evidence regarding the objective that the chief financial officers of faith-based charities say that they pursue, and found that cash position and cash flow management are becoming more prominent. We then recommended as a primary financial objective striving to meet an "approximate liquidity target" over time. This entails running surpluses in some years, possibly deficits in other years. We develop the idea of liquidity management, including monitoring the cash position and managing cash flow, in greater detail in Appendix 1A and in Chapter 2.

In the remainder of this book, we provide guidance on how this cash position and cash flow management focus translates into financial policy and practices. In our next chapter we turn to a fuller investigation of why these concerns should be at the top of a nonprofit organization's financial concern list.

Notes

1. IRS, Instructions for Form 1023 (n.d.), p. 2.
2. From Independent Sector, *The New Nonprofit Almanac and Desk Reference* (2002), at www.independentsector.org. Accessed: 10/2/2005.
3. Jane Lampman, "Robust economy = robust giving", *Christian Science Monitor* (June 20, 2006). Accessed online at: http://www.csmonitor.com/2006/0620/p25s01-lign.html. Accessed: July 17, 2006.
4. John Zietlow, "Organizational Goals and Financial Management in Donative Nonprofit Organizations," (Terre Haute, IN: Indiana State University, 1992–1994). This research project was sponsored by Lilly Endowment, Indianapolis, IN.
5. Richard F.Wacht, "A Financial Management Theory of the Nonprofit Organization," *The Journal of Financial Research* 7 (1, 1984): 37–45.
6. John Zietlow and William Hopkins, "Treasury Management in the Nonprofit World: Best Practices from the Christian Children's Fund," Presentation to the Annual Conference of the Association for Financial Professionals, November 8, 2002 (New Orleans, LA).
7. For our take on financial accountability, see, John Zietlow, "Developing Financial Accountability and Control," in *Serving Those in Need,* ed. Edward Queen (San Francisco: Jossey Bass, 1999).

THE LILLY STUDY FINDINGS

THE LILLY STUDY

We have seen much hyperbole about the true state of financial management in nonprofit organizations. This is especially the case regarding perceptions of social services charities, religious, and art organizations—and all nonprofits outside the health and education sectors. A large group of these donative organizations, which depend on gifts for 60 to 100 percent of their annual operating revenues, was the focus of a two-phase study completed in 1992 to 1994. This study was funded by the Lilly Endowment, Inc. as part of a project entitled "Organizational Goals and Financial Management in Donative Nonprofit Organizations" conducted by John Zietlow.

More than 1,000 religious or religiously based organizations in four categories were selected for study: denominational headquarters, denominational foreign missions (where the headquarters was separate), independent foreign mission agencies, and localized rescue missions. The latter are often called homeless shelters, but their work goes beyond sheltering.

Treasury management topics were studied in detail in Phase 1 of the project. Questions were asked on a 12-page mail survey about organizational and financial goals and all "short-term financial management" (STFM) areas: cash management, cash forecasting, inventory management, accounts receivable and accounts payable management, bank selection and relations, fundraising evaluation, short-term investing, short-term borrowing, risk management, and organizational attributes. Logical organizational characteristics were studied to better understand why certain organizations functioned more effectively or efficiently than others: size, age of the organization, role and interest of the board of directors, and formal training and experience of the chief financial officer.

Completed surveys were received from 288 (29 percent) of the surveyed organizations, a good response rate for a survey that is lengthy and difficult to complete. Based on the survey responses, and with the help of an expert advisory panel, each organization's survey responses were scored based on the STFM sophistication portrayed in the answers provided. For each of the four categories listed, the "best in class" organization was visited in person, as was an "average-rated" organization. How and why CFOs followed specific approaches and used various financial management techniques was the focus of in-depth interviews and additional decision making and board evaluation questionnaires. Interviews were conducted with the CFO, CEO, and the outside (nonemployee) board member most familiar with that organization's financial management.

The typical organization was small, having an annual revenue of only $800,000, on average. One-half of the CFOs had related business experience, with the one-half having eight years or more. The "best of the best," those organizations having the highest overall STFM score in their respective categories, were:

Independent Foreign Mission: Campus Crusade for Christ (Orlando, FL—John Webb, Director of Finance)

Denominational Mission: (1) Church of God Missionary Board (Anderson, IN—Darryl Smith, CFO); and

(2) Southern Baptist Board of Missions (Richmond, VA—Carl Johnson, CFO)

Rescue Mission: Peoria Rescue Ministries (Peoria, IL—Reverend Jerry Trecek, CEO and CFO)

Denominational Headquarters: Church of the Brethren (Elgin, IL—Darryl Deardorff, CFO)

The findings provided in the next section are mostly linked to survey results, although our understanding of these findings was enriched by what was learned in the onsite visits. We now turn to what the survey results revealed.

KEEP THE MISSION FIRST!   The first principle that the survey results revealed cannot be emphasized strongly enough: Mission first! Nonprofit organizations do not answer to stockholder owners but instead must adhere to the charter and mission of the organization. *Finance sustains mission.* Regrettably, some organizations allow that a proposed new program take precedence over existing programs, simply because corporate or foundation or government grant money is easier to get for the proposed program (which often is not closely linked to the charter or mission of the organization).

MANAGEMENT AND FINANCIAL OBJECTIVES

Management Objectives   Maximizing the quality and quantity of service was selected by most respondents, followed by maximize quality. Mission-minded organizations are service-minded, as one would expect.

Financial Objectives   Break-even (total revenues equal to total expenses) was the dominant choice selected as descriptive of the organization (111 of the 288 respondents), followed by maximize net revenue (59 respondents). As a secondary objective, respondents indicated a concern for cost minimization (34 respondents), avoiding financial risk (25 respondents), and maximizing net donations (20 respondents).

The main observation we make in light of these results is that financial risk avoidance is justifiably gaining attention by religious nonprofit organizations. Break-even and cost minimization are inadequate as primary financial objectives, in our view. It would be much better to focus on net revenue, financial risk, and net donations—all of which represent more focused attention to the positive contribution the finance function can make to mission achievement. In Chapter 1 we proposed and in Chapter 2 we defend an objective that supersedes these objectives, that of achieving an approximate liquidity target. One must recognize the overlap between the break-even and cost minimization and maximizing net revenue, as shown in Exhibit 1A.1. Maximizing net revenue or attempting to break even will force attention on cost control. Accordingly, net revenue may retain the best of the other two objectives while adding to them. This in no way negates the importance of program outreach and quality attainment, but it indicates ways in which resources will be allocated to carry out the mission.

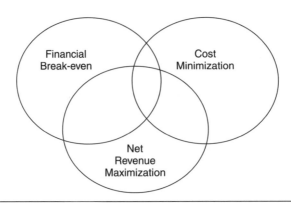

EXHIBIT 1A.1   OVERLAP OF SEVERAL POPULAR FINANCIAL OBJECTIVES

Achievement of Financial Objective: How Well Are You Doing, Regardless of Objectives Pursued?   Self-ratings on the achievement of the stated financial objective were: excellent (14 percent of respondents), very good (43 percent), good (30 percent), fair (10 percent), and poor (4 percent). This self-rating was one of the best indicators of the organization's overall Short-Term Financial Management (STFM) Score, which is based on a careful evaluation of each question in terms of its ability to indicate proficient financial management. An expert advisory panel, assembled under guidance of the Lilly Endowment, assisted in this process. Primitive financial management process and techniques are unlikely to achieve effectiveness in an organization's financial management outcomes. Individual questions within the survey were differentially rated, based on appropriateness for the size and type of organizations studied. Most respondents had a fairly accurate idea of how effective their financial management process was, and the tabulated results indicate that sophistication (what the questionnaire was really measuring) had a strong correlation with perceived effectiveness (as measured by the respondent's self-assessment).

Is the Indicated Financial Objective Really Operational?   A hypothetical decision was posed to the respondent to find out whether the financial objective was actually being pursued or was merely a stated objective. A new or expanded program recommended by the CEO or board clearly conflicts with the financial objective: What would most likely be done? In 46 organizations (17 percent), the program would be fully implemented anyway; in 68 organizations (24 percent), it would be scaled down somewhat, but the financial objective would still be set aside; and in 166 organizations (59 percent), the objective would be met by scaling down the program adequately or not implementing it at all. In other words, the finance function imposes essentially no discipline on 46 of the organizations that responded, and in an additional 68 organizations, that discipline is weak. Possibly this is due to ignorance among the officers regarding either the proper role of finance or the importance of sound financial management.

Some nonprofit executives would object to our conclusion that forging ahead with a new program despite the fact that it causes the organization to fall short of meeting its primary financial objective implies poor management because faith must be exercised. For organizations with a religious orientation, this response may be legitimate. Finance staff would carefully monitor such program initiatives to ensure that additional funds are ultimately raised to vindicate that faith. Where sufficient funds do not materialize during program implementation, this fact should be made apparent to the CEO and board in order to (1) ensure that the organization does not unduly expand those programs (draining resources from other important program areas) or add new ones until cost coverage is attained, and (2) inform decision makers of the types of situations about which to be more cautious in the future.

ON-SITE INTERVIEWS, QUESTIONNAIRES, AND ARCHIVAL STUDIES   The second phase in the Lilly study involved field studies of eight selected organizations. In-depth interviews, study of archived documents such as board meeting minutes and financial reports, and statistical study of cash flows were executed for each of the eight organizations. A pattern of financial decision making appeared from these studies, particularly for those organizations that were scored highly on the financial management proficiency scoring that we applied to the survey results. Bear in mind that the organizations studied were noncommercial, donative nonprofits. These results and the conclusions we garner from them are not necessarily applicable to commercial nonprofits such as hospitals or colleges.

THE APPROXIMATE LIQUIDITY TARGET MODEL   We call the model the "Approximate Liquidity Target" model of financial decision making. Exhibit 1A.2 provides a graphical presentation of the hierarchy of factors influencing decision making in this model. Notice

Donative Nonprofit Decision-Making Influence Spheres

EXHIBIT 1A.2   MISSION AND FINANCIAL OBJECTIVES

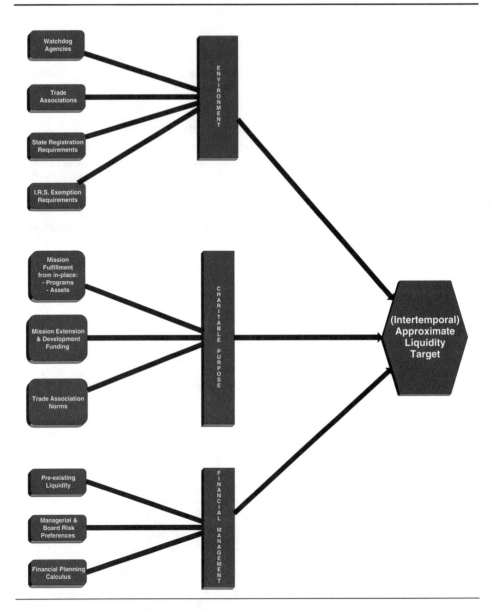

EXHIBIT 1A.3   INTERTEMPORAL APPROXIMATE LIQUIDITY TARGET MODEL

that the central concentric circle depicts the primacy of the organization's mission—its charitable purpose.

Note the financial objective nearest to the center—"liquidity target." It appears that organizations strive to maintain, within some range they are comfortable with, a certain amount of liquidity—an Approximate Liquidity Target (ALT). This target is managed intertemporally, meaning that the liquidity may dip below or shoot above the targeted range in any given year, but the organization will attempt to return the level of liquidity to the prescribed range in the following year(s). What might be an acceptable amount of liquidity for one organization could well be too high or low for another, very similar organization.

The ALT model suggests that (1) the liquidity target range is actually the chief financial objective of the donative nonprofit organization, and (2) mission-related program initiatives may actually be managed in such a way to assist the organization in meeting its target. That items 1 and 2 hold is masked by two factors: (1) it does not necessarily happen each year, but over time, and (2) the level of mission-related program initiative may be managed more with new program development and expansion/reduction of existing programs than with a given year's "output" level of program services. This fact seems to imply that the cart (financial resources) is driving the horse (mission-related program delivery). However, it may simply be that the managers of these organizations are well aware of the inability to tap external equity and the limited ability to utilize long-term debt (and, in many cases, a disinclination to use short-term debt) and are thus assigning more importance to liquidity and its linkage to survival. Without financial health, and with a threat to survival, the organization's ability to deliver its mission in the future is impaired.

The Approximate Liquidity Target model can be expanded to show behavioral aspects of managerial decision making. The joint effect of three categories of variables drives the programmatic and resource allocation decisions as the donative nonprofit organization strives to reach its ALT. We can see the environmental, mission, and financial management categories in Exhibit 1A.3.

Although not shown in the exhibit, the model allows for feedback effects from the realized liquidity position in any given year to the mission delivery (for assets and programs in place), mission expansion or growth path, and preexisting liquidity for following periods.

The box labeled "financial planning calculus" needs further explanation. This "calculus" involves the philosophy as well as technology employed for cash budgets, operational budgets, and *pro forma* financial statements. So it encompasses both short-run and long-run financial planning methodologies, including (for faith-based organizations) the decision maker's view of the relevance of faith in developing the coming years' output levels.

Throughout the remainder of this book, we provide guidelines regarding how to set the liquidity target and how to manage cash flows to best ensure the maintenance of that target and the continued financial vitality of the organization.

LIQUIDITY MANAGEMENT

2.1 INTRODUCTION

We need to set the financial context for nonprofit financial management and for the special importance of liquidity management in the nonprofit sector. In this chapter we lay out the reasons behind our continuous emphasis on liquidity by profiling the legal, environmental, and institutional constraints on nonprofit financial managers. We then move into a critical analysis of the financial ratings available from charity watchdog agencies, which we find overly constraining with regard to liquidity management.

Nonprofits that do not have enough accessible financial resources may divert their attention from mission accomplishment to coping with financial pressures.[1] We often hear of donation-dependent nonprofits thrust into a cash crunch or cash crisis due to the loss of a key donor or part of their donor base. However, contract-based nonprofits are at least as vulnerable if not more so: Managers may underestimate the costs of carrying out the contract, unexpected increases in cost elements such as rent, energy, benefits, or insurance may occur, or several years of inflation may turn what was once an adequate contract revenue amount into an insufficient sum. Consider this observation from Stephen Rathgeb Smith:[2]

In short, the cash flow problem is not an idiosyncratic occurrence or primarily due to mismanagement; instead it is built into the very structure of the contracting regime. Cash flow problems are to be expected. Nonprofit managers are in the position of coping with chronic cash flow concerns. Managers respond with a variety of strategies. They may delay their payments to their vendors, ask their bankers for easier terms on their loans, request that staff take unpaid leave or vacation time, temporarily lay off employees or freeze hiring, even in cases of staff of staff members leaving. In particularly serious cases, agency executives may forego some of their salary or decide to suspend payment of the agency's payroll taxes.

The latter tactic would end the agency in legal problems, if detected. Rathgeb Smith suggests that nonprofits try to deal with the chronic cash flow concerns by one or more of the following funding strategies:

- Obtain a line or credit or win an increased line from their bank
- Gather donations from individuals or grants from corporate foundations
- Tap into the principal of their endowments

Most nonprofits find that these strategies fail them however.[3] Only nonprofits with collateral—something like inventories that can be sold to recoup dollars not repaid—or a longstanding reputation are viewed favorably by bank lending officers. Significantly increasing private gifts is difficult at best, and many foundations prefer to fund capital expenditures or projects, not operating expenses. Relatively few agencies can tap the local United Way funding stream, and that only after a lengthy application and review process. Mid-sized and small nonprofits rarely have endowments. For all of these reasons, new monies are difficult to come by, and government administrators may prefer to contract with large agencies.

We see cash flow problems as endemic to the nonprofit sector. From a managerial perspective, we believe that liquidity management is one of the most important yet least studied areas in the management of nonprofits. *Liquidity* may be defined as financial flexibility[4] or the ability of the organization to augment its future cash flows.[5] A more popular, but deficient view, is to look at the *solvency* of the organization—the extent to which its assets exceed its liabilities. *Many managers and board members, as well as charity watchdog agencies, have either ignored liquidity management or have limited their analysis of nonprofit finances to solvency.* We demonstrate the weakness of the solvency view in this chapter and offer guidance on how your organization can set its desired liquidity level.

(a) IMPORTANCE OF LIQUIDITY.　Liquidity policy and practice has been almost totally overlooked in nonprofit management periodicals and textbooks. Notable exceptions are Wacht, discussed later in this chapter, and Grønbjerg, who notes that growing donative human service organizations require access to liquid reserves to cope with cash flow problems.[6] Recently, two practitioner's guides to making cash flow projections, an important facet of liquidity management, have become available.[7] In most instances when cash or marketable securities are discussed, the problem of inadequate liquidity is briefly mentioned but the possibility or desirability of excess liquidity is not addressed. The coverage gap is surprising for two reasons. First, nonprofit managers, employees, and board members commonly lament the perennial cash crunch or ongoing cash crisis faced by their organizations (see Hall).[8] Second, this area of financial management is one that shares very much in common with business. The views of Aaron Phillips, former director of research of the Association for Financial Professionals, are worth quoting at length:

> The one unifying consideration all organizations share, whether publicly held, privately held, government, or not-for-profit, is the concern over liquidity management. It is a safe assumption that a for-profit entity will not remain in business long if it either lacks liquidity or does not effectively manage its liquidity. Empirical research has documented that corporate financial liquidity measures are important for assessing and/or pricing credit, determining bond ratings, forecasting bankruptcy, etc. Similarly, a not-for-profit organization cannot continue to meet its mission objectives, or at the very least risks jeopardizing its relationship with its stakeholders, if it lacks prudent liquidity management. In short, liquidity management is a major concern for every organization.[9]

Agency theory motivates us to better understand organizational liquidity. The argument is that managers build excess liquidity, or slack, because they are overly concerned about risk. For businesses, managerial risk aversion exceeds stockholder risk aversion, because stockholders are well diversified. The same argument *may* extend to donative nonprofits. To the extent that there are multiple organizations engaging in similar services (and with the same or very similar values and philosophies), the probability of organization failure and dissolution is of less concern to donors than to the organization's managers. Donors may simply reallocate donations to surviving organizations when one of the existing organizations fails.

(b)   ARE NONPROFITS OVERLY RISK-AVERSE?   The difficulty in assessing whether nonprofit managers are too risk-averse comes when trying to jointly assess (1) the probability of organizational failure relative to the amount of liquidity held and (2) the relative risk aversion of donors versus boards and managers of donative organizations. Implicitly, charity watchdog organizations have made this joint assessment. These public watchdog organizations, in their desire to provide tangible, quantitative benchmarks of the effectiveness and efficiency of nonprofits, have adopted the solvency view of liquidity in their evaluative guidelines. Of the three major organizations—BBB Wise Giving Alliance, which is the result of a 2001 merger of the Council of Better Business Bureaus Philanthropic Advisory Service and the National Charities Information Bureau, the American Institute of Philanthropy, and Charity Navigator—two have explicitly adopted a prescribed *maximum* level of reserves (unrestricted net assets) that organizations may hold. A fourth information provider, Philanthropic Research, Inc. (GuideStar), also makes two financial measures available to interested parties, while withholding judgment on "how much is too much."[10]

When a watchdog agency prescribes a maximum, what it is saying is that beyond this level, the organization is holding excess resources that should instead be used for current program or service provision. The reason we must tackle and understand these prescriptions is that they have financial policy implications that have not been identified. These policy guidelines may be appropriate for commercial nonprofits but will severely limit the management style of small donative religious organizations.

But first it is necessary to understand what the policy implications of these agency standards are. The implications fall into two major categories: (1) capital structure—some organizations prefer to self-fund future acquisitions, capital projects, and major program expansions, which implies a large buildup in cash reserves; and (2) liquidity management—not only do two-thirds of religious nonprofits avoid short-term borrowing (see Section 2.5; yet note that borrowing is the primary source of backup liquidity for corporations, according to Kallberg and Parkinson)[11]—but they may hold their assets in a very illiquid form, such as pledges receivable.

Next we need to know whether these standards rest on a sound financial management foundation. One might use one of three approaches to document and test the liquidity management approaches used by donative religious nonprofits and the degree of impact of the watchdog agency liquidity prescriptions.

1. A survey approach to data collection may be used. Survey evidence collected from 288 donative religious organizations provides information on the espoused liquidity management objectives, how liquidity is measured, and the policy toward and utilization of debt financing.

2. A nonprofit financial database may be used to study the incidence of "problem organizations," defined as those having more than the prescribed amount of reserves.

3. One could use simulation modeling or scenario analysis to show how the maximum liquidity limits the financial management options for small donative nonprofits that:

    (a) Do not use debt financing

    (b) Do not typically generate positive operating cash flows (first category on statement of cash flows)

    (c) Are unable to launch capital campaigns

    (d) Have no endowments

To the best of our knowledge, no one has yet employed either the second or third approach to study liquidity or to help set the desired liquidity level.

Before we go any further with our liquidity analysis, we must explain what we mean by donative organizations and survey some early studies of liquidity management in healthcare and educational organizations.

2.2 DONATIVE NONPROFIT ORGANIZATIONS

Nonprofit organizations often rely on donors (20 percent of total revenue overall, 44 percent for arts, culture, and humanities organizations),[12] or granting agencies for much of their operating revenue. Some types of nonprofit organizations, religious organizations, gather over 90 percent of their revenues from donations. Some call these donative organizations because of their primary income source, while others view these as organizations having a high collectiveness index, where "collectiveness" refers to gifts and grants as a percent of total resources. In this chapter we introduce liquidity management, which may also be referred to as working capital management or short-term financial management. Initially, our special focus is donative nonprofit organizations: We illustrate practice and inform policy by providing evidence regarding the financial management practices of a group of donation-dependent nonprofits. We then broaden the focus to commercial organizations, such as private schools and colleges and healthcare organizations. We show how the popular watchdog agency standards may be misguided and detrimental to your organization's financial health and conclude by demonstrating a checklist that assists in setting liquidity policy.

(a) GUIDANCE FROM FINANCE THEORY.   While corporate finance theory is well developed for businesses, it is still in the earliest stage of development for nonprofits. In fact, the only broad-range financial theory of nonprofit organizations was developed over 20 years ago by Richard Wacht.[13] Wacht prescribes for all nonprofit entities the financial goal of "cost minimization, subject to the absolute constraint of maintaining organizational liquidity and solvency over time."

Wacht advocates a cash flow balancing approach to nonprofit financial management. He states at one point that "the financial manager must ensure that actual cash inflows and outflows are balanced and operations are proceeding according to plans."

(b) EVALUATION OF FINANCE THEORY.   We commend Wacht as the true pioneer in the field of nonprofit financial management theory development. He recognized the importance of liquidity along with cost control. Furthermore, he is the only one to ever devise a full-blown model of how mission and finance may work together in a nonprofit organization.

Wacht is somewhat vague on the specific implementation of the financial goal. He does note that new project implementation or existing program expansion can prevent the organization from meeting its financial goals of liquidity and solvency, and may plunge the organization into a financial crisis. Implied in his framework is the ability of an organization to develop and correctly utilize a fairly detailed financial model. Without such a model, there would be no way for the financial manager to back or reject proposed capital projects or program expansion initiatives. In our view, liquidity management should be more proactive than reactive, and organizations should start liquidity planning right from the start-up of the organization.

Wacht overlooks the cash position and short-term securities components of an organization's liquid reserve by arguing that financial uncertainties must be dealt with by having "sufficient flexibility built into the budgets and financing arrangements to avoid jeopardizing the solvency of the organization." Put simply, only by managing down the cost structure (and increasing the amount of operating cash flow) or taking out a loan can the organization deal with a possible revenue shortfall. Again, we believe that proactive liquidity management may forestall these more drastic measures if that management is implemented properly.

2.3 EVIDENCE ON LIQUIDITY MANAGEMENT IN THE NONPROFIT SECTOR

Three groups surveyed nonprofit liquidity-related management practices in nonprofit organizations previously. The surveys focus on health care, education, and faith-based donative organizations. These surveys, though dated, are the best gauges we have of actual policies and practices.

(a) LIQUIDITY MANAGEMENT IN THE HEALTHCARE SECTOR.   The first survey, by Hahn and Aggarwal, focus on healthcare organizations. It dealt primarily with the receivables management of hospitals.[14] That survey detected areas of possible improvement in receivables monitoring and collections that would increase organizational liquidity. Some of the key findings are:

- Working capital management (primarily current assets and current liabilities) is primarily handled by the controller (24 percent) or finance or fiscal director (18 percent).

- Most responding managers spend between 5 percent and 10 percent of their time on working capital management, with about one-quarter of the managers spending 11 percent to 15 percent of their time on such topics—a surprising response compared to similar business manager survey results, which show much larger percentages.

- Only 36 percent had a cash planning horizon under one year, with 45 percent using a year or more as their horizon.

- Cash budgets are revised yearly by 14 percent, semiannually by 7 percent, quarterly by 20 percent, monthly by 36 percent, biweekly by 2 percent, weekly by 13 percent, and daily by 3 percent of the respondents.

- Checks are processed by 93 percent of the respondents in a day or less.

- About 77 percent of the hospitals regularly invested surplus cash in the money market, meaning almost one-quarter do not.

- While 24 percent of respondents stated that they could achieve an average days of receivables of 30 to 45 days, only 7 percent of the firms actually achieve that collection experience.

- Average days of receivables is listed as the primary measure of receivables monitoring.

- Fully 96 percent of the hospitals took advantage of trade credit and cash discounts offered.

- Inventory management was the weakest part of working capital management.

(b) LIQUIDITY MANAGEMENT IN COLLEGES AND UNIVERSITIES.   Another survey, conducted in 1982 by the National Association of College & University Business Officers (NACUBO) and summarized in Marsee, investigated cash and investment management in colleges and universities.[15] The information that follows is representative of that study's findings.

Of the 453 survey responses, 208 colleges and universities (46 percent) indicated that their depository institution was the primary financial institution used when making investments such as certificates of deposit or repurchase agreements.

The responses also indicated that the typical cash manager:

- Handles both the cash management and investment decisions (70 percent), usually as the chief financial administrator

- Is operating under the guidelines of an institutional investment policy (65 percent)

- Feels relatively free of local politics when making investment decisions (82 percent)

- Works primarily with in-state banks (83 percent)

The NACUBO study did not address the role of or the objective for liquidity management.

(c) LIQUIDITY MANAGEMENT IN FAITH-BASED DONATIVE ORGANIZATIONS.   We believe the greatest insight regarding the uniqueness of nonprofit organizations should come from the subgroup(s) that is (are) most purely nonprofit. In this section we briefly recap the methods used in the Lilly research study (see Appendix 1A for background and more detail on that study). Donative nonprofits—those relying on donors for much or all of their operating revenues—were selected for study on this basis. Four types of religious organizations served as the sampled group of nonprofit organizations: (a) denominational headquarters, (b) denominational foreign mission headquarters (where operated separately), (c) independent mission agencies, and (d) domestic rescue missions.

The study, funded by the Lilly Endowment, was conducted in two phases over the period 1992 to 1994. Survey evidence collected by John Zietlow from 288 donative religious organizations provides information on the espoused liquidity management objectives, how liquidity is measured, and the policy toward and utilization of debt financing. The topics covered include those mentioned above along with other short-term financial management topics, such as inventory management and bank relations. Field studies also were conducted at eight selected organizations. Two organizations were selected from each of the four subtypes, with ensuing individual on-site visits for approximately two and a half days. During the field studies, archival data were collected (budgets, variance reports, board minutes, financial policies, audited financial statements, and forecasts) and in-depth personal interviews were conducted. The interviews were with the chief financial officer (CFO), chief executive officer (CEO), and usually also with the board member most involved with financial decisions. Bear in mind that the "key informant" responses are from the vantage point of just one person, with the most extensive questioning done with the CFO.

(i) Study Findings.   This section presents several of the main findings regarding liquidity management. Many of the findings are provided later in the section on the importance of liquidity management, in that they bear on the factors determining the vitality of liquidity.

Organizations manage by planning (including policy setting), executing, and controlling. The finance function focuses mostly on the planning and controlling activities. We profile the survey responses in planning first, then executing (one measure), and controlling. Then we turn to early field study findings, including a basic model of the apparent operational financial objective.

(ii) Short-Term Policies and Planning.   Only one in four organizations (24.3 percent) has an explicit overall policy for the liquidity management (worded in the questionnaire as "the management of its current assets and liabilities—working capital"). Most of those organizations that do have such a policy (56 percent) indicate that it is risk-avoiding ("current asset and liability levels selected to keep risk to a minimum"), with the second most common response (28 percent) being situational ("current asset and liability levels selected depending on the financial position of the agency"). Interestingly,

only 10 percent of those organizations having a policy consider that policy to be risk-accepting ("current asset and liability levels selected to increase interest income, while accepting the possibility that short-term borrowing may be needed.") Sixty percent of the organizations have an investment policy, which all organizations should have.

Surveyed organizations scored better on operating budget practices than on cash forecasting practices. Eighty-nine percent of the organizations have (and presumably use) an operating budget, leaving 11 percent with a handicapped short-term planning system. Forty-four percent of the surveyed organizations develop a cash forecast—an exercise that is absolutely vital for liquidity management. Based on a survey by Campbell, Johnson, and Savoie, Fortune 1000 treasurers consider short-term cash flow projections to be one of the most valuable tools for liquidity management.[16] Beginning to project cash inflows, cash outflows, and the resulting cash position, is the first place to start in improving short-term financial management for over one-half of our surveyed organizations.

More liquid organizations typically have a greater degree of their assets in the form of short-term, or current assets. Current assets are those that are either already in the form of cash or will be converted to cash within a year. A mere 13 percent of responding organizations have a target current assets-to-total assets (CA/TA) ratio value. This ratio is recommended for practitioner use by Herzlinger and Nitterhouse and others.[17] This ratio, a solvency measure, measures the *relative liquidity* of the organization's asset investment. In his 1989 ratio compilation study, Chris Robinson found a wide range of actual values for this "asset ratio" for faith-based organizations: Churches had a median ratio value of 0.06, while foreign mission agencies invested about one-half of their assets in current ratios.[18] (The latter are "conduits," in our framework, presented later.)

It is a slightly different ratio, but data compiled in 2006 by Dan Busby and his staff at the Evangelical Council for Financial Accountability (ECFA) indicates that the cash-to-revenue ratio for the 1,200 faith-based organizations holding membership in ECFA is 0.21.[19] That value implies that an organization could survive for about $2\frac{1}{2}$ months, on average, if revenues were interrupted ($2.5 = 0.21 \times 12$ months). Assuming revenues (or total income) equals expenses for this group overall, this demonstrates that these organizations hold less in cash reserves than the commonly advocated target of 3–6 months of expenses. Bear in mind that the latter guideline is strictly for operating reserves, and does not include additional amounts that should be held for prefunding capital assets or new programs.

(iii) Executing Liquidity Management.   One measure of liquidity management execution is provided by a question regarding whether the organizations practice daily active cash management. Daily active cash management involves setting the day-ending cash position early in the day (before noon), then making short-term investing and borrowing decisions in light of that cash position. About one-half of the organizations state that they do this, which would be considered quite good given their size ($800,000 median annual revenue).

(iv) Controlling.   Organizations do well at calculating monthly budget variances (actual amount versus budget), with four in five organizations doing so, and another 8 percent making quarterly comparisons. Unfortunately, only two in five organizations compute and analyze financial ratios, and half of those organizations do so on a monthly basis. The asset ratio is monitored by almost one-half of the organizations, although as mentioned earlier, most of these do not manage it toward a specific target value. Possibly the best news is that 78 percent of the organizations say that they use a computer to monitor and/or forecast their cash positions.

(v) Primary Financial Objective: Lessons from the Field Studies.   The second phase in the Lilly study involved field studies of eight selected organizations. In-depth interviews, study of archived documents such as board meeting minutes and financial reports, and statistical study of cash flows were executed for each of the eight organizations. A pattern of financial decision making appeared from these studies. From the perceived pattern, a new model of organizational financial decision-making has been developed. The model, which we call the "Approximate Liquidity Target" model of financial decision making, provides a descriptive theory of donative nonprofit organizations. (See Appendix 1A for more on this model.)

Interestingly, charity watchdog agencies now include some facets of liquidity in their ratings of nonprofits. Before we see what the charity watchdog agencies prescribe for your organization's solvency and liquidity, we must establish just how critical liquidity management is for nonprofits. The next section is one of the most important in this book, because it provides the arguments for our central financial objective of managing the organization's target cash position and cash flows.

2.4 FACETS OF LIQUIDITY MANAGEMENT

Liquidity management in the business sector is defined as "the allocation of liquid resources *over time* to meet resource needs for payment of obligations due and for various investments that management undertakes to maximize shareholder wealth."[20] Changing the last phrase to read "to attain its mission" recasts the definition for nonprofit organizations. Gallinger and Healey allege that the failure of managers to provide adequate liquid resources to both meet near-term bills and finance growth initiatives has been the cause of as many business failures as have economic recessions. They indicate that the most fundamental objective of liquidity management is to ensure corporate solvency (pay bills as they become due) or ensure corporate survival. The key issues in liquidity management are to minimize "insolvency risk" by (1) determining how much to invest in each component of current assets and allocate funding needs to each component of current liabilities, and (2) managing these investments and allocations effectively and efficiently.

(a) LAYERS OF LIQUIDITY.   We can view liquidity management in a way useful to managers by establishing "tiers of liquidity."[21] Here the organization's liquidity is viewed in tiers of decreasing liquidity, with six major layers of liquidity (see Exhibit 2.1).

For our discussion of nonprofit liquidity management, it is helpful to distinguish among solvency, liquidity, and financial flexibility.

(b) SOLVENCY.   An organization is *solvent* when its assets exceed its liabilities. The larger the degree to which assets exceed liabilities, the more solvent the organization is. In the nonprofit context, this difference has been labeled positive fund balances or equity fund balances and more recently positive net assets (see Chapter 6 for definitions of these items). When evaluating solvency, we usually go one step further by computing *net working capital*, which equals current assets minus current liabilities. This data is available on the organization's balance sheet, which we also detail in Chapter 6.

(c) LIQUIDITY.   Further, an organization is *liquid* when it can pay its bills on time without undue cost. Clearly an organization is illiquid if it is consistently unable to take cash discounts (e.g., 2 percent cash discount if one pays an invoice within 10 days) or must constantly engage in interfund borrowing.

Liquidity Tier	Comments
Tier 1: Cash flow, cash balances, and the investment portfolio.	Most liquid.
Tier 2: Short-term credit.	This, more so than cash balances and ST investments, provides the majority of the liquidity reserve for businesses.
Tier 3: Management of cash flows.	Examples are to delay payments, offer services at lower prices, offer easier credit terms, or alter inventory positions.
Tier 4: Renegotiation of debt contracts.	Some lenders are more flexible than others.
Tier 5: Asset sales.	The organization is beginning to liquidate valuable assets simply to provide cash to stay afloat.
Tier 6: Bankruptcy.	The purpose of bankruptcy is to buy time to reorganize by protecting the organization from creditors. Bankruptcy may culminate in reorganization or liquidation.

EXHIBIT 2.1 THE SIX LAYERS OF LIQUIDITY

(d) FINANCIAL FLEXIBILITY. Finally, an organization possesses *financial flexibility* when its financial policies (use of debt, excess of revenues over expenses, and relationship of revenues to assets) are consistent with its projected increase in revenues. The Financial Accounting Standards Board (in Financial Accounting Standard 117) defines financial flexibility operationally, indicating that it is measured by the ability of the organization to "use its financial resources to meet program needs, pay maturing debt, or meet any unexpected cash requirements or opportunities."[22]

Correspondingly, the organization should provide information on restrictions on the use of assets, compensating balances that must be maintained in checking accounts, and the maturity structure of long-term assets and liabilities.

2.5 IMPORTANCE OF LIQUIDITY MANAGEMENT

The importance of liquidity management is partly self-evident. It makes sense to have enough funds to pay bills; the converse is to be in a cash crunch or, if the shortfall is ongoing, a cash crisis. A cash crisis eventually arises whenever an organization is not bringing in adequate revenues to offset its expenses. The significance of liquidity management to nonprofits seems clear from the ongoing discussion of how to cope with these cash shortfalls.[23] Cash flow problems might simply be the result of mismanagement in selected, but visible, nonprofits. Here the contrary position is taken that liquidity management is the single most important financial function of the donative nonprofit.[24] This is so because of two sets of factors: institutional factors and managerial philosophy ones. There is some obvious overlap between these factor sets.

(a) INSTITUTIONAL FACTORS.

(i) Primary Financial Objective. Businesses attempt to maximize shareholder wealth as their primary financial objective. This objective drives businesses to constantly increase cash flow, given a particular risk posture. Liquidity tends to take care of itself, except in the cases in which (1) growth is combined with low profit margins and long product development, inventory, or credit sales-collection periods, or (2) the organization is

in decline. In nonprofit organizations, without the shareholder wealth objective, what is the appropriate financial objective, and what are the liquidity implications? Other sources have traditionally advocated as the primary objective striving for financial break-even (revenues just covering expenses), which implies that the stock of liquid resources remains relatively constant, all other things being equal. Increasingly, calls are made for organizations to attempt to earn a small positive net revenue, which would provide a boost to the organization's liquidity, at least for some seasons of the fiscal year. We argue that this is appropriate as a means to an end—the end being maintaining a liquidity target adequate to protect the organization and its mission against seasonal and cyclical cash shortfalls and to build a financial resource base for future program and facility expansion. We revisit actual practices a bit later.

(ii) Limited and Volatile Revenue Stream. Commercial nonprofits are much like businesses, but donative nonprofits have no price lever with which to earn revenue on their core services. Correspondingly, they cannot increase or decrease price—selecting the appropriate change based on how responsive customers' purchases are to price—in order to increase revenue when facing present or potential cash flow shortfalls. (Quantity-cost relationships are important here too to define the *net* revenue effects.) Furthermore, the natural and almost automatic coupling between cash outflows to pay for supplies and labor and the ensuing cash inflows from sales is nonexistent in donative nonprofits. To make matters worse, while a slowdown in revenue from sales for a business triggers a quick downward adjustment in cash outflows for production, cash outflows will be difficult to adjust downward for a donative nonprofit, and the cash position may actually be further depleted if the organization ratchets up its fundraising investment to try to offset the recent decline in donations. Even then, human service organizations pursuing various levels or varieties of donation efforts often are not able to increase the predictability or size of donation revenues.[25] Donations may change in volatile and unpredictable ways, seemingly in spite of intensive development efforts or the existence of natural constituencies (except in cases of institutionalized relationships, such as United Way or religious federations). Further evidence of the unpredictable stream of donated funds is provided by Kingma, whose research indicates that increased financial risk arises from donation revenue streams. Liquidity thus has greater value for the donative nonprofit.[26] If an organization raises funds in advance of program and service delivery, it is engaging in a liquidity management strategy that explicitly recognizes the need for and value of a greater degree of liquidity. *For most organizations, this proactive liquidity management approach of prefunding future needs is the advisable approach.*

Organizations may partly offset the revenue limitations by turning to supplemental earned income ventures, but this implies four greater barriers than are commonly recognized: (1) These ventures deploy already-scarce resources (which would actually exacerbate a cash flow crunch or crisis), (2) they may and often do defuse the organization's mission focus, (3) quite often the managerial team and/or board does not possess competencies requisite for profitably managing the ventures, and (4) even when successful, there is a long time lag between launching the venture and achieving positive net revenue. Numerous nonprofit organizations attempt these ventures, as noted in studies by La Barbera and in Froelich and Knoepfle, but La Barbera finds that, in the small nonrandom sample studied, raising funds was an objective in only a minority of the faith-based organizations.[27]

(iii) Inability to Issue Stock to Raise Equity Capital.   Donative nonprofit organizations face an additional funding constraint in that they cannot issue stock. An important permanent source of financing is therefore unavailable to them. Internal equity is available to these organizations to the extent they take in operating surpluses, engage in capital campaigns, or build endowments. On an ongoing basis, the only means of accumulating equity (nonborrowed) capital is to earn a surplus (profit equivalent) on operations. Yet, as noted earlier, most faith-based donative organizations consider financial break-even to be their chief financial objective, which implies that they are unwilling to earn significant surpluses.

A partial offset to the capital limitation is the institutional reality that no cash dividends are allowed or expected. In this sense, nonprofits operate much like a start-up or other rapidly growing business that reinvests all of its profits in order to self-fund its growth as much as possible. Added assistance comes from the 501(c)(3)'s tax exemption, implying that all "before-tax" net revenue is available as "after-tax" addition to equity.

(iv) Time-Restricted and Use-Restricted Donations.   Possibly the most significant impediment to matching cash inflows to cash outflows comes from the large proportion of time-restricted or use-restricted donations. Cash outflows for expenditures that are not easily or currently funded by donors pose a significant threat to the liquidity position of the donative nonprofit. Fullmer estimates that 75 percent of donations to nonprofits are restricted (primarily to a specific use), and in the Lilly study of donative nonprofits, we find a self-reported average of 72 percent of their current/operating fund donations come with donor designations or other restrictions.[28] This factor alone accounts for a more difficult management task when comparing liquidity management for donative versus other nonprofits, governmental agencies, or businesses. In fact, in Statement 117 the Financial Accounting Standards Board tacitly recognized the organizational impact of restricted gifts on liquidity, motivating the new (unrestricted, temporarily restricted, permanently restricted) breakdown in net assets. Our survey of donative faith-based nonprofits indicates that interfund borrowing is a necessary evil practiced by many organizations: When asked "how frequently does your organization temporarily transfer funds from its current restricted or other restricted funds to meet a shortfall in your current unrestricted (general) fund?" 13 percent said on a monthly basis (!), 14 percent said on a quarterly basis, 10 percent said once a year, 19 percent said less than once a year, and 44 percent said never. The problem is compounded for those organizations that are striving for financial break-even as opposed to a positive net revenue (the former should have a smaller cash inflow, all other things equal) or that have small or nonexistent cash reserves (stock of cash), illustrating the overlap and often cumulative effect of these institutional and managerial philosophy factors.

(v) Operating Characteristics of Donative Nonprofits.   Financial processes of nonprofit organizations can be accurately characterized as a cash flow system. Many charities and churches receive cash in from gifts and grants, hold onto the cash for a while, and then disburse the cash to other organizations, members, clients, or other beneficiaries. Colleges and schools and food and medical care charities, which transform cash into services or products, also benefit greatly from liquidity management, as demonstrated in the cash flow system model (see Exhibit 2.2).

Organizations that primarily transfer funds from donor or grantor to clients or beneficiaries are called *conduits*. Examples include foundations, religious denomination and

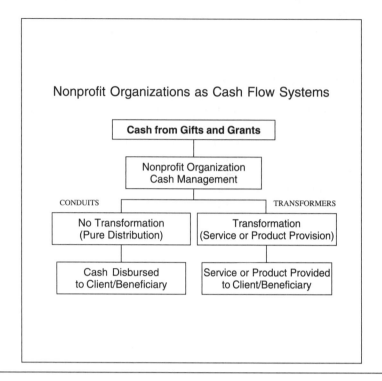

EXHIBIT 2.2   CASH FLOW MODEL OF DONATIVE NONPROFIT FINANCES

association headquarters operations, and multinational agencies sending personnel abroad to deliver a service. Proficient cash management is absolutely essential to the success of conduits in that they are primarily cash-gathering and distributing machines. *Transformers*, in turn, convert cash into one or more products or services and distribute those outputs to clients and other beneficiaries. Transformers include churches, arts organizations, many healthcare organizations, educational institutions, and most human service organizations and other charities. Cash management proficiency is still important prior to the conversion process, but since the organization is also delivering a product or service, the quality and quantity of product/service delivery assumes greater importance. Overall working capital proficiency is the appropriate focus in transformers. Net working capital includes cash, receivables, inventories, payables, accrued expenses, and short-term loans. Whether conduit or transformer, management must focus on liquidity management, which encompasses cash management and the broader aspects of working capital management.

(b) MANAGERIAL PHILOSOPHY FACTORS

(i) Major Reluctance to Earn Surpluses.   When asked what their main financial goal is, donative faith-based organizations have predominantly selected financial break-even.[29] What is not as clear is whether this goal is operative. Intriguing evidence regarding actual surpluses is provided by Chang and Tuckman, who find that charities earned no surplus while other nonprofits were averaging a 10 percent surplus (as a percent of total

revenues).[30] By forgoing the accumulation of positive net revenues, these organizations are bypassing the major source of liquidity in businesses (especially those with high profit margins, such as Microsoft). Profits are also considered by some to be a nonprofit's most reliable source of cash.[31]

(ii) Resistance to Engage in Short-Term Borrowing. Although Tuckman and Chang indicate that 71 percent of nonprofits included in the 1986 IRS 990 database engaged in some borrowing, we do not know how many of these organizations used short-term debt.[32] Many organizations that use mortgage loans for plant and equipment will resist short-term borrowing, in that it is risky to become dependent on borrowed funds to finance operations. Short-term debt, as noted by Kallberg and Parkinson's model, is the second tier of liquidity for an organization. The surveyed donative faith-based organizations are disinclined to use short-term loans:

- Two-thirds of the respondents never do short-term external borrowing.
- 21 percent do short-term borrowing, but not every year.
- 13 percent do short-term borrowing every year.

For the one-third of the organizations that do borrow, the *primary* use is:

- As a regular and constant part of total financing (11 percent)
- As a cyclical part of total financing (15 percent)
- As a seasonal part of total financing (29 percent)
- To meet irregular needs (45 percent)

About 4 in 10 (38 percent) of the borrowing organizations are never asked to provide security (collateral) for their short-term loans, while 34 percent are occasionally required to collateralize and 27 percent must always collateralize the borrowings. Although lenders much prefer to collect loan interest and principal repayment from cash flows realized by the borrower, the security stands as a backup to protect the lender in the event of default.

Finally, although most leasing is long-term in duration, 19 percent of the surveyed organizations arrange leases for financing purposes.

(iii) Insufficient Liquidity Monitoring, Management, or Projection. With one exception, the survey evidence shows that most donative faith-based organizations are insufficiently attentive to available techniques for liquidity monitoring, management, and projection. As shown in the responses for the 1992 to 1994 survey reported earlier, less than one-half of the organizations are doing the minimal tasks necessary to properly monitor, manage, and project liquidity needs.

(c) LIQUIDITY IMPLICATIONS OF INSTITUTIONAL AND MANAGERIAL PHILOSOPHY FACTORS. There are two main implications for liquidity management and related financial policies from the foregoing analysis:

- *Implication #1* : The capital structure decision favors reinvested surpluses as the primary means of financing assets. These organizations are obviously quite risk-averse, based on the survey findings reported here, and will use only limited long-term debt to supplement equity. These organizations should be encouraged to operate at a surplus.

- *Implication #2*:   Liquidity management is critical to survival of the donative non-profit. This is true for short-term solvency, liquidity, and financial flexibility as well as for long-term solvency, or what is sometimes termed "strategic liquidity."[33] This term refers to the ability to seize new strategic opportunities, expand into new services or markets, build infrastructure, or make other large-dollar invest-ments. It focuses on liquidity on a longer-term basis, recognizing the possibility of conceivable risks in the form of unexpected and potentially adverse operating conditions.

To recap, it makes sense for organizations that are constantly pressed for funds and are locked out of equity markets and greatly limited in the use of debt to investigate the behavioral implications of funding sources. Emphasis on funding sources is not new.[34] However, a new and logical implication is a greater value for liquidity, which up to this point has only been mentioned by Gronbjerg.

Summarizing our discussion, the advantages to the donative nonprofit of having a high degree of liquidity are the ability to fund disbursements, earn interest revenue, protect against adverse developments, manage funding risk, and seize unforeseen opportunities. That is not to say that more is always necessarily better. Too much liquidity is disad-vantageous to the organization because it absorbs funds that could be used in program delivery. Furthermore, donors may react negatively and give elsewhere. An organization is considered liquid "if it has enough financial resources to cover its financial obligations in a timely manner with minimal cost."[35] The implication? There is a desirable level of liquidity for each organization that balances benefits and costs. We propose the following as the primary financial objective for most nonprofits: "To ensure that financial resources are available when needed, as needed, and at reasonable cost, and are protected from financial impairment and spent according to mission and donor purposes." The first part of that objective implies that there is a target liquidity level that organizations should set and strive to achieve.

Before addressing your internal view of that liquidity target, it is important to know that outside parties are imposing a one-size-fits-all to externally assess the appropriate liquidity range. These "charity watchdog agencies" have spoken on the topic of liquidity management, so we survey and critique their views.

(d) WATCHDOG AGENCY STANDARDS ON SOLVENCY AND LIQUIDITY.   Among the three major charity watchdog agencies, only the Council of Better Business Bureaus does not prescribe a maximum liquidity level. In the standards set by the BBB Wise Giving Alliance, a maximum liquidity (actually solvency) standard is applied, and the American Institute of Philanthropy (AIP) prescribes a maximum liquidity (again solvency) standard that is similar to the BBB standard.

(i) BBB Wise Giving Alliance Standard.   In its Standard 10, the BBB Wise Giving Alliance states:

> Avoid accumulating funds that could be used for current program activities. To meet this standard, the charity's unrestricted net assets available for use should not be more than three times the size of the past year's expenses or three times the size of the current year's budget, whichever is higher.[36]

It is interesting to note that this standard has been revised upward: The BBB standard upon which this standard is based formerly limited organizations to two years or less of liquid funds. Now Standard 10 states that net assets available for use in the following fiscal year are not usually to be more than three times the current year's expenses or three times the next year's budget, whichever is higher. To arrive at available assets, BBB makes this calculation: Available assets = (unrestricted assets + temporarily restricted assets + deferred revenue − liabilities).

(ii) American Institute on Philanthropy Standard. The AIP is very unforgiving of organizations that have more than three years of budgeted expenses on hand. It downgrades organizations to increasingly severe degrees the farther over three years those available assets are (see Exhibit 2.3). Organizations which have been downgraded are shown in Exhibit 2.4.

(iii) Charity Navigator Standard. Of all of the charity watchdog agencies, Charity Navigator has done the most work in evaluating the liquidity needs of various types of nonprofit organizations.

The most important deficiency in Charity Navigator's framework is its inclusion of long-term investments in its working capital ratio. Charity Navigator recognizes this shortcoming but points out that IRS Form 990 does not allow one to distinguish between short-term and long-term investments. Its comment, regarding this is, that it uses this all-inclusive measure consistently and thus treats all organizations fairly is an overstatement: Consistency when one has an impaired measure of what one is trying to measure (short-term investments) does not guarantee fairness. An organization with all of its investments in 3-month Treasury bills is certainly more liquid than one with all of its investments in 30-year Treasury bonds, but this fact is hidden by the equal treatment in the ratio.

In Charity Navigator's defense, we argue that organizations *should* be able to self-fund capital investments, and at times this includes investing in some longer-term investments—particularly when one begins the funding 5 or 10 or more years in advance of a major capital investment. This fact suggests that the exact breakdown of short-term (one year or less in maturity) and long-term (more than one year in maturity) is not as important as it might at first appear. Second, to its credit, Charity Navigator does not penalize an organization with very large amounts of cash and investments, choosing

---

Charities with Large Asset Reserves

AIP strongly believes that your dollars are most urgently needed by charities that do not have large reserves of available assets. AIP therefore *reduces* the grade of any group that has available assets equal to three to five years of operating expenses. In AIP's view, a reserve of less than three years is reasonable and does not affect a group's grade.

These reductions in grades are based *solely* on the charities' asset reserves as compared to budget. If you agree with these charities that reserves greater than three years' budget are necessary to enhance their long-term stability, you may wish to disregard the lower grades that AIP assigns on the basis of high assets.

AIP's definition of "years of available assets" includes funds currently available for the charity's use, including investments that the charity has set aside as a reserve but could choose to spend if it wanted to do so.

Source: http://www.charitywatch.org/.

EXHIBIT 2.3 AMERICAN INSTITUTE OF PHILANTHROPY STATEMENT ON CASH AND INVESTMENTS

	Grades Reduced for Charities with Large Asset Reserves	🎁	✋$	⧗	🏛 in 000's	🎖	⬇
1.	Army Emergency Relief	93	3	17.6	307,288	A+	F
2.	Research to Prevent Blindness	89–90	7–15	13.8	233,405	A	F
3.	Shriners Hospitals for Children	94	1	12.7	8,620,682	A+	F
4.	Air Force Aid Society	93	3	10.1	172,209	A+	F
5.	YWCA of the USA-N.O.	66	25	8.9	63,006	B-	F
6.	Guide Dogs for the Blind	79–80	8–10	8.8	253,342	A-	F
7.	Cal Farley's Boys Ranch and Affiliates	74	30	8.7	429,738	B	F
8.	Diabetes Trust Foundation	82–83	9–10	8.4	5,259	A	F
9.	Seeing Eye	82	10	8.4	208,700	A	F
10.	Hole in the Wall Gang Fund	86	8	6.8	50,375	A	F
11.	Give Kids the World	80	7	6.3	78,659	A-	F
12.	Southern Poverty Law Center	51–67	20–34	6.2	152,866	C-	F
13.	Amer Action Fund for Blind Children and Adults	59–77	18–33	5.5	19,563	C	F
14.	Girls and Boys Town/Fr. Flanagan's	86–88	29–36	4.9	916,494	B	D
15.	Brookings Institution	78	6	4.8	248,204	A-	C-
16.	Navy-Marine Corps Relief Society	94	2	4.8	158,722	A+	C
17.	Omaha Home For Boys	74	48	4.8	101,873	C+	D
18.	Ploughshares Fund	87	10	4.7	26,033	A	C
19.	Fresh Air Fund	75	23	4.4	104,514	B+	C-
20.	ACLU Foundation	81	8	4.3	175,910	A	C
21.	Accuracy in Media	85	11	4.2	5,922	A	C+
22.	Hadassah	83	9	3.8	579,425	A	C+
23.	Japan Society	71	19	3.8	90,183	B	C
24.	Boy Scouts of America - National Council	90	6	3.7	597,503	A+	B-
25.	Human Rights Watch	75	15	3.5	88,593	A-	C+
26.	Rosebud Educational Society (Little Sioux)	61–68	33–42	3.5	16,941	C	C-
27.	Asian Relief/World Villages for Children	44–54	27–35	3.4	33,555	D	D
28.	Carter Center	70	14	3.4	286,497	B+	C+
29.	American Printing House for the Blind	77	19	3.0	83,350	A-	B-
30.	Resources for the Future	81	16	3.0	30,066	A-	B-

Left margin: August 2006 — American Institute of Philanthropy — AIP

Source: American Institute of Philanthropy (AIP).

EXHIBIT 2.4   ORGANIZATIONS DOWNGRADED BY AIP DUE TO "EXCESS SOLVENCY"

instead to cap its score on the working capital ratio at a value of 10 no matter how high the organization's working capital ratio (see Appendix 7B.2).

(iv) Philanthropic Research, Inc. Standard.   Although technically not a watchdog agency, Philanthropic Research, Inc. (PRI) publishes financial data useful to and possibly used by the same audiences as those targeted by BBB, AIP, and Charity

- **Savings Ratio**

  (Total Revenue − Total Expenses) ÷ Total Expenses

The savings ratio reveals the rate of the nonprofit's savings by measuring the relationship between total annual savings and total expenses. Although the savings ratio is an important component of longevity, high ratios may indicate excessive savings.

  The savings ratio should be considered in combination with the liquid funds indicator. If the nonprofit has low liquid funds, a higher savings ratio may be desirable.

- **Liquid Funds Indicator**

  ([Fund Balances − Permanently Restricted − Land, Buildings, and Equipment]

  × 12) ÷ Total Expenses

The liquid funds indicator measures an organization's operating liquidity by dividing fund balances (other than an effectively frozen endowment and the land, building, and equipment fund) by an average month's expenses. These are the financial resources a nonprofit may legally and reasonably draw down. A high liquid funds indicator could point to low cash-funding urgency and excessive savings.

Chuck McLean and Suzanne E. Coffman, June 2004
© 2004, Philanthropic Research, Inc. (GuideStar)

Source: Guide Star, www.guidestar.org.

EXHIBIT 2.5 PRI's (GUIDESTAR) FINANCIAL RATIOS AND INTERPRETATIONS

Navigator. Philanthropic Research, Inc. publishes its findings on its outstanding Web site (www.guidestar.org). Two ratios provide liquidity-related information:

1. The savings ratio, which is essentially a profit margin (except instead of total revenues, total expenses is in the denominator)

2. The liquid funds indicator, which is a solvency ratio

Consult Exhibit 2.5 for these two ratios and the interpretations PRI places on them. Notice again the negative spin put on high liquidity (savings ratio) and solvency (liquid funds indicator) in the conclusions drawn for each ratio. Positively, PRI does note that organizations with higher savings ratios enhance their survival chances and that if they have a lower Liquid Funds Indicator ratio, a higher savings ratio should be acceptable.

(e) ASSESSMENT OF WATCHDOG STANDARDS. Ideally, the information provided by these charity watchdog agencies and PRI can reduce the unobservability dilemma: Donors cannot observe the effectiveness or efficiency with which their funds are managed. More and better publicly available information affects public image. By doing so, it increases the likelihood that potential effects on an organization's public image and reputation may align the decisions and behavior of the nonprofit's managers with donors' and society's best interests. This is especially important in cases in which boards are ineffective because they are weak, disinterested, or uninvolved. Boards can potentially provide an information mechanism to deal with mismanagement. For example, a greater proportion of outside directors and possibly a greater proportion of directors having business experience might thwart opportunistic, self-seeking behavior on the part of managers.

Regardless of possible usefulness, the standards of BBB and AIP, in particular, are open to criticism on five grounds:

1. All four sets of standards focus on solvency, leaving out the more valuable insights from liquidity or financial flexibility (which includes strategic liquidity) perspectives. Put differently, the agencies are using the weakest measures available for what they are trying to measure. In their defense, it is difficult for these agencies to get the necessary information to make their assessments.

2. Apparently the BBB and AIP agencies believe that the agents (managers) are too risk-averse—and are more risk-averse than typical donors. Why not hold liquid reserves in the form of cash and marketable securities instead of used or unused borrowing capacity? We view this as an unjustified value judgment on the part of the watchdog agencies. Possibly the value judgment has not been recognized due to the solvency focus taken.

3. When donors restrict long-term investments (an endowment fund) instead of the board (quasi-endowment), the result is a lower number for "net available assets," which reduces the probability that the organization will be flagged by BBB or AIP for excess liquidity. However, from a strategic liquidity perspective, it is preferable to have these funds in a board-designated endowment. For some interesting thinking on this, see Ashworth.[37]

4. The most serious indictment is that the BBB and AIP standards are focusing nonprofit managers too much on excessive liquidity when most organizations are grappling with insufficient liquidity. The BBB standard 6d does deal with insufficient liquidity, but again uses the weakest (solvency) type of measure. Even if their organization is never rated by any of the charity watchdogs, most of the over 1.5 million nonprofits in the United States, their boards, donors, and local media may utilize these widely available standards to castigate the organization's managerial policies. This possibility alone may provide the wrong signals to financial managers and boards of these organizations.

5. The BBB and AIP organizations indicate that they make exceptions in applying their liquidity standard, but evidently only very rarely. One should look at *present-year* capital investments (which are not shown in the present year's budgeted expenses) as well as future capital investments in determining when to make exceptions in the application of standards. A similar argument is made by a consultant writing anonymously for the National Federation of Nonprofits, who stated that the operating plan should be consulted instead of mindlessly calculating financial ratios to assess the appropriate level of liquidity.[38]

2.6 WHAT IS THE APPROPRIATE LEVEL OF LIQUIDITY?

It is very helpful to have a bird's-eye view of the organization's liquidity, solvency, and financial flexibility. The actual and potential sources of cash flow are identified in Exhibit 2.6. Projections of anticipated cash position to six-month, one-year, three-year, or five-year horizons will provide strong indications of the adequacy of the organization's current liquidity situation. Two diagnostic tools to assist in this assessment will be presented shortly.

We advocate considering the role of environmental uncertainty in setting liquidity targets. As an aside, faith-based organizations, because of their trust in divine provision, may not be as concerned about outcome uncertainty relative to other donative nonprofit organizations, so they might select lower levels of liquidity. An organization receiving a high proportion of restricted gifts will want to establish higher liquidity targets. An

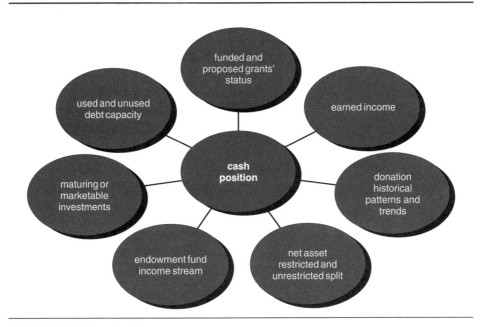

EXHIBIT 2.6 FINANCIAL MANAGER'S VIEW OF THE CASH FLOW AND REVENUE STREAM

organization that is also donative (highly donation-dependent) will have to ratchet the liquidity target even higher.

(a) ESTABLISHING THE LIQUIDITY POSITION BASED ON FINANCIAL VULNERABILITY.
What factors should help set the appropriate level of liquidity? Chang and Tuckman provide a short list in an analysis of financial vulnerability.[39] Their view of vulnerability centers on the ability of the organization to insulate itself from unanticipated financial shocks or financial unpredictability, and include:

- Organization's equity
- Level of administrative costs
- Operating margin
- Diversified revenue sources

Higher levels of each of these factors give the organization more flexibility to cope with financial shocks. The first item, equity, is somewhat misleading: Actually what should be measured here is equity balances in conjunction with liquid assets. If all of the organization's equity is tied up in fixed assets or endowment principal, the organization will be illiquid even if solvent. Added to this short list, one should ideally measure the variability and comovement of revenue sources (how closely they move in tandem through time), based on Bruce Kingma's findings.[40]

(b) DIAGNOSTIC TOOLS TO ASSIST IN SETTING THE APPROXIMATE LIQUIDITY TARGET.
Exhibit 2.7 provides a more exhaustive list of factors helpful in setting your organization's target liquidity, using a diagnostic questionnaire we developed. In the exhibit,

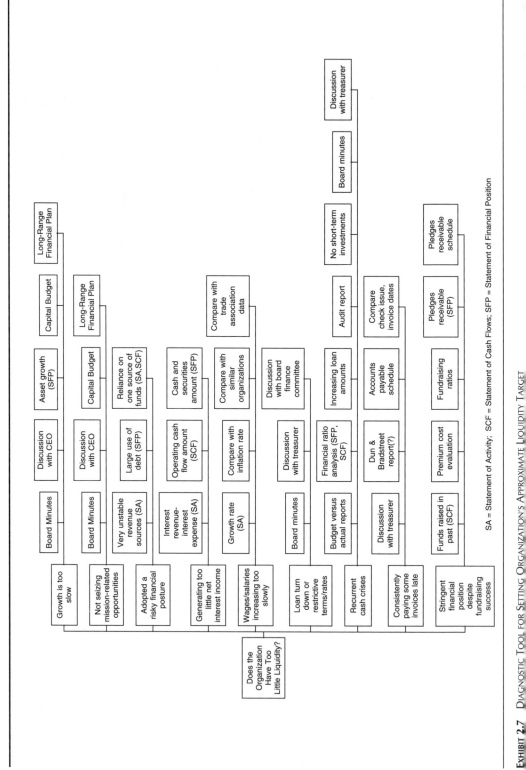

Exhibit 2.7 Diagnostic Tool for Setting Organization's Approximate Liquidity Target

SA = Statement of Activity; SCF = Statement of Cash Flows; SFP = Statement of Financial Position

SA denotes the organization's Statement of Activity, SFP denotes the Statement of Financial Position (or Balance Sheet or Statement of Net Assets), and SCF denotes the Statement of Cash Flows.

2.7 CONCLUSION

Liquidity policy and practice, so vital for an organization's financial management, has received far too little attention in nonprofit periodicals and textbooks, with the exception of two recent cash flow guides by Dropkin/Hayden and Linzer/Linzer. And where the management of cash and short-term investments is discussed, the problem of excess liquidity is not addressed. In this chapter we have provided our insights regarding the financial standards developed by watchdog agencies. We showed that these standards do not recognize the relative liquidity of an organization's asset holdings, use an inferior balance sheet or solvency approach, and are more appropriate for commercial nonprofits than donative nonprofits. We provide compelling reasons why your organization should build up large amounts of solvency, liquidity, and financial flexibility. We provide a checklist to determine if your organization has too much or too little liquidity. Our view of proficient nonprofit financial management suggests that the primary financial objective appropriate for most nonprofits is: "To ensure that financial resources are available when needed, as needed, and at reasonable cost, and are protected from financial impairment and spent according to mission and donor purposes." The first part of that objective implies that there is a target liquidity level that organizations should set and strive to achieve.

Many organizations have too little liquidity. Many nonprofits are either setting their liquidity targets too low or not reaching their liquidity targets. We do not share the view of some critics that nonprofits are too risk averse. To other observers who would argue that cash reserves should be minimized in order to maximize current service provision, we respond with this observation made by Carl Milofsky: There may be management practices that appear objectionable to some—"pointless, cumbersome, and inefficient"—but that "actually serve to protect important styles of practice that run against the grain of traditional management practice."[41]

Notes

1. One of the first places this mission diversion was noted was in Katherine Gallagher and Charles B. Weinberg, "Coping With Success: New Challenges for Nonprofit Marketing," *Sloan Management Review* 33(Fall 1991): 27–42.
2. Steven Rathgeb Smith "Managing the Challenges of Government Contracts" pp 325–341 in Robert Herman & Assoc, (eds) *Jossey Bass Handbook of Nonprofit Leadership and Management* (San Francisco: Jossey Bass Publishers, 1994): 329–330.
3. Id.
4. Jarl Kallberg and Kenneth Parkinson, *Corporate Liquidity: Management and Measurement* (Homewood, IL: Richard D. Irwin, 1993).
5. Terry S. Maness and John T. Zietlow, *Short-Term Financial Management* (Cincinnati: Thomson/South-Western, 2005), p. 31.
6. Richard F. Wacht, "A Financial Management Theory of the Nonprofit Organization," *Journal of Financial Research* 7 (Spring 1984): 37–45; R. F. Wacht, *Financial Management in Nonprofit Organizations* (Atlanta: Georgia State University Press, 1984); Kirsten A. Grønbjerg, "How Nonprofit Organizations Manage Their Funding Sources," *Nonprofit Management & Leadership* 2, no. 2 (1991): 159–175.

7.   Murray Dropkin and Allyson Hayden, *The Cash Flow Management Book for Nonprofits: A Step-by-Step Guide for Managers, Consultants, and Boards* ((San Francisco: Jossey-Bass, 2002); also consult Richard Linzer and Anna Linzer, *The Cash Flow Solution: A Nonprofit Board Member's Guide to Financial Success* (San Francisco: Jossey-Bass, 2007).

8.   Henrietta Hall, "When Cash Doesn't Flow," *Chronicle of Philanthropy,* June 1, 1995: 31–33.

9.   Aaron L. Phillips, "Treasury Management: Job Responsibilities, Curricular Development, and Research Opportunities," *Financial Management* 26, no. 3 (1997): 69.

10.   Philanthropic Research, Inc., *Guidestar Directory of American Charities 1996 Index* (Williamsburg, VA: Author, 1996).

11.   Kallberg and Parkinson, *Corporate Liquidity.*

12.   National Center for Charitable Statistics, cited in Independent Sector, "Facts and Figures about Charitable Organizations," May 9, 2006. Downloaded from www.independentsector. org/programs/research/Charitable_Fact_Sheet.pdf. Accessed: 7/17/06.

13.   Wacht, 1984.

14.   David Hahn and Raj Aggarwal, "More Emphasis Should Be on Working Capital Management," *Hospital Financial Management* (December 1977): 13–14, 16, 18, 79–80.

15.   Jeff Marsee, *Cash Management for Colleges & Universities* (Washington, D.C.: NACUBO, 1986).

16.   David R. Campbell, James M. Johnson, and Leonard M. Savoie, "Cash Flow, Liquidity & Financial Flexibility," *Financial Executive* 52, no. 8 (1984): 14–17.

17.   Regina E. Herzlinger and Denise Nitterhouse, *Financial Accounting and Managerial Control for Nonprofit Organizations* (Cincinnati: South-Western Publishing Co., 1994).

18.   Chris Robinson, "Financial Ratios of Christian Organizations," Master's thesis, University of San Francisco, 1989.

19.   Dan Busby, personal correspondence, 2/21/06. This data is based on 1,202 member organizations. Average total income, or revenue, equaled $11,957,408. Average cash reserves equaled $1,332,196. Taking each organization's cash reserves and dividing that by the organization's total income gives the 21.00% average cash-to-revenue ratio. Many of these organizations achieve break-even or very close to break-even operating results each year, so the assumption we make that expenses equate to revenues is probably fairly accurate.

20.   George Gallinger and P. Basil Healey, *Liquidity Analysis and Management* (Reading, MA: Addison-Wesley, 1987), p. 3.

21.   Kallberg and Parkinson, *Corporate Liquidity,* pp. 17–19.

22.   Mary F. Foster, Howard Becker, and Richard J. Terrano, *1998 Miller GAAP for Not-For-Profit Organizations* (San Diego: Harcourt Brace Professional Publishing, 1998), p. 43.

23.   Hall, "When Cash Doesn't Flow."

24.   If the fundraising function is considered as a financial function, this statement would have to be altered to say that the single most important financial management function is liquidity management. Development offices are separate from the finance department in almost all nonprofits of which we are aware.

25.   This was noted by Kirsten Grønbjerg in her studies of human service organizations: "How Nonprofit Organizations Manage Their Funding Sources."

26.   Bruce R Kingma, "Portfolio Theory and Nonprofit Financial Stability," *Nonprofit and Voluntary Sector Quarterly* 22, no. 2 (1993): 105–119.

27.   Priscilla La Barbera, "Enterprise in Religious-Based Organizations," *Nonprofit and Voluntary Sector Quarterly* 21, no.1 (1992): 51–67. Karen A. Froelich and Terry W. Knoepfle, "Internal Revenue Service 990 Data: Fact or Fiction?" *Nonprofit and Voluntary Sector Quarterly* 25, no. 1 (1996): 40–52.

28.   Vincent A. Fullmer, "Cost/Benefit Analysis in Fund Raising," *Harvard Business Review* 51, no. 2 (1973): 103–110. J. T. Zietlow, "Organizational and Financial Goals and Policies in Religious Organizations," Paper presented at the annual conference of the Association for Research on Nonprofit Organizations and Voluntary Action (ARNOVA), December 4–6, 1997, Indianapolis.

29.   John T. Zietlow, "Capital and Operating Budgeting Practices in Pure Nonprofit Organizations," *Financial Accountability & Management* 5, no. 4 (1989): 219–232. Zietlow, "Organizational and Financial Goals and Policies in Religious Organizations."

30. Cyril F. Chang and Howard P. Tuckman, "Why Do Nonprofit Managers Accumulate Surpluses, and How Much Do They Accumulate?" *Nonprofit Management & Leadership* 1, no. 2 (1990): 117–135.

31. Thomas A. McLaughlin, "In Cash There Is Opportunity," *NonProfit Times* vol. 9 (March 1995): 35.

32. Howard P. Tuckman and Cyril F. Chang, "How Well Is Debt Managed by Nonprofits?" *Nonprofit Management & Leadership* 3, no. 4 (1993): 347–361.

33. Wacht, "A Financial Management Theory of the Nonprofit Organization," and Wacht, *Financial Management in Nonprofit Organizations.*

34. Kirsten A. Grønbjerg, "How Nonprofit Organizations Manage Their Funding Sources," *Nonprofit Management & Leadership* 2, no. 2 (1991): 159–175. S. Shapiro and D. Grunewald, "Improving Decision Making in Nonprofit Organizations," *Thought* 63 (March 1988): 52–68.

35. Maness and Zietlow, *Short-term Financial Management.*

36. Downloaded from www.give.org/standards/newcbbbstds.asp. Accessed: 11/5/05.

37. E. Ashworth, "Endowments: Preparing for a Financially Secure Future," *Federation Folio* (National Federation of Nonprofits) 1, no. 1 (1997): 4–7.

38. National Federation of Nonprofits, "Financial Reserves: How Much Is Enough? How Much Is Too Much?" *Federation Folio* 1, no. 1 (1997): 1–3.

39. Cyril F. Chang and Howard P. Tuckman, "A Methodology for Measuring the Financial Vulnerability of Charitable Nonprofit Organizations," *Nonprofit and Voluntary Sector Quarterly* 20 (1991): 445–460.

40. Bruce R. Kingma, "Portfolio Theory and Nonprofit Financial Stability," *Nonprofit and Voluntary Sector Quarterly* 22, no. 2 (1993): 105–119.

41. Carl Milofsky, "Tradition" (Editorial), *Nonprofit and Voluntary Sector Quarterly* 26, no. 3 (1997): 261–268.

MANAGING MISSION AND STRATEGY

Twenty years ago a nonprofit financial management guide would have scarcely mentioned strategy or strategic management. In their new roles as strategic business partners, however, financial managers and board finance committees are increasingly involved in strategy development, evaluation, and implementation. According to the 2003 Association for Financial Professionals survey of high-level corporate finance professionals:

> As treasury continues to perform many of its traditional functions, it has taken on additional responsibilities that are outside the traditional definition of treasury. These new activities play a greater strategic role for the company and can include... internal consulting, strategic financial planning and technology implementation/management. **Seventy-one percent of senior treasury professionals indicate that their Treasury department is playing a greater strategic role for their company than it did five years ago.** A slightly greater percentage of survey respondents (77 percent) expect their company's Treasury department to increase its strategic role in the coming five years....[1]

Senior-level treasury professionals believe that their treasury staff needs to be better prepared for the role that they will take on in the future. Just 31 percent of survey respondents "strongly" agree that today's treasury professionals are prepared for their future role in their company. Sixty-two percent of survey respondents only "somewhat" agree to the statement that treasury professionals are prepared for their future role.

We see this same trend emerging in the nonprofit world. Rarely are the individuals filling financial roles in nonprofits well versed in strategy concepts and techniques. This chapter will help fill the knowledge gap.

The chapter first develops an understanding of mission, vision, and strategy. It then profiles a major shortcoming of management practices: failure to implement strategic decisions properly. Using information from some of the best available sources, the chapter next provides an overview of strategic planning. The last part of the chapter presents some of the performance management systems that may be used to diagnose current strategies and how well they are being executed by the organization. The balanced scorecard, which is being used by more organizations each year, is prominent within these performance management systems. However, several portfolio models are also available to use, and both types of models offer great promise to financial managers and boards wishing to make better strategic decisions and better meet the mission, vision, and goals of their organizations.

3.1 VALUE OF STRATEGIC PLANNING

Before delving into the specifics of strategic planning, let us consider some motives for engaging in planning. The process of strategic planning and evaluation is as important, or more important, than the plan itself. Expect your organization to glean these benefits from the planning process. Successful strategic planning:

- Leads to action
- Builds a shared vision that is values-based
- Is an inclusive, participatory process in which board and staff take on a shared ownership
- Accepts accountability to the community
- Is externally focused and sensitive to the organization's environment
- Is based on quality data
- Requires an openness to questioning the status quo
- Is a key part of effective management[2]

Regrettably, while almost all nonprofits say that they are involved in strategic planning when asked, too often the planning that is practiced is mired in the budgeting process. This is not strategic thinking; it is merely bean counting. To plan successfully, an organization must have a strategic thinker at its helm and an environment that infuses strategic thinking into all of its endeavors. Regardless of line and staff relations, everyone from the executive director down must adopt a planning philosophy. Planning is not merely an extension of the budgeting process; good planning identifies the key issues to which the appropriate numbers can later be attached.

3.2 WHAT IS STRATEGIC PLANNING?

Strategic planning is "the process of deciding on the goals of the organization and on the broad strategies that are to be used in attaining these goals,"[3] involving "a disciplined effort to produce fundamental decisions and actions that shape and guide what an organization (or other entity) is, what it does, and why it does it."[4] Strategic planning involves deciding how to combine and employ resources. It is not a one-time exercise but rather an ongoing process. The numerous of objectives and customers in the strategic decision-making environment of a nonprofit often disorient business professionals who join nonprofit boards.

Why do nonprofit organizations present unique managerial problems? Six complex factors affect decision making in nonprofit organizations:

1. Intangibility of services

2. Weak customer influence

3. Strong professional rather than organizational commitment by employees

4. Management intrusion by resource contributors

5. Restraints on the use of rewards and punishments

6. The influence of a charismatic leader and/or organizational mystique on choices[5]

Nonprofit decision-making complexity certainly contributes to the primary cause of failure in at least one-half of strategic decisions: poor decision-making processes.[6] Together these six influences weaken decision making and augur inefficiency and ineffectiveness for the nonprofit. Financial managers and finance-oriented board members may improve decision making by ensuring that, at a minimum, financial aspects of decisions are included and properly appraised. Less obvious is the tendency for some nonprofits to lose their program focus and overemphasize revenue generation: The joint effect of (1) constantly needing to seek resources, (2) not having a profit motive, and (3) not being able to accurately measure service quality is to make nonprofit organization managers concentrate more on fundraising than on the needs of service users.[7] It is a struggle that the typical organization with too little liquidity will constantly have to grapple with. That tendency is compounded when the vision and mission of the organization are unclear, unfocused, or forgotten.

3.3 WHAT ARE THE ORGANIZATION'S MISSION, VISION, AND GOALS/OBJECTIVES?

We will use these definitions of mission, vision, and goals/objectives:[8]

- *Mission* is purpose (why the organization exists, the end result the organization is striving to accomplish), the "business" the organization is in as it tries to achieve its purpose, and possibly a statement of guiding values or beliefs; this is captured in the "mission statement."

- *Vision* is a mental image of what successful attainment of the mission would look like or how the world would be different if and when the organization's mission is accomplished.

- *Goals/Objectives* are either (1) program goals/objectives—program-by-program statements of the organization's plan of action, telling what it intends to do over a several-year period; or (2) management goals/objectives—organization development plan of action for each function or area within the organization for which there is a strategic initiative being implemented.

Examples of an organization's mission, vision, and goals come from the American Medical Association:[9]

- *Core Purpose* To promote the science and art of medicine and the betterment of public health.

- *Mission* To ensure a strong, vibrant, and influential professional association with a culture of excellence in all that we do.

- *Vision* By 2008 be recognized by physicians as an essential part of their professional lives. Our organization will center around four basic themes.

1. AMA is seen as the unifying leader and voice of American medicine;

2. An organization that physicians value, support, and join;

3. Focus the association around core areas of competence and value to members.

4. An AMA with a stable financial position and the resources to meet current and future needs.

Notice two things from the AMA's statements: First, it separates its purpose and mission statements, while many organizations combine those. Second, it includes as its fourth vision theme financial strength and resources. The primary financial objective we recommend, an approximate liquidity target, would meet this visionary theme perfectly.

Next, notice AMA's goals/objectives embodied in its statement of strategic direction, which it calls critical objectives:

- *Overall Strategic Direction. The overall strategic direction of the AMA as it looks ahead to 2005–2008 includes the following key areas where impact is critical:*

   o Creating a vision-centric and membership-oriented workforce and culture

   o Achieving substantial and visible advocacy success in exerting AMA influence on key issues affecting patient care and physicians, and effectively communicating those achievements to members, potential members, the public, and other key audiences

   o Stabilizing and improving AMA membership through successful advocacy and communications as well as enhanced product and service offerings that deliver value

   o Pursuing increased non-dues revenue through AMA's business operations by enhancing and diversifying the product line and using sound business practices

   o Implementing governance and operational efficiencies that optimize the use of AMA resources

Here again, it is interesting to note that the first, fourth and fifth goals are really management goals/objectives (functional, departmental, or internal group/area) goals, while the second and third goals are the program goals/objectives. The AMA is to be commended; a common deficiency in business and nonprofit goal/objective sets is focus on program goals/objectives to the exclusion of management ("functional") goals/objectives.

Peter Drucker indicates that there are three "musts" to the development of a successful mission; consider whether your organization has incorporated these items into its mission development:

- Study your organization's *strengths* and its *past performance*. The idea is to do better those things you already do well—if it's the right thing to do. The belief that your organization can do *everything* is just plain wrong. When you violate your organization's values, you are likely to do a poor job.

* Look outside at the *opportunities* and *needs*. With the limited resources you have (including people, money, and competence), where can you really make a difference? Once you know, create a high level of performance in that arena.

* Determine what your organization *really believes in*. Drucker notes that he has never seen anything being done well unless people were committed. One reason why the Edsel failed was that nobody at Ford believed in it.[10]

We will cover some specifics of strengths-weaknesses-opportunities-threats (SWOT) analysis later in the chapter. In implementing your organization's mission, you should ask several questions when viewing possible activities and programs to get involved with. Determine what the opportunities and needs are. Then ask if they fit your organization. Are you likely to do a good job at meeting them? Is there organizational competence in these areas? Do the opportunities and needs match the organization's strengths? Do the board, the staff, and the volunteer contingent really believe in this?

(a) STRATEGY AND THE "BOTTOM LINE."   Nonprofit organizations have no "bottom line." They seem to consider everything they do to be righteous and to serve a cause, so they are not willing to insist that if a program does not produce results, then perhaps resources should be redirected. Nonprofits need the discipline of organized abandonment and the critical choices that involves. Organized abandonment involves a carefully planned reevaluation of programs and activities, with a pruning process applied to certain of those programs in order to free up resources for reapplication. Later in the chapter we provide a tool to guide these organized abandonment decisions.

In addition to overall strategic direction, functional, area-specific strategies are necessary. In his studies of nonprofit organizations, Drucker noted a critical missing ingredient: the lack of a fund development strategy. He notes that the source of money is probably the greatest single difference between the nonprofit sector and business and government. The nonprofit institution has to raise money from donors. It raises its money—at least, a large portion of it—from people who want to participate in the cause but who are not beneficiaries or clients. Money is scarce in nonprofits. In fact, many nonprofit managers seem to believe that their difficulties would be solved if only they had more money. Drucker mentions that some of them come close to believing that raising money is really their mission! As an example, he cites the presidents of private colleges and universities who are so totally preoccupied with raising money that they have neither the time nor the thought for leading their organizations. What happens then? In his words:

> But a nonprofit institution that becomes a prisoner of money-raising is in serious trouble and in a serious identity crisis. The purpose of a strategy for raising money is precisely to enable the nonprofit institution to carry out its mission without subordinating that mission to fund-raising. This is why nonprofit people have now changed the term they use from "fund-raising" to "fund development." Fund-raising is going around with a begging bowl, asking for money because the need is so great. Fund development is creating a constituency which supports the organization because it deserves it. It means developing what I call a membership that participates through giving.[11]

Innovative organizations, both businesses and nonprofits, generally look outside and inside for ideas about new opportunities. A primary example, cited by Drucker, is the megachurch. The pastoral church looks at changes in demographics, at all the young, professional, educated people who have been cut off from their roots and need a community, assistance, encouragement, and spiritual strength. The change seen outside is an opportunity for organizations that are observant. Look *within* the organization and identify the most important clue pointing the way to strategic venturing: Generally, it will be the unexpected success. Most organizations feel that they somehow deserve the unforeseen major successes and engage in self-congratulation. What they should be doing is seeing a call to greater outreach and action.

The Girl Scout Association found that the social phenomenon of "latchkey kids" became a tremendous opportunity, which spawned the Daisy Scouts. When doing anything new, do not leap directly from "idea stage" to "fully operational stage." Test the idea, possibly with a limited rollout (often called the pilot stage). A great idea can be labeled a failure when tiny and easily correctable flaws destroy the confidence of your clients, volunteers, or employees.

As a final note, Drucker has noted how persistence can breed improved performance and yet sometimes the best thing to do is cut your losses:

> When a strategy or an action doesn't seem to be working, the rule is, "If at first you don't succeed, try once more. Then do something else." The first time around, a new strategy very often doesn't work. Then one must sit down and ask what has been learned. "Maybe we pushed too hard when we had success. Or we thought we had won and slackened our efforts." Or maybe the service isn't quite right. Try to improve it, to change it and make another major effort. Maybe, though I am reluctant to encourage that, you should make a third effort. After that, go to work where the results are. There is only so much time and so many resources, and there is so much work to be done.[12]

(b) WHAT ARE STRATEGIC DECISIONS?   Examples of strategic decisions are:

- Deciding to offer a new product line or service
- Deciding to serve a new clientele
- Deciding to deliver services abroad for the first time

Whenever organizations significantly alter their activities, the strategic management process is at work.

Three factors distinguish strategic decisions:

1. Strategic decisions deal with concerns that are essential to the livelihood and survival of the entire organization and usually involve a major portion of the organization's resources.

2. Strategic decisions involve new initiatives or areas of concern and usually address issues that are unusual for the organization rather than issues that are easily handled with routine decision making.

3. Strategic decisions could have major implications for the way other, lower-level decisions in the organization are made.

Henry Mintzberg, one of the great management thinkers of our day, views strategy as a pattern in a stream of decisions. There are two ramifications for the organization:

1. Strategy is not one decision but must be viewed in the context of a number of decisions and the consistency among them.

2. The organization must be constantly aware of decision alternatives.

Think about strategy as the reasoning that guides the organization's choices among its alternatives.

Is an organization's strategy always the result of a planned, conscious effort toward goals that results in a pattern? *Not at all.* This is called *deliberate* strategy; *emergent* strategy emerges from the bottom levels of the organization as a result of its activities. Or it may result from the implementation process—in which changes in goals and "reorienting" may produce strategies that are quite different from what the organization originally intended. As a starting point in diagnosing an organization, study the decisions themselves and infer strategy from the strategic decisions.

3.4 STRATEGIC MANAGEMENT PROCESS

Strategic management refers to the entire scope of strategic decision making in an organization; as it can be defined as the "set of managerial decisions that relates the organization to its environment, guides internal activities, and determines the long-term performance of the organization."[13]

There are three steps in the strategic management process; thus far in this chapter, the first step has been our focus:[14]

Step 1. Strategy formulation. The set of decisions that determine the organization's mission and establishes its goals/objectives, strategies, and policies

Step 2. Strategy implementation. Decisions that are made to put a new strategy in place or to reinforce an existing strategy; includes motivating people, arranging the right structure and systems (see Chapter 4), establishing cross-functional teams, establishing policies, and maintaining the right organizational culture to make the strategy work

Step 3. Evaluation and control. Activities and decisions that keep the process on track; include following up on goal accomplishment and feeding back the results to decision makers.

In their studies of organizational development, Stahl and Grigsby have noted regularities that help us understand the progression of strategic management. The organization will likely have to go through the phases, with each one showing increasing effectiveness, shown in Exhibit 3.1.

- *Phase 1:* Basic Financial Planning: Meet Budget
  - Controlling operations
  - Setting annual budget
  - Focusing on the various functional areas (such as development) in the organization

- *Phase 2:* Forecast-Based Planning: Predict the Future
  - Improved planning for growth
  - Environmental analysis
  - Multiyear forecasts
  - Static resource allocation

- *Phase 3:* Externally Oriented Planning: Think Strategically
  - More responsive to markets and competition

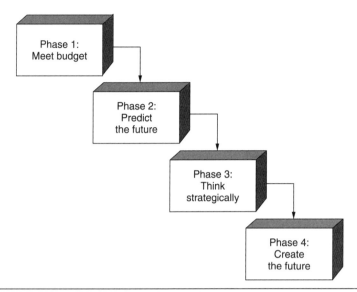

EXHIBIT 3.1 STRATEGIC MANAGEMENT PHASES

- Better analysis of situations and assessment of competition
- Evaluate strategic alternatives
- Dynamic resource allocation

- *Phase 4*: Strategic Management: Create the Future

  - Create competitive advantage using all resources as a group
  - Strategically select planning framework
  - Planning process is creative and flexible
  - Value system and culture support planning and plans

You may immediately apply this framework to your organization in two ways:

1. In which phase do you find your organization? Based on where your organization is, how will this help or hinder strategic decision making?

2. What step(s) might you take to help move your organization and its leadership to the next phase?

(a) SWOT ANALYSIS. When formulating your organization's strategic plan, the board and management team must analyze conditions inside the organization as well as conditions in the external environment. This analysis is now so conventional in strategic management that it is referred to as analysis of internal *strengths* and *weaknesses* and external *opportunities* and *threats* (or *challenges*)—in a word, *SWOT*. Exhibit 3.2 provides the worksheet that includes all components of SWOT analysis. You may wish to duplicate it and use it to diagnose your organization's present situation.

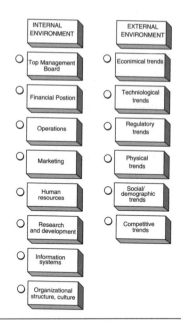

EXHIBIT 3.2   WORKSHEET FOR STRENGTH, WEAKNESS, OPPORTUNITY, AND THREAT (SWOT) ANALYSIS

(b) WHAT ARE INTERNAL STRENGTHS AND WEAKNESSES?   Issues that are within the organization and usually under your management's control are internal strengths and weaknesses. A *strength* is anything internal to the company that may lead to an advantage relative to your funding or service competitors and a benefit relative to your clients. A *weakness* is anything internal that may lead to a disadvantage relative to those competitors and clients. These internal items may have been inherited from past management teams.

A talented and experienced top management team is a great internal asset, especially when the organization is in a rapidly changing or very competitive environment. If your board brings a fresh and questioning perspective to strategic issues, instead of rubber-stamping management's ideas, as so many boards do, count your board as an internal strength.

Financial management is an area in which strength can advance most decisions management might implement. But a weak financial position (usually signaled by very low levels of liquidity and/or very high levels of debt) weakens the organization. For example, the Chrysler Corporation was in such bad shape financially in the early 1980s that even the high hopes of the new chairman, Lee Iacocca, would have led nowhere if the U.S. government had not provided loan guarantees. A weak financial position can prevent an organization from responding to even the most attractive, mission-enhancing external opportunities.[15] Weaknesses often give rise to functional (management) strategies.

(c) USING ENVIRONMENTAL SCANNING TO DETECT EXTERNAL OPPORTUNITIES AND THREATS.   External opportunities and threats (or challenges) are social, economic, technological, and political/regulatory trends and developments that have implications for your services, your clients, your donors, or other key parts of your organization.

Your organization should be continually engaging in *environmental scanning* to recognize these trends and developments and how they will affect revenues and expenses as well as risks. The terrorist attacks of September 11, 2001, meant a significant decline in donations for many organizations, as monies were donor-directed to the rescue effort and organizations like the American Red Cross. Hurricanes Katrina and Rita in 2005 had much the same effect, with the Salvation Army, World Vision, and the American Red Cross seeing revenues and expenses shift upward, while many organizations experienced donation declines. Organizations holding larger liquidity were very glad they had built up their liquidity positions above those levels of most organizations and above the commonly given advice of only three months of operating expenses. (Refer to Chapter 2 for reasons to hold larger cash reserves and operating reserves.)

(d) STRATEGIC MANAGEMENT IS AN ONGOING PROCESS. Strategic management is a process, not just a one-time product of some long meetings. Yesterday's ideal plan will sometimes become substandard due to some changed or just-discovered internal factor (a strength or weakness, possibly a technological innovation helping you in a key service area) or by a difference in the external environment (such as a new service provider moving into a key service arena). A good manager not only plans but also continually reassesses those plans while maintaining openness to opportunities. The manager then evaluates these opportunities evaluated against the manager's honest appraisal of the company's strengths and weaknesses, resulting in a well-founded decision on whether to pursue the opportunity or not, and, if so, in what time span. Do not even begin this procedure until you have asked yourself this basic question: What is our organization?

3.5 IMPLEMENTING THE STRATEGIC PLAN

(a) THREE STEPS IN IMPLEMENTATION. Many nonprofit organizations plan but very few excel when it comes to the implementation of those plans. Many times politics or board–chief executive dynamics, which may be disguised as "organizational realities," get in the way. Three vital ingredients increase the likelihood of working the plan:

1. Unqualified and vocal top management and board support
2. Communication
3. Teamwork

Both top management and the board must continue their overt support of the plan. Change is almost always resisted, so any plan that alters the status quo must be championed.

Communication of the plan and its related program initiatives is also essential. Most important, all volunteers, staff, donors, and regulatory authorities must remain confident that strategic initiatives are consistent with the mission and the organization's tax-exempt purpose. Also, service delivery and staff personnel must be aware of both continuing and new program directives. Gaining a sense of relative importance of the various program activities will enable people to concentrate their efforts on the key areas.

Teamwork is fostered by top management and board support as well as careful and consistent communication. Additionally, teamwork can be bolstered by setting up teams. Quality circles and use of employee suggestions for continuous service delivery improvement are illustrative of what can be done to harness teamwork.

(b) CUTBACK STRATEGIES. Many times, often as a result of having set an inadequate target liquidity level, organization revenues decline and/or expenses increase, and a cash crunch occurs. Or perhaps a major funding source stops supporting the organization permanently, triggering a cash crisis—an ongoing imbalance between revenues and expenses. Either event spurs the financial management team (chief executive officer, chief financial officer, and board) to initiate cutback strategies. Exhibit 3.3 profiles numerous strategies for coping with either a temporary cash crunch or more serious ongoing cash crisis. Notice that many of these are functional strategies—such as purchasing, facilities-related, or fundraising—rather than changes in product or service strategies.

Excerpted from: *Coping with Cutbacks: The Nonprofit Guide to Success When Times Are Tight*

Authors' notes:

We offer this checklist as a thinking tool and as a route to direct action. A more in-depth list is in the book. We hope that you can use this list to help you think creatively about your organization, its culture, its mission, its future, its response to immediate financial crises, and its long-term preparation for the changing culture.

Use these suggestions as a starting point for your own brainstorming, and use the categories to help you organize your thinking and analyze your current approach to fulfilling your mission. But don't get locked into any one strategy—cut them up, pull them out of a hat, mix and match them. Do whatever helps you spur new ideas that fit your specific situation.

Here's our caveat: Just because we've listed a strategy, don't think we endorse it. In fact, we dislike some, and some may conflict with your mission, values, or human resource policies.

FINANCIAL STRATEGIES A: CUT OR CONTROL COSTS

Analyze purchasing

1. Improve purchasing procedures
2. Seek in-kind contributions
3. Network to get better prices on supplies
4. Seek new competitive bids and new suppliers
5. Analyze purchases to see if they are necessary
6. Simplify paperwork and forms; use electronic files
7. Refurbish and reuse supplies

Adjust payables

1. Consolidate or restructure debt
2. Negotiate delayed or reduced payments
3. Barter for needed services

Evaluate facilities and infrastructure

1. Share space or maintenance costs
2. Delay maintenance
3. Save space by moving, reducing size, using home offices, or using split shifts
4. Negotiate a decreased rent with your landlord
5. Find a cheaper phone system; eliminate toll-free lines
6. Eliminate or consolidate newsletters and brochures
7. Eliminate vehicles or shift to less costly vehicles
8. Save energy

Exhibit 3.3   Cutback Strategies

Modify staffing and related costs

1. Reduce hours or work week
2. Cut, freeze, or delay wages
3. Lay off staff; offer voluntary separation; offer unpaid leave; remove poor performers
4. Freeze hiring
5. Share jobs, consolidate staff, increase workload
6. Use volunteers and graduate interns
7. Hire temporary staff or consultants
8. Remove management layers; don't funnel high performers into management merely to reward them
9. Reduce benefits, staff training, and staff development
10. Limit or eliminate travel
11. Cancel subscriptions; use the Internet and libraries
12. Cancel professional association memberships
13. Switch to a direct reimbursement status for unemployment compensation
14. Ask board not to submit expenses for reimbursement
15. Convert some paid staff to volunteers
16. Share staff with other organizations

Reduce services

1. Analyze your programs and services against your mission and financial goals
2. Reduce or eliminate non-core programs
3. Limit eligibility for programs; reduce the number of clients served
4. Reduce or eliminate core programs
5. Temporarily shut down some or all services
6. Plan to go out of business humanely

FINANCIAL STRATEGIES B: INCREASE REVENUES

Manage money differently

1. Speed the inflow of cash by invoicing promptly or offering incentives
2. Try to get grants in the door earlier than the promised date
3. Change management of cash reserves to improve unearned income
4. Sell assets
5. Spend down reserves
6. Borrow money
7. Diversify your sources of income

Increase fees

1. Analyze all the costs of providing a service
2. Change fee structure to result in increased income

Initiate or accelerate fundraising

1. Research the larger community and current donors to improve response
2. Hire development director or staff
3. Add special events, fund drives, charitable gambling
4. Increase board involvement in fundraising
5. Increase planned giving
6. Build an endowment
7. Find new donors and diversify funding base
8. Reach out to under-asked populations
9. Collaborate on fund drives; join a federated fund drive
10. Mobilize everyone in the search for new resources

EXHIBIT 3.3   CUTBACK STRATEGIES (*continued*)

11.   Link with a business or credit card company to receive a percentage of sales
12.   Seek in-kind contributions that can be converted to cash
13.   Increase the search for foundation and government grants

Expand or add services

1.   Boost enrollment in or expand offerings of successful services
2.   Sell staff expertise and time
3.   Add income-generating product or service that fulfills mission
4.   Rent office space or equipment to others
5.   Sell valuable information that others need
6.   Seek related niche markets
7.   Charge others for a service you also use (for example, maintenance)
8.   Develop a catalog of products used by your organization and other nonprofits
9.   Charge a fee to serve as the fiscal agent for other organizations

Increase productivity

1.   Provide incentives for productive staff
2.   Simplify production or service without loss of quality
3.   Invest in an educated staff; provide training as needed
4.   Research and implement "best practice" in all functions
5.   Upgrade staff while cutting back
6.   Invest in technology that improves productivity

STRUCTURAL STRATEGIES

Modify the mission

1.   Reexamine the mission and realign the organization accordingly
2.   Modify the mission to build clients' capacity to solve their own problems
3.   Change the mission to enable the organization to respond to rapidly changing conditions
4.   Move out of direct support services and into prevention services
5.   Be a pilot site for some foundation, academic, or government program

Modify the organization's structure

1.   Eliminate programs that are redundant with those of other organizations or combine them to improve services
2.   Position yourself higher in the "food chain" when intense competition accompanies a changing environment
3.   Respond to a changing environment by changing programs
4.   Spin off a struggling or "orphan" program to another organization where it has a better chance to thrive
5.   Merge with or acquire a competitor's or an ally's program
6.   Relocate with a group of related organizations to form a one-stop shop
7.   Become a for-profit; add a for-profit subsidiary; be acquired by a for-profit

Modify the organization's culture

1.   Enlist the support of potential funders as you modify your programs, and then request funds to support changes
2.   Share resources and expenses with other organizations that have similar needs
3.   Make your services more culturally sensitive
4.   Educate the board of directors to make them more effective
5.   Mobilize everyone in the organization to help market its mission, message, services, and needs
6.   Tear down bureaucracies that interfere with the creative flow of ideas

Exhibit 3.3   Cutback Strategies (*continued*)

7. Replicate rather than reinvent
8. Link with a complementary but different organization to bring resources into the organization
9. Take a more entrepreneurial approach to accomplishing your mission

ENGAGEMENT STRATEGIES

Engage other nonprofits

1. Work with state and national nonprofit associations
2. Form associations to negotiate with contracting agencies as a block
3. Establish cooperative programs with other nonprofits to increase the number of stakeholders in each other's organization
4. Collaborate with like-minded nonprofits; seek funding to support collaboration
5. Develop a bartering resource system among nonprofits
6. Create a nonprofit organization to insure nonprofits; return surplus income to policyholders
7. Pool funds with other nonprofits to get a better return on the investment of capital
8. Acquire or merge with another nonprofit whose services complement yours
9. Establish national goals and standards for nonprofits to increase sector quality, public awareness, and public support
10. Form a consortium with other nonprofits to take advantage of federal block grants
11. Facilitate networks and collaboration by making your space available for such activities
12. Find ways to work with local providers of educational services at all levels

Engage the community

1. Seek funding to help those constituents least able to represent themselves have a voice
2. Involve all members of the community in teaching children the value of community involvement and philanthropy
3. Connect with local media to inform the community about issues related to your mission
4. Show the community that your crisis is a community crisis
5. Hold community issues forums; discuss community goals

Engage the business community

1. Form partnerships with businesses; find a host that will provide space, staff, funds, resources, or technical assistance
2. Advocate for your organization's values and goals while seeking business involvement
3. Know the people, values, and goals of the businesses you are engaging
4. Share your vision of the future with businesses so they can see how they and their community will benefit
5. Link with businesses that will benefit from the positive public relations your organization's cause will generate
6. Network with small and midsize businesses with a personal stake in the local community
7. Show businesses how to get involved in community issues that affect them
8. Collaborate with businesses and other nonprofits to create "incubators" for new, innovative organizations
9. Form nonprofit/for-profit partnerships to advocate for common interests

EXHIBIT 3.3 CUTBACK STRATEGIES (*continued*)

Engage the public/government sector

1. Advocate for tax incentives that encourage businesses to be involved in community efforts
2. Use the public schools to teach philanthropy; set up student-operated philanthropies at schools and universities
3. Seek ways to work with educational institutions at all grade levels, public and private, nonprofit and for-profit
4. Advocate for a nonprofit contribution checkoff on tax forms
5. Advocate for making charitable giving a tax credit rather than a deduction
6. Use publicly owned facilities as a site for delivering nonprofit community services

---

Reprinted from *Coping with Cutbacks: The Nonprofit Guide to Success When Times are Tight*, pages 73–75 by Emil Angelica and Vincent Hymam copyright 1997 Fieldstone Alliance. Used with permission. For more information on Fieldstone Alliance publications or to order this book, visit www.fieldstonealliance.org. *Source:* http://www.fieldstonealliance.org/.

EXHIBIT 3.3   CUTBACK STRATEGIES (*continued*)

Next we examine the areas in which financial managers and financially oriented board members may contribute to strategic decision making and implementation.

3.6 PERFORMANCE MANAGEMENT SYSTEMS

Managers need techniques to enable them to diagnose the fit and appropriateness of programs and service offerings. Organizational inertia in many nonprofits, particularly educational institutions and hospitals, means that programs take on a life of their own, which necessitates a disciplined method for diagnostic evaluation. As Peter Drucker notes:

> All organizations need a discipline that makes them face up to reality.... All organizations need to know that virtually no program or activity will perform effectively for a long time without modification and redesign. Eventually every activity becomes obsolete.... Hospitals and universities are only a little better than government in getting rid of yesterday.... All organizations must be capable of change. We need concepts and measurements that give to other kinds of organizations what the market test and profitability yardstick give to business. Those tests and yardsticks will be quite different.[16]

Action point: Make sure your nonprofit organization has rigorous tests and yardsticks to measure performance.

We first provide several performance tests and yardsticks, especially financial ones, in our presentation of the balanced scorecard. We then introduce measurement tools to assist in your evaluation of service and program offerings. These tools go under various names: portfolio model, matrix, or grid. *The financial manager should have a central role in helping to apply and interpret a scorecard or diagnostic model and to integrate either into the organization's strategic decision making.*

(a) BALANCED SCORECARD.   Strategies need to be reassessed from time to time for one of four main reasons:

1. Even though the strategy was originally sound, insufficient resources were allocated to its implementation, so the goal/objective has not been achieved.
2. The problem being addressed by a strategy has changed, necessitating a revised strategy.

3. The policies and strategies being implemented by this and other organizations may be interacting in unanticipated ways, prompting a review and possible revision of strategies.

4. The political and cultural environment may change, causing a loss of stakeholder support and/or loss of leadership support and zeal in strategy implementation.[17]

Additionally, we cannot manage strategies by simply reviewing past financial results. We need a method that enables us to monitor and manage the financial and nonfinancial indicators that together will drive our future operating and financial results. In short, we need a performance management system—and the balanced scorecard fits the bill.

A performance management system or strategic management system consists of "ongoing organizational mechanisms or arrangements for strategically managing the implementation of agreed-upon strategies, assessing the performance of those strategies, and formulating new or revised strategies."[18] The balanced scorecard is the most popular performance management system in corporate, nonprofit, and public sectors.

(i) Balanced Scorecard. Businesses face the dilemma of how to manage to produce tomorrow's desired operating and financial results. Robert S. Kaplan and David P. Norton developed the balanced scorecard in response to this need. Kaplan revised the corporate balanced scorecard to meet the needs of nonprofit and public sector organizations that have only slightly different operating and financing objectives.

The essential principle behind the balanced scorecard system is this: *Only by maintaining organizational focus on four perspectives can the organization survive and thrive in the future.* These four perspectives, in turn, must have measures or metrics that are monitored and managed by decision-makers to ensure that the organization stays on course.

The four perspectives are: customer, internal business systems and processes, employee learning and growth, and financial. Each of these is tied to the others by the vision and strategy of the organization, and each addresses a different question:

1. *Customer.* "How can we create value for our donors and clients?"

2. *Internal Business Processes.* "To satisfy our donors and customers, which business processes must we excel at?"

3. *Innovation and Learning.* "How can we improve and change to better meet our mission?"

4. *Financial.* "How do we add value for our clients and donors while controlling costs?"[19]

We would rephrase the financial perspective as: "How do we accomplish revenue enhancement and cost control while achieving our target liquidity?" Any organization that does so clearly adds value for both clients and donors.

Exhibit 3.4 illustrates a nonprofit balanced scorecard with a human services organization. The scorecard shows the objectives that this organization attached to each of the four perspectives. Beyond this, and not shown in the exhibit, the management team should develop measures, targets, and initiatives for each of the four perspectives. Paul Niven, whose book serves as the standard source for nonprofit balanced scorecards, recommends no more than 8 to 10 objectives and no more than about 20 measures.[20]

(ii) Financial Objectives and Measures/Metrics Useful for a Balanced Scorecard. The financial team's primary area of balanced scorecard development is selection and communication of the financial objectives and measures, or metrics, to gauge progress

Vinfen's Balanced Scorecard

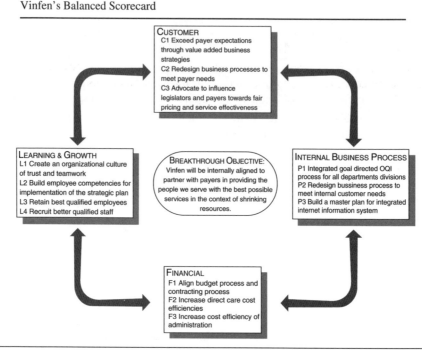

Source: "Vinfen Corporation's strategy map as part of the organization's Balanced scorecard. Vinfen is a leading human services nonprofit headquarted in Cambridge, Mass".

EXHIBIT 3.4   EXAMPLE OF HUMAN SERVICES ORGANIZATION BALANCED SCORECARD

in reaching those objectives. As Robert Anderson, balanced scorecard consultant and former chief financial/chief operating officer of Prison Fellowship Ministries, notes: "Properly communicated measurements that support the [strategic] plan become powerful tools to achieve dramatic results in bringing organizational alignment, motivation and greater customer satisfaction."[21] Before developing or revisiting your organization's financial objectives and measures, collect or construct records of your organization's cash flows, reserves, financial position statements, revenue-expense statements, and endowment. Then compile a brief history of budgets, income growth, key events (including capital campaigns and large one-time gifts), and liquidity levels.[22] These items will provide a backdrop for financial objective and measure development or refinement.

While some of the nonprofit scorecards or dashboards do include a liquidity target, many do not, and this is probably the single largest deficiency in scorecard implementation to date. In arts organizations, for example, the push by executive directors to achieve the artistic mission has caused some organizations to deplete almost all available liquid funds to finance short-term artistic thrusts, threatening the survival of their organizations.[23] Significantly, this problem is compounded by the fact that many nonprofits are very illiquid. Most nonprofit professional theaters, for example, have little endowment or cash reserves.[24] This lack of liquid resources puts added pressure on the CEO who is already facing funding concerns:

> ... the most fundamental problem facing many of the leaders of nonprofit organizations is the continuing effort needed to fund and sustain financial resources sufficient

to carry out the mission of the organization during a time of declining government support and intensifying competition for available funds.[25]

Financial objectives indicate what your organization must do well, related to finances and financial management, in order to implement your strategy. Financial measures or metrics are specific indicators that track or measure strategic success related to these financial objectives. We have already seen a social service agency's objectives; Exhibit 3.5 provides seven additional examples of scorecard financial objectives of nonprofits.

We include the first organization shown in Exhibit 3.5 to illustrate a public sector, not private nonprofit, agency. The slightly different management environment and objectives of public sector agencies possibly justifies the budget target as an objective.

Naval Undersea Warfare Center Newport	• Balanced budget. • Revenue sources. • Value.
Dallas Family Access Network	• Secure adequate funding to operate the organization.
United Way of Southeastern New England	• *External growth:* Increase net amount of funds raised. • *Internal stability:* Balance internal income and expenses to maintain our 100 percent guarantee to others. • *Community building:* increase amount of funds that go to services; Increase amount of funds that go to proprietary products.
Duke Children's Hospital	• Achieve continued improvement in net assets and liquidity to support new service development. • Effectively link clinical and financial data systems and decisions. • Effectively link staff compensation, performance, and service delivery. • Sufficient funding support for all programs/services
New Profit Inc. (a venture capital philanthropic fund)	• *Fund capitalization:* Secure $5 million in fund commitments from investors using pyramid strategy. • *Operating revenues:* Secure $500 thousand operating funds from foundations and friends for FY99 & FY00. • *Sustainability:* Manage cash flow to maintain an operating surplus with 3 months' cash on hand. • *Efficiency:* Maintain ratio of 1:4 staff $/*pro bono* $, optimize *pro bono* and volunteer resources.
Hood College	• Survive. • Succeed. • Prosper.
American Society of Mechanical Engineers (ASME)	• Grow revenue through new products and global growth. • Sunset lower-value programs. • Run a cost-effective operation.

EXHIBIT 3.5 NONPROFIT SCORECARD FINANCIAL OBJECTIVES

As far as specific measures/metrics go, here is the set of measures articulated by the fifth organization shown in Exhibit 3.5, New Profit Inc.:

1. Raise $4.5 million.
2. Maintain operating cash flow with 3-month surplus.

The second measure used by New Profit is clearly an approximate liquidity target (refer to Chapter 2 for more on this). Regardless of the ebb and flow of operating cash flows, the organization strives to achieve a liquidity level of three months of expenses. For many nonprofits, six months or more is ideal, depending on prefunding of maintenance expenses or new programs.

Hood College, the sixth organization portrayed in Exhibit 3.5, had these progressively aspirational measures to monitor achievement of its general objectives:

1. *Survive:* Budget excess (deficit) as a percent of total revenues.
2. *Succeed:* Percent increase in enrollment of students.
3. *Prosper:* Percent increase in the quality of students of students (as measured by a quality index).

While balanced scorecard codeveloper Kaplan asserts that financial perspective items are almost always constraints rather than objectives, we believe that the two most essential financial perspective objectives are funding the mission—however stated—and achieving target liquidity levels. We agree with Kaplan that balancing the budget and achieving a slight surplus are not true effectiveness measures. Anderson documents how a short-term budget focus tends to spawn incremental thinking by staff and tends to put a ceiling on growth hopes and a floor under cost reductions.[26] Finance staff and board finance committee members are uniquely positioned to champion adoption of a scorecard and the appropriate financial objectives and measures for it.

(b) PORTFOLIO APPROACHES.   Because of their multiple, often conflicting, objectives, nonprofits benefit greatly from diagnostic tools that help them map their programs or services in a rows-and-column format. It could be something as simple as the "BSC SWOT Analysis" grid, developed by Patricia Bush and her colleagues at the Balanced Scorecard Collaborative. Exhibit 3.6 shows the grid, as used by Niven in his consulting work. Niven argues that it highlights many potential issues and opportunities that may be translated into balanced scorecard objectives. Furthermore, by having to place each strength, weakness, opportunity, and threat into one of the four perspective boxes, the exercise provides real-time learning regarding the differences as well as overlap between

	Strengths	Weaknesses	Opportunities	Threats	Wild Card
Customer					
Internal					
Learning & Growth					
Financial					

Source: Adapted from Exhibit 8.7, BSC SWOT Analysis, in Paul R. Niven, *Balanced Scorecard Step-By-Step for Government and Nonprofit Agencies* (Hoboken, NJ: John Wiley & Sons, 2003): 173.

EXHIBIT 3.6   BALANCED SCORECARD SWOT ANALYSIS GRID

the perspectives on the scorecard. The fifth column, termed "wild card," is for any item that does not appear to fall neatly into one of the SWOT categories but is an important strategic issue.

(i) Generic Portfolio Modeling. Using some type of grid of rows and columns to visually compare an organization's various services is especially helpful for any organization that operates multiple programs or two or more earned income ventures or "businesses." In general terms, one can place programs or services into a grid that has contribution to the mission on the vertical axis and contribution to financial viability on the horizontal axis. An example of a basic type of product portfolio map is provided by Sharon Oster in her nonprofit strategic management textbook.[27]

(ii) Diagnosing the Services Portfolio. Chris Lovelock and Charles Weinberg were the first to take the concept of business product portfolios and modify them to make them useful for service strategy evaluation.[28] Their model is useful for commercially oriented nonprofits, such as hospitals and universities. Every service program can be placed in one of four categories:

1. Raise more funds or cut costs to support it.
2. Maintain the program or spin it off as a for-profit corporation.
3. Phase out the program in total.
4. Phase out parts of the program.

One factor is "profitability" or cost coverage. Revenues from general fundraising campaigns are not included here, as they help offset nonspecific overhead (fixed) costs. If a cost can be linked to a specific service program, even if it is a fixed cost, it is included in the cost for purposes of this analysis. The other indicator is the extent to which the service offering contributes to the advancement of the organization's mission.

To help classify products or services as to their degree of mission advancement, it is helpful to distinguish among three distinct types: core products, supplementary products, and resource-attraction products.

Core products or services are those that have been created to advance the organization's mission. Supplementary products are often added to either enhance the appeal of the core products or to facilitate their use. A restaurant in a children's museum illustrates this.

Resource-attraction products may be developed to foster the organization's ability to attract added funds, volunteers, and other donated resources. These products are started and developed to contribute to the organization's financial solvency or liquidity. Sometimes these are called social ventures or social enterprises, or comprise activities that go under the heading "social entrepreneurship." If an organization opens a food stand in a location other than one of its normal facilities, with the goal of making a significant amount of net revenue, this would be a resource-attraction "product."

If an organization is operating with persistent deficits, it would try to add a venture that would support the mission at the same time that it brings in adequate revenues so that costs are covered to a greater degree. Quite often, the dual achievement of these objectives is not so easily accomplished.

(iii) Financial Return and Financial Coverage Matrix. The Financial Return and Financial Coverage Matrix (FRFCM) is another portfolio approach. It is primarily useful for diagnosing the effects of new earned income ventures and their likely effect on the organization's liquidity target.[29] For any organization having or considering adding

social entrepreneurship ventures that may be mission-related and will add net revenue financially, this framework may prove helpful. As it involves financial calculations in support of capital allocation decision making, we cover it in Chapter 9, on capital project analysis. At this point, we simply note that other portfolio models share a common deficiency: None specifically incorporates the effect of programs or services on the organization's liquidity.

(iv) Three-Dimensional Portfolio Model. A recent modification and extension of the Lovelock and Weinberg services portfolio model is the Three-Dimensional Portfolio developed by Krug and Weinberg.[30] Shown in Exhibit 3.7, this is an elaborate and fascinating model of nonprofit program effectiveness. In addition to the mission and financial contributions of a program, the model assesses a third dimension of "merit"—how well our organization does at performing the program.

The first dimension, at the left of the diagram, is "Contribution to Mission"—or: Is the organization doing the right things? The second dimension, on the horizontal axis at the bottom of the diagram, is "Contribution to Money," or the degree to which a program covers all direct and indirect expenses associated with it. This is also termed "revenue/cost coverage." Finally, the third dimension, shown extending toward the back directionally, on the far right of the diagram, is "Contribution to Merit." This measures whether the program is high quality, with failing assigned a zero score, satisfactory a score of 5, and outstanding a score of 10. The size of the bubbles for the various programs reflects the amount of cost, or resources invested, in the program. The star that appears near the middle of the diagram is an overall composite measure encompassing all programs for this hypothetical museum.

The model's developers have interpreted it in their account of actual field experience.[31] Ideally, the more programs are toward the back, top, and right of the cube, the better off the organization (although it is very unlikely that a program would be in this location). In organizations observed by the model's developers, subjectivity among program staff and managers regarding likely revenues and costs was an issue, and the CFO had the authority

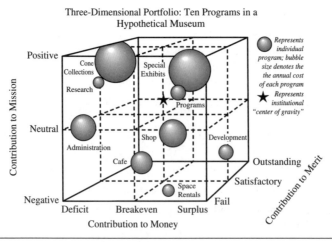

Three-Dimensional Portfolio: Ten Programs in a Hypothetical Museum

Source: "Mission, Money, and Merit", by Kerstikrug and Charles Weinberg, *Nonprofit Management & Leadership*, Spring 2004 pp. 325–342.

EXHIBIT 3.7 THREE-DIMENSIONAL PORTFOLIO

to overrule the estimates made by program staff of revenues and costs. The dialogue engendered by the application of this model to an actual museum proved valuable, as differing perceptions were brought to light.

(v) Organized Abandonment Grid® (Boschee). A final tool for enabling disciplined evaluation of ongoing programs is provided by social entrepreneurship pioneer Jerr Boschee. This Organized Abandonment Grid® is motivated by Peter Drucker's observation of inertia and the need to "sunset" obsolete programs. Exhibit 3.8 shows the grid.

For each product or service, the management team must ask two questions:

1. Regardless of who pays for it or whether anyone can pay for it, how many clients in the community truly need the product or service, and how critical is their need? A "critical need" is scored a 5, "significant need" is a 4, "some need" is a 3, "minimal need" is a 2, and "no need" is a 1.

2. What are the financial implications of offering this product or service? Will it result in losses, or can it be profitable?[32]

The grid does allow for some judgment call decisions regarding whether more resources should be allocated to the program, less resources, or none at all (eliminate the program). For those boxes labeled "probably," for example, these programs probably deserve more resources because they are high on either their social purpose or their financial impact scale. Boschee notes that more nonprofits are now looking to earned income ventures as a primary funding source for the overall organization.

3.7 STRATEGIC PLANNING PRACTICES: WHAT DOES THE EVIDENCE SHOW?

There have been several studies of actual strategic planning practices in the nonprofit sector. A brief survey of their key findings follows.

Melissa M. Stone, Barbara Bigelow, and William Crittenden synthesized the nonprofit strategic management literature from 1977 to 1998, focusing on any real-life findings (sometimes called empirically based research studies).[33] Here are their findings, beginning with the adoption and usage of formal strategic planning methods:

- Many nonprofits have not adopted formal strategic planning.
- Organizational size, board and management characteristics, prior agreement on organizational goals, and funder requirements regarding planning all correlate with whether the organization does formal strategic planning.
- Mission, structure, and board and management roles may change after formal planning occurs.
- The relationship between formal planning and organizational performance is not clear but is often associated with who takes part in the planning process (board, CEO, and possibly others) and with the occurrence of growth.

Regarding strategy content, the real-world findings were:

- Resource environments and existing funder relationships had much to do with strategic plan content.
- Nonprofits engage in cooperative and competitive strategies, with varying outcomes.

The Organized Abandonment Grid®

Copyright® the Institute for Social Entrepreneurs

Notes: "Profits" and "losses" are for annual operations and include all direct and indirect costs; "profits" are pre-tax and prior to capital re-investment

		SOCIAL PURPOSE				
		CRITICAL	SIGNIFICANT	SOME	MINIMAL	NONE
		5	4	3	2	1
PROFITS	7 — 21% OR MORE	DEFINITELY	DEFINITELY	DEFINITELY	PROBABLY	MAYBE
	6 — 11% – 20%	DEFINITELY	DEFINITELY	DEFINITELY	MAYBE	MAYBE
	5 — 0% – 10%	DEFINITELY	DEFINITELY	PROBABLY	MAYBE	PROBABLY NOT
LOSSES	4 — 1% – 10%	PROBABLY	PROBABLY	PROBABLY	PROBABLY NOT	DEFINITELY NOT
	3 — 11% – 40%	PROBABLY	PROBABLY	MAYBE	DEFINITELY NOT	DEFINITELY NOT
	2 — 41% – 70%	MAYBE	MAYBE	PROBABLY NOT	DEFINITELY NOT	DEFINITELY NOT
	1 — 71% – 100%	MAYBE	PROBABLY NOT	DEFINITELY NOT	DEFINITELY NOT	DEFINITELY NOT

(Vertical axis label: FINANCIAL — PROFITS / LOSSES; Horizontal axis label: IMPACT — SOCIAL PURPOSE)

Source: "Keep or Kill? Score Your Progress" by Jerr Boschee, Nonprofit World, Sept/Oct. 2003. *Used by permission.*

EXHIBIT 3.8 ORGANIZED ABANDONMENT GRID

Regarding strategy implementation, Stone, Bigelow, and Crittenden found evidence that:

- External shocks cause the organizational structure to change.

- Leader behavior, the structure of authority, values, and the interaction among these items affected implementation activities.

- Interorganizational networking was important for gaining good implementation outcomes

William Crittenden also studied the strategic processes, funding sources, and growth and financial strategies used by 31 nonprofit social service organizations.[34] He noted that most of these organizations were very small and very resource-constrained. His findings included:

- Organizations typified by the use of marketing and high competitor awareness tended to do better at gaining increased funding.

- Formal planning processes tend to coincide with high levels of donation funding.

- Organizations balancing their budgets and reaching their funding goals tended to also have strong marketing and financial orientations (the latter evidenced by evaluation of sources and uses of funds, revenue and expense forecasting, and predecision detailed financial projections).

- Organizations with no clear funding strategy and without strategic direction tended to falter financially.

- Nonprofit founders play an important role in an organization's strategic decisions.

- Staying focused in product/service offerings and avoiding the addition of many related or unrelated offerings are both strategically important, as was a willingness to move away from the past as direction became refocused.

Most recently, Crittenden, Crittenden, Stone, and Robertson surveyed 303 nonprofit organizations to determine the linkage, if any, between strategic planning and various measures of performance. Strong relationships were not evident in the data, but the study did come out with two significant findings:

> The findings also have implications for board members and executives. First, governing bodies can foster management satisfaction by formalizing the processes involved with forecasting, objective-setting, and evaluation and ensuring that the executive director is involved with these activities. Providing latitude for executives to utilize their personal leadership and decision-making style regarding non-strategic issues will also enhance management satisfaction. However, broad participation by external constituencies is needed for strategic issues involving expanding the volunteer base or adding programs. Managers can deal with external interdependence issues by using planning boards to gather and share information among outside agencies and clients. Such boards provide a buffer between managers and what might be perceived as undue intervention.[35]

3.8 CONCLUSION

Strategic planning is a vital part of ensuring a prosperous and mission-achieving future for your organization. We have focused on the role of financial staff in the development, evaluation, and implementation of these plans. Financial personnel will stand as the first line of defense to avert financial catastrophes when the organization attempts to move too quickly or when necessary funds do not come in on a timely basis. As importantly, financial strategies and policies can be developed or revised by the finance staff.

We conclude with a warning about balancing the role of financial position in strategic planning:

> Nonprofits must resist as much as possible the tendency to make the financial situation the most important determinant of the organization's capabilities. Financial matters are an important element of the strategic plan, but they need to be balanced with other elements. At times, this may mean narrowing the scope of operations. Fulfillment of the mission is of primary importance. If the organization is on a constant treadmill of financial crises, it can easily compromise the mission in the interests of survival. But survival is meaningless if the mission is forgotten. Nonprofits should not hesitate to use the mission to say no.[36]

Notes

1. The Evolving Role of Treasury: Report of Survey Results, November 2003 (Bethesda, MD: Association for Financial Professionals): 4, 6. Downloaded from www.afponline.org. Accessed: 11/2/2005.
2. Alliance for Nonprofit Management, "What Are the Key Concepts and Definitions in Strategic Planning?" Downloaded from www.allianceonline.org/FAQ/strategic_planning/what_are_key_concepts.faq. Accessed: 11/12/05.
3. Robert Anthony et al. *Management Control Systems,* 11th ed. (New York: Irwin/McGraw-Hill, 2004).
4. John M. Bryson, *Strategic Planning for Public and Nonprofit Organizations,* 3rd ed. (San Francisco: Jossey-Bass, 2004), 6.
5. William H. Newman and Harvey W. Wallender, III, "Managing Not-For-Profit Enterprises," *Academy of Management Review* 3 (January 1978): 24–31.
6. Paul C. Nutt, *Why Decisions Fail* (San Francisco: Berrett-Koehler, 2002).
7. Sol Shaviro and Donald Grunewald, "Improving Decision Making in Nonprofit Organizations," *Thought* 63 (March 1988): 52–68.
8. The definitions for mission, vision, and goals/objectives are from the Alliance for Nonprofit Management (downloaded from www.allianceonline.org). Accessed: 11/12/05.
9. From "2005 AMA Strategic Plan"; downloaded from www.ama-assn.org. Accessed: 11/12/05.
10. Peter F. Drucker, *Managing the Non-Profit Organization: Practices and Principles* (New York: Harper Collins, 1992), 56.
11. Id.
12. Id.
13. Michael J. Stahl and David W. Grigsby, *Strategic Management for Decision Making* (Boston: PWS-Kent Publishing Co., 1992), 20.
14. This section is based on a presentation in id., 20–24.
15. There may be a noneconomic reason why an organization would proceed here, despite the financial shortcomings of the proposal. If the project is implemented, however, the board should recognize that the project would be a drain on the organization's financial resources.
16. Peter Drucker and Joseph A. Maciariello, *The Daily Drucker* (New York: Harper-Collins, 2004).
17. Bryson, *Strategic Planning for Nonprofit Organizations,* 264–265.
18. Id., 270
19. Robert S. Kaplan and David P. Norton, "Using the Balanced Scorecard as a Strategic Management System," *Harvard Business Review* 74 (January/February 1996): 75_85. The nonprofit adaptation is from www.balancedscorecard.org, as profiled in Reznick Group, "Measuring Up," *Nonprofit Advisor* (Fall 2004): 3.

20. Paul R. Niven, *Balanced Scorecard Step-By-Step for Government and Nonprofit Agencies* (Hoboken, NJ: John Wiley & Sons, 2003).

21. Robert D. Anderson, "The Balanced Scorecard: How to Make Your Vision a Reality," *Christian Management Report* (December 2002): 14.

22. Thomas J. Reynolds, "Leadership of the Nonprofit Strategy Development Process," in *Improving Leadership in Nonprofit Organizations,* ed. Ronald E. Riggio and Sarah Smith Orr (Hoboken, NJ: John Wiley & Sons, 2004): 207–218.

23. Joanne Scheff and Philip Kotler, "Crisis in the Arts: The Marketing Response," *California Management Review* 39(September 1996): 28–52.

24. Zannie Giraud Voss, Glenn B. Voss, Judith Cooper Guido, and Christopher Shuff, "Theatre Facts," *American Theatre* (July/August 1999): Special Insert Section, 1–12.

25. Robert D. Herman and Richard D. Heimovics, *Executive Leadership in Nonprofit Organizations* (San Francisco: Jossey-Bass, 1991).

26. Robert D. Anderson, "Beyond Scorecard Reporting", www.robandms.com/article-beyond-scorecard.html. Accessed: 11/19/05.

27. Sharon M. Oster, *Strategic Management for Nonprofit Organizations: Theory and Cases* (New York: Oxford University Press, 1995), 93. Oster recommends using the size of the dot, for each program, to represent some measure of the program's size–revenues, employment, or clients served.

28. Christopher H. Lovelock and Charles B. Weinberg, *Public and Nonprofit Marketing* (New York: John Wiley & Sons, 1980).

29. John Zietlow, "Social Enterprise Financial And Nonfinancial Evaluation," Paper presented at the Association for Research on Nonprofit and Voluntary Action (ARNOVA) 29th Annual Conference, New Orleans, LA, November 16, 2000.

30. Kersti Krug and Charles B. Weinberg, "Mission, Money, and Merit: Strategic Decision Making by Nonprofit Managers," *Nonprofit Management & Leadership* 14 (Spring 2004): 325–342. This article was available online, at the time of this writing, at: www.sauder.ubc.ca/faculty/divisions/marketing/docs/MissionMoneyMerit-KrugWeinbergNMLfinal.pdf.

31. Id.

32. Jerr Boschee, "Keep or Kill? Score Your Programs," *Nonprofit World* 21 (September/October 2003): 12

33. Melissa M. Stone, Barbara Bigelow, and William Crittenden, "Research on Strategic Management in Nonprofit Organizations: Synthesis, Analysis, and Future Directions," *Administration & Society* 3 (July 1999): 378–423.

34. William Crittenden, "Spinning Straw Into Gold: The Tenuous Strategy, Funding, and Financial Performance Linkage," *Nonprofit & Voluntary Sector Quarterly* 29 (Supplement 2000): 164–182

35. William F. Crittenden, Victoria L. Crittenden, Melissa Middleton Stone, and Christopher J. Robertson, "An Uneasy Alliance: Planning and Performance in Nonprofit Organizations," *International Journal of Organizational Theory and Behavior* 6 (Spring 2004): 81–106.

36. Katherine Gallagher and Charles B. Weinberg, "Coping with Success: New Challenges for Nonprofit Marketing," *Sloan Management Review* (Fall 1991): 33.

CHAPTER 4

MANAGING STRUCTURE, ACCOUNTABILITY, AND ETHICS

4.1 FINANCIAL TOOLS AND SUPPORT STRUCTURE

The success of a nonprofit organization is dependent on its workforce and governing body and structure it assembles to accomplish its mission. The passage of the Sarbanes-Oxley Act in 2002 has revolutionized governance and internal controls in the business world, and its effects are rapidly being integrated into nonprofit management processes. Nonprofit organizations provide unique challenges in this area. In the story that unfolded after the Washington, D.C., United Way scandal and forced the resignation of the chief executive officer (CEO)/executive director (ED), a task force was convened with the charge to "help formulate a code of ethics and a set of financial and other business procedures that reflect best practices among not-for-profit organizations"[1] Key attributes for nonprofits surfaced: ethics, governance, transparency, and the constant building of trust. An important enabler of each of these is your organization's financial structure.

(a) ELEMENTS OF THE FINANCIAL STRUCTURE. In order to be useful, the financial structure of both nonprofit and for-profit organizations must reflect the nature and needs of the organization. It consists of these components, some of which are accounting issues and others of which we cover in other sections of this volume:

- Organizational structure it is established to support (see the next section)
- Financial component of the organizational structure
- Chart of accounts created to record financial transactions
- Financial plan
- Fundraising plan
- Cash-flow plan
- Systems to support the processing of financial transactions and internal controls
- Financial reporting system
- Distribution system for financial reports
- System for producing all financial and management reports
- System for reviewing financial results
- Communication of roles, responsibilities, and accountabilities related to the financial activity
- System for evaluating and adjusting the system to coincide with organizational goals and objectives
- External reporting and relations

(i) Importance of Financial Structure. Financial resources allow organizations to accomplish their missions and achieve their goals. They are needed to raise funds, hire and reward people, acquire property and equipment, and fund many types of expenses incurred in pursuit of the organization's mission.

Resources can be maximized by planning, recording, and reporting the financial activity in a manner that is meaningful and useful to the organization. Technical expertise as well as managerial and communication skills are required to design a financial system which serves all the organization's constituents.

(ii) Development of Financial Structure. The board of directors of a nonprofit organization is responsible for ensuring that its financial structure is appropriate and meets the organization's needs. Specifically, the CFO develops a proposed structure and presents it to the board for review and approval. After this occurs, the financial structure is

periodically reviewed to ensure its continued ability to meet the internal and external requirements of the organization. It is the responsibility of the board to ensure that these periodic reviews are conducted.

(iii) Financial Structure Soundness.   A financial structure is sound when it serves the needs of all internal and external constituents of the organization, including primarily the following:

- Board of directors
- Program directors
- Fund managers
- Staff
- Volunteers
- Internal Revenue Service
- Banks
- Auditors
- Investment service providers
- Grant agencies
- Donors
- Independent contractors
- Suppliers

(b) INTERNAL CONTROLS.   It is essential for the financial structure of the nonprofit organization to be safeguarded by a system of internal controls, which requires the delegation of roles and responsibilities in such a way that no one person has control over more than one function. We return to this important topic in Chapters 5, 10, and 13.

(c) FINANCIAL POLICY.   Every nonprofit organization that raises and expends financial resources should have written financial policies readily available to those who carry out roles and responsibilities on behalf of the organization and its mission. These policies are determined by the board of trustees or its designee and are statements of the nonprofit organization's requirements in the financial areas of managing cash, investing, fundraising, budgeting, expending, and reporting financial results. We detail the types and nature of these policies in Chapter 5.

(d) FINANCIAL PROCEDURES.   The financial structure of the nonprofit organization should be supported by written financial procedures that provide detailed descriptions of how financial transactions are to be processed to ensure compliance with the organization's financial policy. Examples are documented procedures for handling cash, making deposits, managing funds, and developing budgets. We shall deal with these in later chapters.

Financial procedures provide information on what is required to process various types of financial transactions successfully within the financial structure and system of the specific nonprofit organization. They contribute to the ongoing integrity of financial data and reports and ensure the correct processing of financial transactions with existing and/or new staff, volunteers, boards, committees, and other constituents.

4.2 ORGANIZATIONAL STRUCTURE AND GOVERNANCE

One person should be placed in charge of the financial health and integrity of a non-profit organization. However, financial responsibility is ultimately shared by everyone in the organization with decision-making responsibilities: the board of directors/trustees, councils and committees, ED/CEO, and other managerial and program staff. According to IRS laws governing nonprofit organizations, any of the above-mentioned persons can be held *liable* for financial errors as long as there is sufficient evidence to presume that they should have known about the errors and could have acted to avoid them. It is therefore important to have a clear definition of responsibilities for different roles in the organization, with an accompanying set of checks and balances. The topics of this chapter—organizational structure and governance, the finance function, financial and accountability structures, and ethics—will help to ensure an organizational focus on ethical conduct and trust building, while enabling the nonprofit to carry out its financial management in an effective and efficient manner.

Vulnerability to fraud is an issue that motivates the importance of governance, structure, accountability, and ethics. Nonprofits are especially vulnerable to employee-perpetrated fraud because of these six characteristics:

1. An environment of trust, implying that the guard may be down

2. Large degrees of control by a founder, CEO/ED, or substantial donor

3. Failure to include individuals with financial oversight expertise on the board of directors/trustees

4. Nonreciprocal transactions (contributions) that are easier to steal than other forms of income because when fraudulent they are more difficult to detect

5. Failure to devote sufficient resources to financial management

6. Program and financial reports, particularly with respect to government grants, may determine job security and possibly even compensation[2]

We shall develop fraud issues more completely in Chapter 10, but note that items 2, 3, and 5 each bear on governance and organizational structure issues. *Governance* is the set of responsibilities that ensures accountability, achieves legitimacy with all key internal and external constituencies, and establishes the mission as well as sustains the organizational well-being necessary to pursue that mission.[3] We provide a brief glossary of governance terminology in Exhibit 4.1.

(a) **BOARD OF TRUSTEES/DIRECTORS.**   The board of trustees/directors of a nonprofit organization determines the mission and sets the parameters under which the organization operates. The board's major areas of responsibility are

- Determine the organization's mission and establish policies for its operation, ensuring that its charter and bylaws are written and being followed
- Develop the organization's overall program on an annual basis and engage in long-range and strategic planning to establish its future course

These are some of the most commonly used terms used in the nonprofit sector, with working definitions:

Board of Trustees	Governing board of the nonprofit corporation (trust or charity); see Board of Directors
Articles of Incorporation	Legal document used to create a nonprofit organization
Bylaws	Set of rules that govern a nonprofit organization's internal affairs (see Appendix 4A for a sample)
Board of Directors	Two or more individuals who serve as the governing body of an organization
Tax exempt	Not subject to income taxes
501(c)(3)	Section of IRS code that defines this type of tax-exempt, nonprofit corporation
Nonprofit	Corporation that is not allowed to distribute profits or surpluses to its Board or those in control of the organization
Treasurer	Chief Financial Officer of nonprofit organization
Secretary	Officer of nonprofit Board responsible for preparing Board agendas, minutes, and other documentation of business of nonprofit Board
Officer of Corporation	Legal representative of the Board of nonprofit corporation; President, Vice President or Treasurer, Secretary
Chair of Board	Person selected by Board to be its leader
Volunteer	One who does meaningful, but unpaid, work for the nonprofit organization
Fiduciary	One who is legally bound to oversee the affairs of another using the same standards as one would employ to look after his or her own assets
Stewardship	Holding something in trust for another
Philanthropy	Good will, active effort to promote human welfare
Endowment	An accumulation of contributions that is held for investment; earnings, if any, can be distributed to programs
Deferred giving	A charitable gift made before one's death
Restricted fund	A fund that has been contributed to a nonprofit organization for a specific, designated purpose and cannot be used for general operations
Unrestricted fund	A fund contributed to a nonprofit organization whose use is determined by the Board of Directors
Fund accounting	Technical accounting term that refers to a system of accounting for funds by project
Permanent fund	A fund in which the principal is never spent
Conflict of interest	State of affairs that looks suspicious and raises questions of appearance

EXHIBIT 4.1   THE LANGUAGE OF NONPROFIT GOVERNANCE

- Establish financial policies and procedures, and set budgets and financial controls
- Provide adequate resources for the activities of the organization through direct financial contributions and a commitment to fundraising
- Select, evaluate, and if necessary, terminate the CEO

- Develop and maintain a communication link to the community, promoting the work of the organization

The board of trustees/directors must keep the nonprofit organization focused on its mission. Board members do not ordinarily participate in day-to-day operational decisions—although the board's level of participation has changed slightly since 2002 when Sarbanes-Oxley was enacted—but they approve operating budgets and may assess the productivity of the operational managers. Ordinarily, they receive no compensation, whereas operational managers are usually on the payroll of the organization.

Yesterday's board practices and today's best practices in a Sarbanes-Oxley world are quite different. Orientation regarding financial documents and the strategic plan, importance of the financial viability of the organization, ability to read and analyze financial statements, the unethical nature of conflicts of interest, and the increased importance of an audit or financial review are key differences. *Consult Exhibit 4.2 for more on these differences and how they can usher in an improved culture in your organization.* Today's regulatory environment, in which fines and penalties for self-dealing appear to be increasing and the IRS is honing in on certain other violations by private foundations, as well as excess benefit transactions by public charities, makes these issues even more pressing.

Since the board of trustees/directors can be held responsible for the operations of the nonprofit, it is vital for each member to fully understand the oversight role and for the organization to protect all members through the purchase of board liability insurance. We discuss this in greater detail in Chapter 10.

(i) Choosing Trustees/Directors. It is critical for nonprofit organizations to choose trustees who have the experience, skills, and knowledge base needed for the board to carry out its fiduciary and programmatic responsibilities. The board, as a whole, must work well together and demonstrate strengths in these areas:

- Vision
- Strategic thinking and planning
- Program high-level decisions
- Oversight of but not intrusion into day-to-day operations
- Organizational development
- Fundraising
- Financial management
- Accounting and auditing
- Human resources management
- Legal and risk management issues related to nonprofits, contracts, human resources
- Conflict-of-interest avoidance
- Public relations
- Community representation

(ii) Board Financial Responsibility and Liability. Accountability is an important concept for members of nonprofit boards of trustees to understand, and they should be well informed about the full extent of the liability, both personal and organizational, resulting from their service. Since accountability laws vary from state to state, legal advice should

Yesterday's Board Practices	SOX Best Practices for Today's Board
Board members selected without screening process.	Nominating committee rigorously screens prospective members and submits nominations to full board for vote.
Either board members do not receive orientation or the orientation is a social gathering.	Board members receive extensive orientation, including job description, performance expectations, bylaws, complete financial documentation, strategic plan, and other relevant documents.
Board members are expected to be passive at board meetings; agenda is primarily staff-driven.	Board members are expected to review all materials in advance of the board meeting and come fully prepared to analyze, deliberate, and debate, if necessary, the issues at hand. Board members know how to read and analyze financial reports and spot important trends.
Board culture reflects belief that the nonprofit is a "Mom and Pop" operation governed by well-meaning volunteers.	Board culture reflects the reality that the nonprofit is a financially viable business enterprise governed by competent directors and their leaders whose primary allegiance is to the mission of the organization.
Board members are known to have profited from their position on the board through the nonprofit's contracts with their businesses.	Board members are required to sign a conflict-of-interest statement on an annual basis for the purpose of identifying any existing, or possible, conflicts of interest. Board members are prohibited from having contracts of any kind with the nonprofit or other types of self-dealing.
Board members are the nonprofit's "aristocracy" and are permitted to order the staff about and/or demand favors.	The board orientation clearly articulates that the board's only employee is the executive director (ED) and stipulates that all board members will conduct themselves in a professional manner at all times.
Directors' and officers' insurance is only for large nonprofits.	All boards are indemnified through the purchase of D&O insurance.
Audits are only for large organizations.	An audit or financial review is required on an annual basis. An audit may be stipulated depending on the organization's budget and relevant state legislation. However, smaller nonprofits should arrange for a review of their financial records.

EXHIBIT 4.2   BEST BOARD PRACTICES IN A SARBANES-OXLEY ENVIRONMENT

be sought by all boards of trustees to ensure that they have the correct information for their organization in their particular state. Nine general guidelines follow.

1. The standards established for the conduct of trustees of nonprofit organizations are found in corporate law rather than trust law and are therefore less strict than those governing other types of trustees. Because nonprofit boards do not have the wide range of delegation powers and outside resources found on corporate boards, they are required to exhibit "prudent man" behavior in carrying out their responsibilities and are only liable for gross negligence.

2. Trustees are not likely to be held liable for business or financial decisions, provided they are made through informed judgments. However, they can be found liable if they never attend meetings, approve financial or business transactions with no background information, or engage in illegal financial or business activity.

3. Liability claims can be filed against trustees who place their personal financial interest above that of the nonprofit corporation, use corporate property for personal gain, take advantage of a financial opportunity at the expense of the nonprofit corporation, or self-deal without appropriate disclosure.

4. Trustees are liable for ensuring that the corporation is carrying out its mission, as documented by federal and state law. Trustees are accountable for ensuring that donors' funds are used for the purposes of the organization, as prescribed by the donors.

5. Liability for ensuring that their nonprofit organizations comply with the rules and regulations set by federal, state, and local governments that have jurisdiction over them rests with the board of trustees. These organizations must file tax returns with the IRS and applicable state agencies. Fulfilling legal requirements as an employer, including the payment of payroll taxes for the organization's employees, is the ultimate responsibility of the board of trustees.

6. The financial health of a nonprofit organization also rests with its board of trustees, but it can best be achieved when all stakeholders are assigned some segment of responsibility and accountability. The trustees fulfill this obligation within the context of their broader set of responsibilities, which include the following:

   o Determine and guard the organization's mission.

   o Set policies for ensuring that the organization operates according to its bylaws (see Appendix 4A for a sample set of bylaws), the law, and ethical standards while pursuing its mission.

   o Develop the organization's overall program, and engage in long-range strategic planning to establish its general course for the future.

   o Establish fiscal policy and boundaries, with budgets and financial controls.

   o Provide adequate resources for the activities of the organization through direct financial contributions and a commitment to fundraising.

   o Select and evaluate the performance of the ED/CEO.

   o Develop and maintain a communication link with the organization and the community in promoting the work of the nonprofit.

   o Monitor the performance of the organization to maximize the welfare of the public, not individuals.

   o Raise funds for the organization.

7. Trustees should avoid these types of activities:

   o Engage in the day-to-day operations of the organization.

   o Hire staff other than the ED/CEO.

   o Make detailed programmatic decisions without staff consultation.

8. The financial plan of an organization must be properly aligned with the organizational structure and program needs in order to be meaningful and useful.

Since all organizations require resources to operate, it is critical for the financial development, implementation, monitoring, and reporting activities to involve the program stakeholders.

9. In the process of addressing its financial responsibilities to the nonprofit organization, the board should pursue these tasks:

- Create a vision.
- Raise funds.
- Communicate.
- Set policy and include the rationale.
- Assign responsibility.
- Establish a budget.
- Project cash flow.
- Monitor and amend the budget.
- Review financial statements.
- Report results.
- Watch the trends.
- Develop long-range plans.
- Evaluate results.
- Ensure internal control.

The board's financial responsibilities should be taken seriously. New York's assistant attorney general notes that the "duty of care requires that trustees, directors and offices. . . be attentive to the organization's activities and finances and actively oversee the way in which its assets are managed. . . . This includes. . . insuring that funds are properly managed, asking questions, and exercising sound judgment."[4]

(b) OFFICERS OF THE NONPROFIT ORGANIZATION.   State laws vary, but they generally require a nonprofit organization's board of trustees to have at least three officers: a chair (or president), a treasurer (or chief financial officer), and a secretary. Some organizations include additional officers. The number of officers and their titles, powers, and duties are spelled out in the bylaws (see Appendix 4A for an example), along with the timetable and process by which officers are elected.

The selection of the right individuals to serve on the board of a nonprofit organization is a critical task. Only the most qualified persons should be considered for officer positions, with no one appointed on an honorary basis.

(i) President/Chair of the Board.   The president/chair of a nonprofit board should be a person of authority who is respected by the other board members, the organization, the staff, and the community and who has the time and other resources needed to complete the required work. Ordinarily, the president has previously served in several other board positions and is familiar with and informed about the mission and operation of the organization.

(ii) Treasurer/Chief Financial Officer. The treasurer must be a person with financial experience related to the operation of nonprofit organizations. Accountants and business professionals are generally preferred for these jobs; however, many lack experience with nonprofits and may not be sensitive to the special needs and characteristics of financial management in this sector. It is most advantageous for these organizations to find a treasurer with nonprofit experience. Also, many accountants are lacking in training in cash and treasury management topics, due to a deficiency in most accounting curricula in colleges and universities. This shortcoming may be partially corrected as new accounting graduates take more finance courses to reach the revised 150-hour CPA educational requirement, although the majority of collegiate finance programs nationwide do not teach cash and treasury management topics.

In smaller organizations, the treasurer also serves as the CFO. (The role and responsibilities of the CFO are discussed more in section h, "Finance Function.") Quite often, as organizations grow, they split the board treasurer role from the CFO role. A qualified and dedicated CFO is a great asset to the organization and indispensable to the proficient financial management advocated in this book. As an example of this arrangement, notice in our example in Appendix 4A that "The vice president-finance shall serve as chief staff officer of the executive committee and chief financial officer of the foundation, and act as the foundation's secretary and treasurer."

(iii) Secretary. The secretary must be well organized and able to record information accurately since this position is usually responsible for maintaining all records of the nonprofit, including the preparation of board meeting agendas and minutes. Since minutes serve as the official record of board deliberations and decisions, they must reflect the actual motions, who made and seconded them, and how they were voted.

The secretary should draft the board meeting minutes and distribute them to board members in advance of the next meeting for review and correction, as necessary. After all corrections are noted, the board votes to accept the minutes and make them part of the corporate record. Their importance cannot be overstated because, when the minutes are approved, the board's action is official and binding.

(c) BOARD COMMITTEES. When a nonprofit organization reaches a certain size, its operation becomes more complex and its board may experience difficulty in meeting all of its responsibilities. When this occurs, the board may decide to pursue its work in smaller groups or committees, permitting a more detailed analysis of specific functions or areas, such as executive, finance, staff, fundraising, investment management, property management, and planning. The role of these committees is to delve into the issues in their respective areas in a detailed way and to bring the results of these activities to the full board for discussion. The board may require a recommendation for action from the committee, based on its in-depth review.

Advantages of a committee structure are the division of workload and the promotion of a more informal discussion of the pros and cons of matters before the board. It also allows an organization to bring experts into the deliberation process without appointing them to the board.

In general, such committees should be chaired by a trustee or board member and have a majority of board members serving in combination with outside resource people and staff members, who are assets to the process.

The committees listed next are common in nonprofit organizations. The actual number of committees depends on the size of the organization.

- *Executive Committee*. Mandated to strengthen the efficiency and effectiveness of the governing board
- *Trustee Committee*. Reviews recommendations from the nominating committee and makes final recommendations to the board for new trustees
- *Development Committee*. Develops sound policies and tasks that support successful fundraising and related programs
- *Nominating Committee*. Identifies potential trustees for the board of directors and may also focus on getting people involved in the nonprofit organization (see also *Trustees Committee*.)
- *Planning Committee*. Develops long-range strategic plans for the organization
- *Building and Grounds Committee*. Makes policy for the physical plant and addresses issues, such as deferred maintenance
- *Marketing/Public Relations*. Determines policy for how the organization will be marketed and presented to the public
- *Program Committee(s)*. Assumes general responsibility for one or more major events that may involve mobilizing volunteers to plan and work the event
- *Personnel/Human Resource Management Committee*. Sets human resource management policies

In schools, colleges, and universities, two additional committees are common:

- *Student Affairs Committee*. Deals with issues related to the welfare of students
- *Academic Affairs Committee*. Ensures that an institution's actions and policies reflect its priorities, mission, and character

We have reserved the three committees deserving most of our attention for last: the finance committee, the audit committee, and the investment committee.

(i) Finance Committee.   This committee determines how the board should oversee the fiscal operations of the institution most effectively. The finance committee is responsible for providing a detailed review of financial statements and audit reports, internal as well as external, and reporting the results to the board of trustees. The committee also makes recommendations to the board on policy matters such as target liquidity and issues related to the financial management functions of the organization.

(ii) Audit Committee.   A well-managed audit committee, which some argue should not be a board committee at all in order to ensure total independence, oversees regular audits of financial activities and adherence to laws and regulations and monitors the organization's conflict of interest policies. The audit committee is responsible for overseeing audit functions of the nonprofit organization. The wave of the future for nonprofits is now on the horizon in the form of Securities and Exchange Commission (SEC) rules for business audit committees. Pursuant to the charge given by Sarbanes-Oxley to develop improved audit committee rules, SEC rules include stipulations that the audit committee

- Must have "direct responsibility for the appointment, compensation, retention, and oversight of the work of the company's independent auditor..."
- May have the company pay for any experts or advisers that it determines are necessary

- "Is also responsible for establishing procedures for the receipt, retention and treatment of complaints regarding accounting, internal accounting controls, or auditing matters, as well as for establishing appropriate procedures to handle any anonymous employee complaints about questionable accounting or auditing issues"

- Be made up of truly independent members, meaning that no member may directly or indirectly (including through any family member) accept any compensatory fee related to consulting or advisory services[5]

Organizations such as the Red Cross have already adopted Sarbanes-Oxley guidelines, even though they are not mandated for nonprofits.

KPMG, a "big four" accounting firm, prescribes five "Basic Principles for Audit Committees," which are worthy of quoting:

1. Recognize that the dynamics of each organization and its board are unique—one size does not fit all.

2. The board must ensure that its audit committee comprises the "right" individuals to provide independent and objective oversight.

3. The board and audit committee must continually assess whether the "tone at the top" embodies insistence on integrity and accuracy in financial reporting.

4. The audit committee must demand and continually reinforce the ultimate accountability of the external auditor to the audit committee as the board's representatives of external stakeholders.

5. Audit committees must implement a process that supports their understanding and monitoring of the

   ○ Specific role of the audit committee in relation to the specific roles of the other participants in the financial reporting process (oversight)

   ○ Critical financial reporting risks

   ○ Effectiveness of financial reporting controls

   ○ Independence, accountability, and effectiveness of the external auditor

   ○ Transparency of financial reporting[6]

Related to the fourth point, the external auditor should report directly to the audit committee.

(iii) Investment Committee.   The investment committee develops strategies and guidelines to support the board's short-term and long-term investment programs. The investment committee is responsible for reviewing and managing all the organization's investments, developing or revising and gaining full board approval of the investment policy statement, ensuring full compliance with policies and guidelines applying to nonprofit organizations, and reporting its findings to the board.

An outstanding source of board information, with broad coverage of nonprofit organizational types, is BoardSource®(formerly National Center for Nonprofit Boards):

BoardSource®
1828 L Street NW Suite 900
Washington DC 20036-5114
Phone: (202) 452-6262 or toll-free: 877-89BOARD (877-892-6273)
www.boardsource.org

Another important and useful printed resource on the roles and responsibilities of board committees is "Board Basics," available from

Association of Governing Boards of Universities and Colleges (AGB)
One Dupont Circle
Suite 400
Washington, D.C. 20036
Phone: (202) 296-8400
www.agb.org

Exhibit 4.3 profiles a quick check on board effectiveness that you should use to evaluate your board's governance periodically, at a minimum every two years. Items 4 and 6 are financial effectiveness gauges. Item 4 may be measured by the degree of achievement of the approximate liquidity target as well as the establishment of and board concurrence on a cash flow plan of 12 to 18 months that shows no impairment of that liquidity target. Item 6 suggests some comparison of benefits to costs for the various programs and services delivered, not merely balancing or running a slight surplus in the budget. Additionally, one might compare costs element increases, year over year, to the inflation rate for that year (as measured by the CPI: specifically, gather the number for the Consumer Price Index for All Urban Consumers [CPI-U] for the U.S. City Average for All Items, 1982–84=100; see the first check box at http://data.bls.gov/cgi-bin/surveymost?cu).

(d) EXECUTIVE DIRECTOR/CHIEF EXECUTIVE OFFICER.   The character of every nonprofit organization is largely determined by its executive director/chief executive officer, who speaks for the organization publicly and hires the staff who deal with the organization's constituents on a daily basis. Because this position is crucial to the nonprofit, the selection process should follow the next guidelines:

- Trustees should agree on the kind of person they are seeking, the special qualifications desired, and their expectations of the executive director prior to the actual selection.

- The board must outline everything that needs to be accomplished by the ED in managing the day-to-day operations of the nonprofit organization by responding to these four questions:

  1. What tasks are being performed now, and are they necessary?
  2. What tasks are not being performed now that should be?
  3. What new activities are being added that will require additional work?
  4. What specific tasks are required to accomplish the new work?

The ED/CEO is charged with reviewing and understanding the financial operations of the nonprofit organization as part of his or her overall responsibility for day-to-day operations.

The ED/CEO should appoint individuals who are responsible for various components of financial management, such as internal control, reviewing the financial statements, and monitoring all of the financial details in the organization to ensure their accuracy and integrity. She or he should ask questions until satisfied that answers make sense and are in sync with the mission and related activities of the organization. Individuals with these responsibilities will be held accountable.

Rating Scale: Agree Strongly (5); Agree (4); Agree Somewhat (3); Disagree Somewhat (2); Disagree (1); Disagree Strongly (0)

1.	This organization's orientation for board members adequately prepares them to fulfill their governance responsibilities.	—
2.	This board is actively involved in planning the direction and priorities of the organization.	—
3.	The board does a good job of evaluating the performance of the ED/CEO (*measuring results against objectives*).	—
4.	This organization is financially sound (*viable and stable*).	—
5.	Board members demonstrate clear understanding of the respective roles of the board and ED/CEO.	—
6.	The organization's resources are used efficiently (*good value for money spent*).	—
7.	The board has high credibility with key stakeholders (*e.g., funders, donors, consumers, collateral organizations or professionals, community, staff*).	—
8.	Board members demonstrate commitment to this organization's mission and values.	—
9.	Board members comply with requirements outlined in key elements of the governance structure (*bylaws, policies, code of conduct, conflict of interest, traditional/cultural norms, etc.*).	—
10.	The board's capacity to govern effectively is not impaired by conflicts between members.	—
11.	There is a productive working relationship between the board and the ED/CEO (*characterized by good communication and mutual respect*).	—
12.	I am confident that this board would effectively manage any organizational crisis that could be reasonably anticipated.	—
13.	Board meetings are well-managed.	—
14.	The board uses sound decision-making processes (*focused on board responsibilities, factual information, efficient use of time, items not frequently revisited, effective implementation*).	—
15.	This organization has a good balance between organizational stability and innovation.	—
	Total of the 15 items	—
	Overall Score (Total divided by 15)	—

Source: Mel Gill, Robert J. Flynn, and Elke Reissing, "The Governance Self-Assessment Checklist," *Nonprofit Management & Leadership* 15 (Spring 2005): 271–294. Based on the 32 organizations the authors studied, the mean overall score was 4.06, out of a possible maximum score of 5.00, with a standard deviation of 0.3. The authors also administer a proprietary instrument that has 144 different questions; the 15 items included here correlate highly with those 144 items, and represent the items in the board literature that are especially linked to effective board governance.

EXHIBIT 4.3 THE GOVERNANCE EFFECTIVENESS QUICK CHECK

(e) STAFF.   The ED/CEO is responsible for hiring the staff. Before doing so, he or she must determine the tasks to be performed and distribute them among the salaried employees, volunteers, independent contractors, and outside service providers. The best workforce mix is one that achieves the organization's mission in the most effective and efficient way. Usually a number of configurations will achieve the goal, and each has its own set of advantages and disadvantages.

In addition to financial support functions for the board, assistance from the financial function is needed to support the staff program managers and operational directors in their financial responsibilities. We consider separately the program/fund managers, marketing director, and strategic/long-range planning staff.

(i) Program Managers.   Program managers are responsible for the financial management functions of their programs including budgeting and expending resources and raising funds for their programmatic activities as well as the delivery of the program as a whole within the organization.

The treasurer/CFO helps program managers by providing the financial and nonfinancial information needed to develop and maintain their programs. The treasurer is also responsible for sharing interrelated program information that can be used to benefit the entire organization.

Financial operations and expertise play an integral role in a number of other critical functions within the organization. Some of these contributions and interrelationships are discussed later.

(ii) Marketing Director.   The financial and marketing functions of an organization are separate and distinct. According to one leading scholar in marketing, a marketing professional uses research and understanding of the client to develop an offering to meet the client's needs in a way that the client would value, communicates this to the client, and offers it to the client at the proper time and place. Proficiency in doing this means the marketing staffer has a keen understanding of the service and the organization delivering the service. Applied to donor marketing, marketing involves knowing the various ways in which gifts can be made and selecting the best alternative for each potential donor. The main marketing function of the CFO in this context is to assist in the development of a convincing presentation on the best vehicle for making a gift.

In an organization that has a separately identified marketing director, this marketing director is concerned with making the services of the nonprofit organization attractive to the client, developing client awareness, distributing information to stimulate new clients and contributions, and designing programs to attract new constituencies. The financial function is responsible for ensuing money flows.

The financial function serves the marketing director by providing information and services needed to determine a final marketing budget. Finance also assists in pricing programs, products, services, and contract offers to be presented in the marketplace, in developing effective fundraising strategies, and in constructing valid fundraising effectiveness analyses after the fact.[7]

(iii) Strategic Management/Long-Range Planning.   Planning for the future is critical to the success of a nonprofit organization. We profiled the growing role of the finance function in assisting in the strategic thinking and planning process in Chapter 3, and we cover long-range planning in Chapter 9. CFOs are typically called on to be internal business consultants because of their ability to analyze situations and to perform numerical and financial analyses. By providing *accurate* information that is *useful*, the finance staff becomes more highly valued by other organizational units. For an example from the business world, Intel's CFO asks participants from outside finance to evaluate the contribution the finance area has made in strategic decisions after those decisions have been made; if that contribution is equal to 25 percent or greater, that is considered "on target." Arbitrary? Unquestionably. A good first step toward ensuring finance's strategic contribution? Absolutely.

Businesses now expect their CFOs to (1) understand the markets their companies work within, (2) take part in general management, (3) help construct business strategy, and (4) work hand-in-hand with operating personnel.[8] These attributes apply equally to educational and healthcare organizations, and if we restrict the markets in (1) to "labor markets" and "donor markets," all four attributes may be applied to any nonprofit CFO. A key finance educator role for any CFO includes helping all employees understand that tying up funds has a cost, and that the lost interest revenue or added interest expense reduces the organization's net revenue. Just as importantly, using these funds impairs the organization's liquidity position.

Every organization needs to be financed before it can accomplish its mission, and nonprofits are no exception. Programs have short-, mid-, and long-range financial needs to be used for salaries, benefits, supplies, travel, space, furniture, buildings, and other resources. Nonprofit organizations raise the money to support their activities through strategic, financial, and programmatic planning.

(f) VOLUNTEERS. Volunteers are a source of uncompensated labor that can be extremely useful to the nonprofit organization. The process of recruiting, training, and retaining volunteers is complex, and volunteer interaction with paid staff must be handled with care. Many nonprofits would be unable to function without volunteers, who want meaningful responsibility. Smaller organizations often rely on a volunteer treasurer to serve as the organization's CFO. A volunteer may also do the bookkeeping/accounting work in the nonprofit. Unpaid interns from a local college or university may gain valuable work-related experience while providing the organization with assistance on financial data entry, reports, and receipting and other record keeping. Providing ways to reward and recognize volunteers is one of the significant challenges of the nonprofit organization.

(g) INDEPENDENT CONTRACTORS. Independent contractors are often retained to perform work for the nonprofit organization because they have special expertise that is not available in existing staff, provide that expertise at a cost lower than hiring additional long-term staff to fill a short- to medium-term need, enable organizations to focus on core activities, and increase organizational flexibility.

Outsourcing to independent contractors initially began as a strategy used solely by large corporations, but the practice has become widespread among organizations of all types and sizes. Services commonly outsourced include payroll, taxes, employee benefits, claims administration, investment services, graphic services, organizational restructuring, and organizational development. Accounts payable, remittance processing, and new donor development are areas in which outsourcing is growing.

(h) CONSTITUENTS. Constituents are responsible for requiring and reviewing financial reports and asking the right questions. They also have a fundraising role which includes making contributions of time and money as well as using their networks to provide additional support of all kinds to the organization.

(i) FINANCE FUNCTION.

(i) Chief Financial Officer. In larger organizations, the CFO is typically responsible for selection of those assigned responsibility for the day-to-day financial operations. In midsize organizations, the finance chief may carry the title of controller, with a large accounting and reporting focus. In smaller organizations, the CFO may have the title of business director or finance director, and must perform many of the finance-related

functions rather than delegating them and also perform some responsibilities not normally considered to be part of the finance function. In the smallest organizations, there may only be a bookkeeper or accountant, possibly only part time (or outsourced), and the board treasurer must wear the CFO hat.

Ideally, the CFO of the organization possesses:

- training and experience in financial management (including basic elements of treasury management), generally accepted accounting principles, and internal control systems
- knowledge about the organization's mission and programs and their relationship to financial requirements and components; and
- technical expertise and procedures for developing budgets and preparing financial statements

We next detail the CFO's role and activities, noting the differences in small and large organizations.

1. The role of the CFO in nonprofits is to:

   ○ Make and enable others to generate prudent and appropriate decisions regarding program and asset investments.
   ○ Safeguard financial and other assets.
   ○ Arrange for financing and provide helpful evaluation for fundraising efforts in support of the mission.
   ○ Optimize the level and uses of cash and other forms of liquidity.
   ○ Help ensure that funds providers' wishes are honored.
   ○ Report financial results.

2. The CFO is traditionally responsible for these activities related to that role:

   ○ Maintaining financial records
   ○ Preparing timely, meaningful, and accurate financial statements
   ○ Budgeting
   ○ Safeguarding organizational assets
   ○ Providing effective internal controls
   ○ Complying with external reporting requirements
   ○ Anticipating financial needs
   ○ Reacting to operational changes that affect finances
   ○ Maintaining appropriate communications with the ED/CEO and board of trustees/directors[9]

3. In the small- to medium-size organization, these roles are often expanded; for example, in a private school or college they may include such activities as:

   ○ Fundraising
   ○ Management of physical plant
   ○ Information technology
   ○ Food service management

○ Theater management

○ Human Resource Management (HRM)

4. All these functions, and more, have impacts on the finances of the institution and are required to meet its volunteers' expectations and its mission. Much depends on the size of the nonprofit organization and on the skills of the incumbent in the position. There is no single best way to distribute functions to finance staff members. These assignments should be constantly evaluated and changed when it makes sense to do so. In large organizations, many of the responsibilities are delegated to a controller or accountant.

5. The role of a CFO in today's nonprofit corporations is in a constant state of flux. Over the past decade we have seen these developments for this position:

○ Operational expertise is one of the primary criteria in the selection process.

○ Skills in interpersonal communication, influencing others, and related areas have become as important as technical skills.

○ Principles and values are used to define appropriate standards of behavior and the finance function in the organization.

○ While numerical integrity and the corporate audit process remain a priority, there is an increased emphasis on employee empowerment and softer controls (although this has been offset somewhat by Sarbanes-Oxley initiatives) as long as employees understand that a level of control is needed and does not constitute a negative reflection on their integrity or capabilities.

○ Empowerment has implicit boundaries and demands greater responsibility and accountability.

○ Finance people transcend their functional identities within the organization by serving as key participants in teams engaged in addressing multifaceted organizational problems.

○ Remaining competitive in today's global market requires internal and external information sharing and the development of systems to empower people with the information they need.

○ While cultural change is most effective when it begins at the top of the organization, the finance function may serve as a catalyst because it interacts with every other function. The finance function may also initiate cultural change in companies experiencing financial difficulty.

○ Finance people play an integral role in organizational decision making and focus their efforts on finding creative solutions to issues and problems.

○ Organizations depend on finance people to clarify the business impacts during every step of the planning and budgeting process and to act as advocates rather than merely naysayers. Their early involvement in the decision-making process prevents unnecessary surprises.

○ Beyond providing financial reports, the CFO should present to the ED/CEO and board a balanced picture of what is happening, where the problems lie, and what actions need to be taken. The person in this position is also responsible for working with program heads in order to represent their interests and explain the story behind the numbers.

○ The finance function (in larger organizations) is largely decentralized and matrix managed (e.g., use of multidisciplinary project teams with a finance representative along with individuals such as a program director and someone from the fund development office).[10]

Over the coming years, Tom McLaughlin expects these developments:

- More equality in ED/CEO and treasurer/CFO roles because of the growing insistence by government forces (especially IRS and state attorneys general) to have accurate and reliable IRS informational tax returns (Form 990)

- Greater separation between the ED/CEO and treasurer/CFO as the ED/CEO requires assurance of financial report integrity and accuracy and as the finance person adheres more and more to professional (such as CPA) behavioral norms

- More technology focus for the treasurer/CFO because of growing insistence and possible ensuing legislation regarding electronic financial control standards and the need for the finance director to document effectiveness and accuracy of electronic financial information flows

- More emphasis on long-range strategic input and analysis (documented in Chapter 3 of this book)[11]

Financial managers find their position increasingly important and more complex in today's nonprofit environment. Several developments explain why:

- Increased role for the CFO in strategic initiative evaluations

- Reduced governmental grant or aid provision, necessitating alternative revenue development and/or cost reduction

- Increased competition for donor dollars and "donor fatigue", accompanied by increased demands for accountability regarding efficiency and effectiveness

- Increased availability of new financial instruments, enabling risk management to better contribute to fiscal stability

- Enhanced information technology and increased opportunities for automation, such as electronic information and cash management systems, with a proper emphasis on using these developments to make better decisions on a timely basis—with many nonprofits housing (locating) the information technology (IT) function in the finance office

- Related to the IT revolution, the increased harnessing of information to create and maintain competitive advantage and further mission accomplishment for the nonprofit

- Increased ability of CFOs to document proper control over information flows

Notice the common thread running through each of these forces—information: information about the impact of proposed strategic initiatives on the organization; information about the decline of traditional revenue sources and the availability of alternative revenue sources; information about cost-reduction opportunities; information provided to present and potential donors; information-producing and processing technologies; information provided to program directors and senior management; and the harnessing of information to expand the organization's programs, flexibility, and resourcefulness. Information gathering and dissemination must be coordinated, and the financial and accountability structures enable the nonprofit to do just that. In other words, these structures are not only for cash-flow management but for information-flow management as well. Using computers enables one to meet both objectives simultaneously.

Information management is also a cornerstone of a turn-around strategy in struggling organizations. Business turnarounds have CFOs engage in these practices, which can be adapted to the nonprofit situation:

- *Shift the information mode.* Involve operating managers in financial analysis and reporting so that they will acknowledge financial problems usually brought to their attention by the CFO and so that they have a better feel for the implications of the financial information.

- *Improve the reporting system.* Making small, hardly noticeable changes to the information system may conserve financial resources at this critical time, while providing faster and more accurate operating and financial data.

- *Communicate with candor.* Since employees, donors, clients, and suppliers will learn the truth sooner or later anyway, gain support of the stakeholders by publicly working through the difficulties, enhancing your chances of success as you gain support of critical constituencies.

- *Form a "tiger team" in larger organizations.* This small, motivated group of middle managers can make suggestions and help implement them; it should focus on major plans and permanent solutions, not quick fixes.

- *Be creative in tapping sources of cash.* Tax refunds, restructuring of bank debt, asset-based financing (e.g., selling receivables), negotiating with suppliers, aligning with sympathetic donors or customers, and selling off idle assets are all sources of cash in tight times.

- *Enlist employees' aid.* In difficult times, employees may be enlisted to accept work rule changes, temporary compensation reductions or deferrals, or benefit reductions.

- *Protect earned income and grant and fundraising sources.* It is tempting to engage in across-the-board spending reductions, but this may be tantamount to a high-tech company eliminating its research and development budget: Maintain or even increase your investment in revenue-augmenting activities.

- *Eliminate or automate administrative functions.* Assuming you have already done everything possible to reduce overhead expenses, look for administrative functions that may be trimmed or eliminated: using outside fundraising counsel and out-sourcing payroll are two examples. A key question is whether volunteer resources are already doing some of these tasks, or whether they are required.[12]

The financial manager may have any of a number of formal titles. In smaller organizations, the person holding the title "finance director" or "director of finance" often holds a part-time position, sometimes voluntary. In larger organizations, the finance director or treasurer may make many of the financial policy decisions, with executive director and board committee or entire board approval.

(ii) Treasurers Office and Controllers Office. In larger organizations, separation of controllership and treasury functions is possible. The structure might result in the organizational chart in Exhibit 4.4.

Some of these areas, such as capital budgeting or IT, can be found in either the controller's office or treasurer's office, depending on the organization's preferences. There are two noteworthy differences in the focuses of the two offices: (1) the controller's office assumes responsibility for most of the bookkeeping, reporting, and compliance issues; and (2) the treasurer's office handles most of the areas requiring management decisions, such

Controller's Office	Treasurer's Office
Financial Accounting	Long-Range Financial Planning
Operational Budgeting (shared)	Cash Management (including forecasting)
Financial Reporting	Bank Selection and Relationship Management
Payroll	Tax Management
MIS	Fundraising
Payables	Employee Benefits
Receivables	Pension Fund Management
Audit and Internal Control	Insurance and Risk Management
Regulatory Compliance	Foreign Exchange
	Investing
	Borrowing
	Capital Budgeting
	Strategy Involvement

EXHIBIT 4.4   CONTROLLER'S FUNCTION VERSUS TREASURER'S FUNCTION

as when and how much money must be raised (this timing and amount determination may be delegated to and surely is executed by the development office); how to best manage cash inflows, mobilization, disbursement, and forecasts; how to invest pension fund management (or who will do the investing, if outsourced); whether to self-insure risks, which bank(s) to use and how to compensate the bank(s); which capital projects to accept; whether to hedge foreign exchange exposure; and whether a fundraising event provides enough additional revenue to repeat it, even when taxes must be paid on the net revenue. Our useful oversimplification is then:

- *Controller's focus*:   Get the financial numbers right and conserve the organization's resources.

- *Treasurer's focus*:   Increase financial resources and manage financial resources.

Many organizations deviate from the just-described organizational structure in two significant ways:

1. The organization may try to combine the controller and treasury functions into one office.

2. The organization may divorce fundraising from the finance function altogether. Apparently, organizations view fundraising vis-à-vis finance in the same way a business would view marketing and finance. However, finance may aid and help evaluate the fundraising function, which is typically housed in a "development office."

Why not consolidate the controller's and treasurer's offices? In smaller organizations (up to $1 million in annual revenues), it is necessary to combine the controller's office and treasurer's office. However, larger organizations that keep the offices together often end up with a "second-best" setup that does not allow the organization to work at its full capacity. There are eight reasons why combining the offices places larger organizations at a disadvantage:

1. The control focus ends up dominating, leading to ever-stronger financial reporting and internal control (e.g., use of internal auditors), and more detailed financial reports.

2. The "reports in search of a user" phenomenon may surface; conciseness is sacrificed for level of detail, with no improvement in usefulness. Very few of the reports are true management accounting outputs, such as break-even analyses. Operating personnel may receive larger and more frequent requests for data and explanations to feed the exception reporting (variance analysis) process. On the positive side, management may gain a better idea of corrective actions to take, and there may be more protection against employee fraud.

3. The treasury function invariably suffers, as financial management tasks are important but less urgent than getting the monthly, quarterly, and annual statements compiled, and keeping up with recurring payroll and payables tasks.

4. Capital projects that place ruinous financial burdens on the organization are approved.

5. Planning is sacrificed in favor of overemphasis on financial reporting and auditing. The problem area is not budget development, except to the extent budgets are not linked to carefully developed long-range strategies and plans. What suffers is long-range financial planning (see Chapter 9).

6. Short-term financial management areas suffer from benign neglect: Cash management procedures are archaic, bank relationships are never reevaluated and rebid (costing anywhere from $2,000 to $200,000 in unnecessary fees annually), idle funds are left in low-interest or noninterest-bearing accounts.

7. Risk management is not considered due to inadequate time and expertise: Interest rate and exchange rate exposures go unhedged, and the organization overpays for or has inadequate insurance coverage.

8. Financial investments are made in inferior or inappropriate vehicles: Some organizations invest in overly conservative vehicles (much like the State of Indiana until a 1996 ballot proposition allowing stock investments was passed), shortchanging employees due to underfunded and/or inadequate pension fund coverage for its employees. Other organizations invested in extremely risky mortgage-backed securities because they did not have the in-house expertise to evaluate these investments and have not retained outside counsel.

Why do so many nonprofits suffer from these easily avoidable predicaments? One of the main reasons for the consolidation of controller and treasury functions is the selection of accountants for the CFO position. The emphasis in academic accounting programs at colleges and universities in the United States is financial reporting. Ironically, due to separation of accounting and finance in the academic world, accounting students get very little financial management training. The result? The graduates of these types of programs rarely get any training in the financial aspects of cash management, banking selection and relationship management, receivables management, investments, borrowing, or pension or endowment fund management.

Because of the historical inattention to the treasury function, additional guidance will be provided regarding what treasurers can contribute. Birkett and Sharpe have identified five treasurer competencies in the corporate sector, which provides a checklist for you to evaluate your own organization. These competencies and our added commentary for nonprofits' unique situations are provided in Exhibit 4.5.

Competencies	Nonprofit Implementation
1. Must understand domestic and international financial market institutions, processes, linkage to governmental economic policies, and the legal/regulatory environment	1. Engage in a study of interest rates and foreign exchange rates (if have global operations), and how changes in them affect your organization's statement of activity and statement of cash flows. Recognize the linkage of gross domestic product (GDP) and your donors' local economies with your donations and earned income.
2. Must understand how financial instruments and financial markets are shaped by the legal environment	2. Study the trends in nationwide banking and electronic payment methods. Project their impact on your cash collections (e.g., of mailed donor checks) and your methods of paying bills and collecting funds. Conduct a feasibility study of electronic debits for donor remittances and as a means of stimulating donor retention and upgrading.
3. Must understand how investment and financing interrelate	3. Projected financial statements are the key here. Your financial needs are closely linked to program expansion, and the projected statements will depict this clearly. Statements to forecast: the statement of activity and statement of (financial) position to start with, then add the statement of cash flows. The cash flow statement will show to what degree operational surpluses fund investment needs, negating the need to borrow money.
4. Must understand the strategic aspects of the organization's activity, and how strategy links to the organizational structure and management processes	4. Revisit your organization's mission statement to start with. Is it still applicable? If not, revise it. Then, convene the board and top management to detail strategies (see presentation in Chapter 3). Consider how to build organizational structure to facilitate the implementation of your strategies. Is bureaucracy the best approach, or should participative decision making be facilitated with a flat organization?
5. Must possess the necessary intellectual and instrumental skills for carrying out treasury activities.	5. Hire carefully for both top-level and support staff. Then, train and empower, providing resources necessary to carry out the responsibilities professionally and efficiently. Provide training at regional or national Association for Financial Professionals conferences. Provide the technology infrastructure (primarily PCs and local area networks) to financial personnel.

Source: Competencies in the left column are from W.P. 8irkett and Ian G. Sharpe, "Professional Specialisation in Accounting VIII: Treasury," *Australian Accountant,* February 1997, 49–52.

EXHIBIT 4.5   TREASURY PROFESSIONAL COMPETENCIES

(iii) Financial Function: Service Center or Profit Center? Traditionally, departmental or other units in the organization have been identified as responsibility centers. Managers are then held responsible for the results of their units. This generally meant that departments were considered cost centers or service centers, although some organizations also designated some units as profit centers or investment centers. The distinction has to do with what the unit has control over and responsibility for. Cost or service centers cannot generate revenue directly, so they are held responsible for the level of cost they incurred. They are doing something necessary for the organization's survival but are consuming scarce resources, which must be conserved. A print shop or telecommunications area in a private school or college would be a cost center. "Physical plant" or "buildings and grounds" activities function as cost centers in most organizations.

To control costs, manufacturing businesses determine benchmarks (standard costs) for labor and material, which indicate costs on a per unit basis. The benchmark cost of a unit of output is often based on time studies or engineering estimates. It represents what the cost of production should be under attainable good performance, and thus serves as a basis for measurement or comparison.[13] Cost overruns are then identified, the cost or service center made aware of them, and the manager of the cost or service center is expected to implement corrective action(s).

If the unit also generates revenues and has a high degree of control over the amount of revenue generated, it may be treated as a *profit center*. Net revenues are then the focus of periodic evaluations. An *investment center* is held responsible for net revenues *and* the amount of resources (usually measured as assets) used by the area. Think of its results as "return on investment."

Why discuss profit centers in a book about nonprofits? Because there is some disagreement over whether the treasury area in either a company or a nonprofit should be treated as a profit center. Advocates argue that it is legitimate to assume that the treasury department can be held responsible for net interest revenue. First, note the calculation of net interest revenue:

$$\text{Net interest revenue} = (\text{interest revenue} - \text{interest expense})$$

Investments generate interest revenues, while amounts borrowed result in interest expense. The treasury area controls interest revenue by choices on short-term versus long-term investments, the instruments chosen for investment, and the interest rates earned. Treasury controls interest expenses by their choices on amounts of short-term versus long-term borrowing, the degree of utilization of credit lines, and the interest rates negotiated when borrowing money. Therefore, the argument is to hold the treasurer's office responsible for net interest revenue, particularly in an investment foundation or endowment.

The counterargument is that treasury should be a service center. Proponents of this idea are concerned that the treasurer will take undue risks by investing in inappropriate instruments (such as the Orange County debacle) or simply not arrange enough financing. It also is argued that treasurers cannot control the overall level of interest rates earned or paid. The service center approach has been the accepted approach for most nonprofit treasury operations to date.

Profit center advocates' rejoinder is that (1) the investment policy controls risk, and (2) the absolute level of net interest revenue may not change much because investment and borrowing rates move up and down together.

There are reasons for and against the profit center approach to treasury management. As a profit center or a service center, the function should maintain accountability so that idle funds are invested and prudent risks are taken to enhance returns. Normally, the service center is the most prudent, but for conduit organizations such as investment foundations, a profit center approach is defensible.

Focus on activities. Nonprofit organizations may not be able to develop standard costs, but they may still *estimate* what good cost performance on an *activity* should be. Using a three-pronged approach, your organization can find innovative ways to increase contributions and accomplish its mission for less cost instead of using the current period's performance as a barometer of success:

1.   Tackle the fundamental problems and eliminate "nonproductive structured cost."

2.   Redesign services, activities, and business processes to reduce cost.

3.   Make major improvements in effectiveness.[14]

Organizations should focus on streamlining business processes and activities and managing and reducing the *workload,* not just the workforce. Other fundamental activities include asking clients' and donors' advice, continually improving every process (e.g., donor communications), eliminating wasteful activities, reducing workload in each area where feasible, classifying items as utilized or unutilized (as opposed to fixed and variable cost splits), and controlling the process instead of the results. Involving the individual who performs the activity means one is able to tap that person's expertise. Wherever possible, set a target as a minimum level of performance. What may be the most important idea, and most radical, is to focus on outputs and outcomes, not inputs. While outputs and outcomes are difficult to measure and quality is complex, effort should be made to quantify outputs and outcomes where possible. Automate, simplify, and computerize processes wherever possible to reduce human error and mistakes.

Correctness of your cost analysis. Evaluating cost center performance depends closely on a correct appraisal of costs. An example of mistaken cost analysis is the evaluation of fundraising events. Are all of the costs incorporated into the evaluation? Quite often, even in organizations that computed and reported the event's net revenue (revenue less expenses), the cost of staff time and services necessary to put the event on was not included in the expense total. Instead, only rent, music, food, and prize expenses were considered.

Let us consider another activity: paying a supplier's invoice. The activity cost includes all resources used (e.g., people, equipment, travel, supplies, computer systems) in paying that invoice. The cost of the process of "payables" would be narrowed down to the cost per invoice paid. Quality, cost, and time would be looked at jointly, so as to prevent a myopic cost-only approach to managing the payables function. Always look for a measure that should capture costs directly for the particular activity you are studying. "Per invoice" works well as the key measure for payables. The activity focus enables one to spot "cost drivers," in which you identify a root cause or an earlier activity that has a great impact on an important activity's cost, such as the processing and payment of an incorrect invoice. Identification of these cost drivers can lead to prevention rather than costly rework. One is always on the lookout for non–value-added cost, which means some amount above the minimum amount of time, supplies, or space absolutely essential to add value to the organization.

So how does this "activity management" approach differ from traditional cost accounting? When each organizational unit accumulates costs by cost category and controls costs on this basis, we have traditional cost accounting. When costs are accumulated and controlled by activity, we have progressed to activity-based management. Partially processed "works-in-progress," such as opened but undeposited donation checks, tie up funds that would otherwise be available.

(iv) How Can Finance and Accounting Activities Be Evaluated? Consider the finance and accounting function and the activities it is involved in. Effective organization of that function can reduce waste and provide impetus to the rest of the organization to engage in activity analysis. For example, the accounts payable area engages in these activities: answering inquiries, receiving invoices, and paying vendors. Calculating a cost per activity for each of these is a logical starting point for more effective management of the payables area. "Cost per bill paid" is one such measure. Similarly, the payroll area collects/maintains employee data and issues checks. Those two activities provide a logical focus for cost analysis and cost management.

(j) INTERFACE OF CFO WITH CEO. Close and regular communication must take place between the CFO and the CEO. As partners in the overall management of the organization, a good working relationship is also vital. As a strategic business partner and internal business consultant, the CFO is an important part of the CEO's support team. The CFO is also in the best position to question assumptions as well as to rein in a free-spending culture where it exists.

(k) INTERFACE OF CFO WITH THE BOARD. Occasionally the CFO is an *ex officio*, nonvoting member of the board of directors. In all organizations, the CFO should serve as a financial advisor, financial educator, and sounding board for the directors. Well-run nonprofits have CFOs who are not simply focused on merely dumping financial reports in the lap of the board treasurer and disappearing until the next meeting's reports are due. Explaining what the numbers mean, why they are at these levels, and what possible means the organization may pursue to achieve and maintain its liquidity target are all key responsibilities of the CFO. The CFO does not inherit the board's financial responsibility, but is an invaluable ally in enabling the board to carry out that responsibility. The best CFOs also help board members perceive the risks that the organization faces, and how those risks may impede programmatic and financial objective accomplishment.

This concludes our discussion of financial structure. Next we turn to a discussion of accountability structure, in which individuals are held accountable for their duties and responsibilities.

4.3 ACCOUNTABILITY STRUCTURE

(a) ACCOUNTABILITY STRUCTURE. The many changes in progress in business today, transforming the way in which we do business, require new financial policies, procedures, and techniques. An accountability structure is a way of documenting and clarifying the responsibilities everyone has in this new environment.

(i) Definition. An *accountability structure* details each of the tasks or processes within a unit and identifies the roles of each person in accomplishing the task or process. Our focus is on the accountability structure for the finance office.

(ii) Purpose. Businesses are reviewing how they give authority to their units and their staff, with an eye to empowering and streamlining operations. One important aspect of an accountability structure enables the movement toward giving a unit full responsibility

and accountability for its business transactions, by removing the middleman as much as possible. In addition, an accountability structure:

- Eliminates any confusion about roles and responsibilities
- Details for all parties within the unit how the work is performed
- Verifies compliance with company, government, and any other regulatory agency regulations and guidelines
- Provides a method of reviewing the accountabilities in the unit to ensure they are kept current and accurate
- Serves as a guide for measuring performance

(b) ESTABLISHING AN ACCOUNTABILITY POLICY.   To set up an accountability structure, you first need to be clear about your objectives and goals, and have a method of sharing and conveying those goals to the company, staff, donors, customers, regulatory agencies, and others. Developing a formal policy about accountability can achieve this objective. As with any policy, your policy on accountability should include a general policy statement, core principles, and an interpretation of policy.

(i) General Policy Statement.   A policy statement presents a brief description of the goal of the policy, such as:

> The President/CEO delegates the accountability for the financial management of resources to functional units. Consequently, each unit is responsible for properly managing the financial resources of the unit for which they have been provided jurisdiction to include identifying a designee (normally the Chief Administrative Officer) responsible for formulating an accountability structure for each area. This structure depicts the delegation to initiate, process, and review business transactions by only qualified individuals in accordance with the guidelines put forth by the President/CEO and monitored for compliance by various other units (to be specified).

(ii) Core Principles.   Core principles further define the policy statement. They are the rules or practices adhered to in order to comply with the policy statement, such as:

> Setting the appropriate accountability delegations to conduct business transactions affecting nonprofit organization funds begins with the core principles listed below.

(iii) Interpretation of Policy.   Policy is often written in a language that is technical and not easy for everyone to understand. Policy is a legal document; however, an interpretation of the policy can assist others in applying the policy properly. A policy interpretation can look like this:

A.   Individuals delegating accountability can do so only to the extent that this same accountability has been delegated to them.

B.   Individuals delegating accountability are responsible for ensuring the qualifications of the individuals to whom they delegate as well as the proper fulfillment of their responsibilities.

C.   Qualified individuals are those who:

   1.   Are actively involved with the activities being conducted

2. Possess a working knowledge of the budget, an adequate level of technical skills required to use the various application systems involved, and an awareness of policies, rules, laws, regulations or other restrictions on the use of funds sufficient to either ascertain compliance or seek additional assistance

3. Have sufficient authority to fulfill their responsibilities so they can disallow a transaction without being countermanded or subjected to disciplinary action

D. Each organizational head must officially record all accountability delegations as well as any cancellations or modifications of such delegations, once established.

E. Each business transaction (including commitments) must be reviewed on a timely basis by the individual accountable for the affected accounting unit(s). In instances where this individual prepared the transaction, a second qualified individual must review that transaction and, in so doing, accepts responsibility for the accuracy of the transaction and compliance with all applicable policies, rules, and regulations.

F. Each organizational head (or designee) must regularly review its official record of accountability delegations and related maintenance procedures, to ensure that it remains secure, accurate, and current.

G. Each organizational head (or designee) must monitor the effectiveness of the accountability delegations to ensure that all accountable individuals are performing their functions in accordance with all policies, guidelines, laws, regulations, and related training instructions.

The chief administrative officer is responsible for the financial resources within his or her operating unit. This officer may delegate responsibility to others. These delegations must be recorded in a document that specifies:

- The kind or type of work the employee performs (e.g., purchasing, accounts payable, payroll, personnel)

- The qualifications, training, and/or credentials of the individual that justified the assignment of their duties

- The individuals responsible for reviewing work (including type and conditions) performed by others (e.g., review all Purchasing transactions performed by the department, or all Purchasing transactions for a specific account)

- An alternate to serve when an individual normally assigned to perform this work is not available (vacation or other absences)

- The accountability structure must reflect universally accepted business practices:

  o Separation of duties (the person who receives cash should not also deposit it or reconcile the transaction)

  o No conflict of interest

- Individuals must understand to whom and where they go when they suspect irregularities. In addition, management must set a tone that encourages and supports individuals contacting superiors and others when suspicious of irregularities.

(c) CHECKLIST FOR ASSIGNING RESPONSIBILITY.   The list that follows details the tasks and responsibilities in the financial arena. Each item on the list that is performed at your organization needs to be assigned to a specific individual.

Task or Responsibility	Performed By
❐ Collect past-due accounts	
❐ Design and maintain cash management systems	
❐ Determine appropriate financing vehicles and techniques	
❐ Determine return on investment (ROI) on technology	
❐ Develop and train staff	
❐ Develop long-term organizational financial strategies	
❐ Distribute expenses to subsidiaries and other units	
❐ Establish and monitor service provider performance standards	
❐ Establish borrowing policies and strategies	
❐ Establish communication strategy	
❐ Establish contingency plans	
❐ Establish corporate objectives and strategies	
❐ Establish credit policies of the organization	
❐ Establish employee benefit, pension, and other funds	
❐ Establish financial policies	
❐ Establish investment policies	
❐ Establish lending limits of the organization	
❐ Establish policies and standards for technology	
❐ Establish pricing and compensation	
❐ Establish reporting standards	
❐ Establish risk-management policies	
❐ Establish service quality of the organization	
❐ Establish technology policies with respect to security and standards	
❐ Evaluate industry standards/benchmarks	
❐ Evaluate outsourcing opportunities	
❐ Evaluate technological solutions	
❐ Evaluate the financial strength of the organization	
❐ Forecast cash flows	
❐ Forecast international cash flows	
❐ Implement security and fraud prevention programs	
❐ Implement technological plans	
❐ Implement technological solutions	
❐ Initiate fund transfers	
❐ Initiate loans	
❐ Maintain relationships with creditors	
❐ Manage accounts payable	
❐ Manage accounts receivable	
❐ Manage bank balances	
❐ Manage brokerage relationships	
❐ Manage cash	
❐ Manage collections	
❐ Manage compliance with audit requests and recommendations	

Task or Responsibility	Performed By
❐ Manage corporate liquidity	
❐ Manage daily cash position	
❐ Manage disbursements	
❐ Manage insurance	
❐ Manage foreign exchange	
❐ Manage fund assets	
❐ Manage general ledger	
❐ Manage interest rates	
❐ Manage international financial institution relationships	
❐ Manage international investments	
❐ Manage lease requirements	
❐ Manage leases	
❐ Manage long-term investments	
❐ Manage mergers, acquisitions, and divestitures	
❐ Manage property	
❐ Manage relationships with analysts and investors	
❐ Manage risks	
❐ Manage tax and legal issues	
❐ Manage trade financing	
❐ Mentor donor relationships	
❐ Monitor compliance with financial policies	
❐ Monitor compliance with corporate objectives and strategies	
❐ Monitor compliance with risk management policies	
❐ Monitor compliance with technology policies	
❐ Monitor employee benefit payments	
❐ Negotiate acquisitions and mergers	
❐ Negotiate credit arrangements	
❐ Perform float analysis/cash optimization reviews	
❐ Prepare financial reports	
❐ Reconcile and submit corrections for errors	
❐ Report on significant industry changes and directions	
❐ Select technology vendors	

(d) DESIGNING AN ACCOUNTABILITY STRUCTURE.   There are six steps to designing a structure:

Step 1.   Determine which tasks or processes are performed in your unit.

To determine which tasks or processes are performed in your unit, you may need to survey the staff concerning what they do. Other potential resources are job descriptions, job cards, products, and reports.

These major categories might include:

- ○   Purchasing
- ○   Accounts payable
- ○   Payroll
- ○   Personnel
- ○   Accounts receivable

Step 2. Determine where and how these tasks or processes can be divided into steps among individuals to enable appropriate separation of duties.

- Purchasing
  - ▷ Price quotations/bids
  - ▷ Order placement
  - ▷ Document preparation
  - ▷ Receiving
- Accounts payable
  - ▷ Document preparation
  - ▷ Document review
  - ▷ Invoice matching
  - ▷ Reconciliation
- Accounts receivable
  - ▷ Receipt of cash or other monies
  - ▷ Tally sheets
  - ▷ Document preparation
  - ▷ Transport to bank
  - ▷ Reconciliation

Step 3. Determine which staff members have the skills necessary to perform the tasks, processes, or steps.

An example of this process is presented in Exhibit 4.6.

Step 4. Determine which role the individual will perform as well as the pre-parer/performer or reviewer/auditor of the action or process.

When determining the role an individual will play in a process or action, the person with the most knowledge should generally be given the responsibility to review the entire action. The decision is often based on the supervisory or management position the individual holds. While it may appear contrary to tradition, the best reviewer of an action is the person with the most knowledge, regardless of his or her ranking within the area.

Establish guidelines or rules that each role requires. After establishing these rules and guidelines, detail how individuals should properly perform their functions, to whom they go for advice or training, and how they can properly question a transaction, process, or action without fear of reprimand. A primary and a backup should be assigned to each step (see Exhibit 4.7).

Step 5. Determine whether the workload is distributed appropriately or reasonably.

After determining who has primary responsibilities and backup responsibilities, review the structure to assure that work is distributed evenly across the unit and make adjustments as necessary. Be sure to factor in work schedules, seasonal fluctuations, and attrition (impacts of retraining and cross-training).

	Jeff	Michael	Tricia	Jenny	Nancy
Purchasing					
Price quotations/bids	X	X			
Order placement	X	X	X	X	X
Document preparation	X			X	X
Receiving	X	X	X	X	X
Accounts payable					
Document preparation		X		X	
Document review		X		X	
Invoice matching		X	X		
Reconciliation		X	X		
Accounts receivable					
Receipt of cash or other monies			X	X	X
Tally sheets/counting					X
Document preparation		X			X
Transport to bank	X	X	X	X	X
Reconciliation				X	X

EXHIBIT 4.6 DETERMINING STAFF MEMBERS' STRENGTHS AND WEAKNESSES

	Jeff	Michael	Tricia	Jenny	Nancy
Purchasing (review)	PP			PB	
Price quotations/bids		PP		PB	
Order placement			PP		PB
Document preparation			PP		PB
Receiving		PP		PB	
Accounts payable (review)		PP	PB		
Document preparation				PP	
Document review				PP	
Invoice matching			PB		
Reconciliation			PB		
Accounts receivable (review)				PB	PP
Receipt of cash or other			PP	PB	
Tally sheets/counting				PB	PP
Document preparation		PP			PB
Transport to bank	PP		PB		
Reconciliation				PP	PB

EXHIBIT 4.7 DETERMINING TASK PREPARER AND AUDITORY

Step 6. Review the structure for accuracy.

Before implementing your accountability structure, review it carefully to make certain that all tasks or processes have been included and that the staff assignments are consistent with the individual's abilities. (Cross-training may be necessary.)

(e) MONITORING AN ACCOUNTABILITY STRUCTURE. After you have developed developing an accountability structure, begin to monitor its effectiveness. Initially monitor the structure to determine that the initial design works in principle. You may need to make adjustments to the initial design.

(i) Types of Reviews. After the basic structure has been implemented and determined to be reasonably accurate and functional, periodic reviews of the structure should be performed. Several types of reviews or factors that should be performed or included follow:

1. Determine whether additional processes or tasks have been added to the units' responsibilities.
2. Determine whether changes in workload have affected the quality of the work performed.
3. Determine whether individuals are performing their role and responsibilities as intended.
4. Determine that policies and procedures are being followed.

(ii) Schedule of Reviews. The accountability structure should be reviewed at regular timed intervals and as necessary. The uniqueness of your organization will determine how often changes in workload or responsibilities occur. Use these guidelines:

- *Monthly*: Review or scan products, reports, and output to determine that all tasks and processes are being performed.

- *Quarterly*: Review or scan products, reports, and output for quality, accuracy, and compliance with policy.

- *Annually*: Provide performance reviews to all staff members detailing how effective their work has been during the previous year. Where necessary, make changes to the individual's performance objectives and responsibilities, and provide counsel and training where needed.

As you implement these reviews, you are achieving a solid internal control structure.

Notice that our accountability structure discussion has focused on things that the CFO and others can do internally to better ensure effectiveness, efficiency, and adherence to policies and procedures. Together these goals should enhance external accountability to stakeholders. We return to some specifics that your organization can implement in our chapter conclusion. First, though, we delve further into the arena of ethics.

4.4 ETHICS

A thorough discussion of business ethics is beyond the scope of this book. However, since ethical conduct is interwoven with governance and accountability, we offer some guidelines.

Operating and financial decisions are often subject to interpretation. Consequently, a decision maker may often find him- or herself in a quandary over how to ensure compliance. Our best advice is to do your best to thoroughly understand the rules and regulations that apply to the particular issue at hand. Use this information, along with your best judgment and possibly another's opinion, to make your decision. Guard against the tendency to rationalize and apply "situational ethics," which simply means engaging in dishonesty or other unethical behavior "because this case is different." The accounting scandals in the corporate sector have forcibly reminded us that there are moral absolutes of right and wrong that need to be adhered to in personal and organizational decision making.

A simple example illustrates the point that judgment must be combined with an understanding of rules and policies:

A problem is discovered in the way the organization is accounting for planned gifts. The chief administrative officer must determine how broadly to make adjustments without impacting future gifts or embarrassing people and/or the institution. Questions that must be answered in the process of determining corrective action are: What is the responsible person's duty to inform, to fix, to improve, and to control? The ability to make these hard calls comes from a strong base of experience.

Another challenge is red tape, because bureaucracies are inherently complex and confusing. When faced with the realities of the red tape affecting the ability to get things done, individuals may feel it is their ethical responsibility to cut through it. This dilemma places the individual in a gray area between the ethical responsibilities of complying with the regulation or law and our society's push to cut through red tape. Being professional, though, implies doing what is in the client's best interests and what adheres to the mission, above even loyalty to the organization and its norms.[15] In many such cases one is best served by getting a superior's view of the ethics of a decision before forging ahead with it.

(a) ETHICS CHECK. As indicated in the audit and audit committee sections of this book, audit as a means of assuring compliance is necessary when reviewing all business transactions. Exhibit 4.8 reinforces the fact that a decision that is not illegal or fraudulent may still be unethical.

It is also necessary to perform an audit of decision-making within your organization. Constantly review and monitor the interpretations of regulations and laws and assist individuals forced to make these difficult ethical decisions with the stress that this creates. Further, the manager should be certain that individuals have not determined they can decide arbitrarily to ignore all laws, rules, and regulations out of habit because of "special circumstances." Once an individual has seen a possible need to make an exception, will the individual know how far he or she may go before the action becomes immoral or illegal?

Discussions about ethics do not occur often. Many times the ethics issue is ignored for fear that even broaching the subject might cause or raise suspicion. Certainly formal, established policy on how far an individual can go in deviating from internal rules and regulations would be unreasonable, but a discussion or pamphlet outlining the company's attitude toward compliance is certainly advisable. It is also possible to teach or monitor company ethics using analogies. Most important, individuals within the company must understand the basic assumption that all rules, laws, and regulations must be adhered to and that only when the situation or task makes it absolutely necessary to deviate from

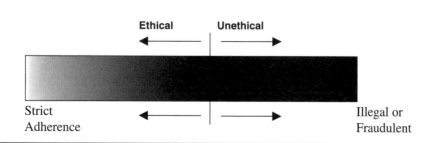

EXHIBIT 4.8 RANGE OF ETHICS

the strict interpretation are they to consider such an option, and that they need to seek the advice of the department head, CFO, or ED/CEO when making these decisions.

(b) MAKING ETHICAL DECISIONS.   It is especially tempting to break the rules when the organization is financially strapped. One recurring problem for businesses and nonprofits alike is stretching payables beyond their due date. How can boards and top management instill a culture dedicated to integrity in the organization? A starting point is instruction on the three tiers of ethical standards by which employees and volunteers can judge their actions, as shown in Exhibit 4.9.

In the first tier, the concern is whether the action is legal or at least consistent with the relevant law's intent. This requirement would be the minimal one of all employees and volunteers. The middle tier moves beyond this to ask whether an impartial observer would judge the organization's decisions, way of conducting business, and reasons for its actions to be both prudent and mutually beneficial to all parties. The Golden Rule applies here. It is clear that stretching payables violates the middle-tier standard. Going beyond this, the top tier requires a commitment to enhancing the well-being of the people with whom business is conducted, even if there is a cost to the organization. As one moves from lower to higher tiers, a greater commitment to relationship enhancement is necessitated. Summarizing, do what is legal, but always strive to make decisions that build and strengthen relationships rather than tear them down.[16]

Individuals within the organization need to be reminded constantly that compliance with regulations, rules, and laws (lower tier) is consistent with the mission of the company. The development and periodic review of an accountability structure, as a regular, integral part of day-to-day business, provides a mechanism for accomplishing this.

(c) ETHICAL CHALLENGES FACED BY NONPROFITS.   We are all familiar with the episodes of abuse of power by those in the ED/CEO role at nonprofit organizations. Many times these involve shirking of responsibility (in effect, overdelegating roles and responsibilities to underlings) or subverting organizational resources to private benefit. Organizations diverting funds raised for one purpose to a different use represent another obvious ethical breakdown. Although we do not wish to minimize these scenarios, the

---

Top Tier

Make a commitment to enhance the well-being of our neighbors, even when it requires some self-sacrifice.

Middle Tier

Subject all decisions and actions to the "sunlight test" and ask, Would both interested and impartial observers of the decisions and actions find them to be mutually beneficial to all affected parties, and prudent, practical, sound, discreet, circumspect, wise, informed, etc.?

Lower Tier

Does this decision obey the intent and letter of the law and respect the cultural mores that bear on this action?

Source: Adapted from Richard Chewning, *Biblical Principles and Economics: The Foundations* (Colorado Springs, CO: NavPress, 1989), p. 278.

EXHIBIT 4.9   TIERS OF ETHICAL STANDARDS

three categories we focus on here should be of special interest to the CFO and to the board:

1. *Conflicts of interest.* A conflict of interest exists in any "situation in which a person has a private or personal interest sufficient to appear to influence the objective exercise of his or her official duties as, say, a public official, an employee, or a professional."[17] Such conflicts corrode the trust donors, volunteers, and clients have in the organization. Board members may wish to steer business to their banks, insurance companies, or law firms. The nonprofit organization may spawn a for-profit subsidiary and then wish to use the parent organization's tax-exempt status to build a brand that is capitalized on to aid in the marketing of the products/services delivered by the for-profit. Conversion from nonprofit to for-profit status is alleged by some to represent a similar ethical breach. Allowing an association's name and/or logo to be placed on a company's product packaging—apparently endorsing this company's product over competitors' offerings—and affinity credit cards appear to some to represent similar misuse of the organization's brand name. Earned-income ventures bring with them ethical conflicts along with the incremental revenue stream.

2. *Fundraising.* In order to maintain the trust that comes from cultivating and maintaining donor relationships, fundraisers have an ethical obligation to understand the donor's intentions and obligations as well as to provide assurance that donations are used as and where intended. Accordingly, many organizations now subscribe to the "Donor's Bill of Rights," which includes a number of items of which both the finance staff and the board finance committee should be aware and supportive:

   ○ Donors should be informed of the donation's intended use and the organization's capacity to use the monies effectively for that use.

   ○ Donors should reasonably expect the board to exercise prudent judgment in its stewardship responsibilities.

   ○ Donors should have access to the organization's most recent financial statements.

   ○ Donors should have assurance that all gift-related information is handled with respect and confidentiality.

   ○ Donors should feel free to ask questions and receive prompt, truthful, and forthright answers.[18]

Approximately 1,200 faith-based organizations hold voluntary membership in the Evangelical Council for Financial Accountability (ECFA), which indicates that the organization subscribes to seven standards, including the following:

7.1 Truthfulness in Communication:

All representations of fact, description of financial condition of the organization, or narrative about events must be current, complete, and accurate. References to past activities or events must be appropriately dated. There must be no material omissions or exaggerations of fact or use of misleading photographs or any other communication which would tend to create a false impression or misunderstanding.[19]

3. *Budgeting.* The "fixed performance contract" built into the budget-setting and budget-approval processes may lead to gaming and deception, especially in commercial nonprofits, such as healthcare and educational institutions. Higher-level

managers may push hard to get better financial results, while lower-level personnel may attempt to gain easier targets to reduce stress and increase the chance of gaining favorable performance evaluations and even performance-based incentives. (We address budget ploys in more detail in Chapter 8.) Awareness of this conflict is an important first step; some organizations have gone to a "Beyond Budgeting" approach that includes several changes in managerial principles:

o   Replace goals with targets, focusing on relative improvement instead of incremental numbers, and disconnect goals from evaluations and rewards.

o   Adopt a two-year to five-year time frame rather than the traditional one-year time frame.

o   Base goals on relative performance improvement that is ethical and sustainable.

o   Give out rewards based on teams' relative success as compared to external benchmarks, and do this in hindsight based on a formula

o   Link any bonus pool to key performance indicators that are consistent with goals and strategies.

o   Engage in action planning as a continuous and inclusive process, not as an annual top-down event.

o   Make resources available as required rather than being allocated in advance and base allocations on key performance indicators that serve both as goals and controls (often in ratio format).

o   Establish internal agreements for service provision within the organization that facilitate spending coordination, with the agreements being demand-driven.

o   Base controls on key performance indicators, rapid information updates, and a "coach and support" leadership style.[20]

(d) AN EFFECTIVE ETHICS AND COMPLIANCE PROGRAM GOES BEYOND A CODE OF ETHICS/CONDUCT.   One thing businesses and nonprofits have learned in recent years it that it is not enough to have a code of ethics, or what some call a code of conduct. This is partly due to the day-to-day behavior that employees see around them, which they assume to be rational and normal.[21] A code communicates a clear set of expectations to employees but does not prevent ethical lapses. Enron had a wonderful code of ethics. Realistically, no organization can prevent every conceivable instance of unethical behavior, but it can greatly reduce the chance of such behavior occurring and possibly forestall repeated occurrences.

Joan Dubinsky, drawing on work done with Dawn-Marie Driscoll and W. Michael Hoffman at the Center for Business Ethics at Bentley College, has devised steps and related diagnostic questions that comprise an effective ethics and compliance program. These steps follow a values-oriented rather than a rules-focused approach. We have adapted the framework slightly in Exhibit 4.10. Notice that having a code of ethics/conduct is only one of the 10 steps. Your management team and board should run through the questions periodically to ensure the steps are being implemented.

Every nonprofit manager has a moral responsibility to ensure that the organization's objectives are satisfactorily achieved. Saying "we are nonprofit, therefore not businesslike" is not an excuse for ineffectiveness or inefficiency. In his classic management guide, Chester Barnard noted that the ED/CEO is responsible for creating "moral codes

Step 1: **Conduct a Rigorous Self-Assessment**

- o   What are our organization's espoused core values?
- o   What do employees believe are our real values?
- o   What elements of an ethics and compliance program are already in place?
- o   What must we create anew?

Step 2: **Ensure Commitment from the Top of the Organization**

- o   What outcomes does senior management want to achieve?
- o   How do they describe what will be different once this program is in place?
- o   How does senior management demonstrate its dedication?
- o   Are our leaders ethically neutral or ethically committed?

Step 3: **Publish and Distribute**

- o   Do we have written guidance that explains our rules and expectations for all employees and stakeholders?
- o   Do employees know what they can expect from their organization?
- o   Can employees find, read and apply this guidance?
- o   Are the policies and procedures that employees need to do their jobs readily available?
- o   Are these procedures written at the average employee's reading level?

Step 4: **Communicate, Communicate, and Communicate Once Again**

- o   How are our messages communicated?
- o   Do employees hear and believe us?
- o   What are the key messages that must be repeated over and over?
- o   How well do we handle change?
- o   Are we using multiple channels to get our messages across?

Step 5: **Training**

- o   How are our messages reinforced?
- o   Do employees get timely training that helps them use our rules and values?
- o   Are we building a capacity among all employees to exercise moral judgment?

Step 6: **Provide Confidential Resources**

- o   Where can employees go with problems, concerns, and allegations of misconduct?
- o   How reliable and trusted are those resources?
- o   Must employees channel all concerns through a supervisor, or is there an alternative confidential resource, such as a help line or hotline?
- o   Are confidences maintained?
- o   Can reports be made anonymously?
- o   What happens after a call is made?

EXHIBIT 4.10   TEN STEPS TO AN EFFECTIVE ETHICS AND COMPLIANCE PROGRAM

Step 7:	**Ensure Consistent Implementation**	
	o	Do our processes work smoothly and efficiently?
	o	Do we work effectively across program and organizational boundaries?
	o	Are roles and responsibilities clear and well documented?
Step 8:	**Respond and Enforce Consistently, Promptly, and Fairly**	
	o	Are we consistent in applying our values, standards, and rules?
	o	Is appropriate conduct recognized and rewarded?
	o	How are our internal investigations conducted?
	o	Is discipline uniformly applied?
	o	How do we treat high performers who fail to conduct dealings and activities according to our values?
Step 9:	**Monitor and Assess**	
	o	How do we measure success?
	o	Do employees receive feedback on our own internal controls?
Step 10:	**Revise and Reform**	
	o	Do we periodically update our values, rules, and program content?
	o	Are we committed to continuous improvement?

Source: Adapted from Joan E. Dubinsky and Curtis C. Verschoor, "10 Steps to an Effective Ethics and Compliance Program," *Strategic Finance* (December 2003): 2, 4.

EXHIBIT 4.10   TEN STEPS TO AN EFFECTIVE ETHICS AND COMPLIANCE PROGRAM (*continued*)

for others," establishing morale and employee loyalty, and "the morality of standards of workmanship."[22] As Peter Drucker commented in a 1999 interview, "The vast majority of nonprofits are not so much badly managed as not managed at all."[23]

4.5 STRUCTURE, ACCOUNTABILITY, AND ETHICS IN PRACTICE

Several surveys have been conducted to help us draw a profile of actual practices in today's nonprofit. We include Grant Thornton's most recent nonprofit board governance survey, the Association of Executive Search Consultants senior executive pay survey, a survey of Canadian recreation associations, and a survey of U.S. healthcare executives.

Grant Thornton surveyed 700 nonprofits in 2004 and determined that:

- Two-thirds of the nonprofits' boards have discussed the implications of Sarbanes-Oxley for their organizations.

- Almost half of the organizations have made changes in corporate governance policies in the past years, largely due to the new law and possible state and local government initiatives.

- 84 percent of the organizations now have audit committees, up from 77 percent in 2003.

- 55 percent of the organizations have a combined committee handling audit and finance, even though this is not a recommended practice due to the different functions that are served by audit committees and finance committees.

- Although it is recommended that the audit committee meet with external auditors at least twice a year, 62 percent of the audit committees met with auditors either once or not at all.

- 83 percent of the organizations maintain a conflict-of-interest policy; of these, 85 percent have board members sign the policy, 49 percent have executive managers sign, and 39 percent have all employees sign.

- The CEO or CFO of 36 percent of the organizations hires the external auditor, even though the best practice is for the audit committee or the board of directors hire and oversee the external auditor.[24]

More senior executives now trust for-profit companies more than nonprofit organizations regarding honesty in administering pay practices. This startling finding was unearthed by the Association of Executive Search Consultants worldwide survey: 48 percent of executives state that for-profits have a better reputation for honesty in executive pay practices, as opposed to 40 percent asserting that nonprofits have a better reputation.[25] This study suggested that businesses' stakeholders demand disclosure, unlike those holding a stake in nonprofits, who tend to scrutinize nonprofits less. In our opinion, this is probably less true for larger organizations like the Red Cross or American Heart Association, however.

Malloy and Agarwal surveyed a large Canadian sports federation with 70 affiliates and inquired into the factors driving one's perception of ethical work climate.[26] They found that length of service, existence of ethical codes, organization size, and the degree of peer pressure do *not* effectively influence that ethical perception. Instead, the level of education (more educated workers tended to rate the organization higher on a scale of "Machiavellianism"), decision style (autocratic style led to a greater perception of "Machiavellianism"), and superior and volunteer influence *do* influence one's perception of an ethical work climate. Since climate has been shown to influence ethical conduct, these are important findings.

Jurkiewicz surveyed 1,069 senior and midlevel nonprofit health executives in the United States and found that these individuals perceived intense ethical tensions. These tensions were linked to many factors, including the level of care provided by the institution, budget improprieties, lying, and personnel issues. The higher-level executives felt they were unable to change their organizations' ethical environments. The majority (59 percent) stated that they knew of overtly unethical business practices in their organizations. The top five issues they listed when asked what unethical practices they were aware of and would eliminate if they could were: privacy/confidentiality violations, discrimination, hiring and personnel matters, board members' preferential treatment, and lying to clients. These executives also expressed a strong desire to get rid of these practices, but the fact that many of the conflicts arose between them and either higher-level executives or board members may have led to an inability to right the wrongs.[27]

4.6 CONCLUSION

Regardless of how well an organization's finance function is managed in areas such as budgeting, strategic decision making, cash management, investing, and risk management, breakdowns in accountability and ethics can do irreparable damage to the organization's reputation and fundraising ability. Wise decisions regarding the organizational structure, accountability structure, and ethics code and oversight reduce the chance of serious problems.

We conclude with several pointers that bring this chapter's material together. Drawing on work done by Sheldon Whitehouse, who argues that Sarbanes-Oxley guidelines serve as a useful benchmark for nonprofits (even though most of these provisions do not legally bind the nonprofit), here is a final checklist:

1. **Ethics statement**

   ❏ Are all relevant areas addressed?

   ❏ Do we have it in written form, updated as appropriate?

   ❏ Do all board members read and sign the statement when joining the board, and regularly thereafter?

   ❏ Do board members also sign a statement affirming that they have neither a criminal record nor personal bankruptcy record?

2. **Conflict of interest**

   ❏ Has a thorough policy, including policy planks regarding disclosure, been adopted?

   ❏ Are loans to directors or senior staff forbidden in this policy?

   ❏ (For any conflicts not forbidden) Are any apparent conflicts of interest reviewed and approved through a careful reporting and recusal process?

3. **Audit review**

   ❏ Is the organization large enough to have an annual outside audit? [We would add: If it is not, is a compilation or review done instead?]

   ❏ Is there an audit committee?

   ❏ Does the audit committee meet Sarbanes-Oxley independence and expertise standards?

   ❏ Is the audit committee made up solely of individuals who are not board members?

   ❏ Is at least one audit committee member a financial expert?

   ❏ Does the organization consider rotating its outside auditor every five years or so? [For some organizational types, particularly faith-based organizations, very few audit firms possess the needed interest and expertise to serve audit, compilation, and review needs.]

4. **Certified financials**

   ❏ Does the ED/CEO sign off to the board on the financial statements?

   ❏ Does the board comprehend, review, and approve the IRS Form 990 through appropriate committees?

   ❏ Does the board have a policy requiring appropriate disclosures?

5. **Education**

   ❏ Is there an education policy for board members?

   ❏ Do policies specify fiduciary and governance obligations and the necessary financial expertise to make prudent decisions in areas pertinent to this organizational type?

6. Whistleblowers

    ❏ Has a means been established for whistleblowers [employees having become aware of and now reporting illegal or unethical conduct] to identify problems to management an to the organization's legal counsel?

    ❏ Is the policy communicated clearly and regularly to staff?

    ❏ Has the organization established a non-retaliation policy, and is it communicated to staff and carefully followed?

7. Document retention

    ❏ Is there a policy stipulating which documents should be retained and for how long, and for the destruction of documents?

    ❏ Does the policy allow for the protection of the privacy of confidential information, including personal financial or medical information as well as sensitive business information?

8. Attorneys

    ❏ Has the board requested and received from the organization's attorney a review of the attorney's reporting and disclosure obligations related to the Rules of Professional Conduct? Does the board understand the contents of this review?

    ❏ Has the board examined the new SEC reporting requirements for attorneys and adopted portions deemed appropriate?[28]

Careful attention to the foregoing issues goes a long way toward ensuring that your organization's governance, accountability, and ethical stance will aid its reputation and fundraising ability in the years to come. Appendix 4A provides a sample set of bylaws for an educational foundation. Appendix 4B portrays the responsibilities and qualifications you should look for in your board, board chair, ED/CEO, treasurer/CFO, board secretary, board nominating committee, board finance committee, and volunteers.

Governance and accountability structures depend on a sound set of financial policies for their implementation,. We turn next to a survey of the policies that will support the control and treasury functions in achieving and maintaining financial management proficiency.

Notes

1. Michael G. Daigneault, *Executive Update* (Washington, D.C.: Greater Washington Society of Association Professionals, May 2004).
2. Gerard Zack, *Fraud and Abuse in Nonprofits: A Guide to Prevention & Detection* (Hoboken, NJ: John Wiley & Sons, 2003).
3. Ada Demb and F.-Friedrich Neubauer, *The Corporate Board: Confronting the Paradoxes* (New York: Oxford University Press, 1992).
4. Jeffrey Haas, "When the Endowment Tanks," *Business Law Today* 12(May/June 2003).
5. Larry W. Sonsini and David J. Berger, "Creating an Effective Board," *Global Corporate Governance Guide 2004: Best Practices in the Boardroom* (London: Globe White Page Ltd., 2004): 121–25.
6. "Not-for-Profit Audit Committees Broaden Their Focus," *KPMG FlashPoint* (December 2002): 8.

7.   Herrington J. Bryce, *Financial and Strategic Management for Nonprofit Organizations: A Comprehensive Reference to Legal, Financial, Management, and Operations Rules and Guidelines for Nonprofits*, 3rd ed. (San Francisco: Jossey-Bass, 1999).

8.   Miriam Bensman, "The Big-Picture CFO Comes of Age," *Institutional Investor* (May 1992): 29–34.

9.   Malvern J. Gross, Jr., John H. McCarthy, and Nancy E. Shelmon, *Financial and Accounting Guide for Not-for-Profit Organizations,* 7th ed. (Hoboken, NJ: John Wiley& Sons, 2005): 2.

10. Henry A. Davis and Frederick C. Militello, "The Empowered Organization: Redefining the Roles and Practice of Finance," Financial Executives Research Foundation (FERF), 1994.

11. Thomas A. McLaughlin, "Changes—Meet Your New CFO," *NonProfit Times Weekly,* September 26, 2005. Online at: www.nptimes.com/enews/Sep05/news/news−0905₄.html. Accessed: 9/26/2005. For more on the CFO role in a nonprofit, see: John T. Reeve, "So You've Been Elected Treasurer," *Management Adviser* (November/December 1972): 38–42; also, an insightful association CFO panel interview moderated by Andrew Lang, documented in Keith C. Skillman, "CFO Q&A," *Association Management* (December 2004): 44–51, 84; and a broad-ranging interview of two nonprofit CFOs by Tom McLaughlin, "Today's Finance Folks Aren't Full of Beans," *NonProfit Times Financial Management Edition*, October 15, 2000, available online at:www.nptimes.com/fme/oct00/oct1.html; for more current thinking on the role of the CFO in the business sector, consult Don Durfee, "Striking a Balance: Can Finance Departments Be Cost-Effective and Smart at the Same Time?" *CFO* 21(November 2005): 52–62; Ann Monroe, "Fidelity Discovers the Bottom Line," *CFO* 11(September 1995): 46–54; Don Durfee, "Profile of the CFO," *CFO* 21(November 2005): 30; and Miriam Bensman, "The Big-Picture CFO Comes of Age," *Institutional Investor* (May 1992): 29–34.

12. Adapted from John S. Purtill and Robert L. Caggiano, "How the CFO Can Lead a Business Turnaround," *Journal of Accounting* (June 1986): 108–113.

13. L. Gayle Rayburn, *Principles of Cost Accounting Using a Cost-Management Approach,* 4th ed. (Homewood, IL: Irwin, 1989).

14. James A. Brimson and John Antos, *Activity-Based Management for Service Industries, Governmental Entities, and Nonprofit Organizations* (New York: John Wiley & Sons, 1994).

15. See the insightful discussion of today's ethical environment and some possible cures in Ronald F. Duska, "Six Cures for Current Ethical Breakdowns," *Journal of Financial Services Professionals* (May 2004): 23–26. "Be professional" is one of the six cures Duska prescribes, along with "constrain self-interest", "don't be greedy", "keep worthwhile goals in mind", "avoid hubris", and "don't misplace loyalty".

16. See Mary L. Woodell, "Fraud? Imagine You're in the Spotlight," *New York Times,* November 24, 1991, F11. Woodell offers three tests to help make the right decisions: the "smell" test, the "what would your parents say" test, and the "deposition" test. The Association for Financial Professionals, Bethesda, MD, has a code of ethics that applies equally well to financial staffers in businesses and nonprofits; consult www.afponline.org.

17. Chris MacDonald, Michael McDonald, and Wayne Norman, "Charitable Conflicts of Interest," *Journal of Business Ethics* 39(August 2002): 67–74.

18. For the full Donor Bill of Rights, as well as the Association for Fundraising Professionals' Code of Ethics, see www.afpnet.org/ethics. For a fuller discussion of fundraising ethical issues, consult Paulette V. Maehara, "Let Ethics Be Your Fundraising Guide," *Association Management* 54 (July 2002): 30–34, 36–37.

19. Quoted from www.ecfa.org/ContentEngine.aspx?Page=7standards. Accessed: 12/10/05. World Vision's fundraising policy was available for download at the time of this writing at: www.ecfa.org/Pdf/TopicFundRaising/FR_WrldVsnPhilosophy.doc.

20. Steve Player, "How Does Your Budgeting System Impact Ethical Behavior?" *Cost Management* 18 (May/June 2004): 15–21.

21. See, for example, John Dobson, "Why Ethics Codes Don't Work," *Financial Analysts Journal* 59 (December 2002): 29–34.

22. Chester I. Barnard, *The Functions of the Executive, 30th Anniversary Edition* (Cambridge, MA: Harvard University Press, 1938): 279. We are indebted to Michael O'Neill for bringing this to our attention (see Michael O'Neill, "Responsible Management in the Nonprofit

Sector," in *The Future of the Nonprofit Sector,* ed. Virginia A. Hodgkinson and Richard W. Lyons and Associates (San Francisco: Jossey-Bass, 1989).

23. Quoted in Eric Schmuckler, "The Better Angels," *Barron's* (December 18, 2000), P6,P9-P10.

24. "Sarbanes-Oxley Prompts Nonprofits to Take Action," *Association Management* (June 2005): 22. Also see the archived press release entitled "Not-for-Profits' Reputation at Risk: National Survey Finds Only 26 percent of Not-for-Profits Have a Whistle-Blower Policy," available online at www.grantthornton.com.

25. Steve Watkins, "As Honest as Necessary?" *Investor's Business Daily,* December 3, 2004, A3.

26. David Cruise Malloy and James Agarwal, "Factors Influencing Climate in a Nonprofit Organization: An Empirical Investigation," *International Journal of Nonprofit and Voluntary Sector Marketing* 8 (August 2003) 224–250.

27. Carole L. Jurkiewicz, "The Trouble with Ethics: Results of a National Survey of Healthcare Executives," *HEC Forum* 12 (June 2000): 101–123.

28. Sheldon Whitehouse, "The Sarbanes-Oxley Act and Nonprofits: 'But I Thought That Didn't Apply to Us,'" *Nonprofit World* (September/October 2004): 10–11, 13.

BY-LAWS OF THE ABC EDUCATIONAL FOUNDATION—A CALIFORNIA NONPROFIT PUBLIC BENEFIT CORPORATION

ARTICLE I. NAME

The name of this corporation is THE ABC EDUCATIONAL FOUNDATION ("the Foundation").

ARTICLE II. OFFICES

SECTION 1. EXECUTIVE OFFICE   The executive office of the Foundation is hereby fixed and located at _____. The Board of Trustees is hereby granted full power and authority to change from time to time said executive office from one location to another. The location of the executive office of the Foundation need not be in the state of California. Any such change shall be noted in the By-Laws by the Secretary, opposite this section, or this section may be amended to state the new location.

SECTION 2. OTHER OFFICES   Other business offices may at any time be established by the Board of Trustees at any place or places where the Foundation is qualified to do business.

ARTICLE III. PURPOSES AND POWERS

SECTION 1. PURPOSES   The Foundation is a nonprofit public benefit corporation and is not organized for the private gain of any person. It is organized under the California Nonprofit Public Benefit Corporation Law for public and charitable purposes to do the following:

    a. Broaden participation in and access to higher education within the State of California.

    b. Promote a better understanding of the community's role in improving access to higher education.

c.   Provide financial assistance to schools and colleges, support groups, faculty, and students in support of activities to improve access to higher education.

d.   Engage in a variety of activities related to the above purposes.

SECTION 2. POWERS   In furtherance of the purposes herein above set forth, the Foundation shall have and shall exercise, subject to any limitations contained in its Articles of Incorporation, these By-Laws, applicable law, or applicable policy statements, all powers of a natural person and all other rights, powers, and privileges now or hereafter belonging to, or conferred upon, corporations organized under the provisions of the California Nonprofit Public Benefit Corporation Law, including without limitation, the power to do the following:

a.   Adopt, make, use, and at will alter, a corporate seal, but failure to affix such seal shall not affect the validity of any instrument.

b.   Adopt, amend, and repeal By-Laws.

c.   Qualify to conduct its activities in any other state, territory, dependency, or foreign country.

d.   Issue, purchase, redeem, receive, take, or otherwise ac-quire, own, sell, lend, exchange, transfer, or otherwise dispose of, pledge, use, and otherwise deal in and with real and personal property, capital stock, bonds, debentures, notes and debt securities, and money market instruments of its own or others.

e.   Pay pensions, and establish and carry out pensions, deferred compensation, saving, thrift, and other retirement, incentive and benefit plans, trusts and provisions for any or all of its Trustees, officers, employees, and persons providing services to it or any other subsidiary or related or associated corporation, and to indemnify and purchase and maintain insurance on behalf of any fiduciary of such plans, trusts, or provisions.

f.   Make donations for the public welfare or for community funds, hospital, charitable, educational, scientific, civic, religious, or similar purposes.

g.   Assume obligations, enter into contracts, including contracts of guaranty or suretyship, incur liabilities, borrow or lend money or otherwise use its credit, and secure any of its obligations, contracts, or liabilities by mortgage, pledge, or otherwise encumber all or any part of its property and income.

h.   Participate with others in any partnership, joint venture, or other association, transaction, or arrangement of any kind whether or not such participation involves sharing or delegation of control with or to others.

i.   Act as a trustee under any trust incidental to the principal objects of the Foundation, and receive, hold, administer, exchange, and expend funds and property subject to such trust.

j.   Receive endowments, devises, bequests, gifts, and donations of all kinds of property for its own use, or in trust, in order to carry out or to assist in carrying out, the objects and purposes of the Foundation and to do all things and acts necessary or proper to carry out each and all of the purposes and provisions of such endowments, devises, bequests, gifts, and donations with full power to mortgage, sell, lease, or otherwise deal with or dispose of the same in accordance with the terms thereof.

SECTION 3. DEDICATION OF ASSETS   This corporation is organized and shall be operated exclusively for educational purposes (meeting the requirements for exemption provided for by California Revenue and Taxation Code Sec. 214), within the meaning of
Section 501(c)(3) of the Internal Revenue Code of 1986, as amended, and Section 23701d
of the California Revenue and Taxation Code, as amended. The property, assets, profits,
and net income of this corporation are irrevocably dedicated to said educational purposes (meeting the requirements for exemption provided for by California Revenue and
Taxation Code Sec. 214), and no part of the profits or net income of this corporation
shall ever inure to the benefit of any Trustee, officer, or to any individual. Upon the
dissolution of this corporation, the assets remaining after payment of, or provisions for
payment of, all its debts and liabilities, to the extent not inconsistent with the terms
of any endowment, devise, bequest, gift, or donation, shall be distributed to an organization which is organized and operated exclusively for educational purposes (meeting
the requirements for exemption provided for by California Revenue and Taxation Code
Sec. 214), and which is exempt from taxation under Section 23701d of the California
Revenue and Taxation Code, as amended (or the corresponding provision of any future
California Revenue Law), and Section 501(c)(3) of the Internal Revenue Code of 1986,
as amended (or the corresponding provision of any future United States Internal Revenue
Law), or to the federal government or to a state or local government.

Notwithstanding any other provision of these By-Laws, the Foundation shall not carry
on any activities not permitted to be carried on:

a.   By a corporation exempt from Federal Income Tax under Section 501(c)(3) of
the Internal Revenue Code of 1986, as amended (or the corresponding provision
of any future United States Internal Revenue Law) *or*

b.   By a corporation, contributions to which are deductible under Section 170(c)(2) of
the Internal Revenue Code of 1986, as amended (or the corresponding provision
of any future United States Internal Revenue Law)

No substantial part of the activities of the Foundation shall consist of the carrying on
of propaganda or otherwise attempting to influence legislation, nor shall the Foundation
participate in, or intervene in (including the publishing or distributing of statements) any
political campaign on behalf of any candidate for political office.

ARTICLE IV. MEMBERSHIP CORPORATION

SECTION 1. MEMBERSHIP   The Foundation shall be a membership corporation as provided in Chapter 3 of the Nonprofit Public Benefit Corporation Law (California Corporations Code Sections 5310 et seq.). One class of voting membership is hereby created and
all persons who are eligible and active members of the Board of Trustees or as Advisory
Trustees on the date this By-Law becomes effective will constitute the membership of
the Foundation for the remainder of the terms to which they were originally elected or
appointed.

There shall be no multiple or fractional memberships, nor members who are not natural
persons.

SECTION 2. MEMBERS CALLED TRUSTEES   The members of the corporation shall be
called "Trustees" and the membership as a whole the "Board of Trustees" (and are
so referred to hereinafter) in recognition of the long association of these terms with

the Foundation. The use of these terms implies no other or different relationship or responsibility than that provided for members in the Nonprofit Public Benefit Corporation Law and these By-Laws.

SECTION 3. PERSONS ASSOCIATED WITH THE FOUNDATION   By resolution, the Board of Trustees may create any advisory boards, councils, honorary memberships, or other bodies as it deems appropriate. The Board of Trustees may also, by resolution, confer on any persons not already Trustees in such classes all of the rights of a member of the corporation under the Nonprofit Public Benefit Corporation Law other than the right to vote.

SECTION 4. LIABILITY OF TRUSTEES   Trustees of the Foundation are not personally liable for the debts, liabilities, or obligations of the Foundation.

ARTICLE V. TRUSTEES

SECTION 1. POWERS   The Trustees shall have all of the powers conferred by law, the Articles of Incorporation, or these By-Laws on members of nonprofit public benefit corporations. Notwithstanding any other provision in these By-Laws, the Board of Trustees legally has the exclusive and nondelegable power to do the following:

a. Elect the Board of Trustees of the Foundation.

b. Elect the President.

c. Dispose of all or substantially all of the assets of the Foundation.

d. Approve a merger or dissolution.

e. Amend or repeal the Articles of Incorporation or the By-Laws of the Foundation.

SECTION 2. NUMBER AND QUALIFICATION OF TRUSTEES   The authorized number of Trustees shall be not less than twenty (20), with no upper limit on the number of Trustees.

SECTION 3. MANNER OF SELECTION OF TRUSTEES   The composition of the Board of Trustees shall be as follows.

3.1 Elected Trustees   Trustees (except for ex-officio Trustees as provided in Section 3.2) shall be elected by majority vote of the Trustees in attendance in person or by proxy at the meeting held to conduct such election, provided that there is a quorum (as provided in Section 11 of this Article), or a majority vote of mail-written ballots, provided the requisite number of votes are cast (as provided in Section 12 of this Article), and may be reelected. No more than twenty (20) new Trustees may be elected each year. The election of Trustees shall take place at the last meeting of the Board of Trustees each fiscal year. The Board of Trustees shall vote upon the nominations submitted by the Nominations Committee and such other nominations as may have been submitted by *any* member of the Board of Trustees eligible to vote not later than a date set by the Board sufficiently in advance of the vote to enable the inclusion of such nominations on proxy forms or mail-written ballots.

3.2 Ex-Officio Trustees   The following persons shall be ex-officio Trustees:
   Former presidents of the ABC Educational Foundation

SECTION 4. TERM OF OFFICE   All elected Trustees shall serve on the Board of Trustees for a term of three (3) years and may be reelected. Terms of office shall commence on the first day of the Foundation's fiscal year.

SECTION 5. HONORARY TRUSTEES   Subject to the provisions of Section 3 of Article IV (relating to Persons Associated with the Foundation), the Board of Trustees may from time to time invite individuals to serve as Honorary Trustees. Such Honorary Trustees shall serve at the pleasure of the Board of Trustees and shall have all rights and privileges of Trustees other than the right to vote.

SECTION 6. RESIGNATION AND REMOVAL OF TRUSTEES

6.1 Resignation   A Trustee may resign at any time. Such resignation shall not affect the Trustee's obligation for any liabilities already or thereafter incurred to the Foundation.

6.2 Expulsion, Suspension or Termination   A Trustee may be expelled or suspended, or membership on the Board of Trustees or any of the rights associated therewith may be terminated or suspended, for just cause and upon the delivery of notice to such Trustee no later than fifteen (15) days prior to the date of intent to take such action, by first-class or registered mail, postage paid, addressed to such Trustee's last known address. Such notice shall indicate the reasons for the proposed action to be taken, the proposed effective date thereof, and shall inform the Trustee of his or her right to a hearing, orally or in writing, no sooner than five (5) days before the proposed effective date of this action.

The intent to take such action against a Trustee shall be submitted on the motion of any Trustee to the Nominations Committee at a meeting specifically called to consider such action, and must be approved by the majority of the quorum in attendance at such meeting.

If the intent to take such action is approved by the Nominations Committee and notice is duly mailed to the affected Trustee, the President (or, if the President is the affected Trustee, the Vice President–Finance) shall appoint an *ad hoc* hearing committee of not fewer than ten (10) Trustees who are not members of the Nominations Committee to provide for the hearing, if one is requested, pursuant to Corporations Code §5341. The decision of the Nominations Committee, or, if a hearing is held, of the *ad hoc* hearing committee, shall be final.

SECTION 7. VACANCIES

7.1 Elected Trustees   There is no limit to the number of elected Trustees, and therefore the resignation, removal, or death of a Trustee shall not cause a vacancy unless the number of Trustees thereby falls below twenty (20), in which case a majority of the remaining Trustees shall fill the vacancy, or all of the vacancies shall be filled by a sole remaining Trustee.

7.2 Ex-Officio Trustees   Vacancies created by the removal, resignation, or death of ex-officio Trustees shall be filled by the persons who succeed them in the offices that qualified them as Trustees.

SECTION 8. REGULAR MEETINGS The Board of Trustees shall meet at least two times during each fiscal year. Notice of such regular meetings shall be given pursuant to the provisions of these By-Laws.

SECTION 9. SPECIAL MEETINGS Special meetings of the Board of Trustees may be called for any purpose at any time by the Chairman of the Board, the President, the Vice President–Development, the Vice President–Finance, or any five Trustees by delivering written notice to the President or Vice President–Finance. Notice of such special meetings shall be given pursuant to the provisions of these By-Laws for notice of regular meetings.

SECTION 10. NOTICE AND PLACE OF MEETINGS Meetings of the Board of Trustees shall be held at the place which has been designated in the notice of the meeting, if any; or if not stated in such notice or if there is no notice, at the place designated by resolution of the Board; or, absent any other designation, at the executive office of the Foundation located at—.

Whenever a notice of a meeting of the Board of Trustees is required to be given, the Vice President–Finance shall cause notice of such meeting to be delivered by personal service, first-lass mail, or telegraph to each Trustee. In case notice is given by mail or telegram, it shall be sent, charges prepaid, ad-dressed to the Trustee at his address appearing on the Foundation's records, or if it is not on these records or is not readily ascertainable, at the place where the regular meetings of the Board of Trustees are held. Such notice shall be given not fewer than ten (10) nor more than ninety (90) days before the date of the meeting to each Trustee who is entitled to vote; provided, however, that if notice is mailed, it shall be deposited in the United States mail at least twenty (20) days before the meeting.

Such notice shall state the date, place, and hour of the meeting and, whenever practical, the general nature of the business to be transacted. Any other business which properly comes before a meeting may be transacted, notwithstanding the preceding sentence.

SECTION 11. ACTION AT A MEETING: QUORUM AND REQUIRED VOTE One-third of all the Trustees eligible to vote shall constitute a quorum. Only Trustees eligible to vote may hold and vote proxies. A majority of those present in person or by proxy at a duly held meeting with a quorum may perform any act or make any decision vested in the Board of Trustees, unless a greater number, or the same number after disqualifying one or more Trustees from voting, is required by law or the Foundation's Articles of Incorporation or By-Laws, and may continue to transact business notwithstanding the withdrawal of enough members to leave less than a quorum.

SECTION 12. ACTION WITHOUT A MEETING: MAIL-WRITTEN BALLOTS Any action which may be taken at any regular or special meeting of Trustees may be taken without a meeting if the Foundation distributes a mail-written ballot to every Trustee entitled to vote on the matter. Such ballot shall set forth the proposed action, provide an opportunity to specify approval or disapproval of any proposal, and provide a reasonable time within which to mail or otherwise return the ballot to the Foundation.

Approval by mail-written ballot shall be valid only when the number of votes cast by ballot within the time period specified equals or exceeds the quorum required to be present at a meeting authorizing the action, and the number of approvals equals or exceeds the number of votes that would be required to approve the action at a meeting at which the total number of votes cast was the same as the number cast by ballot.

Ballots shall be solicited in a manner consistent with the notice requirements of these By-Laws. All such solicitations shall indicate the number of responses needed to meet the quorum requirement and, with respect to ballots other than for the election of Trustees or Directors, shall state the percentage of approvals necessary to pass the measure submitted. The solicitation must specify the time by which the ballot must be received in order to be counted.

Mail-written ballots may not be revoked. Trustees may be elected by mail-written ballot if the Board so determines, in which case the Board shall also fix a date for the close of nominations a reasonable time before the printing and distribution of the mail-written ballots.

The use of a written ballot at a meeting of the Board of Trustees, which is intended to be voted upon at the meeting where it is distributed, does not invoke the provisions of this section as to mail-written ballots.

SECTION 13. VALIDATION OF DEFECTIVELY CALLED OR NOTICED MEETINGS   The transactions of any meeting of the Board of Trustees, however called or noticed or wherever held, shall be as valid as though transacted at a meeting duly held after regular call and notice, if a quorum is present and if, either before or after the meeting, each of the Trustees not present or who, though present, has prior to the meeting or at its commencement protested the lack of proper notice to him, signs a written waiver of notice or a consent to holding such meeting or an approval of the minutes thereof. A waiver of notice need not specify the purpose of any regular or special meeting of the Board of Trustees. All such waivers, consents, or approvals shall be filed with the Foundation's records or made a part of the minutes of the meeting.

SECTION 14. ADJOURNMENT   A majority of the Trustees present in person or by proxy, whether or not a quorum is present, may adjourn any meeting to another time and place. If the meeting is adjourned for more than thirty (30) days, notice of the adjournment to another time or place shall be given prior to the time of the adjourned meeting to the Trustees who were not present at the time of the adjournment.

SECTION 15. FORM OF PROXY OR MAIL-WRITTEN BALLOT   Any form of proxy or mail-written ballot shall afford an opportunity on the proxy form or mail-written ballot to specify a choice between approval and disapproval of each matter or group of related matters intended, at the time the proxy or mail-written ballot is distributed, to be acted upon at the meeting for which the proxy is solicited or by such mail-written ballot, and shall provide that where the person solicited specifies a choice with respect to any such matter the vote shall be cast in accordance therewith.

In any election, any form of proxy or mail-written ballot in which the Trustees to be voted upon are named therein as candidates and which is marked by a Trustee "withhold" or otherwise marked in a manner indicating that the authority to vote for the election of Trustees is withheld shall not be voted either for or against the election of a Trustee.

SECTION 16. FEES AND COMPENSATION   Trustees shall not receive compensation for their services as such. Trustees may, however, be reimbursed for reasonable out-of-pocket expenses incurred by them in the performance of their duties as Trustees.

SECTION 17. COUNCIL OF PRESIDENTS   The president and all the former presidents of the Foundation shall constitute a Council of Presidents whose primary function shall be to recommend to the Nominations Committee a person to be President-elect at the appropriate time. The Council of Presidents shall meet on the call of the President and may serve to advise the President on other matters of importance to the Foundation as the President may from time to time request.

ARTICLE VI. STANDING BOARDS OF THE FOUNDATION

The Board of Trustees shall have certain Standing Boards as set forth herein.

SECTION 1. EXECUTIVE COMMITTEE   The Executive Committee is a Standing Board of the Foundation.

1.1 Composition   The Executive Committee shall have not fewer than twenty-four (24) nor more than thirty (30) members, the exact number to be fixed from time to time by resolution of the Board of Trustees. All members of the Executive Committee shall be members of the Board of Trustees. Except for ex-officio members, and except as otherwise provided in these By-Laws, the Executive Committee shall be elected annually by the Board of Trustees in accordance with the nomination and election procedures for Trustees in these By-Laws. Vacancies of elected members on the Executive Committee arising during the term of office may be filled by the Board of Trustees at a special election to be held at the discretion of the President, unless such vacancies reduce the number of Executive Committee members below twenty-four (24), in which case the President shall call for a special election to be held at the next regularly scheduled meeting of the Board of Trustees. The remaining members of the Executive Committee may temporarily fill vacancies until an election is held.

Any other provision of these By-Laws notwithstanding, at no time shall more than forty-nine (49) percent of the persons serving on the Executive Committee be any of the following: (i) persons compensated by the Foundation for services rendered within the previous twelve (12) months (whether as an employee, contractor, or otherwise) other than reasonable compensation paid to a member for his service as an Executive Committee member, or (ii) the spouse, an ancestor, sibling, or descendent to the first degree of consanguinity, or any person married to such relative of any person so compensated.

1.2 Ex-Officio Executive Committee Members   The following Trustees are designated ex officio as members of the Executive Committee, to serve until their successors are named:

   a.   The Chair of the Board of Trustees
   b.   The President of the Foundation (who shall serve as the Chief Executive Officer and Chair of the Executive Committee)
   c.   The President-elect of the Foundation (when one exists)
   d.   The Vice President–Finance of the Foundation (who shall serve as Chief Staff and Financial Officer of the Executive Committee)
   e.   The Vice President–Development of the Foundation
   f.   The General Counsel of the Foundation

Any other provision of these By-Laws notwithstanding, at no time shall more than one-third of the persons serving on the Executive Committee be ex-officio members as designated herein.

1.3 Term of Office   Elected members of the Executive Committee shall serve for a one-year term and may be reelected for not more than six consecutive one-year terms. Ex-officio members of the Executive Committee shall serve so long as they hold the positions that qualify them as members

1.4 Duties and Powers   The Executive Committee shall manage the activities and affairs of the Foundation and have the full authority to act thereon except as limited by law, the Articles of Incorporation, and except as certain functions may be reserved to the Board of Trustees or may be delegated by the Board of Trustees to Standing Boards or special committees of the Foundation pursuant to these By-Laws.

Notwithstanding any other provision of these By-Laws, the Executive Committee is vested with the full fiduciary responsibility for the following:

a.   The prudent investment of and accountability for the assets of the Foundation.

b.   The adoption of the Foundation's annual budget.

c.   The power to approve self-dealing transactions, the power to issue checks, drafts, and other orders for the payment of money, notes or other evidence of indebtedness and to receive the same on behalf of the Foundation, with such signature or endorsement authority as the Executive Committee determines.

d.   The power to authorize any officer or officers, agent or agents, to enter into any contract or execute any instrument in the name of, and on behalf of, the Foundation. Such authority may be general or confined to specific instances and, unless so authorized by the Board of Trustees, no officer, agent, or employee shall have any power or authority to bind the Foundation by any con-tract or engagement or to pledge its credit or to render it liable for any purpose or any amount, except for con-tracts or commitments in the regular course of business of the Foundation executed by an officer within the scope of his authority.

Subject to any limitations of law, or the Articles of Incorporation, the Executive Committee shall manage and carry out the fiduciary responsibility vested in it by these By-Laws and in so doing shall have all the rights, powers, and authority of the Board of Trustees.

1.5 Regular Meetings   Meetings of the Executive Committee shall be held at such times and at such places as the President may determine, but in no event fewer than three (3) times during each fiscal year of the Foundation. Notice of such meetings shall be given in the manner set forth in Section 8 of Article V of these By-Laws (relating to Notice and Place of Meeting), except that notice may be given by telephone not less than twenty-four (24) hours prior to the meeting and that notice sent by mail shall be given not less than forty-eight (48) hours prior to the meeting.

Actions may be taken without a meeting of the Executive Committee if all members individually or collectively consent thereto in writing. Such consents shall be filed with the minutes of the proceedings of the Executive Committee, and shall have the same force and effect as an action taken at regularly noticed meetings of the Executive Committee.

1.6 Quorum   Twelve (12) members present in person shall constitute a quorum for the transaction of business, except as expressly provided otherwise in the Articles of Incorporation, these By-Laws, or by resolution of the Board of Trustees. The Executive Committee shall not conduct business by proxy or mail-written ballot.

1.7 Meetings by Conference Telephone   Members of the Executive Committee may participate in a meeting through use of conference telephone or similar communications equipment, so long as all members participating in such meeting can hear one another. Participation in a meeting in this manner shall constitute presence in person at such meeting.

1.8 Special Committees and Organization   In discharging its responsibilities, the Executive Committee will establish appropriate policies for the investment and management of funds, for the conduct of audits, for the acceptance and management of planned gifts, for the grants and allocations of Foundation funds, and for the nomination of persons for election to the various posts established in these By-Laws for election by the Board of Trustees. The Executive Committee shall create special committees on investment, audit, grants and allocations, and nominations for the exercise of these respective responsibilities and may delegate to these committees such responsibility to act on behalf of the Executive Committee, to the extent permitted by law, as it deems appropriate, and each such committee shall report all actions taken to the next regular meeting of the Executive Committee. The Executive Committee from time to time may create such other committees and delegate to each such authority as the Executive Committee deems appropriate.

The Executive Committee shall, by resolution, establish the number of members, responsibility, title, and rules governing any special committees established hereunder. The members, and Chair, of all such special committees shall be appointed annually by the President, subject to approval by the Board of Trustees. The President, the Vice President–Development, and the Vice President–Finance shall be ex-officio members of all special committees (except the Audit Committee); all other members of the special committees shall be appointed from the membership of the Board of Trustees, provided that the majority of each committee is comprised of Trustees who are not ex-officio members.

The President shall appoint the Chairs and members of such committees established by the Executive Committee and shall assure that each committee shall have representatives of the Executive Committee and other groups represented on the Board of Trustees as a whole.

The Executive Committee shall establish rules and procedures for the conduct of its business and, except as already provided for in these By-Laws, appoint such officers as it deems appropriate for the conduct of its business.

1.9 Removal with Cause   The Board of Trustees may remove from office by majority vote an Executive Committee member who has been declared of unsound mind by final order of a court, or convicted of a felony, or found by final order of a court to have violated a duty under Article 3 of the Nonprofit Public Benefit Corporation Law.

1.10 Removal without Cause   Any Executive Committee member may be removed from office without cause by the vote of a majority of the Trustees then in office.

SECTION 2. BOARD OF DEVELOPMENT   A Standing Board to be known as the Board of Development shall be vested with the Foundation's authority to raise private funds and other gifts to support its mission.

The composition of the Board of Development is intended to reflect the breadth of the development effort, with representatives from diverse areas of the community as well as central development activities. Its purpose is to serve as the senior advisory and volunteer management body for development. The President shall be Chair of the Board of Development.

2.1 Ex-Officio Members of Board of Development: Term of Office   The following persons are designated ex officio as members of the Board of Development, to serve so long as they hold the position designated below, or as otherwise provided herein:

1.   The Chairman of the Board of Trustees

2.   The President of the Foundation (who shall serve as Chair)

3.   The President-elect of the Foundation (when one exists)

4.   The Vice President–Development of the Foundation

5.   The Vice President–Finance of the Foundation

6.   The General Counsel of the Foundation

2.2 Other Members of the Board of Development: Term of Office   The President may appoint other members of the Board of Development who may or may not be Trustees, to serve at the pleasure of the President. Consideration in making such appointments should be given to the person's strong history of financial support for the Foundation or whose experience, ability, and leadership would be of great value to the Board of Development.

ARTICLE VII. OFFICERS

The Foundation shall have certain officers as set forth herein. The Foundation may also have such other officers as the Executive Committee may from time to time establish in order to conduct the business of the Foundation. Each officer of the Foundation shall have such authority and perform such duties as provided in the By-Laws or as the Executive Committee may from time to time prescribe.

SECTION 1. CHAIR OF THE BOARD   The Chair of the Board shall be the immediate past President of the Foundation. He or she shall preside at meetings of the Board of Trustees, the Executive Committee, and the Board of Development in the absence of the President.

SECTION 2. PRESIDENT   The President shall be an elected Trustee of the Foundation and is elected by the Board of Trustees as provided in these By-Laws for a term of two years, and may not be reelected to a second consecutive term. The President shall be the Chief Executive Officer and shall preside at all meetings of the Board of Trustees, the Board of Development, and the Executive Committee. A vacancy in the presidency will be filled by the President-elect or, if there is none, by special election of the Board of Trustees. An ex-officio Trustee shall not serve as President.

SECTION 3. PRESIDENT-ELECT   The President-elect shall be an elected Trustee of the Foundation and is elected by the Board of Trustees at the last meeting of the fiscal year before the anniversary of the President's assumption of office, and shall take office as President at the expiration of the President's term of office, or upon a vacancy in the office of President. The President-elect shall preside at meetings of the Board of Trustees in the absence of both the President and Chairman of the Board and shall perform the other duties of the President in the President's absence.

SECTION 4. VICE PRESIDENT–DEVELOPMENT   The Vice President–Development shall serve as Chief Staff Officer of the Board of Development.

SECTION 5. VICE PRESIDENT–FINANCE   The Vice President–Finance shall serve as chief staff officer of the Executive Committee and Chief Financial Officer of the Foundation, and act as the Foundation's Secretary and Treasurer.

SECTION 6. GENERAL COUNSEL   The General Counsel shall be the legal advisor to the Foundation and all of its boards and committees, and shall exercise such other powers and perform such other duties as the Board of Trustees may from time to time determine. The President shall appoint the General Counsel, who shall serve at the pleasure of the President.

SECTION 7. REMOVAL AND RESIGNATION   Any officer elected by the Board of Trustees or appointed by the President may be removed at any time with or without cause either by the Board of Trustees, by the President, or by any officer upon whom the power of removal has been conferred by the Board of Trustees, subject to the rights, if any, of the officer under a contract of employment with the Foundation. Without prejudice to the rights, if any, of the Foundation under any contract to which the officer is a party, any officer may resign at any time by giving written notice to the Foundation. Unless otherwise specified therein, any such resignation shall take effect at the date of the receipt of such notice.

SECTION 8. VACANCIES   A vacancy occurring in any office shall be filled in accordance with the procedure for the regular selection or appointment of that officer under these By-Laws, although the President may appoint a person to act as that officer in the interval of time reasonably required before a regular appointment can be made.

SECTION 9. COMPENSATION   Officers may receive such compensation for their services or such reimbursement for their expenses as may be determined by the Executive Committee to be just and reasonable. The Board of Trustees may, at the Foundation's expense, bond any officer and employee for the faithful performance of his duties in such amount and with such surety or sureties as it may determine.

ARTICLE VIII. PROCEDURES

The Board of Trustees, the Executive Committee, and the Board of Development may each prescribe appropriate rules.

SECTION 4. STANDING ORDERS   Standing orders and rules of practice consistent with the Articles of Incorporation and the By-Laws may be prescribed from time to time by the Board of Trustees in order to facilitate and expedite the carrying on of the business of the Foundation. The Vice President–Finance shall keep such orders and rules, if any, in permanent written form, properly indexed, and same shall be part of the permanent records of the Foundation and shall govern and control the administration of the activities and affairs of the Foundation as far as applicable.

SECTION 5. INDEMNIFICATION OF AGENTS OF THE CORPORATION: LIABILITY INSUR-ANCE

5.1   Subject to any limitations contained in the Articles of Incorporation and to the extent permitted by the California Nonprofit Public Benefit Corporation Law, the Foundation may indemnify any person who was or is a party or is threatened to be made a party to any proceeding by reason of the fact that such person is or was a Trustee, officer, employee, member of a committee, or other agent of the Foundation, against expenses, judgments, fines, settlements, and other amounts actually and reasonably incurred in connection with such proceeding and the Foundation may advance expenses in connection therewith.

5.2   The Foundation may purchase and maintain insurance on behalf of any Trustee, officer, employee, or other agent of the Foundation against any liability asserted against or incurred by such person in his or her capacity or arising out of his or her status as such, whether or not the Foundation could indemnify such person against such liabilities under the provisions of Section 5.1 of Article IX. Notwithstanding the above, the Foundation shall not purchase and maintain such insurance for a violation of Section 5233 of the California Nonprofit Public Benefit Corporation Law (with respect to self-dealing transactions).

5.3   Section 5 of Article IX (relating to Indemnification of Agents of the Corporation: Liability Insurance) does not apply to any proceeding against any Trustee, investment manager, or other fiduciary of any employee benefit plan in such person's capacity as such, even through said person may also be a Trustee, officer, employee, or other agent of the Foundation for purposes of Sections 5.1 and 5.2 of Article IX. The Foundation may indemnify such Trustee, investment manager, or other fiduciary to the extent permitted by Subdivision (f) of Section 207 of the California General Corporation Law.

SECTION 6. SUPPORT GROUP POLICY   Notwithstanding any provision of these By-Laws to the contrary, the Foundation shall comply with policies relating to support groups as set forth in policy statements in effect from time to time.

ARTICLE IX: MISCELLANEOUS

SECTION 1. INSPECTION OF CORPORATE RECORDS   Every Trustee shall have the absolute right at any reasonable time to inspect and copy all books, records and documents of every kind and to inspect the physical properties of the Foundation. Such inspection may be made in person or by agent or attorney and the right of inspection includes the right to copy and make extracts.

SECTION 2. REPRESENTATION OF SHARES OF OTHER CORPORATIONS   The Chair of the Board, the President, the Vice President-Finance or another Trustee designated by the Executive Committee is authorized to vote, represent, and exercise on behalf of the Foundation all rights incident to any and all shares of any other corporation or corporations standing in the name of the Foundation, unless the Board of Trustees designates another person to exercise such rights, or unless the By-Laws of the other corporation otherwise provide. The authority herein granted may be exercised either in person or by proxy or power of attorney duly executed.

SECTION 3. FISCAL YEAR: AUDIT   The fiscal year of the Foundation shall be from July 1 to June 30. The financial books and records of the Foundation shall be audited at least once during each fiscal year by reputable and independent certified accountants.

ARTICLE X. AMENDMENTS TO BY-LAWS

The Board of Trustees may adopt, amend, or repeal these By-Laws. Any proposed amendment, repeal, or revision of these By-Laws shall be submitted in writing to the Vice President–Finance not fewer than fifteen (15) or more than ninety (90) days prior to the meeting at which the same is to be considered. At least ten (10) days prior to such meeting, the Vice President–Finance shall mail or cause to be delivered copies of any such proposal to each Trustee in the manner provided in Section 10 of Article V (relating to Notice and Place of Meetings) of these By-Laws.

SUMMARY OF RESPONSIBILITIES
AND QUALIFICATIONS

BOARD OF TRUSTEES SUMMARY OF RESPONSIBILITIES

Members of the board of trustees of a nonprofit organization must assume their role with a full understanding of the accountability and liability, both personal and organizational, resulting from their service in their particular state. Specific responsibilities include but are not necessarily limited to:

- Determine the organization's mission and ensure that it is being carried out, as documented by federal and state law.
- Set policies for ensuring that the organization operates according to its bylaws, the law, and ethical standards.
- Ensure compliance with the rules and regulations set by federal, state, and local governments that have jurisdiction over it (e.g., filing tax returns with the IRS).
- Make certain that donated funds are used for the purposes of the organization, as prescribed by the donor.
- Fulfill the legal requirements of the organization as an employer, including the payment of payroll taxes for the organization's employees.
- Develop the organization's overall program and engage in long-range strategic planning to establish its general course for the future.
- Oversee the financial health of the organization and establish fiscal policy and boundaries with budgets and financial controls.
- Provide adequate resources to operate the organization through direct financial contributions and a commitment to fundraising.
- Select and evaluate the performance of the executive director/chief executive officer.
- Develop and maintain a communication link between the organization and the community in promoting its work.
- Monitor the performance of the organization to maximize the welfare of the public.

QUALIFICATIONS   Trustees must possess these qualifications:

- Strong commitment to the mission, goals, and objectives of the organization

- Time, energy, and expertise required to make a significant contribution
- Skills and experience in organizational, financial, and human resource management and strategic planning
- Ability to address issues and problems analytically, creatively, and decisively
- Strong leadership, interpersonal, and networking skills
- Familiarity with federal, state, and local laws and regulations governing nonprofit organizations
- Honesty, integrity, dedication, and positive attitude

BOARD CHAIR

SUMMARY OF RESPONSIBILITIES   The chair's overarching responsibility is to lead and motivate the board of trustees in concert with the ED/CEO. Specific responsibilities include:

- Focus the board on fulfilling its short- and long-term responsibilities and developing a clear vision for the future.
- Provide strong leadership and direction to the board, and develop ways to enhance its effectiveness.
- Represent and speak on behalf of the board concerning its decisions, actions, and related activities in interactions with the media, donors, and other constituencies of the nonprofit organization.
- Serve as the board's conscience and disciplinarian in order to control inexperienced or misguided trustees, prevent factionalism and other practices harmful to the board's reputation, promote teamwork and collegiality, and uphold ethical standards.

QUALIFICATIONS   The chair must demonstrate these qualities:

- Exemplary record of service and contributions to the board that has earned the respect and trust of the membership
- Clear understanding of the respective responsibilities of the chair and the ED/CEO, and the ability to work cooperatively with the ED/CEO toward common goals
- Excellent command of all aspects of the nonprofit organization, including strengths and weaknesses, and the ability to focus the board's attention on both short-term needs and a long-term vision
- Close ties with business leaders, potential donors, government agencies, and others who can be of assistance to the nonprofit organization
- Strong organizational, communication, listening, motivating, decision-making, and public speaking skills
- Sensitivity, objectivity, foresight, loyalty, and discretion

EXECUTIVE DIRECTOR/CHIEF EXECUTIVE OFFICER

SUMMARY OF RESPONSIBILITIES   The ED/CEO of a nonprofit organization is appointed by and reports to the board of trustees and has primary responsibility for the day-to-day operations. Specific responsibilities are to:

- Manage the financial operations of the organization to include internal control, review of financial statements, and monitoring of all financial details to ensure their accuracy and integrity.
- Ensure that all programs, services, and activities contribute to and are in sync with the organizational mission, goals, and objectives.
- Implement and monitor compliance with policies related to the organizational bylaws, the law, and ethical standards.
- Select, supervise, and evaluate the performance of key positions including the treasurer/chief financial officer.
- Develop and maintain close working relations with trustees, staff, donors, and the community at large.

QUALIFICATIONS   The ED/CEO must possess these qualifications:

- Master's degree in business or the equivalent in a related field
- Extensive skills and experience in providing leadership and direction for all aspects of a large, complex nonprofit organization
- Proven ability to effectively manage financial, human, capital, and other organizational resources
- Excellent organizational, motivational, and interpersonal skills
- Familiarity with federal, state, and local laws and regulations governing nonprofit organizations
- Honesty, integrity, dedication, and positive attitude

TREASURER/CHIEF FINANCIAL OFFICER

SUMMARY OF RESPONSIBILITIES   The role of treasurer/chief financial officer of a nonprofit organization entails these responsibilities (assuming that the organization does not have a separate chief financial officer):

- Develop a financial structure for the review and approval of the board of trustees.
- Safeguard the financial assets and maintain the financial records.
- Define appropriate standards of behavior for fulfilling the finance function within the organization.
- Prepare timely and meaningful financial statements.
- Plan and implement fundraising programs and explore planned giving opportunities.
- Comply with external reporting requirements.
- Develop and implement appropriate budgeting practices and procedures.
- Respond to operational changes affecting financial needs.
- Report financial results to the ED/CEO and board of trustees.
- Supervise and empower employees engaged in the organization's financial activities.
- Serve as a key participant in teams engaged in addressing multifaceted organizational problems.

- Play an integral role in organizational decision-making and creative problem solving.
- Develop and implement systems for internal and external information-sharing related to the organization's finances.
- Work with program heads to represent their interests, explain the story behind the numbers, and clarify the business impacts during every step of the planning and budgeting process.
- Present to the ED/CEO and board of trustees a balanced picture of what is happening, where the problems lie, and what actions need to be taken.

QUALIFICATIONS   The treasurer/chief financial officer must possess these qualifications:

- Training and experience in financial management, and knowledge of the treasury function, generally accepted accounting principles, and internal control systems
- Knowledge about the organization's mission and programs, and their relationship to the financial requirements and components
- Technical expertise in developing budgets and preparing financial statements
- Operational expertise
- Interpersonal communication and decision-making skills
- Honesty, integrity as evidenced by background check and ability to be bonded, and commitment to the organization's mission, values, and goals

SECRETARY

SUMMARY OF RESPONSIBILITIES   The responsibilities of the secretary are reflected in the nonprofit organization's bylaws and standing orders and include these major functions:

- Plan board meeting calendar and individual meetings, develop and distribute agendas, and provide for the staffing needs of the board and its committees.
- Prepare and disseminate minutes, resolutions, policy statements, and board correspondence.
- Review and maintain bylaws and standing orders.
- Serve as custodian of official corporate documents and records.
- Coordinate and facilitate all board meeting arrangements, including travel, hotel, meals, and other logistical details.
- Foster effective communication and good personal relations between the board of trustees and the ED/CEO.

QUALIFICATIONS   The secretary must possess these skills/strengths:

- Understanding of the secretary's unique role and commitment to developing and enhancing it
- Experience in managing and organizing all aspects of the work environment
- Knowledge of the history and mission of the nonprofit organization
- Familiarity with the legal and ethical issues of concern to trustees
- Superior writing, coordinative, and interpersonal skills
- Efficiency, flexibility, and attention to detail

NOMINATING COMMITTEE

SUMMARY OF RESPONSIBILITIES   Members of the nominating committee must devote their efforts to ensuring that the board of trustees possesses the optimal mix of skills, experience, and influence needed to meet the board's wide-ranging challenges. Particular responsibilities include:

- Assist the board in determining the desired composition with respect to skills, abilities, experience, diversity, and influence and in making periodic adjustments to meet the changing needs of the organization.
- Develop and cultivate a list of top-notch candidates who possess the desired qualities and are willing and able to serve.
- Design, implement, and oversee a program for orienting, educating, and motivating new trustees.
- Oversee the successful integration of new trustees onto board committees and other activities.
- Assess the effectiveness of individual board members at the end of their terms, and determine their reelection status.
- Identify and acknowledge meritorious contributions to the board on the part of individual trustees.
- Coordinate periodic reviews of the overall performance of the board.
- Nominate the officers of the board, and evaluate their performance on an annual basis.

QUALIFICATIONS   Members of the nominating committee must possess these qualifications:

- Track record of strong, effective, and dedicated service on the board
- Access to prominent individuals in the business, financial, and other communities who are prospective recruits
- Clear understanding of the board's role and the importance of its composition to the organization's future
- Excellent planning, networking, and persuasive skills
- Patience, perseverance, and commitment to the task at hand

FINANCE COMMITTEE

SUMMARY OF RESPONSIBILITIES   The finance committee is charged with these tasks:

- Undertake a detailed review of all financial statements and audit reports (unless the latter is done by a separate audit committee), and convey the results to the board.
- Make recommendations to the board on policy matters and issues related to the financial management function of the nonprofit organization.
- Provide assistance and support to the treasurer/chief financial officer in the development of long-range plans for raising, managing, and safeguarding organizational funds in an optimal manner.

QUALIFICATIONS   Members of the finance committee must have these qualifications:

- Clear understanding of the mission, goals, and respective roles of the finance committee and treasurer/chief financial officer for the nonprofit organization
- Skills and experience in the areas of financial management, communication, and planning
- Integrity, good judgment, and adherence to sound financial principles

VOLUNTEERS

Volunteers are invaluable resources who contribute to the mission of nonprofit organizations in a variety of important ways. They can assist in an optimal manner under these conditions:

- All volunteers are required to participate in an orientation program in order to gain a thorough understanding of the mission, goals, and activities of the nonprofit organization as well as learn about available involvement opportunities.
- Volunteers are assigned to activities that match their particular experience, talents, and areas of interest.
- Staff members are assigned to oversee specific tasks performed by volunteers as well as to provide guidance and answer any questions that may arise.
- Job descriptions are used to clarify the specific tasks, duties, responsibilities, expectations, chain of command, and other details of the various volunteer positions.
- Background checks are administered where appropriate.
- Liability insurance coverage is held where appropriate.
- Periodic meetings with volunteers are held to solicit feedback on the progress made, problems encountered, and changes needed.
- Close working relations between volunteers and professional staff are fostered to ensure maximum effectiveness and productivity.
- Volunteers are treated with the utmost respect and appreciation, and complete their assigned tasks with thoughtfulness, flexibility, enthusiasm, and dedication.

CHAPTER 5

DEVELOPING FINANCIAL POLICIES

5.1 INTRODUCTION

"Use your own best judgment at all times." Nordstrom, a nationwide fashion specialty retail chain, encapsulates its entire policy manual in eight words, highlighting the importance of careful recruitment, training, and retention of qualified and ethical employees. However, the extreme brevity of Nordstrom's policies also implies a limit to policy and raises the question of why an organization would want to have an elaborate set of policies.

We respond in two ways. First, wisdom is enshrined in carefully developed and well-thought-out policies. Second, policies precede practices, just as beliefs lead to behaviors.

Establishing and complying with policy is the fundamental charge of the director, chief financial officer (CFO), or fund manager. *Internal policies* are your organization's set of policies. *External policies* are provided by outside organizations and are agreed to as part of the acceptance of their funds

(a) WHAT IS POLICY?   There are two general definitions for policy and procedure: authoritative and practical:

	Authoritative	**Practical**
Policy	A definite course of action adopted as expedient or from other consideration	A set of guidelines or principles defining an organization's philosophy toward how business shall be conducted
Procedure	The act or manner of proceeding in any action or process; conduct	Steps and/or actions to be taken to comply with a specific policy

Policy has regrettably been associated with red tape or bureaucracy. Phrases such as "I'm sorry, that's not our policy" as a method of telling someone no contributes greatly to the perception that policy interferes with productivity, efficiency, and good customer relations. Certainly, in many instances, the negative association with policies is legitimate; many governmental bodies and regulatory agencies are mired in policy that is ineffective and out of date. Also, many policies have become a method of preventing lawsuits rather than what they are intended to be: a set of guidelines (laws, rules) or principles for how day-to-day business should be performed.

(b) WHY ARE POLICIES REQUIRED?   Policy is the rule of law for an organization. Policies establish a common understanding of the overriding principles behind all that we do. Good policies merge all of the laws, rules, and regulations from all sources (both internal and external) into a cohesive instrument. Rather than providing new staff members with copies of all the various laws, codes, and policies from all of the agencies and organizations that they may work with, policies condense all that information into one set of guidelines, eliminating inconsistencies and redundancies.

Even if policies are not written down, all organizations have policies. Sometimes, to avoid the negative association with the term, organizations may refer to them as guidelines, work rules, or job instructions. Regardless of what they are called or the form they take, they do exist.

If we did not have policies, a method or plan would have to be established each time someone needed to do something. If we needed to buy something, we would have to find out what rules applied and what steps or actions needed to be taken every single time. In addition, policies enable us to share information by requiring that certain actions be performed and information be gathered in a consistent manner.

Summarizing, we see four benefits to having policies, preferably written ones:

1. Policies communicate and reinforce valued standard operating procedures (SOP) and philosophies to board members, staff, volunteers, and donors or grant agencies.

2. Policies help in the management of the organization, as the executive director (ED)/chief executive officer (CEO) cannot be there for every decision that must be made, and are the vehicle through which the board influences and governs the organization. (We often hear that boards are "responsible for policy.") Good policies may help prevent micromanagement on the part of the board

3. Policies protect the organization, particularly those set for financial position, fraud prevention, risk management, investments, debt, employment (background checks), and employee relations (harassment, confidentiality, discrimination, bonding); as a set, good policies make an organization more "bankable" as well.

4. Policies serve as an orientation tool for new board members and new staff or volunteer.

Do current organizational practices give more or less emphasis to the benefits of policy? In Exhibit 5.1 you will see ten board member cautions related to finance. As you read this listing of areas of nonprofit board financial malfeasance (misconduct or wrongdoing) and nonfeasance (failure to perform an official duty), think of how policy could prevent or limit the degree of harm.

(c) COMPLYING WITH AND ESTABLISHING POLICY AND PROCEDURE.   One of the jobs of the CFO, as well as all the leaders in an organization, is to promote and establish

---

1. **Ineffectually scrutinizing the overall enterprise**, from not receiving or reading financial statements, receiving them late or incomplete, not receiving or distributing to other board members the IRS Form 990, unawareness of how functional allocations are made (program, management, and fundraising expenses), or not discussing the auditor's management letter.
2. **Failing to monitor key indicators, allowing the organization to drift into financial trouble**, from not matching revenues and expenses, not monitoring debt ratios, overspending some budget categories, or not being informed by the ED/CEO when income is delayed or under-budget.
3. **Failing to pay sufficient attention to whether the organization's financial resources are being effectively spent on programs**, from not having documented program results related to outcomes, not merely the clients served or dollars spent.
4. **Being too trusting of staffers who handle money**, meaning that activities are verified, and other appropriate internal controls are used, and possibly involving establishment of a financial control committee.
5. **Lacking strong external checks on financial reporting**, including not having a CPA firm conduct an audit (which should be done by many organizations, particularly those with budgets of $350,000 or more), since only three states require registered charities to have an audit.
6. **Emphasizing executive compensation at the expense of other employees**, offering competitive salaries and benefits to top-level executives while offering substandard compensation packages to all other staffers, resulting in poor morale and higher turnover [and, we would add, perceived inequity].
7. **Failing to "bid out" the sale of organizational assets**, such as hospital conversions, and building, camp, and religious television station sales that are made to a single bidder and without the board assessing fairness of the sales price.
8. **Failing to scrutinize outside service contracts sufficiently**, including fundraising, direct mail, and telemarketing consulting services, which should normally be rebid at least every three years [we would add your primary banking and service providers to this list].
9. **Spending funds restricted by time or purpose**, including meeting cash flow shortfalls with special project dollars, capital funds, or even endowment funds, even though temporary uses of restricted funds are technically a violation of law in every state; this situation reveals that the board has allowed the organization to get into a financial hole, linking back to pitfall #2.
10. **Mixing charitable and business interests**, which is arising more and more as a conflict of interest that comes out of a partnership of some kind, and appears to emerge from the very board members who were recruited because of their connections.

Source: Jon Pratt, "Financial Malfeasance and Nonfeasance: Ten Pitfalls Boards Should Avoid," *Board Member* (September/October 1996);3. Used by permission.

EXHIBIT 5.1   BOARD MEMBER CAUTIONS RELATED TO FINANCES

a positive attitude toward the compliance with policy, either external or internal. If there is no support at the top, there will be no compliance at the bottom. Before staff and managers will comply with policy, they need to receive a clear message from executive management that the organization supports and actually insists on compliance with policy.

Depending on the nature of your organization and the specific policy, internal or external noncompliance can range from fraud to poor business management, from felony to raised eyebrows.

Office of Management and Budget (see Exhibit 5.3)	
National Institutes of Health (NIH)	**Department of Defense—Agencies**
Center for Information Technology	Defense Advanced Research Projects Agency (DARPA)
Center for Scientific Review	Defense Commissary Agency (DECA)
National Cancer Institute (NCI)—Center for Cancer Research	Defense Contract Audit Agency (DCAA)
	Defense Contract Management Agency (DCMA)
Etc.	Defense Finance and Accounting Service (DFAS)
	Etc.

EXHIBIT 5.2   SIMPLIFIED DIAGRAM OF THE HIERARCHY OF POLICY WITHIN THE U.S. GOVERNMENT

(d) WHO SETS POLICY?

- *Internal.* Internal policies are those that are in effect within your organization. These policies must indicate compliance with external policies. (See Exhibit 5.12 later in the chapter for methods to develop these policies.) The board establishes policy, and each department within the organization develops a set of policies that detail compliance with the policy established by the board.

- *External.* External policies are those that affect day-to-day operations but are in the charge of an entity outside of the organization, such as the government or other regulatory agency.

Policies are very similar to laws: They have a hierarchical structure. Your organization has some form of hierarchy. The board of directors sets the mission and goals of the institution; it communicates this mission to the executives who, in turn, communicate it to the units under their jurisdiction, and so on. At each step in the process, policy is being established.

Organizations that are part of the U.S. government, or do business with it, are required to comply with all U.S. government policies. Within the U.S. government, there is a hierarchy of policies. A simplified diagram of this hierarchy is shown in Exhibits 5.2 and 5.3.

Exhibit 5.2 illustrates how the Center for Cancer Research must comply with the policies in the Office of Management and Budget (OMB) as well as the National Institutes of Health (NIH) and the National Cancer Institute (NCI). The Center for Cancer Research also has its own set of policies with which it must comply. Any organization doing business with it must comply with this same set of policies. If each time staff members in an organization dealing with the Center for Cancer Research had to decipher all of the policies in the hierarchy, they would not be able to do anything productively; however, if they had a set of policies that included the requirements of the Center for Cancer Research as well as any other agency with which they did business, work could be conducted both efficiently and effectively.

When the NIH developed its policies, it interpreted the policies provided by the OMB. In turn, the NCI developed its policies from the interpretation of the OMB policy produced from the NIH. Each time the OMB makes a policy change, it causes a ripple effect throughout the entire U.S. government as well as in all the organizations that do business with the government. To see more about the OMB's oversight role in this structure, see Exhibit 5.3.

Office of Management and Budget Mission

   OMB's predominant mission is to assist the President in overseeing the preparation of the federal budget and to supervise its administration in Executive Branch agencies. In helping to formulate the President's spending plans, OMB evaluates the effectiveness of agency programs, policies, and procedures, assesses competing funding demands among agencies, and sets funding priorities. OMB ensures that agency reports, rules, testimony, and proposed legislation are consistent with the President's Budget and with Administration policies.

   In addition, OMB oversees and coordinates the Administration's procurement, financial management, information, and regulatory policies. In each of these areas, OMB's role is to help improve administrative management, to develop better performance measures and coordinating mechanisms, and to reduce any unnecessary burdens on the public.

Source: http://www.whitehouse.gov/.

Exhibit 5.3   OMB's Role

Unfortunately, many organizations within and outside of the U.S. government have not devoted the time and resources to maintaining their policies, eliminating old policies, or incorporating new policies. Policies within the U.S. government—or any organization—can proliferate and become meaningless.

(e) WHERE TO START?   Since policies are very often an interpretation of another policy, the core meaning of the policy is often lost after multiple iterations—and the original intent may have been largely forgotten.

   With the proliferation of policies without proper maintenance, it is important to start with the original policy statement in developing new policies (or updating of existing policies). Only in the original document, not in the interpretations, can the policies in effect be found. If your organization has dealings with the U.S. government, obtaining copies of the OMB publications is one of the best places to start. (See the most recent listing in Exhibit 5.4.) Even if you do not have business dealings with the U.S. government, the policies from the OMB may be a good model for some of the policies you develop, such as your payables policy.

   Of particular interest to the CFO or treasurer is the way in which the federal government has codified and implemented the Prompt Payment Act provisions. The details are included as Exhibit 5.5. We include this not as a model example of the level of detail to which your policy should go—yours will be much briefer and simpler—but to reflect the thoughtfulness and care with which some organizations craft financial policy. Notice how the policy writers included such details as defining the invoice receipt dates and whether to consider cash discounts.

5.2 FINANCIAL POLICIES

Financial issues are among the greatest source of stress for your organization's CEO/ED. According to the 2001 Illinois statewide survey of all types of arts organizations, finances/fundraising is the single most frustrating aspect of being a CEO/ED, and finances (apart from fundraising) have the most adverse effect on these individuals in their current position, as seen in Exhibit 5.6.[1] We cannot help but wonder how many of these organizations

OMB Circular A-1, System of Circulars and Bulletins to Executive Departments and Establishments (08/07/1952)

OMB Circular A-4, Regulatory Analysis (09/17/2003)

OMB Circular A-11, Preparation, Submission and Execution of the Budget (Revised 11/02/2005)

OMB Circular A-16, Coordination of Geographic Information, and Related Spatial Data Activities (08/19/2002)

OMB Circular A-19, Legislative Coordination and Clearance (09/20/1979)

OMB Circular A-21, Cost Principles for Educational Institutions (05/10/2004)

OMB Circular A-25, Transmittal Memorandum #1, User Charges (07/08/1993)

OMB Circular A-34, Instructions on Budget Execution (Rescinded 6/27/2002; superseded by *OMB Circular No. A-11, Part 4*)

OMB Circular A-45, Rental and Construction of Government Quarters (10/20/1993)

OMB Circular A-50, Audit Followup (09/29/1982)

OMB Circular A-76, Performance of Commercial Activities (05/29/2003) (includes technical correction made by OMB Memorandum M-03-20, 08/15/2003)

Implementing the FAIR Act:

Transmittal Memorandum #20 (06/14/1999)

Transmittal Memorandum #21 (04/27/2000)

Transmittal Memorandum #22 (08/31/2000)

Transmittal Memorandum #23 (03/14/2001)

Transmittal Memorandum #24 (02/27/2002)

Transmittal Memorandum #25 (03/14/2003)

Proposed Revised OMB Circular A-76 of November 14, 2002

Historical Circular A-76, Performance of Commercial Activities, (08/04/1983) (Revised 06/14/1999)

Supplemental Handbook (04/01/1996) (Revised 06/14/1999)

OMB Circular A-87, Cost Principles for State, Local and Indian Tribal Governments (05/10/2004)

OMB Circular A-89, Catalog of Federal Domestic Assistance (08/17/1984)

OMB Circular A-94, "Guidelines and Discount Rates for Benefit-Cost Analysis of Federal Programs" (10/29/1992):

Text of OMB Circular No. A-94 (10/29/1992)

Appendix C: Discount Rates for Cost-Effectiveness, Lease-Purchase, and Related Analyses for OMB Circular No. A-94 (01/31/2005)

Table of Past Years Discount Rates from Appendix C of OMB Circular No. A-94 (01/05/2005)

Memorandum M-05-07, 2004 Discount Rates for OMB Circular No. A-94 (01/31/2005)

OMB Circular A-97, (08/29/1969)

Transmittal Memorandum #1, Specialized or Technical Services for State and Local Governments (03/27/1981)

OMB Circular A-102, Grants and Cooperative Agreements With State and Local Governments (10/07/1994) (further amended 08/29/1997) *Where is the Grants Management Common Rule? Where are the Attachments to A-102?*

OMB Circular A-110, Uniform Administrative Requirements for Grants and Other Agreements with Institutions of Higher Education, Hospitals and Other Non-Profit Organizations (11/19/1993) (further amended 09/30/1999)

OMB Circular A-119, Transmittal Memorandum, Federal Participation in the Development and Use of Voluntary Standards (02/10/1998)

OMB Circular A-122, Cost Principles for Non-Profit Organizations (05/10/2004)

OMB Circular A-123

–Management's Responsibility for Internal Control (Effective beginning with Fiscal Year 2006) (Revised 12/21/2004)

–*Appendix A Implementation Plans* (August 1, 2005)

–*Appendix A Implementation Guide* (July 2005)

–*Appendix A Frequently Asked Questions* (August 22, 2005)

–*Appendix B Improving the Management of Government Charge Card Programs* (August 5, 2005)

–Management's Accountability and Control (Effective through Fiscal Year 2005) (Revised 06/21/1995)

EXHIBIT 5.4   OMB CIRCULARS IN NUMERICAL SEQUENCE

OMB Circular A-125 was rescinded and replaced by the Prompt Pay regulations at 5 CFR Part
    1315.
OMB Circular A-126, Improving the Management and Use of Government Aircraft (05/22/1992)
    –Attachment A
    –Attachment B
OMB Circular A-127, Financial Management Systems (07/23/1993)
    Transmittal Memorandum #3 (12/01/2004)
    Transmittal Memorandum #2 (06/10/1999)
OMB Circular A-129, Managing Federal Credit Programs (11/2000)
OMB Circular A-130, Transmittal Memorandum #4, Management of Federal Information
    Resources (11/28/2000)
OMB Circular A-131, Value Engineering (05/21/1993)
OMB Circular A-133, Audits of States, Local Governments, and Non-Profit Organizations
    (06/24/1997) (includes revisions published in Federal Register 06/27/2003)
    –Appendix A: Data Collection Form (Form SF-SAC)
    –Appendix B: 2005 OMB Compliance Supplement
     Update
    –March 2004 Compliance Supplement
OMB Circular A-134, Financial Accounting Principles and Standards (05/20/1993)
OMB Circular A-135, Management of Federal Advisory Committees (10/05/1994)
OMB Circular A-136, Financial Reporting Requirements (Revised 08/23/2005)

EXHIBIT 5.4   OMB CIRCULARS IN NUMERICAL SEQUENCE (*continued*)

are underfunded and possibly understaffed in the finance function, possibly due to the
lack of appropriate financial policies and financial strategies. Financial policies are absolutely essential to organizational health and well-being in the current landscape of U.S.
nonprofits.

(a) ROLES OF BOARD, BOARD TREASURER, AND CEO/ED.   The board treasurer is a key
resource in enabling your organization as it devises or revises financial policies. The board
as a whole is responsible for setting policy. Whether your organization has adopted John
Carver's policy governance model or not, an underpinning philosophy for your policies is
that the board governs the organization and is the sole voice overseeing the CEO/ED. The
key is not to put more authority in the board treasurer than is warranted, as Carver notes:

> Board Treasurers, as commonly used, threaten CEO accountability as well as the
> one voice principle. Treasurers are typically expected to exercise individual judgment
> about the financial dealings of the organization. But Policy Governance boards do not
> allow Treasurers to exercise authority over staff. (Rendering an official judgment of
> performance against one's own individual criteria has the same effect as exercising
> authority.) By creating a role with supervisory authority over the CEO with respect
> to financial management, the board cannot then hold the CEO accountable for that
> topic. The board should accept responsibility for financial governance (setting policy,
> then comparing performance) and require the CEO to be accountable for managing
> finances so that performance compares favorably to policy. The typical use of a
> Treasurer, when a Policy Governance board is required by law to have one, is to
> assist the board in making financial policy, never to judge CEO compliance against
> the Treasurer's own expectations.

Unfortunately, many boards are handicapped when it comes to setting policy. Partly
this is due to their limited understanding of the dynamics of the organization and
the markets in which it operates—especially donor and grantor markets. However,

Sec. 1315.4 Prompt payment standards and required notices to vendors.

Agency business practices shall conform to the following standards:

(a) Required documentation. Agencies will maintain paper or electronic documentation as required in Sec. 1315.9.

(b) Receipt of invoice. For the purposes of determining a payment due date and the date on which interest will begin to accrue if a payment is late, an invoice shall be deemed to be received:

   (1) On the later of:

      (i) For invoices that are mailed, the date a proper invoice is actually received by the designated agency office if the agency annotates the invoice with date of receipt at the time of receipt. For invoices electronically transmitted, the date a readable transmission is received by the designated agency office, or the next business day if received after normal working hours; or

      (ii) The seventh day after the date on which the property is actually delivered or performance of the services is actually completed; unless–

         (A) The agency has actually accepted the property or services before the seventh day in which case the acceptance date shall substitute for the seventh day after the delivery date; or

         (B) A longer acceptance period is specified in the contract, in which case the date of actual acceptance or the date on which such longer acceptance period ends shall substitute for the seventh day after the delivery date;

   (2) On the date placed on the invoice by the contractor, when the agency fails to annotate the invoice with date of receipt of the invoice at the time of receipt (such invoice must be a proper invoice); or

   (3) On the date of delivery, when the contract specifies that the delivery ticket may serve as an invoice.

(c) Review of invoice. Agencies will use the following procedures in reviewing invoices:

   (1) Each invoice will be reviewed by the designated agency office as soon as practicable after receipt to determine whether the invoice is a proper invoice as defined in Sec. 1315.9(b);

   (2) When an invoice is determined to be improper, the agency shall return the invoice to the vendor as soon as practicable after receipt, but no later than 7 days after receipt (refer also to paragraph (g)(4) of this section regarding vendor notification and determining the payment due date.) The agency will identify all defects that prevent payment and specify all reasons why the invoice is not proper and why it is being returned. This notification to the vendor shall include a request for a corrected invoice, to be clearly marked as such;

   (3) Any media which produce tangible recordings of information in lieu of "written" or "original" paper document equivalents should be used by agencies to expedite the payment process, rather than delaying the process by requiring "original" paper documents. Agencies should ensure adequate safeguards and controls to ensure the integrity of the data and to prevent duplicate processing.

(d) Receipt of goods and services. Agencies will ensure that receipt is properly recorded at the time of delivery of goods or completion of services. This requirement does

Exhibit 5.5 Federal Agency Prompt Payment Policy

> not apply to interim payments on cost-reimbursement service contracts except as otherwise required by agency regulations.
>
> **(e)** Acceptance. Agencies will ensure that acceptance is executed as promptly as possible. Commercial items and services should not be subject to extended acceptance periods. Acceptance reports will be forwarded to the designated agency office by the fifth working day after acceptance. Unless other arrangements are made, acceptance reports will be stamped or otherwise annotated with the receipt date in the designated agency office. This requirement does not apply to interim payments on cost-reimbursement service contracts except as otherwise required by agency regulations.
>
> **(f)** Starting the payment period. The period available to an agency to make timely payment of an invoice without incurring an interest penalty shall begin on the date of receipt of a proper invoice (see paragraph (b) of this section) except where no invoice is required (e.g., for some recurring payments as defined in Sec. 1315.2(dd)).
>
> **(g)** Determining the payment due date. (1) Except as provided in paragraphs (g)(2) through (5) of this section, the payment is due either:
>
>   (i) On the date(s) specified in the contract;
>
>   (ii) In accordance with discount terms when discounts are offered and taken (see Sec. 1315.7);
>
>   (iii) In accordance with Accelerated Payment Methods (see Sec. 1315.5); or
>
>   (iv) 30 days after the start of the payment period as specified in paragraph (f) of this section, if not specified in the contract, if discounts are not taken, and if accelerated payment methods are not used.

Exhibit 5.5 Federal Agency Prompt Payment Policy (*continued*)

even in businesses, many of which have compensated boards, key decision-makers may not comprehend the risks. Recent evidence gathered by consulting agency McKinsey finds that 44 percent of directors only partly understand the main drivers of value for their organizations, and 43 percent cannot state what the organizations' key risks are.[2] We project even lower percentages for nonprofit boards based on our observations and the studies we have read. Accordingly, the template of policies we offer here may serve as a valuable starting point for board members. As their understanding of their organization grows, they can modify and amplify various aspects of these policies.

(b) FINANCIAL POLICIES: PRESCRIPTIVE OR RESTRICTIVE? A natural tendency, but one that must be resisted, is to prescribe what the organizational management can or should do in many conceivable scenarios. This *prescriptive* approach to policy is doomed to failure for two reasons:

1. One can never anticipate all important future scenarios or their probability of occurrence (witness the donation fall-offs in late 2001 and 2002 after 9/11 and then again after the tsunami and after Hurricanes Katrina and Rita in 2005).

2. One would not wish to limit the flexibility of managers because new solutions become available over time for dealing with given scenarios.

A better approach is to have a *restrictive* set of policies, limiting to a prudent degree the responses that may be taken for generic events, such as funding shortfalls. Again, the

Question: What are the Two Most Frustrating Things About Your Current Job as Executive Director?

Finances/fundraising: 50%; Staff problems: 40%; Overworked/stress: 36%; Board conflict/complacency: 23%.

Question: To What Degree Are These Factors Adversely Affecting You in Your Current Position?

Scale of 1 = not much at all to 5 = very much.
Mean: 2.8

Finances	3.6
High stress/long hours	3.4
Funding requirements	3.0
Audience	3.0
Fundraising	2.8
Personnel problems	2.8
Isolation	2.7
Low compensation	2.5
Conflict with the Board	1.8

EXHIBIT 5.6 CEO/ED FRUSTRATIONS WITH FINANCIAL POSITION OF THE ORGANIZATION

goal is to put some limits on response categories, not prescribe exact measures to take in each future eventuality. This becomes much clearer with an example; Carver offers a good one:

> ... consider an Executive Limitations policy in which the board is putting certain financial conditions and activities "off limits." At the broadest level, the board might say: "With respect to actual, ongoing financial condition and activities, the CEO shall not allow the development of fiscal jeopardy or a material deviation of actual expenditures from board priorities established in Ends policies [about the changes for persons to be made outside the organization, along with their cost or priority]." That covers the board's concerns about the organization's current financial condition at any one time, for there is likely nothing else to worry about that isn't included within this "large bowl" proscription.

> However, most boards would think such a broad statement leaves more to CEO interpretation—even if reasonable interpretation—than the board wishes to delegate. Hence, the board might add further details, such as saying the CEO shall not: (1) Expend more funds than have been received in the fiscal year to date except through acceptable debt. (2) Indebt the organization in an amount greater than can be repaid by certain, otherwise unencumbered revenues within 60 days, but in no event more than $200,000. (3) Use any of the long term reserves. (4) Conduct interfund shifting in amounts greater than can be restored to a condition of discrete fund balances by unencumbered revenues within 30 days. (5) Fail to settle payroll and debts in a timely manner. (6) Allow tax payments or other government ordered payments or filings to be overdue or inaccurately filed. (7) Make a single purchase or commitment of greater than $100,000, with no splitting of orders to avoid this limit. (8) Acquire, encumber or dispose of real property. And (9) Fail to aggressively pursue receivables after a reasonable grace period.

> A given board might go into less or more detail than in this example.[3]

Accountability Delegations	The <Chancellor/Board/President> delegates the accountability for the financial management of resources to functional units within <Organization>. Consequently, each unit is responsible for properly managing the financial resources of the <Organization> for which they have been provided jurisdiction (e.g., earnings from sales and services, appropriations into accounting units assigned to their departments, etc.) to include identifying a designee (normally the Chief Administrative/ Financial Officer) responsible for formulating an accountability structure for each area. This structure depicts the delegation to initiate, process, and review business transactions by only qualified individuals.
Financial Management	Each operating unit requires financial resources in order to conduct their respective role in the <Organization>'s overall mission. Each organizational head or their designee is responsible for ensuring that the units under their direction manage <Organization> funds in an efficient and cost-effective manner by adopting proven financial management practices.
Data Integrity	Financial management decisions affect each organizational unit, the <Organization>, and interested outside parties. In order to make these decisions appropriately, timely, accurate, and complete data is imperative. Additionally, systems must be in place that contain and generate reliable financial information to help facilitate this decision-making process. Each unit must adopt proven data-integrity practices which provide reasonable assurance that transactions which occur are in accordance with management's general and specific authorization, and that all financial activities which occur are recorded in the financial records of the <Organization>. Each organizational head or their designee is responsible for establishing a system that ensures data integrity.
Regulatory Compliance	All individuals conducting business transactions affecting <Organization> funds must comply with all laws and regulations as well as any restrictions on the use of those funds. Each organizational head or their designee is responsible for ensuring that these units under their direction commit funds only in accordance with legal and regulatory requirements

EXHIBIT 5.7   SAMPLE OF CORE FINANCIAL MANAGEMENT POLICIES FOR OPERATING UNITS

We recognize that there are general areas of guidance that are part of policy statements, as we will illustrate when we get into policy specifics. To the extent possible, though, try to state policy statements restrictively.

(c) CATEGORIES OF FINANCIAL POLICIES.   For organizations not already having policies, we shall provide categories for these policies and some examples. Larger organizations may wish to establish a second level of policies for operating units. Exhibit 5.7 provides a sample of core financial management policies for operating units.

We focus mainly on the first two categories in our presentation of organizational policies, but note that many nonprofits are viewing Sarbanes-Oxley legislation as a good guide for the "Regulatory Compliance" category, even though the legislation is nonbinding for nonprofit organizations. Accordingly, we will group "Regulatory Compliance" with "Accountability" in our presentation.

(d) ACCOUNTABILITY AND REGULATORY COMPLIANCE POLICIES.   Public perception of nonprofit ethics today requires that your organization seriously consider adopting policies that promote and convey an accountable, ethical organization that merits trust on the part of all stakeholders and complies with appropriate legislation and regulation. A Michigan survey finds that only 75 percent of people agree with the statement "Most charitable organizations are honest and ethical in their use of funds."[4]

(i) Accountability Policies.   Your policy here may be as simple as "using all appropriate communication media to demonstrate XYZ organization's adherence to mission and efficiency." For example, this may be evidenced by how well the organization meets "charity watchdog" standards—although, as suggested in Chapter 2, some of these standards may be dysfunctional for your organization's financial health and development. As an example, Exhibit 5.8 is a screen capture from World Vision's donor Web site, taken from a 2005–2006 Sudan campaign conducted by the relief agency. Notice that World Vision, in the right column, gives percentages of expenses going to program, fundraising, and administration, signals membership in the Evangelical Council for Financial Accountability (ECFA), and has icons with hyperlinks to the organization's reports and rating as judged by Charity Navigator and the BBB Wise Giving Alliance. To review the financial standards promoted by these charity watchdogs, refer back to Chapter 2.

Here are some items that prepare your organization for accountability and for writing accountability policies:

- Are our Form 990 reports easily available?
- Do we publish our annual reports with financial data and outcomes measures?
- Do we rely on annual independent audits?
- Do we create necessary policies and enforce them regularly?
- Do we avoid and manage conflicts of interest?
- Do we understand our board's role and responsibility?
- Are we familiar with intermediate sanctions, and do we have policy to prevent situations that would cause them to be levied?
- Do we keep accurate, timely, and well-organized records?
- Do we know applicable federal regulations and our state's laws?[5]

Conflicts of interest are a huge front-burner issue today; we include in Exhibit 5.9 an example of such as policy.

(ii) Regulatory Compliance Policies.   Some of the items here overlap with accountability, as you will see in the next list of items to consider in your policies:

- *Form 990 and other financial reports.* While you may not formally address this aspect of your external financial reporting in a policy statement, your organization may show accountability and market itself at the same time through the Form 990. Nonprofit auditing and consulting firm Capin Crouse LLP offers some wise counsel in this regard, which we have included as Exhibit 5.10.

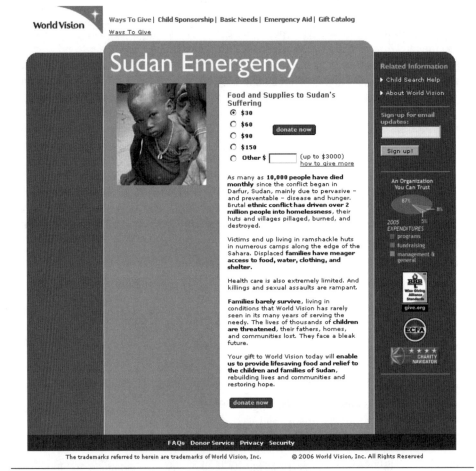

EXHIBIT 5.8   ACCOUNTABILITY AND CHARITY WATCHDOG STANDARDS COMPLIANCE

The standard of behavior at the_____Organization is that all staff, volunteers, and board members scrupulously avoid conflicts of interest between the interests of the_____ Organization on one hand, and personal, professional, and business interests on the other. This includes avoiding potential and actual conflicts of interest, as well as perceptions of conflicts of interest.

I understand that the purposes of this policy are to protect the integrity of the_____ Organization's decision-making process, to enable our constituencies to have confidence in our integrity, and to protect the integrity and reputations of volunteers, staff, and board members. Upon or before election, hiring or appointment, I will make a full, written disclosure of interests, relationships, and holdings that could potentially result in a conflict of interest. This written disclosure will be kept on file and I will update it as appropriate. I understand that the purposes of this policy are to protect the integrity of the_____ Organization's decision-making process, to enable our constituencies to have confidence in our integrity, and to protect the integrity and reputations of volunteers, staff and board members. Upon or before election, hiring or appointment, I will make a full, written disclosure of interests, relationships, and holdings that could potentially result in a conflict of interest. This written disclosure will be kept on file and I will update it as appropriate.

In the course of meetings or activities, I will disclose any interests in a transaction or decision where I (including my business or other nonprofit affiliations), my family and/or my significant other, employer, or close associates will receive a benefit or gain. After disclosure, I understand that I will be asked to leave the room for the discussion and will not be permitted to vote on the question.

I understand that this policy is meant to supplement good judgment, and I will respect its spirit as well as its wording.

Signed:

Date:

Source: From "Boardroom Dancing," a handbook for nonprofit boards written by Jan Masaoka and Jude Kaye of CompassPoint Nonprofit Services (February 2000).

EXHIBIT 5.9 SAMPLE CONFLICT-OF-INTEREST POLICY

- Audits
- Outcomes measures (that these will be developed, measured, and managed)
- Human resource management policies (see Chapter 14)

  ○ IRS tax withholding from wages and salaries

  ○ Hiring policy, including use of background checks (e.g., credit checks or criminal record checks)

  ○ Performance review and promotion policy

  ○ Sexual harassment policy

  ○ Nepotism policy

  ○ Diversity and nondiscrimination policy

  ○ Exclusion to discrimination on religious grounds if faith-based organization

  ○ Grievance policy

  ○ Other relevant laws, statutes, guidelines

For example, here are the guidelines for internal control for National Endowment for the Arts (NEA) grant recipients:

Your annual Form 990 is now a higher profile document than ever before. The fact that anyone can get a copy of your Form 990 from sources such as GuideStar.org has long frustrated many charities, because these forms include personal information about key employees and board members. But Form 990 also allows you to market your organization, because it gives details about your mission and program service accomplishments. Nonprofits vary dramatically in the amount of data they provide here, but this is definitely an opportunity to shine.

Form 990 asks for your primary exempt purpose and specific information for each of your four largest programs, including a description of programs' service accomplishments using measurements such as the number of clients served, units of service or publications issued. It also requires that you describe the activities, as well as current and long-term objectives.

Don't feel constrained by the few lines of space on the form. You may simply state "see attached" and provide more detailed information about your activities, accomplishments, staff expertise and innovations. Volunteer services don't get included as expenses, but you can report them on the form. You may also attach an explanation about everything that you've accomplished thanks to volunteers' generosity. Clearly, a detailed Form 990 can be a great marketing tool for your organization.

Source: http://www.capincrouse.com/.

Exhibit 5.10   Marketing Your Organization Through Your Form 990

Internal Control Standards

Organizations must provide safeguards for all grant property, whether cash or other assets, and assure that it is used solely for authorized purposes. Control will be enhanced if the duties of the members of the organization are divided so that no one person handles all aspects of a transaction from beginning to end. Although a complete separation of functions may not be feasible for the small organization, some measure of effective control may be obtained by planning the assignment of duties carefully.

Many of the most effective techniques for providing internal control are very simple. Some examples are:

- Cash receipts should be recorded immediately and deposited daily.
- Bank accounts should be reconciled monthly by someone other than the person who signs the checks.
- A petty cash fund should be entrusted to a single custodian and used for all payments other than those made by check.
- Checks to vendors should be issued only in payment of approved invoices, and the supporting documents should then be cancelled.
- The person who is responsible for the physical custody of an asset should not also have responsibility for keeping the records related to that asset.
- The person who has authority for placing employees on the payroll and establishing wage rates should not be the same person who signs the checks.[6]

- *Optional items.* These items are not mandatory but are "best practice," such as those related to Sarbanes-Oxley legislation.

We recognize that human resource management policies are not financial policies *per se*, yet they have important financial repercussions, and someone in the organization will have to ensure that these policies are developed, communicated, and enforced.[7]

(e) FINANCIAL AND FINANCIAL MANAGEMENT POLICIES. We strongly believe that a well-articulated set of financial policies will be your organization's key driver to achieve maintenance of its target financial position—the primary financial objective of a nonprofit, as noted in Chapter 2—and a contributory driver for mission achievement as well as accountability substantiation.

Here are the areas for which we would like to see policy established. Some of these are board-level policies, others are functional or operating unit policies:

- Liquidity target policy (see Section 2.6 in Chapter 2 and Section 15.8 in Chapter 15)

  Limitation on number of months of expenses held in cash reserves (typically a minimum of three months, but normally at least six months is prudent)

  ○ Limitations on use(s) of operating reserve, including purpose(s) and dollar target and basis for establishing that target (e.g., prefund one-third of the forthcoming church building capital expenditure)

  ○ Limitations on use of quasi-endowment (if a board-designated quasi-endowment is held), basis for that quasi-endowment, and how large it should be

- Accounting policies (see Chapter 6)

  ○ Cash basis or generally accepting accounting principles (GAAP) accounting?

  ○ Audit policy

- Cash management policies (see Chapter 11)

  ○ Cash collection and receivables, including cash handling policies

  ○ Cash mobilization, including cash access and wire transfer policies

  ○ Cash disbursement and payables, including fraud and payment method policies

- Cash forecasting policies (see Chapters 8 and 11)

  ○ Horizon

  ○ Interval

  ○ To whom forecasts are disseminated and in what time frame

  ○ Allowable forecast error

- Banking relations policies (see Chapter 11)

  ○ Limitation on how depository bank(s) is selected (e.g., competitive bids must be used)

  ○ Limitation on maximum number of depository relationships

  ○ Limitation on target balance or fee compensation (if any)

  ○ Limitation on maximum account balance (usually for FDIC insurance purposes)

  ○ Preference for relationship approach or transactional approach

- Insurance and risk management policies (see Chapter 14)

- o Specific identification of all the risks that the organization faces, how these will be monitored, and how a "global" or comprehensive risk profile shall be developed, monitored, and managed
- o Limitations on types of insurance that will be used or coverages that will be carried
- o Use of employee bonding
- o Use of directors' and officers' policies
- o Use of liability policies
- o How volunteer risk exposures will be handled
- o Use of property and casualty policies

- Purchasing policies
  - o Restrictions on how few vendors can bid
  - o Restrictions on how final vendor decision and pricing may be established
  - o Restrictions on how quickly vendor contracts can be negotiated or renegotiated
  - o Restrictions on how long before a contract must be rebid
  - o Restrictions on board or manager relationships with service providers used

- Financial planning and budgeting policies (see Chapters 8 and 9)
  - o Development of operating budget and frequency of board review of budget versus actual
  - o Capital budget development and limitations on evaluation techniques (e.g., must have at least 15 percent return on invested capital for new earned income venture to be approved)
  - o Maximum dollar expenditure that various positions can authorize without higher-level, including board, approval(s)
  - o Use of windfalls (e.g., midyear unexpected bequest comes in)

- Investment policies (see Chapter 12)
  - o Internally managed or outside management preference
  - o Short-term investment policy
  - o Long-term investment policy
  - o Endowment policies (if applicable)
  - o Pension policies (if applicable)
  - o Limitation on use on derivatives and swaps

- Debt/borrowing policies (see Chapter 10)
  - o Limitation on short-term borrowing
  - o Allowable uses
  - o Disallowable uses
  - o Arranged financing (e.g., bank loans)
  - o Spontaneous financing (e.g., accounts payable and accrued wages)
  - o Debt reduction policy
  - o Limitation on long-term borrowing

- o Allowable uses
- o Disallowable uses
- o Use of swaps and other derivatives to manage principal and interest

- Internal controls and reporting policies

  - o Conflict-of-interest policy
  - o Whistleblower policy
  - o Fraud prevention policy
  - o Audit policy
  - o Others

- External reporting policies

  - o Donors
  - o Grantors
  - o Community
  - o Other stakeholders
  - o State attorney general
  - o IRS
  - o Other

- Fundraising policies

  - o Donation use and receipting
  - o Use of restricted funds for restricted period or restricted purpose
  - o Policy to solicit unrestricted donations
  - o Policy in event donor intent cannot be honored
  - o Gift conversion policy (e.g., will stocks or bonds be sold immediately upon receipt of ownership?)
  - o ECFA (or similar fundraising standards compliance)
  - o Others

For more specifics on a number of these policies, consult the online sources listed in Appendix 5A.

In support of a liquidity target policy (or liquid reserve policy), we note the many underfunded organizations and how severe the effects of underfunding are. We hear often of service cutbacks due to financial shortfalls. Yet if organizations had sufficient liquid reserves, current-year funding shortfalls would not necessitate service cutbacks. The reality is that many organizations are cutting back on programs and laying off staff due to such shortfalls. Study Exhibit 5.11, noting these effects on New York City nonprofits.

(f) DATA INTEGRITY POLICIES. Areas that you may wish to cover in your policies related to data and data integrity include:

- Privacy
- Confidentiality
- Records retention

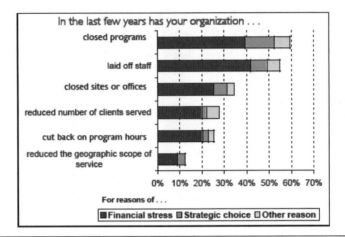

Source: New York City Nonprofit Executive Outlook Survey. Baruch College, Spring 2005. Used by permission.

This survey was conducted by Jack Krauskopf and Gregg Van Ryzin at Baruch College, and co-sponsored by the Nonprofit Group and Survey Research Unit in the Baruch College School of Public Affairs, Human Services Council of New York City, Federation of Protestant Welfare Agencies, UJA-Federation of New York, and United Neighborhood Houses of New York.

EXHIBIT 5.11   RESULTS OF INADEQUATE LIQUID RESERVE POLICY FOR NEW YORK CITY NONPROFITS

- E-mail
- Access and sharing limitations
- Security
- Data backup
- Disaster recovery
- Separation of duties

Consult Chapter 13 for more on these topics.

5.3 PUTTING POLICIES INTO PLACE

After collecting required copies of external policies, such as those imposed by grant agencies or governmental agencies, we must determine which internal policies will be developed or modified. Then the process of developing internal policies can begin, as detailed in Exhibit 5.12. In cases involving high-level policies, which are largely our focus in this chapter, the committee (Step 1) would be either a board committee or an advisory committee, and the approval would come from the entire board (Step 4), not organizational management. Clearly, the board would want to gather input on proposed policies from some managers before voting new policy into place, but it should be clear that this is just that—input—and the board is the body making high-level policy decisions.

For policies that are not high level in nature but address accountability and financial management for monies that have been allocated to operating units, an internal committee of management and staff can work on policy review. At one university, a policy review

1. Establish a small committee with individuals who have a thorough understanding of existing internal policies within your organization and have the insight and knowledge necessary to understand the essential elements of these policies.
2. Charge this committee with the responsibility of simplifying existing policies.
3. Provide the committee with all of the existing rules, laws, policies, and other external documents that affect your business operations.
4. Present these new policies to your organization for review and approval and make changes as necessary.
5. Submit a draft of the policies to your regulatory bodies, if applicable, to seek their acceptance of your new policies; based on their feedback, incorporate changes if necessary.
6. Distribute the new policies to your organization.
7. Establish training to assure compliance and understanding of the new policies.
8. Monitor compliance of the new policies.

Exhibit 5.12 Steps to Develop and Introduce New Policies

committee was established to produce a new streamlined set of policies as well as to reconcile the inconsistencies and redundancies in their existing policies. The charge of the review committee was to develop policies that were true to the original spirit of the policies established at the OMB and to comply with all of the various agencies within the government and nongovernmental organizations. After several months, the committee found that these departmental/program financial management policies could be divided into four main categories, as shown earlier in Exhibit 5.7.

5.4 ESTABLISHING PROCEDURES

The purpose of policies is to combine all rules (external and internal) into one set of rules that do not conflict with one another. After policies have been established, the procedures for complying with policy can be developed.

It is important to distinguish between policies and procedures as well as the difference between work instructions and procedures. Procedures are the steps that must be taken to comply appropriately with policy. Work instructions are the suggested steps that should be taken to comply with procedures.

Very often, individuals feel constricted by procedures because they confuse the literal procedure with the work instructions they have been taught. They are unable to respond dynamically to changes within the organization or special needs of constituents because they are attempting to comply with outdated job instructions.

At one nonprofit institution, a class was presented in contract and grant accounting. One of the attendees had been performing her duties in the same manner for more than 20 years. She had always saved a copy of each invoice and packing slip she received and filed it with the original purchase order documents. During the delivery of the course, where the use of a new technology was introduced that would allow her to maintain a checklist of this same information, allowing her to throw the invoices and packing slips away. Visibly upset, she confronted the instructor, claiming that this change was not appropriate and violated policy. What had happened was this:

The institution had a procedure that specified that all invoices, prior to payment, must be reconciled to the original purchase order. In addition, the merchandise must be received in good condition and as ordered (reconciling the packing slip to the order).

1. Establish a committee who will be responsible for developing procedures. The group should include individuals who perform the work as well as individuals who must audit the work.
2. Review each policy and determine if a procedure needs to be established. Some policies may not require an associated procedure.
3. Detail the requirements for compliance as indicated by the policy.
4. Verify that the steps outlined in step 3 can be performed. If not, review the steps or consult with the policy makers to better understand their intent.
5. Submit the procedure draft to your organization for review and acceptance. Make changes or modifications, as necessary.
6. Submit a copy of the procedures to your regulatory agencies, if applicable.
7. Incorporate changes and modifications.
8. Distribute procedures.
9. Develop training and/or work instructions (e.g., job aids).
10. Audit compliance.

EXHIBIT 5.13   DEVELOPING AND MAINTAINING PROCEDURES

Her department had complied with this procedure by saving a copy of the invoice and packing slip. The stapling of the documents indicated that they had been reconciled.

The woman had confused the procedure with the steps with which she had been taught to comply; therefore, she refused to believe that a log would suffice as a method of complying with the procedure. This example illustrates how staff may interpret work rules as procedure and also how careful an institution must be about mandating how work should be performed.

Procedures should contain only those steps that are required by policy. If work rules or job aids are produced, staff members need to understand that those rules or aids are not policy or procedure, but only a method of compliance. Refer to Exhibit 5.13 for the steps to develop procedures.

5.5 FINANCIAL POLICIES AND PROCEDURES IN PRACTICE

The Johns Hopkins Listening Post Project is a good source for current practice in relation to policies and procedures. Over 200 respondents provide evidence of fairly widespread implementation of board-level oversight and policy making. "Highly" or "significantly" involved boards were found engaged in these practices:

1) Board roles.

- Reviewing auditing and accounting policies and practices (83 percent).
- Approving significant financial transactions (81 percent).

2) Financial disclosure. The overwhelming majority (97 percent) of sampled organizations have undergone an independent audit within the past two years and comparable proportions (95 percent) regularly distribute their financial reports to their boards.

3) Ethics protections. The overwhelming majority of responding organizations also already have other policies and procedures in place to promote accountability and ethical behavior. This includes:

- Internal controls on finances and financial accounting (98 percent);
- Records retention policies (84 percent);
- Conflict of interest policies (83 percent);
- Travel expense policies (81 percent);
- Compliance programs for regulation (81 percent); and
- Codes of ethics for board and staff (73 percent).

Even among smaller organizations, a majority have such policies in place.[8]

We offer a caution regarding interpreting some other results from this survey. The Study noted that 83 percent of the boards were heavily involved in reviewing auditing and accounting policies and practices, and we would surmise that accounting policies and practices would include many of the policies addressed in this chapter. No doubt respondents were not entirely sure as to what is meant by "basic management policies"; some respondents would interpret this as program-level or unit-level policy. As a result, only 40.5 percent of all organizations reported having boards "highly" or "significantly" involved in setting basic management policies. Here are several of other pertinent findings about the differences seen in board practices at large organizations versus small organizations:

> Boards at large organizations (expenditures over $3 million) were more involved in organizational finances than those at small organizations (expenditures under $500,000). Included here were functions such as establishing, reviewing, and approving compensation for the executive director (96 percent of large organization boards highly involved vs. 72 percent of small organization boards); and approving significant financial transactions (81 percent vs. 60 percent).

> On the other hand, the boards of the smaller organizations tended to be more heavily involved in some of the more detailed managerial functions, such as setting basic management policies (72 percent of small organization boards highly or significantly involved vs. 42 percent of large organization boards); setting program objectives (56 percent vs. 38 percent); setting program performance measures (56 percent vs. 34 percent); setting compensation for staff other than the CEO (48 percent vs. 23 percent). Clearly, as organizations grow in size and complexity the capacity of the board to remain intimately involved in organizational management declines.[9]

The J.H. Cohn accounting and consulting firm surveyed 524 New York City nonprofit organizations, and the 123 responses indicate that annual ethics code compliance reports, conflict-of-interest policies, and quarterly actual versus budget comparisons have been or are being implemented by the majority of nonprofits. Exhibit 5.14 profiles the responses to this 2003–2004 survey.

Significantly, one of the main conclusions from the University of Wisconsin-Milwaukee study of Milwaukee-area nonprofits is that boards limit their policy-making prerogative mainly to auditor engagement and conflicts of interest. While laudable, the study advocates that boards go beyond these two areas to construct policies in other areas. Quoting the survey's findings:

> Setting policy has long been associated with good governance, and the majority of local Boards have determined that policies are critical with regard to engaging an external auditor and protecting against conflict of interest. Yet, many other aspects of risk management or protecting the public's interest should also be addressed with guidance from policies. Recommendation: Produce templates and offer consultation to assist Boards in developing policies suitable to their level of sophistication.

Three has been much discussion about not-for-profit entities adopting practices from the Sarbanes-Oxley Act. Please indicate your current thoughts about implementing the following practices in your organization:

Report annually on the organization's compliance with its code of ethics, including applicable federal and state laws:

Plan to Implement		22%
Already Implemented		41%
Implement Once Required		37%

Develop and/or revise a conflict of interest policy for all personnel, including directors:

Plan to Implement		16%
Already Implemented		67%
Implemented Once Required		17%

Provide a quarterly comparison of actual as. budgeted results:

Plan to Implement		11%
Already Implemented		77%
Implement Once Required		12%

Source: J.H. Cohn LLP, 2003/2004 NonProfit Survey Report.

Exhibit 5.14   New York Survey of Nonprofit Changes Subsequent to Sarbanes-Oxley

We have endeavored to help your organization to construct a useful set of policies to better enable it to achieve its mission. By restricting management's actions appropriately and establishing an adequate liquidity reserve, your organization will be well on its way to achieving financial management proficiency.

5.6 ADDITIONAL RESOURCES

The development of effective policies and procedures is not a simple task. If you do not have the resources to devote to this effort, networking with other similar organizations may yield a solid set of policies that can be modified. In addition, government institutions must provide copies of their policies. Many policies of government and private organizations may be found in your local library and on the Internet. Appendix 5A lists some of the best policy Web sites available at the time of this writing.

Notes

1.   Illinois Facilities Fund and Donors Forum of Chicago, *Getting It Right: How Illinois Nonprofits Manage for Success* (Chicago: Illinois Facilities Fund and Donors Forum of Chicago, 2004).

2. McKinsey April-May 2002 U.S. Directors Survey, cited in Michael E. Nagel and Chris Rigatuso, "Improving Corporate Governance: A Balanced Scorecard Approach," Balanced Scorecard Collaborative, Inc., 2003. Available for download at www.bscol.com. Accessed: 12/16/05.

3. John Carver and Miriam Carver, "Le Modele Policy Governance et les Organisms sans but Lucrative," *Gouvernance—Revue Internationale* 2 (Winter 2001): 30–48.

4. Mark I. Wilson and Neal R. Hegarty, "State of the State Survey: Public Perceptions of Nonprofit Organizations in Michigan," Briefing Paper 97-28, Institute of Public Policy and Social Research, Michigan State University (November 1997).

5. Adapted from Board Member, Special Edition, *Accountability: The Buck Stops Here* (Washington, D.C.: *BoardSource*, Publication #322).

6. Available online at: www.nea.gov/about/OIG/FMGNPO.pdf. Accessed: 12/19/05.

7. An excellent source of information on human resource policies is Kathleen Fletcher, *The Policy Sampler: A Resource for Nonprofit Boards* (Washington, D.C.: BoardSource, 2000).

8. Lester M. Salamon and Stephanie L. Geller, *Nonprofit Governance and Accountability*, Center for Civil Society Studies at the Johns Hopkins Institute for Policy Studies Listening Post Project, 2005.

9. Id.

10. These are also available as navigable links at the website that accompanies this book, available at www.wiley.com/go/zietlow.

NONPROFIT FINANCIAL POLICY EXAMPLES ON THE INTERNET[10]

- Guidance on Financial Policies & Procedures from Ontario Ministry of Agriculture, Food, and Rural Affairs:

  www.omafra.gov.on.ca/english/rural/facts/01-047.htm

- Church basic financial policies example:

  www.bcidot.org/chu/5005-01.html

- Fraternity chapter financial policy examples:

  http://csi-net.org/displaycommon.cfm?an=1&subarticlenbr=43 (Chi Sigma Iota) and www.nursingsociety.org/chapters/financial_policy.pdf (Sigma Theta Tau)

- Trade association example (American Association of Law Libraries; includes some nonfinancial policies):

  www.aallnet.org/about/policy_financial.asp

- IdeaAlliance policies, including privacy, ethics, document retention, financial policies:

  www.idealliance.org/about/bylaws&policies.asp

- National Conference of Catholic Bishops internal controls policies:

  www.usccb.org/finance/internal.htm

- Charlotte Diocese parish, mission, and school financial policies and procedures:

  www.charlottediocese.org/customers/101092709242178/filemanager/finance/financial_full.pdf

- Florida Youth Soccer Association financial policies:

  www.usyouthsoccer.org/downloads/treasurers/FloridaFinPol.pdf

- Society of Environmental Journalists financial policies (see especially C, D, and E):

  www.sej.org/about/financial_policies.htm

- PennAEYC Financial Policies (Pennsylvania Association for the Education of Young Children):

  www.pennaeyc.org/governing board_files/FINANCIAL POLICIES AND PROCEDURES.doc

- American Heart Association comments on its financial accountability:
  www.americanheart.org/presenter.jhtml?identifier=4556

  The next four items are all investment policy statements:

- American Society for Engineering Education investment policy:
  www.asee.org/about/investment.cfm
- IEEE Investment Operations Manual:
  www.ieee.org/portal/cms_docs/about/whatis/policies/investopsmanual.pdf
- LA Society of Financial Analysts investment policy statement:
  www.lasfa.org/attachments/LASFA-Investment-Policy-2003.pdf
- Investment Policy of New Life Corporation of America:
  www.natcf.org/webforms/investmentpolicy.pdf

CHAPTER 6

UNDERSTANDING ACCOUNTING BASICS AND FINANCIAL STATEMENTS

6.1 INTRODUCTION

Financial statements communicate the most important financial information to your organization's stakeholders. Financial statements and ratio analysis based on those statements are very valuable. For example, they can be used to predict financial "vulnerability" (three-year decline of 20 percent or more in net assets), as noted in one study.[1] Another study determined that the amount of assets financed by borrowed money, the reliance on a single source of revenue, the "profit margin" (revenues less expenses divided by total revenues), the size, and which sector a nonprofit organization is in all help to predict the chances the organization will become financially vulnerable.[2]

Before we can analyze a nonprofit's financial information, we need to gain a basic understanding of the statements. In this chapter, we survey the major financial statements, what they show, how accurately they portray the financial situation, who uses them and for what, and some differences across organizational types. In Chapter 7, we show how to develop metrics and summary reports and conduct financial ratio analysis using these financial statements and the data they contain.

One very important point before we launch into financials: Your organization's most important outcomes are *nonfinancial* (unless your organization is a foundation, endowment, or credit union or other financial cooperative, in which mission achievement is intertwined with financial outcomes). *Mission accomplishment is the single reason why your organization exists.* Having said that, financials *do* give a reading on your organization's financial performance and indicate whether and how it is meeting its primary financial objective of achieving a target liquidity level. *Financial management supports and enables mission accomplishment.* We begin our presentation by finding out who uses financials and for what purposes. At the conclusion to the chapter, we return to this topic of mission-related outcomes.

(a) FINANCIAL STATEMENT USERS AND USES.   Let us start with the results of a fascinating survey conducted by the Maryland Association of Nonprofit Organizations. In the survey (see Exhibit 6.1), which was made of the general public and not donors or other stakeholders of specific organizations, respondents were asked what factors would increase their confidence in charities.

The response percentages changed very little over the period in which the two identical surveys were administered (1999 and 2001) to the 800 randomly selected respondents from the general public residing in Maryland. Most important, notice two things about this survey response:

1. According to this survey, program outcomes and effectiveness—as we alluded to earlier—were ranked most important for the public to increase its trust in charities.

2. All of the remaining top-five factors for trust-building have to do with your financial records, financial administration, and financial policies.

Failing to disclose and be accountable for financial records, items 2 and 5, costs an organization a greater level of public trust. This risk must be weighed against the increasingly significant costs of developing, auditing, and disseminating that information. For example, the Salvation Army is exempted from having to file financial reports with the IRS as it is part of "houses of worship and affiliated organizations," yet it invests resources in developing and getting audits of its financial reports and makes them available at its regional headquarters offices for those who may be interested in viewing them. We view financial disclosure as a "best practice" and prudent principle of management. We have yet

Impact of Standard on Confidence in Charities			
2001 % Reporting that Standard would increase trust in charities	2001 Rank	Standard	1999 % Reporting that Standard would increase trust in charities
90%	1	Standard requiring charities to evaluate programs in relation to mission to see if they are working	85%
89%	2	Standard requiring charities to have their financial records audited yearly	89%
87%	3	Standard requiring charities to have a conflict of interest policy	87%
85%	4	Standard requiring charities to set limits on how much is spent on fundraising and administration	81%
84%	5	Standard requiring charities to publish and distribute financial information	85%

Source: Maryland Association of Nonprofit Organizations, "Protecting the Trust: Revisiting Public Attitudes About Charities in Maryland," 2002. www.marylandnonprofits.org.

EXHIBIT 6.1   PUBLIC DESIRE FOR FINANCIAL STATEMENT DISCLOSURE

to see a well-crafted fundraising and administration expense limitation (item 4). A "one size fits all" fundraising and administration expense is unworkable because start-up organizations necessarily will have high ratios, and many donative organizations prefund large expenditures for a series of years. In those years the fundraising (and possibly administrative) expenses appear abnormally high relative to current-year program expenses.

We see some level of interest in nonprofits' financials from each of these groups, and the breadth and diversity of interested parties is noteworthy:

- Board members
- Clients
- Funding and other resource sources

  o Donors, especially major ones making deferred gifts

  o Donors' representatives: GuideStar, BBB Wise Giving Alliance, Charity Navigator, American Institute on Philanthropy, Wall Watchers

  o Lenders

  o Investors (e.g., social enterprise venture funds)

  o Grant agencies

  o United Way and other federated campaigns

  o Large contractors or suppliers/vendors (particularly when an organization is buying on credit terms from them)

- Workforce

    ○ Volunteers

    ○ Employees

- Regulators and tax authorities

    ○ State attorneys general offices

    ○ IRS

    ○ Public officials (e.g., the Senate Finance Committee)

    ○ Courts (e.g., in excessive compensation cases)

- Independent Sector, Urban Institute, and Indiana University Center on Philan-thropy (mostly for research purposes, but these organizations are also called on to share their expertise by public policy makers)

(b) WHAT DO DONORS' REPRESENTATIVES SAY? Donors often delegate their finan-cial evaluations to others. This delegation can happen in many ways. They may tap the expertise of trust officers, knowledgeable acquaintances, magazine ratings (e.g., *Money* magazine), a trade association, or the ratings of the charity watchdog organi-zations—GuideStar, BBB Wise Giving Alliance, Charity Navigator, American Institute for Philanthropy, or Wall Watchers. Religious donors and grant agencies may look favor-ably on organizations that meet the accountability and management standards of the Evangelical Council for Financial Accountability (ECFA). We limit our coverage of these standards mostly just to the portions of the BBB Wise Giving Alliance and ECFA standards that are relevant to financial reporting and financial outcomes.

(i) BBB Wise Giving Alliance Standards. We see in the "Measuring Effectiveness" section of the BBB standards (Exhibit 6.2) that program effectiveness *internal reporting* is an issue that is evaluated. In the "Finances" section, notice that relative expenses for program, fundraising, and management are scrutinized. We'll address the issue of allo-cations of fundraising expense later in this chapter and the calculation and interpretation of ratios in the next chapter. We have already profiled our disagreement with Standard 10 in Chapter 2. Although we disagree with the specifics of the implied definition of liquidity and with the ceiling amount stated in BBB Standard 10, the upside is that at least this standard forces boards and management teams to discuss and set policy in the area of liquidity, solvency, and financial flexibility.

(ii) ECFA Standards. The ECFA standards of financial accountability and integrity are voluntarily subscribed to by approximately 1,100 faith-based 501(c)(3) organizations, including religious, missionary, social, and educational organizations. Notice in Exhibit 6.3, which includes only the parts of the standards relevant to our discussion, the requirements for an annual audit by a CPA firm with generally accepting account-ing principles (GAAP)–based financials and generally accepted accounting standards (GAAS)–based audits, financial disclosure of current audited financial statements as well as project financial information when soliciting funds for a project, and current, com-plete, and accurate presentation of the organization's financial condition if that aspect of the organization is included in an fundraising appeals. Regarding Standard 3, in 2005

MEASURING EFFECTIVENESS

An organization should regularly assess its effectiveness in achieving its mission. This section seeks to ensure that an organization has defined, measurable goals and objectives in place and a defined process in place to evaluate the success and impact of its program(s) in fulfilling the goals and objectives of the organization and that also identifies ways to address any deficiencies. To meet these standards, a charitable organization shall:

6. **Have a board policy of assessing, no less than every two years, the organization's performance and effectiveness and of determining future actions required to achieve its mission.**

7. **Submit to the organization's governing body, for its approval, a written report that outlines the results of the aforementioned performance and effectiveness assessment and recommendations for future actions.**

FINANCES

This section of the standards seeks to ensure that the charity spends its funds honestly, prudently and in accordance with statements made in fund raising appeals. To meet these standards, the charitable organization shall:

> **Please note that Standards 8 and 9 have *different* denominators.**

8. **Spend at least 65% of its total expenses on program activities.**

> **Formula for Standard 8:**
>
> $$\frac{\text{Total Program Service Expenses}}{\text{Total Expenses}} \text{ should be at least 65\%}$$

9. **Spend no more than 35% of <u>related</u> contributions on fund raising.** Related contributions include donations, legacies, and other gifts received as a result of fund raising efforts.

> **Formula for Standard 9:**
>
> $$\frac{\text{Total Fund Raising Expenses}}{\text{Total Related Contributions}} \text{ should be no more than 35\%}$$

10. **Avoid accumulating funds that could be used for current program activities. To meet this standard, the charity's unrestricted net assets available for use should not be more than three times the size of the past year's expenses or three times the size of the current year's budget, whichever is higher.**

An organization that does not meet Standards 8, 9 and/or 10 may provide evidence to demonstrate that its use of funds is reasonable. The higher fund raising and administrative costs of a newly created organization, donor restrictions on the use of funds, exceptional bequests, a stigma associated with a cause and environmental or political events beyond an organization's control are among factors which may result in expenditures that are reasonable although they do not meet the financial measures cited in these standards.

EXHIBIT 6.2   BBB WISE GIVING ALLIANCE STANDARDS RELEVANT TO ACCOUNTING AND FINANCIAL REPORTS

11. **Make available to all, on request, complete annual financial statements prepared in accordance with generally accepted accounting principles.** When total annual gross income exceeds $250,000, these statements should be audited in accordance with generally accepted auditing standards. For charities whose annual gross income is less than $250,000, a review by a certified public accountant is sufficient to meet this standard. For charities whose annual gross income is less than $100,000, an internally produced, complete financial statement is sufficient to meet this standard.

12. **Include in the financial statements a breakdown of expenses (e.g., salaries, travel, postage, etc.) that shows what portion of these expenses was allocated to program, fund raising, and administrative activities.** If the charity has more than one major program category, the schedule should provide a breakdown for each category.

13. **Accurately report the charity's expenses, including any joint cost allocations, in its financial statements.** For example, audited or unaudited statements which inaccurately claim zero fund raising expenses or otherwise understate the amount a charity spends on fund raising, and/or overstate the amount it spends on programs will not meet this standard.

14. **Have a board-approved annual budget for its current fiscal year, outlining projected expenses for major program activities, fund raising, and administration.**

FUND RAISING AND INFORMATIONAL MATERIALS

A fund raising appeal is often the only contact a donor has with a charity and may be the sole impetus for giving. This section of the standards seeks to ensure that a charity's representations to the public are accurate, complete and respectful. To meet these standards, the charitable organization shall:

15. **Have solicitations and informational materials, distributed by any means, that are accurate, truthful and not misleading, both in whole and in part.** Appeals that omit a clear description of program(s) for which contributions are sought will not meet this standard.

    A charity should also be able to substantiate that the timing and nature of its expenditures are in accordance with what is stated, expressed, or implied in the charity's solicitations.

16. **Have an annual report available to all, on request, that includes:**

    a. **the organization's mission statement,**

    b. **a summary of the past year's program service accomplishments,**

    c. **a roster of the officers and members of the board of directors,**

    d. **financial information that includes (i) total income in the past fiscal year, (ii) expenses in the same program, fund raising and administrative categories as in the financial statements, and (iii) ending net assets.**

17. **Include on any charity websites that solicit contributions, the same information that is recommended for annual reports, as well as the mailing address of the charity and electronic access to its most recent IRS Form 990.**

Source: Excerpted from http://www.give.org/. See that website for the complete set of standards. Used by permission. Accessed: 12/20/05.

EXHIBIT 6.2 BBB WISE GIVING ALLIANCE STANDARDS RELEVANT TO ACCOUNTING AND FINANCIAL REPORTS (*continued*)

the ECFA as a standard-setter caught the eye of the Panel on the Nonprofit Sector, a group of 175 experts convened by Independent Sector. In particular, in its report to the Senate Finance Committee the panel cited the guidance the Evangelical Council for Financial Accountability (ECFA) gives organizations regarding having an audit done by

---

STANDARD 3—AUDITED FINANCIAL STATEMENTS:

Every member organization shall obtain an annual audit performed by an independent certified public accounting firm in accordance with auditing standards generally accepted in the United States of America (GAAS) with financial statements prepared in accordance with accounting principles accepted in the United States of America (GAAP).

STANDARD 5—FINANCIAL DISCLOSURE:

Every member organization shall provide a copy of its current audited financial statements upon written request and provide other disclosures as the law may require. An organization must provide a report, on request, including financial information, on the specified project for which it is soliciting gifts.

STANDARD 7—FUND-RAISING:

Every member organization shall comply with each of the ECFA Standards for fund-raising:

7.1 TRUTHFULNESS IN COMMUNICATION:

All representations of fact, description of financial condition of the organization, or narrative about events must be current, complete, and accurate. References to past activities or events must be appropriately dated. There must be no material omissions or exaggerations of fact or use of misleading photographs or any other communication which would tend to create a false impression or misunderstanding.

Source: Excerpted from http://www.ecfa.org/. See that website for the complete set of standards. Used by permission. Accessed: 12/20/05.

EXHIBIT 6.3 EVANGELICAL COUNCIL FOR FINANCIAL ACCOUNTABILITY (ECFA) FINANCIAL STANDARDS

a CPA firm: "Organizations with less than $500,000 in annual revenues may periodically obtain a compilation and review of financial statements in lieu of an audit."[3] We shall return to the differences between these three forms of review later.

(c) EXTERNAL AND INTERNAL FINANCIAL STATEMENTS.   Our primary focus in this chapter is external financial statements. However, these statements are also used internally by the board, chief executive officer (CEO)/executive director (ED), chief financial officer (CFO), other top managers, and program managers. In Chapter 7 we consider additional internal reports that your board and management team will find useful.

(d) WHO DOES THE ACCOUNTING?   One of the issues each organization must face is who will do the bookkeeping work, which involves recording financial transactions as they occur, as well as who develops external financial reports and whether the organization will contract for an annual audit of its financial statements.

(i) *In-House versus Outsourced.*   Small organizations typically have a bookkeeper, who is either a part-time employee or a volunteer—possibly the board treasurer. The expenses of the bookkeeping/accounting function are kept to a minimum, but accuracy, timeliness, and report usefulness may and often do suffer as a result. Another alternative is to outsource some or all of the bookkeeping and accounting report function to an accounting firm that specializes in doing this work. The greater expense of outsourcing is often more than offset by the quality and timeliness of the record-keeping and report-generation functions, and there is less chance of fraud because small organizations have difficulty in placing record-keeping and cash-handling or bank reconciliation functions in the hands of different individuals. It is rare to find midsize and large organizations without at least one full-time staff person handling accounting and possibly including some financial functions as well within his or her work responsibilities. Even so, outsourcing is an alternative here as well. Or the small or midsized organization may outsource the CFO position, saving in annual expense $60,000 to $150,000 in salary, and as much as 40 percent more in benefits and support expenses.

Businesses outsource for four reasons, each of which also pertains to nonprofits, according to a Hewitt Associates survey: (1) to increase a process's cost-effectiveness, (2) to reduce administrative costs, (3) to capitalize on a third party's technology and/or expertise, and (4) to focus on core business functions.[4] The three possible outsourcing options include: (1) replace the accounting department in its entirety with an accounting/consulting firm's people; (2) replace the CFO with an accounting/consulting firm's person; (3) replace the entire accounting and finance functions (not including the board treasurer, of course) with an accounting/consulting firm's people. Many of these outsource providers will work on a per-hour basis; those that do so typically charge a one-time setup fee, then an annual fee. The Girls Scouts of Chicago, for example, pays an accounting/consulting firm $400,000 per year (above the one-time set-up fee) to handle the accounting, budgeting, and financial analysis needs of the organization's entities.[5]

(ii) Accounting Software.   Nonprofit accounting software continues its impressive evolution at the low end, significantly improving both in terms of becoming less expensive and easier to use for bookkeeping and financial statement and report generation. Quickbooks may be the most popular accounting software used by nonprofits. We also mention Nonprofit Books not as a product promotion, but simply as an example of how a business software product (Quickbooks) has been developed and now migrated into a fairly powerful nonprofit accounting package.

For those wanting more advanced features, companies such as Blackbaud, Sage, Serenic, Cougar Mountain, Logos Management, and Shelby Systems (for churches) are software providers. Your organization should thoroughly investigate all of the options before making purchase decisions. Getting a broad overview of the software available entails the need to network with others in your industry (e.g., museums have collections accounting needs that are specialized) and also consult software reviews to compare software features, including: ease of use; installation/training/upgrade/license costs; allowable number of users; upgrade frequency; customer support; web interface; payables/receivables; bank account, vendor, donor receipting, and customer interfaces; and other important buying decision criteria.[6]

Enterprise resource planning (ERP) systems are coming to the nonprofit world, so prudent larger organizations would find out what vendors such as PeopleSoft can offer them to tie accounting and other business process systems together as seamlessly as possible.

(e) ROLES OF THE CONTROLLER AND TREASURER.   In today's environment emphasizing efficiency and doing more with less, is the controller still chief accountant? Yes, but that is not the only role the controller plays. The paradigm shift is for the CFO, the controller, and the treasurer to all see themselves as servicing the organization and helping it to meet its goals, financial and nonfinancial. Clearly, this implies that the CFO, controller, and treasurer shoulder both an educational role and an internal business consultant role. At the risk of being redundant, bookkeeping and reporting have long been primary emphases in nonprofits, and we believe Sarbanes-Oxley and today's regulatory environment will intensify that emphasis along with a greater internal control emphasis. As important as these roles are, the downside is that treasury duties may receive too little attention.

What role should the board treasurer have, if the organization does not have a staff person serving as head over the treasury function (say, as director of treasury operations)? In this case, the board treasurer must help staff interpret financial data and statements, guide establishment and ensure maintenance of the organization's liquidity target (and that this gets calculated correctly, as noted in Chapter 2, and featured prominently on internal financial reports), and project cash flow (perhaps using the statement of cash flows as a forecasting template). This is in addition to the normal expectation that he or she ensures that the finance committee understands the financials, including the Form 990 where applicable, and is carrying on its other roles, as profiled in Chapter 5.

6.2 ACCOUNTING BASICS

In our overview of accounting basics, we look first at financial standards and who sets these standards for external financial reports. We then briefly discuss fund accounting and consolidation. Cash basis and accrual basis accounting approaches are touched on next, and finally we contrast an audit, a review, and a compilation.

(a) FINANCIAL STANDARDS AND STANDARDS SETTERS.

(i) Financial Accounting Standards Board.   The Financial Accounting Standards Board (FASB) sets the standards that nonprofits are expected to adhere to in their accounting. Its guidelines are called standards, including two especially important ones for most nonprofits, Standard (or SFAS or FAS) 116 and Standard (or SFAS or FAS) 117. Organizations such as public agencies and universities that are part of a governmental entity abide by a different set of standards, those developed by the Governmental Accounting Standards Board (GASB). By having all nonprofits abide by FASB's standards, users are more certain of the information being conveyed in financial statements and comparisons between organizations are facilitated. Yet there is some discretion or judgment allowed in the application of the standards, and different organizations sometimes differ in important ways—meaning that such comparisons must be made carefully and conclusions tempered by the discretion and differences.

The American Institute of Certified Public Accountants (AICPA) provides guidance to accountants and auditors through technical practice aids, statements of position (abbreviated SOP), Statements on Auditing Standards (abbreviated SAS), and accounting and auditing guides. Its role is secondary in authority to FASB, however. SOP 98-2, *Accounting for Costs of Activities of Not-for-Profit Organizations and State and Local Governmental Entities that Include Fund-Raising,* is the AICPA position statement most readers will likely hear about and consult for guidance. Healthcare finance staff should be aware of SOP 02-2, *Accounting for Derivatives and Hedging Activities by Not-for-Profit Health Care Organizations, and Clarification of the Performance Indicator.*

For users accustomed to business financial statements, the biggest difference in nonprofit accounting is in accounting for contributions, which we take up in our later discussion of Standard 116.

(ii) Generally Accepted Accounting Principles.   Not all FASB accounting standards apply to nonprofit organizations, although most have at least some applicability. The relevant body of accounting pronouncements from FASB, the AICPA Audit and Accounting

Guide that applies to an organization's industry, and certain AICPA SOPs constitute generally accepted accounting principles to which your auditors will expect your organization to adhere. In order to have a CPA audit your organization and give your organization an unqualified opinion on your financial statements, you *must* present those statements according to GAAP. For example, faith-based ministry organizations are expected to adhere to FASB Statements 116, 117, 124, 136, the AICPA Audit and Accounting Guide, for Not-for-Profit Organizations, and SOP 98-2 at the time of this writing.[7]

(b) FUND ACCOUNTING VERSUS CONSOLIDATION.   Before 1995, organizations typically reported financials internally and externally using an approach called "fund accounting." This method of accounting was firmly grounded in the stewardship principle: If the donor restricted donations, these restricted amounts were being provided to the organization on the presumption that the organization would be careful to use them as directed by the donor. The way to ensure that the organizations adheres to those wishes and then to evidence this fidelity is to use separate, self-balancing accounts or sets of accounts called "funds." Many organizations continue to use funds for internal bookkeeping purposes—for example, the current operating fund, plant fund, scholarship fund, endowment fund—but when doing external financial reports, the organization must report a more combined, consolidated picture of the organization as a whole. The new requirement, enshrined in FASB Statement 117, must be followed in order for your external financial statements to receive an unqualified opinion from your CPA audit firm. FASB made the change because fund accounting reports were just too difficult for nonaccountants to understand and use.

Organizations are now required to focus on the entity as a whole, not merely report separate fund groups. Fund balances (assets less associated liabilities; see below in the discussion of the Statement of Financial Position) are now called "net assets."

(c) CASH BASIS VERSUS ACCRUAL BASIS ACCOUNTING.   It is fine to use cash basis accounting (perhaps your organization has insignificant receivables, payables, and inventories, and no depreciable assets) during the year, as long as you or your accountant restates the results to accrual basis at year-end when presenting your external financial reports. In cash basis accounting, revenues are recorded when cash comes in and expenses are recorded when cash is expended. The problem is that revenues and expenses are not properly matched during the year. This mismatch becomes serious whenever your organization has significant dollar amounts of payables, receivables, inventories, or depreciable assets.

Accrual basis accounting better shows a period's operating results by virtue of the fact that it has revenues recorded when earned (e.g., when you ship a product or perform a service), and expenses are recorded when incurred. The biggest downfall of accrual basis accounting, which is mandated by GAAP, is that it may not portray how your organization's cash position is changing. It is for this reason that we place so much emphasis in this chapter on the statement of cash flows, even above the statement of activity. We return to this important distinction later.

(d) AUDIT, REVIEW, OR COMPILATION?   Does your organization need to pay the $20,000 or possibly much more for a full-blown audit? The final report of the Panel on the Nonprofit Sector, convened in 2005, recommended to Congress that audits be mandated for charities having annual revenues of $1 million or more, but an independent accountant's review is acceptable when an organization's annual revenues are between $250,000 and $1 million. That audit threshhold is higher than that recommended by some other sources.

An audit is the broadest in scope, with an auditor expressing an opinion that the financial statements fairly present activities of the organization in according with GAAP. An auditor may help your organization express its financials in the most clear and understandable way, including statements about the adequacy of internal controls. Your organization may send a request for an audit proposal to several CPA firms that would seem to have the appropriate industry experience and interest. Meet with members of each firm so that they better understand your management team and organizational culture and context prior to submitting their bids. The final selection of the auditor should be done by the board or audit committee, not by management.[8]

A review involves less than an audit but more than a compilation. It means that the accountant reviewed the financial statements, but all information in those statements is the representation of management. The review is based primarily on inquiries made of company personnel; some analytical procedures are applied to financial data, but the review is substantially less detailed in scope than an audit done in accordance with GAAS. The accountant performing the review will not express any opinion regarding whether the financial statements are in accordance with GAAP. The accountant will state whether he or she is aware of any material modifications that should be made to the statements to bring them into conformity with GAAP. The accountant may comment about the likelihood of misstatement and inadequacies in the underlying data upon which the statements are based. However, it is not an audit and may not be called an audit, regardless of what accounting firm does the review. No statements will be made about internal controls.

A compilation is the most limited of engagements, and involves assembling financial statements in good form. It is not an audit and may not be called an audit, regardless of the identity of the accounting firm doing the compilation.

6.3 THREE FINANCIAL STATEMENTS

You will have three financial statements to present to external users unless yours is a voluntary health and welfare organization, in which case you will also have a fourth statement to present. The three statements are the statement of financial position, statement of activity, and statement of cash flows. They also are called the balance sheet, statement of net revenues, and cash flow statement, respectively. As a financial manager or board finance committee member, you would want to devote serious attention to the statement of financial position and the statement of cash flows, because they depict how and why your target liquidity position is changing and whether you are achieving that target. Your ED/CEO and program managers will key in more on the statement of activity, in that it most closely mirrors their operating budget. Part of your financial education agenda for these managers is to convince them to "watch the cash flow," not merely a certain period's revenues and expenses.

(a) STATEMENT OF FINANCIAL POSITION OR BALANCE SHEET.   The statement of financial position (SFP), often called the balance sheet by businesses and some nonprofits, shows what resources the organization owns or has control of and how those are being financed, all at a certain point in time. *Assets* are the items that the organization possesses, with which it carries out its programs and services. *Liabilities* are amounts of borrowed money, or debt, that the organization has used to finance some of those assets. Some of those assets are financed by *equity,* or *net assets*, in the nonprofit world; these are funds that were used to establish the nonprofit at its inception or monies "earned" by the nonprofit through subsequent years as it brought in more money than it paid out for expenses. Often, in donative nonprofits, the lion's share of assets is funded by equity that represents contributions made through the years in response to annual campaigns (and perhaps also capital campaigns).

Consult our SFP, shown in Exhibit 6.4, as we work through some of the important accounts on that statement. We selected an organization that would have a statement of functional expenses—World Vision, a well-known faith-based relief agency with world-wide service provision.

(i) Assets. *The assets are listed in order of decreasing liquidity.* This means that the farther down the listing one goes, the farther from cash that item is, or the slower it would be expected to turn into cash. *Cash and cash equivalents* include bank deposits and any investment made with an original maturity (at the time your organization purchased them, how long until the issuer pays back the amount of the investment) of less than

World Vision Inc.		*consolidated statements of financial position*	
		*In Thousands of Dollars	September 30, 2003 and 2004*	
Assets	**Notes**	**2003**	**2004**
Cash and cash equivalents		$4,936	$ 5,000
Accounts receivable from the United States Agency for International Development		3,368	16,102
Accounts, notes, and other receivables, net		10,349	11,131
Marketable securities	note D	7,249	6,676
Investments in pooled funds	note C	52,172	86,403
Donated real estate held as investment		3,237	2,072
Inventory, net of allowance of $ 6,987 and $ 5,999	note E	55,439	41,390
Other assets		2,736	17,825
Fixed assets, net	note F	42,944	53,059
Assets held in trust		20,141	18,121
TOTAL ASSETS		**$202,571**	**$257,779**
Liabilities and net assets	**Notes**	**2003**	**2004**
Liabilities:			
Accounts payable and accrued expenses		$20,018	$22,654
Due to World Vision International		4,482	58,726
Notes payable	note I	10,297	10,002
Obligations under capital lease	note H	545	497
Charitable gift annuities		4,056	3,559
Deferred revenue		11,687	17,603
Amounts held for others		10,604	10,630
Total liabilities		61,689	123,671
Net assets:	note K		
Unrestricted		106,150	108,085
Temporarily restricted		34,097	25,388
Permanently restricted		635	635
Total net assets		140,882	134,108
TOTAL LIABILITIES AND NET ASSETS		**$202,571**	**$257,779**

The accompanying notes are an integral part of these consolidated financial statements.

Source: Downloaded from World Vision website at www.worldvision.org. Used by permission.

Exhibit 6.4 Example of a Statement of Financial Position (or Balance Sheet)

three months. This is a form of solvency, as noted in Chapter 2, and may also be a key part of your organization's liquidity. Smaller organizations may look at trying to hold larger cash reserves, having a bank credit line, or identifying donors (i.e., often board members) who may step in when cash does not flow.

Recapping, "cash equivalents" (listed along with cash) are typically short-term investments in which you get your interest and principal (amount invested) back within three months. The financial policy idea behind investing reserves in cash equivalents instead of 30-year bonds is that you may need the money on short notice. Looking at the organization as a whole, a liquid organization is one that has a ready ability to pay its bills without incurring undue cost. A target liquidity measure (see Chapter 7) is a numerical measure of this, but the analyst must still apply judgment as to whether the number calculated constitutes adequate liquidity.

One of the biggest financial management issues is hinted at in the item just below "cash"—receivables. Nonprofits may have one or both of two types of receivables. *Accounts receivable* are sales an organization makes on credit to its customers (gave them 20 days to pay, perhaps), but it has not received the check or electronic payment yet. *Pledges receivable* are pledges that have been made (unconditionally promised) but not yet collected. The similarity among the two forms is that neither is cash yet; one cannot cover payroll with either form of receivables.

Pledges receivable will be listed as either short term (expect these to be collected within one year) or long term (collected next year and years following, and someone will have to estimate the present value of the future pledges or what these are worth if expressed in today's money). Most well-run organizations are careful to set up a best-estimate reserve for pledges deemed not likely to be collected, in order to more accurately record on the balance sheet the "true" pledges receivable. Membership organizations also typically have a third form of receivable, *dues receivable*. World Vision has evidently arranged some loans to a third party, as it also has *notes receivable* shown as part of its receivables. The modifier "net" connotes that it has netted out any amounts it does not reasonably expect to ever receive.

Many receivables transacted during this period count as revenues this period—so an organization can grow rapidly and suddenly find itself in a cash flow crisis even though its budget is balanced and its net revenue (revenue less expense) positive.

Some organizations have classified financial statements, in which current and non-current or long-term assets are separated and subtotals are shown. If done for assets, it should also be done for liabilities (current and long-term liabilities).

If not classified, the financial statement user must try to determine which asset listed is the last current asset and which asset begins the listing of long-term, or fixed, assets. It is for this reason that experts usually recommend that organizations develop and report classified financial statements.

Of course, property, plant, and equipment, the last asset, represents a very large investment for some charities and most churches.

(ii) Liabilities.   For every $1 of assets, you must have $1 of financing from somewhere—which leads us to liabilities and "net assets." *Liabilities* represent a category of items that is equivalent to debt, which is equivalent to money borrowed. Every board member, in his or her orientation, should be asked to repeat this slogan slowly, with emphasis: "D—debt, D—dangerous!" The flip side of the financial vulnerability concept of being undercapitalized is being overleveraged, which simply means that sooner or later, the organization takes on too much debt given its risks and operating characteristics.

Every dollar in the liability section is a dollar that will have to be paid back—with current liabilities paid back within the year and long-term liabilities paid back over a series of years.

Consider first *current liabilities*. Just as current assets, other than cash and cash equivalents, are expected to be converted to cash within one year, current liabilities are expected to drain cash from your organization within one year. The often-overlooked liabilities that we need to focus on briefly are accounts payable and accrued expenses.

Accounts payable (A/P) are amounts borrowed from your suppliers; they are the mirror image of the supplier's accounts receivable. They gave you 30 days to pay, and you will take it! The great thing about A/P it is that it is interest-free (unless you pay late, in which case you may owe an additional 1.5 percent per month, which annualizes to 18 percent per year, ignoring compounding). So take the 30 days to pay unless you are offered a cash discount (say 2 percent taken off the invoice) for early payment.

Accrued expenses are monies owed (think "borrowed") from employees, bondholders, or Uncle Sam—money you know you owe but you do not have to write a check for just yet. Realize that, ethically, the organization does not want to be in the position of maximizing accruals (by, say, paying its workforce consistently three months after work was completed). Used appropriately, as a normal course of business, however, accrued expenses improve the organization's cash position (deferring cash outlays) and constitute interest-free financing.

Explicit interest is paid when your organization borrows from a bank or other lender. Amounts owed within the year on these short-term loan arrangements are called *notes payable*. (World Vision does not have any short-term notes payable.) Study the notes accompanying the financial statements to see to what degree a credit line that the organization has arranged is fully used ("taken down")—this becomes important when evaluating liquidity and the achievement of the target liquidity level. In the notes to the financial statements not shown, World Vision indicates it has a $7 million revolving line of credit, to be used for operating purposes if and when needed, but it had not used any of that at the end of either fiscal year shown.

Bonds and other *long-term liabilities*, such as capital leases (the organization may prefer to lease a piece of equipment rather than issue debt to buy it outright), long-term notes payable (all of World Vision's notes payable are long term, according to the notes, not shown), and mortgage loans comprise the remaining liabilities that you may see on the statement of financial position. We return to the management aspects of these in Chapter 10 on liability management.

(iii) Net Assets.   Now what about this idea of "net assets"? We call it equity in the business world. Think of it, policy-wise, as less risky to use this type of financing because you do not have to repay it. Ever. Unlike business equity, which is technically permanent financing but has implicit requirements to eventually pay dividends or perhaps repurchase shares of stock when the organization generates a great deal of cash and may not have profitable avenues in which to deploy it, a nonprofit gains permanent use of net asset amounts with no requirement to repay it (ignoring net asset amounts related to certain annuities or pensions, of course). Think of this as the seed capital the organization started with, plus any "profit" (change in net revenue that is positive) accumulated through the years the organization has been in existence.

The whole right-hand side or bottom part of the statement of financial position (liabilities plus net assets) is what we call "capital structure." The strong balance sheet is one with much more net assets and much fewer liabilities in the financing mix.

Briefly, when people donate money, they may restrict it for a particular use (use restriction) or time period (time restriction). Unrestricted means you can spend it as you desire. Temporarily restricted items are typically donations given for a special project, and in the period in which that money is spent the money moves from "restricted" to "unrestricted." Other donations may never become unrestricted. For example, endowment giving and museum pieces (normally) are permanently restricted.

One more caution: "Net assets" is *not equivalent* to cash. There is way too much confusion on that—even among sources that should be knowledgeable. That is, you cannot immediately spend even the total amount of the unrestricted net assets—that amount has already been distributed ("invested") across the assets of the organization, some in equipment. How much can you spend now? Only the amount of unrestricted cash and cash equivalents that is on the asset side of the balance sheet.

Every asset is financed by some mix of liabilities and net assets. Consider a car owned by your organization. The car is a long-term, fixed asset, possibly financed by borrowed money (liability) or possibly by money donated or "profit" made in the past (net assets, in either case). The point is, your net assets are already invested in various assets, some of which are very illiquid, such as that used car.

(iv)   *Financial Strength and Target Liquidity.* Recapping the SFP, a "financially strong" organization has a relatively large amount of cash and investments (preferably short term, meaning they mature within a year) and little debt (borrowed money). The most "liquid" (nearest to cash, or immediately spendable funds) assets are listed first. Then assets are listed in order of decreasing liquidity as you move downward under assets.

How would we compile a measure of target liquidity from this balance sheet? Let us consider a simple hypothetical example. Generic Charity has $450,000 in cash, $500,000 in short-term investments, and an unused credit line of $1 million. It therefore has target (where actual amount held is assumed to equal its targeted figure) liquidity of $1,950,000 (sum of the three components). Without knowing more about upcoming bills and cash flow patterns, it is tough to know whether this is adequate. Someone familiar with the organization should be able to make that call, however (see Chapter 7 on how they might do this). Looking at World Vision's SFP, cash and cash equivalents are approximately $5 million in each year, cash and equivalents related to its operating funds that are included in its pooled funds (this is documented in Note C, not shown) of $8.6 million in 2003 and approximately $26 million in 2004, and the unused credit line is $7 million in each year. Thus, target liquidity in 2004 would be cash + marketable securities + unused credit line, or $5 million + $26 million + $7 million = $38 million. The target liquidity increased significantly from 2003 ($5 million + $8.6 million + $7 million = $20.6 million). As many faith-based organizations, and a considerable number of other nonprofits do, this organization may be prefunding a capital investment or a significant program expansion anticipated in the 2005 or 2006 fiscal years.

(b)   STATEMENT OF ACTIVITIES OR STATEMENT OF NET REVENUES.   The statement of activity (SA) indicates to what extent an organization's revenues exceeded its expenses in a given period, resulting in an increase in its net assets. Exhibit 6.5 has our example, showing World Vision's 2003 and 2004 operating results. Revenues consist of contributions, grants, gifts-in-kind (e.g., donated foodstuffs, clothing, health supplies, or building materials), interest income, appreciation in investments, and other income. Notice that some of these are unrestricted, some are temporarily restricted, and some are permanently restricted.

World Vision Inc.

consolidated statements of activities
In Thousands of Dollars | September 30, 2003 and 2004

	Notes	2003				2004			
		Unrestricted	Temporarily Restricted	Permanently Restricted	Total	Temporarily Unrestricted	Permanently Restricted	Restricted	Total
Contribution and revenue									
Contributions		$19,839	$257,964	$—	$277,803	$21,708	$274,894	$—	$296,602
Public cash and food commodity grants	note L	198,079	—	—	198,079	284,880	—	—	284,880
Gifts-in-kind		203,917	—	—	203,917	215,281	—	—	215,281
Other income—net		3,893	2,078	—	5,971	9,216	864	—	10,080
Net assets released due to expiration of time: split-interest agreements		4,775	(4,775)	—	—	913	(913)	—	—
Net assets released due to satisfaction of program restrictions		256,078	(256,078)	—	—	283,554	(283,554)	—	—
TOTAL CONTRIBUTIONS & REVENUE		686,581	(811)	—	685,770	815,552	(8,709)	—	806,843
Expenses									
Program services									
Funding of World Vision International :									
Child sponsorship		117,299	—	—	117,299	134,554	—	—	134,554
Relief and rehabilitation, community development, and Christian impact and leadership projects		235,822	—	—	235,822	254,254	—	—	254,254
Gifts-in-kind		38,998	—	—	38,998	90,964	—	—	90,964
Other international relief & development programs		119,387	—	—	119,387	161,381	—	—	161,381
Domestic programs		25,825	—	—	25,825	54,384	—	—	54,384
Public awareness and education		4,632	—	—	4,632	5,524	—	—	5,524

EXHIBIT 6.5 EXAMPLE OF A STATEMENT OF ACTIVITY (OR STATEMENT OF NET REVENUE)

	Notes	2003				2004			
		Unrestricted	Temporarily Restricted	Permanently Restricted	Total	Temporarily Unrestricted	Permanently Restricted	Restricted	Total
Sponsorship programs		1,880	—	—	1,880	2,105	—	—	2,105
Gifts to other ministries		9,359	—	—	9,359	5,720	—	—	5,720
Total program services		**553,202**	—	—	**553,202**	**708,886**	—	—	**708,886**
Supporting services									
Management and general		32,542	—	—	32,542	42,004	—	—	42,004
Fund raising		63,279	—	—	63,279	62,727	—	—	62,727
Total supporting services		**95,821**	—	—	**95,821**	**104,731**	—	—	**104,731**
TOTAL EXPENSES		**649,023**	—	—	**649,023**	**813,617**	—	—	**813,617**
CHANGE IN NET ASSETS		37,558	(811)	—	36,747	1,935	(8,709)	—	(6,774)
Net assets, beginning of year		68,592	34,908	635	104,135	106,150	34,097	635	140,882
NET ASSETS, END OF YEAR		**$106,150**	**$34,097**	**$635**	**$140,882**	**$108,085**	**$25,388**	**$635**	**$134,108**

The accompanying notes are an integral part of these consolidated financial statements.

EXHIBIT 6.5 EXAMPLE OF A STATEMENT OF ACTIVITY (OR STATEMENT OF NET REVENUE) (*continued*)

All expenses are always shown as unrestricted items. This makes sense, because it is donor-stipulated restrictions that lead to the three categories of revenues (and net assets), and donations are revenues, not expenses. Notice the breakdown of expenses into program expenses and supporting services—and the further breakdown of supporting services into the two components of "management and general" and "fundraising."

World Vision experienced a significant increase in net assets in 2003, as its change in net assets (total contributions and revenue less total expenses) was almost $37 million. However, in 2004, it saw total expenses of $814 million slightly exceed total contributions and revenue of $807 million, resulting in a reduction in net assets of almost $7 million. As a result, it ended up with $134 in net assets at the end of 2004, down from about $141 million the previous fiscal year. Be careful if comparing this to another organization—its fiscal year may not end September 30, as does the World Vision fiscal year. Some nonprofits use the calendar year as their fiscal year, and many—especially colleges and universities—use a July 1 to June 30 fiscal year. Their 2006 fiscal year would start on July 1, 2005, and run through June 30, 2006.

Not to confuse you, but some organizations have yet another name for this statement: the statement of revenues, expenses, and changes in net assets." Businesses call it their income statement or their "P&L" (profit and loss statement), but since changes in net assets are not identical to income in a business, and are more like equity, one can think of this statement as being like a combination of the business income statement and the business statement of retained earnings.

Here is a handy formula to help you navigate, and guide your users, through this statement:

$$\text{Net Revenue} = \text{Revenue minus Expenses}$$

Notice we are not separating out contributions from other revenues, as was done in the statement in Exhibit 6.5.

Income, technically, is the same as profit (revenue minus expense), even though many in the nonprofit world incorrectly say "income" when they really mean revenues.

In our World Vision example, there are contributions and public cash and food commodity grants plus quite a bit of "Gifts-in-kind" (perhaps donated foodstuffs) income making up the revenue. Without going into a lot of detail, often you will see a nonprofit reporting significant revenue, but a large chunk of that is either not for operations (money for buildings but not specifically restricted by the donor) or it is noncash.

Compared to the SFP, which profiles an organization's financial strength at a point in time (a snapshot), the SA looks at the nonprofit's ability to cover its expenses. Instead of a snapshot at the end of a time period, it measures the flow of revenue over (under) expense during a time period.

We looked in our Lilly study (Appendix 1A and Chapter 2) at organizations striving to break even—that would imply a $0 increase (or decrease) in net assets. We would call it "$0 profit" (revenues just cover expenses) in business.

You see in Exhibit 6.5 that many donors have restricted their contributions. And the accountability function of the finance department includes ensuring that those wishes are honored.

Notice again that expenses are broken into two (really three) categories, and all expenses are always "unrestricted." Program expenses (that one will put you on the cover of *Money* magazine if it's high relative to other expenses) is shown first, then management and general (your salary!), and finally fundraising expenses are listed. The sum of management and administrative and fundraising is "Total supporting services."

So-called efficiency experts will scrutinize your program expenses compared to your supporting services expenses.

Notice one final thing from this SA: At the bottom right of the SA, the increase or decrease in net assets ties directly to the change in net assets recorded on the SFP (Exhibit 6.4) Compare the bottom right of this statement with the total net assets on the SFP. It is interesting, and of some concern, to note that the entire $50 million expansion in assets was debt-financed by World Vision in the 2004 fiscal year.

(c) STATEMENT OF CASH FLOWS.   Astute financial managers, we believe, manage cash flow first, not net revenue or balances. They do so knowing that the only way to ensure an approximate liquidity target will be achieved and maintained over time is to carefully manage cash inflows and cash outflows. Unfortunately, neither the SFP nor the SA shows cash flows. To get that picture, let's go to the statement of cash flows.

The statement of cash flows (SCF) shows us how the cash and cash equivalents amount changed from one year (or quarter) to the next. Our example is in Exhibit 6.6.

Refer for a moment to the SFP (Exhibit 6.4). Note the cash and cash equivalent dollar amounts for 2003 and 2004. Now turn back to the SCF and see the bottom line: same numbers! And the SCF does that very effectively by breaking down cash flows into three categories: O = operating, I = investing, F = financing. This is not a case where one category is as good as another—for most years an organization would strive to have positive operating cash flow, by and large.

Some organizations may not have any financial cash flows for the period. And if the organization does not like to borrow, that implies that increases in its plant and equipment (such as "Additions to furniture and equipment") have to be self-financed. If the organization has a nice positive operating cash flow this year, which World Vision does for 2004, it can "self-finance" capital expenditures during the same period or during subsequent periods. If not, it will have to sell off some investments, unless it engages in external financing through, say, bond issuance.

When looking back at the balance sheet, an item's *change* from one period to the next represents a cash inflow or outflow. Increases in asset investment represent a *use* of cash (you are using up cash to buy the asset), and increases in liabilities or net assets represent a *source* of cash.

Example:

We pointed out earlier that accounts payable and accrued expenses may be thought of as borrowing from suppliers and workers. That is a source of cash. But it is the change in that amount that represents a current-period source of cash. From 2003 to 2004 on the SFP, A/P and accrued expenses together increased from $20.018 million to $22.654 million. On the SCF, "Accounts payable and accrued expenses" shows us the $2.636 million difference as an "operating-related" source of cash in the 2004 fiscal year. By being granted extended payment terms and not having to pay workers before or immediately at the time work is performed, the organization has an additional $2 million in cash.

Some organizations also look at the match-up between how much they have in receivables, at a point in time, and how much they have in payables. This figure shows the degree to which your suppliers (payables are unpaid credit purchases) are financing your receivables. More generally, we look at the degree to which a $1 of assets is financed by borrowed money (liabilities) versus permanent contributed capital and accumulated past "profits" or surpluses.

In Thousands of Dollars | September 30, 2003 and 2004		
Operating activities	**2003**	**2004**
Change in net assets	$36,747	($ 6,774)
Adjustment to reconcile change in net assets to net cash		
provided by operating activities:		
Depreciation and amortization	3,839	5,792
Realized and unrealized (gain) loss on investments	(1,100)	(1,445)
Loss on sale of donated vehicles	200	2
Loss on disposal of equipment	1,756	—
Non-cash contributions	(7,367)	(6,560)
Changes in operating assets and liabilities:		
Accounts receivable from USAID	3,127	(12,734)
Accounts and other receivables	(555)	282
Inventory	(43,721)	14,049
Other assets	(11,790)	(14,958)
Assets held in trust 2,020	9,953	2,020
Accounts payable and accrued expenses	7,251	2,636
Due to World Vision International	(695)	54,244
Charitable gift annuities (497)	(17)	(497)
Deferred revenue	10,033	5,916
Amount held for others (net)	(5,662)	26
Net cash provided by operating activities	1,999	41,999
Investing activities		
Acquisition of fixed assets	(12,710)	(16,662)
Proceeds from sale of equipment	693	1,029
Purchase of marketable securities	(1,904)	(1,504)
Proceeds from the sale of marketable securities	6,522	5,524
Purchase of investment in pooled funds	(213,077)	(196,649)
Proceeds from the sale of investment in pooled funds	214,164	163,525
Proceeds from sale of donated real estate held as investment	6,452	2,893
Proceeds from the sale of donated vehicles	623	744
Decrease in notes receivable	960	(218)
Net cash provided by (used in) investing activities	1,723	(41,318)
Financing activities		
Proceeds from line of credit and notes payable	2,004	—
Principal payments on line of credit and notes payable	(2,601)	(295)
Principal payment under capital leases	(145)	(322)
Net cash (used in) financing activities	(742)	(617)
Net increase in cash and cash equivalents	2,980	64
Cash and cash equivalents, beginning of year	1,956	4,936
CASH & CASH EQUIVALENTS, END OF YEAR	$4,936	$5,000
Cash paid during the year for interest	$465	$394

EXHIBIT 6.6 EXAMPLE OF STATEMENT OF CASH FLOWS

Depreciation is a noncash charge that causes operating cash flow to be larger than the change in net assets for that period, *all other things equal*. The FAS 117 accounting standard has almost all nonprofits showing depreciation on their SA. It shows up, also, on the SCF to help one see that the period's net revenue *understates* the amount of cash generated by the operations. By adding back an expense that is noncash (you do not write a check for the depreciation expense amount recorded in that period), it gives a truer picture of cash from operations.

We show changes in receivables and payables on the SCF because some revenues have not been collected in cash yet (so receivables are building up), and as accounts payable increase, they provide us with cash (we did not write a check for the amount owed yet, so we have more in our cash account for awhile).

Finally, note the supplemental disclosure at the bottom of the SCF, indicating that the organization paid out about $4 million in cash each year in interest.

(d) FINANCIAL ACCOUNTING STANDARDS 116 AND 117

(i) SFAS 116.   Some of the key aspects of this standard for financial managers and users are:

- Contributions are "unconditional, nonreciprocal transfer of assets," so if a donor imposed a condition, such as the amount needed to be matched before gifted, no recognition of the contribution should be made until the match is achieved.

- Contributions are recorded when pledges are made, not just when cash is received. (Record pledge receivable and contribution revenue *before* getting the cash.)

- Even if donor restrictions have not been met for unconditional contributions, record the contribution then as revenue. (The related expenditure to satisfy the restriction may yet occur in a future time period.)

- There are restrictions on volunteer time contributed services being recorded—if that time is spent building an asset for the nonprofit or the volunteer has a legal or accounting skill, for example, that the nonprofit would have had to have paid for otherwise, this contributed service may be recorded.[9]

The entire text may be found at www.fasb.org/pdf/fas116.pdf.

(ii) SFAS 117.   Statement 117 indicates how nonprofits are to present financial statements and that organizations need to show the SCF (and voluntary health and welfare organizations must show the statement of functional expenses). The entire text may be found at www.fasb.org/pdf/fas117.pdf.

Some of the key aspects of this standard for financial managers and users are:

- Contributions and net assets are now separated into three categories, with the distinction simply based on donor-imposed restrictions, if any. If there are no donor-imposed restrictions, the funds are considered to be, and reported as, "unrestricted." If the funds are donor-restricted as to time ("may not be spent until … ") or use ("must be spent on capital since given to the capital campaign"), they are classified as "temporarily restricted." When the restriction expires or is met, the amounts are reclassified, which means they are subtracted from the temporarily restricted category and added to the unrestricted category. If a donor stipulates that a donation is to go to an endowment, in which the principal is never to be spent but income from that principal may be spent for operations, the gift amount goes into "permanently restricted" net assets.

- All expenses are listed in the unrestricted category even if the source of funds may have been restricted

- Pledges payable in later periods need to be reported as "temporarily restricted."

- If donors restrict contributions that are also spent in the same period, these may be reported as unrestricted support. (There is no need to reclassify across period, in other words.)

- All board-designated unrestricted amounts ("quasi-endowments": board designated for some purpose but not donor-restricted) must be shown as unrestricted net assets—only donors may restrict monies.

- Unless donor-stipulated otherwise, capital gains on investments are reported in the unrestricted net assets.

- Show revenues "gross," or not having the expenses associated with raising those funds subtracted before reporting as revenues. (Show those expenses separately.)[10]

(e) WHAT ABOUT THE IRS FORM 990 TAX RETURN? Why should we care? Because in evaluating charities, the public primarily works from Form 990s. Despite its weaknesses, the Form 990 will continue to get much scrutiny from users.

(i) Who Files a 990 or 990-EZ? Other than small organizations (less than $25,000 in annual gross receipts) and houses of worship and specific related institutions, it is standard procedure for nonprofit organizations that are exempt from federal income tax to file a Form 990, Form 990-EZ, or Form 990-PF (for private foundations) information "tax return" with the IRS each year.

(ii) Do 990s Have the Same Financial Statements as GAAP? In a word, no. Some information is present in the Form 990 but not in your SA or SFP. Other information is in the SA or SFP but not in the Form 990. There are also significant differences in the way in which amounts are compiled or reported as compared to GAAP practices. These are summarized in Exhibit 6.7.

(iii) Problems with 990s. Researchers from Urban Institute and the Indiana University Center on Philanthropy conducted a study of 1,500 nonprofit organizations' Form 990 filings and found the following items which the researchers labeled as "implausible":

- 37 percent of IRS Forms 990 reporting over $50,000 in private contributions report zero dollars in fundraising or special event costs.

- Zero fundraising or special event costs were also reported for about 25 percent of nonprofits reporting $1 to $5 million, and 18 percent reporting over $5 million, in contributions.

- About one-fourth of nonprofits reporting some fundraising costs report over $15 in contributions for each dollar spent; this implies a fundraising expense ratio of less than 7 cents per dollar raised.

- About one in eight Forms 990 report zero dollars in management and general expenses.[11]

When the study authors did nine follow-up case studies, they discovered after-the-fact yearly allocations of personnel expense and suspect accuracy due to, to use their wording:

PRESENT IN THE FORM 990 BUT NOT REQUIRED FOR AUDITED FINANCIAL STATEMENTS:

- Information on officers, directors, and compensation
- Description of mission and program services (optional in audited financials)
- Responses to yes/no questions about compliance with legal requirements
- Analysis of income-producing activities (used to determine whether the firm is fulfilling operational tests required to maintain exempt status)
- Ownership information on taxable subsidiaries

PRESENT IN AUDITED FINANCIAL STATEMENTS BUT MISSING FROM FORM 990:

- Information whether the statements are audited and received a qualified or unqualified opinion
- Accounting principles used to prepare the statements
- Description of the entity being audited
- Cash-flow statement
- Amounts, timing, and conditions associated with restricted funds

PRACTICES IN FORM 990 THAT ARE NOT CONSISTENT WITH GENERALLY ACCEPTED ACCOUNTING PRINCIPLES:

- Accounting method for many accounts is not disclosed
- Use of an indeterminate basis for allocating joint costs to program activities rather than to administrative or fundraising activities
- Unrealized gains and losses on investments and the equity in the audited financial statements
- Recognition of most contributed goods and services cannot be included, while certain noncash contributions can be included in the audited financials
- Limited or no information is disclosed about revenues and expenditures associated with restricted funds
- Indirect costs of selling merchandise (such as selling, general and administrative costs) can be included in cost of goods sold
- The 990 requires that nonprofits carry revenues from sales of merchandise, special events, and rental activities net of expenses as a gain/loss included in revenue rather than as separate components shown in revenues and expenses. GAAP accounting allows netting only for incidental or peripheral activities.

Source: Elizabeth K. Keating and Peter Frumkin, "Reengineering Nonprofit Financial Accountability: Toward a More Reliable Foundation for Regulation," *Public Administration Review* 63 (January/February 2003): 3–15. Used by permission.

EXHIBIT 6.7   HOW DOES FORM 990 DIFFER FROM AUDITED FINANCIAL STATEMENTS?

- "Glaring functional expense reporting errors."
- "Nonprofits responding to pressure to keep real and reported overhead low."
- "Capital gifts and in-kind donations create unique reporting problems."
- "Form 990 offers a different picture than GAAP for conglomerates and those leveraging donated space and services."[12]

One might logically conclude that these pitfalls and inaccuracies drives users away from any reliance on Form 990 data. In actuality, usage is high and increasing.

(iv) Continued Reliance on 990s by Users. Despite these shortcomings, the Form 990 informational return continues to be the primary financial disclosure made by nonprofits in the United States. As a board member, ED/CEO, or financial manager, knowing these shortcomings and being able to steer information users to the information they need that is accurate and timely are the keys. One decision to make: Should our organization use the new "e-Docs" feature at GuideStar to voluntarily make audited financials available to the 20,000 inquirers who visit GuideStar's Web site daily and are otherwise finding primarily just Form 990 data available?[13]

(f) HEALTHCARE AND HUMAN SERVICE AGENCY FINANCIAL STATEMENTS. FASB Statement 117 requires a voluntary health and welfare organization to present, as part of its external financial statements, a statement of functional expenses. See Exhibit 6.8 for an example. Users find the natural expense categories to be helpful in assessing expense control and expense trends.

(g) EDUCATIONAL INSTITUTION FINANCIAL STATEMENTS. As with other types of organizations, there are some college-specific or academy/school specific financial reporting standards that accreditation or certification agencies will require or strongly recommend for the reports you file with them. Representative of these is Standard 7, part of which we reproduce in Exhibit 6.9, from the Northwest Commission on Colleges and Universities. This commission oversees, for the states of Alaska, Idaho, Montana, Nevada, Oregon, Utah, and Washington, educational quality and institutional effectiveness of colleges and universities. Notice that some information beyond what the organization may have provided in its audited financials must be provided, and also that calculated ratios of some of the statement items are also required. We will include the latter in Chapter 7.

This accrediting body also requires, as part of its standards, a general policy requirement related to liquidity:

> 7.B.7 The institution maintains adequate financial reserves to meet fluctuations in operating revenue, expenses, and debt service.[14]

(h) CAUTIONS FOR FINANCIAL STATEMENT INTERPRETATION.

(i) Accounting Standards Issues. Accounting standards are in a state of flux, so always be sure that the most recent standards and pronouncements are available to your organization. Consult with your accounting firm on this issue periodically.

More serious for users is the fact that there are judgment calls in the application of accounting standards. For example, how much in pledges should be considered uncollectible? Unconditional pledges must be recorded as assets, but "condition" is defined as "future and uncertain"—and there is judgment involved in determining whether an event is uncertain or not. (When the donor pledges based on "if X happens," the accountant must assess the likelihood of X actually occurring in the future.) Also, how certain information gets presented may vary across organizations even in the same industry. For example, comparative financial statements are not required, but it is most helpful to see two years together, as we saw with the World Vision statements.

World Vision Inc. consolidated schedule of functional expenses

In Thousands of Dollars | For the Year Ended September 30, 2004 (with comparative totals for 2003)

	2004 Program Services					2004 Supporting Services			Totals	
	International Programs	Domestic Programs	Public Awareness & Education	Sponsorship Programs	Total Programs Services	Management & General	Fund Raising	Total Supporting Services	2004 Total	2003 Total
Funding of World Vision International and U.S. domestic programs:										
Child sponsorship	$134,554	$ —	$ —	$ —	$134,554	$ —	$ —	$ —	$134,554	$117,299
Relief and rehabilitation, community development, and Christian impact and leadership projects	246,035	4,299	—	—	250,334	—	—	—	250,334	231,422
Gifts-in-kind	90,964	41,543	—	—	132,507	—	—	—	132,507	52,748
Other international relief & development programs	155,471	—	—	—	155,471	—	—	—	155,471	113,953
Gifts to other ministries	—	5,720	—	—	5,720	—	—	—	5,720	9,359
Salaries and benefits	8,036	4,907	1,951	1,364	16,258	22,183	21,480	43,663	59,921	55,696
Professional services	1,097	545	1,153	2	2,797	5,630	7,978	13,608	16,405	13,160
Media and advertising	149	26	1,153	1	1,329	360	12,353	12,713	14,042	14,113
Freight and postage	76	47	194	142	459	373	6,002	6,375	6,834	6,399
Printing	31	77	208	—	316	237	7,345	7,582	7,898	8,843
Travel	1,715	830	374	11	2,930	1,208	3,294	4,502	7,432	6,463
Telephone and communication	272	209	73	25	579	463	727	1,190	1,769	1,557
Occupancy	540	1,128	153	312	2,133	1,657	1,619	3,276	5,409	5,210
Supplies	212	256	173	109	750	344	638	982	1,732	1,433
Equipment	176	171	40	63	450	656	291	947	1,397	874
Repairs and maintenance	71	182	4	12	269	1,375	105	1,480	1,749	1,752
Interest	87	35	9	11	142	140	112	252	394	146
Depreciation	610	112	39	52	813	4,395	584	4,979	5,792	3,839
Other	1,057	17	—	1	1,075	2,983	199	3,182	4,257	4,757
TOTALS	$641,153	$60,104	$5,524	$2,105	$708,886	$42,004	$62,727	$104,731	$813,617	$649,023

TABLES FOR PRIVATE INSTITUTIONS

Effective with fiscal year 1995–96, most private colleges and universities were required to report financial conditions according to Financial Accounting Standards (FAS) 116, *Accounting for Contributions Received and Contributions Made*, and FAS 117, *Financial Statements for Not-for-Profit Organizations*. These standards, **which are not applicable to public institutions**, significantly affect the appearance of the audited financial statements that accompany institutional self-study reports. In order to enable the Commission to interpret these new financial reports, the Commission modified its financial reporting forms for private institutions and requires additional materials to be submitted with audited financial statements.

ADDITIONAL REQUIREMENTS FOR FINANCIAL REPORTING FOR PRIVATE/INDEPENDENT INSTITUTIONS:

All member and candidate institutions submitting audited financial statements under FASB are also required to supply:
1. A breakdown of all net assets; e.g., unrestricted, plant, loan, life income funds, endowment funds, and agency funds.
2. A breakdown of all pledges by year of expected collection.
3. Data, if not already contained in the audited financial statement, on:

   a. Net investment in plant

   b. Unappropriated net gain on endowment

   c. Scholarship and fellowship expense funded from tuition revenue

   d. Cumulative unrealized appreciation (depreciation) of investments

   e. Annual excess of endowment total return over (under) spending policy

   f. Maximum aggregate annual debt service

4. Copies of the institution's Federal Form 990 (required of tax-exempt organizations).
5. For purposes of internal comparisons, certain ratios for each of the three years prior to the year of the comprehensive evaluation. These ratios are important to the Commission in determining the financial health of the institution.
   ….. [Section partially omitted.]
If the institution's internal financial reporting system does not accommodate an item in any of the ratios, the institution is advised to calculate the ratio using data as approximate as possible and to indicate where and how modifications have been made in the calculations.

Source: http://www.nwccu.org/.

EXHIBIT 6.9 FINANCIAL TABLES REQUIRED BY EDUCATION ACCREDITATION BODY

(ii) Cost Allocation Choice Issues. From a joint Urban Institute and Indiana University Center on Philanthropy study, we have these statistics regarding nonprofit accounting practice, related to the Form 990:

- Of the two-thirds of nonprofit organizations under $500,000 in annual revenues, 16 percent reported no management and general expenses and 3.4 percent reported 100 percent of their expenses as management and general expenses.

- 12 percent of all nonprofit organizations reported all staff expenses as management and general expenses, while 13 percent reported all staff expenses as program expenses.

- Less than half of nonprofits report salaries for officers in Line 25; of those that do, 12 percent reported it as all program expense, and about one-third as all management and general expense.

- About 7 percent of the nonprofits charged all accounting fees to program expense, and about 20 percent split accounting fees across categories.

The investigators concluded that "underreporting of overhead spending nonprofits is significant and widespread." They also noted that:

- "Comparisons based on reported numbers can easily lead to flawed conclusions."
- Reporting problems come from:

  - "Weak accounting staff and systems."
  - "Intentional underreporting."
  - "Unique nonprofit accounting issues."[15]

(iii) Comparison Data and Issues.   When different organizations use different cost allocations and varying conservatism in their judgments, it is difficult for users to compare numbers across these organizations. Yet data are now becoming available to compare organizations' Form 990 results. GuideStar is a primary source, and now we are seeing state-level sources become available, as in Ohio. For Ohio charities filing Form 990, data have been compiled at the Center for Community Solutions' Web site (www.communitysolutions.com) so that you can see ranges of financial data for a particular industry. For example, you can access the ratio of fundraising expenses to total expenses" for all "Religion Related, Spiritual Development" charities that report to the IRS. (As of this writing, there are 516 such charities in Ohio.)[16]

6.4 THE AUDIT AND THE AUDIT COMMITTEE

We addressed audit policy in Chapter 5 and earlier in this chapter we contrasted the differences among an audit, a review, and a compilation. One additional decision your organization must make is whether and how often to change audit firms or rotate audit partners.

What about rotating audit firms? Even though Sarbanes-Oxley legislation has not yet been applied to nonprofits, many nonprofits are adopting some provisions from its governance platform. Regarding audit partner rotation, we concur with this advice:

> Sarbanes-Oxley requires mandatory rotation of audit partners after five years, with a five-year timeout period during which the former audit partners can have no decision-making authority with respect to the audit. However, the limited availability of audit firms with knowledge of nonprofit organizations, and of experienced partners within those firms, could make a five-year rotation difficult to implement. In addition, because nonprofit organizations do not typically have the same frequency or intensity of partner involvement as public companies, it is reasonable to consider a longer time period before rotation. Consequently, NACUBO and other national associations recommend rotation of the lead partner every seven years, with a two-year timeout provision. For organizations that use high quality single-partner firms, rotation is impossible, in which case manager or staff rotation is advisable.[17]

6.5 FINANCIAL STATEMENT USERS AND USES IN PRACTICE

Earlier we mentioned the public's desire to know about your mission achievement and have access to your financial statements.[18] We also addressed user needs and how the financial statement could be interpreted to address those needs. To recap, organizations need to consider internal and external needs.

Internally, your management team and board needs good financial data in order to assess liquidity and set and monitor the target liquidity level, as well as to balance cash inflows and outflows over the near future and longer-term future. The SFP and the SCF, including projections of the latter into the future, are instrumental in accomplishing these objectives.

Externally, you will need to satisfy three major categories of interested parties with your external financial reports: donors and grantors, lenders, and investors (for organizations launching earned income ventures, particularly social entrepreneurship ventures).

6.6 SOCIAL ACCOUNTING

Space does not permit an in-depth discussion of social accounting, the inclusion in financial reports of program inputs and outcomes in nonmonetary terms. These reports might include information about volunteer contributions and social benefits.[19] There are various approaches to constructing social account measures, none of which is well developed at this time. These approaches include social return on investment (SROI), socioeconomic impact statements, and a reformulated statement of activity called an "expanded value-added statement."[20] In our experience, the SROI is a difficult concept to apply.[21]

6.7 ADDITIONAL RESOURCES

(a) SOURCES FOR NONPROFIT ACCOUNTING AND ACCOUNTING STANDARDS. The best presentations on nonprofit accounting methods are found in books and manuals.

The single best guide, in our opinion, is:

- Malvern J. Gross, Jr., John H. McCarthy, and Nancy E. Shelmon, *Financial and Accounting Guide for Not-for-Profit Organizations,* Seventh Edition (Hoboken, NJ: John Wiley & Sons, 2005).

The best place to start for someone with no accounting background or training would be these two guides:

- Debra L. Ruegg and Lisa M. Venkatrathnam, *Bookkeeping Basics: What Every Nonprofit Bookkeeper Needs to Know* (St. Paul, MN: Amherst H. Wilder Foundation, 2003).
- Warren Ruppel, *Not-for-Profit Accounting Made Easy* (Hoboken, NJ: John Wiley & Sons, 2002).

For more guidance on GAAP and their application, see this source:

- Richard F. Larkin and Marie DiTommaso, *Wiley Not-for-Profit GAAP 2005* (Hoboken, NJ: John Wiley & Sons, 2005).

For more on nonprofit audits, see these sources:

- AICPA, *Not-for-Profit Organizations—AICPA Audit and Accounting Guide* (Jersey City, NJ: AICPA, 2005).
- Robert N. Anthony and David W. Young, *Management Control in Nonprofit Organizations,* Seventh Edition (Boston: McGraw-Hill Irwin, 2003), Chapter 3, "Published Financial Statements."
- Evangelical Joint Accounting Committee, *Accounting and Financial Reporting Guide for Christian Ministries,* 2001.
- Warren Ruppel, *Miller Not-For-Profit Organization Audits with Single Audits (2005–2006)* (Riverwoods, IL: CCH, 2005).

The FASB standards are available online; the two standards that are most essential to study are:

- FASB 116: www.fasb.org/pdf/fas116.pdf
- FASB 117: www.fasb.org/pdf/fas117.pdf

(b) SOURCE FOR NONPROFIT ACCOUNTING SOFTWARE REVIEWS.   Various issues of *Faithful Finances*, a very fine bimonthly newsletter edited by Dan Busby, CPA. Also, see the most recent survey done by *Nonprofit Quarterly* magazine.

(c) SOURCE FOR NONPROFIT ACCOUNTING FIRM CONTACTS.   With the trend by the big four accounting firms to only focus on the largest nonprofit clients, finding audit firms can be a challenge. For faith-based clients, ECFA helps by offering this link:

www.ecfa.org//

Other resources are also available; See the FASB and AICPA Web sites: www.fasb.org and www.aicpa.org.

(d) SOURCES FOR NONPROFIT AUDIT COMMITTEE TOOLKIT.   The AICPA makes available a number of resources for free download. These may be accessed at: http://www.aicpa.org/Audcommctr/toolkitsnpo/homepage.htm.

(e) SOURCES FOR SOCIAL ACCOUNTING INFORMATION AND TECHNIQUES.   A book on this topic is now available:

- Jack Quarter, Laurie Mook, and Betty Jane Richmond, *What Counts: Social Accounting for Nonprofits and Cooperatives* (Upper Saddle River, NJ: Prentice-Hall, 2003).

Online resources include:

REDF Good introductory paper (Word document): www.redf.org/download/sroi/goodshipsroi2.doc.

REDF: Listing of a number of SROI reports, including actual applications to social enterprise ventures:www.redf.org/results-sroi.htm.

New Economics (nef): Builds on the REDF framework: www.neweconomics.org/gen/newways_socialaudit.aspx.

The Centre for Social and Environmental Accounting Research (CSEAR), housed in the School of Management at the University of St. Andrews in Scotland, has a number of resources on its Web site. Start with some of the discussion papers to get an overview and idea of some of the newest social accounting developments: www.st-andrews.ac.uk/management/csear/researchresources/dps-socenv. html.

Notes

1. John Trussel "Revisiting the Prediction of Financial Vulnerability," *Nonprofit Management & Leadership* (Fall 2002): 17–31.
2. Janet S.Greenlee and John J. Trussel, 2000). "Predicting the financial vulnerability of charitable organizations," *Nonprofit Management and Leadership* 11(Winter 2000): 199–210.
3. Panel on the Nonprofit Sector, "Interim Report presented to the Senate Finance Committee," March 1, 2005. Available online at: www.nonprofitpanel.org/interim/PanelReport.pdf. Accessed: 12/20/2005.
4. Stuart Kahan, "Outsourcing NonProfits' Financials," *Practical Accountant* 33(May 2000): 53–55.
5. Id.
6. See Jeanne Peters, "Accounting Software: A Buyer's Guide" and "Directory of Nonprofit Accounting Software," *Nonprofit Quarterly* 11 (Winter 2004).
7. Evangelical Joint Accounting Committee, *Accounting and Financial Reporting Guide for Christian Ministries* (Author, 2001).
8. Malvern J. Gross, Jr., John H. McCarthy, and Nancy E. Shelmon, *Financial and Accounting Guide for Not-for-Profit Organizations,* 7th ed.(Hoboken, NJ: John Wiley & Sons, 2005).
9. "What You Need to Know About FASB 116 and FASB 117," idealist.org, June 11, 2005. Available online at: www.nonprofits.org/npofaq/0/1501.html. Accessed: 12/21/2005.
10. Several of these items were highlighted in Nonprofit Financial Center, "Statement of FAS 117: Financial Statements of Nonprofit Organizations," 2000. Available online at: www. nfconlilne.org/downloads/fas17req.pdf. Accessed: 12/23/05.
11. Ken Wing, Mark Hager, Tom Pollak, and Patrick Rooney, "Reporting Nonprofit Overhead: Problems and Solutions," Presentation to the 2004 Annual Conference of ARNOVA, Los Angeles, CA, November 2004.
12. Id.
13. With the eDocs service, nonprofits "can add their annual reports, audited financial statements, letters of determination, and other documents" to the information present at GuideStar's website. Source: www.guidestar.org.
14. Northwest Commission on Colleges and Universities, "Standard Seven: Finance," downloaded from: www.nwccu.org/Standards percent20and percent20Policies/Standard percent207/ Standard percent20Seven.htm. Accessed: 12/22/05.
15. Ken Wing, Mark Hager, Tom Pollak, and Patrick Rooney, "Toward a Theory of Limited Nonprofit Organizational Effectiveness," Presentation to the 2004 Annual Conference of ARNOVA, Los Angeles, CA, November 2004.
16. See Janet M. Kelly, "Indicators of Financial Performance for Northeast Ohio and Cuyahoga County Nonprofit Organizations," Prepared in collaboration with the Center for Community Solutions (Maxine Goodman Levin College of Urban Affairs, Cleveland State University (October 2004). Available online at: www.communitysolutions.com/images/upload/resources/final-with-security.pdf. Accessed: 12/23/05.
17. Gary McGee, "Sarbanes-Oxley Act: What Nonprofit's Need To Know," Presentation to the Oregon Society of CPAs Not-For-Profit Conference, May 10, 2004. Excerpts reprinted at: www.tacs.org/qa/dirtemplate.asp?pID=123. Accessed: 12/21/2005.
18. For more about nonprofit financial statement presentation practices, including cost allocations, see the research done by Robert Yetman and others; for example, consult

www.newyorkfed.org/research/conference/2004/governance_papers/desaiyetman0925.pdf. Also see Robert Yetman, "Tax Motivated Expense Allocations by Not-for-Profit Organizations," *Accounting Review* (2001); Michelle Yetman and Robert Yetman, "The Effect of Nonprofit's Taxable Activities on the Supply of Private Donations," *National Tax Journal* 16, no. 1 (2003); Tom Omer and Robert Yetman, "Near-Zero Taxable Income Reporting by Nonprofit Organizations," *Journal of the American Taxation Association* 25 (Fall 2003); and Robert Yetman, "Nonprofit Taxable Activities, Production Complementarities, and Joint Cost Allocations,'' *National Tax Journal* 56 (December 2003): 789–799.

19. For a public sector social accounting guide, see Governmental Accounting Standards Board, *Reporting Social Performance Information* (Norwalk, CT: Author, 2003).

20. Jack Quarter, Laurie Mook, and Betty Jane Richmond, *What Counts: Social Accounting for Nonprofits and Cooperatives* (Upper Saddle River, NJ: Prentice-Hall, 2003). Also see the review of this book by Elizabeth K. Keating, *Nonprofit and Voluntary Sector Quarterly* 32 (2004).

21. For more on the topic of SROI, see Alison Lingane and Sara Olsen, "Guidelines for Social Return on Investment," *California Management Review* 46 (Spring 2004): 116–135.

CHAPTER 7

DEVELOPING FINANCIAL REPORTS AND RATIOS

7.1 INTRODUCTION

How are things going with the finances of your organization? Is there enough financial strength to expand or add new programs? Or will there be another cash crisis this year? Financial reports and financial ratios provide answers to these questions. It is hard to overemphasize the importance of accurate and timely financial reports for *internal* financial decision making. Additionally, donors, the IRS, and charity rating services such as the BBB Wise Giving Alliance, Charity Navigator, the American Institute on Philanthropy, and Philanthropic Research, Inc. will scrutinize your financial position and policies and judge your organization as to whether it is "support worthy." When you go to the bank for a mortgage or short-term loan, the lending officer scrutinizes your financial reports before making the lending decision. Bond underwriters and investors will do the same. Because the rating service bureaus, information providers, lenders, and investors will be looking at some of the same things you should be looking at periodically in your internal financial process, we will focus primarily on internal reporting and financial ratios that anyone could monitor.

7.2 MAJOR DIFFERENCES FROM FOR-PROFIT BUSINESS REPORTS

Nonprofit financial reports may look much like business reports, but the focus and emphases are different. Business professionals on the board may not be aware of these differences, and it takes some effort on the part of the chief financial officer (CFO) to explain why things are different.

(a) FINANCIAL RESULTS ARE NO LONGER THE PRIMARY FOCUS IN MANAGEMENT REPORTS.

In businesses, if the stock price is going up and the organization is profitable, the organization is deemed a success. In nonprofits, financial results no longer have primacy, because shareholder wealth or profit maximizing no longer serve as the overarching objectives. In a study of nonprofit effectiveness and excellence, in which more than 900 staff officers and board chairs were surveyed from a national sample of nonprofits, the mission and related goals were found to dominate in effectiveness assessment:

- When asked to list characteristics of an effective organization, most gave an answer that indicated a clear sense of mission accompanied by goals to carry out that mission.

- When asked how a nonprofit can improve, most gave the highest priority to "making mission central."

- A strong mission orientation is the chief criterion used by board chairs to judge the effectiveness of the chief executive officer (CEO).[1]

One of the more interesting interviews conducted in the major study of faith-based organizations (the Lilly study, profiled in Appendix 1A) was with Darryl Smith, CFO of the Church of God Missionary Board. Prior to coming to the Church of God, Darryl was a plant controller for a chemical company. When asked the difference between the mind-set and practices of the charitable organization compared to a corporation, he replied:

> I guess the biggest difference is the mission. Even a corporation has a mission orientation—they should. I think the mission direction of the not-for-profit, or at least the Church of God board here, is primarily that of trying to have an impact in people's lives around the world almost at times regardless of the cost. I'm not trying to say that we're not concerned about the finances related to that, but that seems to be an area that the church relies on faith and relies on individuals to support that. So it's not

necessarily looking at your one-year plan, your three-year plan, your five-year plan, and trying to implement that. I think in the private sector without question you've got a shareholder that you've got to relate to, you've got an operating board that is held accountable by the shareholders ... and many times the primary focus of the private business sector is the operating results related to that. I know in the chemical industry, maximizing your inventories (your turnover rates), your profit and loss statement, those were the biggest areas .... So I think the biggest change, the biggest thing I can see is that the mission is not related primarily to the financial strength. I think it's more related to the vision and the direction that the board or any of the staff feels that needs to be done around the world.

CFO's role: Use the financial reports to show how the financial results facilitated and enhanced present and future mission achievement.

(b) PRIMARY FINANCIAL OBJECTIVE IS TARGET LIQUIDITY, NOT PROFIT OR SHAREHOLDER WEALTH. The very different financial dynamics of businesses and nonprofits are highlighted when their life cycle pattern under financial stringency is considered.

A business that is not making money is closed to conserve shareholder capital; thus the financial reports focus on the organization's ability to make a profit and a positive operating cash flow, with stewardship defined as greater profits and cash flows.

A nonprofit, however, will operate until insolvent, and can be in the red for some years without any corrective action being taken; thus the financial reports focus on organization's net assets or what used to be called its fund balance (and, ideally, on the amount of that which is spendable in the sense of unrestricted cash and investment securities balances), with stewardship on maintaining some target level: *too little* jeopardizes the organization's future both in the sense of limiting its ability to respond quickly to new opportunities and in the sense of providing an insufficient buffer against a bad fiscal year; *too much* indicates "hoarding," which brings into question both why the organization is not spending more on meeting critical societal needs and whether the organization really merits the same level of donor or grantor support.

CFO's role: Use financial reports to show how the organization uses its financial policies, especially its primary financial objective of a target liquidity level, to add stability and further the organization's potential for future mission achievement. Consider this example from the business community: White Castle ("Buy 'em by the sack") states that it intentionally slows its growth rate in order to finance growth only with reinvested profits "so we can provide a stable company for our 9,500-plus employees." An example from the nonprofit arena: Salvation Army includes in its annual report this statement: "About 73 percent of the Army's net assets consist of land, buildings and equipment ($2.87 billion), *plus invested board-designated reserves for future capital expenditures, ongoing facilities maintenance and specific programs ($2.1 billion).*" [Emphasis added.]

At the program level, for most programs, strive to meet the secondary objective of *cost coverage* (revenues cover cost). A program not raising adequate donor funds within a certain time frame must be scaled back or ultimately ended. New programs are always welcome; just make sure to begin building financial support as you move toward implementation. In some cases, as we noted in Chapter 4, programs that do not cover their costs should be maintained, with reliance on earned income or subsidization from other programs that more than cover their costs. Some organizations have unethically diverted monies raised for one purpose to another purpose.

(c) FEWER EXTERNAL USERS, WITH A DIFFERENT ACCOUNTABILITY FOCUS.   Users often have a great deal of difficulty in interpreting nonprofit financial statements. Some years ago, a group of Harvard Business School master's degree students were given typical fund accounting-based statements to review. After much time and effort, they were unable to analyze and draw correct conclusions from the statements. With the new reporting format prescribed by FASB Statement 116, the statements are consolidated and look more like business financials, yet the meanings of such terms as "unrestricted," "temporarily restricted," "permanently restricted," "pledges receivable," and "net assets" are still confusing to many users.

Despite the difficulties, the general public and present and potential donors want accountability from nonprofits. As a result, quite often effectiveness and efficiency are judged from the service delivery observed (or read about in press reports such as those in *Forbes Magazine* that are appearing with increasing frequency), or a rating service report. For example, BBB Wise Giving Alliance and the American Institute on Philanthropy (AIP) each rate 500 charities, Charity Navigator rates 3,700 organizations, and reports are now available on 1 million organizations at www.guidestar.org.[2] There must be a strong case for your organization's financial position if one of the rating service agencies rates the organization's cash reserves as "excessively high." And be ready to justify administrative expenses if they are fall above a normal percentage of total expense. Not that these external groups are mere negative influences: how an outside party perceives an organization often conveys valuable information back to your management team and board. And many times the reports are positive (see Exhibit 5.8 for an example).

One other problem: External reporting requirements or needs may dictate internal reporting and budgeting formats, as nonprofits are too hard pressed to do two sets of reports.[3]

Stakeholders may raise a number of far-ranging questions about your organization's performance, as noted in Exhibit 7.1. Notice that the first two categories reflect mostly nonfinancial aspects and outcomes, while the last four categories include items that can be assessed by studying financial reports and developing and interpreting financial ratios.

Internal uses (the reports for which are sometimes called managerial accounting) at times may differ from uses outside the organization. Showing the difference between planned or budgeted amounts and actual reported results is an important input into whether the organization needs to initiate corrective action and whether it is heading toward a financial crisis.

CFO's role: Establish a work-around to provide helpful internal and external reports. Set up a financial spreadsheet to automatically link your management report form to your external reports. This way, your management forms are automatically updated each month (quarter or year) as you fill in the board, grant agency, state, IRS, or annual financial statement external reports. From there, customize the data into the framework most helpful for your management team.

(d) DIFFERENT FUNDS AND THE (TEMPORARILY OR PERMANENTLY) RESTRICTED VERSUS UNRESTRICTED NET ASSET DISTINCTION.   Fund accounting, still used for internal record keeping by many nonprofits, is not a problem in itself. Essentially, it is no different from divisional or department reporting in a business. A problem arises in cases in which (1) fund accounting reports may be provided to board members or major donors who request additional information, and these external users are not accustomed to the format; (2) internal decision makers do not specify how liquid resources in the plant fund or other funds might be tapped by the organization in an emergency; or (3) there are frequent interfund loans or transfers.

1. **Mission**

   ○   What is your organizational mission?

   ○   Is the mission consistent with the stakeholder's values?

   ○   How does that translate into goals and objectives?

   ○   What is the business model/strategy?

   ○   What are present obstacles to fulfilling the mission?

2. **Service Delivery**

   ○   What is the demand for these services?

   ○   What type, volume, and quality of services are delivered?

   ○   Are these services compatible with mission?

   ○   Are they meeting goals and objectives (are $ spent on right stewardship things)?

   ○   What are present obstacles in service delivery?

3. **Organizational Management**

   ○   What is the experience and expertise of management?

   ○   What is the quality of internal support systems?

   ○   What is the administrative efficiency?

   ○   What is the appropriateness of compensation?

4. **Organizational Funding**

   ○   What cash funds are available?

   ○   What non-cash contributions (goods, services, volunteers) are used and available?

   ○   How financially supportive are board and community?

   ○   How financially supportive are commercial activities?

   ○   Is there continuity of support and diversity of income streams?

   ○   How compatible is the funding with the mission?

   ○   How efficient is fundraising and development?

   ○   What are present obstacles in funding and support?

5. **Financial Health**

   ○   What is the cash flow position?

   ○   How financially stable is the organization?

   ○   Does it have accumulated wealth to sustain it if funding is reduced?

6. **Financial Management**

   ○   What is the quality of internal control system?

   ○   How prudent is the cash and investment management?

   ○   Are non-financial assets prudently managed?

Source: Keating & Frumkin (2001), ''How to Assess Nonprofit Financial Performance.'' Working Paper, Northwestern University and Harvard University.

EXHIBIT 7.1   QUESTIONS ASKED TO ASSESS PERFORMANCE

The relatively recent accounting distinction between temporarily restricted net assets and permanently restricted net assets should be more helpful than simply reporting items as "restricted." Here is an example that has been clarified by accounting rules that require moving such items to "unrestricted": In the past some organizations reported board-designated funds as restricted "endowment" funds, when in fact they should have been called "quasi-endowment" as they could be spent at the board's discretion at anytime. Even so, there are questions about how "restricted" these items are or when they will move from the restricted category to unrestricted and become spendable funds. Furthermore, there is an important distinction that may be masked in the classification. Some items are time-restricted, meaning they cannot be spent at the present. Other items are designated for a specific use and cannot be spent for general operations at any time. The financial manager must determine how much fits either category, and when (if at all) funds will be spendable and can be included in the cash budget to cover needed expenditures. This determination may be impossible for an outside statement user, however.

7.3 OBJECTIVES OF FINANCIAL REPORTS

There are four main reasons why the organization puts together financial reports: (1) to represent the organization's financial situation accurately and on a timely basis, (2) to support mission attainment, (3) to evidence accountability, and (4) to facilitate turnaround management. These reasons overlap, but each has unique aspects the CFO and treasurer will want to emphasize.

(a) ACCURATE AND TIMELY REPRESENTATION OF FINANCIAL SITUATION.   Ideally, weekly reports should be available one to two business days after the week's close and monthly reports within five business days of month-end. If reports are unavailable, issue control totals without the detail in order to speed the information flow. Use flash reports to get quick readings of key financial success indicators (KFSIs) such as donations. Use your financial situation analysis of year-to-date and yearly totals to guide new budget development and your long-range financial plans.

(b) MISSION ATTAINMENT SUPPORTIVE ROLE.   The financial reports should mirror the role of the finance department: Proficient financial management enhances mission attainment. Remember that in striving for your target liquidity level, the purpose is preserving and providing financial resources for the organization to carry out its mission. The fact that financial results are no longer the primary focus in management reports triggers three action points to guide your financial reporting and analysis:

1. *Serve the mission achievement end, recognizing that the report is not an end in itself*. Although the usual situation in nonprofits is inadequate financial analysis, resist the tendency to make financial affairs the dominant focus of top management and board attention while correcting the deficiency.

2. *Emphasize report usability*. Depth interviews and/or focus groups may go a long way to orient you to the informational needs and information processing capabilities of your financial report "customers." Benchmarking, total quality management (TQM), and the new reporting metrics that will be discussed later in this chapter have evolved partly in order to see through internal customers' eyes.

3. *Focus your reporting and analysis thrust mainly for internal users*. Necessary IRS and regulatory filings take time and attention from your development of management-oriented, donor-oriented or grantor-oriented financial information.

Most nonprofits fall far short of making the necessary managerial information available in the right form on a timely basis. Recognize that few businesses in the same size classes as typical nonprofit organizations have strong internal reporting systems either. Focus on a process of continuous improvement. Initially and at periodic reevaluation points, concentrate on the *process* (procedures and methods) of making decision-making information available, and think through the formats of reports carefully before releasing new or modified reports. One of your first objectives, which we will help you with later in the chapter, should be to improve on your presentation format (including graphics and annotations attached to the numbers) and variance analysis.

(c) **EVIDENCE OF ACCOUNTABILITY.**   Organizations must not only be accountable; increasingly they must persuade skeptical regulators, newspaper reporters, and donors of that accountability. What does "being accountable" mean? Look the word "accountable" up in a dictionary and you will see it is defined as "liable to being called to account; answerable." The financial and moral scandals over the past 15 years involving PTL Ministries, several United Way organizations, the Episcopal Church, the Roman Catholic Church, and New Era Philanthropy as well as those involving corporations, such as Enron, Adelphia, WorldCom, and Tyco have heightened Society's calls for accountability. In response, charities are becoming answerable to go-between rating service groups, such as the BBB Wise Giving Alliance, Charity Navigator, American Institute on Philanthropy, and MinistryWatch; we looked at their standards in Chapters 2 and 6. For these standards setters, accountability in philanthropy means providing complete financial statements that are prepared in a standard format with full disclosure both of resources and obligations as well as the expenses for program and administration. These guidelines constitute an excellent start; and you will notice that some of the other standards, even though not labeled as accountability standards by the groups, also bear on the issue. We need a broader framework, though, and one is outlined in Exhibit 7.2.

Who are the key stakeholders in your organization? Are you evidencing accountability as a good steward to each of the stakeholder groups? Can you provide a coherent response to a given stakeholder group that contends you are not doing enough for them (and maybe benefiting another stakeholder group to do so)? If so, *your* organization, speaking generically, is well on the way to being accountable.

Your key accountability, ultimately, is to the mission founders (upon whose vision the organization received approval to exist as a charity) and the present and potential donors. These stakeholders and their requirements are the boundaries structuring your provision of accountability-related information. In developing your reports, consider two things:

1. What information evidences fidelity to and achievement of the original (or revised) mission? If the mission changed, how did the change mesh with the original vision of the founders? Data to include:

    o   Program effectiveness
    o   Program efficiency
    o   Program controls (including financial)
    o   Program resource commitment

    In each category, pick one or two key indicators so as not to overwhelm your audience.

EXHIBIT 7.2 ACCOUNTABILITY AND YOUR FINANCIAL REPORTS

2.   Are donors' desires being honored? Donors want all of the items just listed, but also want to know:

○   What is your primary financial objective, and how are you doing in reaching it?

○   If you budget for other than break-even, why? Did you make budget this year? If not, why not?

○   Are you voluntarily providing information to clearinghouse Philanthropic Research, Inc. (GuideStar)?

○   How are you rated by BBB Wise Giving Alliance, Charity Navigator, American Institute on Philanthropy, MinistryWatch? If any of these bodies identifies a "problem area" how are you addressing it (or if you do not see it as a problem, have you clearly indicated why not)?

○   Designated funds spent as directed

○   Waste eliminated

○   A process of continual improvement (which usually means you admit some areas of weakness)

○   Entrepreneurial and creative initiatives to find new resources and to better use existing ones

○   More and better information about your organization's fundraising function:

▷   Some key ratios

▷   The philosophy and how it was honored

▷   Integrity first, last, and in between

▷   Evidence that you are not overly dependent on one source of funds, particularly if that source is "expensive" (in terms of costs and in terms of diverting attention from other, preferable sources of funds)

This brief outline gives some ideals that informed donors might hold. They would be delighted to get all of this information, but would not be surprised that you did not provide all of it because at times you do not have the data (yet, anyway) and you realize you don't want to overload them. So, parcel the information out over time in your various communications. Perhaps most important is that your attention to detail and to staying in touch shows a professional, dedicated, and informed management approach.

Note: For more on this topic, see John Zietlow, "Developing Financial Accountability and Control," chapter in *Serving Those in Need: A Handbook for Managing Faith-Based Human Services Organizations,* Edward L. Queen II, ed. (San Francisco: Jossey-Bass, 2000).

Exhibit 7.2   Accountability and Your Financial Reports (*continued*)

Note that accountability starts with staying true to the mission. Next, be able to answer to those asking about effectiveness (doing the right things and doing them in a way that achieves desired end results) and efficiency (doing those right things with a minimum of resource consumption). Is there a viable risk management framework in place? It is much better to *prevent* scandal, fraud, and mismanagement than to *control the damage* after the fact (see Chapter 14). Donors have needs and desires that your organization is also answerable to: They will need to know about your future expansion plans if you have a huge stockpile of cash reserves, for example. They will not understand your funding cycle unless you explain it in terms they can understand. What's more, the larger and more involved and astute present or potential donors will watch your operating administration and policy-setting actions for signs of accountability and proficiency. In the past, the visible nature of and organization's services and meeting of client needs in the community seemed to cover a multitude of financial and managerial sins; few organizations have that sort of community and donor loyalty today. Besides, why wait to be pressed into accountability when you can enhance your image by taking the initiative to be in the forefront of organizational stewardship? We saw in Chapter 6 how World Vision does this using its Internet web page. That stewardship principle is increasingly evidenced in all sectors of the nonprofit economy.

(d) TOOL FOR TURNAROUND MANAGEMENT. One of the best-kept secrets in the nonprofit financial management sector is the role financial reporting plays in the financial turnaround of struggling organizations. In the Lilly study, we were intrigued to find that two of the four top-performing organizations had recruited CFOs from the corporate sector who had radically redesigned financial policies and reporting. Both brought an emphasis on financial control and financial reporting that is rarely seen in nonprofits. Maybe the situation at your organization is not severe, but turnaround management is just a special case of transformational leadership that every organization can adopt. Remember: The process of continuous improvement is the path to take you to proficient financial management.

(i) Church of the Brethren. The Church of the Brethren, in Elgin, Illinois, had hired their top financial manager from the Dayton Press newspaper. Darryl Deardorff, CPA, who was CFO at the time of the study, had inherited a situation that was almost out of control. The previous CFO had totally given up on a deteriorating financial situation, in which expenses consistently outstripped revenues. The first thing Deardorff did was to convince the top management and board of the necessity to maintain a balanced or surplus budget. Although it took a while to persuade them, the reports he prepared portrayed the seriousness of the situation. Then, on an ongoing basis, he used periodic actual versus budget reports to monitor progress toward meeting the budget goal. In this way, the Church of the Brethren avoided a much more serious crisis that could have jeopardized the survival of the headquarters operation and shaken the confidence of members worldwide.

(ii) Church of God Missionary Board. The transformation at the Church of God Missionary Board, in Anderson, Indiana, is no less impressive. The board had been running deficits for a number of years, with no sign of improvement. Darryl Smith had worked in the chemical industry for 26 years with various organizations, and at the time he was recruited by a Church of God board member he was plant controller for Mobay Chemical. Smith, a Certified Management Accountant, had college training in finance and sociology and an MBA in finance. The competitive, profit-oriented focus on the chemical industry turned out to help Smith in his work at the Church of God. In our interview with him, he recounted the relative overemphasis on mission, to the exclusion of financial affairs, at the time he came to the Missionary Board:

Q: Why did you pick financial break-even as your primary financial objective?
A: I think the past has reflected a very difficult financial direction for the board because the primary focus has been to maximize the ministry opportunities and then to determine methods of financing those. I think what is happening now with the organization is that we are saying "Wait a minute, let's not only maximize our ministry but let's also be able to finance that ministry to a point of break-even."

One of the things we don't want to do is to have a whole bunch of money sitting here to draw interest off of. That's not one of the board's directives. They're saying we can break even, which means that we are maximizing the use of our resources for the ministry, for the needs of the people around the world. So, I believe break-even would be the primary objective.

Interestingly, in the four years Darryl had been in the CFO position, he still had not seen break-even achieved, but he felt confident that in one or two years the organization would be there. The moral of the story: Be patient in implementing change. Furthermore, there must be buy-in to the mission by the CFO and other financial professionals. The CEO and board must be assured that the CFO is not in a mindless "shut-the-door" mode—even though the CFO and board treasurer both are tasked with maintaining fiscal prudence.

We will return to this issue in two later sections of this chapter. Next we turn to a brief discussion of reporting system design and then we survey the main financial reports and financial ratios.

7.4 REPORTING SYSTEM DESIGN

For those organizations considering reporting system redesign, here are several developmental principles to follow:

1. Keep the end users in mind, and consider their technical knowledge and time constraints.
2. Either the accounting system provides the needed data, or you must revise it.
3. Provide management information on an accurate and timely basis.
4. Provide two display formats: program-by-program detail and natural expense elements (e.g., salaries in total).
5. Be able to get data *out of* accounting system and other databases into a financial spreadsheet.
6. Very important: The finance director or board treasurer must be able to extract liquidity detail including projection of future liquidity.

7.5 MAJOR REPORTS

When most people think of nonprofit financial reports, they picture the statement of activity, the statement of financial position (or balance sheet), and the statement of cash flows. Donors usually think of the Form 990 submitted to the IRS. These reports do double duty, as internal and external users find them helpful for understanding the organization's financial position and how it has changed during the year, and whether the organization can cover costs from all funding sources. However, our primary focus here is managerial: We emphasize the internal reports upon which management decisions will be based. To do this we must talk about variance analysis, in which actual revenues and expenses are compared to budgeted amounts, followed by corrective action when necessary. We begin our discussion with internal reports, looking at the annual reports first, then quarterly, monthly, and daily reports that organizations might use. Within that discussion we talk about the CFO's involvement in overseeing fundraising evaluation. Then we turn to a brief discussion of external reports. Finally, we get into the core of proficient financial management: managing off of the budget and using financial ratio analysis to gain insight from the financial reports.

7.6 INTERNAL REPORTS

Because your chief concern should be with management reports, we start with the internal reports. Even small organizations should develop budgets and do some annual budget comparisons at a minimum. We will start, then, with some of the annual reports you should prepare for the top management team and for the board. We include financial ratios and fundraising evaluation in our annual reporting framework. Then we move to quarterly reports, monthly reports, and daily reports. Finally, in our internal reporting framework, we turn to internal financial management processes, including how the manager interprets financial reports and financial ratios.

(a) ANNUAL.   To set up our annual reporting commentary, study Exhibit 7.3. Even the smallest organization should cover the base-level responsibilities, which involve a commentary and possibly graphs explaining why the actual revenues and expenses came in at the levels they did. Included here are highlights of significant dollar and/or percentage differences for the various revenue and expense items. Cause-and-effect discussion is vital, in order for users to assess the likelihood of recurrence for good news and bad news. Staff resources and time permitting, then move to the second level of the pyramid, which involves financial ratio analysis. Included here are basic views of net revenue, liquidity, borrowing, and degree of dependence on funding sources. If these ratios are being calculated, you are ready for financial input into the fundraising process, in which you assist and provide accountability to the development office. Finally, and very importantly for demonstrating the highest level of financial proficiency, conduct refined cash and liquidity analysis. Very few nonprofit organizations have gotten very far with level 3 fundraising evaluation, much less the refined, sophisticated analysis represented by level 4. We should also mention here that you have two separate but overlapping audiences: the top management team (other than the CFO) and the board of directors. How will

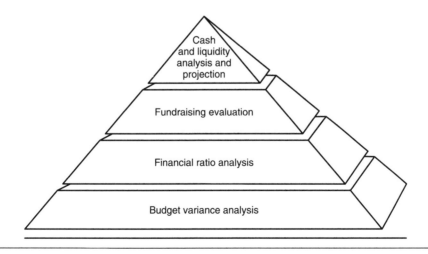

EXHIBIT 7.3 FINANCIAL REPORTING PYRAMID

your presentation differ? Show more detail for the top management presentation, but present the cause-and-effect discussion to the board as well. If yours is more than a policy-making board, such as in the case of local rescue missions, share much of the information that goes to the CEO.

(b) LEVEL 1: BUDGET VARIANCE ANALYSIS.   First in importance for managerial usefulness is the budget variance analysis (BVA) report. Typically, the BVA is associated only with the operating budget (see Chapter 8), and we begin our discussion with that budget.

(i) Operating Budget.   As we discuss in Chapter 8, this process has been ongoing on a monthly basis during the year, so there should be few surprises at year-end. Variances are the difference between actual (what happened) and budgeted (what was expected). A variance is a symptom that may be linked to many different problems, some more severe than others. Someone must identify the reason(s) behind any significant favorable (actual better than budget, which would be revenues greater than budget, expenses less than budget) or unfavorable variance.

We return to the specifics of presentation format and what generic actions your organization can take if revenues are below budget or expenses are running above budget in Chapter 8.

(ii) Capital Budget.   The capital budget is presented in Chapter 9. Compile a summary report at year-end to show what projects were totally or partly implemented during the year. Compare that to the capital budget(s) approved in the past year(s). Postaudit the actual project expenditures, by project, to find out if they matched anticipated amounts and if not, why not. What you learn from these postaudits will greatly help your organization in future capital project analyses.

(iii) Cash Budget.   The cash budget preparation is shown in Chapter 8. How may it be used to do after-the-fact analysis? Quite simply, it is used to check the accuracy of your year-earlier forecast and see if seasonal or trend patterns emerge in the actual cash flows that occurred. Determine in which months your forecast was farthest off, and why. Use that information to guide your development of next year's cash budget. Of chief importance, determine whether the target liquidity should be adjusted based on the past year's variance. It may be that your organization is heading for chronic deficits and a rapidly eroding cash position. Your organization may also need to change its programming, if fees are part of the revenue base, or engage in earned income ventures to supplement donations. If your organization is growing rapidly, the problem is compounded, because quite often funds are disbursed to finance the growth before the donor base responds to the increased outreach. You will gain additional ideas as we work through levels 2, 3, and 4 of the annual financial reporting pyramid.

(iv) Supplemental Report: Deferred Giving.   Has the organization ever done a complete report on the status and revised projections of deferred gifts? If not, it's time to start, and your office can give input to the development office or do the projection in your shop. The idea is to bring all funding sources into the picture as you evaluate the significance of your just-completed budget year. As we did with capital projects, compare gifts received with gifts projected. Recognize that bequests are just about the most difficult item to project in the entire spectrum of forecasts, except in the case where an estate is almost settled and you have some basis on which to project a remittance.

Recap of Level 1 Budget Comparisons. The budget variance analysis you do is extremely important. Too many organizations either do not conduct these comparisons, or seize on an asserted explanation but then do nothing to correct important deficiencies or to build on unexpected success. Work hard at improving your analysis and the clarity of presentation to the executive team and to the board.

(c) LEVEL 2: ANNUAL FINANCIAL STATEMENTS AND RATIOS.   We ordinarily think of the annual financial statements as being prepared for external users. However, there are useful insights to be gleaned from them beyond what you found with the budget variance analysis. First, comparisons can be made with the statements themselves or with a restatement of them ("common-size statements"). Second, financial ratios can be calculated from them that will give added insight.

Let's begin by looking at the statements themselves and their restatement.

(i) Statements of Activity, Financial Position, and Cash Flows.   The statement of activity shows us the degree of cost coverage of the organization's operations during a certain time period. We are interested in the degree to which all costs are covered. If costs are not covered, we find out the shortfall (deficit), and if they are more than covered, the surplus is identified. We want to know whether this was a planned or unplanned outcome, and if unplanned, the reason(s) for the deficit or surplus. Study Exhibit 7.4 carefully before going any further.

Habitat for Humanity International, Inc.
Consolidated Statements of Activities and Changes in Net Assets

| | Year ended June 30, 2004 | | |
	Unrestricted	Temporarily Unrestricted	Total
Revenues and gains			
Contributions	$ 86,796,589	$33,106,487	$ 119,903,076
Government grants	15,727,356	—	15,727,356
Other income, net	14,450,289	—	14,450,289
Donations-in-kind	914,365	19,742,126	20,656,491
Total revenues and gains	117,888,599	52,848,613	170,737,212
Satisfaction of program restrictions	51,512,333	−51,512,333	—
Total	169,400,932	1,336,280	170,737,212
Expenses			
Program services:			
U.S. affiliates	63,759,122	—	63,759,122
International affiliates	47,027,203	—	47,027,203
Public awareness and education	10,776,364	—	10,776,364
Total program services	121,562,689	—	121,562,689
Supporting services:			
Fund raising	33,292,354	—	33,292,354
Management and general	6,243,564	—	6,243,564
Total supporting services	39,535,918	—	39,535,918
Total expenses	161,098,607	—	161,098,607
Losses on contributions receivable	—	2,421,939	2,421,939
Total expenses and losses on contributions receivable	$ 161,098,607	$ 2,421,939	$ 163,520,546
Change in net assets	$ 8,302,325	$ (1,085,659)	$ 7,216,666
Net assets at beginning of year	$ 4,915,733	$ 59,213,202	$ 64,128,935
Net assets at end of year	$ 13,218,058	$ 58,127,543	$ 71,345,601

Source: Habitat for Humanity International, Inc.

EXHIBIT 7.4   EXAMPLE OF STATEMENT OF ACTIVITY FOR INTERPRETATION

Notice that for the 2004 fiscal year, the change in net assets is $7.2 million, so net revenue is in a surplus position. Revenue and gains were more than adequate to cover all expenses in this fiscal year. Also, there are no permanently restricted items, indicating the absence of donor-restricted endowment gifts in which the principal must be held in perpetuity and only the income (or some percentage of the amount in the endowment) may be used by the organization in a given fiscal year (assuming donors have not also restricted the returns from the endowment).

Beyond simply looking at the statement dollar amounts, we would like to compare this year's results to those of recent years, and we would also prefer to know what percent of revenue is attributable to each cost element. The way to do this is with a common-size statement of activity, as shown in Exhibit 7.5.

In our abbreviated example, we did not show the revenue mix breakdown. To illustrate how you would compute these revenue percentages, contributions represent $119,903,076 of the total revenue of $170,737,212, which equals 70.2 percent of total revenue. This percentage can and should be compared to percentages from previous years. Notice also in our example that the total of the expenses, when subtracted from 100 percent, do not add to the surplus percentage of 4.2 percent (change in net assets divided by total revenue). The reason for this is that a loss on contributions receivable—due to a write down of contributions that Habitat does not expect to receive—reduces the amount of contributions revenue that the organization will be able to retain.

The common-size SA is condensed, and a user may wish to know more about the line-item detail. Expressing total revenue as 100 (for 100%), we can then see what percent of total revenue arises from various revenue sources and is taken by the various expense line items (e.g., public awareness and education). If we divide public awareness and education expense of $10,776,364 by total revenue of $170, 737,212, we get 6.31 percent. We compare this to other expenses that same year, and also see if that expense category accounted for a larger percentage of revenues or smaller percentage, compared to previous years (2003, 2002, etc.). Further, some organizations calculate a three-year average of each item's expense percentage, to offset one-time spikes that may not be expected to represent a change in trend.

Health benefits expense has constituted of the larger increases in recent years for many nonprofits, and we do not even see this listed on the SA. We will need to gather that data elsewhere. For voluntary health and welfare organizations such as Habitat for Humanity, we will use the statement of functional expenses, which breaks program, management, and fundraising expenses down into "natural" categories, such as salaries, fringe benefits, office-related, utility, insurance, and so on. Using the basic functional expense example in Exhibit 7.6, we can readily see how this is done. Again, simply divide each expense amount by total revenue. Not only does this reveal the program, management, and fundraising ratios that philanthropic bureaus closely watch, but also it

Item	Dollar Amount	Percent
Total revenue	$170,737,212	100.0%
Program expense	121,562,689	71.2
Management and general expense	6,243,564	3.7
Fundraising expense	33,292,354	19.5
Surplus/(Deficit)	$7,216,666	4.2

EXHIBIT 7.5   COMMON-SIZE STATEMENT OF ACTIVITY—EXPENSES ONLY

Habitat for Humanity International, Inc.
Consolidated Statements of Functional Expenses

Year ended June 30, 2004

	Program Services				Supporting Services			
	U.S. Affiliates	International Affiliates	Public Awareness and Education	Total Program Services	Fund Raising	Management and General	Total Supporting Services	Total
Program and house building transfers	$25,417,932	$25,557,290	$ 169,718	$ 51,144,940	$ —	$ —	$ —	$ 51,144,940
Donated assets distributed	18,190,272	—	—	18,190,272	—	—	—	18,190,272
Salaries and bene...	12,322,084	14,741,084	4,765,332	31,828,500	5,192,025	3,222,710	8,414,735	40,243,235
Payroll tax expense	814,832	366,591	281,671	1,463,094	290,314	176,811	467,125	1,930,219
Professional services – direct mail	—	—	—	—	22,439,933	—	22,439,933	22,439,933
Professional services – other	714,185	921,098	730,432	2,365,715	1,783,445	603,100	2,386,545	4,752,260
Postage and freight	213,486	119,029	1,407,798	1,740,313	1,200,057	64,578	1,264,635	3,004,948
Travel	1,455,801	2,534,138	918,699	4,908,638	480,255	195,593	675,848	5,584,486
Printing	118,312	110,920	1,194,405	1,423,637	298,302	21,466	319,768	1,743,405
Service agreements and utilities	900,159	467,608	601,931	1,969,698	703,511	1,027,959	1,731,470	3,701,168
Insurance	824,646	174,942	142,696	1,142,284	141,226	146,435	287,661	1,429,945
Interest, service charges and taxes	1,240,878	160,531	31,477	1,432,886	64,213	76,595	140,808	1,573,694
Of e and equipment	275,086	707,288	223,714	1,206,088	179,418	52,334	231,752	1,437,840
Depreciation and amortization	449,363	361,673	160,976	972,012	300,426	198,078	498,504	1,470,516
Other	822,086	805,011	147,515	1,774,612	219,229	457,905	677,134	2,451,746
Total	$63,759,122	$47,027,203	$10,776,364	$121,562,689	$33,292,354	$6,243,564	$39,535,918	$161,098,607

See accompanying notes.

EXHIBIT 7.6 STATEMENT OF FUNCTIONAL EXPENSES FOR INTERPRETATION

Total expenses	100.0%
Program and house building transfers	31.7
Donated assets distributed	11.3
Salaries and benefits	25.0
Payroll tax expense	1.2
Professional services—direct mail	13.9
Professional services—other	2.9
Postage and freight	1.9
Travel	3.5
Printing	1.1
Service agreements and utilities	2.3
Insurance	0.9
Interest, service charges, and taxes	1.0
Office and equipment	0.9
Depreciation and amortization	0.9
Other	1.5

EXHIBIT 7.7   COMMON-SIZE STATEMENT OF FUNCTIONAL EXPENSES

gives us an idea of relative magnitude of our expenses and can be monitored from year to year and from quarter to quarter. Consult Exhibit 7.6 to see the Statement of Functional Expenses (SFE) for Habitat for Humanity, then Exhibit 7.7 to see the common-size SFE. Because Habitat for Humanity presents comparative statements (showing more than just the most recent year), we can do a more valid and refined analysis.

We would first survey this common-size statement to see what the major expense categories are for Habitat. Two stand out: program and house building transfers and salaries and benefits. After this, professional services—direct mail and donated assets distributed show up as large expense items. (Accounting treatment for donated items is to show the dollar value of those items as both a revenue and an expense in the same period.) Then we would compare this percentage breakdown with the previous year's as well as the fiscal year two years prior. The key is to look for a trend. For example, for Habitat, salaries and benefits expense for 2003 was $32,103,414/$161,472,096 = 19.9$ percent of total expenses, and for 2002 it was $28,215,811/$159,576,400 = 17.7$ percent of total expenses. This indicates that not only is salary and benefit expense increasing in absolute terms (from $28 million to $40 million), but it is so growing rapidly in relative terms. As a percentage of total expenses, this one item has swelled from less than 18 percent of total expense to 25 percent of total expense. Nonprofits are normally "labor-intensive," so in absolute terms this 25 percent figure is unsurprising: large churches average 40 percent and small churches 46 percent on this measure, for example.[4] Management would want to assess the reason(s) for this, and whether the main reason is increased employee headcount, large pay increases, or benefit cost increases. It is most likely the latter, as benefit costs have spiraled at most nonprofits. A caution for your general interpretation of this percentage: This percentage will normally increase in any year when total expenses decline, as salaries and benefits are relatively fixed in dollar amount, and a nonprofit operating with a lean staff has difficulty in reducing headcount or scaling back on benefits when it needs to reduce expenses. Finally, many analysts would average each row's expense for the past three years to get an average. Then, next year, the analyst would drop out the oldest year's value, include the most recent previous year's value, and recompute the three-year average for each expense item. These "moving averages" are useful to note trends and to reduce the influence of an abnormal year on the three-year average.

Habitat for Humanity International, Inc.
Consolidated Statements of Financial Position

	June 30	
	2004	**2003**
Assets		
Cash and cash equivalents	**$ 17,342,999**	$ 10,892,596
Investments at fair value	**21,285,517**	19,856,232
Receivables:		
Contributions and grants, net	**37,754,292**	37,658,645
Affiliate notes, net	**25,657,510**	24,392,837
Due from affiliates, net	**6,929,830**	7,358,880
Other, net	**2,222,121**	525,565
Total receivables	**72,563,753**	69,935,927
Inventories, net	**610,182**	1,083,115
Prepaids and other assets	**1,930,994**	959,876
Land, buildings, capital leases and equipment—net of accumulated depreciation and amortization	**10,435,509**	9,370,410
Total Assets	**$124,168,954**	$112,098,156
Liabilities and net assets		
Accounts payable, accrued expenses and capitalized lease obligation payable	**$ 14,642,554**	$ 11,151,940
Notes payable	**3,173,282**	3,573,032
Annuity obligation	**6,312,034**	5,355,866
Investor notes payable	**28,695,483**	27,888,383
Total liabilities	**52,823,353**	47,969,221
Net assets:		
Unrestricted	**13,218,058**	4,915,733
Temporarily restricted	**58,127,543**	59,213,202
Total net assets	**71,345,601**	64,128,935
Total Liabilities and net assets	**$124,168,954**	$112,098,156

Source: Habitat for Humanity International, Inc. Used by permission.

EXHIBIT 7.8 STATEMENT OF FINANCIAL POSITION EXAMPLE FOR INTERPRETATION

The statement of financial position (SFP) (also called the statement of financial condition [SFC] or balance sheet) shows us items owned or over which the organization has control and how they are financed. Notice the Habitat for Humanity SFC in Exhibit 7.8. To the extent the organization use borrowed funds to finance assets, it is in a riskier position due to the necessity to pay interest and ultimately repay principal. The use of past surpluses reduces risk because this amount represents permanent financing that does not have to be repaid. We will return to these issues in Chapter 10 on liability management.

Once again, as we did with the SA, we will also prepare a common-size statement of financial position (Exhibit 7.9) to see the relative magnitude of each asset item (divide each line item by the total assets dollar amount) and for each liability or net asset item (again dividing each item by total assets). Compare the percentages over several years to see how much is being invested in each asset, how assets are being financed, and the trends affecting your organization. Especially note any reductions in cash and equivalents as a percentage of total assets (remember our liquidity target and the key role cash and equivalents has in liquidity) or an increasing reliance on borrowed funds when analyzing an SFP common-size statement.

Exhibit 7.9 shows the common-size SFP with both the most recent year and the prior two years (2004 and 2003 in this case). Immediately, we note that cash and equivalents

Common-Size Percentages	2004	2003
Total assets	100.0%	100.0%
Cash and cash equivalents	14.0%	8.8%
Investments	17.1%	16.0%
Receivables:		
Contributions and grants, net	30.4%	30.3%
Affiliate notes, net	20.7%	19.6%
Due from affiliates, net	5.6%	5.9%
Other, net	1.8%	0.4%
Total receivables	58.4%	56.3%
Inventories, net	0.5%	0.9%
Prepaids and other assets	1.6%	0.8%
Land, buildings, capital leases		
and equipment—net	8.4%	7.5%
Liabilities and net assets:		
Accounts payable, accrued expenses and		
capitalized lease obligation payable	11.8%	9.0%
Notes payable	2.6%	2.9%
Annuity obligation	5.1%	4.3%
Investor notes payable	23.1%	22.5%
Total liabilities	42.5%	38.6%
Net assets:		
Unrestricted	10.6%	4.0%
Temporarily restricted	46.8%	47.7%
Total net assets	57.5%	51.6%

EXHIBIT 7.9   STATEMENT OF FINANCIAL POSITION COMMON-SIZE STATEMENT

has spiked up significantly, from 8.8 percent of total assets to 14 percent of total assets. Affiliate notes have increased, which may well be the evidence of a policy decision being implemented as national headquarters provides an increasing degree of financing to regional affiliates. About 4 percent more of assets are financed with debt, but this increase in reliance on debt financing is less serious than it at first appears because notes payable dropped slightly as a percentage of sales and some of the 3 percent increase in liabilities was from non–interest-bearing liabilities (accounts payable–which is a credit extension from suppliers–accrued expenses, which are wages, salaries, interest–and taxes that are owed but funds have not yet been disbursed). Nevertheless, one would want to watch the use of debt financing (liabilities) to see if the cash flow burden of interest payments and principal payments continued to be manageable. We can assess this further by looking at the SCF.

The SCF is still not well understood by most nonprofit managers or board members. It shows how cash was received to support operations, how cash was disbursed to provide programs, and it reconciles the change in cash on the SFP. In our view, it is probably the most valuable of the three statements for showing how target liquidity was met. Because that is the primary financial objective of the proficient organization, we will want to tap into the usefulness of this statement. Once again, we look at the line items by themselves to observe the big-dollar amounts. Beyond that, we look (1) at the sign of each of the three categories (operating, investing, financing), and (2) the operating cash flow dollar amount relative to both the investing dollar amount and relative to the financing dollar amount. Study the Habitat for Humanity SCF, shown in Exhibit 7.10.

Habitat for Humanity International, Inc.
Consolidated Statements of Cash Flows

	Year ended June 30	
	2004	**2003**
Operating activities		
Change in net assets	$ 7,216,666	$ (7,019,085)
Adjustments to reconcile change in net assets to net cash provided by operating activities:		
Depreciation and amortization	1,470,516	2,844,006
Net loss (gain) on disposal of land, building, and equipment	29,093	(48,756)
Losses on contributions receivables	2,421,939	3,972,414
Losses on other receivables	199,200	—
Change in reserve for inventory obsolescence	109,668	1,364,042
Net realized and unrealized gains on investments	(306,340)	(23,342)
Changes in operating assets and liabilities:		
Increase in receivables	5,678,015)	(1,822,870)
Decrease (increase) in inventories	363,265	(200,197)
(increase) decrease in prepaids and other assets	(971,118)	108,538
Increase in accounts payable and accrued expenses	3,490,611	4,925,901
Net cash provided by operating activities	8,545,488	4,100,651
Investing activities		
Purchases of investments	(11,557,732)	(14,815,195)
Proceeds from sales and maturities of investments	10,434,787	7,486,415
Loans to affliates	(2,662,251)	(2,714,676)
Repayments from affliates	3,091,301	3,733,241
Purchases of land, buildings and equipment	(2,575,086)	(2,083,436)
Proceeds from sale of land, buildings, and equipment	10,378	70,254
Net cash used in investing activities	(3,258,603)	(8,323,397)
Financing activities		
Proceeds from notes payable	2,341,741	374,573
Principal repayments on notes payable	(2,741,491)	(2,430,623)
Increase in annuity obligation	1,332,844	1,214,388
Payments or annuity obligation	(376,676)	(368,518)
Proceeds from issuance of investor notes payable	6,678,300	8,414,200
Payments on investor notes payable	(5,871,200)	(5,924,329)
Net cash provided by financing activities	1,363,518	1,279,691
Increase (decrease) in cash and cash equivalents	6,450,403	(2,943,055)
Cash and cash equivalents:		
Beginning of year	10,892,596	13,835,651
End of year	$ 17,342,999	$ 10,892,596

Source: Habitat for Humanity International, Inc.

EXHIBIT 7.10   STATEMENT OF CASH FLOWS FOR INTERPRETATION

Before interpreting the SCF, it is instructive to compare the operating cash flow dollar amount to the change in net assets from the SA for the same year. Referring to Exhibit 7.4, we see that Habitat had a surplus of $7,216,666 for 2004. Its increase in cash and equivalents in 2004, $6,450,403, was pretty close to this amount. In this case, then, the surplus was a pretty good indicator of the increase to the organization's cash position. This is quite unusual, however, as we see by referring back to Habitat's earlier financial results (not shown here). In 2001, Habitat had a deficit of $(1,213,656) but operating cash flow plunged by $(8,049,243). In 2002, Habitat had a deficit of $(3,774,322) and an operating cash flow of $4,975,945. In 2003, Habitat had a deficit of $(7,019,085) and operating cash flow of $(2,943,055). Clearly, one cannot base a prediction on how the cash position will change from operating results simply on whether a surplus or deficit is achieved in that year. The cash and equivalents amount may also change from investing activities and financing activities, neither of which is captured by the SA for that period. This also motivates our study of cash forecasting, which we present in Chapter 8.

If the sign of the operating cash flows is negative, your operations have reduced your cash and liquidity during the year. To meet the reduction, either your organization drained cash and cash equivalents (and you will see that change at the bottom of the SCF) or it funded this amount by selling assets (literally liquidating part of the organization's asset base, possibly by selling off some short-term investments that were not accounted for as cash equivalents) or taking on additional financing. *None of the three mechanisms for covering operating cash deficits is sustainable.* Take a negative operating cash flow *very* seriously if you have one. Be vigilant to eliminate this situation immediately.

Looking at the operating cash flow dollar amount relative to the investing or financing cash flow can also be instructive. A brief discussion will show what we mean. Let's assume that the operating cash flow is zero or positive. If zero, your operations "broke even" on a cash basis. If positive, you will want to compare the operating cash flow (OCF) to the investing cash flow (ICF): Simply divide the dollar amount of the operating cash flow by the dollar amount of the investing cash flow. For a healthy business, this generally results in a positive numerator divided by a negative denominator, as the growing business uses some of its surplus cash from operations to finance growth in plant and equipment investments. If such is the case for your organization, you might have this situation:

$$OCF = \$50; ICF = -\$25;$$

$$\text{Then } OCF/ICF = \$50/-\$25 = -2.0.$$

What this means is that you generated enough cash to cover the investing needs twice over. Many nonprofits, especially faith-based organizations (FBOs) and conservatively managed nonprofits, self-finance investing outflows with one or more years of positive operating cash flows. This comes largely due to a financial policy stance regarding debt and the risk it entails. Caution: If OCF is negative or ICF is positive, do not calculate the ratio because the interpretation would be nonsensical; in neither case would operating cash inflows be covering investing cash outflows. Another SCF ratio we have seen is to take OCF and divide by current liabilities from the SFP. This gives an indication of the organization's ability to cover its near-term obligations. We have more to say about ratios in the next section.

We can do a similar analysis by comparing operating cash flow to financing cash flow (FCF) in cases in which OCF is negative and FCF is positive. A temporary use of financing to fund deficits is acceptable, which might result in this situation:

$$OCF = -\$25; FCF = \$25;$$

$$\text{Then } OCF/FCF = -1.0.$$

The ratio value of -1.0 tells us that the operating cash outflow was just covered by a financing cash inflow. One year or perhaps two years of this pattern might be acceptable, but we would not want this pattern to persist because we are experiencing ever-greater reliance on restricted gifts (which cannot be tapped to meet cash crisis needs) and/or borrowed money.[5]

(ii) Financial Ratio Analysis. Financial ratios are relative measures of an organization's financial position. We compute a financial ratio by taking an amount from the SA or SFP and dividing it by a different amount from either of those two statements. Ratios are useful for seeing (1) where our organization has been over time financially, (2) the organization's financial strength at this point in time, and (3) how it compares to other organizations in the same industry of the same approximate size.

Despite their value, we found that only four of ten organizations use ratios as part of their financial management process (Lilly study), and our contacts with nonprofits suggest that many charities outside of the education and hospital sectors still do not develop and utilize ratios.

We present basic ratios and their calculation formulas next.[6] If you have never computed ratios before, start with these ratios and work with them until you and your management team and board are comfortable with them. We show an example of their calculation in Appendix 7A for the Habitat for Humanity SFP and SA presented earlier. We will primarily use the set of financial ratios highlighted by Chris Robinson in his pioneering work with faith-based organizations. Robinson focused on a set of ratios that includes 11 ratios and one level (dollar amount) measure. To that we will add three target liquidity level measures. In Appendix 7B we briefly cover several other ratios that have been presented by analysts over the past 15 years. In Appendix 7C we profile some ratings important to bond ratings agencies, with a special focus on those applicable to educational institutions.

The basic ratios fall into three categories: liquidity, funding, and operating. One of the difficulties that has plagued the nonprofit sector is the absence of industry standards (average values for other organizations serving the same clientele as your organization). Robinson calculated standards for faith-based organizations spanning organizations from churches to radio/TV stations, social welfare organizations, colleges and private secondary schools, associations, and camps and conference centers; however, as these standards are over 15 years old, they may or may not accurately portray these industries. Arts and healthcare organizations are advised to check with their trade association or one of the Big Four accounting firms or private debt rating organizations for comparative data. Charity Navigator makes ratio distributions available online, but it is unclear for how long these will be publicly available. For some organizations, the best approach is to develop a network with five or six similar organizations and then share data in order to develop their own comparative data and standards.

Liquidity ratios. Maintaining liquidity is crucial for your organization, because cash is the lifeblood of your organization's finances. Running a donative nonprofit is especially risky, in that you are basically raising your financing from ground zero each and every year. Having liquid resources helps you bridge the dry seasons and gives some breathing room when contributions resulting from your fundraising shows year-over-year declines. These resources also provide the fuel for program expansions and provision of emergency needs such as natural disaster relief aid, one-time or short-term opportunities, and acquisitions or strategic alliances. The basic liquidity ratios are cash ratio, cash reserve ratio, current ratio, asset ratio, and target liquidity level. An advanced liquidity ratio, target liquidity lambda, is also introduced here. Each measure we will look at gives us a slightly different perspective on the spendable funds of the organization.

$$\text{Cash ratio} = \frac{\text{cash and cash equivalents*}}{\text{current liabilities}}$$

$$\text{Cash reserve ratio} = \frac{\text{cash and cash equivalents*}}{\text{total annual expenses}}$$

$$\text{Current ratio} = \frac{\text{current assets}}{\text{current liabilities}}$$

$$\text{Asset ratio} = \frac{\text{current assets}}{\text{total assets}}$$

$$\text{Target liquidity level} = (\text{cash and cash equivalents} + \text{short} - \text{term investments}$$
$$+ \text{ total amount of credit line**} - \text{short-term loans})$$

$$\text{Target liquidity level lambda} = \frac{\text{Target liquidity level} + \text{Projected OCF}}{\text{Uncertainty of OCF}}$$

Where:

Projected OCF is the operating cash flow amount for the next year.

Uncertainty of OCF is the standard deviation of the organization's historical OCFs for at least the past three years.

For the first four ratios, all items in the numerator and denominator are found in the SFP, except total annual expenses, which is in the SA.

Cash ratio.   The cash ratio shows us the organization's coverage of near-term financial obligations with its cash and near-cash investments. The typical financial obligations are accounts payable, accrued interest, wages, salaries, possibly taxes, and principal repayments due within one year. We usually interpret a ratio value by expressing it per unit of whatever item is in the denominator. For example, if the ratio value is 2.0, and both numerator (let's say, cash and cash equivalents) and denominator (say, current liabilities) are in dollars, we interpret the ratio as $2 of cash and equivalents per $1 of current liabilities.[7] Recognize that your organization is giving something up by having more money in the cash and cash equivalent category. Interest rates on cash (most of this would be in interest-bearing checking accounts) and on cash equivalents (investments purchased with original maturities of three months or less, which would include some treasury bills, commercial paper, money market mutual funds, and certificates of deposit) are normally lower than on one-year treasury bills or two-year treasury notes. This is one reason not to have too much of your liquidity in cash and cash equivalents, and also the reason your organization's target liquidity level will include all short-term investments.

Cash reserve ratio.   The cash reserve ratio uses the same numerator as the cash ratio, cash and cash equivalents, but compares it to a year's worth of operating expenses instead of what liabilities happen to be listed as current at this moment of time. Not only does it avert seasonality of liabilities (you may be measuring liabilities at a low point in the year), but it also provides a "time to ruin" measure for the organization. It tells us how long, as a fraction of a year, the organization could meet operating expenses if revenues

*Use unrestricted and temporarily restricted cash and cash equivalents in any case in which organization has a portion of its cash and equivalents that is permanently restricted.
**This item is not included in the SFP, but should be in the notes accompanying the financial reports.

were totally shut off. For example, a ratio value of 0.75 tells me that my organization can operate for nine months without additional revenues. This measure provides a very conservative measure of liquidity, but the key point is that it is giving you another perspective on your organization's liquidity. Your organization can compare its figure to past values and to other similar organizations.[8] While you may not experience any month in the year in which you receive *no* revenues, there are months when donations trickle in, and your organization is plunged into a cash crunch because of the low level of cash as compared to daily expenses. Measure expenses on a cash basis when doing this calculation, but you will have to use the accrual-based SA total expense amount if that is the only data you have available. We are not aware of benchmark data on the cash reserve ratio, but a similar ratio based on Form 990 data (cash, savings, and investments securities) across 6,600 organizations finds that cash plus investments ranges from a low of 0.21 for mental health organizations to a high of 2.05 for social science research organizations. Most nonprofit industries had ratios between 0.61 and 1.13. A frustration analysts have is that the Form 990 and the SFP using GAAP accounting do not split out investments by restriction category (although supplemental disclosure in GAAP accounting requires a footnote disclosure of maturity ranges of investments if no current/noncurrent disclosure is shown in the SFP).[9]

Current ratio.   The current ratio measures the coverage of near-term obligations, again, but with a broader measure of "ability to pay." This ratio includes near-term pledges receivable, accounts receivable, inventories, and prepaid expenses in the numerator. The ratio is not as conservative as the cash ratio, but more correctly matches up near-term obligations with the resources that will be available to meet those obligations. A ratio value of 3, for example, means the average organization had between $3 and $4 of cash and other liquid resources with which to pay its obligations coming due within the next year. One large-scale study of nonprofits finds a median current ratio value for nonprofits of 33.33, while the average, or mean, ratio value is 0.61. There is a significant amount of variation in this ratio across the spectrum of nonprofit organizations.[10] Again, this is a positive sign of strong liquidity. We would want to compare our organization's current ratio against other organizations of the same type and approximately the same size. A value of 2.0 or above is generally thought to signal adequate liquidity in for small businesses and in some industry segments—although many companies now are amply liquid with a current ratio of 1.0 or even less because of reliable backup credit line availability and very sophisticated cash management. If funds are being held on a semipermanent basis, such as in a capital fund for a building project, they should be invested in longer-term investments (and these investments are not accounted for as current assets).

Asset ratio.   The asset ratio serves as both a liquidity ratio and an investment strategy ratio. It looks at the asset investment as a whole and asks what percent of the total asset "pie" is placed in near-term assets. To the extent that *more* of the assets are placed in the current items (cash and cash equivalents, accounts receivable, inventories, short-term investments, prepaid expenses, contributions receivable), they are nearer to cash; therefore, the organization is more liquid. But if *less* is invested in current assets, this implies greater long-term assets such as plant and equipment or pension assets. These cannot be readily turned into cash to pay bills that come due or to meet unexpected emergencies.

Beyond the liquidity aspects, though, lies the investment strategy element. As we said, short-term investments are sometimes made when longer-term investments are more appropriate. The organization enhances its liquidity at the price of the higher interest revenue and operating net revenue it could have had, based on the normally higher interest rates of the longer-term investments. Furthermore, nonfinancial long-term assets such as plant and equipment can often be rented or leased out or used otherwise to generate earned income. This income might far exceed the low interest rates paid on interest-bearing checking accounts or near-term investments.

Lower values for this ratio signal greater capital intensity, typically bringing with them higher fixed operating costs and higher debt levels to finance those long-term assets. Higher values signal less capital intensity, fewer fixed operating costs, and lower debt levels to finance the long-term assets. They are also a sign of more liquidity as the current assets are nearer to cash, and should soon be converted to cash. While it is not the same ratio, a broad-ranging study of nonprofits finds a median ratio of net working capital to assets (where net working capital is current assets minus current liabilities) of 0.41, while the mean or average ratio value is 0.39.[11]

Target liquidity level.   The target liquidity level shows us whether we have reached our goal for liquid resources, and may be measured in several ways. Our formula (cash and cash equivalents + short-term investments + total amount of credit line − short-term loans) is one way of measuring the target liquidity level. Many nonprofits do not have an established credit line with a bank or other financial service provider, so the third term in the formula is often $0. The fourth term, short-term loans, may represent either the amount of an established credit line that is currently borrowed (or "taken down"), or it could be another type of note payable (even a loan from an affiliated organization or national umbrella organization, or a working capital loan received from a nonprofit loan fund or foundation). Include only short-term loans in this formula; mortgage loans and other long-term borrowing are not part of our target liquidity calculation, as they do not normally affect our liquidity in the near future. (If due within one year, you may opt to include it in a modified formula calculation, however.) We are not aware of any benchmark data for this ratio to which you might compare your liquidity level.

An alternate formula for target liquidity might include only the first two terms, leaving setup of a credit line or other short-term loans as one of several *ways* of providing the liquidity desired. We'll call this "target liquidity level-alternate." The reason we prefer the first formula is that it shows us how much liquidity we have *after* paying back arranged financing.

We can see how these two measures differ with a hypothetical example. Let's say that when that the liquidity of World Symphony Orchestra (WSO) falls short of its target level, it uses short-term loans to increase the liquidity. Would the two measures give the same number when the amount of arranged financing is held in cash or short-term securities? Let's assume WSO's desired target liquidity level is $300,000, but at present it has $175,000 in cash and cash equivalents, $50,000 in short-term securities, and no short-term loans. Assume WSO takes out a loan for the $75,000 needed to get liquidity (cash and securities) up to $300,000. Calculating our formula and the alternate measure for WSO, we get a different result:

$$\text{Target liquidity level} = \$175,000 + \$50,000 + \$75,000 \text{ addition} - \$75,000 \text{ loan}$$

$$= \underline{\$225,000}$$

According to our measure, WSO's liquidity has not really increased, because the increase is not permanent. The loan (and interest) will have to be repaid. Short-term borrowing may be fine to provide for *temporary* needs, such as a seasonal buildup in inventories or receivables, but should not be seen as a source of permanent liquidity financing.

$$\text{Target liquidity level—Alternate} = \$175,000 + \$50,000 + \$75,000 \text{ addition}$$

$$= \underline{\$300,000}$$

According to this alternate measure, WSO's liquidity has increased to the organization's predetermined target level. It will have to plan carefully to have enough funds to pay back the loan at maturity, or if it is a credit line, to pay it down in its entirety during the bank's "clean-up period," when it must pay the loan down to zero.

For many nonprofit organizations, the two measures would give the same reading because their financial policy is to use no short-term debt. Two-thirds of the organizations in the Lilly study never do any short-term borrowing, and only one in eight has short-term loans each year. If you plug a value of $0 in for short-term loans in our formula, you get the same result as you would with the alternate formula. We will provide more detail on evaluating, liquidity when we get to the level 4 analysis, and we address short-term borrowing dos and don'ts in Chapter 10.

Target liquidity level lambda.   Although not used before in the nonprofit arena, there are a number of more sophisticated solvency, liquidity, and financial flexibility measures that may be adapted for our purposes. Chief among these are the cash conversion period and lambda.[12] Lambda is a measure of liquidity that assists the analyst in determining if the organization has enough liquidity. It also brings into the picture, to some degree, the organization's near-term financial flexibility. For hospitals or other entities having significant inventories and credit sales, the cash conversion period may prove useful; we introduce it in Appendix 7B. For all nonprofits, target liquidity level lambda (TLLL), our modified version of lambda may prove a useful measure. Let's take a closer look at the formula:

$$\text{TLLL} = \frac{\text{Target liquidity level} + \text{Projected OCF}}{\text{Uncertainty of OCF}}$$

Where:

Target liquidity level (as defined earlier):

Target liquidity level = (cash and cash equivalents + short-term investments + total amount of credit line − short-term loans)

Projected OCF is the operating cash flow amount you predict for the next year

Uncertainty of OCF is the standard deviation of the organization's historical OCFs for at least the past three years

Notice that two estimates are required here to calculate TLLL:

1. Someone must forecast your organization's OCF. You may wish to look at last year's SCF to see what the OCF amount was and perhaps plug that in as a naïve forecast. Or perhaps reduce that amount by some arbitrary amount (say, 25 percent) for a more conservative estimate. A third option is to take the average of your organization's past three years of OCFs. A fourth option, if your organization has been growing, is to project a somewhat higher level of OCF. (But be careful: often growth causes higher investment levels in receivables and perhaps in inventories or prepaid expenses, so OCF will not grow as much as revenues

and may actually decline somewhat). Careful study of the relationship between past years' changes in net assets and OCF (as we contrasted with Habitat for Humanity earlier) is very helpful here.

2. The uncertainty of OCF reflects the financial vulnerability your organization faces. It only makes sense, if your organization has large fluctuations in its cash revenues and/or cash expenses, to need a higher level of liquidity. Placing risk of your operating cash flows in the denominator, TLLL indicates through the resulting lower calculated value (quotient) that you have less liquidity. Two ways to estimate this uncertainty: Calculate the standard deviation of the past 7 to 10 years of OCFs, perhaps using the STDEV function built into Microsoft Excel™; or take the highest OCF in the past 7 to 10 years, subtract from it the lowest OCF in that same time frame, then divide that amount by 6. The latter is an approximation of the standard deviation of your organization's OCFs, based on the idea that there are six standard deviations of numerical values in an entire range (or distribution) of numbers.[13]

Calculating TLLL is extremely helpful to your analysis for three reasons:

1. It demonstrates to your policy-making team that steady, dependable cash flows require holding less liquidity and that highly risky cash flows may be offset by having more cash and equivalents, more short-term (unrestricted) investments, a higher unborrowed credit line, the ability to borrow quickly for working capital on an as-needed basis (rare for nonprofits), or a positive and high inflow of funds over the upcoming period. (But watch for seasonality—if yours is a donative organization, much of that is likely to materialize between Thanksgiving and Christmas, when a very high percentage of cash donations are made.).

2. If your calculated number turns out too low for comfort (see #3)—meaning it is below your financial policy for target liquidity, as discussed in Chapter 2—you can plug in different numbers for credit line amounts or short-term investment amounts, and then see the impact. Doing this helps you to know how much is enough for liquidity-filling investing or borrowing actions.

3. Used with a standard normal table (or the Excel™ NORMDIST function), the TLLL tells you the probability of running short of cash over the forecast period. A particular value for TLLL is associated with a 5 percent chance of running out of cash, a different value for TLL matches to a 1 percent chance, and so on. No other liquidity measure provides decision makers with this type of information.

Let's illustrate TLLL with our earlier WSO example. Assuming that WSO was successful in taking out the loan for $75,000, we found TLL was $225,000. We need two additional pieces of information: the forecasted OCF for the next year and the uncertainty of WSO's OCF amounts over time. The treasurer tells us that she is looking for OCF of $8,500 in the upcoming year. The past five years, OCF has been shown, according to the table provided to us by WSO's bookkeeper:

Year	OCF
1	($30,500)
2	($75,000)
3	15,000
4	7,000
5	($15,000)

Just looking at the numbers, it is apparent that WSO has experienced significant fluctuation in its annual cash flow. We need to convert that into a statistical measure, called standard deviation. We will do it using both techniques listed earlier; we'll call the first one SD_1 and the second one SD_2.

Standard deviation using a financial spreadsheet (SD_1).   We keyed the data into an Excel spreadsheet, then used the $[f_x]$ key to pull up the functions menu. We selected, from the statistics functions, STDEV. This function will calculate a sample standard deviation from numbers in the spreadsheet. Doing so, we got a standard deviation of $35,755. (Note that we have very little data, and preferably we would have 7 to 10 years to use in this calculation.)

Standard deviation using a range estimate (SD_2).   We took the highest OCF in the series, $15,000, and subtracted from it the lowest value, $-$75,000$. We got $90,000 (= $15,000 $-$75,000$). Next, we divided this by 6, and arrived at $15,000 (= $90,000/6) for our estimate of standard deviation. Notice that our standard deviation estimates are quite different here; this spread arises both because of the small sample of OCFs and because OCF is not normally distributed.

Now let's calculate TLLL using each of these standard deviation estimates; we'll call these ratio values $TLLL_1$ and $TLLL_2$:

$$TLLL_1 = (\$225,000 + \$8,500)/\$35,755$$

$$= \$233,500/\$35,755$$

$$= \underline{6.53}$$

$$TLLL_2 = (\$225,000 + \$8,500)/\$15,000$$

$$= \$233,500/\$15,000$$

$$= \underline{15.57}$$

What is the probability of running short on cash for each of these calculated values for TLLL?[14]

$$\text{Probability of running short of cash for } TLLL_1 = \underline{0.00\%}$$

$$\text{Probability of running short of cash for } TLLL_2 = \underline{0.00\%}$$

In WSO's case, then, the probability of financial vulnerability is insensitive to the uncertainty estimate. In other words, regardless of which standard deviation we used, WSO does not face even a 1 percent chance of running out of cash in the upcoming year. The target liquidity level is sufficient *for covering likely operating cash outcomes.* This does not mean that the target liquidity is sufficient to cover maintenance, new programs, very large negative cash flow spikes (as we saw with the Red Cross in 2005), or large plant and equipment outlays. Any of these that apply to WSO would have to be subtracted out of the target liquidity level, then the analysis redone, to get an accurate picture of financial vulnerability. Only the historical pattern of OCF and the best estimate of next period's OCF is taken into account in our analysis.

Funding ratios.   The second group of ratios is funding ratios. This group includes a ratio that indicates the dependence on donated funds (contribution ratio) as well as one that measures the degree to which we use borrowed money to finance assets (debt ratio). Risk is the central focus here. First, using the contribution ratio, how "donation dependent" is our organization for each year's expenses? Second, based on the debt ratio, are our assets in place funded with borrowed money, which has to be paid back with interest, or net assets, which are permanent contributions or earned income retained in the organization? The greater the value of either number, the more risk we have in the organization's structure. In the corporate sector, the first measure would be called operating risk or business risk and the second measure would be labeled financial risk.

$$\text{Contribution ratio} = \text{total contributed revenue}/\text{total revenue}$$

$$\text{Debt ratio} = \text{total liabilities}/\text{total assets}$$

Contribution ratio.   Projections of donations for donative organizations drive the financial planning process for these organizations. High levels of donation dependence, resulting in contribution ratios of 0.65 or above, imply risk because of possible donor fatigue or because of high-profile urgent situations such as the Asian tsunami and the Gulf Coast hurricanes in recent years. If donations are expected to taper off, the organization must move quickly to replace the lost funds or face a financial crisis. Fundraising is obviously very critical for these organizations, and we emphasize in the level 3 discussion later the vitality of having the CFO involved in the fundraising management and evaluation process. One recent study finds, using Form 990 data, an average contribution ratio of 0.14, or 14 percent for a broad spectrum of 4,500 nonprofits (but skewed toward healthcare and educational organizations).[15] Another category of funding that is considered "soft money" is grants. A high degree of reliance on grants also places the organization at risk. Some analysts calculate a "contribution and grants ratio," combining these two items in the numerator of the ratio.[16]

Debt ratio.   The debt ratio measures the degree to which our assets are funded with borrowed money rather than equity capital that was contributed or accumulated through past years' operating surpluses. A ratio of 0.25 indicates that one-fourth of all assets are funded by borrowed funds; a ratio of 0.50 indicates more risk, as one-half of the assets are financed with borrowed money, which often has to be repaid with interest. What gives rise to higher reliance on borrowed money? Often it's the longer-term asset investment in plant and equipment, which drives the long-term mortgage loans that figure largely in these higher ratio values. Asset intensity turns into financial leverage risk as the long-term fixed assets are financed with borrowed funds. The borrowing puts a strain on the organization as it has to pay interest and repay principal. We return to this subject in Chapter 10. A large-scale study of nonprofits finds a median debt ratio of 0.07, or 7 percent. (The average, or mean ratio, is 40 percent.)[17]

Operating ratios.   Our final category of ratios is a set of six operating ratios. We want to assess the cost coverage, expense composition, and "return on investment" in our operations. We use the return ratio, the net operating ratio, the net asset reserve ratio, the program expense ratio, the support service expense ratio, and the net surplus level.

$$\text{Return ratio} = \frac{\text{total revenue}}{\text{total assets}}$$

$$\text{Net surplus} = \text{total revenues} - \text{total expenses}$$

$$\text{Net operating ratio} = \frac{\text{net surplus}}{\text{total revenue}}$$

$$\text{Net asset reserve ratio} = \frac{\text{net assets}}{\text{total expenses}}$$

$$\text{Program expense ratio} = \frac{\text{program expenses}}{\text{total expenses}}$$

$$\text{Support service expense ratio} = \frac{\text{support service expenses}}{\text{total expenses}}$$

Return ratio.   The return ratio is generally considered to be an efficiency measure. The term "efficiency" here is used not in the sense of being cost-effective, but in how well our asset investment translates into revenues and gains, or financial resources, brought into the organization. In a business, it is called "total asset turnover" because it shows how often the investment in total assets "turns over" into sales. For nonprofits, we are measuring the ability of an organization to generate or raise revenue from its asset base. In another sense, it is a "return on investment," where the return is revenues flowing into the organization each year per dollar invested in assets. Another way to view it is a size-adjusted measure of revenue-generating ability, because organizations of different sizes (asset bases) will all be measured on a "per dollar of assets" basis. If the ratio value is 1.25, the organization receives $1.25 in revenue per $1 invested in assets. For donative organizations, you are largely measuring the efficiency of the fundraising function. For schools or healthcare organizations, you are mainly gauging the efficiency of earned income ventures. In any case, you are also measuring asset intensity; an organization with a small fixed asset investment will tend to have a higher ratio. We again emphasize: Measure yourself against similar organizations (type of service, location, revenue mix, mix of services offered, cost structure) or against your own past values. One large-scale study found that the median return ratio for nonprofits is 1.11 (while the average, or mean, ratio value is 4.18).[18]

Net surplus.   Net surplus is the "profit" on operations for a given period. For a business, profit is a primary measure of effectiveness and success. Nonprofits don't like to talk about profit, so they call it net revenue. On the SA, it is identified as the change in net assets. How does the manager view it? As the relative cost coverage by revenues for the period. If positive, then revenues more than covered costs. If zero, the revenues just covered cost, a situation most call "financial break-even." Recall from our Chapter 2 discussion that most respondents in the Lilly study selected this as their primary financial objective, even though we advocate target liquidity level as a better objective, and one that is practiced by the best-managed organizations. Obviously, a negative value suggests that in this period the revenues did not cover costs. The key question to ask: Was it planned? If so, no problem. If not, we have to go back to the budget variance analysis to find out why not and how to avoid the situation next year. Many data sources look at samples of nonprofits, both magazine-published lists and academic research lists, and find that many nonprofits are running surpluses. A quick look at the financial results of the 200 largest charities published annually in *Forbes* magazine reveals that very few large charities run a deficit, and those that do typically only have a very small deficit (as a percentage of revenues). The largest and most recent academic study finds that, over many years, charities earn a median surplus that amounts to 6 percent of revenues and 5 percent of assets.[19] Because many organizations do raise money in advance of planned expansion or to build up to the target liquidity level, running surpluses in some periods may simply show good managerial foresight. However, persistent surpluses by a no-growth organization may reflect hoarding and inadequate provision of much needed services. Yale University became famous for its inability to properly plan for renewal of its crumbling infrastructure, and we again urge you to put into practice the strategic and long-range financial planning tools presented in Chapter 9.[20]

Net operating ratio.   The net operating ratio gives us the same information as the net surplus, except in relative terms. Its analog in business is the net profit margin. For an organization pricing its services, such as schools/colleges and camps/conference centers, we get insight into pricing and its degree of cost coverage. For all organizations, it gives cost coverage feedback as scaled to the total revenue. Again, as we saw with the return ratio, you can view the denominator as a scaling factor to put different-size organizations on an equal footing: Surplus or deficit is expressed per dollar of revenue. A broad study of nonprofits finds a median value for the net operating ratio of 6 percent, with an average, or mean, ratio value of 9 percent.[21]

Net asset reserve ratio.   The net asset reserve ratio (formerly called the fund balance reserve ratio) is very similar to the cash reserve ratio we discussed in the liquidity section. We can therefore view it as both an operating ratio and a liquidity ratio. The difference between this ratio and the cash reserve ratio is that we are looking at what would be similar to equity in a business and asking in relative terms how it compares to total yearly expenses. We're not thinking that we would "liquidate" net assets to pay a year's expenses, but instead are wondering how much of a cushion of permanent financing we have built up relative to annual expenses. From the flip side, a combined view of the cash reserve ratio and the net asset reserve ratio provides us with another view of *operating risk*. The larger the cash reserve ratio and the net asset reserve ratio, the less risky the operating posture of the organization. A broad sample of 4,500 nonprofits, weighted toward healthcare and educational institutions, finds an average ratio value of 3.17, but with much variation across organizations (the standard deviation is 6.75 percent).[22]

Program expense ratio and support service expense ratio.   Program expense ratio and the support service expense ratio show the split of expenses into program and the sum of management/general and fundraising. We are asking if most of our annual expenses are program-related or if too much of our resource allocation is going to "overhead" activities that are necessary but are not providing services to our clientele. These ratios are complementary: Added together, they equal 100 percent. So, if the program expense ratio is 80 percent, the support service expense ratio is 20 percent. Recognizing the arbitrariness of accounting allocations, we still have a valuable indicator when comparing this year's values for a specific organization to its prior year values, and *possibly* when comparing to other organizations using similar accounting practices.[23] Be aware that your organization may get positive or negative publicity based on your ratios for these categories. Periodicals such as the *Chronicle of Philanthropy, Forbes* (www.forbes.com), *Consumers Digest*, and *Worth Magazine* annually report on expense ratios for large nonprofits, along with statements that those organizations with higher program expense ratios are more efficient. Implicitly, these higher program expense ratios suggest that these organizations are more worthy of donor support. However, recognize that organizations getting government grants and large quantities of donated goods will look better on their support services ratio in many of these ratings schemes, unless adjustments are made for those two items.[24]

Ratios as a way of assessing financial vulnerability. We introduced target liquidity level lambda as one measure of financial vulnerability. Some interesting multiple-ratio attempts have been made recently in modeling a nonprofit's vulnerability to financial exigency. One recent study finds that these financial statement items and financial ratios are helpful in predicting financial vulnerability:

- Size (larger organizations had a lower risk of insolvency)
- Debt ratio (higher debt ratio increases risk of insolvency)
- Negative change in net assets (when negative in a given year, this increases the risk of insolvency a year later)
- Two-year difference in change in net assets, scaled by the average net income in the prior and current years (larger relative changes in change in net assets amounts in consecutive years increase the probability of insolvency in the subsequent year)[25]

The authors of this study noted that they still do not have a highly accurate way of predicting year-ahead financial vulnerability, however.

As we bring our discussion of ratio analysis to a close, we remind you to *always exercise caution when drawing conclusions*. Ratios are but one piece in your overall evaluation, and you must look at what is special or unique about your organization or those to which you are comparing yourself.[26] Furthermore, even with the growing standardization of accounting treatment and financial statement presentation, there are still judgment calls to be made, and some organizations disclose more about their policies and financial estimates than others.[27] It is usually safest to begin with a trend analysis of your own organization, which studies how your organization has changed from year to year. Then find a group of similar organizations to which to compare your organization. Ideally, put both comparisons on the same graph, so you have a given ratio for your organization and others plotted for at least three years. Once you get comfortable with that, you are ready to move to level 3, involvement in fundraising management and evaluation. Some CFOs and board treasurers have no choice but to get involved, regardless of their mastery of levels 1 and 2, because of their expanded job responsibilities.

(d) LEVEL 3: FUNDRAISING MANAGEMENT AND EVALUATION. Fundraising management and evaluation is an area in which nonfundraising, financial personnel can and should be involved. It is an area in which the organization may be forced to rely on the CFO, because it cannot afford and chooses not to hire a development officer. Or, although rare, the CFO may also hold the title of development officer. We contend that it is also an area in which nonprofits can learn from businesses. First, recognize that in businesses, the treasurer is the fundraiser. The treasurer is responsible for arranging funding, typically from leases, debt, and equity. Second, she or he has a global view of many interlocked facets of the organization:

- Organizational strategy
- Long-range financial plans
- Present and anticipated financial position
- Cash flow characteristics
- Alternate sources of revenue and liquidity

  ○ Investments maturing
  ○ Investments ready for sale

- o Debt financing
- o Grant proposal and status
- o Business income
- o Historical pattern and trends of donation revenue
- o Split of restricted and unrestricted funds
- o Time until temporarily restricted funds become unrestricted (i.e., until certain time period elapses or certain use of funds as expenses occurs)

We show the global viewpoint of the treasurer in Exhibit 7.11. It is apparent that the financial manager has a panoramic, integrated perspective that no one else in the organization has—at least at this level of detail and with this degree of comprehension.

Third, we contend that the organization benefits from having the nonprofit CFO increase his or her involvement in fundraising objectives, planning, execution, and post-campaign evaluation. Doing so:

- Better integrates the entire spectrum of financial resource utilization
- Assists the fundraising office in communicating its objectives, methods, and resource needs across the organization
- Provides improved strategic direction and continuous improvement to the fundraising office/function

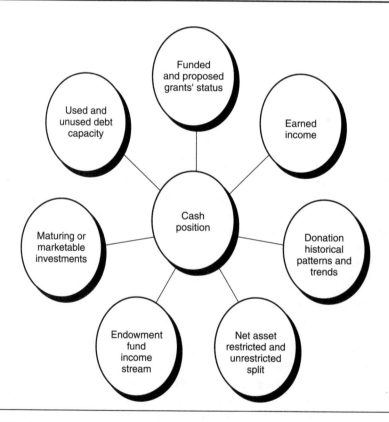

EXHIBIT 7.11   FINANCIAL MANAGER'S VIEW OF THE CASH POSITION AND REVENUE STREAM

Summarizing, proficient organizations have CFOs with hands-on authority and/or oversight over the organization's revenue stream. How can we put these ideals into operation? The CFO should pursue four strategic involvements, in this order of priority: (1) ensure adherence to the correct philosophy and major objective of fundraising; (2) plan and then schedule the campaign expenditures; (3) assist in the midcampaign evaluation and redirection; and (4) oversee postcampaign effectiveness and efficiency ratio analysis. We will expand on each of these briefly.

(i) Setting the Philosophy and Major Objective of Fundraising. The fundraising expenditure must be viewed as an investment, like other capital expenditures, not as an expense. An appropriate philosophy for the annual campaign may be to proactively raise money *this* year for *next* year's operations, instead of scrambling this year to try to fund this year's operations. Failure to recognize this explains why so many nonprofits are living hand-to-mouth and experiencing recurrent cash crises. A major objective of fundraising is to do its part to help meet the service provision objective, which is spelled out in it's budget (see Chapter 8) and in its long-range financial plan (see Chapter 9). Remember: The investment in annual campaign fundraising is derived from the anticipated service provision spelled out in the budget and is a direct output of the budgeting process.

There is one important modification/amplification: Looking back at our hub and spokes diagram (Exhibit 7.11), we must adjust up or down the annual campaign dollar goal based on the relative revenue contributions of those other revenue sources. Our ultimate goal is to achieve a liquidity target that is based on transactions needs for cash, which increase along with service activity. See the cash management discussion in Chapter 11 regarding setting the liquidity target to account for other factors that may reduce the liquidity target, such as reengineered bank relations and/or using controlled disbursement account.

The organization should have fundraising policies that spell out its philosophy of fundraising to prospective donors. While details of such policies are beyond the scope of our presentation, we suggest checking with other organizations to find out what they are doing. Prison Fellowship, the Washington D.C.-based organization founded by Chuck Colson to provide an outreach to prisoners, has an outstanding set of policies that might serve as a model for your organization.[28]

(ii) Plan and Then Schedule the Campaign Expenditures. Instead of prolonging the start of the annual campaign or doing it at the development office's convenience, use your knowledge of the organization's cash flow cycle and current cash position to provide direction to the effort. Also recognize and help others on the management team understand the timing of the underlying cash flow cycle in an annual campaign:

Cash outflow for materials and labor $\rightarrow$ Cash inflow from campaign

The annual campaign is a cash-draining activity for some period. The financial implications? Expenditures must be anticipated, and enough cash must be on hand prior to the campaign to fund the campaign. The most important reason for not achieving their organization's financial objective, according to financial officers surveyed in the Lilly study, was *inadequate and/or ineffective fund raising.* We emphasize: Fundraising must be looked at as an investment, not as an expense, regardless of the accounting treatment. It is vital that you work with the development officer to convey this mind-set to your CEO and board and ultimately your donors or grant sources. Some CFOs or board treasurers counter: "But we don't have the cash to do the level of fundraising that we really need to undertake." Maybe Bill Levis, a fundraising expert associated with Baruch

College in New York City, was thinking of these especially when he recommended that organizations go one step further with the cash flow cycle analysis and raise funds this year to fund next year's expenses. Think about that: Takes a planning mind-set, doesn't it? What are some likely repercussions of such a policy? It results in having the equivalent of one year's operating expenses in unrestricted liquid assets (in addition to the money for a rainy day you already hold in cash reserves) by the end of this year.[29] In turn, that may require educating the donors, and it will also in some cases result in a red flag raised by one of the philanthropic oversight bureaus—particularly if you have sizable reserves saved up for planned program expansion or for a merger/acquisition.

(iii) Assist in the Midcampaign Evaluation and Redirection.   Here is an example of using reports gathered within the year to help guide management for the remainder of the year. As results start coming in, the financial office can work with the development office, if separate, to interpret the results to management and the board. With its global view of the organization, the finance office knows how critical a shortfall is at any given point in time and can provide guidance as to the best use of a surplus when positive results are achieved.

(iv) Oversee Postcampaign Effectiveness and Efficiency Ratio Analysis.   In the past, it was very difficult to find good information on measuring fundraising efficiency and effectiveness, but this is changing.[30] Here are some of the general guidelines offered by expert James Greenfield:[13]

Activity	Reasonable Cost Guideline
Direct mail acquisition	$1.00 to $1.25 per $1.00 raised
Direct mail renewal	$0.20 per $1.00 raised
Membership organization	$0.25 per $1.00 raised
Donor club program	$0.20 per $1.00 raised
Benefit events	$0.50 per $1.00 raised
Volunteer-led annual giving individual major gift programs	$0.10 to $0.20 per $1.00 raised
Capital campaigns	$0.10 to $0.20 per $1.00 raised
Planned giving/estate planning	$0.10 to $0.20 per $1.00 raised
	$0.20 to $0.30 per $1.00 raised

A three-year study of 51 American colleges and universities found that on average it costs 16 cents to raise a dollar, with a median cost of 11 cents and the middle 50 percent of campuses experiencing costs of between 8 and 16 cents.[32] This figure covers all direct fundraising staff and programs, but does not include any allocation for president or dean's salaries or space or utility overhead costs. The study was conducted by CASE and the National Association of College and University Business Officers and funded by Lilly Endowment, Inc. It also found that, on average, colleges spend just over 2 percent of their educational and general (E&G) budgets for raising money, with gifts raised for operations meeting 10 percent of that budget.[33] The report made an important observation: "The objective of an institution's program should not be to spend as little as possible each year to raise money, but to maximize the net. A program that annually produces $2 million at a cost of $160,000, or 8 percent, may look good and is indeed efficient, but one that produces $3 million at a cost of $300,000, or 10 percent, is presumably of more help to the institution—it is bringing in $860,000 more."

As a financial officer, offer assistance to the development office in developing cost standards and efficiency and effectiveness reports. Offer assistance to the CEO and board in interpreting those reports and making resource allocation decisions related to fundraising. Fundraising analysis is most effective if it is relevant (your organization may need to hire a consultant or marketing agency to do a file audit to see if your annual campaign donors are segmented and grouped appropriately), measures of efficiency and cost effectiveness are clearly understood and reviewed quarterly, and benchmarks such as those provided above are used to gain context, perspective and reprioritization of future fundraising goals.[34] Above all, help your management team and board understand the concept of return on fundraising investment. Once you are there, you are ready to embark on the final achievement: level 4.

(e) LEVEL 4: CASH AND LIQUIDITY ANALYSIS AND PROJECTION. Moving to the next level is not too difficult once the financial manager gains the global perspective we viewed in the fundraising involvement in level 3. The tasks we have in mind here are:

1. Refine the analysis of cash and liquidity that you did in levels 1, 2, and 3. Specifically:

   o Look at your historical cash flow patterns to see which months have the highest net cash inflows (cash receipts minus cash disbursements), the lowest net cash inflows, and the longest period within a fiscal year for which you are in a "net borrowed position" (i.e., showing a bottom-line cash shortage that persists across several months).

   o List all of the sources of cash your organization has tapped in the past, and to what degree, to weather cash crunches.

   o Estimate the variability of net cash flow by statistical estimation of the range and standard deviation of your historical figures.[35]

2. Work through a review of factors that should cause your organization to have a higher or lower level of liquidity. (We offer a diagnostic questionnaire in Chapter 8 in our cash budgeting discussion.) Use the results of your analysis to determine if your target liquidity level is set too low or too high.

3. Develop a refined cash projection model by incorporating your findings from steps 1 and 2. Begin to use this model alongside your present forecasting method until you gain confidence in it. If funds are available, check into advanced forecasting computer software such as Forecast Pro for Windows™ (Business Forecast Systems).

4. Once you are comfortable with your model in step 3, go beyond the single-case model to develop scenarios. These are built in the newer releases of the financial spreadsheet programs, such as Microsoft Excel™ or Lotus 1−2−3™. If you have the capability, or can arrange a college internship with a business student from a local college or university, also utilize simulation analysis to simulate your monthly cash budget.

5. Attempt to revisit and possibly "retune" your organization's target liquidity level based on your findings in steps 1 to 4 (refer to Chapter 2, Section 2.6, for further guidance).

6. Develop a prioritized listing of cash sources that your organization will tap when it faces its next anticipated or unanticipated cash shortfall. Indicate dollar amounts

for your first source, second source, and so on. Be sure to contact banks to prescreen them for availability of funds if you intend on using credit lines to cover some or all of a shortfall.

7. Strategize with your executive director (ED)/CEO and board on potential strategic alliance or merger partners that would be able to provide funding for expanded or new program initiatives that are the most "cash-intensive" of all your anticipated program offerings.

As for the optimal level of target liquidity, you will have to do the analysis yourself because the Robinson study did not address this issue. As a starting point, take a look at the low point in your fiscal year, which for many nonprofits is late September or early October. Set a liquidity level for your peak season, probably early January, that is sufficient to cover your organization through the dry season. This is where your annual cash budget reevaluation, covered as part of level 1, is so helpful. Study past cash flow patterns carefully and note when the cash crunches came as well as how much liquidity should have been held earlier in the year to prevent each cash crunch. The degree of flexibility your organization has in managing off of the budget (see Chapter 8) will also help you determine the size of your safety buffer of liquidity.

We now conclude our internal reporting coverage with brief discussions of monthly or quarterly reporting, daily or flash reporting, and a final reporting checklist.

(i) Monthly or Quarterly Reports.   Much of what we have to say here is redundant with the annual reporting cycle. Obviously, you will not have as much time to do thorough analysis of the monthly or quarterly data. And you will not need to do as much thinking about the impact of variances on next year's budget or the long-range financial plan. However, some boards meet monthly, especially for nonprofits with a localized scope of service provision. Others meet quarterly or semiannually, and they will require a concise and insightful presentation from you. At a minimum, provide:

- Budget reports (BVAs)
- Financial ratio analysis
- Statement of activity
- Updated cash forecast

Ideally, these reports are the same as the annual reports in scope and coverage, but practically they more limited. Include:

- Variance analysis and the likelihood of meeting full-year budget target
- Capital campaign and deferred giving reports, if applicable, to give the bigger picture
- Target liquidity scorecard to show how you are doing in maintaining or reaching the target liquidity level

Graphs and explanatory comments are very much appreciated by report users. The ED/CEO may also ask for information regarding nonfinancial data (meals served, persons housed) that you will need to merge or have someone else merge with this financial data.

(ii) Daily or Flash Reports.   What kinds of information should be provided to you or others on a daily basis? Some reports that would serve a useful purpose on a daily or weekly basis include:

- Cash position, including bank deposits and withdrawals
- Donation report
- Receivables (accounts receivable and contributions receivable) and payables updates (use to give a better picture of near-future cash receipts and disbursements)

As with the monthly or quarterly reports, the ED/CEO or board may also request information regarding nonfinancial data (meals served, persons housed) that you will need to merge or have someone else merge with this financial data.

7.7 EXTERNAL REPORTS

(a) STATEMENTS OF ACTIVITY, FINANCIAL POSITION, AND CASH FLOWS. Organizations are already well aware that they must provide financial reports adhering to the appropriate financial accounting standards. Because we already addressed internal uses of these statements earlier, we provide a brief review of the financial statements here. As noted in Chapter 6, that Financial Accounting Standards Board (FASB) Statements 116 and 117 guide the reporting for most of the organizations we are addressing in this book. As discussed, the three required statements for all types of 501(c)(3) organizations, per FASB 117, are the statement of activity, the statement of financial position (or statement of net assets), and the statement of cash flows. The intent and purpose of FASB 117 was to bring uniformity to the financial statements of nonprofits, mostly for the benefit of external users. Statement 117 also requires voluntary health and welfare organizations (and encourages other nonprofits) to prepare an additional financial statement that portrays expenses in natural classifications (e.g., salary expense), as well as the functional (program, fundraising, etc.) classifications required of all nonprofits. The three classes of contributions recognized in Statements 116 and 117 (permanently restricted net assets, temporarily restricted net assets, unrestricted net assets) should give readers a better idea of the organization's liquidity and financial flexibility.

(b) FORM 990 AND OTHER PUBLIC REPORTS. Briefly, your external reports should be accurate, timely, show the appropriate level of detail, and provide supplemental commentary if done in the context of an annual report. Studies of museums and environmental organizations in 2001 indicate that about 10 percent of the typical nonprofit annual report addresses financial information.[36] Graphs are also helpful, as we discussed earlier.

(i) Forms 990, 990-EZ, and 990-T. In addition to the three reports just mentioned, most sizable (gross receipts of $25,000 or more) non–church-related nonprofits are required to file a Form 990 (or if gross receipts during the year are less than $100,000 and total assets at year-end are less than $250,000, Form 990-EZ) with the IRS each year, and if they have unrelated business income (gross income of $1,000 or more), the Form 990-T with accompanying payment of taxes owed. Information on filling these forms out is beyond our scope, but extensive information is now available at the IRS Web site on the Internet.[37]

(ii) Donor Mailings and "Publicly Available" Reports. Another outside party that has great interest in your organization is the base of present and potential donors. Accountability is provided by the organization that supply useful and accurate information to donors on a timely basis. Scandals and charity watchdog ratings (see Chapter 2) have had a positive effect on organizational accountability, but there are still some organizations that have not been forthcoming with their financial reports when requested. Form 990 should be made available *freely* to anyone interested. Clearly, many organizations in the nonprofit sector have room to improve in their reporting to donors.

What should we tell donors.   Donors want to know about effectiveness (results attained with their money), efficiency (including waste and how you're eliminating it), and steps of progress (innovation, new initiatives, creative approaches). They are especially interested in high-level indicators such as the program expense ratio, discussed earlier. Because the results attained are sometimes difficult to quantify, they may use your financial data to infer effectiveness—much as a stockholder would look at a company's profits.

Annual report.   Using pie charts or bar graphs to portray financial data to donors is very helpful. You may wish to refer to Exhibit 5.8. The key idea is to focus on the main ideas, without overwhelming your nontechnical audience.

Mail appeal "stuffer" reports.   Don't overlook the opportunity to use your mail appeals as an opportunity to showcase your main accomplishments and financial results. You may wish to include in your mail-outs a pamphlet or single-page summary in which you presents key elements of your financial policy, your sources of support, your budget situation (possibly including charts for both funds received and funds distributed), and your statement of financial accountability.

(iii) State Requirements.   State reporting requirements vary tremendously. Check with your secretary of state or attorney general's office for the specific requirements in your state and each state in which you raise funds. At a minimum, raising funds in a state generally requires that you register with the appropriate state agency.

(iv) Granting Agency Reports.   Again, granting agencies have specialized formats that they want to have used for grant requests and periodic follow-up reports. The key point is to follow the format and provide the necessary information, just as you would to donors in general.

   As a final comment on external reporting, guard against the tendency to evaluate performance based only on easily measured input measures (hours worked) or output measures (clients served). Go the extra mile to define the appropriate measure(s) of effectiveness, then educate donors and grantors on how you will be presenting that information to them.

7.8 CONCLUSION

In this chapter, we have presented the major internal financial reports and how they might be compiled. We focused on usefulness and practicality. We recognized that although your reporting might now be geared primarily to the IRS or grantor needs, the greatest benefit comes to the organization that harnesses its financial reporting to management and board decision-making needs. The emphasis should be on budget variance analysis, financial ratio analysis, and constant vigilance over the target liquidity level. Once financial strains begin to appear, take steps to ward off the problems, and use stopgap measures when necessary. Begin benchmarking treasury management performance and processes now. Exhibit 7.12 presents a final reporting checklist that you may apply to your organization's reporting cycle, as provided by the Alliance for Nonprofit Management.

What reports should we prepare and how often?

The answer will depend on several factors, including the extent to which the organization is financially stable, the degree and extent to which the financial picture changes during the period, the availability of cash to meet financial obligations, the availability of staff or other professionals to prepare reports, etc.

A mid-sized human service organization in reasonably good shape financially might consider the following schedule of reports:

Monthly Reports

☑   Statement of Position (Balance Sheet)
What is our financial health? Can we pay our bills?

☑   Statement of Activities (consolidated) showing budget to actual information
What has been our overall financial performance this month and to date?

☑   Departmental Income and Expense Statement showing budget to actual information
How does actual financial experience compare with the budget? Is specific action called for, such as limiting expenses in certain areas? Does experience indicate a change in the budget is appropriate?

☑   Narrative report including tax and financial highlights, important grants received, recommendations for short term loans, or other means of managing cash flow
An executive summary of financial highlights, analysis, and concerns.

Quarterly Reports

☑   Fundraising Reports; actuals vs. projections for donations; status report on all foundation proposals.
Are fundraising results on track?

☑   Cash flow projections for the next six months
Do we anticipate a cash surplus or shortage?

☑   Payroll tax reports
Have payroll tax reports been submitted on time and tax deposits been made?

☑   Fee for service report showing number of fee-paying clients and revenue against projections
Are we servicing approximately the same number and type of clients as we had anticipated? If not, what action or change is appropriate?

Annual Reports

☑   Annual Federal forms, including 990 and Schedule A; State Reports
Has the organization fulfilled its reporting responsibilities to federal and state governments?

☑   Draft financial statements for year: Statement of Activities; Statement of Position; Income Statement for each program. Aggregated financial statements with narrative showing key trends
Focus: Internal management decision-making. What was our financial performance over the past year? In what ways and for what reasons was performance different from the budget? What financial implications must be taken into account when planning the upcoming year?

☑   Audited financial statements for the entire organization, including Statement of Position, Statement of Activities, Statement of Cash Flows, Statement of Functional Expenses
Focus: External accountability and financial disclosure to funders and the public

☑   Management letter from the auditor
What recommendations has the auditor made related to the accounting system, internal controls, and financial planning?

Source: http://www.allianceonline.org/, FAQ/financial_management/what_financial_statements_1.faq. Used by permission.

EXHIBIT 7.12   FINAL CHECKLIST OF ITEMS FOR FINANCIAL REPORTS

Notes

1. E. B. Knauft, Renee A. Berger, and Sandra T. Gray, *Profiles of Excellence: Achieving Success in the Nonprofit Sector* (San Francisco: Jossey-Bass, 1991).

2. For more on these charity rating services, including a critical evaluation, see Stephanie Lowell, Brian Trelstad, and Bill Meehan, "The Ratings Game," *Stanford Social Innovation Review* (Summer 2005): 38–45. They argue that (1) the financial data upon which these reports are based needs to be improved, made more reliable, and evaluated in a more sophisticated manner; (2) the strength of the organization's reputation, management team, human resource function, and board should be included; and (3) the organization's social impact (mission achievement) should be quantified.

3. Richard S. Wasch, "Budgeting in Nonprofit Organizations," in *Handbook of Budgeting*, 3rd ed. (New York: John Wiley & Sons, 1993)

4. From study of 277 U.S. churches by Christianity Today International. See "The Finances of Faith," *Church Business* (September 2005). Available online at: www.churchbusiness.com/articles/591feat10.html. Accessed: 12/30/05.

5. The exception here is the case in which equity is issued for a for-profit subsidiary, which shows up as a financing flow for the consolidated organization.

6. Many of the ratios we cover were first applied to nonprofit organizations by Chris Robinson. His study of 479 audited financial statements, done as part of his master's thesis at the University of San Francisco, is the finest we have seen because of its careful study of ratios and their value. Robinson was also controller at Partners International, a faith-based organization located in San Jose, CA, while conducting this study.

7. Overall, Robinson found faith-based organizations had a ratio of about 1.4; this implies that every $1 of near-term obligations was covered by $1.40 of cash or near-cash investments, which is quite good. The mean (average) and median (midpoint value, with one-half of the organizations having values above or below it) were quite different for some industry groups, however: Medians ranged from 0.72 for schools and colleges to 2.41 for foreign missions and social/medical agencies.

8. The median ratio across the groups studied by Robinson was 0.09, which implies that these organizations could last only 33 days (0.09×365 days) if their revenues were cut off. From this vantage, liquidity is very poor. In his sample of faith-based organizations, only professional associations (0.19, or 69 days) had a median ratio value above 0.13 (47 days). Again, while we would not expect a complete shutdown of the revenue stream, we have evidence here of relatively low levels of liquidity.

9. John E. Core, Wayne R. Guay, and Rodrigo S. Verdi, "Agency Problems of Excess Endowment Holdings in Not-for-Profit Firms," Working paper, Wharton School, University of Pennsylvania, September 24, 2004. Other high values were 1.81 (civil rights/social action), 1.66 (environmental quality), 1.44 (arts/culture/humanities), and 1.38 (medical research). Religious organizations had a value of 0.86. Other low values were 0.22 (health), 0.23 (employment/job-related), 0.27 (food/agriculture), 0.28 (crime/legal-related), and 0.25 (housing/shelter).

10. Elizabeth K. Keating, Mary Fischer, Teresa P. Gordon, and Janet S. Greenlee, "Assessing Financial Vulnerability in the Nonprofit Sector," KSG Working Paper No. RWP05-002 (Harvard University), January 2005. The overall average was 4.08, but the overall median value was 3.09 (some high numbers skewed the average). The sector is important here: Church median current ratio was 0.97 but denominations/denominational groups had a median value of 10.85. Most nonprofit sectors studied had medians of 2 or 3, which corresponds closely with what we see in business enterprises. The very large value for denominations is partly linked to inventory held for churches and outreach ministries, but it also reflects the pooling of liquid assets as funds are "upstreamed" from member congregations. These funds are held longer than they should be, in some cases, prior to being disbursed or invested in pensions or buildings.

11. Id. Robinson's study finds the overall mean and median for the asset ratio of about 0.35, meaning that 35 percent of the assets of sampled organizations were in the current category, with the remainder of 65 percent in long-term assets. The sector that the organization is

in matters greatly: churches had a median current asset investment of only 6 percent and camps and conference centers only 14 percent, while foreign missions had 51 percent, denominations had 62 percent, and professional associations had 78 percent in short-term assets.

12. See Chapter 2 of Terry S. Maness and John T. Zietlow, *Short-Term Financial Management: Text and Cases*, 3rd ed. (Cincinnati: Thomson/South-Western, 2005). Lambda was developed by Kenneth Cogger and Gary Emery; further information and interpretation of this measure are provided in the referenced chapter.

13. This range approach to estimating standard deviation assumes a normal distribution, or the familiar bell-shaped curve, for your organization's operating cash flows. Since your cash flows are most likely not normally distributed, this estimate must be viewed as a rough approximation.

14. We calculated these by using the NORMDIST function built into Excel™: Probability of cash shortfall $= [1 - \text{NORMDIST(TLLL)}]$. For TLLL_1, this gives us: Probability $= [1 - \text{NORMDIST}(6.53)] = [1 - 1] = 0.00$. Use the percent format to turn this into a percent, which gives us 0.00% in this case.

15. Raymond Fisman and R. Glenn Hubbard, "The Role of Nonprofit Endowments," in *The Governance of Not-for-Profit Organizations*, ed. E. Glaeser (Chicago: University of Chicago Press, 2003).

16. The median value for the contribution ratio in the Robinson study was 0.84. Fully 84 percent of total revenues were from donated funds, showing a heavy reliance on such funds. Schools/colleges and camps/conference centers were the least reliant on donations, with median values of 0.28 and 0.37, respectively. This makes sense given that they can charge for their services. Churches, foreign mission agencies, and social and welfare agencies all had ratios of around 0.90 or above, showing extreme reliance on donated funds.

17. Keating et al., "Assessing Financial Vulnerability in the Nonprofit Sector." In their study of FBOs, the median value for the debt ratio across all organizations was 0.24. As you would expect, the sector again has much to do with the debt usage: social/medical agencies, camps/conference centers, foreign mission agencies, domestic missions (such as homeless shelters), and schools/colleges all had ratios of 0.17 to -0.25; publishers and radio/TV organizations had ratio values in the mid-thirties, and churches and denominations had ratios of 0.47.

18. Id. The median value was 1.34 in the data, but here this disguises a great deal of variability. Schools/colleges (0.5), camps/conference centers (0.68), and churches (0.65) were at the low end, and domestic missions (1.99), professional associations (2.38), and foreign missions (2.8) were considerably higher. For further comparison, for the 128 varied nonprofit organizations registered with the State of Oregon in 1993, the average return ratio was 0.89 (1993 fiscal year data, Oregon Department of Justice).

19. Id.

20. Robinson's data indicate that regardless of espoused objectives, most FBOs were running surpluses. The median was $16,000, with only one subgroup (professional associations) running a deficit (median loss of $3,000). Organizational types running surpluses were publishers and radio/TV ($2,000), domestic missions ($5,000), foreign missions ($10,000), and churches ($16,000). At the high end, again using median values, were social/medical ($34,000), camps/conference centers ($40,000), denominations ($46,000), and schools/colleges ($75,000). One caution: At the time of Robinson's study many organizations were not depreciating assets, and surpluses would be in some cases deficits were restatements made.

21. Keating et al. The overall median for the sample of FBOs was 0.02 (a 2 percent surplus), with the same relative ranking as we saw with the net surplus. The differences, though, are not nearly as great. The highest values were achieved by camps/conference centers at 0.05 (5 percent). Schools and colleges (0.03) and social/medical agencies (0.03) are next in line. The "profits" reported above appear to be much more modest when scaled by revenue.

22. The overall median for the net asset reserve ratio in Robinson's sample was 0.49, meaning one-half a year's expenses are built up as permanent, non–interest-bearing financing. At the low end are professional associations (0.27), domestic and foreign missions

(0.34), and publishers (0.35); at the high end we find camps/conference centers (1.24) and schools/colleges (1.27). Robinson et al. (1988, p. 83) point out that the latter organizations may hold these net assets in liquid form for capital renovation and construction.

23. The overall median for FBOs is 75 percent for program expenses and 25 percent for support services. The highest program percentages were achieved by denominations (81 percent) and foreign missions (79 percent); the lowest were camps/conference centers (71 percent) and social/medical (73 percent). Camps and conference centers battle the limited-year phenomenon, in which they generally receive revenues and provide programs for only part of the year, and yet have administrative and fundraising expenses pretty much year-around.

24. This bias, which the American Institute of Philanthropy (AIP) adjusts for in its calculations, may have a significant effect. See "AIP's Method Better Judges Charity Efficiency: Why Oxfam Compares Better and UNICEF Worse," 2005. Available online at AIP's Web site: www.charitywatch.org/articles/airpmethod.html. Accessed: 11/5/2005.

25. Id.

26. See Chuck McLean and Suzanne E. Coffman, "Why Ratios Aren't the Last Word" (June 2004). Available online at: www.guidestar.org/news/features/ratios.jsp. Accessed: 11/5/2005.

27. For example, organizations may or may not separate out operating and nonoperating activities in their SA presentation, allowing them to report a measure of operating income. See a study of private college practices in this regard in Mary Fischer, Teresa P. Gordon, Janet Greenlee, and Elizabeth K. Keating, "Measuring Operations: An Analysis of U.S. Private Colleges and Universities' Financial Statements," *Financial Accountability & Management* 20 (May 2004): 129–151. The authors noted that: "Among the schools that chose to display operating income and operating revenue we found wide differences in definition and computation" (p. 147).

28. See the pamphlet "The Ministry of Fund Raising," by Whitney Kuniholm, pp. 39–47; it is published by Prison Fellowship, P.O. Box 17500, Washington, D.C., 20041-0500.

29. Your organization may already be there without consciously planning such a strategy. Does it have both (1) cash reserves significantly greater than next year's anticipated operating expenses (and will you still have it at the end of the fiscal year) and (2) a policy that allows the organization to draw down cash reserves to some minimum level in order to fund operations? If so, it is in the same financial position as an organization which consciously adopts this forward-year annual campaign strategy.

30. We gratefully acknowledge the assistance of Philip M. Purcell, J.D., Director of Planned Giving and Development Counsel, Rose-Hulman Institute of Technology, Terre Haute, IN, on this section. A very helpful resource for those wishing to conduct self-assessment of fundraising is *Fundraising Cost Effectiveness: A Self-Assessment Workbook*, by James M. Greenfield (New York: John Wiley & Sons, 1996). More recent information on fundraising efficiency percentages is available in James M. Greenfield, *Fund Raising: Evaluating and Managing the Fund Development Process* (AFP/Wiley Fund Development Series), 2nd ed. (Hoboken, NJ: John Wiley & Sons, 2001); James M. Greenfield, ed., *The Nonprofit Handbook: Fund Raising* (AFP/Wiley Fund Development Series), 3rd ed. (Hoboken, NJ: John Wiley & Sons, 2001); and James M. Greenfield, ed., *The Nonprofit Handbook: Fund-Raising 2003 Cumulative Supplement* (Hoboken, NJ: John Wiley & Sons, 2003).

31. Greenfield, *Fundraising Cost Effectiveness,* 676.

32. Ellen Ryan, "The Costs of Raising a Dollar," *Case Currents* (September 1990): 58–62.

33. Id., 58.

34. From Mary Beth McIntyre of the Target Analysis Group; cited in "Benchmarking. . . Understanding how all data works together," *NPT Instant Fundraising e-newsletter*, January 5, 2006. McIntyre suggests that organizations compare their fundraising results to industry-wide resources available from Giving USA, Target Analysis Group National Index, Paradyz Matera Performance Watch, Campbell Rinker, and industry surveys.

35. Once you have your daily cash receipts and cash disbursements in a financial spreadsheet, use the statistics functions to do this for you.

36. Saleha B. Khumawala, Teresa P. Gordon, and M. M. Kraut, "Not-for Profit Financial Reporting at the End of the 20th Century: Environmental Organizations," 2001. Working Paper, University of Houston and University of Idaho; and Anne L. Christensen and Rosanne M.

Mohr, "Not-for-Profit Annual Reports: What do Museum Managers Communicate?" *Financial Accountability & Management* 19 (May 2003): 139–158. In the latter study, the authors found that 22 percent of the museum annual reports included complete financial statements with footnotes.

37.   Instructions for Form 990 and Form 990-EZ are located at: www.irs.gov/pub/irs-pdf/i990-ez.pdf.

SAMPLE RATIO CALCULATIONS

HABITAT FOR HUMANITY

Here are snapshots of the worksheet in which we calculated the financial ratios from Chapter 7 for Habitat for Humanity's financial statements.

RATIO CALCULATIONS FOR HABITAT FOR HUMANITY, 2004 Fiscal Year:

Here are the calculations of the 2004 financial ratios from Chapter 7 statements.
Items gathered from the notes to the financial statements in italics.

Liquidity Ratios:

		2004	*Interpretive Comment(s):*
Cash Ratio = (Cash and Cash Equivs. / Current Liabs.) =	=	1.07	We could cover upcoming year's obligations almost 1.1 times, or we could have about a 7% drop in cash and still cover our near-term financial obligations.
Note 7 says short-term N/P = $1,506,480			
Cash Reserve Ratio = (Cash and Cash Equivs. / Total Annual Exps.) =			Cash and equivalents from the SFP; Annual Expenses from SA.
	=	0.1077	More conservative measure than cash ratio:
	=	10.77%	We can only cover 11% of year's expenses with cash and very short-term investments (keep the revenues coming!!!)
Current Ratio = (Current Assets / Current Liabilities) =	=	4.81	Almost three times as many current assets as current liabilities, representing good bills-paying ability.
Note 7 says short-term N/P = $1,506,480; Note 3 ST Invest =>$ 4,844,508			
Note 4 ST grants & contribs. receivable =>$18,138,969			
Asset Ratio = (Current Asset / Total Assets) =	=	0.626	
	=	62.6%	Almost 2/3 of all assets owned or controlled are Short-Term ("Working Capital").
Target Liquidity Level = (Cash & Cash Equivs. +		$ 17,342,999	(See pg. 185 on **why** to use.)
Short-Term Investmts. + Total Short-Term Credit Line		$4,844,508	
- Short-Term Loans)		$1,506,480	
Note 3 ST Invest =>$ 4,844,508	=	**$ 20,681,027**	Compare to management target, which
Note 7 says short-term N/P = $1,506,480; credit line not disclosed, so $0.			we don't know in this case.

Funding Ratio:

		2004	
Contribution Ratio = (Total Contributed Revenue / Total Revenue)			Both items are from the Statement
Numerator: Contributed Revenue (Indiv. + Corp./Foundation)		119,903,076	of Activities.
Denominator: Total Revenue		170,737,212	
Contribution Ratio =	=	0.7023	
and in %, Contribution Ratio =	=	70.2%	So almost exactly 70% of total revenues are from contributions and corp/foundation grants. Higher % represent more risk, since uncertain $.
Debt Ratio = Total Liabilities / Total Assets			Both items from SFP.
Numerator: Total Liabilities (from SFP)		52,823,353	
Denominator: Total Assets (from SFP)		124,168,954	
Debt Ratio =	=	0.42542	
and in %, Debt Ratio =	=	42.5%	Fairly risky, since over 40% of assets are financed with borrowed money (debt). That means 60% (100%-40%) is financed with net assets, or contributed capital plus accumulated surpluses from the most recent and all prior fiscal years.

Operating Ratios:

	2004

Note: other than the return ratio (which is analogous to total asset turnover in the business world) and net asset reserve ratio, the numerator and denominator for each ratio comes from the Statement of Activity.

Return Ratio = (Total Revenue / Total Assets)
Numerator: Total Revenue (see Stat. Of Activ.)   170,737,212
Denominator: Total Assets (SFP, above)   124,168,954
   Return Ratio =   =   **1.38** Org. brings in $1.38 in rev. for every $1 in assets.
                    Higher is more efficient, given the asset base.

Net Surplus = (Total Revs. – Total Expenses)
It is available directly, without calc., from Statement   = **$ 7,216,666** Want it to be positive. Compare to
of Activities. It will typically be listed as "change   prior years to see trend.
in net assets" or "net revenue".

Net Operating Ratio = (Net Surplus / Total Revenue)
Net Surplus (just shown in prior formula)   7,216,666
Total Revenue (this denominator is same as numerator in return ratio above)   170,737,212
   Net Operating Ratio =   0.0423 This is the similar to profit margin on sales in business.
   in %, Net Operating Ratio =   =   **4.2%** Habitat for Humanity "makes" 4.2 cents per $1 of revenue.

Net Asset Reserve Ratio = (Net Assets / Total Expenses)
Net assets is listed on the SFP: 71,345,601
Total Expenses seen in Cash Reserve Ratio above.   161,098,607
   Net Asset Reserve Ratio =   0.44 Don't put too much emphasis on this ratio, generally.
   in %, Net Asset Reserve Ratio =   =   **44.3%** We have 44% of expenses "covered" by capital
                    that has been infused by past year surpluses (but the
                    question is how much of that capital, or net assets,
                    is truly spendable if needed for covering expenses when
                    revenues are unavailable or insufficient for that purpose?)

Program Expense Ratio = (Prog. Exps. / Total Expenses)
(**we want this number to be high, in %)
Program Expenses (Statement of Activity)   121,562,689   <= "Total program services" from SA
Total Expenses (already in net asset reserve ratio formula above)   161,098,607
   Program Expense Ratio =   0.75
   in %, Program Expense Ratio =   **75.5%** Interesting to see that about 76 cents
                    per dollar expended by organization is for program instead
                    of fundraising, general salaries, or other "overhead".
                    This value is very typical for charities, so no surprise.

Support Service Expense Ratio =(Support Service Exps. / Total Expenses)
this is 100% minus the program expense ratio   0.25
**or, 1 minus the program expense ratio
     in decimal form (cell several rows above)
In %, the Support Service Expense Ratio =>   =   **24.5%** Compare to similar agencies in same service arena.
                    Same information as we got in program
                    expense ratio, except we want this to be low.

ADDITIONAL FINANCIAL RATIOS

We presented our core financial ratios in Chapter 7. However, there are additional ratios that you may wish to calculate to better evaluate the financial position and operating results of your organization. Or, you may have a for-profit subsidiary, and you wish to apply some business ratios to that subsidiary's operating results. We will present some liquidity and operating ratios that are commonly used by businesses, and many of these could be applied by health care organizations as well as to the for-profit subsidiaries of other nonprofits. We then look at some ratios calculated by charity rating agencies (Charity Navigator and GuideStar). We follow this with some ratios making use of the information in the Statement of Cash Flows. We then profile some Form 990 ratios that have benchmark data available for your comparison. Finally, we present some of our own faith-based organization benchmark data compiled from audited financials.

7B.1 BUSINESS LIQUIDITY, FUNDING, AND OPERATING RATIOS

(a) **LIQUIDITY RATIOS.** We briefly list average collection period (ACP), inventory conversion period (ICP), average payment period (APP), operating cycle (OC), and the cash conversion period (CCP) here. For more details, see Maness and Zietlow (2005), cited in the Chapter 7 references.

ICP (also called Days Inventory Held, or DIH) measures the length of time it takes to convert your inventory into sales. Again, shorter is better, because inventories also tie up your cash. The denominator has Cost of Goods Sold, not sales, because inventories are accounted for at cost. To use sales there would also distort the measurement because it includes the mark-up added to your cost.

$$ICP = (Inventory \times 365)/Cost\ of\ goods\ sold$$

ACP (also called Day Sales Outstanding, or DSO) measures the length of time it takes to collect credit sales. You want this to be as close to your offered credit period (commonly 30 days) as possible, and higher numbers tie up more of your cash.

$$ACP = (Accounts\ receivable \times 365)/Total\ sales$$

Your operating cycle (OC) is the sum of the elapsed times for converting inventories to sales and then collecting on those sales (so that you once again have cash):

$$OC = ICP + ACP$$

Fortunately, you are not out-of-pocket for cash that long, normally. This is because you buy inventories on credit, normally. We adjust for this by first calculating the average payment period (APP), then subtracting that from the operating cycle to get the cash conversion period.

APP (also called Days Payable Outstanding, or DPO) measures the length of time it takes to pay for your credit purchases. You want this to be as close to your suppliers' offered credit periods (commonly 30 days) as possible, but some businesses stretch payables unethically because higher numbers tie up less of their cash as it ties up more of their suppliers' cash.

$$APP = (\text{Accounts payable} \times 365)/\text{Total purchases}$$

Many times purchases data are not available to an external analyst, and cost of goods sold is used in the denominator instead.

We may now calculate the cash conversion period (CCP), which shows us for how long the organization has its cash tied up in its operations:

$$CCP = OC - APP$$

or

$$CCP = ICP + ACP - APP$$

Illustrating, if ICP is 70 days, ACP is 45 days, and APP is 30 days, CCP would be:

$$CCP = 70 + 45 - 30$$

$$CCP = 85 \text{ days}$$

We can use this information to estimate minimum operating cash (MOC) for an organization. First, we calculate cash turnover (CT), which measures how many times per year cash cycles through the organization:

$$CT = 365/CCP$$

In our example, since CCP = 85 days:

$$CT = 365/85$$

$$CT = 4.29$$

Think of this as similar to inventory turnover, but the turnover is in your inventory of cash. Some organizations estimate their minimum cash by taking some percent of their sales (for example, if set to 8% of sales, and sales are $2 million annually, minimum cash = $160,000 = .08 \times $2,000,000$). Our CT data, coupled with annual cash expenses, gives us another way to estimate minimum operations-related cash, or MOC (you would hold cash for other reasons, as well, as noted in Chapter 2):

$$MOC = \text{Annual cash expenses}/CT$$

If annual cash expenses are $1,600,000, using our CT of 4.29, we get MOC:

$$MOC = $1,600,000/4.29$$

$$MOC = $372,960.37$$

To monetize the effect of this on your annual interest expense, multiply this by your annual cost of capital. Assuming this is 10%, or 0.10 in decimal form, we get an annual interest expense related to our cash conversion period of $37,296:

Annual interest expense of MOC $=$ MOC $\times$ Annual cost of capital

Annual interest expense of MOC $= \$372,960.37 \times 0.10$

Annual interest expense of MOC $= \$37,296$

If we could convert our inventories more quickly, collect our receivables more quickly, or renegotiate more favorable payment terms, we could reduce our CCP, increase our CT, reduce our MOC, and thereby reduce the interest expense related to our operating cycle. When the CCP increases, we get the opposite effect, as shown in the following chain reaction diagram:

Longer Cash Cycle Ties Up Funds, Lowers Interest Income

(b) **FUNDING RATIOS.**   The two funding ratios we present here are times interest earned (TIE) and the current liquidity index (CLI). Both ratios reflect on our organization's ability to cover its fixed, financing-related obligations. Higher ratio values are better as they reflect a greater ability to cover those obligations:

TIE $=$ Earnings before interest and taxes/Interest expense

(Cash and equivalents $+$ Short-term investments $+$ Projected OCF)

$$\text{CLI} = \frac{(\text{Cash and equivalents } + \text{ Short-term investments } + \text{ Projected OCF})}{(\text{Short-term notes payable } + \text{ Current portion of long-term debt})}$$

(c) **OPERATING RATIOS.**   Several profitability ratios that businesses use are return on assets (ROA), return on invested capital (ROIC), and return on equity (ROE). Each measures profits (or what nonprofits call net revenue, typically measured by change in net assets, which may be adjusted by the analyst) relative to an important variable: assets invested in the business (ROA), long-term capital invested in the business (ROIC), or stockholder equity invested in the business (ROE). Higher values show greater profitability, and this is positive so long as a company is not underinvesting in training, advertising, new product development, and other forms of research and development:

ROA $=$ Net income/Total assets

ROIC $=$ Net income/(Long-term debt $+$ Stockholders'equity)

ROE $=$ Net income/(Stockholders'equity)

7B.2 OTHER RATIOS USED BY CHARITY RATING SERVICES

(a) **CHARITY NAVIGATOR.**   Charity Navigator (CN) assigns scores to charities' financial condition based on numerous financial ratios. The pros are: (1) great ratios selection; (2) great scaling of ratio values based both on logic and on the industry (e.g., daycare centers have a different scaling than food banks); (3) its reports draw from a database of peer data that provides good benchmark data (although charities, like businesses, are sometimes diversified and therefore not purely operating in one industry, so the benchmark may be partly inapplicable for comparison purposes); and (4) its scoring system rewards, rather than penalizes, organizations for holding higher cash reserves (see our discussion of liquidity and CN in Chapter 2).

The primary con is: CN's reports and scoring are based only on one year of data, and this is based on the organization's most recently filed, sometimes inaccurate (and non-GAAP), Form 990.

Especially helpful for us in our focus on liquidity, solvency, and financial flexibility is Charity Navigator's focus on "organizational capacity," which it measures with three ratios:

1. Average annual growth of program expenses.

    ○   This is what many would call a compound annual growth rate of program expenses.

    ○   You may calculate this with a financial calculator or in Excel™ or using one of the free Internet online calculators.

2. Average annual growth of primary revenue.

3. Working capital ratio.

> *Numerator:* (Cash and equivalents + Savings accounts + Pledges receivable
>
> + Grants receivable) − (Accounts payable + Grants payable
>
> + Accrued expenses).
>
> *Denominator:* Total expenses, including payments to affiliates.

(b) **GUIDESTAR.**   GuideStar uses the following ratios, most of which we presented in Chapter 7:

$$\text{Accounts payable aging indicator} = (\text{Accounts payable} \times 12)/\text{Total expenses}$$

$$\text{Contributions and grants ratio} = (\text{Contributions} + \text{Grants})/\text{Total revenue}$$

$$\text{Debt ratio} = \text{Total liabilities}/\text{Total assets}$$

$$\text{Fundraising ratio} = \text{Fundraising expenses}/\text{Total expenses}$$

$$\text{Liquid funds indicator} = \frac{([\text{Net assets} - \text{Permanently restricted net assets} - \text{Land, buildings, and equipment}]}{\text{Total expenses}}$$

$$\text{Program ratio} = \text{Program service expenses}/\text{Total expenses}$$

$$\text{Savings ratio} = (\text{Total revenue} - \text{Total expenses})/\text{Total expenses}$$

7B.3 STATEMENT OF CASH FLOWS RATIOS

Notice that all of the other ratios we present in Chapter 7 and the appendixes take information from the Statement of Activity and Statement of Financial Position, but not the Statement of Cash Flows (SCF). The ratios in this section take information from the SCF as well as the SA and SFP, and are helpful for lenders, rating agencies, and other analysts doing evaluations of businesses. Some of these ratios, such as the OCF ratio, will be helpful for all organizations. The others may be helpful in your evaluation of health care and education nonprofits, as well as earned income ventures. These are presented by John R. Mills and Jeanne H. Yamamura, in "The Power of Cash Flow Ratios," *Journal of Accountancy* (October 1998).

Liquidity and Funding Ratios

   1. Operating cash flow (OCF) ratio:

$$\text{OCF ratio} \ = \ \text{OCF/Current liabilities}$$

where OCF is taken off of the SCF (the subtotal that you will see at the end of the first category of items on the organization's SCF). Current liabilities are on the SFP, but many nonprofits do not classify their SFP, so take A/P + Accrued expenses + Deferred revenue + Short-term portion of N/P to get CL in this case. Compare to similar organizations.

   2. Funds flow coverage (FFC) ratio:

$$\text{FFC ratio} = \text{EBITDA/(Interest expense } + \text{ Debt repayment)}$$

EBITDA is earnings (or change in net assets) before interest, taxes, depreciation, and amortization. So add back the latter items to the change in net assets to arrive at EBITDA. Interest expense should be the cash amount of interest paid (which may be provided as a supplemental disclosure below the SCF) and debt repayment is the sum of short-term debt and any current maturities of long-term debt (which may represent bonds issued 19 years ago with an original 20-year maturity, so they are now within one year of repayment).

     In our presentation here, we have modified the original FFC ratio for nonprofits' tax-exempt status. Done for a business, this ratio has both debt repayment and preferred dividends in the denominator, and each must be divided by (1 − marginal tax rate) to "gross up" the amount to enable the organization to both pay taxes and meet the financial obligation.

     Rationale for this ratio, relative to SCF ratio: OCF has interest and taxes already subtracted out; EBITDA does not. Compare the calculated value to that of similar organizations.

   3. Cash interest coverage ratio:

$$\text{Cash interest coverage ratio} = \text{(OCF } + \text{ Interest paid}$$
$$+ \text{ Taxes paid)/Interest paid}$$

Again, use cash interest paid and if the ratio value is less than 1.0, there is an immediate risk of potential default on debt obligations.

   4. Cash current debt coverage ratio:

$$\text{Cash current debt coverage ratio} = \text{(OCF − Cash dividends)/Current debt}$$

where, since nonprofits do not have dividends, the numerator is just OCF, and the denominator is all debt maturity within one year, just as in the funds flow coverage ratio (#2 above). Higher ratios are better, but appropriate minimum value depends on the industry (health care would differ from education, for example).

Measures of Ongoing Financial Health

5. Capital expenditure ratio:

$$\text{Capital expenditure ratio} = \text{OCF/Capital expenditures}$$

This ratio is similar to our OCF/ICF measure in Chapter 7. It separates out from ICF the line item representing additional investment in property, plant, and equipment. If the ratio value is greater than 1.0, the organization has enough cash to cover all capital expenditures and has money left over to meet debt obligations.

6. Total debt (cash flow to total debt) ratio:

$$\text{Total debt ratio} = \text{OCF/Total debt}$$

where total debt includes all short-term and long-term arranged debt. This gives the amount of time it would take to pay off all debt from the organization's operating cash flow, assuming all OCF was to be dedicated to debt repayment. Lower ratio values signal less financial flexibility and potential problems in the future. Compare value to those of similar organizations.

7. Total free cash (TFC) flow ratio:

Numerator: Total free cash = (Change in net assets

+ Accrued and capitalized interest expense + Depreciation and amortization

+ Operating lease and rental expense − Capital expenditures)

Denominator: Total fixed obligations = (Accrued and capitalized interest

expense + Operating lease and rental expense + Current portion of long

− term debt + Current portion of capitalized lease obligations)

Total free cash(TFC)flow ratio = Total free cash/Total fixed obligations

The numerator is some definition of free cash, and net free cash flow is defined differently by different analysts. The denominator is the sum of many fixed financial and operating obligations. Because there are so many items in the numerator and denominator, we show them separately. We modified the numerator slightly to change "net income" to "Change in net assets" and to eliminate dividends. This ratio looks much like a fixed-payment coverage ratio, with the numerator using mostly SA items. The capital expenditures number may include only those capital expenditures necessary to maintain the organization's operating assets (maybe some percentage of total assets, such as 2%, or some percentage of property, plant, and equipment, such as 5%). For assessing long-term growth, you may use actual capital expenditures from the SCF, however.

Organizational Credit Quality

8. Cash flow adequacy (CFA) ratio:

(EBITDA − Taxes paid − Interest paid − Capital expenditures)

Cash flow adequacy (CFA) ratio = (Average annual debt maturities scheduled over next 5 years)

EBITDA is the same as in the FFC ratio (ratio # 2 above). A high ratio means the organization has good cash flow relative to upcoming debt obligations, and is therefore a high credit-quality borrower from the vantage point of a lender or bond rating agency.

7B.4 RATIOS WITH COMPARATIVE BENCHMARK DATA AVAILABLE (BASED ON FORM 990)

Greenlee and Bukovinsky (using Form 990 data) have developed a very helpful set of financial ratios, and along with it, benchmark data by industry. We include this by including several exhibits from their analysis.

In Exhibit 7B.1, you see the ratios used for determining whether the nonprofit has adequate resources. PPE refers to property, plant, and equipment. Notice that these are liquidity and funding ratios.

In Exhibit 7B.2, we see the ratios used for evaluating the uses to which funds are put.

In Exhibit 7B.3, we see the industries into which nonprofits were categorized for purposes of displaying benchmark ratio standards.

Finally, in Exhibits 7B.4 and 7B.5, we have the comparative ratio benchmarks. Compare your organization's Form 990–based ratios to these benchmarks to give a sense of how your organization matches up.

Ratio Definitions	
Adequacy of Resources to Support the Mission of the Charity	
Name	**Formula**
Defensive Interval (DI)	$\dfrac{\text{Cash + Marketable Securities + Receivables}}{\text{Average Monthly Expenses}}$
Liquid Funds Indicator (LF)	$\dfrac{\text{Fuand Balance–Restricted Endowment–Land–PPE}}{\text{Average Monthly Expenses}}$
Accounts Payable Aging Indicator (AP)	$\dfrac{\text{Accounts Payable}}{\text{Average Monthly Expenses}}$
Saving Indicator (S)	$\dfrac{\text{Revenues–Expenses}}{\text{TotalExpenses}}$
Contributions & Grants Ratio (CG)	$\dfrac{\text{Revenue from Contributions \& Grants}}{\text{Total Revenue}}$
Endowment Ratio (E)	$\dfrac{\text{Endowment}}{\text{Average Monthly Expenses}}$
Debt Ratio (D)	$\dfrac{\text{Average Total Debt}}{\text{Average Total Assets}}$

Source: Janet S.Greenlee and David Bukovinsky, "Financial Ratios for Use in the Analytical Review of Charitable Organizations," *Ohio CPA Journal* (Jan–Mar 1998): 32–34, 36, 38. Used by permission.

EXHIBIT 7B.1   GREENLEE AND BUKOVINSKY RESOURCE ADEQUACY RATIO DEFINITIONS

Ratio Definitions	
Use of Resources to Support the Mission of the Charity	
Name	Formula
Fundraising Efficiency (FE)	$\dfrac{\text{Total Contributions (other than Government Grants)}}{\text{Fundraising Expense}}$
Fundraising Expense (FX)	$\dfrac{\text{Fundraising Epense}}{\text{Total Expense}}$
Management Expense (MX)	$\dfrac{\text{Management \& General Expenses}}{\text{Total Expense}}$
Program Service Expense (PX)	$\dfrac{\text{Program Services Expense}}{\text{Total Expense}}$
Program Service Expense to Total Assets (PA)	$\dfrac{\text{Program Service Expense}}{\text{Average Total Assets}}$

Source: Janet S. Greenlee and David Bukovinsky, "Financial Ratios for Use in the Analytical Review of Charitable Organizations," *Ohio CPA Journal* (Jan–Mar 1998): 32–34, 36, 38. Used by permission.

EXHIBIT 7B.2   GREENLEE AND BUKOVINSKY RESOURCE UTILIZATION RATIO DEFINITIONS

Charitable Sector Classification	
Sector	**Description**
Arts, Culture Humanities	Education & Services; Museums & Galleries; Performing Arts
Education	Early Childhood; Special Education; Vocational Education; Adult Continuing Education Facilities; Libraries, Archives; Remediation Testing and Services to Dropouts, Financial Aid Scholarships; Student Support Services
Human needs	Employment, Food; Shelter; Housing; Social Services; Civil Liberties/Human Rights; Recreation
Community Services	Public Preparedness; Public Safety; Legal System, *Justic Services; Citizen Safety, Youth Activities;* Government Services; Philanthropy (private foundations, federated giving)
Health	Hospitals, Outpatient Clinics; Reproductive Health-Services; Rehabilitative Services; General Health Support Services; Mental Health Treatment; Mental Health Disorders; Physical Diseases, Prevention/Treatment; Medical Disiplines; Prevention; Public Health

Source: Janet S. Greenlee and David Bukovinsky, "Financial Ratios for Use in the Analytical Review of Charitable Organizations," *Ohio CPA Journal* (Jan–Mar 1998): 32–34, 36, 38. Used by permission.

EXHIBIT 7B.3   INDUSTRY CLASSIFICATION FOR GREENLEE AND BUKOVINSKY RATIOS

Charitable Ratios—By Sector and Quartile

Quartile Revenues	Are there adequate resources to support the mission of the charity?**						How are the resources used to support the mission of the charity?***					
	DI	LF	AP	S	CG	E	DT	FE	FX	MX	PX	PA
Arts, Culture, Humanities												
1 > $1,122,929	3.496	.886	.663	.031	.463	4.824	.299	6.920	.053	.187	.750	.581
2 $435,638 – 1,122,929	3.034	1.169	.351	.037	.459	3.506	.269	7.455	.047	.221	.735	.876
3 $236,575 – 435,637	2.621	1.114	.225	.017	.422	3.775	.181	8.115	.045	.231	.735	.934
4 < $236,575	4.003	2.134	.141	.012	.409	7.141	.081	8.241	.049	.205	.753	.824
Median for sector	3.226	1.209	.330	.028	.441	4.534	.214	7.520	.049	.206	.746	.776
Number of charities	2,503	2,161	2,399	1,940	2,503	578	2,369	1,346	1,346	2,503	2,503	2,052
Community Needs												
1 > $1,089,319	4.312	1.884	.441	.034	.851	2.554	.269	9.875	.063	.097	.844	.799
2 $464,870 –1,089,319	3.775	1.973	.334	.021	.868	3.139	.257	10.483	.063	.124	.832	1.049
3 $247,034 – 464,870	3.757	1.779	.182	.013	.790	3.850	.190	9.596	.059	.126	.836	1.036
4 < $247,034	4.419	2.413	.090	.055	.728	10.001	.085	11.772	.055	.138	.826	.621
Median for sector	4.091	2.107	.269	.029	.817	3.253	.201	10.267	.061	.118	.837	.902
Number of charities	1,899	1,651	1,784	1,451	1,904	280	1,779	939	939	1,899	1,899	1,583
Education												
1 > $1,852,881	2.552	1.273	.721	.031	.172	3.608	.290	5.409	.022	.112	.875	1.280
2 > $702,670 – 1,852,881	2.598	1.203	.462	.032	.632	2.056	.306	7.566	.034	.125	.856	1.679
3 $317,897 – 702,669	2.983	1.902	.260	.026	.705	7.228	.159	12.269	.018	.128	.860	1.409
4 < $317,897	4.587	2.760	.069	.047	.505	25.816	.057	12.762	.050	.109	.866	1.064
Median for sector	3.014	1.703	.375	.032	.464	5.062	.215	9.097	.024	.120	.866	1.314
Number of charities	1,143	978	1,083	924	1,146	162	1,074	343	343	1,143	1,143	979

Source: Janet S. Greenlee and David Bukovinsky, "Financial Ratios for Use in the Analytical Review of Charitable Organizations," *Ohio CPA Journal* (Jan–Mar 1998): 32–34, 36, 38. Used by permission.

EXHIBIT 7B.4 RATIO BENCHMARKS FOR ARTS/CULTURE/HUMANITIES, COMMUNITY NEEDS, AND EDUCATION

Quartile Revenues	Are there adequate resources to support the mission of the charity?					How are the resources used to support the mission of the charity?						
	DI	LF	AP	S	CG	E	D	FE	FX	MX	PX	PA
Health												
1 >$2,900,639	2.514	1.796	.966	.027	.099	.823	.416	5.528	.019	.128	.861	1.325
2 $1,005,523-2,900,639	2.601	1.706	.652	.028	.486	1.969	.318	6.159	.047	.148	.829	1.567
3 $394,551-1,005,523	2.974	2.004	.455	.027	.580	2.563	.224	7.899	.052	.148	.823	1.504
4 <$394,551	3.248	1.809	.257	.018	.612	2.512	.129	6.788	.065	.154	.810	1.229
Median for sector	2.695	1.812	.659	.027	.406	1.447	.315	6.155	.042	.140	.840	1.391
Number of charities	4,930	4,428	4,759	4,006	4,943	414	4,719	1,393	1,393	4,830	4,930	4,182
Human Needs												
1 > 1,621,921	2.007	.883	.834	.015	.476	1.196	.482	7.798	.015	.108	.885	1.632
2 $ 665,363-1,621,921	2.251	.872	.639	.014	.478	1.549	.420	8.576	.023	.111	.878	1.228
3 $324,778-655,362	2.232	.878	.521	.012	.474	2.806	.342	11.293	.025	.118	.870	1.231
4 < $324,778	2.562	1.089	.342	.012	.505	5.401	.263	14.410	.025	.114	.873	1.069
Median for sector	2.239	.915	.615	.013	.483	1.705	.389	9.483	.021	.111	.878	1.290
Number of charities	8,792	7,861	8,517	7,241	8,821	634	8,471	2,063	2,063	8,792	8,826	7,542

*DI = Defensive Interval
CG = Contribution and Grants Ratio

**FF = Fundraising Efficiency Ratio
PA = Program to Assets Ratio

LF = Liquid Funds Indicator
E = Endowment Indicator

FX = Fundraising expense ratio

AP = Accounts Payable Aging Indicator
DT = Debt Ratio

MX = Management Expense Ratio

S = Savings Ratio

PX = Program Expense Ratio

Source: Janet S.Greenlee and David Bukovinsky, "Financial Ratios for Use in the Analytical Review of Charitable Organizations", *Ohio CPA Journal* (Jan–Mar 1998): 32–34, 36, 38. Used by permission.

EXHIBIT 7B.5 RATIO BENCHMARKS FOR HEALTH AND HUMAN NEEDS CHARITIES

7B.5 COMPARATIVE BENCHMARK DATA FOR FAITH-BASED ORGANIZATIONS (BASED ON SA AND SFP)

RATIO MEDIANS: FAITH-BASED ORGANIZATIONS

Here are some ratio Medians we have compiled with the assistance of Capin Crouse LLP for Faith-based organizations.

Median Ratio Values - 2004 Fiscal Year					
Organizational Type:	**Churches**	**Faith-Based Colleges**	**Independent Missions**	**Other Mission Organizations**	**All Organizations:** *Avg. of Medians*
Number in sample:	10	9	8	21	
Ratio Categories:					
LIQUIDITY RATIOS					
Cash ratio	1.43	0.78	1.16	1.00	*1.09*
Cash reserve ratio	0.13	0.06	0.07	0.09	0.09
Current ratio	2.14	2.72	6.28	4.62	*3.94*
Asset ratio	0.13	0.12	0.43	0.46	0.28
Target liquidity level	$725,469	$2,409,082	$1,873,769	$1,999,101	$1,751,855
Liquid funds indicator	-1.18	2.02	3.09	3.56	1.87
Cash Flow to Total Debt	0.06	0.08	0.42	0.13	*0.17*
Cash Flow from Operations	$415,897	$892,510	$569,218	$151,790	$507,354
Cash Cycle	-177.80	6.39	90.90	-8.39	*-22.23*
Cash Turnover	-0.90	9.21	2.86	0.95	3.03
Net Liquid Balance	$725,469	$308,871	$980,177	$944,478	$739,749
Working Capital Requirements	($230,843)	$420,435	$3,304,002	$497,681	$997,819
Current Liquidity Index	26.28	15.78	2.14	13.04	*14.31*
Lambda	NA	NA	NA	NA	*NA*
Defensive Interval	74.31	95.60	74.87	114.77	*89.89*
FUNDING RATIOS					
Contribution ratio	0.92	0.17	0.70	0.75	*0.64*
Debt ratio	0.14	0.28	0.17	0.26	0.21
Self-Funding Ratio	0.53	0.38	2.51	1.27	*1.17*
Operating-Funding Balance Ratio	0.11	0.64	-1.23	3.53	0.76
Times Interest Earned	4.56	3.94	36.15	17.55	*15.55*
Long-Term Debt to Capital	0.35	0.21	0.08	0.09	0.18
OPERATING RATIOS					
Return ratio	0.61	0.43	2.77	1.44	*1.32*
Net surplus	$514,382	$394,683	$1,639,383	$232,188	$695,159
Net operating ratio	0.08	0.03	0.06	0.04	*0.05*
Return on assets (ROA)	0.08	0.02	0.14	0.06	0.07
Return on equity (ROE)	0.11	0.02	0.16	0.09	*0.10*
Net Asset reserve ratio	1.09	1.62	0.32	0.50	0.88
Unrestricted Net Asset reserve ratio	0.85	1.10	0.33	0.39	*0.67*
Program expense ratio	0.42	0.82	0.82	0.80	0.72
Support service expense ratio	0.21	0.18	0.18	0.20	*0.19*

Note: NA means not available; lambda requires a forecast of the next period's operating cash flows.

CREDIT RATINGS AGENCIES AND DOE RATIOS

Education organizations have a number of specialized ratios by which they are evaluated. Bond rating agencies and the U.S. Department of Education (DOE) use these specialized ratios in order to assess creditworthiness. Many of these were developed originally by accounting firm Peat Marwick, now part of KPMG LLP. Bank lenders may also use some of these ratios in evaluating your loan requests. We include here a summary done by Fischer, Gordon, Greenlee and Keating, as well as website information for your further study.

In Exhibit 7C.1, note the key ratios that the DOE, KPMG, and the three largest ratings agencies (S&P, Moody's, and Fitch) use in their analysis of private colleges and universities. Exhibit 7C.2 gives the definitions of the items in the ratio numerators and denominators. Following these exhibits, we provide the web addresses for the five nationally recognized statistical ratings organizations (NRSROs) in the United States.

WEBSITES FOR CREDIT RATING AGENCIES

Educational institution and health care ratings are based largely on financial ratios, and credit ratings agencies have specialized ratios on which they rely. Each credit rating agency has a website with information about its ratings criteria and definitions or ratings guidelines. Several of these require a free registration, and each may limit advanced research materials to paid subscribers. The following three credit ratings organizations have been rating public sector (or "public finance") organizations for a number of years:

1. Moody's (www.moodys.com)
2. Standard & Poor's (S&P) (www.standardandpoors.com)
3. Fitch Ratings (www.fitchratings.com)

The following credit ratings organization has started to rate businesses, and may choose to also rate public sector organizations:

A.M. Best (www3.ambest.com/ratings/default.asp)

The following credit ratings organization rates Canadian businesses and a few Canadian "public finance" organizations, is beginning to rate U.S. businesses, and may choose to also rate U.S. public sector organizations:

Dominion Bond Rating Service (www.dbrs.com/intnlweb/)

	Liquidity Ratios	Operating Performance Ratios	Debt and Leverage Ratio
US Department of Education	$\dfrac{\text{Adjusted Expendable Net Assets}}{\text{Total Expenses}}$	$\dfrac{\text{Change in Unrestricted Net Assets}}{\text{Total Unrestricted Revenue}}$	$\dfrac{\text{Modified Net Assets}}{\text{Modified Assets}}$
KPmG et al. (1999)	$\dfrac{\text{Expendable Net Assets}}{\text{Total Expenses}}$	$\dfrac{\text{Change in Unrestricted Net Assets}}{\text{Total Unrestricted Revenue}}$ $\dfrac{\text{Operating Revenue} - \text{Operating Expense}}{\text{Total Unrestricted Operating Revenue}}$	$\dfrac{\text{Expendable Net Aseets}}{\text{Long-Term Debt}}$
Standard & Poor's (2002a)	$\dfrac{\text{Expendable Resource}}{\text{Total Operating Expenses}}$	$\dfrac{\text{Change to Unrestricted Net Assets}}{\text{Total Unrestricted Operating Revenues}}$	$\dfrac{\text{Expendable Resources}}{\text{Total Debt}}$ $\dfrac{\text{Maximum Annual Debt Service}}{\text{Total Operating Expenses}}$
Moody's (2002)	$\dfrac{\text{Expendable Financial Resources}}{\text{Annual Operating Expenses}}$	$\dfrac{\text{Adjusted Unrestricted Income}}{\text{Total Adjusted Unrestricted Revenues}}$	$\dfrac{\text{Expendable Financial Resources}}{\text{Debt}}$ $\dfrac{\text{Adj. Unrest. Income} + \text{Interest} + \text{Depreciation}}{\text{Annual Principal} + \text{Interest Payments}}$ $\dfrac{\text{Available Funds}}{\text{Total Debt}}$
Fitch (2001)	$\dfrac{\text{Available Funds}}{\text{Unrestricted Expenses}}$	$\dfrac{\text{Change to Unrestricted Net Assets}}{\text{Unrestricted Operating Revenues}}$	$\dfrac{\text{Maximum Annual Debt Service}}{\text{Unrestricted Revenues}}$

Source: Mary Fischer, Teresa P. Gordon, Janet Greenlee, and Elizabeth K. Keating, "Measuring Operations: An Analysis of U.S. Private Colleges and Universities' Financial Statements," *Financial Accountability & Management*, 20 (May 2004): 129–151 (Table 1). Used by permission.

EXHIBIT 7C.1 KEY RATIOS FOR EVALUATING PRIVATE COLLEGES AND UNIVERSITIES

Definitions

Adjusted expendable net assets = (unrestricted net assets) + (temporarily restricted net assets) − (annuities, term endowments, and life income funds that are temporarily restricted) − (intangible assets) − (net property, plant and equipment) + (post-employment and retirement liabilities) + (all debt obtained for long-term purposes).

Adjusted unrestricted income = adjusted unrestricted revenues − adjusted unrestricted expenses. Adjustments to revenues include removing sponsored and unsponsored scholarships, including 1.5% of beginning cash and investments instead of investment income and gains, and removing net assets released from restrictions if related to gifts for capital projects. Expenses are adjusted by removing scholarships and followships.

Available Funds = unrestricted and temporarily restricted cash and investments. Fitch says it does not use net assets because of the uncertainty related to the liquidity and value of some assets.

Expendable net assets = expendable resources = expendable financial resources = (total net assets) − (permanently restricted net assets) − (net investment in plant).

Net investment in plant = (net property, plant and equipment) − (long-term debt).

Modified net assets = (unrestricted net assets) + (temporarily restricted net assets) + (permanently restricted net assets) − (intangible assets) − (unsecured related party receivables).

Modified assets = (total assets) − (intangible assets) − (unsecured related-party receivables).

Total unrestricted operating revenue includes only investment income to the extent of the school's endowment spending policy. If there is no policy, investment gains and losses are excluded.

Unrestricted operating revenues (Fitch) = total unrestricted revenues less investment gains (if investment income is a significant source of revenue).

Source: Mary Fischer, Teresa P. Gordon, Janet Greenlee, and Elizabeth K. Keating, "Measuring Operations: An Analysis of U.S. Private Colleges and Universities' Financial Statements," *Financial Accountability & Management*, 20 (May 2004): 129–151 (Table 1, Continued). Used by permission.

EXHIBIT 7C.2 DEFINITIONS FOR KEY RATIOS FOR EVALUATING PRIVATE COLLEGES AND UNIVERSITIES

CHAPTER 8

DEVELOPING OPERATING
AND CASH BUDGETS

8.1 INTRODUCTION

At the core of proficient financial management is the budget. A *budget* is a plan stated in dollar terms. The budgeting process is important because it allocates resources, in turn revealing the program preferences of the parties involved in budgeting. After the budget is developed, a nonprofit organization should use periodic reports to compare budgeted revenues with actual revenues and budgeted expenses with actual expenses. Improving your budgeting and financial reporting processes is a key part of achieving financial management proficiency. The highest award for excellence in management in the Chicago area in 2003 was for an organization that revamped its budgeting and financial reporting processes and then began to solicit foundation grants:

> The move toward greater fiscal responsibility is just one of a series of steps taken in the last year by... [Ivan Medina, executive director of Onward Neighborhood House, a Chicago social-services group] and the board of Onward Neighborhood House, which provides day care and other programs to low-income immigrants in a Chicago neighborhood that is in the midst of gentrification.
>
> In addition to soliciting foundations in order to reduce its reliance on government funds, the group also revamped its accounting and budgeting systems and trimmed costs. The settlement house, founded in 1868, posted deficits for seven of the 10 years before Mr. Medina arrived in 2002. However, in the fiscal year ending in June, the charity had a surplus of about $3,337 on a budget of $1.9-million, says Frank Arredondo, Onward's director of finance. A massive leap in Onward's foundation grants—up more than ninefold in the 2003 fiscal year—is largely responsible for closing the gap.
>
> The turnaround garnered an award for financial-management excellence from the Nonprofit Financial Center, a Chicago group that helps charities improve their management. Onward distinguished itself by adopting a new budgeting system with good financial reporting and accounting controls, says Kenneth Tornheim, a director at the Chicago accounting firm of Ostrow Reisin Berk and Abrams, which sponsored the award. Such solid financial management, Mr. Tornheim says, is particularly important in today's difficult economic times. "If organizations are watching expenses and budgeting properly," he says, "they can stay on course."[1]

There are actually three types of budgets: operating budgets, cash budgets, and capital budgets. When we use the word "budget" without stating which type, we are referring to the operating budget. An *operating budget* shows planned revenues and expenses for a period of time, usually one year. Proficient managers manage not only revenues and expenses but also cash flows, so a cash budget is developed. A *cash budget* shows planned cash inflows, cash outflows, and the amount and duration of cash shortages or surpluses for a certain period of time, usually the next 12 months. Its main value is highlighting the periods of imbalance between cash coming in and cash going out, so that the manager can take early action to manage the cash position. As we saw in Chapter 3, a *capital budget* shows planned fixed asset outlays and other large-dollar, long-lived capital acquisitions such as mergers and acquisitions. This chapter will assist you with the key aspects of the operating and cash budgets.

8.2 OVERVIEW OF THE BUDGETING PROCESS

Before any budgeting takes place, your organization should have formulated its mission, objectives, and strategic plan. In Chapter 3, the basics of these processes were presented. Even if your organization does no formal planning, inertia alone places your organization in a strategic path for specific programs and initiatives. These are translated into operating

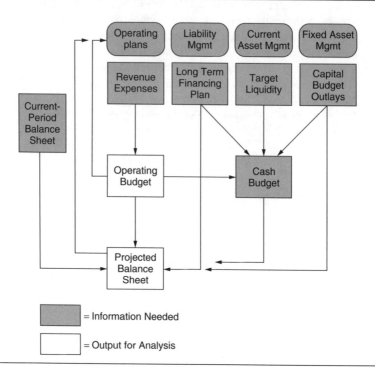

= Information Needed

= Output for Analysis

EXHIBIT 8.1   BUDGETING PROCESS

plans. Those plans, and donors' willingness to support them, give rise to revenues and expenses.

The development of the cash budget is a little more complex. Exhibit 8.1 shows that in addition to operating plans and policies and plans arising from liability management (see Chapter 10), current asset management (see Chapters 11 and 12) and fixed asset management (see Chapter 9) are key inputs.

These same policies and the just-prepared operating budget and cash budgets, along with the current-period statement of financial position (SFP) (or balance sheet), provide the input for projecting the upcoming balance sheet. *If the projected SFP (balance sheet) is unacceptable based on inadequate liquidity or overly high use of borrowed monies this should trigger a revised operating plan.* A projected balance sheet that is "too weak" arises when an organization's capital budget outlays are partly self-funded (reducing cash) and partly financed (increasing borrowing). The remainder of this chapter outlines the context and actual development of the operating and cash budgets.

8.3 ARE NONPROFIT ORGANIZATIONS DOING THEIR BUDGETING PROPERLY?

There is much room for improvement in nonprofit budgeting. In a classic in-depth study of 17 large nonprofit arts, educational, and healthcare agencies, the authors concluded that the budgets were developed in a very basic, even simplistic, fashion, and the budgets were not used for control. Briefly, the study established that budget development and use were deficient.[2]

(a) OPERATING BUDGETS IN PRACTICE.   In Chapter 1 and Appendix 1A, the performance of financial management in faith-based charities was outlined as part of the Lilly study. While 85 percent of responding organizations in the study develop and use an operating budget (showing revenues and expenses), the concern is that 15 percent do not. Budget revisions occur within the fiscal year by 60 percent of the budget-using organizations. This is good practice when uncontrollable external events make previously budgeted amounts useless as standards, but may indicate that budgeting control is largely absent in some organizations. The use of supplemental financial data other than "budget versus actual" variances is seriously lacking. Only 53 percent of budget users monitor their current asset amount on a monthly basis (and merely 12 percent have a target for their current assets), and 41 percent evaluate financial ratios periodically. The fact that roughly 60 percent, or three of five, do not utilize the insights of ratios points to the significant opportunity for improved financial management in the nonprofit sector. There is no good reason for these deficiencies now that personal computers are widely available.

(b) CASH BUDGETS IN PRACTICE.   Nonprofit organizations were rated only fair in their cash forecasting. The most reliable indicator of how an organization rated overall (in all short-term financial management areas) was whether the organization used a computer to monitor or forecast its cash position. Seventy-eight percent *did use* the computer for one or both of these purposes. Using a computer facilitates cash forecasting, which is one of the ways to implement daily active cash management—a practice of most of the Fortune 500 corporations. Short-term investing and borrowing decisions are improved because of a better understanding of how much excess cash exists now and in the future. With longer maturities yielding higher interest rates, the organization is rewarded for knowing how long it can tie excess funds up. Furthermore, we noted that the organization's cash control is facilitated by computer use, because now it may tie its records via personal computer to its bank(s), regularly updating balances and being able to check yesterday's closing balances at the beginning of today's workday.

Only 8 out of 288 organizations developed daily cash forecasts, whereas 22 projected cash using weekly intervals and 94 developed monthly forecasts. At a minimum, your organization should attempt a weekly forecast. If your organization is sizable, make a daily forecast your ultimate goal. The higher short-term interest rates go, the greater the rewards for your effort.

8.4 DEVELOPING AND IMPROVING YOUR BUDGETING PROCESS

This part of the chapter provides guidance on how to develop or improve the budgeting process. It starts with what is needed to prepare an organization for budgeting, then moves to actual budget development, and finally concludes with comments about budget refinements such as zero-based budgeting (ZBB), program budgeting, and rolling budgeting.

(a) PREPARATION FOR BUDGETING (OPERATIONS).   The chief financial officer (CFO) (or board treasurer in small organizations) should attend to the organizational and procedural prerequisites before launching into the actual budget development. The budget director's function shows us what must happen organizationally to get ready for the budget process. The procedural prerequisites show us how the organization mobilizes specific information to ensure successful budget development.

(i) Function of the Budget Director. The individual heading up the budgeting process, whatever his or her title, is generally the CFO of the organization. It is the budget director's responsibility to ensure that a comprehensive oversight system be set up to include these four areas:

1. Make sure everyone involved gets the information he or she needs. This includes any and all forecasts, organizational goals and policies, guidelines, performance data and standards, and any organization-unit plans that impinge on budget items.

2. Set up and maintain the appropriate planning system. The necessary information package includes channeling of appropriate information, plan formulation scheduling, and subunit as well as organization-wide checking of adherence to economic and financial guidelines and to organizational goals. Certainly you would not want one unit using an inflation rate of 2 percent for its forecasts while another assumed a 5 percent rate.

3. Set up and oversee use of models. These models test for the effect of inside and outside forces on achievement of organizational goals. For example, what would happen if interest rates suddenly went up by 2 percent? Down by 2 percent? One multinational nonprofit had to scale back its headquarters operation by 20 percent during a two-year period due to an unexpected *decline* in interest rates; interest revenue earned on cash reserves was funding a significant portion of those operations. Poor endowment performance in the early 2000s brought another reminder to endowed organizations of the value of considering the downside of investment performance.

4. Collect and analyze performance data. For each organizational responsibility center, data should show how plans are or are not being attained over time, and that analysis is made of variances, especially for large expense overruns or large revenue shortfalls. See the section on managing off the budget in Section 8.8 later in this chapter).[3]

Ultimately, the budget director may assume responsibility for each of these four tasks. Indeed, in smaller organizations, he or she may perform each task himself. The organization suffers as the latter two tasks are often left undone due to time constraints. Furthermore, department heads may view the budget negatively because it is imposed on them without adequate input on their part.

(ii) Procedural Prerequisites. Before "budget time" rolls around each year, there are three preparatory steps that you may need to take.

1. *Establish budget policy.* This step does not need to be done annually, but if your organization has never thought these concepts through, it is time to do that before setting another budget.

2. *Gather archival data.* This step involves assembling necessary documents from the financial reporting system and fund development office.

3. *Initiate data collection.* We perform this step to get the appropriate offices working on collecting data that are not normally part of the financial reporting process.

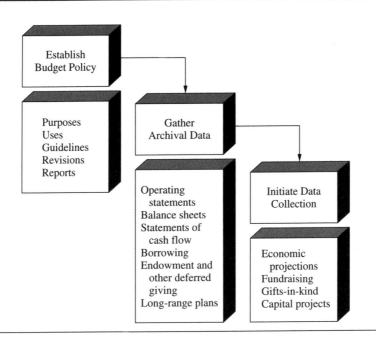

EXHIBIT 8.2   STEPS PRIOR TO BUDGET DEVELOPMENT

Please study Exhibit 8.2 to set in your mind the sequence of these activities as a framework for our discussion.

(b) STEP 1: ESTABLISH A BUDGET POLICY.   Every organization should have a budget policy that spells out the purposes of its operating budget, the uses for that budget, guidelines for budget development, revision policy, and the frequency and nature of budgetary reports.

(i) Purposes of a Budget.   Reviewing the purposes of an operating budget will convince financial and nonfinancial personnel of the indispensability of budgets. Recall that your operating budget sets out your organization's plan, expressed in monetary terms. Both revenue and expense budgets should be carefully developed and detailed. Some funders will even address budget preparation in their legal contracts.

Budgets are also necessary administrative, financial, and program management tools for nonprofit managers. In most cases, there should be individual budgets for each program or separate activity, which fold into a single, consolidated budget for the organization as a whole.[4] In general, the main purposes for operating budgets are

- Priority control

  o Budget setting should follow mission and program establishment and should not be done simultaneously with those activities.

  o Budgets reveal priorities because they indicate resource allocations and reallocations.

- Fiscal control

  ○ Limited funds means need for effective controls over revenue and expenses. Budgets serve this purpose best, in that they allow for regular comparison of budgeted to actual expenditures.

- Administrative control

  ○ Nonprofit organizations established to serve public purposes that are often intangible or expensive to measure.

  ○ Detailed budgets provide administrators with monetary control where traditional for-profit controls (price-less-cost profit margin targets) are neither possible nor practical.

- Program control

  ○ Outside funders may require separate budgets for each program they support.

  ○ Funding sources may limit spending flexibility by restricting expenditures to specified categories and line items, and they may request that written budget modifications be approved in advance.

- Audit control

  ○ Outside funds often have specific expenditure restrictions and compliance requirements.

  ○ These restrictions and requirements apply particularly for organizations receiving government funds, where budgets are utterly essential to ensure that the annual audit will determine that the nonprofit organization complied with funding-source guidelines.

- Survival

  ○ If the organization makes unallowable expenditures that must be repaid to the funding source, liquidity problems will ensue.

  ○ How will you know if expenses are going to be covered until it is too late, if you have no budgetary projection?

(ii) Uses of the Budget.   Lack of a budget has several negative repercussions; the organization may face one or more of these situations:

- *Overspending.* This leads to the situation in which the organization is hit with unexpected operating deficits and a cash crunch, as spending quickly outruns incoming revenues.

- *Underspending.* This results in the need to return unspent funds to funding sources.

- *Mistimed spending.* Mistimed spending is the failure to meet required program or activity goals on time, possibly resulting from the fear that revenues are inadequate to cover expenses.

- *Misappropriated spending.* This includes spent funds outside allowable cost categories, or when spending is audited it is discovered that questioned costs may have to be repaid to funding sources.

(c) BUDGET PREPARATION PHILOSOPHY AND PRINCIPLES. Several decisions related to budget philosophy and principles are to be used in revising and reporting budget-related data. *Budget philosophy* involves what approach will be taken, what level of aggregation to use, and the "bottom-line" target to strive for.

The budget approach may be top-down or bottom-up, or a combination of both. The approach used will drive the assignment of budget development responsibilities and level of participation. We advocate the combination approach. When organizations impose budgets on departments, the approach is definitely *top-down*. When department heads submit their budgets, and these are added together to arrive at a consolidated budget, we have a purely *bottom-up* approach. *A combination approach* involves communication of economic and organizational assumptions to be made by all budget participants (to ensure consistency), but department heads have great latitude in establishing budgetary amounts. These are subject to review and mutually agreed adjustment. Participation and involvement of budget managers is essential, and the absence of their involvement leads to budgets that are weak and ineffective as control tools.

The budget's *format and level of aggregation* also must be determined. The minimum requirement here is to have a *consolidated budget* (organization-wide). This budget, sometimes called *a line item budget,* should list the major sources of revenues and the expenses by type. The expenses are listed by what are sometimes called "natural expense elements": rent, utilities, salaries and wages, insurance, and so forth. Budgets done at this aggregated level of detail help prevent overspending or underspending and provide the minimal planning, coordination, and control functions. In the revenue and expense budget illustration later in this chapter (Exhibit 8.5), we will show how an organization develops a consolidated budget.

As organizations grow and add support staff and accounting and computer systems, they begin to develop a *subunit budget* for each program, department, or activity. Let's take a look at two logical subunit budgets that you may wish to develop: Program budgets and functional budgets.

Program budgets spell out revenues and expenses for each of the organization's major programs. Having information in this format is tremendously helpful for two reasons: it makes program allocations and reallocations obvious, and it makes cost-benefit comparisons for individual programs much easier. We will return to program budgeting later in the chapter. If each program is operated by a different division or department within the organization, the divisional or departmental budgets accomplish the same thing as program budgets.

Functional budgets show revenues and expenses for each separate functional area. In a business, the major functional areas are marketing, finance, and production. In a non-profit, these might be development, finance, and services. The services subunit can then be further broken down into program subunits, if desired. The main advantage is that each area can be held responsible for costs, revenues versus costs (net revenue), or net revenue versus investment. After-the-fact comparisons not only can pinpoint efficiency or inefficiency in areas such as fundraising, but also provide needed input for redeployment of resources for the following year. Although they are not considered major functional areas, support areas such as human resources and information systems can also be budgeted for separately in the functional budgeting system.

Consider as your budget target the level of net revenue the organization strives for. On a consolidated budget, should we budget a surplus, break-even, or deficit? Peoria Rescue Ministries, the highest-rated homeless shelter in the Lilly study, strives for and achieves a budget surplus each year. This provides internal funding for program expansion and related capital projects.

Some other organizations project a "balanced budget," even though operating revenues exceed operating expenses. The "plug figure" that balances the budget is called something like "Contingencies," which may be a means of forced savings to help build up cash reserves over a period of several years. If all goes as planned, these organizations will report a surplus for the year (positive change in net assets) on its statement of activity (SA), assuming there are not non-operating items such as capital campaigns or investment gains or losses.

Here is another way of having a balanced budget but saving for known future expenditures: Assuming that your organization includes an expense account for depreciation, it could be using a balanced budget target, and the amount reported as depreciation expense (which is a noncash charge, merely a bookkeeping adjustment to match the using of equipment with the revenues it helps generate) could be set aside each year in a special fund. When new capital equipment must be purchased, the monies saved in the fund can provide the financing. If all goes as planned, your organization would be reporting a break-even ($0) SA at the end of the year, using accrual-based accounting, since depreciation expense will be shown on the SA.

In some years, you may actually budget a deficit. An organization with long-term financial problems, but that has a significant liquid reserve built up, may continue its essential programs while it repositions itself over a period of several years. Eventually, it should plan to break even or even run a surplus.

Anthony and Young in their budgeting presentation, provide some excellent guidance on the subject of how to set a budget target.[5] They argue that in most years we should plan spending to match the available resources, by not overspending or underspending. Therefore, a balanced budget should be the rule, with some acceptable exceptions. (It is assumed that the nonprofit is recognizing the depreciation of fixed assets.) They offer five reasons why most organizations *should not consistently* plan a sizable budget *surplus*, because that may indicate:

1. To clients that are probably not getting the service quality or quantity they might desire.

2. To donors that possibly they gave too much.

3. To all stakeholders a lack of achievement on the part of the organization, rather than good management, given that most nonprofits have much greater demand on services than they can possibly meet.

4. To clients that the organization is charging too high a price, in cases where it is charging for services.

5. To management that it may need to consider the possibility of the organization becoming a for-profit business.

None of the reasons should preclude your organization from planning a small surplus, however, which we view as a superior target as compared to a balanced budget.

What about consistently projecting a deficit? On the surface, it appears that many nonprofits are in a perpetual financial squeeze, using their revenue shortfall as an effective fundraising ploy. Budgeting a deficit is not advisable as a normal practice, with some years being exceptions. For one thing, if budgeted amounts are realized as actual amounts, you are reducing the flexibility you would have had for spending the income from your endowment, or draining cash from your liquid reserve, which you must replenish (i.e., run a surplus or do extra fundraising appeals) later. Some faith-based organizations and some nonsectarian nonprofits operate under what Peter Drucker terms the "God will provide" mind-set. Certainly events can turn out better than expected, and God does provide—but as a principle, we should prefer receiving God's provision of the funds *beforehand* in response to faith to receipt after/during a certain period. Second, it is interesting that some colleges have had to retrench and even close down because of a failure to recognize the need to prefund expenditures. If an organization is impelled to initiate or expand programs for which it does not have anticipated revenues to cover, it can build a preventive mechanism into place. As the organization moves toward the end of its fiscal year, and if it has not received sufficient funds to meet the shortfall, it needs to immediately (1) reduce spending on the new program(s), and (2) recognize that it has suffered from a misdirection.

The practical reality for many organizations is that they have not fully exploited their fundraising ability, either through underinvestment in fundraising or unfocused fundraising. This underinvestment issue came out loud and clear in the Lilly study. Most organizations indicated that the main reason they do not do better in reaching their financial objective is "insufficient or ineffective fundraising." If new opportunities arise that match potential donors' desires to help, the development office may be able to raise additional funds to cover the added program expenses. This ability to raise additional funds is plausible, despite the "full mailbox" and "donor fatigue" syndromes, and appears to be more characteristic of faith-based organizations than of other charities.

In technical terms, think about your organization having a "fundraising net revenue function"—although there are "diminishing returns" to additional expenditures for fundraising, certainly the funds raised are almost always greater than the costs to raise them. The implication: Your organization can often raise more money if particular opportunities present themselves, in particular, one-time "golden opportunities." Fundraising experience shows that people give more freely to great opportunities than to great needs. However, this is much easier done over a long period of time, not on a short-run, late-in-the-fiscal-year basis.

Anthony and Young do recognize these exceptions to their recommendation that organizations propose a balanced budget:

- *Discretionary revenue.* Basically, this refers to occasions when intensified fundraising can raise more funds. The key is not to rely on this too often or for large amounts (unless you are really thinking about doing this to fund a one-time opportunity).

- *"Hard money" versus "soft money"*
  - Revenue from annual gifts or short-term grants for research are both considered "soft money" in that onset of recession or other factors may cause severe declines; a recent survey of nonprofits in the Philadelphia metro area found that donations were their single most risky source of funds. Another survey of Oregon nonprofits found: "despite successful fund-raising efforts, 30 percent of nonprofits reported they have reduced services to meet operational costs."[6]
  - One implication might be to budget surpluses during economic booms.
  - Another implication is to build up loyalty and close relationships with clients and/or donors.

- *Short-run fluctuations.* Count on reserves to tide you through any unexpectedly lean years, in which a proposed deficit might be budgeted; this is why it is not somehow immoral or unethical to run a surplus in some years as well.

- *The promoter.* This is the idea of budgeting more expense than revenue, knowing hotshots can make up the difference; probably not wise, as nothing goes up forever!

- *Deliberate capital erosion.* Part of your permanent capital is being depleted by operational overspending. This approach is acceptable in limited circumstances, e.g., a cure has been found, so this program can be dissolved.

We would add this: If an organization is really program-driven, it might see unfunded needs and foresee anticipated new service delivery several years ahead. It will then build up a "critical mass" of financial resources with which to launch the new service(s). Doing this implies running surpluses for several years.

(i) Budget Revisions. Your organization should have a policy on what circumstances occasion a budget revision. Strike a balance here—don't make it so easy to get a revision approved that you lose the expense control of a budget, but recognize that environmental changes make some budget plans unreasonable. The budget serves best as a control device when targets are difficult but achievable. We address using the budget as a management and control tool later.

(ii) Interim Reports. Again, you should prescribe what reports will be made to compare actual revenues and costs to budgeted amounts, and with what frequency. Financial reports are also covered in the next chapter.

To recap our discussion of the first step preparatory to budget development, establishing budget policy, we addressed the purposes of its operating budget, the uses for that budget, guidelines for budget development, the budget revision policy, and the frequency and nature of budgetary reports. Not every organization thinks these issues through, but your budgeting process will be more valuable in supporting program delivery and run more smoothly if you have done the groundwork. We move into the data collection phase next.

(d) STEP 2: GATHER ARCHIVAL DATA.   You will consult a number of data sources in your budget development. Here are some of the basic ones:

- Strategic plan and long-range financial plan
- Operating statements: past budgets and statements of activity

  o   Revenues

  o   Expenses

- Statements of financial position (also called balance sheets)
- Statements of cash flows, if any have been completed
- Mortgage and other borrowing data
- Endowment and deferred giving data
- Previously done projections

(e) STEP 3: ASSIGN OR BEGIN COLLECTION OF OTHER AREA DATA INPUT OR PROJECTIONS. The degree of delegation possible in getting necessary economic, labor, fundraising, gifts-in-kind, and capital budget data will depend on the budget approach profiled earlier (top-down, bottom-up, or combination). Allow some lead time for this step in the process—some organizations start this process six months before the budget approval date.

- Economic projections[7]

  - Income and discretionary income, such as local information if your scope is localized (e.g., you operate single local symphony, homeless shelter, retirement center, or "meals on wheels"). Maybe the best you can do is extrapolate, so get recent historical buying power index data from a recent issue of *Sales & Marketing Management* (buying power indexes are published in a special issue once a year).

  - Interest rates, including short-term bank rates,[8] mortgage rates, and charitable gift annuity rates[9] (if applicable).

  - Inflation, such as economy-wide inflation rates and key input (e.g., commodity) price trends.[10]

  - Labor cost and productivity, including wages and salaries, nonprofit differentials, local differentials, and productivity.

  - Charitable giving (gives check on fundraising, covered below), including national data, regional or state data (if available), and trends.[11]

  - Exchange rates if your organization operates internationally.[12]

- Fundraising

  - Projected annual campaign receipts
  - Projected special appeal receipts
  - Projected capital campaign receipts
  - Projected bequests and other deferred gifts

- Gifts-in-kind
- Capital projects

Once the appropriate assignments for these vital inputs are made, it is important to follow up to ensure that the worksheets are finalized on a timely basis. If the preparatory work lags, the whole budget process is held up. Budget preparation is stressful enough without having analysts working excessive overtime.

8.5 SETTING THE BUDGETARY AMOUNTS

(a) WHAT DO I NEED TO KNOW ABOUT FORECASTING? A budget is a plan, and any plan involves an implicit forecast. How much in donations and other revenues will we take in next year? How much should we project for expenses, given our operating plans? These questions motivate the planner to gain a basic understanding of forecasting techniques. We use Exhibit 8.3 to profile the basic forecasting methods. Space does not permit a thorough treatment of these techniques, but we present the basics.[13]

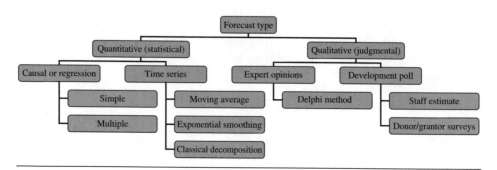

EXHIBIT 8.3   FORECASTING METHODS

Quantitative, or statistical, forecasting methods may be divided into causal (or regression) methods and time series methods. A *causal method* is one in which the analyst has identified a cause factor for the item he or she is trying to forecast. In the case of simple regression, we have only one causal variable. For example, donations (forecast variable) may be linked to personal income (causal variable). *Regression analysis* may be used to "fit" an equation to make the relationship precise and usable for generating a forecast. In our example, we might find that the following relationship for donations and disposable income, if we measure donations and (average household) disposable income in thousands of dollars:[14]

$$\text{Donations} = \$500 + 1.2(\text{disposable income})$$

Let's say that disposable income is $40,000. Donations would then be:

$$\text{Donations} = \$500 + 1.2(40) = \underline{\$548}$$

Our forecast for donations would be $548,000. Notice that because we are forecasting current donations based on current disposable income, the only way to generate a forecast for donations is to get a (hopefully accurate) forecast of disposable income.

A *multiple regression model* illustrates the case of multiple causal factor models. Here, instead of one causal variable, we have two or more. Donations might now be linked to the number of individuals in the "empty nest" stage of the family life cycle, along with our original disposable income variable.

Time series models, in which a pattern from the past is extended into the future, are often more complex. Of the group, a *moving average* is the easiest to understand. A three-day moving average is just the arithmetic average of the most recent three actual values. If your donations for the past three months are $45,000, $50,000, and $60,000, then the moving average forecast would be:

$$\text{3-day moving average} = \frac{(\$45,000 + \$50,000 + \$60,000)}{3}$$

$$= \underline{\$51,666.67}$$

When the next month's actual value comes in, you update the moving average by adding the new value and dropping the oldest value. In our example, if the new value is $65,000, the 3-day moving average becomes:

$$3\text{-day moving average} = \frac{(\$50,000 + \$60,000 + \$65,000)}{3}$$
$$= \underline{\$58,333.33}$$

The moving average has increased by $6666.66 (=$58,333.33 − $51,666.67), as the most recent number ($65,000) is significantly higher than the earlier number that has now dropped out of the calculation ($45,000).

Exponential smoothing and *classical decomposition* models are beyond our scope, but information on them may be found in any forecasting book.[15] As with moving average methods, these time series methods basically extrapolate the past into the future.

There are three occasions in which to use times series models. One is when you cannot figure out what logical causes affect your forecast variable. Another is when whatever causes your forecast variable to change in value also steadily increases or decreases with the passage of time. The time variable (e.g., 2006 is year 1, 2007 is year 2) tends to capture the ongoing effects of the undetected cause variable(s), so in this situation go ahead and use a time series model. Finally, time series models make sense when you have many small-dollar items to forecast, making the application of causal or qualitative modeling too time-consuming and expensive.

(b) REVENUES. Before budgeting expenses, a reasonable amount for revenues should be estimated to set the revenue budget. An accounting definition of revenues is "inflows or other enhancements of assets of an entity or settlements of its liabilities (or a combination of both) from delivering or producing goods, rendering services, or other activities that constitute the entity's ongoing major or central operations."[16] Be careful, though, when laying out the revenues for the operating budget. The items included are slightly different from the SA we presented in Chapter 6. *Excluded* from the SA are increases in the entity's net assets that result from "peripheral or incidental transactions." These are considered "gains," not revenues. However, *do include* both revenues and anticipated gains or losses when estimating budgetary sources of funds to cover expenses. We will reinforce the importance of including both of these later in the section on cash budgeting.

Many organizations budget for revenues and other inflows an amount some percentage above last year's, if that's been the pattern of growth historically. This policy is dangerous in recession or when important drivers of your operating results change. Besides, as we have shown in the forecasting section, you may gain accuracy with the aid of computer-based statistical forecasting models. Applying statistical modeling is one of those projects that are ideal for a college intern or for college course consulting, as most college and university business schools offer business statistics courses to provide basic training to their students in the art and science of forecasting.

(c) EXPENSES. Technically, "expenses are outflows or other using up of assets or incurrences of liabilities (or a combination of both) from delivering or producing goods, rendering services, or carrying out other activities that constitute the entity's ongoing major or central operations,"[17] When arriving at budget amounts, look at inflationary increases, those changes in the environment that you can foresee, program changes you anticipate, additional resources required, and labor cost increases. Remember that labor-related expense is usually your big-ticket item and should be estimated carefully.

Because the budget may have to be adjusted when significant environmental changes occur within the year or when establishing flexible budgets, we need to understand variable, semivariable, and fixed costs.

- *Variable costs.* Costs that vary with each unit of activity—labor in manufacturing process (if production increases 10 percent, total labor costs will increase 10 percent because labor cost per unit does not change). Of course, when the cost of the labor increases, total labor costs will rise proportionally.

- *Semivariable costs.* These costs increase as activity increases, but not in direct relationship to it; for example, maintenance costs—machinery may have some base level of maintenance that must be performed regardless of how intensively it is used, and beyond that maintenance expense varies with machinery usage; the latter component may not be proportional—doubling the usage may only increase the maintenance expense by 1.5 times.

- *Fixed costs.* These costs remain the same regardless of the level of activity: for example, rent, insurance, top management salaries, property tax for a facility, depreciation expense on previously purchased fixed assets. Even if service delivery is doubled, the amount of this cost element will not change. It is important to note that fixed costs are fixed within the short term—say, one year. Over the long run, there are no fixed costs. In areas experiencing high inflation rates, even those costs considered to be fixed costs may spiral upward quickly (as in the case of rent or salaries).

What is the relevance of these cost types to expense budgeting? We have already noted that a budget is a plan. When laying out the planned expenses, our method is simple:

- State expected level of activity (number of units of items produced or delivered).

- Then estimate how much of the costs will be based on this activity level, so that the budgeted amount accurately reflects whether this item is a variable, semivariable, or fixed cost. Overhead costs are especially important to estimate if your budget development is in support of a grant proposal.[18]

- This whole process takes on added importance when doing *flexible budgeting,* because in that method of budgeting one must calculate the amount of each expense element for various levels of activity—not just the "most likely" or projected level of activity. (See Section 8.6)

(d) EXTENDED EXAMPLE OF ACTUAL BUDGET DEVELOPMENT.   We use the actual budget development of Peoria Rescue Ministries (PRM) to illustrate revenue and expense projections. PRM was one of the top financial management performers identified in the Lilly study.[19]

Before portraying the operating budget, we first demonstrate PRM's capital budget worksheet in Exhibit 8.4. (See Chapter 9 for more on capital budgeting.) We include the capital budgeting template (Exhibit 8.4) to show how the capital budget is incorporated into the operational budgeting process. Exhibit 8.5, the operating budget, shows the prior year (year-to-date actual plus prior December's actual amount), the current budget, and the projected budget. The "rationale" column is especially helpful for your study: It gives background or the person responsible for developing the figure, as well as factors considered in developing the budgeted amounts. Information from both the operating

CAPITAL BUDGET 20XX			
MINISTRY MONTH	PURPOSE FOR ITEM	PRIORITY*	AMOUNT

*PRIORITY   1 = MUST HAVE TO CONTINUE MINISTRY

2 = NOT ESSENTIAL IN THIS YEAR, BUT WILL NEED NEXT YEAR

3 = MINISTRY EXPANSION

prm www.peoriarescue.org

EXHIBIT 8.4 PEORIA RESCUE MINISTRIES CAPITAL BUDGET TEMPLATE

budget and capital budget will be necessary for development of the cash budget, which is discussed next.

Note from our example schedule several things that will help you develop an operating budget.

1. Some items are *estimated,* others are *calculated.* Estimations involve subjective judgment. Calculations involve (a) finding a historical relationship between one variable (some measure of activity) and the expense element, or (b) simply extrapolating the historic growth rate.

2. The feedback from this year's year-to-date actual (which is annualized by adding in the 12-month prior year actual amount) is used to help estimate the new year's proposed budget. That is, we don't simply make a mindless adjustment based on a historical growth pattern, but adjust up or down the calculated amount where appropriate.

Description	Dec94 Plus Ytd/Nov/95	Rationale	Budget95	Budget96
Income				
Individual Contributions	471099	Development & General Director Plans Based upon Previous Year	500000	480000
Church Contributions	110898	Same as Above	85000	115000
Business Organizations	57237	Dev & Gen Director Plans Based upon Trend and Business Contacts	65000	60000
Restricted Gifts	28230	Spec Projects Planned for Coming Year. Dev Director Input	75000	80000
Gifts in Kind	16624	Past History and Planned or Known Gifts Coming	25000	15000
Misc.	5184	Gifts Too Small to Identify, of Unknown Nature. Past History Guidelines	7000	7000
Education Contribution	450	Based upon Past History and Planned Appeals. Gen Director and Dev Director	10000	500
Internation. Aid Contrib.	11954	Only Budget Known Entities in Next Year and Past Trends	0	15000
Vending	3042	Based upon Our Vending Machines, New Additions, and Projected Prices	3000	3000
Speaking	11064	Gen Director Input Based upon Previous Years and New Contacts for 1996	8000	10000
Evening Offering	5017	Based Entirely on Past History with Alterations for Additional/Fewer Services	5000	5000
Life Ins. Premium	4135	Gen Director Input Based upon Board History and New Projected Policies	4000	4500
Interest	4256	Bank Interest Based upon Projected Rates and Our Cash Flow	3000	4000
Sale of Goods	10889	Dev Director Input and Input from Special Items for Sale	100000	10000
Pallet Sales	43078	Entirely on New Projections—New Contracts for Pallets—History Not App)	0	50000
Livestock Sales	12546	Farm Director/Gen Director Input on Planned Livestock Sales	13000	5000
Shop Income	2574	Farm Director and Gen Director Plans for Shop Sales	0	2500
Memorials	16834	Past History Guidelines	20000	25000
Special Events	49330	Dev Director. Gen Director Plans for Spec Events and Proj Income	75000	50000
Book Sales	6473	Dev Director Plans for Book Sales Based upon His Plan	1000	6000
Consulting Fees	2911	Use History and Known Contracts	1000	3000
Trusts	3806	Dev Director Known Trust Payouts and New Trusts to Start	5000	4000
Special Appeals	48523	In House Special Appeals Planned Using Last Year as a Guide	10000	50000
Wills & Estates	35000	Dev Director Known Est Plus Est of New Estates Based upon History	5000	35000

EXHIBIT 8.5   PEORIA RESCUE MINISTRIES TOTAL MINISTRIES BUDGET FOR A GIVEN YEAR

Description	Dec94 Plus Ytd/Nov/95	Rationale	Budget95	Budget96
Cilco Mailing	1976	Did Not Use	20000	
New Donor Acq.	36198	Planned by Gen & Dev Directors Using Previous Year Plus Special Plans	20000	35000
Individual Cont. S.A.	45235	Out of House Special Appeals Planned by Development Dir		45000
Sale Wood Prod.	47325	Farm and Gen Director Plans for Wood Chip Promotion and Known Contracts		50000
Sale Wood Chips	9139	Same as Wood Products		20000
Food	7299	Past Trends and Planned Appeals		7000
Meals Thk., Christ	2354	Development Director Plans for Special Thks Christmas Appeal for Dinners		2500
Emergency Assist.	1380	Budgeted Based upon Past History		1000
Total Income	111206		1060000	1200000
Expenses				
Salaries & Wages	407513	Gen Director Review Staffing Needs Factors Increases with Consult Directors	400000	450000
Fringe Benefits	61853	Gen Director Reviews Benefit Costs and Sets Budget	96000	68000
FICA Taxes	30899	Bus Manager Factors Payroll Taxes Based upon Payroll Amounts	32000	34000
Equip Pur. & Rep.	22384	Gen Director with Consultation of Equipment Needs with Ministry Directors	25000	75000
Office Supplies	24937	Gen Director/Bus Manager Review Needs Project Amount	20000	25000
Program Materials	9593	Ministry Directors Determine Program Consult with Gen Director for Amt	16000	10000
Travel & Transportation	19467	Gen Director/Bus Manager Budgets Based on Mileage Allow and Vehicle Expense	18000	20000
Professional Expense	13817	Gen Director Based upon Needs of Ministry with Consult of Ministry Directors	13000	15000
Stipends	9290	Gen Director & Ministry Directors Determine Based on Personnel on Program	10000	10000
Property Tax	1556	N/a Unless We Own Property for Profit Business	1000	
Building Improvement	46	Normally Capital Unless Small in Nature/Gen Director Budgets	20000	
Equipment Repair	0	Gen Director/Ministry Directors Determine Based upon Plan/Needs	4000	
Misc.	25640	Items that Cannot Be Budgeted in Other Areas Bus/Mgr Determines	35000	26000
Insurance	28557	Gen Dir Based on Ins Needs and Projected Ins Coverage-Increases Considered	30000	29000
Building Maintenance	13672	Routine Maint Ministry Directors/Gen Director Projects on Need for 1996	11000	15000

EXHIBIT 8.5   PEORIA RESCUE MINISTRIES TOTAL MINISTRIES BUDGET FOR A GIVEN YEAR (*continued*)

Description	Dec94 Plus Ytd/Nov/95	Rationale	Budget95	Budget96
Conferences	7392	Gen Director Projects Based on Ministry Needs	8000	8000
Electric	32806	Gen Director/Bus Mgr Determine Based on Current Amt and Future Rates	35000	30000
Natural Gas	10706	Same as Above	12000	15000
Water	4398	Same as Above	5000	5300
Telephone	11583	Same as Above	10000	12000
Janitorial Supplies	5006	Gen Director and Ministry Directors Based on Square Footage and Each Building	7000	5000
Life Ins. Premium	4109	Correlates with Life Ins Prem in Income Side Should Be Same or Approx Same	4000	4200
Education Fund	3682	Correlates with Life Ins Prem in Income/Gen Director Determines	10000	4000
Vending	1706	Expense of Vending Income. Correlates with Income for Profit	2000	2000
Food	1995	Determined After Income Budgeted. Determined by Gen Director	6000	2000
Livestock Production	1945	Costs Assoc with Farm Directors Assessment of Income	8000	2000
Shop Expense	3335	Farm Director Based upon Shop Income and His Assessment of Needs	10000	4000
Pallet Production	2679	Farm Director/Gen Director Based upon Production Income and Needs	5000	5000
Promotional Material	74806	Newsletters/Ministry Promotion/ Ads/Brochures-Determined Dev Dir & Gen Dir	45000	80000
Spec. Appeals External	22316	Dev Director Based upon External Appeals Planned	0	25000
Wood Chip Prod. Exp.	13367	Farm Director Cost Associated with Wood Chip Project	0	15000
ADP Charge	1002	Bus Mgr Based on Head Count for Payroll Processing	0	
Book Sales Expense	7554	Dev Director Based on Planned Book Prod Costs	0	1000
Medical Client Expense	2963	Gen Director/Ministry Director Based on Client Load	0	3000
Smart Start Expense	826	WPC Ministry Director/Gen Director	0	2000
International Aid	2526	For Special Int Needs Determined by Plan of General Director	0	3000
International Supp.	20941	For Int Ministries Budgeted by Gen Director Based on Proj Needs and Staff	0	21000
Gift in Kind Expense	2064	For Preparing Merch/Equip Donated for Sale-Projected by General Director	0	2500
Emergency Assistance	1158	Gen Director Based on History and Projected Needs	0	1000
Total Expenses	1005176		1000000	1155000
Net Income/Deficit	106884		60000	45000

Source: Reprinted, by permission, from David L. McFee for Peoria Rescue Ministries.

Exhibit 8.5   Peoria Rescue Ministries Total Ministries Budget for a Given Year (*continued*)

3. PRM budgets for a surplus. Notice that PRM does not show depreciation expense, so some of this surplus will be eventually be used for plant and equipment replacement. Other portions are for (a) intrayear cash receipts versus cash disbursements imbalances, (b) to offset any negative developments on either the revenue (unfavorable variance being less-than-budgeted amounts) or expense fronts (unfavorable variance being greater-than-budgeted amounts), and (c) to fund anticipated growth. PRM is growing, in total revenues, at double-digit percentage rates from year to year.

This example also verifies one of our main points in this chapter: The main uses for operating budgets are to set out a plan in monetary terms, anticipate possible problems, and benchmark actual performance.

(e) BUDGET APPROVAL. Once a budget is agreed on by all parties, assuming some participation has been allowed, a commitment is fostered. The budget agreement itself signals bilateral commitment between an operating unit and top management. The PRM budget approval process is indicative of good practice.[20] After the initial preliminary budget amounts are determined, a budget meeting is set with the PRM board's finance committee. This meeting includes an intensive line-by-line ministry analysis—with input to modify or change programs and budget amounts if warranted. At that meeting, the executive director and the business manager are present, and a financial spreadsheet is "live" on a computer screen so the preliminary figures can be adjusted immediately and a new "bottom line" for the consolidated budget can be arrived at. In this way, the finance committee members can conduct what-if scenarios and see readily how a change to the budget affects the overall budget. At the conclusion of this meeting, each person is given a copy of the proposed budget for further review preparatory to its consideration by the overall board. Copies are mailed to all board members who are not on the finance committee. The overall board receives the proposed budget at its December meeting, which is usually at least two weeks after the finance committee meeting. PRM also prepares its capital budget in conjunction with the operating budget, in order that program personnel may plan for program needs as they develop their future programs.

(f) BUDGET VARIANCE REPORTS AND RESPONSES. We noted in Chapter 7 that the first level of your financial reporting, done for internal users, is the budget variance analysis (BVA) report. This report is first in importance for managerial usefulness. Typically, the BVA is associated only with the operating budget, and we begin our discussion with that budget.

(i) Operating Budget. This process should be ongoing on a monthly basis during the year to avoid surprises at year-end. Variances are the difference between actual (what happened) and budgeted (what was expected). A variance is a symptom that may be linked to many different problems, some more severe than others. Someone must identify the reason(s) behind any significant favorable (actual better than budget, which would be revenues greater than budget, expenses less than budget) or unfavorable variance. Being alerted to ongoing or emerging *significant* problems enables the manager to initiate corrective action. Sometimes the cause of the variance implies an obvious correction: Uncollected pledges receivable suggests more and firmer follow-up contacts and better front-end donor education. Other times the variance springs from uncontrollable factors, such as a change in exchange rates (for which no protection was provided through a

- Weekly or daily variance reports should be prepared for selected items over which management has control and that are vital to the success of the organization. Waiting until month-end is sometimes too late. For example, radio and TV stations conducting telethons give constantly updated totals for management use and for prompting donor response.

- Show month's variance (both % and $) to the left of the revenue line item, and the year-to-date or full-year variance to the right of the account information. A brief explanation can be included to the right of the tabulated variances if space permits; otherwise provide the information below the table.

- Implement management-by-exception by highlighting variances that pass threshold tests—say, greater than 10 percent of the budgeted amount or greater than $500.

- Highlight positive variances as well as negative ones. Usually, show unfavorable variance numbers (lower revenue or higher expense amounts) within brackets; favorable variances should not be bracketed.

- Include in the written explanations not only variance cause(s), but also what will be done to correct the problem.

- Show enough detail so that offsetting variances within an expense category does not disguise underlying problems. For example, if "donations" is shown only in total, a mail campaign positive variance may be offset by a negative variance on face-to-face fundraising, and no corrective action gets triggered for the latter.

- Highlight controllable items for special management attention.

- Recognize that a variance may signal a faulty budget or a change in the environment, which should trigger the development of a revised budget to guide the remainder of the fiscal year.

Exhibit 8.6   Variance Report Checklist

hedge, such as an interest rate swap), or a drop in interest rates earned on cash reserves, and the organization will have to make offsetting adjustments in controllable areas. Of course, information from this year's results feeds back into new budget development even before the year is closed. Generally, the variance reports should conform to the checklist shown in Exhibit 8.6, with some pointers applying to monthly variance reports and others applying to weekly, monthly, or annual variance reports.

In some organizations, the budget development and variance analysis processes are highly political. What can be done to eliminate political conflict? The following five precautions, some of which must be taken at the time the departmental or program budgets are developed, may be helpful:

1. Have final budgets prepared by a cross-departmental committee, and then have everyone affected by the budgets review them.

2. Have the manager that prepared the budget explain the variance. Whoever oversees the reporting process should make sure actuals are not massaged to hit budgeted amounts.

3. Include and retain budget development assumptions in the final budget documentation.

4. Do not blame departments or individuals for variances, but focus attention on positive ideas for reversing the problems.

5. Find the causes of the variances, and to the extent they are linked to a faulty budget, ensure that the next budget that is developed is done on a more accurate basis. Also, instead of blaming someone for the inaccurate budget, develop a

revised budget. Some organizations persist in estimating expenses and then writing down a revenue figure to match total expenses. This practice makes revenue variance analysis almost useless—unless the organization sets within-year targets that serve as control points if and when the revenue forecast is not realized.[21]

We will return to the specifics of presentation format and what generic actions your organization can take if revenues are below budget or expenses are running above budget in the later section in this chapter entitled "Managing Off the Budget."

(ii) Capital Budget. We showed an example of a capital budget request template earlier in Exhibit 8.4 The capital budget evaluation techniques are presented in Chapter 9. Compile a summary report at year-end to show what projects were totally or partly implemented during the year. Compare that to the capital budget(s) approved in the past year(s). Postaudit the actual project expenditures, by project, to find out if they matched anticipated amounts and if not, why not. This will greatly help your organization in future capital project analyses.

(iii) Cash Budget. The cash budget preparation is demonstrated in Section 8.7 below. The variance analysis is similar to that used for the operating budget. How is it be used to do after-the-fact analysis? Quite simply, it is used to check the accuracy of your year-earlier forecast and see if seasonal or trend patterns emerge in the actual cash flows that occurred. Determine in which months your forecast was farthest off, and why. Use that information to guide your development of next year's cash budget. Of chief importance, consider whether the target liquidity should be adjusted based on the past year variance. Let's consider the two cases of positive and negative variances in the net cash flow, which we define as:

$$\text{Net cash flow} = \text{Cash receipts} - \text{Cash disbursements}$$

Case 1: Net cash flow comes in above budget. In this case, the cash position is growing, unless the trend was spotted during the year and additional expenses incurred or assets purchased. Possibly, the liquidity target should be adjusted downward, but whether you do so depends on several considerations. Some of the factors you should look at are:

- If the trend is temporary and is about to be reversed (possibly because of special factors such as one-time undesignated gifts to the organization), do not change the liquidity target, because your cash position will return to its normal level in the near future.
- If some of the cash receipts were simply proceeds from borrowing,[22] the amount must be repaid, bringing the cash position back to its normal level.
- If the trend is permanent, and you do not anticipate increasing service provision, you may reduce the amount of liquidity because you have a level of operations that brings in revenues more than covering expenses.
- If you are not sure as to the cause or permanence of the change, gain interest income and retain flexibility by parking some of the cash buildup in longer-term securities, say with one-year or two-year maturities, making sure to choose those that are readily marketable.
- If your organization is growing rapidly, sit tight with the higher level of liquidity until you have a better idea of how much liquidity you need.

Case 2: Net cash flow comes in below budget. In this case, cash expenses are outstripping cash revenues, and you have less cash at the end of the year than you originally anticipated. Possibly, you borrowed some money to meet the shortfall. To the extent possible, you will probably want to rebuild the drained cash reserves. Recognize now that you will need to discuss increased fundraising activity to meet that target. In some cases, taking the flip side of the list we just looked at, the change is temporary, and possibly self-correcting. More often than not, nonprofit executives and board members blithely assume that such events are self-correcting, but you should take the change seriously. It may be that your organization is heading for chronic deficits and a rapidly eroding cash position. Your organization may also need to change its programming, if fees are part of the revenue base, or engage in earned income ventures to supplement donations. If your organization is growing rapidly, the problem is compounded, because quite often funds are disbursed to finance the growth before the donor base responds to the increased outreach. See additional ideas. In Levels 2, 3, and 4 of the annual financial reporting pyramid presented in Chapter 7.

(g) CAUTIONS.   Anthony and Young note four aspects of budget review that you should recognize:

1. You will face time constraints. Count on it! You won't have time to go into sophisticated budget procedures, or be a perfectionist.

2. There are budget review effects on behavior: Problems arise because so much of nonprofit spending is discretionary. This fact suggests that negotiation be used and that ability, integrity, and forthrightness are not soon forgotten.

3. Politics and gamesmanship often occur.

4. Watch out for the "budget ploys."[23]

(i) Budget Ploys.   The following four budget ploys are prevalent in the nonprofits we have observed:

1. *Foot in the door.*   Here, a modest program is sold initially, but once the constituency has been built and the program is under way, its true magnitude is revealed. Sometimes this is triggered by "resource hunger" in which the budgetee's motivation is to acquire as many resources as possible, especially when output cannot be reliably measured and the output-input relationship is unclear. Your best hope is to detect this ploy up front and disapprove the program. Failing that, force the program advocates to hold to the original cost estimate.

2. *Reverence for the past.*   This ploy is used to maintain or increase an ongoing program. The argument goes that the amount spent last year was necessary to carry out last year's program, so the only thing to negotiate is the increment to add to that base for this year's program. Time for careful consideration is often lacking, so try to implement selective zero-based budgeting (ZBB) over a period of several years; we address ZBB in greater detail later in the chapter.

3. *Make a study.*   Users of this ploy are trying to avoid having their program's budget slashed. The advocate tries to buy time or block the action by demanding that all repercussions of such an action be studied. Sometimes the best response is to make the study and be persistent in cutting the program, assuming the study verifies the original reasoning. Other times, stick with your guns and cut the budget without further delay.

4. *We are the experts.* Here again, the goal is to forestall cuts. Budgetees are arguing that they have superior knowledge that the supervisor or budget director does not have. Professionals (teachers, scientists, physicians, and clergy members) are especially adept at this. The best answer is to insist that the "experts" phrase their reasoning in terminology and expression understandable to all.

(ii) What Hinders an Effective Budget System? Methods and techniques used in the budget system have only limited impact on budget system effectiveness.[24] Of course, methods used should be understood by organizational personnel, budgets need to be done on time (and often are not), and variance reports showing actual-versus-budget differences should be prepared regularly, accurately, and on a timely basis. The key determinant of success or failure is the use made *after* the budget is in place. And the use made is primarily aided or hindered by communication. Communication problems arise in the following relationships:

- Between the budget department and operating management
- Between the different levels of the management hierarchy (e.g., top and middle management)
- Between the manager responsible for the budget (budgetee) and his or her direct supervisor[25]

Budgets are yardsticks, and sometimes they are taken seriously and operate effectively. At other times there is political maneuvering to escape the restraint of the budget. Breakdown in verbal communication is more often the culprit than written communications such as budget variance reports. The way you *use* the budget and the attitudes of top-line management are most important. Some of these problems can be prevented by the budget guidelines.

(iii) Is the Finalized Budget Consistent with Financial Targets and Policies? This reality check is essential before publishing the budget. There should be a direct tie between your strategic plan and the budget as well as between your long-range financial plan and your budget. If done at the same time, there should be a very close correspondence between the first year of your five-year financial plan and your operating budget for next year. If the financial policy is to run surpluses for the next three years, obviously your budget should show revenues exceeding expenses.

8.6 BUDGET TECHNIQUE REFINEMENTS

While technique is not the most important indicator of operating budget effectiveness, some organizations have found value in using newer, refined budget techniques, including nonfinancial targets, flexible budgets, program budgets, and ZBB.

(a) NONFINANCIAL TARGETS. Many businesses include nonfinancial targets in their annual budget reports. We strongly advocate that you consider doing this, assuming your budget development process is running smoothly. What nonmonetary budget targets might you include? Anthony and Young recommend three output measures: (1) workload or process measures, (2) results or "objective achievement" measures, and (3) a framework for the objective achievement measures.[26] The latter framework might be the use of a management philosophy known as management by objectives (MBO), which is defined as the use of quantitative measures for measuring planned objectives, possibly including objectives to maintain operations, objectives to strengthen operations, and objectives to improve operations. In this situation, benchmarking and reengineering studies are helpful.

(b) FLEXIBLE BUDGETING.   Sometimes called variable budgeting, *flexible budgeting* is particularly useful for organizations operating in an uncertain environment, where you plug in the expense budget only after you find out exactly what level of output you're going to be producing or how many clients you plan on treating in a time period. On the expense side, flexible budgeting works well, you might have guessed, only for variable costs. Organizations that do not develop flexible budgets must adapt to changes in the environment "after the fact"—scrambling to prepare a revised budget to fit the new realities. You'll live with the original budget? Not if you want the budget to serve as a control and coordinating device, in which managers are held responsible for meeting or exceeding budgetary amounts.

Let's use a greatly simplified example, which builds on our earlier classification of variable, semivariable, and fixed costs. Recall that labor expense is the major cost to be managed by nonprofits. This is really a semivariable expense in many organizations: New staff and laborers do not have to be added for each additional client served, but perhaps one laborer must be added for each additional five clients. Salaried workers basically represent a fixed cost. Utilities, insurance, and mortgage payments are fixed costs. Supplies used in client engagements are a variable cost; the more clients served, the more supplies used.

Let's start with a base case budget for the year 20XX, based on the "most likely" figure of 1,000 client engagements. We have annotated it to show the cost type for each item in Exhibit 8.7.

To develop a flexible budget, we need to have a way to figure the amount for each variable and semivariable cost expressed as a percent of activity level (services delivered). Recall that the "base case" budget (the one you would have used if you did not go the extra step to develop a flexible budget) was based on 1,000 client engagements. This implies that client supplies cost $40 per client engagement:

$$\text{Variable cost per unit} = \text{Total cost divided by number of units}$$

$$= \$40,000/1,000$$

$$= \$40$$

(1,000 Client Engagements) January 1–December 31, 20XX		
Expense Element		Amount
Variable costs:	Client supplies	40,000
Semivariable costs:	Labor expense	$120,000
Fixed costs:	Salary expense	60,000
	Utilities	5,000
	Insurance	4,000
	Mortgage payments	15,000
Total expenses:		**$244,000**

EXHIBIT 8.7   BASE CASE BUDGET WORKSHEET

Expressed as a formula:

$$\text{Client supplies expense} = \$40 \times (\# \text{ of client engagements})$$

Semivariable costs have both a variable component and a fixed component. To get the fixed component, you need to determine how much of this cost element would be necessary to have a minimal service delivery (say, one or a very few clients). For labor expense, our organization projected $120,000 based on 1,000 client engagements. The staff director suggests that even if the organization had only 20 client engagements (the smallest number it could have and still remain open), the labor expense would be $20,000. What that tells us is that for the remaining 980 clients (1,000 clients assumed in the base case budget, less the 20 minimal-level clients), there would be $100,000 of labor expense ($120,000 base case budget less the $20,000 minimal level). This data implies that the variable component is:

$$\text{Variable cost per unit} = \text{Total variable cost/number of units}$$

$$\$102.04 = \$100,000/980$$

Let's express the relationship we have just discovered in a format we can use to calculate the semivariable cost for *any* level of clients. We saw that labor expense is $20,000 plus $102.04 per client engagement. Our formula is:

$$\text{Labor expense} = \$20,000 + \$102.04 \times (\# \text{ of client engagements})$$

The easy part is estimating the fixed cost. By definition, a fixed cost does not change regardless of the amount of services delivered. So all we have to do is add all fixed costs:

Salary expense	60,000
Utilities	5,000
Insurance	4,000
Mortgage payments	15,000
Total fixed costs	$84,000

Our formula for fixed costs is very simple: Total fixed costs = $84,000.

And now, the grand finale: Let's add the three formulas together to get one overall formula to simplify our flexible budgeting:

$$\text{Client supplies expense} = \$40 \times (\# \text{ of client engagements})$$

$$\text{Labor expense} = \$20,000 + \$102.04 \times (\# \text{ of client engagements})$$

$$\text{Total fixed costs} = \$84,000$$

$$\text{Total costs} = \$104,000 + \$142.04 \times (\# \text{ of client engagements})$$

Using this formula, we can determine the expense budget for any level of activity we desire. For example, if client engagements double to 2,000, total costs could be:

$$\text{Total costs} = \$104,000 + \$142.04 \times (2,000)$$

$$= \$104,000 + \$284,080$$

$$= \underline{\mathbf{\$388,080}}$$

As actual figures for client engagements begin to come in, we can compare actual amounts to an adjusted "flexible budget" amount, which correctly states what the budget is at that particular activity level. This way, managers are not penalized for expenses that are running higher due to a higher caseload. Further, budget revisions based on environmental changes are no longer needed. The change in caseload due to environmental changes is automatically reflected in budget expense levels. In more technical terms, we no longer have to concern ourselves with a "volume variance"—an actual versus budget difference that is strictly due to changes in service activity. We can then limit our concentration on "price variances" that are due to changes in the unit cost of an input, such as a change in the minimum wage, or "mix variances" that are due to a changing composition in the types of clients we serve. One other benefit of doing the extra work involved in flexible budgeting: When cutbacks or expansion of your organization is being considered, you will already be prepared to pinpoint the likely financial effects.

(c) PROGRAM BUDGETING.   Recall that with line-item budgets, the focus is on expense elements. We noted earlier that program budgets may be a type of subunit budget. A program budget may also be your organization's primary budget format as well. With program budgets, instead of concerning ourselves with the type of expense, we focus on programs and their associated expenses. Essentially, think of it as having subunit budgets, one for each program. By directing our attention to individual programs instead of the overall organization, the manager is aided in allocating the right amount of financial and human resources to each activity. Furthermore, from a control and coordination perspective, program budgeting links spending directly to planned activity levels of the organization's product(s) or service(s). An organization with a well-developed strategic planning process will find that it has already done some of the work necessary to establish the program budgets.[27]

(d) ZERO-BASED BUDGETING.   Budgets, whether line item, flexible, or program, are usually arrived at by changing the past year's budget slightly, perhaps based on new economic assumptions or based on noted actual versus budget variances from this year's experience. A more radical, and some would argue superior, approach is to force each program or other subunit to justify its existence and budgetary allocation "from the ground up." This approach to budgeting is known as zero-based budgeting (ZBB). ZBB has five key components:

1.   Identify objectives.
2.   Determine the value of accomplishing each activity or program.
3.   Evaluate different funding levels.
4.   Establish priorities.
5.   Evaluate workload and performance measures.[28]

The idea here is to look at all the organization's discretionary activities and priorities in a fresh way, and then to redo the budget allocations accordingly. Particularly important is the review of all support allocations. Basic or necessary operations are separated from discretionary or optional tasks. Every dollar of discretionary cost must be justified. The finalized money allocation must be based on a cost-benefit comparison of each competing activity's goals, program for attaining those goals, expected benefits and how one will know if they have been attained, alternatives to the program, consequences from *not* approving the activity and its corresponding budgetary allocation, and who will carry out the activity's program(s).

Once the supporting data have been put together, it is time to rank the various activities. This ranking may be done first by program directors for all activities within their programs, then higher-level managers may assemble rankings of organization-wide alternatives. Management must rank order all of the alternatives from most beneficial to least beneficial, then decide how to allocate the overall budget to achieve the greatest good. For example, a charity might decide that for the coming year, computer software training will do more good than the usual in-service client relations training.

Some proponents of ZBB argue that it can actually simplify the budgeting process and bring about better resource allocation of funds. It does so by making managers consider the various priorities and how funds should be allocated to them. With the list of ranked activities, managers have an additional tool for augmenting or reducing activities as the allowable expenditure level changes as the budget year begins.

Very few nonprofits are using this technique, but it would be an excellent technique to use once every 5 or 10 years because of the disciplined look at expenses that it forces on the organization. We recognize the effects of politics and other budget ploys that must be overcome to make this exercise truly effective, however.

(e) ROLLING BUDGETS. Rolling budgets involve redoing the budget within the year and projecting at least the following 12 months (some businesses project out for 18 months). Technically, unless you are updating data and forecasts on a real-time basis based on new financial, operational, and economic information, you are using modified rolling budgets. Exhibit 8.8 provides the rationale and some specifics of rolling budgets that have been gleaned from their use by businesses.

- Many companies are recognizing that the conventional static budget—produced near year-end and then used as a guide for the following year even though it's out of date—is just not good enough.

- Instead, they are turning to rolling budgets—forecasts that are updated every few months—in effect, reassessing the company's outlook several times a year.

- The result: an always-current financial forecast that not only reflects a business's most recent monthly results but also any material changes to its business outlook or the economy.

- Implementing rolling budgets doesn't necessarily require any fundamental change in the way a company has been doing its budgets—except, of course, it no longer does the job just once a year. However, companies that decide to step up to rolling budgets may want to take advantage of the decision to make changes in the way they approach the task. They may search for new ways to speed up the budgeting process and make it more useful.

- In the view of many accountants, traditional budgets too often are useless because they are hopelessly out of date soon after they are assembled.

- When a company uses a traditional static budget process and finds that it misses its sales targets in the first month, it typically pushes those projected sales into subsequent quarters, acting as if the outlook for the full year remains unchanged.

- For rolling budgets to work, management must access and process information more quickly, and that often means acquiring special software that does the job.

Source: Randy Myers, "Budgets on a Roll," *Journal of Accountancy* Vol. 192 (December 2001) 41–46.

EXHIBIT 8.8 FEATURES AND ADVANTAGES OF ROLLING BUDGETS

We believe that rolling budgets keep the organization's eyes on a full-year-ahead horizon, not merely what will happen between this point in the year and the end of the fiscal year. Furthermore, we see rolling budgets as taking advantage of advances in information technology, including web-based budgeting and planning software, web-based banking, improved accounting and record-keeping systems, and more rapid availability of information. They also enable larger nonprofits to decentralize budget setting (after assumptions have been handed down from the main office), as has been done by two nonprofits, International Missions and Mercy Health Partners.[29] A study being conducted by two accounting groups in England and Wales reached this conclusion, which also applies in the United States:

> Part of the reason budgeting has changed and why budgets can be more flexible...
> is that information can be gathered much more easily now than was possible even
> a decade ago. Because data is collected, stored and analyzed more readily, frequent
> reforecasting and adaptation is possible if an organization is willing to invest the
> time to set up the systems. This allows the budget to be forward looking and more
> strategic, and forecasts can be more precise. Some participants in the... budgeting
> forum actually suggested that forecasts are more important than budgets in their
> businesses.[30]

Reforecasting into the next 12 months is a good discipline for any organization, and a best budgeting practice.

Once the operating budget is finalized, it needs to be *calendarized* (distributed across months, as some months are higher-revenue or expenditure months than others), and the cash flow ramifications need to be spelled out. The process for showing when cash comes in and goes out is called cash budgeting.

8.7 CASH BUDGET

If your organization's accounting is done on a cash basis, your operating statement provides the input for the cash budget. The cash budget differs in purpose, in that it highlights the cash available to the organization at various points in the future. It is very revealing, especially the first time it is constructed, because nonfinancial managers typically are unaware of just how unsynchronized cash inflows and cash outflows are.

(a) USES OF THE CASH BUDGET. We start our presentation on cash budgeting with a definition: The cash budget shows the timing of cash inflows and outflows, usually on a monthly basis for the next 12 months. It is sometimes called a cash plan or cash forecast. Exhibit 8.9 shows the value of a cash budget. The cash budget has five major purposes; it shows the:

1. Unsynchronized nature of inflows and outflows (e.g., see October figures in historical cash flow table in Exhibit 8.10)

2. Seasonality of these flows (e.g., donations run high around Easter and especially between Thanksgiving and Christmas)

3. Degree of mismatch (surplus or shortfall)

4. Duration of these surpluses or shortfalls (how long they last, in months)

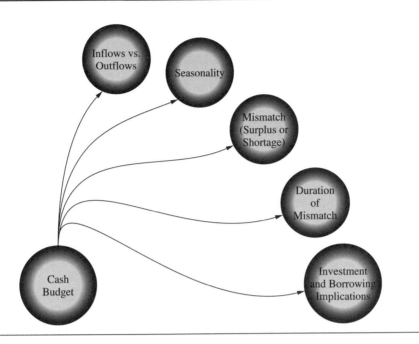

EXHIBIT 8.9 CASH BUDGET: USES

5. Necessary inputs for short-term investment or borrowing planning (together degree and duration of mismatch provide this, with the output being amounts and maturities of short-term investments or borrowing)

(b) STEPS IN CASH BUDGETING. The four steps in developing a cash budget are:

1. Determine which measure of cash to manage and forecast:
   - General ledger cash balance (checkbook balance if that's your only accounting)
   - Bank balance (preferred)
2. Decide on presentation format.
3. Collect historical information (see Exhibit 8.10 for an actual nonprofit's prior year cash flows).
4. Develop cash forecast.

(c) FORECASTING YOUR CASH POSITION. When actually laying out your cash budget, you may choose one or more of several formats. Because you already are probably developing a statement of cash flows (SCF), one alternative is to use the SCF format. You would then show projections for cash from/(to) operating activities, cash from/(to) investing activities, and cash from/(to) financing activities. This works well for an annual consolidated projection but is unnatural for monthly or daily projections. An alternate format, which you may decide to use for your daily or monthly projections, is the cash receipts and disbursements method (see Exhibit 8.11).

Month	Oct.	Nov.	Dec.	Jan.	Feb.	Mar.	Apr.	May	June	July	Aug.	Sep.
Line item:												
Cash Receipts (Total Deposits)	$1,373,317.26	$1,495,458.64	$2,296,298.05	$1,600,345.48	$1,585,68234	$1,455,742.97	$1,474,501.30	$1,410,048.27	$1,528,613.80	$2,872,784.74	$1,928,010.02	$1,405,515.21
−Cash Disbursements (Total Pymts/Withdrawals)	1,866,433.15	1,358,838.60	2,191,922.40	1,826,944.39	1,598,544.96	1,516,459.75	1,417,947.23	1,360,117.18	1,469,020.89	3,064,544.94	1,715,130.63	1,459,922.01
Net Cash Flow	($493,115.89)	$136,620.04	$104,375.65	($226,598.91)	($12,862.62)	($60,716.78)	$56,554.07	$49,931.09	$59,592.91	($191,760.20)	$212,879.39	354,406.80)
+Beg Cash (Beginning Balance)	$626,414.41	$133,298.52	$269,918.56	$374,294.21	$147,69530	$134,832.68	$74,115.90	$130,669.97	$180,601.06	$240,193.97	$48,433.77	$261,313.16
=Ending Cash (Ending Balance or New Balance)	$133,298.52	$269,918.56	$374,294.21	$147,695.30	$134,832.68	$74,115.90	$130,669.97	$180,601.06	$240,193.97	$48,433.77	$261,313.16	$206,906.36

EXHIBIT 8.10 COLLECTING HISTORICAL INFORMATION

	January	February
Beginning cash	$250	$175
+ Cash receipts	100	
− Cash disbursements	175	
= Ending cash	$175	
− Minimum cash	200	
= Cash surplus	—	
OR		
Cash shortage	($ 25)	

EXHIBIT 8.11 BASIC CASH BUDGETING/FORECASTING TEMPLATE

To operationalize this method, we would need to provide the necessary detail for each category of cash flow and for the minimum necessary cash:

- Categories of cash inflows
- Categories of cash outflows
- Needed minimum cash

Basically, all we are doing here is looking back to see what items provided our cash inflows and outflows in the past, and deciding how much detail to show for each category.

Let's look more closely at projecting our cash receipts, and then we'll comment on cash disbursements.

(i) Determine Cash Receipts. The determination of cash receipts proceeds in a logical and orderly, six-step fashion:

1. The operating budget is your starting point.
2. Accrual versus cash basis adjustment may need to be made (if necessary—if already on cash basis, don't worry about adjustments).
3. Watch out for the common oversights:
   - Don't forget prearranged financing inflows.
   - Don't forget (formerly) restricted net assets, such as deferred giving or time-restricted or purpose-restricted prior gifts that will become unrestricted this period.
4. Calendarize the full-year receipts and disbursements by putting the amounts expected in each month.
   - Study history to see seasonal patterns.
   - Consider special factors that may have caused numbers to appear in a different month or quarter in the past than they will most likely occur in the upcoming period.
5. Anticipate changes in the forthcoming 12 months.
6. Show quarterly totals to provide one checks-and-balances monitoring sequence.

(ii) Determine Cash Disbursements. Again, the operating budget expenses are the starting point. Because of accounts payable, you may have to make an accrual-to-cash basis adjustment (if necessary). Do not include depreciation expense. Watch out for the capital budget outlays; many organizations forget to include them in the cash budget. Then calendarize the cash outlays correctly, recognizing seasonal or other ups and downs. Pull together quarterly subtotals to use down the road for comparisons with actual cash flows.

(iii) Put It All Together.   Now we are ready to bring the cash receipts and disbursements together to find the difference ("net cash flow" [NCF]) for each month. Once we have that, we will add it to beginning cash to arrive at ending cash. We compare ending cash to minimum cash required (by subtracting the latter), and see if we have a cash surplus anticipated for the month's end or a cash shortage. Summarizing, we have a three-step sequence that you should carry out at least monthly and probably weekly or even daily.

1.   Compute NCF (Cash inflows—cash outflows), ending position, cash sur-plus/(shortfall) for each month.

2.   Analyze pattern(s). Are there distinct seasonal highs or lows for either cash receipts or cash disbursements? How will this feed back into our cash planning (i.e., building up larger reserves) or fundraising appeal timing?

3.   Make recommendations with regard to both cash reserve buildup (how does the sum of the forecasted amounts of cash, cash equivalents, and short-term investments compare to your target liquidity level) and fundraising campaign timing or frequency, but also for short-term investments (amount and maturity of securities) and short-term borrowing (amount and anticipated maturity of any short-term borrowing, if such borrowing is used).

The cash forecasting exercise is valuable in assisting with your implementation of financial policies, particularly your target liquidity level, and with carrying out your financial management processes.

(iv) Use the Cash Budget to Help Set Target Liquidity Level.   For background on our discussion of how much liquidity an organization should have, you may wish to refer back to our discussion of the target liquidity level in Chapter 2. We also noted, in Chapter 6, some pointers on the optimal liquidity level, which we recap here. As for the optimal level of target liquidity, you will have to do the analysis yourself because no technique will give you that specific target level.

As a starting point, take a look at the low point in your fiscal year, which for many nonprofits is late September or early October. Set a liquidity level for your peak season, probably early January, that is sufficient to cover your organization through the dry season. *This is where your annual cash budget reevaluation is so helpful.* Study past cash flow patterns carefully and note when the cash crunches came as well as how much liquidity should have been held earlier in the year to prevent each cash crunch.

The degree of flexibility your organization has in managing off of the budget (see Section 8.8) will also help you determine the size of your safety buffer of liquidity.

In addition, consult Exhibit 8.12, which provides you with a road map to determine whether your organization has too little liquidity. Work through it carefully, providing answers to the areas listed. Notice the key considerations: slow growth, missed opportunities, risky financial posture, small or zero net interest income (investments income less interest paid on borrowed funds), wage/salary freezes or minute increases, loans turned down or received on unattractive terms, recurrent cash crunches (or cash crises), late invoice payments (or lateness on other amounts paid), and ongoing stringency in financial posture despite successful fundraising campaigns. Once you have worked through these diagnostic questions from the vantage point of evaluating illiquidity, consider the opposite of each of these factors, in order to determine whether your organization might have *too much* liquidity. Readjust your target liquidity level according to your answers.

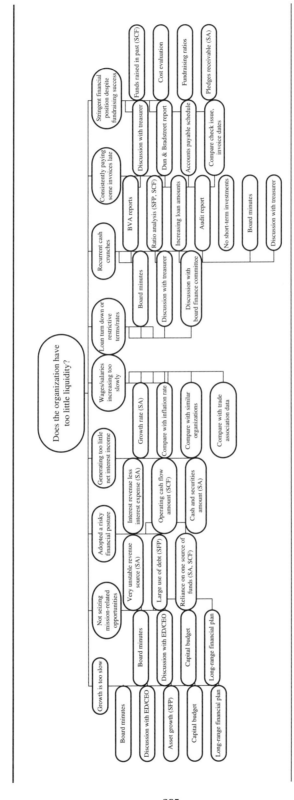

EXHIBIT 8.12 DETERMINING WHETHER ORGANIZATION HAS TOO LITTLE LIQUIDITY

8.8 MANAGING OFF THE BUDGET

We have provided much information on budgetary reports, but up to this point we have not given very much guidance on what to do when the BVA shows a deteriorating financial position. In this section, we will provide some pointers.

(a) BUDGET VARIANCE ANALYSIS REVISITED.   Some organizations either ignore their target liquidity levels or never set them in the first place. An example is the Midwest Finance Association; the association continued to experience operating budget deficits for a series of years without taking any correction action. As it continued to run deficits, what do you suppose happened to its liquidity? Right! The cash reserves continued to dwindle, until the viability of the organization was in jeopardy. Finally, in late 1996, the president of the MFA wrote the members of the chronic deficits and notified them that the dues were being almost doubled in order to bring the organization back to a break-even or surplus position and, more important, to preserve and rebuild the cash reserves. In the MFA's case, the corrective action took place after annual results were evaluated to see how they fit into the past years' established trends. Most organizations can react more quickly by harnessing their ongoing financial reports.

Three reporting principles will help you manage off the budget:

1.   An exception reporting focus will help shine light on the large-dollar or large-percentage items that contribute most to the problems and therefore the likely solutions.

2.   Inclusion of year-to-date (YTD) variances as well as the last month and/or last quarter will give the needed perspective for decision making.

3.   If possible, include actual versus forecast as well as actual versus budget (two comparisons) in your variance analysis reports.

The third principle necessitates more management time for preparation, because each month or quarter you not only have to review the past performance but also do a new forecast, which possibly varies from the budgeted amounts. Organizations that use flexible budgets, if recalculated, may eliminate the need to do an actual versus forecast because the revised budget may have been a new forecast based on how things have changed.

Progressive organizations are moving beyond mere financial reporting and including nonfinancial items in their periodic reports. Let's face it: Your financial results three or five years from now are going to be closely linked to nonfinancial factors and trends.

Accordingly, universities and businesses are adopting a new approach in their monthly or quarterly meetings, in which they highlight key financial success indicators (KFSIs) and possibly cost drivers. KFSIs include contacts made by the admissions office, follow-up letters written by academic unit heads, and the like. Indiana State University board members receive a report of KFSIs at each board meeting based on consultation provided by business students and a faculty member, as refined by the internal auditor.[31]

The focus in a KFSI report is on selected areas of performance in which satisfactory results will ensure the organization's competitive success, meriting top management time and attention.

Several other success factors seem to enhance the potency of your budget reporting and its usefulness to the organization. One is the importance of doing your variance analysis and situation analysis in conjunction with ratios and other indicators. As we saw in Chapter 7, ratios taken as a group provide a composite picture of the organization's financial health.

There are a number of other indicators that can be used beyond what has been presented here, and all the important indicators should be assessed. Gross, McCarthy, and Shelmon provide five classes of indicators of impending financial trouble: (1) reduced community support, (2) decreased financial independence, (3) declining productivity, (4) deferred current costs, and (5) ineffective management practices (i.e., a pattern of budget cost overruns, revenue shortfalls, lower investment returns, higher interest charges, and delayed/unclear/incomplete reports to board or top management).[32] A second success factor we noted in the Lilly study is the importance of the "1,000-word picture," in which graphs or charts are used to depict to top management or the board what is happening to the organization's financial position. For example, board members who work as engineers at Caterpillar in Peoria, Illinois, draw up trend-line charts to show revenue and expense trends for the Peoria Rescue Ministries CEO and other board members. Related to this, a third success factor is to include not only trends but also comparative data if available (peer analysis). This gives a more balanced view of the present situation. Fourth, we noted in the Lilly study the importance of the verbal presentation accompanying the reporting of financial results. Learn to walk your management team and board through the maze of financials that they might not have the time, energy, or expertise to wade through. Finally, you might be surprised at the importance of annotating the financials with brief interpretive comments (because your listeners will forget the verbal presentation and possibly misinterpret the graphs and ratios).

(b) CASH POSITION. As your cash position changes, you will be in the position of advising management and the board of the seriousness of the change and what corrective actions, if any, are needed. You will want to provide this guidance each quarter or, if warranted, more often. Some organizations take a new look at the liquidity weekly or even daily. As cash manager of the organization, assuming you have enough cash to make it worth your while, look each day at the checking account balance to determine whether and how much to transfer to overnight or longer investments.

Now that we have an idea of the role of analysis and reports in "managing off of the budget," we turn to some of the responses you might consider in coping with financial difficulties. You also may wish to look at these as ways to fine-tune your already healthy financial position.

(c) RESPONSES TO FINANCIAL DIFFICULTIES. Many organizations within and outside of the nonprofit sector are engaging in reengineering. This happens when service delivery and internal management processes are opened up for radical redesign instead of just incremental improvements. The approach is much like zero-based review or zero-based budgeting, except it is applied to efficiency of service delivery and internal management processes.

Some organizations are noting the difficulties that similar organizations are getting into and are moving ahead of time to build an endowment income stream or their cash reserves as money for the rainy days. Related to this, financial analysts are planning for the overhaul of aging plant and equipment so as not to be caught short when the time comes for refurbishment or replacement. Residential colleges, churches, and museums must be especially careful to plan for the fixed asset needs for which they will have to plan internal funding or arrange funding. Other organizations are noting the need for pension funding or benefits funding.

But what if it's too late to plan ahead? Let's profile some responses to financial shortfalls:

- Quickly eliminate deficit spending.
- Quickly increase internal control.
- Quickly increase the role and prominence of the finance department. (It sounds self-serving, but it certainly helped the Church of the Brethren and the Church of God Missionary Board, as well the organization highlighted in the beginning of this chapter.)
- Quickly reorient the organization to a more deliberate program expansion (whether new programs or expansion of existing ones):
  - Managed growth, which means a measured, manageable rate of growth (practiced by Cedarville University, Cedarville, Ohio)
  - Sustainable growth rate[33]
  - Internal growth rate[34]

In addition to these stopgap measures, there are some internal and external measures you can take to stem a long-term decline.

(d) INTERNAL MEASURES.   There are six major financial strategies to embark on *within* your organization. Briefly, they are:

1. *A new emphasis on cash forecasting with shorter horizon (month) and interval (weekly)*. 3M's policy is to accurately forecast cash sources and uses and take whatever actions are deemed appropriate so that adequate cash is on hand at all times and so that daily and long-term liquidity needs are met at the best price.
2. *Asset sales*. This might be called "strategic disposition" in order to focus better on core areas of operation.
3. *Expansion strategy*. Land purchase, lease to builder/leaseback to the nonprofit organization: This strategy enables the builder to utilize the depreciation (40-year) expense deduction against income taxes, whereas the nonprofit would be unable to.
4. *Asset redeployment*. Put scarce labor and volunteer resources in critical areas.
5. *Cost reduction/containment*. This is the "downsizing" or "rightsizing" we hear so much about.
6. *Treasury strategies*. Much of what is in mind here involves revising your treasury management approach and operations based on benchmarking. We provide techniques in Chapter 11 and benchmarks to begin using to gauge your treasury operation in Chapter 15.

(e) EXTERNAL MEASURES.   The external measures that organizations may take to cope with financial problems fall into three major categories:

1. *Fundraising*. Increase the intensity and focus of your fundraising efforts.
2. *Bank borrowing*. Document future improvements to merit short-term financing to bridge the gap.
3. *Merger/acquisition partner or strategic alliance*. Join hands with a partner that has deep (or deeper) pockets.

Budgeting practices are most valuable when they are well planned and carefully executed, and include the types of control and follow-up we have discussed.

8.9 CONCLUSION

In this chapter, we have shown how to develop operating and cash budgets. We show the sequence of steps that should be followed, so you can set up the process. We provide warnings of the pitfalls that many nonprofit organizations face along the way. Most notably, budgets are rarely tied to long-range financial plans and strategic plans. Budget enhancements are also discussed; some of them might merit further study on your part. Budgets are valuable management tools for planning and coordinating your service delivery, despite the weaknesses inherent in the budget process and the way it gets implemented in organizations. Organizations that do not budget are losing financial control. Organizations that do budget find the budget system most effective when it is tied to the strategic plan. Once in place, the budget may be compared to actual dollar amounts as the budget year progresses, with management taking action on the corrective actions that are signaled by the budget variances.

Notes

1. Maura Webber, "Turning Red Ink into Black: A Chicago Settlement House Commits to Fiscal Responsibility—and Wins Grants," *Chronicle of Philanthropy,* November 13, 2003. Available online at: http://philanthropy.com/free/articles/v16/i03/03003001.htm. Accessed: 12/31/2005.
2. Anthony J. Gambino and Thomas J. Reardon, *Financial Planning and Evaluation for the Nonprofit Organization* (New York: National Association of Accountants, 1981), 21–35.
3. Budget Executives Institute, "Statement of Duties and Responsibilities of the Budget Director," reprinted in *Readings in Cost Accounting, Budgeting and Control,* 5th ed., ed. William E. Thomas (Cincinnati: South-Western Publishing Company, 1978), 82–83.
4. Most of this section and the next are based on the insights of Gregg Capin, of Capin Crouse, LLP, Atlanta, GA, from a seminar entitled "Financial Management for Nonprofit Leaders," sponsored by the Christian Management Association, Indianapolis, IN, May 12, 1992.
5. Robert N. Anthony and David W. Young, *Management Control in Nonprofit Organizations,* 7th ed. (Boston: McGraw-Hill/Irwin, 2003), Chapter 10.
6. The survey was jointly conducted by Portland-based Collins and the Technical Assistance for Community Services, with over 450 responses. "Survey: Nonprofit Contributions Insufficient to Cover Rising Overhead," *Portland Business Journal,* December 16, 2005. Available online at: http://portland.bizjournals.com/portland/stories/2005/12/12/daily34.html. Accessed 12/31/2005.
7. Here are some Internet Web sites to help you gather economic forecasts and data: www.wachovia.com (then select Corporate & Institutional > Research & Publications > Economic Commentary); www.northerntrust.com (then select Resources, then Economic Research); www.bloomberg.com (then select News & Commentary, then Economy/Politics, then Fed Watch).
8. Current interest rates are available online at: www.bloomberg.com/markets/rates/index.html.
9. Annuity rates are available from the American Council on Gift Annuities, which posts "Suggested Rates."
10. Information on inflation is available online at www.bondmarkets.com (then select Research).
11. Information on giving trends is available online at the Association of Fundraising Professionals Web site: http://www.afpnet.org/research_and_statistics/fundraising_research.
12. Information on exchange rates is available online at: http://finance.yahoo.com/currency; and at: http://money.cnn.com/data/currencies.

13. Although not tailored to nonprofit applications, an excellent source for more help with forecasting methods is Jae K. Shim and Joel G. Siegel, *Handbook of Financial Analysis, Forecasting, & Modeling* (Englewood Cliffs, NJ: Prentice-Hall, 1988).

14. Any financial spreadsheet software will do the trick to analyze the raw data numbers to arrive at an equation of "best fit." Microsoft Excel™, Lotus 1-2-3™, and Quattro Pro™ are all very adept, and one does not have to be a "techie type" to do the analysis.

15. Regression, moving averages, exponential smoothing, and classical decomposition time series techniques are also presented in a cash forecasting framework in Chapter 12 of Terry S. Maness and John T. Zietlow, *Short-Term Financial Management: Text and Cases,* 3rd ed. (Cincinnati: Thomson/South-Western, 2005).

16. Paragraph 78 of Financial Accounting Concepts No. 6, *Elements of Financial Statements,* as cited in AICPA, *AICPA Audit and Accounting Guide, Not-For-Profit Organizations* (New York: AICPA, 2005), 207.

17. From paragraph 80 of FASB Concepts Statement No. 6, *Elements of Financial Statements.*

18. For help in estimating grant proposal overhead, see Elizabeth K. Keating, "Is There Enough Overhead in This Grant?" *Nonprofit Quarterly* 10 (Spring 2003): 41–44.

19. For more on budgeting, consult David C. Maddox, *Budgeting for Not-for-Profit Organizations* (New York: John Wiley & Sons, 1999).

20. For another example of a nonprofit's budgeting practice, showing the budget development schedule, see: http://www.ussailing.org/budget/changeprocess.htm.

21. Michael C. Thomsett, *The Little Black Book of Budgets and Forecasts* (New York: AMA-COM, 1988).

22. This should not be the case if you followed the recommended format offered at the end of this chapter. In that format, each month gives a cash surplus (if positive) or cash shortage (if negative), with the cash shortage reflecting the cumulative shortfall and therefore the borrowed balance at that point in time. So the loan amount does not appear in cash receipts at all.

23. Anthony and Young, *Management Control in Nonprofit Organizations,* 497–517.

24. Geert Hofstede, *Uncommon Sense about Organizations: Cases, Studies, and Field Observations* (Thousand Oaks, CA: SAGE Publications, 1994), 140–153.

25. Id.

26. Anthony and Young, *Management Control in Nonprofit Organizations,* 494, 620–626.

27. For a comparison of a line-item budget to a program budget, see Robert N. Anthony and David W. Young, *Management Control in Nonprofit Organizations,* 7th ed. (Boston: McGraw-Hill Irwin, 2003), 493. For more on program budgeting, see Jerry Soto, "Is Your Program Budget a Monster in the Making?" *Nonprofit Quarterly,* 8 (Fall 2001): 54.

28. Tom M. Plank, Lois Ruffner Plank, and Donald Morris, *Accounting Desk Book with CD (2006)* (Riverwoods, IL: CCH Inc., 2006).

29. Marie Leone, "Rolling Budgets, with a Twist," www.cfo.com (June 3 2003): 1–4. Available online at: http://www.cfo.com/article.cfm/3009422. Accessed: 7/19/06.

30. Robert Colman, "Better Budgeting," *CMA Management* (October 2004). Available online at: http://www.managementmag.com/index.cfm/ci_id/2014/la_id/1.htm. Accessed: 12/31/2005.

31. The key success indicator approach is documented in Mary M. Sapp and M. Lewis Temares, "A Monthly Checkup," *NACUBO Business Officer,* (March 1992): 24–31. We strongly advocate that you evaluate using this approach in your management reporting, regardless of your organizational type.

32. Malvern J. Gross, John J. McCarthy, and Nancy E. Shelmon, *Financial and Accounting Guide for Not-For-Profit Organizations,* Seventh Edition (New York: John Wiley, 2005), pp. 425–426)

33. For information on the sustainable growth rate, see Maness and Zietlow, *Short-Term Financial Management,* Chapter 2.

34. The internal growth rate is profiled in most introductory corporate finance texts.

CASE STUDY: THE CASH CRISIS AT THE CHILDREN'S TREATMENT CENTER*

Loan payments, government contracts, United Way money—sometimes running the not-for-profit Honolulu Children's Treatment Center was nothing but one big headache, thought Ron Williams, executive director of the Center. So many children needed help, and yet more and more time seemed to be spent on a growing number of financial problems. Ron saw that there wasn't enough cash to pay for the services provided by the parent agency, and payments were several years overdue. The temporary bank loan of $100,000 would need renewal soon and interest rates were moving up. The bank was unhappy that a so-called temporary loan had to be refinanced again. The United Way would reduce its support dollar for dollar if the center had an operating surplus of more than $5,000, but without an operating surplus it might not be possible to take care of the overdue payables and the bank loan. Actually, an operating surplus was unlikely to occur. The forecast for 2005/06 was a deficit of $19,000. And if that wasn't enough, today's mail brought yet another letter from the board of directors in California that said "if you just managed things properly, you should be able to pay off the bank loan, eliminate the operating deficit, and get current on payables." The letter ended with the request: "Please explain." The March annual meeting with the board of directors was coming up soon and they would be expecting some answers. "'Managed things properly' indeed," thought Ron. "What did they think he was trying to do?" Life certainly had been simpler in the early days when he was merely a child psychiatrist.

8A.1 THE HONOLULU CHILDREN'S TREATMENT CENTER

The Center was a not-for-profit organization founded in the 1920s to provide a home for dependent and neglected children. Over the years it evolved into a fully accredited residential psychiatric facility with a complete range of professional staff providing care to over 50 emotionally disturbed children. As the only fully accredited and licensed residential setting for the treatment of children with psychiatric disabilities in the Hawaiian Islands, children were received for care from throughout the entire state. Their length of

---

*This Case was written by Steven Dawson, Professor of Finance, Shidler College of Business, University of Hawaii, and W.R. Cozens, Honolulu Children's Treatment Center. Used by permission.

stay, depending upon the severity of their problems, ranged from 5 to 24 months with the average being 16 months. During this time, in addition to treatment for their emotional problems, they received a range of supportive services including special education, medical care, social services, recreation, room and board, and structured leisure time activities.

The Center is a subsidiary of a California-based not-for-profit corporation and operated with its own board of directors that was responsible for reviewing the budget and setting general policy. The directors meet quarterly in California and hold a meeting each March in Hawaii to review the budget for the fiscal year beginning on July 1.

As a not-for-profit organization, its basic objective was to render services. Success was measured by how much service was provided and by how well available resources were used. The Honolulu Children's Treatment Center thus differed markedly from a profit-oriented organization where decisions were intended to increase, or at least maintain, profits or to maximize the value of the firm. This was not to say that not-for-profit organizations did not report profits—there were years when reported revenues exceeded expenses. If this happened over several years, however, it was not a sign of good management but rather a warning signal that the organization was not accomplishing its objective of providing as much service as possible with available resources. Either it should cut the price charged for services or it should provide more services. A not-for-profit organization's usual policy should be to break even in the long run. The equity interests involved would have little incentive to build up an operating surplus since they could not sell or trade their ownership to others and no part of the assets, income, or profit would be distributed to them.

In financial reports for a not-for-profit organization a clear distinction is made between capital costs and operating costs. Capital costs refer to the acquisition of fixed assets, equipment, and real property from which benefits will accrue over a long period of time. Operating costs include labor, materials consumed, and services purchased as part of operating an organization for a given period of time. The two types of costs are handled separately as are the revenues associated with them. Depreciation is not a part of operating expenses.

8A.2 SOURCES OF REVENUES

The Center's operating income the next fiscal year would be close to $1.8 million in 2005/06. Income was expected to come from two primary sources, government agencies and charitable groups. Both of these sources set strict limitations, typically of a line-item nature, for the use of the funds they provided. One of the most stringently enforced rules was the prohibition against the accumulation of an operating surplus. The intent was to have as much as possible of the funds go to the ultimate beneficiary. The income received each fiscal year for funding operations should equal the allowable operating expenses incurred in providing services. Increases in working capital and funds to cover past operating deficits were not an allowable expense. If income was greater than operating expenses, the center would run into considerable difficulty with its funding agencies. If income was less, the Center would soon find its ability to continue operating impaired.

During fiscal year 2005/06, payments from the federal and state governments would constitute the largest sources of operating income, as shown in the following table:

Expected Distribution of 2005/06	Operating Revenues by Source
Federal government	35.8%
State government	34.2
Aloha United Way	14.4
Parents	6.8
Contributions	6.5
Other	2.3
Total	100.0%

Payment was usually received one to three months after billing. At the end of the federal fiscal year, federal regulations required an end-of-contract accounting. Payment for the last month was usually delayed an additional one or two months. The State government was the other major source of income. It, as well as parents who paid a portion of their children's expenses, was billed at the end of the month in which the service was provided and payment was generally received within the next 30 to 60 days:

Sources of Income (%)—Fiscal year ends June 30								
	1997/98	1998/99	1999/00	2000/01	2001/02	2002/03	2003/04	2004/05
State of Hawaii	58	41	38	38	35	34	31	34
U.S. Government	0	25	27	33	36	38	40	37
United Way	32	25	21	18	18	15	15	14
Other*	10	9	14	11	11	13	14	15
Total	100	100	100	100	100	100	100	100

*Local foundations, parents, and other sources.

Aloha United Way was the largest nongovernmental source of funds, providing over 14 percent of the Center's revenue in 2004/05. United Way funds were allocated annually and distributed at the start of each month in 12 equal payments. Although the Center had to apply for funds each year, experience had shown that these funds could be counted on in the future as long as the Center did not make an operating surplus. The United Way reduced its payments, dollar for dollar, for any not-for-profit agency with an operating surplus of more than $5,000 at the end of each year. They reasoned that funds were provided to pay for services, and if any recipient did not need them for that purpose, there were many other recipients who would use them for worthwhile purposes.

Over the years the Center's sources of income had changed dramatically. Starting in the 1980s, payments from the State of Hawaii for children placed at the Center began a slow but steady rise. By 1997/98, the year after Ron Williams became executive director, State payments were 58 percent of total income with no income at all coming from the Federal government. Without federal dollars, the Center was locked into trying to maintain a semblance of quality care for a very small portion of the total number of children needing help. Thus it was with great excitement that Ron and his co-workers viewed the availability of federal funds beginning in 1998. This new source of funds allowed the center to expand rapidly and to more adequately service the pressing needs of the community. A further advantage of federal funds was that they came in the form of signed contracts negotiated each year, which provided a guaranteed source of funding for a specific number of children. A lot of forms and government red tape were involved but Ron and his staff had learned how to handle the administration of the contracts.

From zero in 1997 the federal funds soared to 25 percent of revenues in 1998/99 and 37 percent in 2004/05. The growth of federal money, however, was not matched by a similar rise in funds from other sources. Most of the growth in the center's budget, $682,000 in 1997/98 to $1.6 million in 2004/05, came from the buildup of federal contract dollars.

8A.3 EXPENSES

In simplest terms the Center collected funds from its various sources and used them to pay for the services it provided for the children in its care. In the projected 2005/06 operating budget approximately two-thirds of all outlays would go for payroll expenses (see Exhibit 8A.1). The remaining one-third would be allocated to other operating expenses such as supplies, travel, occupancy/utilities, and equipment. Like many service-oriented businesses, the Center was labor intensive. Payroll outlays were made in the month the services were provided and the other operating expenses typically were paid later—60 percent in the month following purchase and 40 percent the month after that.

The parent agency provided many direct and indirect support services to the Honolulu Children's Treatment Center, and the Center in turn paid 10 percent of its total gross income to the parent agency. These payments, called the "centage" fee, were due the month following billing for the services provided. The centage fee was a major source of operating funds for the parent agency. Principal among the services it provided the center were program consultation, employee retirement and health plan provision and administration, a full range of insurance coverage, auditing services, legal services, public relations, federal-level governmental contract negotiations, fundraising

Honolulu Children's Treatment Center—2005/06 Fiscal Year	
Revenue:	
Federal	$640,350
State	612,600
Aloha United Way	257,500
Parents' payments	121,600
Contributions	116,300
Other	40,947
Total revenues	$1,789,297
Expenses:	
Personnel	$1,207,000
Field service ("centage")	178,870
Professional consultation	45,500
Supplies	90,300
Occupancy	87,100
Awards and grants	54,500
Travel	44,200
Equipment	30,000
Other*	70,905
Total expenses	$1,808,375
Surplus/(deficit)	($19,078)
Includes $10,000 for payment of interest on the $100,000 bank loan.	

EXHIBIT 8A.1   PROJECTED STATEMENT OF EXPECTED OPERATING EXPENSES AND INCOME

for major capital expenditures, long-range fiscal and program planning, and centralized purchasing.

8A.4 THE BANK LOAN

The first signs of impending financial problems came in 2003, with the situation becoming critical a year and a half later. In July 2004, there wasn't enough cash available to meet the payroll. The Center took out a bank loan of $75,000 for three months at 8.25 percent interest secured by federal government receivables. The interest rate was prime plus 4 percent. Everyone, including Ron, thought it was just a temporary problem. As soon as the delayed end-of-fiscal-year payments were received, the loan could be paid back. This was done but to everyone's dismay a similar cash shortage almost immediately reappeared, necessitating another loan. This time the loan was for $100,000 at 8.75 percent interest and a term of six months with similar collateral. This loan was still outstanding, and it was only with some effort that the monthly interest payments had been made.

The size and cause of the loan had been a major source of concern to Ron. The Center was not against borrowing for short-term needs but it was against having a loan that never seemed to get repaid. Although it had been renewed several times, the bank might decide not to renew it again since it had now become obvious this was not just a temporary need for funds. In any case, bank loan interest rates had risen in recent months with the prime reaching 5.5 percent, up 1.25 percent from when the original loan was made. The expectation was for even higher rates as the Federal Reserve Board was tightening credit after a long period of low interest.

To compound the problem, state and federal contract negotiators would not accept interest charges on the loan as a reimbursable expense. Nongovernmental sources expected that their contributions would go toward providing services, not to pay loan costs. The United Way was of no help, either. Since the Center was funded as a not-for-profit organization, it would drop its support, dollar for dollar, for any agency that showed more than a $5,000 operating surplus at the end of the fiscal year. Interest payments were not an allowable operating expense. To date, about half the interest expense had been met by income received from nongovernmental sources and the remainder had shown up as an increase in the operational deficit, which was projected to reach close to $19,000 for 2005/06. Although this was not high in terms of the projected 2005/06 budget of $1.8 million, it was still unacceptable to Ron as well as to his board of directors.

Of even greater concern to Ron and the board was the rise in payables, particularly to the parent agency. The unpaid centage fee was almost $400,000 at the end of 2004. There was no penalty for late payment to the parent agency but most of the other creditors had a discount for early payment, a 1.5 percent per month charge on overdue bills, or both. In 2004 no discounts were taken and late payment penalties were over $1,000.

These overdue payments had become an increasing source of friction with the parent agency and were the cause of a series of letters of concern from the board of directors requesting more information and early repayment of the bank loan and the payables. In their latest letter the board pointed out that they knew the centage collections were now coming in at the rate of 15 percent during the month service was provided, 60 percent the month after, 20 percent the third month, and 5 percent the fourth month. "Agreeably, this should have some initial effect," they wrote, "but surely if you manage things properly you should be able to catch up after four months, and then you can pay the loan and begin to reduce your payables."

Balance Sheets and Total Revenues: 1997, 2001, and 2004			
	12/31/97	12/31/01	12/31/04
Assets:			
Cash	$5,067	$24,221	$20,521
Accounts receivable	22,204	81,036	266,267
Prepaid expenses	—	6,840	11,850
Reserves held by headquarters*	46,649	94,905	47,535
Total assets	$73,920	$207,002	$346,173
Liabilities:			
Accounts payable-trade	$17,484	$137,971	$117,322
Accounts payable-headquarters	31,438	32,819	396,896
Bank loan	—	—	100,000
Accrued expenses and payables	8,314	21,526	22,033
Loan from headquarters	—	15,000	15,000
Total liabilities	$57,236	$207,316	$651,251
Net assets	$16,684	$(314)	$(305,078)
Total liabilities and net assets	$73,920	$207,002	$346,173
Total revenues	$682,090	$1,439,651	$1,566,602

*These reserves are restricted for capital improvements and are not available to the center for operations.

Exhibit 8A.2   Honolulu Children's Treatment Center

Before preparing a response to the board, Ron decided to go over once again the budget for 2005/06 (see Exhibit 8A.1) and the 2004 balance sheet (see Exhibit 8A.2), both previously submitted to the parent agency and the United Way. The formats were mostly consistent with the generally accepted standards of accounting as applied to not-for-profit agencies. Since there were no substantive changes in services provided or purchases forecasted for 2005/06, aside from a somewhat larger volume and cost increases due to inflation, the projections were believed to be reasonably accurate.

As Ron Williams thought about the Center's financial problems and the request from the parent agency, he realized the irony of it all. Ten years ago, when a lower level of services was being provided, there were few financial problems. Now that he had successfully increased the Center's funding, the financial situation seemed to be falling apart. Perhaps in coming up with a response to the parent agency's "please explain" request, he would be able to find a way to resolve the potentially crippling financial situation. There was at least one consoling aspect to all this: With federal funding many more children were receiving much better care than was previously possible. The governmental third-party payments at about 70 percent of total operating revenues were, from all expectations, here to stay.

8A.5 QUESTIONS

1. What are the financial and nonfinancial causes of the situation that the CTC currently faces?

2. How serious are the causes you identified in #1, and do these arise from internal policies and practices or from external sources? Use any appropriate tools from

Chapters 5–8 to assist you in answering this question, using financial analysis where appropriate.

3. What is the most serious problem facing CTC? Are there any other problems that you perceive? Support your answer.

4. Is the California board (which communicate with the parent agency and oversees the Honolulu CTC) right in its assessment of the ability of this situation to self-correct if "things are managed properly"? In addressing this question, for your forward year cash planning you may assume the following:

  a. The organization starts with no cash, no loan, no receivables, and no payables.

  b. Revenues equal expenses and there is no operating deficit or surplus.

5. What is (are) the alternative solution(s) to the problem(s) you identified in #3?

6. What are your top three recommendations for CTC? Give any implementation specifics (actions, timing) that you can to help the board and management team.

CASE STUDY: TRICITY ACADEMY

Assignment: Your task is to complete a cash budget worksheet and a written analysis that interprets the cash budget. Complete both parts of the case study—a cash budget worksheet and an interpretation write-up. The worksheet template follows this assignment prospectus.

Purpose: This assignment requires completion of a partially completed cash budget worksheet, as well as interpretation of the completed cash budget. (For those with access to Microsoft Excel™, an Excel™ worksheet is available for use at the website that accompanies this book.) All individual line items of cash inflows and cash outflows for a private 501(c)(3) nonprofit pre-K–12 school, Tri-City Academy, have been completed. (These data are from a real organization, but the name has been changed for confidentiality purposes.) Remaining to be done are some subtotals, totals, and then transferring the totals to the master cash budget worksheet in order to complete the cash budget (see generic template in Chapter 8). By completing this worksheet and an interpretive write-up indicating what the cash budget shows us, you are demonstrating your understanding of the totaling of various cash inflows, cash outflows, and their compilation to a cash budget.

CASH BUDGET

CONSTRUCTION   First, complete the boxes that are left blank on the cash receipt template. (If you are working from the Excel™ file, click on left tab in the Excel™ file.) You will see the specific locations of those boxes that you need to fill in listed underneath the table, near the bottom of that worksheet. Second, fill in the blank items in the cash disbursements worksheet (if working from the Excel™ file, click on the middle tab to go to that worksheet). Finally, go to the cash budget (rightmost tab if using the worksheet file) template, and fill in the formulas there. Near the top, you will mainly be entering "copy and paste" numbers (or use this type of formula if using the computer spreadsheet) to pull numbers from your now-completed cash receipts and cash disbursements worksheets. [If using the computer spreadsheet, begin your formula by pressing = (the equals key) and then you can click on the appropriate tab (e.g., cash receipts tab) and on the appropriate totals cell within that worksheet (you will see the referenced cell address show up in the formula bar near the top of the Excel™ screen once you do so).] Do the same for other cash receipts items in your cash budget template. The first total has been completed for you. (In the computer spreadsheet as well, the first total has been completed, so you can view that cell formula to see how the formulas look once complete.)

Now work downward in your cash budget by summing columns to calculate each month's net cash flow. Then, as shown in the template in Chapter 8, add this to beginning cash to get ending cash. Subtract the "minimum cash required"—the same amount each month—to get the adjusted cash position. If that number is *negative*, this implies a *shortfall* of cash, and if the organization cannot increase revenues or decrease expenses, this amount would be total dollar amount of the credit line "drawdown" (credit line balance borrowed). If that number is *positive*, a cash *surplus*, this amount would presumably be invested in interest-bearing securities or a money market mutual fund. Note that the number shown in each month's column, for either a shortfall or a surplus, is cumulative. For a surplus, if it is $40,000 one month and $50,000 the next month, an additional $10,000 would have been invested in short-term investments.

CASH BUDGET

ANALYSIS   For each of the questions in (a) through (d), write one short paragraph to answer the question:

a.   What is the largest surplus cash amount, if any, over the four months, and in what month does it occur?

b.   What is the largest shortage cash amount, if any, over the four months, and in what month does it occur?

c.   If there is a surplus in one or more months (refer to your answer in (a)), what could Tri-City Academy do with the surplus (after reviewing pertinent sections of Chapters 7 and 8, give some recommendations for how to utilize or deploy those funds)? If there is no month with a surplus, just put "not applicable" for part (c).

d.   If there is a shortage in one or more months (refer to your answer in (b)), what could Tri-City Academy do to deal with the shortfall (after reviewing pertinent sections of Chapters 7 and 8, give some recommendations for how to obtain or free up the needed funds)? If there is no month with a shortage, just put "not applicable" for part (d).

Projected Cash Receipts for Tri-City Academy (Feb–May 2006)

Month \ Item	Feb	Mar	Apr	May	TOTAL
Tuition	63600	80000	63600	63600	270800
Athletic Fees	500	500	500	500	
Late Fees	300	300	300	300	1200
Telethon Income	0	0	0	17000	17000
Foundation Grant	0	0	0	0	0
State Grant	0	0	0	0	0
Registration Fees	30000	10000	0	0	40000
Club Donations	2000	2000	2000	2000	8000
Pre- & Post-Care	1900	1900	1900	1900	7600
Store Certificate Sales	0	0	0	0	0
Other	0	0	0	0	0
TOTAL:					

Projected Cash Disbursements for Tri-City Academy (Feb–May 2006)

Item / Month	Feb	Mar	Apr	May	TOTAL
Payroll Expense: Faculty & Staff	$72,000	$72,000	$72,000	$72,000	
Substitute Teachers	0	2,656	0	5,000	
Retiremt. Withholding	700	700	700	700	
Subtotal: Payroll & Other Empl. Exp.	72,700				
Payment to Church	6,250	6,250	6,250	6,250	25,000
Other Expenses:					
Copier	500	987	750	750	
PSI & IN Gas	220	562	350	350	
Misc.	500	5,001	1,000	1,000	
Repair & Mainten.	300	100	100	100	
Fundraising Expenses	—	6,625	—	—	
Office Supplies	1,600	5,560	3,000	3,000	
Postage	300	616	450	450	
Athletic	1,000	1,800	1,200	1,200	
Phone	400	272	300	300	
Supplies	3,000	1,080	2,250	2,250	
Yearbooks & Ribbons	—	8,500	—	—	
Sports Banquet	—	2,400	—	2,400	
Testing Evaluation	—	—	1,800	—	
Total Other Exps.	7,820				
Store Certificate Remittances	0	0	0	0	0
TOTAL REGULAR EXPENSES:	86,770				
Capital Expenditures:	0	43,000	0	0	43,000
TOTAL CASH DISBURSEMENTS:					

Projected Cash Budget (Feb–May 2006)

Item / Month	Feb	Mar	Apr	May	TOTAL	
BEGINNING CASH	$5,000				—	
CASH RECEIPTS	0					<-- total
CASH DISBURSEMENTS	0					<-- total
+ NET CASH FLOW						<-- total
= ENDING CASH					—	
– Minimum Cash Balance	25,000	25,000	25,000	25,000	25,000	
= CASH SURPLUS / (SHORTFALL)					—	

Note: The Feb beginning cash was January's ending cash,which was told to us by treasurer.

CHAPTER 9

LONG-RANGE FINANCIAL PLANNING AND CAPITAL BUDGETING

9.1 INTRODUCTION

This chapter outlines the financial manager's role in the long-range financial planning and capital allocation processes. Managing growth is one of the reasons organizations plan and do financial evaluations. The chapter begins by developing the financial plan for existing and already approved programs, then shows how the financial evaluation of new program alternatives such as new ventures are made. We then demonstrate how you may evaluate individual capital expenditures made as part of program implementation. A financial approach to evaluating mergers and acquisitions, partnerships, joint ventures, and strategic alliances follows. We conclude with a survey of actual practices in the areas of long-range financial planning and capital budgeting, to help you see what your peer organizations are doing.

Rhode Islanders Sponsoring Education (RISE) learned the value of long-range financial and program planning when its service demands outstripped its ability to meet those demands. A private nonprofit agency established in Rhode Island to educate the children of imprisoned women as a means of attacking the intergenerational cycle of poverty and violence, it established an 8-member committee (from its 25-member board of directors) to revisit its mission, vision statement, and goals. Then the committee established a long-range plan, which included goals, objectives, and action plans for RISE's future finances, as well as for its evaluation strategies, its role in the network of local nonprofit service providers, its public relations, and its staff and board structure. The six-page long-range plan specifies a cap on how many new students can be admitted each year to the program, with the cap based on the amount of funds raised from sponsors.

Before developing the plan, RISE (as would many nonprofits) took as many students as applied and hoped to later raise the needed funds. As importantly, the plan specified what would and would not be its core services. One of its board members, whose school also partners with RISE, praises it: "One of the beautiful things about RISE is that it doesn't try to be all things to all people."[1] Notice from this example that the strategic plan and the long-range financial plan should be consistent. As a side note, RISE also created a new associate director position, hiring an experienced Salvation Army manager who professionalized the agency by installing new systems and procedures.

Despite such success stories, some nonprofit managers and board members continue to devalue the planning process, perhaps because of (1) a philosophy that planning techniques are corporate-world methods that do not fit the values and philosophies of the nonprofit sector, (2) the often-changing nature of the environment within which they operate, (3) ignorance, or (4) a simple breakdown in their implementation of planning and evaluation techniques. Faith-based organizations, for example, devalued planning skills in the early 1990s, partly because these techniques appeared to go against biblical admonitions to have faith and not be overly concerned about the future. Recent evidence, however, indicates this is changing, as more churches and other ministries are using long-range planning techniques.[2]

Executive directors/chief executive officers (EDs/CEOs) from a broad range of nonprofits indicate that, after fundraising, grant writing, and volunteer administration, the areas that they rate the highest for training needed are planning—which would include program and financial planning—and cooperative ventures.[3] We address both of these topics in this chapter. Partly to deal with these sorts of knowledge/skill gaps, the Panel on the Nonprofit Sector (convened by the Independent Sector) recommends that organizations have individuals with some financial literacy on their boards.

Nonprofit financial planning was formerly limited mostly to the single-year budgeting process. This is neither strategic nor wise, but mere "bean counting." To plan successfully, an organization must have a strategic thinker at its helm and an environment in which it infuses strategic, long-range thinking into all of its endeavors. Regardless of line and staff relations, everyone from the executive director down—and especially the chief financial officer (CFO)—must adopt a planning philosophy.

Planning is not just an extension of the budgeting process. It starts with good strategic planning, which identifies the key issues to which the appropriate numbers can later be attached, as we noted in Chapter 3.

We focus on formal planning, in that most business-sector studies have documented that organizations using formal plans tend to outperform those using informal plans. In the nonprofit arena, a recent study of churches indicates that those engaging in formal planning experienced greater growth in both attendance and finances.[4]

As nonprofits begin contracting with governmental agencies, they find that government oversight places emphasis on planning and reporting. Yet, as noted in the Indiana nonprofit survey done by Gronbjerg and colleagues, 30 percent of nonprofits refer to strategic planning as a major challenge, and 43 percent say that obtaining adequate funding is a major challenge.[5] Considering these results, it is no surprise that long-range financial planning is a difficult task, one that many nonprofits choose not to undertake. But it is a vital part of proficient financial management. With that backdrop, let's turn to the long-range financial planning and capital project evaluation techniques.

9.2 PLANNING FOR THE FUTURE

(a) **IMPORTANCE OF LONG-RANGE FINANCIAL PLANNING.**   A best practices study of community associations documented the importance of long-term financial planning, listing both a plan for major assets (*long-term financial plan*) and for revenues and expenses (*long-term operating budget*) in its profile of best planning practices:

- Establish a long-term financial plan for the association's assets (cash, accounts receivable, replacement fund, investments, etc.) that is reviewed and revised annually.

- Develop written, board-approved investment policies and procedures.

- Commission a reserve study and/or update current reserve study at least every three years and review the report annually.

- Prepare a long-term operating budget covering the next three to five years.

- Include reasonable reserves for future major repairs and replacement of common facilities in assessments as determined by the association's most recent reserve study.[6]

Businesses call the plan for major assets a *pro forma balance sheet*, and the long-term operating budget is *a pro forma income statement*. Think of pro forma as "projected"; its literal meaning is "as a matter of form."

One financial policy that should be addressed periodically, as a best practice, is the specification of the levels of cash reserves held as operating reserves and as strategic reserves. Operating reserves represent money for a rainy day, and buffer against revenue shortfalls or unanticipated expense spikes. Strategic reserves may be called a building reserve in your organization—44 percent of surveyed Denver-area nonprofits have a building reserve, for example.[7] We highlight the needed total cash reserves in our discussion of the target liquidity level, one of the outputs of a well-constructed financial plan.

In addition to helping you establish the appropriate level for your target liquidity level, consisting primarily as cash reserves (including short-term investments), we see at least four other advantages for organizations that engage in long-range financial planning:

1. It enables them to better determine the appropriate amount of net assets, or equity, in the organization's capital structure (which also implies how much debt the organization may carry; see Chapter 10).[8]

2. They more fully benefit from strategic planning, and are able to mesh the strategic plan with financial policies and decisions and with yearly operating budgets.

3. It enables them to portray themselves as well-managed organizations to banks, bond investors, and foundations and agencies providing government grants; in fact, one consultant counsels philanthropists that one way to reduce the risk of their investment in nonprofits is to ensure that recipient organizations are implementing "financial plans for the long-term health of the organization."[9]

4. These organizations are better able to determine a reasonable growth rate for the organization's activities.

A late 2005 survey of Oregon-based nonprofits found that, even though fundraising efforts were deemed successful, 30 percent of the nonprofits were forced to reduce services to meet operational costs, and most nonprofits were concerned about rising healthcare costs for employees, increased costs of other insurance, and increased regulation for nonprofits.[10] Anticipating negative trends such as these by including their likely effect on the organization's financial position would not only cause the nonprofit to hold a higher target liquidity level (to avert service cutbacks), but also help the organization prepare itself for the possible cost increases that lie ahead. The financial plan helps your organization see the effects of these trends on its financial position.

(b) CFO'S ROLE IN FINANCIAL PLANNING AND CAPITAL BUDGETING. In his classic article "Strategy for Financial Emergencies," written 40 years ago, Gordon Donaldson declares, "[T]he financial executive's primary managerial responsibility is to preserve the continuity of the flow of funds so that no essential decision of top management is frustrated for lack of corporate purchasing power." Although written for business financial executives, Donaldson's assertion applies equally to nonprofit finance officers. The board treasurer and the organization's CFO share responsibility for ensuring that the nonprofit plans its financial future and allocates scarce capital to the best uses. Regardless of whether the treasurer is the CFO, he or she retains ultimate responsibility for these processes, so at a minimum the treasurer must oversee this important aspect of proficient financial management. As we have emphasized, doing this includes projecting the organization's liquidity and accumulation of or maintenance of the target liquidity level. Beyond this, there are several key components to the CFO's responsibility:

> The CFO's role seems to be threefold. First, as part of the senior management team, the CFO contributes fully in overall strategic planning for the organization, always with an eye on the financial ramifications. The second role is to drive the capital planning process, maintain the rigor around assessment, keep everyone honest, and serve as "quarterback" of the capital planning team. The third role is the quantitative role: understand debt capacity, provide a consistent methodology for assessing return on individual projects, and generally support the decision-making process.[11]

We developed the strategic planning role in Chapter 3, and we shall return to evaluating debt capacity in the next chapter. Our focus in this chapter is to spell out the long-range financial planning process and the capital budgeting process.

(c) **LONG-RANGE FINANCIAL PLANNING PROCESS.**   Financial projections covering the next five years are developed in an exercise called *long-range financial planning*. These projections should be done periodically as part of the organization's strategic planning process. The main financial planning document should be based on all current programs as well as those future programs already approved. Later planning scenarios can be developed to bring possible new programs or ventures into the picture. The purposes of the long-range financial plan are:

- To tie financial resource requirements to the strategic plan
- To identify any future period with fund surpluses or, much more commonly, fund shortfalls
- To determine approximate funding needs for the shortfall periods, which is the essential information the executive needs for planning capital campaigns, other special fundraising appeals, and endowment building
- To identify the seasonal and cyclical aspects of the organization's cash flows
- To bring together in one place all the interacting sources and uses of funds experienced by the nonprofit organization: operating, investing, and financing cash flows
- To build a financial contingency plan, or what Donaldson terms "a strategy for financial mobility"

We cannot emphasize too strongly the importance of doing a long-range financial plan. Not only will such a plan help a strong organization to become stronger, but it may spell the difference between survival and financial failure and dissolution for your organization. Often nonprofit organizations do a good job of selecting programs, but then fail to plan for the financial requirements of implementing those programs, leading a number of these organizations—especially private colleges—to fail.[12]

Averting a financial crisis from too-rapid or ill-advised expansion is well worth the expense and effort of long-range financial planning. An example to emulate here is Cedarville University (Cedarville, Ohio), which uses its strategic planning process to implement "managed growth." Our chapter-opening vignette of RISE is another positive example.

Further, where programs are vital to the organization's mission but the financial plan indicates significant shortfalls, the ED/CEO is stimulated to search for other organizations to help share the load. Resource sharing may take place through a merger, acquisition, joint venture, or strategic alliance.

The degree of sophistication and level of detail in nonprofit organizations' financial planning varies. Many small organizations, and quite a few larger ones, do no formal long-range financial planning; this situation tends to indicate an organization whose overall financial administration process is poorly managed. The Lilly study found that organizations not using "present and anticipated financial positions" to guide programmatic decisions tended to be those deficient in overall financial management.

Some of these organizations may even engage in strategic planning, but are in the dark about the funding feasibility of these plans and whether they need to begin arranging financing now or can self-finance the program. Capital campaigns cannot be initiated and executed quickly. Other organizations have sophisticated, computerized financial models. Mostly these are larger organizations that can afford to devote staff and computer resources to the task or hire an outside consultant to develop the model. Many organizations, even those otherwise proficient in their financial management processes, fail to anticipate key events that could alter the future financial position of the organization. As a result, these organizations have no strategy for dealing with those events if and when they occur and no financial model with which to project cash flow. At bottom, proficient financial managers anticipate *what could be*, not merely what they think is the most likely financial future.

(d) FINANCIAL PLANNING BASICS.   Here's a simple approach that can be used to get started in financial planning. It is based on three vital inputs:

1. The most recent three years of financial statements
2. The capital budgets for the next five years, insofar as they are known
3. Management and board financial policies regarding investments, debt, and minimum necessary liquidity

How might your organization assess its future capital spending needs? The best general approach is to first specify several categories of the external environment that will affect your organization's future (e.g., competition or regulations), then identify the specific external drivers that will be at work within those categories and that have relevance to your industry (e.g., youth services or performance arts). Then specify the internal goals that will best suit your organization to meet those anticipated developments in the external environment. Finally, detail the capital responses that your organization will have to make to achieve those internal goals: new or refurbished plant or equipment, enhanced information technology, renovation, expansion, upgrades to systems, training investments, increased research and development expenditures, multiyear brand- and image-building investments, and so on. Consult Exhibit 9.1 for a filled-out schematic for the hospital industry.

Armed with these inputs, the financial manager can obtain or develop operating forecasts that will enable the formulation of simple long-range financial plans. While the next year may be somewhat detailed (depending on whether the operating budget has been developed yet), years 2 to 5 will show very little detail—possibly only total revenue and total expense of operations.

The example that follows illustrates the long-range financial plan and the fact that the planning process, when used properly, takes at least two passes or iterations. The first pass takes the strategic plan and preexisting funding strategies as givens and determines each future year's funding surplus or shortfall. The feedback from this exercise provides the organization's managers and board with needed input for possible revisions of the strategic plan and/or the funding strategy—which is the second pass.

To the extent surpluses appear in forward years, the management team can choose whether to:

- Develop program initiatives (expand present programs or add new ones)
- Reduce debt

Responses to External Drivers of Capital Need			
Category	**External Drivers**	**Internal Goals**	**Capital Responses**
Competition	• Strategic efforts by other area hospitals • Emergence of specialty providers • Shift of volume to physician offices and other outpatient centers • Payer shifts of volume to lower-cost providers • Scarcity of medical professionals • Shifting regulated and negotiated payment incentives	• Protect existing volume and market share • Create opportunities to expand market share • Avoid loss of profitable programs to specialty providers • Attract and retain valued employees and physicians • Retool programs that become unprofitable as a result of shifts In reimbursement	• Facilities renovation or construction • Equipment purchases and upgrades • Automation and enhancement of digital capabilities • Information systems and technology up grades
Technology/ Regulation	• Advances in technology • Advances in pharmaceutical therapies • Shift in procedures to outpatient settings • Bio-terrorism preparedness • Privasy and security	• Retain key physicians • Improve physician and patient satisfaction • Enhance quality of care and patient safety • Comply with regulatory mandates • Maintain community safety net services for health emergencies	• Equipment purchases or upgrades • Process redesign around new equipment and treatment modilities • Renovations and expansion of ambulatory capacity • Joint ventures around ambulatory capacity • Implementation of digital capabilities
Consumers	• Rise of consumerism in selection of healthcare providers • External reporting of quality and safety data • Extension of life expectancy • Aging population that uses more services • Shifting regional demographics	• Invest in programs and services for the changing needs of an aging population • Communicate quality externally • Report external information accurately	• Facilities renovation or construction • Equipment purchases or upgrades • IT/IS enhancements to reporting

Source: Financing the Future Healthcare Financial Management Association, Used by permission.

EXHIBIT 9.1   CAPITAL PLANNING EXAMPLE USING THE HOSPITAL INDUSTRY

- Increase investment in existing staff or technology
- Build liquidity (if appropriate, based on financial policies)

Where shortfalls appear, organizations can choose whether to

- Have large cash reserves, draw these down
- Reduce discretionary expenses
- Redirect funds from noncore to core (essential to mission) programs
- Sell investment securities from portfolio
- Initiate capital campaign (if capital spending is the reason for the shortfall)
- Increase interest revenue through the use of appropriate investment vehicles and/or building of endowment
- Increase rental and/or unrelated business income revenue
- Increase investment in fundraising for operations—annual campaign

If there are perpetual problems with shortfalls, permanently reduce expenses and work to initiate or increase investment in planned giving fundraising.

At a minimum, do a projection of the statement of cash flows (SCF) (you may wish to refer to Chapter 6 for a review of this statement). To keep things even simpler, enter the last five or six years of statement of activity data into a computer spreadsheet. Then let the spreadsheet program do a straight-line projection of total revenue (income) and expenses. Exhibit 9.2 shows such a projection using the financials of an anonymous ministry organization.

Notice the deteriorating trend; if the trend had continued, the organization would have ended up out of business. Simply knowing that this is what will occur if corrective action is not taken is well worth the time and effort of the entire planning exercise. If you were the CFO of this organization, and its financial policies rule out the use of short-term debt, how might you close the gap in 2009 to 2011?

As you reflect on the situation, you will likely identify three situational factors that generally act as constraints on your actions:

1. You cannot draw down liquidity without violating the minimum liquidity financial policy (target liquidity level).
2. Short-term debt is forbidden (not uniformly but commonly, in nonprofits).
3. All programs are core (so no program may be eliminated or severely curtailed).

The financial manager might recommend these possible courses of action to the ED/CEO and the board:

- Reduce discretionary expenses.
- Increase the investment in fundraising.
- Increase rental and unrelated business income.
- To extent possible, build endowment and/or shift investment portfolio to higher-yield investment vehicles (within risk parameters).
- Revisit the minimum liquidity target to see if it should be set higher in the future.

The planning exercise is valuable because when shortfalls are projected, they provide early warning of impending financial shortages, and when surpluses are expected, we

Statements of Activity of a Nonprofit Organization

	2000	2001	2002	2003	2004	2006	Projected 2007	Projected 2008	Projected 2009	Projected 2010	Projected 2011
Income:											
Contributions	$5,121,652	$5,088,913	$5,721,854	$5,725,263	$5,852,144	$6,618,502	$6,665,790	$6,945,143	$7,224,496	$7,503,849	$7,783,202
Net gain on disposal of fixed assets	29,733	214,717	85,714	34,816	42,641	78,749					
Investment income	193,319	194,318	227,973	275,187	279,756	364,352					
Sales less cost of goods sold			—	128,116	142,991	149,530					
Total Income	$5,344,704	$5,497,948	$6,035,541	$6,163,382	$6,317,532	$7,211,133	$7,286,914	$7,627,449	$7,967,985	$8,308,520	$8,649,055
Expenses:											
Program Activities:											
Church growth, evangelism	$1,618,616	$1,409,014	$1,526,571	$1,678,493	$1,873,124	$2,456,467					
Media, translation	548,411	469,713	575,519	697,491	875,791	785,726					
Theological, church leadership training	404,940	356,640	414,600	410,305	360,691	289,019					
Education	272,770	199,141	217,979	246,747	334,175	302,764					
Field administration	207,196	192,317	228,145	297,591	347,325	291,803					
Appointees	206,719	209,831	133,666	108,690	108,726	94,001					
Homeland ministries, furlough	671,830	760,737	726,156	615,136	743,129	866,198					
Relief	96,276	44,915	118,758	192,541	133,910	434,442					

EXHIBIT 9.2 FINANCIAL PROJECTION PROVIDING EARLY WARNING OF FINANCIAL DETERIORATION

Statements of Activity of a Nonprofit Organization

	2000	2001	2002	2003	2004	2006	Projected 2007	Projected 2008	Projected 2009	Projected 2010	Projected 2011
Service to missionaries	71,872	59,049	137,027	135,292	182,386	137,644					
Medical	40,448	41,616	38,114	27,428	57,871	40,639					
Subtotal: program exps.	$4,139,078	$3,742,973	$4,116,535	$4,409,714	$5,017,128	$5,698,703	$5,712,065	$6,052,459	$6,392,852	$6,733,246	$7,073,639
Supporting activities: Management and general	$814,414	$996,659	$864,530	$1,046,032	$1,149,552	$1,210,873					
Fund raising	81,585	140,880	193,685	188,453	199,089	172,759					
Subtotal: support exps.	895,999	1,137,539	1,058,215	1,234,485	1,348,641	1,383,632	$1,501,193	$1,593,985	$1,686,778	$1,779,570	$1,872,363
Total expenses	$5,035,077	4,880,512	5,174,750	5,644,199	6,365,769	7,082,335	7,213,258	7,646,444	8,079,630	8,512,816	8,946,002
Excess (deficiency) of income over expenses over expenses	309,627	617,436	860 791	519,183	–48.237	128.798	73.656	(18,995)	(111,6451)	(204,296)	(296,947)
Unadjusted net assets—end of year*	$4,388,295	$5,005,731	$5,866,522	$6,385,705	$6,337,468	$6,466,266	$6,539,922	$6,520,927	$6,409,282	$6,204,985	$5,908,039

*Shows what net assets would be without adjustments or transfers.

Source: This table uses actual data for a ministry organization, but the organization's name has been withheld and the years changed. Projections were done by author using financial spreadsheet Microsoft Excel™. This is done by simply entering the numbers shown for contributions, then highlighting the range, and clicking and holding down the drag handle on the bottom right of the range and dragging it to the right over several cells.

EXHIBIT 9.2 FINANCIAL PROJECTION PROVIDING EARLY WARNING OF FINANCIAL DETERIORATION (*continued*)

may consider opportunities to expand or enhance the mission or build endowment. Furthermore, as noted earlier, you may engage in contingency planning, selecting for further study events that are not expected. Although they are not considered "most likely," and therefore are not incorporated into your normal financial plan, these events may still be quite probable and they could have a significant impact on your revenues, expenses, assets, or liabilities. High-profile natural disasters, such as the Asian tsunami and Gulf coast hurricanes, would be a prime example. These siphoned off significant donation funding from many non-relief U.S. nonprofits, especially food banks, homeless shelters, and after-school programs.[13]

(e) DEVELOP A FINANCIAL MODEL. The next phase in your financial planning process is to develop a full-blown financial model of your organization, its operations, its asset requirements, and how these will be financed. A financial model may be defined as "the financial representation or model of how an organization works and functions, created in such a way that it can productively be used as a means to simulate the real world."[14] This more complete portrait of your organization's financial future adds significant value to the simple forecast we profiled earlier by:

1. Showing asset requirements of growth (or scale-backs), along with the need for financing those asset requirements, by projecting key aspects of the statement of financial position (SFP).

2. Incorporating relationships between the various financial accounts into a cause-and-effect relationships, which is easily done even in a financial spreadsheet model.

3. Showing the true effects of revenue, expense, liability, and net asset changes on the target liquidity level, by backing out noncash effects of depreciation, amortization, and other accounting adjustments such as losses on discontinued operations or restructuring charges.

4. Identifying knowledge and information gaps that must be addressed for the organization to have a better understanding of its financial interrelationships and cash flows—some of which will be discovered in the processes of modeling #1, #2, and #3. Others will be unveiled as banking, payment system, and regulatory policies and constraints (Chapter 11) are built into the model and as loan covenants (Chapter 10) and restricted cash and other restricted net assets are identified in the model.

5. Allowing a view of the financial position, funding need, and revenue coverage of expense changes when any single input to the model changes in value. This what-if scenario analysis function is the most valuable feature of a financial model, in the view of most users. See Appendix 9A for an example.

It is beyond our scope to go into detail on the hows of financial modeling, and there are print and Internet sources to help you to develop a model.[15] We use a publicly available financial planning model developed by PriceWaterhouse Coopers[16] for service businesses to show you the level of detail and interaction between your forward year projections.

Exhibit 9.3 shows the set of assumptions that go into the financial model. Many items are computed as a percent of sales, or total revenues.

Next we see our first projected financial statement, the Income Statement (Exhibit 9.4). It is similar to the nonprofit statement of activity. As you study it, note the level of detail

Financial Model: Assumptions

Labels

Company name to be used on all statements..	
Date projections first begin..	January 1, 2005
Name of 1st product line..	Project Revenues
Name of 2nd product line..	Service Two
Name of 3rd product line..	Service Three
Name of 4th product line..	Service Four
Name of 1st department..	Production Process
Name of 2nd department..	Sales & Marketing
Name of 3rd department..	Administration

Sales

UNITS SALES	2005	2006	2007	2008	2009
Project Revenues	–	–	–	–	–
Service Two	–	–	–	–	–
Service Three	–	–	–	–	–
Service Four	–	–	–	–	–

AVERAGE FEES PER UNIT	2005	2006	2007	2008	2009
Project Revenues	–	–	–	–	–
Service Two	–	–	–	–	–
Service Three	–	–	–	–	–
Service Four	–	–	–	–	–

Balance Sheet

Accounts Receivable (adjustable upto 360days)...........*(in days)*..	45 days
Accounts Payable (fixed at 30 days)................................*(in days)*..	30 days
Salaries Payable (fixed at 15 days)................................*(in days)*..	15 days
Taxes Payable (fixed at 90 days)....................................*(in days)*..	90 days
Available Credit Line...*(as a percentage of net accounts receivable)*....................	0 days
Maximum Credit Line Used..*(amount borrowed not to exceed)*..................................	$0
Capital Equipment Lease Term (1 year minimum)........*(in years)*..	3 years
Long Term Borrowings Term (1 year minimum)...........*(in years)*..	5 years

DEPRECIATION	HARDWARE	SOFTWARE	FURN & FIXTURES
Production Process	3 years	3 years	3 years
Sales & Marketing	3 years	3 years	3 years
Administration	3 years	3 years	3 years

EXPENSES

HEAD COUNT	2005	2006	2007	2008	2009
Production Process	–	–	–	–	–
Sales & Marketing	–	–	–	–	–
Administration	–	–	–	–	–
TOTAL	–	–	–	–	–

PER PERSON EXPENSES	Supplies	Travel & Meals	Phone/Postage
Production Process	–	–	–
Sales & Marketing	–	–	–
Administration	–	–	–

EXHIBIT 9.3   FINANCIAL MODEL ASSUMPTIONS—SERVICE BUSINESS EXAMPLE

EQUIPMENT PURCHASES	Hardware	Software	Furn & Fixtures
Production Process	–	–	–
Sales & Marketing	–	–	–
Administration	–	–	–

Benefits & Taxes..(as a percentage of salaries)..

Salary Increases...(as an annual percentage)..

Sales Commissions...(as a percentage of sales)...

Total Sales Through Commissions..............................(as a percentage of total revenue).................................

Business Insurance...(as a percentage of total revenue).................................

Anticipated Bad Debt...(as a percentage of collections)..................................

Interest Revenue..(as a percentage of cash balance)................................ **4%**

Interest Expense On Credit Line................................(as a percentage of outstanding balance)................... **10%**

Interest Expense On Capital Equipment Lease...............(as a percentage of outstanding balance)............... **10%**

Interest Expense On Long Term Borrowings....................(as a percentage of outstanding balance)............... **10%**

Combined Federal & State Tex Rate..............................(as a percentage of positive cumulative income)...... **40%**

Office Rent...(per square foot)... **$3.00**

Minimum Office Space..(square foot age per person)..

Term of Office Lease...(in months)...

Utilities Expense...(per square foot)...

Expenses for advertising, tradeshows, and collateral are budgeted as indicated in the DETAIL worksheet.

Consultants,Contractors, & Professional Services are employed at market rates and are indicated as needed (see DETAIL worksheet).

Salaries are based on competitive compensation (see DETAIL for individual salaries).

Bonuses and other incentives are paid out as indicated in the income statement. www.pwcv2rform.com. Accessed: 01|21|06 Used by Permission.

EXHIBIT 9.3   FINANCIAL MODEL ASSUMPTIONS—SERVICE BUSINESS EXAMPLE (*continued*)

0-Jan-00 Income Statement ($)

	2005	2006	2007	2008	2009
Revenue					
Project Revenues	$0	$0	$0	$0	$0
Total Revenues	$0	$0	$0	$0	$0
Operating Expenses					
Production Process	$0	$0	$0	$0	$0
% of Revenues	0%	0%	0%	0%	0%
Sale & Marketing	$0	$0	$0	$0	$0
% of Revenues	0%	0%	0%	0%	0%
Administration	$0	$0	$0	$0	$0
% of Revenue	0%	0%	0%	0%	0%
Total Operating Expenses	$0	$0	$0	$0	$0
% of Revenue	0%	0%	0%	0%	0%
Interest Expense	$0	$0	$0	$0	$0
Interest Revenue	$0	$0	$0	$0	$0
Income Before Taxes	$0	$0	$0	$0	$0
Tax Exp	$0	$0	$0	$0	$0
Net Income	$0	$0	$0	$0	$0
% of Revenue	0%	0%	0%	0%	0%

EXHIBIT 9.4   PROJECTED REVENUES AND EXPENSES—SERVICE BUSINESS EXAMPLE

that is appropriate for your long-range financial plan. You may wish to customize it with your organization's Statement of Activities captions, or use it "as is" if you are projecting for a for-profit subsidiary that is involved in generating unrelated business income.

Note that the "Net Income" would be the "Change in Net Assets" for a nonprofit organization and that tax expense ("Tax Exp") might be zero for tax-exempt nonprofits (unless they have to pay some use or excise taxes or taxes on unrelated business income).

Next, we need to project the SFP, or balance sheet. Notice in Exhibit 9.5 the service business projected balance sheet developed by PriceWaterhouseCoopers. Again, modify it to the account categories for your organization, including a breakdown in "Cash" for unrestricted cash and restricted cash. The caption "A/R" is an abbreviation for accounts

Balance Sheet ($)					
	2005	2006	2007	2008	2009
ASSETS					
Current Assets					
Cash	$0	$0	$0	$0	$0
Net Accounts Rec	$0	$0	$0	$0	$0
Total Current Assets	$0	$0	$0	$0	$0
Gross Fixed Assets	$0	$0	$0	$0	$0
Less Accum Depreciation	$0	$0	$0	$0	$0
Net Fixed Assets	$0	$0	$0	$0	$0
TOTAL ASSETS	$0	$0	$0	$0	$0
LIABILITIES					
short Term Liabilities					
Accounts Payable (30 days)	$0	$0	$0	$0	$0
Salaries Payable (15 days)	$0	$0	$0	$0	$0
Taxes Payable (90 days)	$0	$0	$0	$0	$0
Line of Credit (0% of net A/R)	$0	$0	$0	$0	$0
Current Portion of Cap Equip Lease	$0	$0	$0	$0	$0
Current Portion of Long Term Debt	$0	$0	$0	$0	$0
Total Short Term Liabilities	$0	$0	$0	$0	$0
Long Term Liabilities					
Capital Equipment Lease (3 years)	$0	$0	$0	$0	$0
Long Term Debt (5 years)	$0	$0	$0	$0	$0
Total Long Term Liabilities	$0	$0	$0	$0	$0
TOTAL LIABILITIES	$0	$0	$0	$0	$0
Equity					
Preferred Stock	$0	$0	$0	$0	$0
Common Stock	$0	$0	$0	$0	$0
Retained Earnings	$0	$0	$0	$0	$0
Total Equity	$0	$0	$0	$0	$0
LIABILITIES & EQUITY	$0	$0	$0	$0	$0

Source: PriceWaterhouse Coopers. © 2005 Pricewaterhouse Coopers. All rights reserved. PricewaterhouseCoopers refers to the network of member firms of PricewaterhouseCoopers International Limited, each of which is a separate and independent legal entity. Available for download at: www.pwcv2rform.com. Accessed: 01/2/06. Used by permission.

EXHIBIT 9.5   PROJECTED ASSETS, LIABILITIES, AND NET ASSETS—SERVICE BUSINESS EXAMPLE

receivable, which would fit commercial nonprofits but might instead be pledges receivable for the donative nonprofit.

For Equity, use Net Assets, and split out Unrestricted Net Assets, Temporarily Restricted Net Assets, and Permanently Restricted Net Assets.

Finally, and for many organizations possibly the most important projection, is the sources and uses of funds projection. It is similar to a projected SCF, and you may opt to use your SCF format rather than the sources/uses template shown in Exhibit 9.6. Regardless, study it carefully, noting how the financial plan details the needs for funds and the anticipated funding sources. You may leave one category in the latter blank (zero value), using this as the "plug figure" for your projected long-range financial plan. Then strategize on how to meet that shortfall as you view the first-pass projection of your sources and uses. That leads us directly to the target liquidity level assessment, our next topic.

What is the bottom line on the sources and uses of funds projection? Ending cash. If the total of the anticipated sources of cash are inadequate to cover anticipated uses of cash, your ending cash will be eroded over time. Move now to arrange additional sources of funds or reduce anticipated uses of funds to bridge the gap between sources and uses. Furthermore, many organizations will want to intentionally plan to have a smaller total *uses* of cash figure, in order to build toward higher values of ending cash as it targets a higher liquidity level.

Statement of Sources & Uses ($)					
	2005	2006	2007	2008	2009
BEGINNING CASH	$0	$0	$0	$0	$0
Sources of Cash					
Net Income	$0	$0	$0	$0	$0
Add Depr/Amort	$0	$0	$0	$0	$0
Issuance of Preferred Stock	$0	$0	$0	$0	$0
Issuance of Common Stock	$0	$0	$0	$0	$0
Plus Changes In:					
Accounts Payable (30 days)	$0	$0	$0	$0	$0
Salaries Payable (15 days)	$0	$0	$0	$0	$0
Taxes Payable (90 days)	$0	$0	$0	$0	$0
Additions to Line of Credit	$0	$0	$0	$0	$0
Additions to Cap Equip Lease	$0	$0	$0	$0	$0
Additions to Long Term Debt	$0	$0	$0	$0	$0
Total Sources of Cash	$0	$0	$0	$0	$0
Uses of Cash					
Less Changes In:					
Net Accounts Rec	$0	$0	$0	$0	$0
Gross Fixed Assets	$0	$0	$0	$0	$0
Reductions to Line of Credit	$0	$0	$0	$0	$0
Reductions to Cap Equip Lease	$0	$0	$0	$0	$0
Reductions to Long Term Debt	$0	$0	$0	$0	$0
Total Uses	$0	$0	$0	$0	$0
CHANGES IN CASH	$0	$0	$0	$0	$0
ENDING CASH	$0	$0	$0	$0	$0

EXHIBIT 9.6 PROJECTED SOURCES AND USES OF FUNDS—SERVICE BUSINESS EXAMPLE

(f) PROJECT AND REEVALUATE TARGET LIQUIDITY.   Earlier in this book we profiled evaluating the necessary level of liquidity (Chapter 2, 5, and 8) and how to measure liquidity (Chapters 2 and 7). Better yet is an analysis of the target liquidity level that is based also on the projected financial position several years in the future. In this way, we not only know what level of operating reserves to hold, but also the level of strategic reserves to hold. The latter includes amounts accumulated to prefund capital expenditures, funds for unanticipated strategic options (such as new programs or large one-time service needs that may arise), and funds for a board-designated endowment, or quasi-endowment, the income from which may help fund program expenses. These additional funds are necessary because nonprofits typically do not earn enough of a surplus ("profit") of revenues over expenses to self-fund such expenditures on a timely basis.[17]

The beginning point for this analysis is the Ending Cash projection we looked at in our sources and uses projection (refer to Exhibit 9.6). Recall, from our ratios presentation in Chapter 7, the definition of target liquidity level and also a related ratio, target liquidity level lambda:

$$\text{Target liquidity level} = (\text{Cash and cash equivalents} + \text{Short-term investments}$$
$$+ \text{Total amount of credit line}^{**} - \text{Short-term loans})$$

Total amount of credit line is the ceiling amount approved for the bank, or the maximum amount that may be borrowed at any one time. It is similar to the credit limit on a credit card.

$$\text{Target liquidity level lambda} = \frac{\text{Target liquidity level} + \text{Projected OCF}}{\text{Uncertainty of OCF}}$$

Where:

Projected OCF is the operating cash flow amount for the next year
Uncertainty of OCF is the standard deviation of the organization's historical operating cash flows (OCFs) for at least the past three years

The first thing we add to Ending Cash is the amount held in short-term investments. Notice on our projected balance sheets (refer to Exhibit 9.5) that no line item was listed for short-term investments. If your organization has short-term investments (beyond cash and cash equivalents, with the latter being very short-term investments with a maturity at the time of purchase of three months or less), you should list those on your projected balance sheet immediately below the cash row. Then determine the total amount of your organization's negotiated credit line, if any, and add this to the total you had for (Ending Cash + short-term investments). This amount *will not be shown on your projected balance sheet except in the special case in which you plan to have borrowed up to the limit of that credit line at the balance sheet date, say, 12/31/08.* Your organization will find that one of the primary benefits of projecting a balance sheet is to know how much of a credit line to request from a bank. For comparison purposes, if you need to determine what another peer organization has arranged in a *past* year for its credit line you would have to search the notes that accompany the financial statements to find the total amount of the credit line. Finally, subtract also from your projected balance sheet any amount shown under current liabilities for "Credit line" or an equivalent entry, normally "Notes payable." This represent amounts borrowed under a credit line or similar short-term borrowing arrangement with a bank or other short-term lender.

For example, let's say you project Ending Cash of $5,000, short-term investments of $15,500, have arranged a credit line for $100,000, and project a borrowed amount of $45,000. Your projected target liquidity level would be $75,500 ($= \$5,000 + \$15,500 + \$100,000 - \$45,000$).

If your organization typically has significant across-year variability in its operating cash flows (consult your last five SCFs to check this), you will also want to calculate the projected TLLL, or projected target liquidity level lambda, which involves two modifications to the formula: (1) add the next year's projected operating cash flow to projected TLL and then (2) divide the sum from step 1 by the standard deviation of your organization's historical operating cash flows.

Revisiting our previous example, let's say your organization expects an operating cash flow for the next year of $-\$35,000$ and has these historical operating cash flows for the *past* five years:

PAST YEARS	OPERATING CASH FLOW
1	$45,000
2	−25,000
3	5,000
4	−15,000
5	10,000

Clearly, your organization has experienced significant variability in its OCFs. We need to calculate the standard deviation of this sample of cash flows to use in our calculation of projected TLLL. Let's illustrate that calculation by using Microsoft Excel™ and the built-in function for sample standard deviation:

Sample standard deviation = $\boxed{27{,}018.51}$ (Using STDEV function built into Excel™.)

Using this sample estimate for our OCF variability, we get this projected TLLL:

Projected TLLL = (TLL + Projected OCF)/Variability of OCF

Projected TLLL = ($75,500 + −$35,000)/$27,018.51

Projected TLLL = $40,500/$27,018.51

Projected TLLL = 1.50

If your organization's OCFs are approximately normally distributed (appearing as a fairly symmetrical, bell-shaped curve when graphed), we can use this information to estimate our probability of running out of cash.

First, let's assume that "out of cash" is a negative cash balance. This implies we exhaust our Ending Cash, then exhaust our short-term investments, then use up any previously unused credit line availability, and finally burn through any positive OCF that comes in the next period.

Second, in our illustration, next year's projected OCF is forecasted to be a negative $35,000, which we noted should drop our TLL to $40,500. Based on historical OCF variability (a standard deviation of $27,000 plus), what is the chance we will drop below

$0 in cash next year? We take the difference between $0 and our forecast of $40,500 (= TLL + Projected OCF), and divide that by $27,018.51. This gives us how many standard deviations $0 falls below our $40,500 forecast, which is actually called a "z score" in statistics:

$$z = (\$0 - \$40,500)/\$27,018.51$$

$$z = -\$40,500/\$27,018.51$$

$$z = -1.50$$

Notice that this figure is exactly the same as our projected TLLL.

The question is now: What is the probability of our liquidity dropping not just below $40,500, but below $0, in the forthcoming period? The TLLL number of 1.50 tells us that $0 is 1.5 standard deviations below the expected value of $40,500. Visually, looking at Exhibit 9.7, one-half of the possible outcomes fall above $40,500, so these would represent 50 percent of the outcomes, or a 50 percent likelihood. To determine how likely an outcome below $0 is, we need to determine the likelihood of an outcome falling between $0 and $40,500, then add that to the 50 percent likelihood of an "above $40,500" outcome, and finally subtract this sum from 100 percent. We can consult a standard normal table to get the likelihood of the $0 to $40,500 outcome, or use the NORMSDIST function to do this for us, using Excel™. We start by getting the probability of getting an outcome above $0:

Area under the likelihood curve to the right of $0 = NORMSDIST (1.50)

= 0.933059584

Therefore:

Area under the likelihood curve to the left of $0 = (1 − 0.933059584)

Area under the likelihood curve to the left of $0 = <u>0.0669 or 6.69%</u>

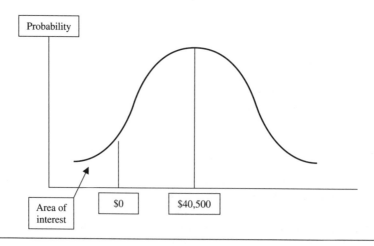

EXHIBIT 9.7   DISTRIBUTION OF TARGET LIQUIDITY LEVEL OUTCOMES USING HYPOTHETICAL EXAMPLE

Interpretation: This calculated value for the area suggests that the chance of our organization running out of cash is less than 7 percent for the upcoming year.

We may decide this probability of running out of cash is too high. If we were to plan based on a slightly larger credit line, say $123,000 instead of $100,000, our TLL jumps $23,000 to $63,500. That gives us a TLLL of $2.35 = \$63,500/\$27,018.51$.

Let's see how this revised credit line amount affects our probability of running short on cash.

$$\text{Area under the likelihood curve to the right of } \$0 = \text{NORMSDIST}(2.35)$$
$$= 0.990619356$$

Therefore:

$$\text{Area under the likelihood curve to the left of } \$0 = (1 - 0.990619356)$$
$$\text{Area under the likelihood curve to the left of } \$0 = \underline{0.00938 \quad \text{or} \quad 0.94\%}$$

The board and CFO may find a probability of less than 1 percent to be acceptable. We see here the value of iterative and interactive financial planning, whereby different values can be plugged in for target liquidity and the preferred policy decision selected. In this case, the organization decided its original TLL was too low and bumped it up by $23,000. It would not have necessarily done this by increasing the credit line amount, however, and may have (given sufficient lead time in the planning process) built up the level of short-term investments instead.

(i) Scenario Analysis and Sensitivity Analysis. Running various scenarios through your financial model to see their likely effect on revenues, expenses, assets, liabilities, and the target liquidity level is very helpful. If you are not prepared to do this scenario analysis, at least vary your revenues up and down by 5, 10, and 15 percent to see the effect on your financials, and do the same with expenses.

We agree with Donaldson that an organization needs a database for a strategy of funds mobility in order to cope with unexpected changes. In Exhibit 9.8 we present a template modified from his business template. It lists items as uncommitted reserves, reduction of planned outflows, and liquidation of assets. This template is related to the tiers of liquidity (Kallberg and Parkinson) that we presented in Exhibit 2.1 in Chapter 2; you may wish to review that diagram before going any further. In Exhibit 9.8, we see an estimate of funds that could be made available from both internal and external sources. Note that these are funds that have not already been committed for use in the next three years. These include:

- *Uncommitted reserves.* This includes instant reserves and negotiable reserves:

   o   Instant reserves (unrestricted cash balances, unrestricted short-term marketable securities, and the unused portion of the bank credit line, if any) are instantly available for any purpose. Buy time for the organization in order that it can mobilize other resources—implying that the size of the instant reserves should be larger the larger an unexpected cash deficit might be and the longer it takes the organization to tap other resources.

Resources	Available for use within:		
	Three months	One year	Three years
I. Uncommitted reserves			
Instant reserves			
Surplus unrestricted cash	$		
Unused line of credit	$		
Negotiable reserves			
Additional bank loans			
Unsecured (no collateral)	$		
Secured (have collateral)	$		
Additional long-term debt		$	
Additional funds raised*		$	$
II. Reduction of planned outflows			
Volume-related			
Change in production or service schedule	$		
Scale-related			
Marketing/promotion program		$	
R&D/New program development budget		$	
Administrative overhead**		$	
Capital expenditures		$	
Value-related			
Fundraising expenditure**		$	
Capital campaign**		$	$
Endowment campaign**		$	$
III. Liquidity of assets			
Shutdown (temporary)		$	
Sale/divestiture of unit			$
SUBTOTAL	$	$	$
TOTAL RESOURCES			$

* It is unusual to be able to raise more funds the same fiscal year when increasing fundraising efforts, although some organizations (especially faith-based organizations) are able to do this at times.

** Generally, pare back or defer, but do not eliminate entirely. If "Additional funds raised" is a Level I objective, this will preclude cost reductions in one or more of the fundraising categories.

Source: Adapted from Exhibit I in Gordon Donaldson, "Strategy for Financial Emergencies," *Harvard Business Review* (November/December 1969): 67–79. Used by permission.

EXHIBIT 9.8   INVENTORY OF RESOURCES FOR FINANCIAL MOBILITY—A TEMPLATE

- ○ *Negotiable reserves* (new short-term bank loans, new long-term debt issues, new fundraising approaches or intensity) involve some form of negotiation and are therefore less certain. Also depend on the degree and type of previous use of these items (long-term debt issues depend on previous use of long-term debt and short-term debt). Consider the sequencing and interrelationships in this category of funding sources.

- ○ Collateral for short-term loans is typically inventory and accounts receivable (ruling out this form of borrowing for many nonprofits), although at times grants and contracts receivable may serve as security for loans.

- • *Reduction of outflows.* Here the view is toward what existing commitments to planned outflows may be reduced and a consideration of whether an unexpected need that arises might better be met through one of these reductions rather than drawing on uncommitted reserves—the wisdom of which depends on how large and pressing the need is, the size and accessibility of the organization's reserves, and the special circumstances related to the unexpected need.

- ○ Value-related expenditures are not directly related to the organization's services, but do affect the donor franchise and donors' perceived value (such as expenditures on an ongoing capital campaign).
- ○ The largest potential fund source here is usually the scale-related outflows, in that they offer the most flexibility regarding expenditure timing.
- ○ Volume-related cuts are best done if service demands are also declining.
- ○ New and unexpected needs are golden opportunities to revisit the organization's priorities, which is a reason why budget cuts may be appropriate as an organizational response.
- ○ "Defending the remaining financial reserves may be more important that defending the budget"—so keep it intact to protect against future totally unexpected and urgent needs whenever possible.[18]
- ○ If your organization is already very lean, and few if any cutbacks are possible without causing service provision cutbacks, rely more on a larger instant reserves level and less on reduced outflows for meeting unexpected needs.
- ○ At times reductions or deferrals in annual campaigns or deferred giving campaigns may be necessary, but recognize the effect on this on your donors and their perceptions, including the loss of additional opportunities to solidify your organization's value proposition in their minds.

- • *Liquidation of assets.* Temporary suspension of the use of property or eventual sale of property, facilities and plant, equipment, and land.

- ○ Recognize that there is a great deal of uncertainty here if assets are sold off, both with respect to amount and length of time to consummate the disposal.
- ○ This requires an estimate of "liquidation value."
- ○ It is best to identify in advance which operations are least "mission-central" and would have the smallest effect on the organization's revenue stream.

Even more valuable, once you have completed Exhibit 9.8, is to do a second inventory of funding resources based on a projection of what you think they are likely to be a year from now. Especially important in that second inventory is the anticipated change in instant reserves: If an erosion in instant reserves is anticipated, take action now to tap negotiable reserves and/or a reduction planned outflows in order to restore your instant reserves. Remember that the primary financial objective of a nonprofit is to maintain its target liquidity level.

(ii) Other Financial Goals and the Organization's Life Cycle. If yours is a commercial nonprofit (can price its services to more than cover costs), you may also adopt some profitability goals for some of your lines of business. Or your organization may be at the point in its life cycle to start or build your endowment fund. For example, the University of North Florida is planning a new student union (cost: $30 to $35 million) but is also building its endowment to $100 million by 2010 in order to (1) increase operations funding with a more predictable annual income, (2) improve its standing in the academic community, and (3) decrease its dependence on the state legislature's funding allocations.[19] Stevens notes that different stages in your organization's life cycle

may occasion different financial priorities; we quote here only the ones that are part of your financial planning objectives.[20]

STAGE IN LIFE CYCLE	FINANCIAL CHALLENGE
Idea Stage	Obtain funding or financing
Start-Up Stage	Create a break-even budget
	Manage cash flow
Growth Stage	Diversify program revenues
	Obtain line or credit or working capital loan
	Recognize that each program has different costs; some will produce surpluses, some will not thoroughly understand and budget administrative costs
	Budget depreciation as an operating expense
	Set aside cash surpluses for working capital reserves
Maturity Stage	Develop net asset (equity) balances
	Create operating reserves from unrestricted income
	Continue to develop working capital reserves to internally finance cash flow and growth
	Set up "repair and replacement" reserves, funded by depreciation allowances
	Possibly develop an endowment, take on a mortgage, or consider other forms of permanent capital
Decline Stage	Use reserves only for regenerating activities, not for deficit spending
	Examine the budget for top-heavy administrative expenses
Turnaround Stage	Create a financial plan to pay off creditors and restore organizational credibility
	Consider and obtain a debt reconsolidation loan to allow you to focus on the future while responsibly handling past debts
	Cut back to minimal expense levels
Terminal Stage	Establish an orderly way to go out of business

Smaller organizations, especially, will find this life cycle framework valuable for prioritizing their financial strategies and long-term financial plans. A key concern that we have not yet addressed, however, is how fast our organization can grow.

(iii) Based on Our Financial Policies and Structure, How Fast Can We Grow?   If you make some simplifying assumptions, you can determine the approximate rate of growth of activity for your nonprofit organization. This framework works much better for a commercial nonprofit (in which revenues tend to bear a direct, causal link to asset investment) than for a donative nonprofit, but it will give insight in either case. The nonprofit version of this "sustainable growth model" was developed in 2003 by Marc Jegers.[21] We base our presentation on his model, beginning with the data inputs needed to estimate the maximum growth rate in service provision. Your organization's maximum rate of growth in service provision jointly depends on its profitability (degree to which revenues more than cover expenses), capital structure (relative use of debt financing), and efficiency.

Inputs.

Operating Variables.

Level of service provision at the beginning of the year, X_0.

Level of service provision at the end of the year, X_1.

Growth rate in service provision, $g = (X_1 - X_0)/X_0$

The efficiency (labeled as α) with which the organization "produces" X, relative to total assets, which we represent as $T : \alpha = X/T$, and the change in α (labeled as $\alpha\prime$) is:

$$\alpha_\prime = \alpha 1/\alpha_0.$$

The profitability of the organization, or the change in net assets, is represented by P. Your organization might normally refer to this as your surplus. P would be equal to total revenues (whether restricted or unrestricted, whether gathered through fees, dues, donations, grants, or sales) less total expenses. Express this profit in relation to total assets (with the ratio labeled as m):

$$m = P/T.$$

Financing Variables.
We know, from the SFP that every dollar of assets must be financed by either debt (borrowed money, liabilities) or net assets. Therefore, we have the SFP identity:

$$T = D + NA$$

The capital structure is the relative use of net assets (what some call equity or used to call fund balance) and debt in financing assets, with d being the ratio of debt to net assets:

$$d = D/NA$$

For consecutive years, just include the year as the subscript:

$$d_0 = D_0/NA_0$$
$$d_1 = D_1/NA_1$$

Projection Model.   What we wish to determine is $g*$, the maximum growth rate in service provision. If you calculate this model using your year-end numerical values, it will tell you the ability to grow your service levels for the upcoming year. (If you do it at the end of 2006, you will see what your maximum growth rate should be for 2007.) You will have to specify, as an input to the model, how your relative use of debt financing will change during the year (d_1) compared to the beginning-of-year (which is, of course, the end of the last year) relative use of debt financing (d_2). The model calculates the maximum growth rate of service provision to be:

$$g* = \frac{(1+d_1)\alpha'}{(1+d_0)(1-(1+d_1)m)} - 1$$

Your growth rate is limited by the use of debt financing for this year and next year (d_0 and d_1), the relative efficiency from this year to next year ($\alpha' = \alpha_1/\alpha_0$), and the "return on assets" (m).

For example, let's say that our charity has a 0.50 debt-to-net-assets ratio that will not change during the upcoming year; its ratio of service provision to total assets is 0.70 and is expected to increase to 0.75; and its ratio of profit (or surplus) to total assets is 0.05. The maximum growth rate of service provision for the upcoming year is:

$$g* = \frac{(1+0.50)(0.75/0.70)}{(1+0.50)(1-(1+0.50)0.05)} - 1$$

$$g* = \frac{(1.50)(1.07143)}{(1.50)(1-0.075)} - 1$$

$$g* = \frac{1.607145}{(1.50)(0.925)} - 1$$

$$g* = \frac{1.607145}{1.3875} - 1$$

$$g* = 1.1583 - 1$$

$$g* = 0.1583 \text{ or } \underline{15.83\%}$$

Interpretation.   The level of service provision for our charity can grow during the upcoming year at a maximum rate of 15.83 percent unless one or more of these events occur: (1) it uses more debt for each dollar of net assets; (2) it increases its efficiency more than the 7.143 percent increase in efficiency already projected (which was based on increasing X/T from a 70 to 75 percent ratio); or (3) it increases its "profit" (change in net assets) as a percent of assets.

Special cases.   Three special cases allow you to simplify this formula:

Case 1: Capital structure and efficiency do not change.   In this case, the formula simplifies to show the effect of financing growth strictly through profits and just enough additional debt to keep the D/NA ratio unchanged:

$$g* = \frac{(1+d)m}{(1-(1+d)m)}$$

Case 2: Capital structure does not change and there are no profits ($m = 0$). In this case, the formula simplifies to show the effect of a change in efficiency on growth:

$$g* = \alpha' - 1$$

Here the growth rate simplifies to being the rate of growth in efficiency.

Case 3: Efficiency does not change and there are no profits ($m = 0$). In this case, the formula simplifies to show the effect of a change in the capital structure on growth:

$$g* = \frac{(d_1 - d_0)}{(1 + d_0)}$$

Minimum required profitability. A very helpful planning formula can be developed from the sustainable growth model. In it, we know the growth rate in service provision that we desire. We project our anticipated capital structure and efficiency level. The question is: What rate of profit (as a percent of assets) must we generate in order to grow at our desired growth rate? We can solve for that profit ratio with this formula:

$$m = \frac{1}{(1 + d_1)} - \frac{\alpha'}{(1 + g)(1 + d_0)}$$

Cautions. We offer four cautions as you apply this sustainable growth model:

1. If you use revenues as your measure of service provision, make sure to subtract any "in-kind gifts," because these will distort the revenue to relationship for planning purposes.

2. Because of the permanently restricted nature of endowments, we recommend that you subtract any endowment-related amounts from revenues, expenses, assets, and net assets.

3. Because of the long-term restrictions on most trusts, either modify your trust-related revenues, expenses, assets, liabilities, and net assets, or subtract any trust-related amounts from these accounts.

4. Related to #3, a messy issue for nonprofits is the degree to which revenues and net assets are restricted versus unrestricted. Particularly, to what degree your organization's gifts restricted versus unrestricted, and what are the revenue implications of this?

If these amounts are insignificant for your organization, you may ignore them in your growth calculations. If any of them are significant, you may either modify your numbers as recommended or ignore these issues but consider the sustainable growth rate as only a very rough approximation of the true sustainable growth rate.

9.3 FINANCIAL EVALUATION OF NEW AND EXISTING PROGRAMS

Up to this point, we have assumed that you knew what programs you would plan for and on what scale you would operate those programs. Now let's shift our focus to how to do program evaluation of the portfolio (or set) of programs your organization offers or could offer. Deciding which activities to engage in and how much in resources each activity will receive is sometimes called *programming*.

An illustration of this concept is a listing (in Exhibit 9.9) of some of one organization's 158 different human services *program elements*, subactivities within the three similar groups of activities called *programs*.

The remainder of this chapter will highlight four interrelated issues: (1) how to determine which programs to engage in, (2) how to determine how much in organization resources (if any) to devote to each program on an ongoing basis, (3) how to evaluate the possible addition of new activities (program elements), and (4) how to evaluate the ongoing investment of organizational resources in the various activities. We begin by analyzing the financial manager's role in programming.

Programming involves four steps:

1. Identifying program alternatives
2. Analyzing program alternatives
3. Making the programming decisions
4. Developing program support

In programming, some major finance-related responsibilities in both the analysis of program alternatives and programming decisions fall on the financial manager. In analyzing program alternatives, the financial manager might assist in four activities:

1. He or she must specify resource (including financial) requirements. Nonfinancial resources include equipment, facilities, materials, and supplies, and staff and professional time.

2. He or she must develop a financial plan, which provides a summary of all the financial consequences of the programming decisions: sources of funds, costs of resource usage, any surplus or deficits to be expected, and a need for special fundraising campaigns or borrowing.

3. The financial manager must see that discounted cash flow analysis is conducted when the projects have revenues associated with them.

4. As profiled earlier in this chapter, the financial manager determines financial feasibility for the organization by projecting cash flows in a long-range planning study. The latter might result in an estimate of the additional grants or donated

Program Structure (Partial Listing)	
Program	**Program Elements**
Human services	Adoption agencies
	Day care centers
	Food banks
	Meals-on-wheels services
	Foster care for abused and neglected children
	Drug and alcohol recovery
Housing	Apartment complex development for low-income families and the elderly
	Specialized housing for disabled persons
Health care	Nursing care facilities (4 states)

Exhibit 9.9   Programs and Program Elements for a Social Services Organization

funds that must be obtained for the organization to remain financially viable if it pursues a given program alternative.

At times the analysis of program alternatives involves consideration of new programs and/or larger resource commitments than usual. The financial manager provides the same kind of assistance as before, but additionally must help the ED/CEO and board see the big picture in financial terms. We need to learn about service portfolios and relative cost coverage to see specifically how the financial professional can contribute to the discussion.

(a) SIMPLE PORTFOLIO ANALYSIS. A good starting point for your program diagnosis that about any ED/CEO, board, and CFO might use is the Dual Bottom-Line Matrix developed by Peters and Schaffer.[22] It is provided in Exhibit 9.10.

Programs in the lower left quadrant, "stop signs," should be closed down soon. At the opposite extreme, "star" programs at the top right are keepers to which you will want to increase resource allocations. Bottom-right programs are "money signs" that may help to fund those "star" programs. Finally, "heart" programs should normally be kept and work should be done to improve the sustainability of these programs.

(b) ADVANCED PORTFOLIO ANALYSIS. We presented some more advanced portfolio models in Chapter 3, which we will not duplicate here. One weakness of most of these

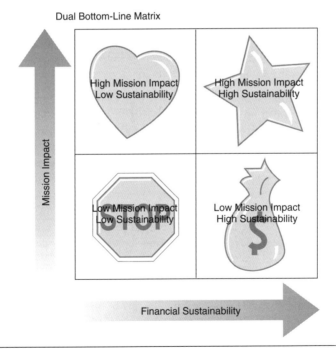

Dual Bottom-Line Matrix

High Mission Impact
Low Sustainability

High Mission Impact
High Sustainability

Low Mission Impact
Low Sustainability

Low Mission Impact
High Sustainability

Mission Impact

Financial Sustainability

EXHIBIT 9.10 DUAL BOTTOM-LINE MATRIX PORTFOLIO ANALYSIS

models is the failure to include liquidity and financial flexibility. Appendix 9B provides one view of how to evaluate "social enterprises" from a financial perspective. In that model, liquidity is a key driving factor in the evaluation, corresponding to our view that achieving and maintaining a target liquidity level is the single most important financial objective of a noncommercial nonprofit and one of the most important variables in commercial nonprofits.

(c) ANNUAL NECESSARY INVESTMENT.   If a program is growing but funding resources are not growing more quickly, the manager is faced with the situation in which that program will be draining an ever-increasing share of investable monies over time. The implication is clear: Other programs being offered or considered will have to have funding cut over time. Very few nonprofit managers foresee this type of situation, and equally few study past financials (laid out by program) to even see this in retrospect. This is just the type of contribution you can make to assist a board and top-management team in diagnosing and strategically positioning an organization for a desired future in which top-priority programs and mission achievement are secure. Compare the organization's future position to its present position.

Once your management team and board have agreed on a set of programs, conduct a final check on the structure of selected programs before making financial and personnel decisions:[23]

- Are the operating plans well developed?
- Have nonfinancial resources been identified?
- Have financial constraints been considered?
- Are the desired results from the program well defined?
- Does the program have a detailed list of objectives?
- Will the program achieve the organizational goals?

It is at this point that a set of pro forma balance sheets and statement of financial activities should be drawn up for one to five years in the future. Possibly a set of four scenarios could be used for each year. Include the status quo (no change in present situation), as well as optimistic, most likely ("base case") and pessimistic scenarios. This will greatly assist in answering the third question ("Have financial constraints been considered?").

The financial manager may also assist in the development of program advocates within the funding sources. The idea here is to procure some stability over the funding source. By demonstrating how the source's funding is critical to a program's long-range financial viability, the organization may be able to gain a deeper, more permanent degree of commitment.

The final duty is budgeting. Financial managers have primary responsibility for the budget process. Our concern here is to ensure that programming decisions are translated into budget line items. (Chapter 8 is dedicated largely to budgeting.) Ideally, as each year progresses, last year's strategic and long-range financial plan becomes the starting point not only for the new strategic and long-range financial plan, but also for the development of next year's operating and capital budget. A warning signal emerges when the long-range financial plan is not used to help develop budgets. Possibly it is too inaccurate, or the organization is unaware of the tie between programming and budgeting. Obviously, those organizations updating long-range plans less frequently than yearly have less direct correspondence between plans and budgets. Plans are most likely to be implemented when they drive the resource allocation embodied in the annual operating and capital budgets. Finally, the process of planning is invaluable, forcing discussion and resolution of the trade-offs and prioritization involved in spending decisions.

9.4 CAPITAL BUDGETING: FINANCIAL EVALUATION OF PROJECTS THAT ARISE FROM EXISTING PROGRAMS

Programs spawn projects, and these projects often involve large capital allocations with multiyear cash flow effects. These will affect your organization's target liquidity level for years to come. Consequently, the next key question when evaluating a capital project is: Will the capital expenditure cover all of its costs *and* provide an adequate return on invested capital? This is a pivotal question for evaluating capital expenditures that bring in revenues as well as for selecting between alternative expenditures that involve only costs. Even donative nonprofit organizations may have to consider both capital expenditure types. Any expenditures bringing in multiyear cash revenues should be evaluated in the way we show next. Not doing so could lead to a faulty decision for projects providing cash revenues (revenue would increase, but with an extremely low return on invested capital) or when selecting between two or more alternatives that have different up-front costs or different life spans. Two simplified examples illustrate this point.

(a) **EXAMPLE 1: NET PRESENT VALUE AND BENEFIT-COST RATIO ILLUSTRATED.**   Youthsave, Inc. occupies a building that is much larger than it needs in the foreseeable future. Youthsave has fixed up the part of the building it occupies, but the other parts of the building are in disrepair and would need major remodeling in order to be usable. Youthsave has received repeated inquiries from other nonprofit organizations wishing to rent the space it renovated. Several have indicated that Youthsave's prime central business district location would lead them to pay $1,000 per month, payable in a lump sum at the end of each year, for an office area of 2,500 square feet. The rental prospects would also pay all utilities used by them. Youthsave has received three sealed-bid remodeling estimates from contractors having strong track records of high-quality work. The lowest bid is $95,000. Assuming it would be 15 years both for the lease and before the area would have to be remodeled again, and ignoring any leasehold improvement considerations, should Youthsave engage in the revenue enhancement project? (Assume the organization will not have to pay tax on the rental income.)

(i) *Approaching a Capital Expenditure Analysis.*   Because the remodeling is an up-front expense and the rent is paid on a monthly basis in the future, it is *incorrect to merely multiply* the revenue per month by the number of months and then subtract the up-front cost. A dollar received or paid today is worth *more* than a dollar received or paid 1, 2, or 12 years from now because it can be invested to earn interest. This fact is recognized as the *time valve of money*. It implies the need for these three steps:

1.   Specify the project's anticipated cash flows: What cash outflows will result and when, what cash inflows will result and when?
2.   Select a discount rate to reflect the time value of money: What rate of return could you have earned per year if you did not tie funds up in this capital project?
3.   Apply the discount rate to future cash flows (those anticipated next year and in following years), then subtract any up-front costs to determine the ROIC and project acceptability.

Step 1.   Let's show a cash flow timeline. Cash outflows are shown as spikes below the horizontal axis, cash inflows are represented by spikes above the axis. We have an initial ("period 0") outflow of $95,000 followed by 12 end-of-year inflows of $12,000 (each end-of-year $12,000 is $12 \times \$1,000$):

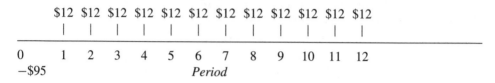

Step 2.   The organization can invest long-term funds at about 10 percent, and the mortgage rate is about 10 percent. So we will use an interest rate of 10 percent to determine the present value (present dollar equivalent) of each of the future cash flows.

Step 3.   We will compute two measures of project acceptability. The first, net present value (NPV), represents the surplus of revenue over expense, if any, after stating all cash flows in today's terms. We "discount" each future cash flow back to today's value by dividing it by (1 + interest rate) raised to a power representing how many years away the flow occurs. Equivalently, multiply the cash flow by 1/(1 + interest rate) raised to the appropriate power.

For example, to discount a cash flow that will occur two periods from now, using a 10 percent discount rate, multiply it by: $1/(1+0.10)^2 = 1/(1.1)^2 = 1/1.21 = 0.8264$. Then subtract the initial remodeling outlay, which does not need to be adjusted to present value because it occurs at present. A table can be set up to show the calculations:

YEAR	CASH FLOW	PRESENT VALUE FACTOR	PRESENT VALUE OF CASH FLOW
0	−$95,000	1.0000	−$95,000
1	$12,000	0.9091	10,909.20
2	$12,000	0.8264	9,916.80
3	$12,000	0.7513	9,015.60
4	$12,000	0.6830	8,196.00
5	$12,000	0.6209	7,450.80
6	$12,000	0.5645	6,774.00
7	$12,000	0.5132	6,158.40
8	$12,000	0.4665	5,598.00
9	$12,000	0.4241	5,089.20
10	$12,000	0.3855	4,626.00
11	$12,000	0.3505	4,206.00
12	$12,000	0.3186	3,823.20

When we sum up the right column, we get a negative value for NPV: −$13,236.80. Because the time value factors in our table are rounded to four decimal places, this estimate is slightly inaccurate.

We could key these numbers into an Excel™ spreadsheet and use Excel™'s built-in NPV financial function to get a more exact NPV. The formula looks like this: =NPV(0.10, range of inflows)−Initial Investment cell. The range of inflows is merely the cell address range in which you entered the year 1–12 cash inflows, which would each be $12,000.

We have to subtract the outflow (or add it, if we entered it as a negative number) to have Excel handle it properly. In Youthsave's case, the exact NPV turns out to be negative:

$$NPV = -\$13,235.70.$$

(ii) Making the Capital Expenditure Decision. What should Youthsave do? After we have calculated NPV, these decision rules tell us what to do:

- If the NPV is positive, the project more than covers all costs, including financing costs (or forgone investing revenues). Approve it.
- If the NPV is zero, the project just covers all costs. Approve it.
- If negative, revenues do not cover all costs. Because the rental contract does not cover all costs in this case, it should be turned down.

If you prefer to think in terms of benefit-cost ratios, you could have expressed the data slightly differently. Add up the present value of all the cash inflows (in the "Present Value of Cash Flow" column), which equal $81,763.20. This is your financial benefit amount. Then divide this by the amount of the initial investment, expressed as a positive amount. The resulting *benefit-cost ratio*, also called the *profitability index*, signals a good project if greater than 1, benefit equivalent to cost project if equal to 1, and a poor project if less than 1:

$$\text{Benefit} - \text{Cost ratio} = \text{PV of all Cash Inflows/Initial Investment}$$

Inserting the numbers for our example:

$$\text{Benefit} - \text{Cost ratio} = \text{PV of all Cash Inflows/Initial Investment}$$
$$\text{Benefit} - \text{Cost ratio} = \$81,763.20/\$95,000$$
$$\text{Benefit} - \text{Cost ratio} = \underline{0.86}$$

In this case, the project would be turned down as the benefit-cost ratio is less than 1. This metric is consistent with the NPV metric. Again, we are looking at the project in purely financial terms, and there may be nonfinancial reasons why you still might implement it. Be aware that you are causing a financial drain on your organization to do so, however.

Now compute a complementary measure that is easier to interpret because it is expressed in percent. This measure, *ROIC*, or return on invested capital, indicates the financial return per year, after adjusting for the timing of project cash flows. Some organizations call it the time-adjusted rate of return. It tells us what interest rate that the initial investment earns per year when generating the cash inflows forecasted for the project. You can use the IRR function built into Excel in order to calculate ROIC.[24] In our example, the ROIC is relatively low:

$$ROIC = \underline{7.06\%}$$

This return is clearly less than the 10 percent annual rate Youthsave can earn if it leaves that money invested. Additionally, the 7.06 percent return is less than the annual interest rate Youthsave would pay a bank to borrow money for a real estate loan to be able to purchase rental property.

Is it worth the effort to calculate NPV or ROIC? What if Youthsave ignored the time value of money? In that case, the analyst would have multiplied the annual inflow of $12,000 by 10 years to get a total project revenue of $120,000. Then the analyst would have subtracted the initial investment of $95,000 to get a $25,000 net return, and the organization might have made the investment. Properly evaluated, this is not a good investment—the ROIC is too low and the investment in remodeling is not cost beneficial.

This same approach of discounting cash flows can be used when evaluating mergers, joint ventures, strategic alliances, or other strategic investment decisions.

Before considering these, let's illustrate a common capital investment scenario: How do we evaluate capital projects that involve only costs?

(b) EXAMPLE 2: EQUIVALENT ANNUAL COST ILLUSTRATED.   Compared to a business, the nonprofit organization encounters many more capital projects that generate no revenues. Some of these projects are "independent" projects that are undertaken in support of service delivery: buying a new van, adding capacity, buying office furniture, and so on. The key here is in getting multiple sealed bids on construction projects or comparing among various vendors for a vehicle or equipment to find the one with the best combination of quality, price, payment terms, warranty, and service after the sale. In some purchasing situations, however, the analyst must select one from between two clearly identifiable alternatives.

Assuming quality, service after the sale, and other nonquantifiable factors are roughly the same, the analyst can find the project having the lowest "cost per year" by once again discounting cash flows. The technique is very similar to the discounting we just illustrated, but is a bit more involved. Called equivalent annual cost (EAC), it may be applied to alternative projects having different life spans and that will be repeated indefinitely (once a machine wears out, it is replaced with another identical machine).

The Trinova Soup Kitchen is considering which of two commercial stoves to purchase. The first, the Everlast model, costing $41,500, would cost $300 per year to operate (including electricity, cleaning, and maintenance) and would last approximately eight years. The second, the Value Miser, costs only $25,000, would cost $450 per year to operate, and would last only five years. Which should Trinova buy, assuming each is equally reliable within its expected lifespan?

First, let's see how someone might do a rough analysis in this example, not taking the time value of money into account.

$$\text{Annual Cost of Everlast} = \frac{\$41,500 + (\$300 \times 8)}{8}$$

$$= \frac{\$43,900}{8}$$

$$= \underline{\$5,487.50}$$

$$\text{Annual Cost of Value Miser} = \frac{\$25,000 + (\$450 \times 5)}{5}$$

$$= \frac{\$27,500}{5}$$

$$= \underline{\$5,450}$$

Based on this approximation method, *which ignores the fact that $1 of cost today is not the same as $1 of cost in later years*, Trinova would select Value Miser because its cost per year is $5,450 (compared to Everlast's $5,487.50). Clearly, however, the advantage is almost insignificant—about $48 a year.

Let's redo the analysis with a correction: (1) discount the annual operating costs to today's present dollar equivalent ("present value"), then (2) spread the sum of all acquisition and operating costs over the life span to arrive at a correct cost per year. The appropriate discount rate is again 10 percent.

Step 1.   Calculate each alternative's NPV.

	EVERLAST		VALUE MISER	
Year	Cash Flow (CF)	Present Value of CF	Cash Flow (CF)	Present Value of CF
0	$(41,500)	$(41,500.00)	$(25,000)	
1	(300)	(272.73)	(450)	
2	(300)	(247.93)	(450)	
3	(300)	(225.39)	(450)	(338.09)
4	(300)	(204.90)	(450)	(307.36)
5	(300)	(186.28)	(450)	(279.41)
6	(300)	(169.34)		
7	(300)	(153.95)		
8	(300)	(139.95)		
NPV		$ (43,100.48)		$ (26,705.85)

Step 2.   Convert the NPV into an equivalent "cost per year." The formula used to make this conversion is beyond our scope,[25] but essentially converts the NPV to an equivalent equal amount ("annuity") for each of the years of the project's life span, using a 10 percent interest factor.

EVERLAST	VALUE MISER
Cost per yr. = $8,078.93	Cost per yr. = $7,044.94

Notice the much larger advantage now demonstrated by Value Miser. Taking into account the time value of money—the fact that costs occur in different amounts at different times and the return on investment given up by the much larger (if less frequent) outlay for Everlast—the annual cost savings jump to about $1,000. Much of this comes from the opportunity to repeatedly invest the difference in the two stoves' initial outlays ($41,500 − 25,000 = $16,500) in securities yielding 10 percent, generating investment income (or avoiding interest expense) that would not be received if Trinova buys the Everlast model. The additional funds can be directed into new programs or into existing program expansion.

Discounted cash flow analysis is a technique used daily in thousands of businesses. Once again you can see the difference that proficient financial management can make in your organization. Even when you are evaluating capital investments that must be made regardless of the financial attractiveness, draw up a cash flow table. Doing so provides the numbers that you will need to do an overall cash budget for your organization, a topic we covered in Chapter 8.

(c) HOW TO MANAGE THE TOTAL CAPITAL BUDGET.   The *capital budget* is the listing of all capital projects that the organization wishes to invest in, typically ranked from best to worst or from most necessary to least necessary. While a business can "in theory" always raise funds when it has a project that will provide an adequate return for shareholders, a nonprofit organization is often limited by the total dollar amount it can invest in capital projects in a given year. This situation, known as *capital rationing,* arises from the inability to raise funds from any kind of stock issue, the unwillingness or inability to borrow funds, and a limited ability to generate funds from revenue-providing activities or capital campaigns. Special capital campaigns work superbly for periodic building or expansion programs (witness the University of Notre Dame's $1.1 billion capital campaign, which was originally targeted for $767 million), but cannot be utilized for every year's capital project funding.

(d) CAPITAL BUDGET AND CAPITAL RATIONING.   Example: There is $150,000 in funds available for capital projects in 2007 at Charity First. First, list the desired capital expenditures from best (or most necessary) to worst (least necessary). The dollar amount of each investment should be included along with a grand total. Projects which generate revenues should have the computed ROIC number listed next to them. To ensure that later year cash flows are included in the long-range financial plan, another column may be included to signify such flows. Exhibit 9.11 provides a sample listing for an organization.

The total capital budget in Exhibit 9.11, $178,000, is then compared to capital available for projects. The "capital available" amount is based first on a portion of the cash reserves, which will be listed on the balance sheet as cash.[26] Second, there may well be some short-term marketable securities that are not included in the cash account. However, some of the total in cash and marketable securities is temporarily restricted (for a certain time period or until some action is taken by the organization) or permanently restricted (permanent endowment or revolving loan funds). The temporarily restricted portion may include funds restricted specifically for the purpose of fixed assets, so some or all of this should be included in capital available. Much care must be applied in arriving in the "capital available" figure because, in many organizations, three-fourths of monies raised are restricted as to purpose or time of availability.

Let's say that the amount of capital available for Charity First is $150,000. Which project(s) should be funded?

Charity First Capital Budget			
Project	**Cost**	**ROIC**	**Future Year Cash Flows?**
New central air conditioning unit	$120,000	N/A*	Y
Repair roof	25,000	N/A*	N
Renovate, rent office space	30,000	12 percent	Y
Buy another copier	3,000	N/A*	Y
	Total $178,000		

*N/A means not applicable; usually this means that the project generates no revenue or cost savings.

EXHIBIT 9.11   AN ORGANIZATION'S OVERALL CAPITAL BUDGET

(e) RATIONING THE CAPITAL. The way to ration scarce capital, assuming the organization cannot free up or raise funds to meet the shortfall, is to consider which set of available projects best utilizes capital available. With the four projects in our example (Exhibit 9.11), there are only 12 combinations available that would keep us within our $150,000 capital limitation:

- 1 only
- 2 only
- 3 only
- 4 only
- 1 and 2
- 1 and 3
- 1 and 4
- 2 and 3
- 2 and 4
- 3 and 4
- 1, 2 and 4
- 2, 3, and 4

For each of these combinations, check to verify that the combination's total capital budget would not exceed capital available. At the same time, make sure donor or fund restrictions are adhered to. This process can be tedious and very time consuming when there are many projects and consequently multiple combinations to evaluate.

If one or more of the top-ranked projects are "must-haves," the analyst's job is considerably simpler because now only the amount of capital available *after* subtracting the cost(s) of the must-have project(s) need be allocated to remaining project combinations.[27] Returning to our example, the first two projects might be must-haves. Together they would use up $145,000 of the available $150,000. Only the copier purchase could be funded with the remaining $5,000.

One very important caution: There is an assumption in the foregoing analysis that each of the proposed projects has roughly equal program or mission benefits; that is, each contributes to the organization's mission to roughly the same degree. Looking back at our list of projects, each is a general office-related investment, and it is not necessary to pinpoint the benefits of the various projects. We are not looking at allocation between various programs, some of which contribute more to mission achievement than others, with these projects.

9.5 FINANCIAL EVALUATION OF MERGERS, JOINT VENTURES, AND STRATEGIC ALLIANCES

(a) MERGERS AND ACQUISITIONS. Some, but not all, mergers and acquisitions in the nonprofit sector are financially motivated. In these, the financial manager's role is pivotal. Either the CFO must do the financial analysis of the proposal, or locate a consultant or board member who can do it. The CFO must translate the financial ramifications of the proposal to top management and the board in either case.

(b) MOTIVES FOR MERGERS AND ACQUISITIONS.   There are numerous reasons why organizations merge with or acquire other organizations, but most fall into one or more of these categories:

- Synergy-programmatic

  - Geographic or service-offering extension
  - Competitive threat
  - Survival

- Synergy-financial

  - Revenue enhancing
  - Cost reducing

(i) Programmatic Synergy.   Synergy is commonly defined as "two plus two equals five," or the whole is greater than the sum of the parts. The combined organizations are in the same or closely related industries. The key in *programmatic synergy* is in program accomplishment-quality and/or quantity. To illustrate, perhaps Alphanumerics has a widespread distribution network and Betaphonics has an advanced and very effective donor acquisition program. Together, the Alphabeta organization can expand the mission achievements beyond what either organization could do on its own.

(ii) Financial Synergy.   When the efficiency of the combined organizations is such as to reduce costs or increase borrowing power, we have *financial synergy*. The enhanced financial strength that results is what propels the merger or acquisition. Quite often, programmatic synergy and financial synergy go hand in hand because effective service delivery and enhanced program achievements usually result in increased donations and the organization's borrowing power increases correspondingly. The factors that bring about financial synergy may be from revenue enhancement or from cost reduction. Exhibit 9.12 illustrates some of these factors.

You should be aware of a couple of issues here. Earned income may be increased not only because of the initiation of ventures related to the core mission of either preexisting organization, but also because existing ventures may be expanded. Additionally, the new organization may take on riskier program activities and ventures (which typically offer greater revenue-expense differentials) due to the facts that (1) the new organization has a larger net asset base, and (2) the overall cash flows of the merged organization are more stable.[28]

Over on the cost reduction side, we key in on economies of scale and economies of scope. *Economies of scale* refer to lowered costs per unit of service delivered as the service quantity increases. Every organization faces some costs that are fixed (e.g., CEO salary), and the greater the output the less the fixed cost per unit of output (e.g., cost per meal served in a rescue shelter). One study in England and Wales finds that most nonprofits are currently too small to fully take advantage of available economies of scale,[29] and we believe this is the case in the United States as well.

Illustrating, let's say salaries are $200,000 at Alphanumerics and $350,000 at Betaphonics; they would not be $550,000 ($200,000 + $350,000) at the combined Alphabeta. Duplicate workers would be let go in some areas (e.g., you don't need two fundraising directors), and as Alphabeta grows, the increased volume of service would not necessitate a proportional increase in workers. Specialization and division of labor account for much

Financial Synergy	
Revenue-Enhancing Factors*	**Cost-Reducing Factors**
• New fund-raising methods (e.g., face-to-face meetings) • Shared expertise • Larger resource base to invest in fund-raising • Initiation of business ventures • Increasingly risky business ventures can be initiated (due to larger net asset base, less-than-perfectly correlated cash flows) • Initiation or expansion of planned giving	• Sale of unneeded assets • Economies of scope (eliminate overlapping service networks) • Shared expertise • Bring fundraising in-house if one or both of the organizations formerly relied exclusively on outside fundraising counsel

*Use "revenue" and "income" interchangeably.

EXHIBIT 9.12   WAYS TO BRING ABOUT FINANCIAL SYNERGY THROUGH COMBINATIONS

of the increased efficiency. Similarly, the land and building requirements of the merged organization might be 50 or 60 percent of the sum of the separate organizations. One area of savings is in the headquarters facilities. Reengineering opportunities have larger payoffs in bigger firms, generally. Summarizing, an organization experiences economies of scale whenever costs per unit fall as the scale of options is expanded.[30]

Economies of scope refer to sharing of costs across various programs. Computer resources can be shared by unrelated programs that two merging nonprofit organizations may offer. Fundraising efforts can be shared. The key is that the costs of producing the products or delivering the services are less when joined in one organization rather than carried out by two separate organizations. Distribution and marketing costs are often given as prime examples of cost elements that can be shared, making the *overall* cost of delivering a given service lower. One example of this, elimination of duplicate service networks, is so important we have pulled it out as a separate item in Exhibit 9.12.

Commercial ventures are appealing not only for the revenues they bring in, but also because often share costs with core service programs. Mergers and acquisitions often promise lower costs both because of scale economies and scope economies. However, businesses have tried to exploit these economies for much longer than nonprofits. Some of the spectacular failures come from unrelated diversification. We can learn three things from the lessons learned from the relative success of the many corporate mergers and acquisitions:[31]

1.   *Trying to gain stability through a merger with or acquisition of an organization whose cash flows are high when your cash flows are low is extremely difficult. The goal here is to find an organization whose cash flows follow a different cycle due to economic risks that are quite different from the merger partner. The combined cash flow stream is more predictable, a safety factor that enhances financial viability for both entities when they join together. This is similar to the pooling-of-risks concept that underlies insurance. When one sector is hitting the skids, the story goes, the other should be doing famously well.*

2.   Why has this concept been so difficult to apply? One reason is that it is most difficult to find organizations with cash flow streams exactly opposite to each other (see Exhibit 9.13). Instead, one may find an industry whose economic cycle turns a little sooner or later than the economy as a whole, or a "defensive" industry, such as soft drinks, which experiences less cyclicality of sales and cash flows. Graphically, the offsets in most cases are not as dramatic, as shown in Exhibit 9.14.

On top of this, it takes considerable skill to put the right mix of business together to achieve a stable cash flow "portfolio" (set of companies or organizations). The ideal merger or acquisition target organization may not be the right size for a match-up with yours, and even if it were, its growth rate may be quite different than your organization's, meaning the combined mix is out of balance in a year or two.

2.   *Related mergers or acquisitions may not be safer.* Although it would seem to be less risky to "stick with the knitting," dealing with business and markets you already know, reaping the benefits may be elusive. The quality of the individual

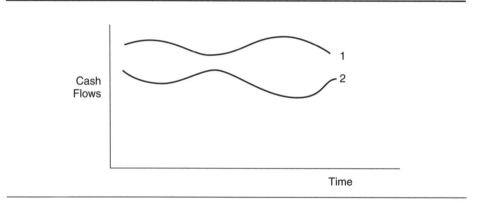

EXHIBIT 9.13   PERFECT OFFSET FOR TWO ORGANIZATIONS' CASH FLOWS OVER TIME

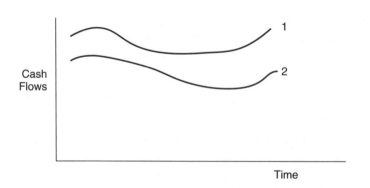

EXHIBIT 9.14   PARTIAL OFFSET FOR TWO ORGANIZATIONS' CASH FLOWS OVER TIME

entities, how much integration it takes to gain the benefits of synergy (can the cultures be merged, e.g.), how real the perceived "relatedness" is, and whether the combination provides improved competitive advantage are all key success factors.

3. *A strong management team at the acquired company is not sufficient.* Having a strong management team at the target company may seem important, but in fact it is the acquiring company's management skill and resources that are essential for realizing merger-acquisition benefits. They must have the financial talent and managers that can conduct strategic analysis of diverse industries and markets.

On the positive side, two basic strategies have been found to work for businesses, and these guidelines should prove helpful to nonprofit organizations as well. Under each we see specific road maps.

Strategy 1: Increase the cash flow stream through synergy.

A. Special skills and industrial knowledge of one partner can be used to solve competitive problems and opportunities the other partner is facing.

B. In the long run, cost per unit can be reduced by investing in markets closely related to current markets. Associations have found this true in their mergers.[32] They are able to benefit from:

  1. Scale effects

  2. Rationalizing of product and other important management tasks

  3. New opportunities for technical innovation

C. Expanding business in an area of competence can lead to the development of a "critical mass" of resources necessary to do well in a market as a threshold size is reached (e.g., banks must be money centers or super-regional banks in order to have the size necessary to offer a broad range of cash management services).

D. Transfer cash from cash-rich to cash-poor units to avert outside borrowing.

  1. Some businesses are always cash-rich (Microsoft); in a nonprofit organization, some programs always need to be subsidized. These may be core programs.

  2. Each area may have different cyclical or seasonal patterns of cash surpluses or cash shortages.

E. If a company is diversified, direct cash-rich areas to provide funding to areas that are currently cash-poor, but soon to be cash generators—increasing long-run profitability (cost coverage) for the organization as a whole.

  1. Low-growth area sends funds to high-growth area.

  2. Internal market intelligence of diversified company can be valuable as information is shared.

F. Through pooling of risks, the diversified company can have lower borrowing costs and do more borrowing, if it so desires.

  1. It gains a larger debt capacity.

  2. It requires a smaller liquid reserve (not including debt).

Strategy 2: Decrease risk.

A.   Reduce variability of the cash flow stream so that it is less than just the average of the variability of the two separate entities. This refers to the offsetting cash flow patterns we graphed in Exhibits 9.13 and 9.14. Down cycles in Organization 1 are partly offset by the up cycles in Organization 2, so that Organization 1 + 2 is on more solid footing than either organization was independently. This feeds back to lower borrowing costs in Strategy 1.F.

What is the bottom line in many business combination failures? Failure comes because companies (1) merge with or acquire what is readily available, not what "meets sound strategic and economic criteria"; (2) pay too high a price for the acquisition; or (3) do not necessarily have the resources and management commitment to exploit the potential advantages.

(c) PARTNERSHIPS, JOINT VENTURES, AND STRATEGIC ALLIANCES.   Cross-organizational strategic alliances, partnerships, and joint ventures provide a less costly or significant change than mergers or acquisitions, while enabling some of the same resource-pooling benefits. We begin our discussion with partnerships and joint ventures.

A formal *partnership* is defined as an association of two or more entities or persons to carry on a business for profit as co-owners.[33] Because it is looked upon by the IRS as a pass-through entity, a partnership is not taxed. Instead, the partners are liable for income tax.[34] A *joint venture* does not involve an ongoing relationship among the two parties but is a one-time setup of at least two persons or entities in a business undertaking. However, a joint venture is treated as a partnership when it comes to federal income taxation. The motives for these combinations are usually to expand and/or diversify program activities.

Often the nonprofit does not have the financial resources to launch or expand some program or service that it wishes to provide. Yet the managers may not want to start a social enterprise or be able to get ongoing grant funding. By setting itself up as the sole general partner in a limited partnership, it can tap the limited partners (e.g., cash-rich pension funds or profit-sharing plans) for needed capital. Most joint ventures have involved healthcare or university organizations. These organizations mostly cite the need to raise capital as the motive for engaging in joint ventures. The primary caution to be noted is that the nonprofit as general partner may jeopardize its Section 501(c)(3) exempt status if the joint venture conducts an activity unrelated to its charitable purpose. The I.R.S. is watching healthcare joint ventures to ensure that the nonprofit partner does not cede control to the for-profit partner.[35] The joint venture should be structured to allow the nonprofit to further exclusively its charitable purposes, protect its exempt assets, and not allow for private individuals' benefit and inurement. Instead of being part of a joint venture itself, the nonprofit may form a subsidiary or affiliate to serve as general partner. Another alternative is for the nonprofit to serve as a limited partner in the joint venture when the partnership does not further the organization's exempt purpose.

Another possible setup, having partnerships with other exempt organizations, must further the exempt purpose of *each* organization in order for each organization to be exempted from paying tax on its share of the income earned. Otherwise, the organization must pay unrelated business income (UBI) tax based on its share of income and expenses.

Why should your organization be interested in partnerships and joint ventures? First, some non–income-producing informal partnerships can be established that help your organization better achieve its mission without added financial or manpower drains. A great example is the Minnesota Housing Partnership, which has seen its role in ensuring that Twin Cities' affordable housing expand in services offered (including financing), geographic scope, and coordination benefits to partner organizations.[36] Another example is in higher education: Colleges and universities may contract with for-profit distance learning providers in order to be able to offer online classes to their students. Second, consider the reasons healthcare organizations give for engaging in joint ventures:[37]

- Raise needed capital.

- Grant service providers (physicians) a stake in a new enterprise or service, thereby increasing physician loyalty and patient referrals.

- Bring a new service or facility to a needy area.

- Share new enterprise risk.

- Pool various areas of medical competency.

- Attract new patients.

- Induce physicians not to refer patients elsewhere.

- Prevent physicians from establishing a competing healthcare operation.

Some of these motivations will pertain to any nonprofit arena, particularly the need to raise capital, the desire to bring a new service or facility to a needy area (such as the low income housing joint ventures that have sprung from the low-income housing tax credit),[38] risk sharing on a new enterprise, and competency pooling. The finance office can make a special contribution to the managerial discussions regarding the need to raise capital, and in fact may have originally surfaced the need for a joint venture by documenting a funding shortfall in the long-range financial plan. At a minimum, the financial manager can assist in determining the amount of capital that should be raised. Also, regarding risk sharing, through the use of computerized scenarios, the finance staff can show the financial effects of uncertain future outcomes of a proposed new venture, helping top management to see the benefit of engaging in a joint rather than a sole venture. Recall that target liquidity is the primary financial objective of the nonprofit, and evidence that there is a high probability that a go-it-alone venture will financially cripple the organization should provide strong impetus to investigate and properly structure a joint venture.

(d) STRATEGIC ALLIANCES.   When two or more organizations agree to pool resources and skills in order to achieve common goals, as well as goals specific to each organization, the pooling creates a *strategic alliance*. These cooperative arrangements are often multiyear—when businesses enter into joint ventures these may last for 30–50 years—and may encompass just one functional area or activity (e.g., marketing) or more than one functional area (e.g., manufacturing and marketing). Let's consider two examples. First, the Fox Cities Children's Museum in Appleton, Wisconsin was given a collection of dolls. The museum did not know how best to exhibit the dolls, so it allied with a local business. The owner of the business, Roxanne's Doll Shop, first volunteered as curator of the doll collection and then came aboard as manager of the museum's gift shop when that shop was later revitalized.[39] Another example is the alliance between The Stairstep Initiative, a grassroots organization commited to building up the African American community on the north side of Minneapolis, and Glory Foods of Ohio. The Stairstep Initiative hopes to brings jobs to an economically distressed area of Minneapolis through economic development. It wanted to start up an inner-city manufacturing partnership, and after initially parnering with General Mills to develop a food packaging factory, it came into contact with Glory Foods of Ohio. Based on mutual interests, the two companies formed an alliance creating a manufacturing plant called Siyeza. This plant employs sixty people from the northside of Minneapolis and produces a family-size meal product line for Glory Foods.[40]

Strategic alliances encompass equity joint ventures, in which two organizations both contribute capital to a third organization, and share in profits and risks. Given our focus on nonprofits, we will focus in this section on nonequity ventures, another form of strategic alliance. Nonequity ventures include initiatives such as a joint service development team or a cooperative advertising campaign. The latter types of ventures are more flexible and can be revised, restructured, or ended more easily. Note the word "strategic"; if a vendor and a customer are simply tying their purchasing and supply systems together, this is an operational partnership as opposed to a strategic alliance. The purpose of strategy is to advance mission achievement through selection of markets served, new service development, and similar activities.

(i) Motives for Strategic Alliances. Adapting from the excellent review of business strategic alliances compiled by Varadarajan and Cunningham,[41] nonprofits may benefit for several reasons. They:

1. Broaden service line/fill service offerings gaps

   • Fill gaps in current service offerings
   • Broaden present line of services
   • Differentiate or add value to the service

2. Enter new services domains/gain a foothold in emerging industries or industry segments

   • Diversify and take advantage of growth opportunities in new services domains (due to traditional market stagnation)
   • Gain foothold in areas where alternative, substitute technologies are developing by allying with organizations already exploiting those technologies

3. Enhance resource use efficiency, lowering costs by taking advantage of:

   • Scale, scope, and experience effects
   • Differential costs of labor, raw materials, or other inputs

4. Extend resources, particularly when a merger (and loss of corporate identity) is unacceptable but the organization cannot manage the internal development or acquisitions

   • Especially for smaller organizations that do not have the resources to invest in research and development (R&D), capital equipment, new products or services, and other activities necessary for meeting the needs of clients

We are most interested in same-industry, or intra-industry strategic alliances. Why would a nonprofit wish to form an alliance with another organization currently competing for resources in the same geographic market(s) or with another organization which constitutes a potential competitor? By pooling product or service development costs, production/delivery costs, and/or marketing resources, the two (or more) organizations may be able to seize new service or market opportunities that neither organization could seize on its own. Many times, however, the perceived competitive threat may not be large because the services provided are geared toward different clienteles or the organizations are separated far enough geographically that their service areas do not (and will not) overlap. Most nonprofits are already members of a trade association (e.g., the homeless shelters holding membership in the Association of Gospel Rescue Missions [AGRM] or the many foundations comprising the Council on Foundations) and understand what the benefits are of banding together when there is no competition between the vast majority of the members.

(ii) Financial Aspects of Strategic Alliances.   Joint fundraising alliances, such as the new donor development program coordinated for faith-based rescue missions by the AGRM, illustrate that the function that a nonprofit alliance is built around may be fund development. Fundraising is part of the treasury function in corporations, and is therefore legitimately characterized as a finance function strategic alliance.[42] In a case such as this, the first task for the finance office should be ready to make the argument for cooperative fundraising, showing the efficiencies (real cost savings) involved as well as the commonly noted potential for more funds to be raised.

Second, the finance office will have to be ready to project the needed financial resources that are the driving force between most strategic alliances (as well as for partnerships, joint ventures, and mergers). Management teams will be naturally reluctant to enter into such arrangements. Management might fear donor attrition, to the extent the alliance partner is either (1) a potential draw to this organization's donors, or (2) viewed negatively by this organization's donors, who will in turn react negatively when hearing of the alliance.

Furthermore, their management may not want to give up operating autonomy. Varadarajan and Cunningham make the point that whenever an organization has financial resources to either acquire or internally develop the skills and other resources needed to exploit a market opportunity, it is quite unlikely to enter into a strategic alliance due to a loss of operational control. The desired resources include assets, capabilities, organizational characteristics and processes, information, and expertise. So alliances are not necessarily cost related; business alliances have been predominant for achieving market or sales growth and for gaining access to new markets.

Third, the risks of strategic alliance should be highlighted by the financial manager, in that she or he has ultimate responsibility for asset protection. Two major risks are the possible "stealing" of skills by the alliance partner and the possibility of becoming overly dependent on alliances. Both of these are lesser issues to nonprofit organizations than for businesses trying to protect and build manufacturing and R&D capabilities.

(iii) Financial Projections of Mergers, Acquisitions, or Joint Ventures.   Financial spreadsheet software is ideally oriented for projecting the before-and-after financial positions of an organization. Spreadsheets have built-in scenario (or version) managers to assist the analyst in quickly generating optimistic, most likely, and pessimistic cases for a proposed merger, acquisition, or joint venture.

As an example, let's look at the before-and-after situations of a private school considering a merger with another private school. After projecting combined enrollments and cost savings due to the larger size and the ability to share costs, the analyst ends up with the data shown in Exhibit 9.15.

Why the cost reductions from a merger? Salaries are fixed up to a point, meaning they do not change with small changes in enrollment. Administration costs (principal's

Item	Present Statement of Activity ($)	Proposed Merger Statement of Activity ($)
Revenues:		
Tuition	$300,000[a]	$920,000 [f,g]
Fundraisers	25,000	65,000
Meal revenue	15,188[b]	40,500[h]
Other	3,200	5,000
Total revenue:	343,388	1,030,500
Expenses:		
Salaries and wages	225,000[c]	325,000[i]
Employee benefits	48,000	72,000
Insurance	30,000	32,000
Materials	35,000	45,000
Rent	20,000[d]	20,000
Utilities	14,400	16,400
Interest	6,000[e]	6,000
Other	3,250	5,000
Total expense:	381,650	521,400
Surplus/(Deficit):	$(38,263)	$509,100

[a]Based on 150 students × $2,000 tuition
[b]Based on $1.25 × 60 students eating on average x 5 days per week x 9 months x 4.5 weeks per month
[c]Based on faculty/administration of eight
[d]The main school building is rented
[e]Offices (with a multipurpose room) constructed with borrowed money
[f]Enrollment projection w/merger: 400
[g]Tuition projection w/merger: $2,300
[h]Meal revenue w/merger: $32,400
[i]Based on faculty/administration of twelve

EXHIBIT 9.15   MERGER ANALYSIS WORKSHEET

salary and benefits) are fixed, and only one principal is needed for the merged institution. Registration and/or certification fees are fixed. Labor, energy, and maintenance expenses are not totally fixed, but rather step-function or semivariable costs. The combined school can order maintenance and office supplies in larger quantities, gaining quantity discounts. Other administrative costs—office related, financing, and purchasing—also decline on a per-student basis as enrollment increases due to the merger. As the number of students increases, these fixed costs, *when figured on a per-student basis*, decline.

The proposed merger is a winner, financially, from the vantage of the merger partner doing this financial analysis. Using scenario analysis (Exhibit 9.16), even the worst-case

Scenario Summary	Most Likely	Worst Case	Best Case
Changing cells			
Enrollment projection with merger	400	325	500
Tuition projection with merger	$2,300	$2,000	$2,400
Result cells			
Surplus or deficit	$509,100	$231,506	$799,225

EXHIBIT 9.16   SCENARIO SUMMARY

scenario is (1) better than the current situation, and (2) a generator of a fiscal surplus, which can be used to replace aging plant[43] and/or build endowment reserves.

9.6   FINANCIAL PLANNING AND CAPITAL BUDGETING IN PRACTICE

We review here some evidence regarding program evaluation capital budgeting and long-range financial planning.

Evaluation may be built into existing programs and can benefit from the use of an external evaluator who brings credibility without adding significant cost. Such program evaluations contribute to organizations' planning efforts, based on a study done by mail, telephone, and on-site investigation.[44] Nonprofits believe they are ill-equipped to conduct program outcome assessment in many cases. Very few nonprofits have received training in outcome measurement, outcome data analysis, or service improvement strategies based on outcome results. This study noted that "most organizations performing outcome measurement are just beginning to become comfortable with it and to use the information to improve programs and support other activities such as marketing or fundraising."[45] Strategic and long-range financial planning have no doubt been hampered by measurement inadequacies, but should improve over time as this information gets used in planning processes.

Those organizations deemed successful based on meeting two financial goals—having a balanced budget without borrowing from an endowment or tapping cash reserves—were more likely to evaluate sources and uses of funds, forecast revenues and costs, and prepare detailed financial projections before making major decisions. This was discovered in a small-sample strategic planning study conducted by William Crittenden.[46]

A major study of hospitals' capital expenditures indicate that there is a significant gap between "have" and "have-not" hospitals: Hospitals with strong balances sheets (good liquidity, reasonable debt) and a "successful strategic capital planning process" are investing enough to more than offset depreciation. Struggling hospitals, however, become less creditworthy, losing access to capital, and struggle to keep current with today's demands but seem unable to build for tomorrow's needs.[47] Another survey finds that 41 percent of hospitals' capital budgets went for major modernization, 14 percent for new programs, 14 percent for medical equipment, 14 percent on information systems, 5 percent on other equipment, and 5 percent on code compliance.[48]

Most of the 254 nonprofits surveyed in the Denver and Boulder areas foresee significant capital expenditures in future years. Of the 254 surveyed nonprofits, 88 percent foresee client population growth within the next 5 years, 60 percent asserted that current facilities would be unable to meet those needs within 5 years, and most said that the reason for this would be inadequate space for future programs. There was also considerable concern regarding the quantity, cost, location, and quality of space available.[49]

Most surveyed Indiana nonprofits *do not* have financial reserves dedicated to projected capital needs or to facility maintenance. These reserves could be used to cope with unexpected outlays for repair or replacement, but only 44 percent of Indiana nonprofits have reserves for maintenance needs and only 35 percent have reserves for capital needs. Faith-based nonprofits were the most likely to have these types of reserves, and arts/culture/humanities and mutual benefit nonprofits were the least likely to have reserves.[50]

With respect to capital budgeting evaluation techniques, an early study indicates that the payback method (how many years to recover the initial investment) was used by 45 percent of faith-based respondents, and 30 percent used cost-benefit analysis. A mere

7 percent used ROIC, and 4 percent used NPV in project evaluation.[51] A recent study, not of nonprofits but of Canadian municipal governments, finds a minority use formal capital budgeting evaluation techniques, and those that do tend to use the payback techniques despite the fact that it ignores the time value of money. More emphasis is placed on quantitative/financial factors than on qualitative/intangible factors.[52] The best news, though, comes from a recent study of U.S. nonprofit agricultural coops: Over 50 percent used NPV, ROIC, or the benefit-cost ratio (profitability index) in their capital project evaluations.[53] We expect to see wider adoption of sophisticated techniques as proficient financial management becomes valued more highly by nonprofits.

9.7 CONCLUSION

Long-range financial planning and proper capital allocation are vital parts of ensuring a prosperous and mission-achieving future for your organization. We have focused on the role of financial staff in the development, evaluation, and implementation of these plans. The power of PCs and financial spreadsheet software for forecasting and proposal evaluation has been demonstrated. We have also seen that nonprofit organizations are increasingly turning to partnering, strategic alliances, and mergers to leverage scarce resources. Informal partnerships, often labeled strategic alliances, abound. These may involve many organizations, underscoring the importance of having all organizational personnel work together as team members to communicate and implement the strategic plan. Financial personnel will be the first line of defense to avert financial catastrophes when the organization attempts to move too quickly or when necessary funds do not come in on a timely basis. Finally, financial strategies and policies can be developed or revised by the finance staff, with appropriate approvals by senior management and the board of directors.

Notes

1. Quote and other details about RISE are from Alessandra Bianchi, "Educators with Borders: Sometimes Nonprofit Workers Have to Learn to 'Just Say No,'" *Stanford Social Innovation Review* (Summer 2005): 52.
2. This was documented in Roy J. Clinton, Stan Williams, and Robert E. Stevens, "Constituent Surveys as an Input in the Strategic Planning Process for Churches and Ministries: Part I," *Journal of Ministry, Marketing & Management* 1(2): 43–55; and Amit J. Shah, Fred R. David, and Zigmont J. Surawski III, "Does Strategic Planning Help Churches? An Exploratory Study," *Coastal Business Journal* 2 (Fall 2003): 28–35. The latter survey asked whether churches engaged in "strategic or long range planning." This study also noted four scriptural admonitions in favor of planning: Proverbs 29:18, Proverbs 15:22, Proverbs 19:20, and Proverbs 20:18.
3. Drew A. Dolan, "Training Needs of Administrators in the Nonprofit Sector: What Are They and How Should We Address Them?" *Nonprofit Management & Leadership* 12 (Spring 2002): 277–292.
4. Shah, David, and Surawski, "Does Strategic Planning Help Churches?"
5. Kirsten A. Gronbjerg and Richard M. Clerkin, *Indiana Nonprofits: Financial and Human Resource Challenges* (Bloomington, IN: Indiana University School of Public and Environmental Affairs, August 2004).
6. Foundation for Community Association Research, *Best Practices: Financial Operations, Report # 4* (Alexandria, VA: Author, 2001). Available online at: www.cairf.org/research/bpfinancial.pdf. Accessed: 1/16/2006.

7. Nonprofit Finance Fund and Technical Development Corporation, *Survey Results: Facilities Needs of Nonprofit Organizations in the Seven-County Denver Metropolitan Area—Final Report,* February 6, 2002. Available online at: http://www.rcfdenver.org/reports/finalNFFsurvey.pdf.

8. See an interesting case study of capital structure policy-making in healthcare organizations in Dick W. Feenstra and G. Jan van Helden, "Policy Making on Reserves of Dutch University Hospitals—A Case Study," *Financial Accountability and Management* 19 (February 2003): 1–20 . "Reserves" in this article are the amount of net assets, not the amount of operating or strategic reserves as commonly referred to.

9. Renata J. Rafferty, "Risk and Return: Defining Your 'Comfort Zone,' " 1999. Available for download at: www.guidestar.org/news/features/rafferty.jsp. Accessed: 12/20/2005.

10. "Survey: Nonprofit Contributions Insufficient to Cover Rising Overhead," *Portland Business Journal,* December 16, 2005. Available online at: http://portland.bizjournals.com/portland/stories/2005/12/12/daily34.html. Accessed: 12/31/2005.

11. Healthcare Financial Management Association, *How Are Hospitals Financing the Future? Capital Spending in Health Care Today* (HFMA's Financing the Future Series) (Westbrook, IL: Author, 2004).

12. Regina E. Herzlinger, "Managing the Finances of Nonprofit Organizations," *California Management Review* 21(Spring 1979): 60–69.

13. Trent Stamp, executive director of Charity Navigator, quoted in Jane Lampman, "Much Has Been Given, Much Is Still to Be Done," *Christian Science Monitor,* November 21, 2005, 11–12.

14. Adapted from a definition of a business model given by Bill Rosser of the Gartner Group, quoted in Thomas Zsolt, *Business Modeling: Ready for Prime Time* (New York: Hyperion, 2001). Available for download at: www.hyperion.com/downloads/wp_busmodel.pdf. Accessed: 4/15/2005.

15. A good Internet source on spreadsheet financial modeling is available at the time of this writing at: www.eusprig.org/smbp.pdf. A good print resource, which goes into detail on the philosophy and techniques of financial modeling, is Chandan Sengupta, *Financial Modeling Using Excel and VBA* (Hoboken, NJ: John Wiley & Sons, 2004).

16. Available for download after free registration at: www.pwcglobal.com/Extweb/industry.nsf/docid/A628BE64CC84BA578 5256AC5007F1B94. Accessed: 1/21/06.

17. For an informative and brief discussion of strategic reserves, see "Information Flyer: Financial Planning and Operating Reserves," California Department of Parks and Recreation (n.d.). Available for download at: www.parks.ca.gov/pages/735/files/financial%20planning%20and%20operating%20reserves.pdf. Accessed: 1/17/2006.

18. Gordon Donaldson, "Strategy for Financial Emergencies," *Harvard Business Review* (November/December 1969): 67–79.

19. Ann C. Logue, "Solving the Financial Planning Puzzle," *University Business* 9(January 2006): 49–52.

20. Susan Kenny Stevens, *Nonprofit Lifecycles* (Long Lake, MN: 2001).

21. Marc Jegers, "The Sustainable Growth Rate of Non-Profit Organisations: The Effect of Efficiency, Profitability and Capital Structure," *Financial Accountability & Management* 19 (November 2004): 309–313.

22. Jeanne Bell Peters and Elizabeth Schaffer, *Financial Leadership for Nonprofit Executives* (St. Paul, MN: Fieldstone Alliance, 2005).

23. Mary T. Ziebell and Don T. Decoster, *Management Control Systems in Nonprofit Organizations* (Ft. Worth, TX: Harcourt Brace Jovanovich, 1991), 164.

24. The format for the IRR function is: *=IRR(range of cash flows).* Make sure your initial investment is in the first cell of that range and has a negative sign, the final cash flow is the last cell in that range, and there are no blank cells in the range. It does not matter whether you data are in single dollars or thousands of dollars, as long as all of the numbers are consistent.

25. This can be done for an EAC calculation in Excel by: *=PMT(rate, years, NPV).* However, you must change the sign of the NPV to a positive sign first.

26. Refer to discussion of liquidity analysis and how to calculate the appropriate liquid balance for your organization in Chapters 2, 5, and 8.
27. A mathematical programming computerized worksheet makes the process much simpler. You may do this using the "Solver" function that is part of the Tools menu in Microsoft Excel™ or another computer spreadsheet program. If you are unfamiliar with this, you might contact a finance professor at a local college or university; this makes an ideal paid or unpaid student internship project.
28. Statistically this is so because the cash flow streams of the two organizations are less than perfectly correlated. When one organization is experiencing a down year, the other may be neutral or up, or vice versa. In fact, the less closely associated the two organizations' cash flows, the better.
29. Noel Hyndman and Donal McKillop, "Conversion Ratios in Charities in England and Wales—An Investigation of Economies of Scale," *Financial Accountability and Management* 15 (May 1999): 135–153.
30. For more on economies of scale, see Sharon M. Oster, *Strategic Management of Non-profit Organizations* (New York: Oxford University Press, 1995), 32–34.
31. See Malcolm S. Salter and Wolf A. Weinhold, *Diversification Through Acquisition: Strategies for Creating Economic Value* (New York: The Free Press, 1979), 38–42.
32. Bronislaw Prokuski, "Anatomy of a Merger," *Association Management* (February 2002): 42–48.
33. Uniform Partnership Act, Section 6(1); Henry Campbell Black, *Black's Law Dictionary: Definitions of the Terms and Phrases of American and English Jurisprudence, Ancient and Modern*, 6th ed. (Minneapolis: West Publishing, 1990): 120. For more on this topic, see Michael I. Sanders, *Joint Ventures Involving Tax-Exempt Organizations*, 2nd ed. (Hoboken, NJ: John Wiley & Sons, 2000) and the annual supplements to that text. We drew on this information for this section.
34. If income is earned on an unrelated business activity, each member is taxed based on his or her distributive share of income, gain or loss, expenses, or credit.
35. This is a major concern with "whole hospital" joint ventures, in which a charity and a private entity each contribute one or more hospitals to a third organization called an operating limited liability company. The nonprofit can lose its tax exempt status if the nonprofit does not retain control in a joint venture. Private inurement is also a concern because of the financial agreements that are crafted as part of these joint ventures. See Sanders, Chapter 11.
36. For more information on the Minnesota Housing Partnership, refer to www.mhponline.org/About%20MHP/history.htm.
37. Reasons offered to the IRS when seeking IRS approval for joint venture arrangements.
38. For information on these low income housing ventures, see Michael I. Sanders, *Joint Ventures Involving Tax-Exempt Organizations*, 2nd ed., *2005 Cumulative Supplement* (Hoboken, NJ: John Wiley & Sons, 2005), Chapter 12.
39. Peter F. Drucker Foundation for Nonprofit Management, Meeting the Collaboration Challenge: Developing Strategic Alliances Between Nonprofit Organizations and Businesses Video, May 2002, Jossey-Bass. This video is referenced at http://leadertoleader.org/collaboration/challenge/appendixe.html. Accessed: July 20, 2006.
40. Id.
41. We draw heavily on the Varadarajan and Cunningham analysis in our discussion of strategic alliances. Refer to P. Rajan Varadarajan and Margaret H. Cunningham, "Strategic Alliances: A Synthesis of Conceptual Foundations," *Journal of the Academy of Marketing Sciences* 23 (Fall 1995): 282–296.
42. See section on finance structure in Chapter 4 for discussion of greater role for the finance area in fundraising planning, implementation, and evaluation.
43. Note that depreciation is not included in the expenses listed.
44. Allison Fine, Colette Thayer, and Anne Coghlan, "Program Evaluation Practice in the Nonprofit Sector." Working Paper. Nonprofit Sector Research Fund (The Aspen Institute), 1998.
45. Elaine Morley, Elisa Vinson, and Harry P. Hatry, *Outcome Measurement for Nonprofit Organizations: Current Practices and Recommendations* (Washington, D.C.: Independent Sector, 2001).

46. William F. Crittenden, "Spinning Straw into Gold: The Tenuous Strategy, Funding and Financial Performance Linkage," *Nonprofit and Voluntary Sector Quarterly* 29S (2000): 164–182.

47. HFMA, *How Are Hospitals Financing the Future?*

48. Ingrid Singer and Betsy Carrier, *Capital Investment in America's Safety Net: Results of the NAPH Capital Expenditure and Financing Survey for FY 2001* (Washington, D.C.: National Association of Public Hospitals and Health Systems, September 2003).

49. Nonprofit Finance Fund and Technical Development Corporation, *Survey Results.*

50. Gronbjerg and Clerkin, *Indiana Nonprofits.*

51. John T. Zietlow, "Capital and Operating Budgeting Practices in Pure Nonprofit Organizations," *Financial Accountability & Management* 5 (Winter 1989): 219–232.

52. Yee-Ching Lilian Chan, "Use of Capital Budgeting Techniques and an Analytic Approach to Capital Investment Decisions in Canadian Municipal Governments," *Public Budgeting Finance* 24 (June 2004): 40–58.

53. John B. White, Morgan P. Miles, and Linda S. Munilla, "An Exploratory Study into the Adoption of Capital Budgeting Techniques by Agricultural Co-operatives," *British Food Journal* 99, no. 4 (1997): 128–132.

APPENDIX **9A**

CASE STUDY: KIAWAH ISLAND COMMUNITY ASSOCIATION*

Size: 4115 properties
Age: 26 Years
Location: Kiawah Island, SC

Kiawah Island is a National Community Association of the Year Award (NCAYA)–winning community in South Carolina. In addition to the board and management's dedication to community spirit and service, they also pay particular attention to financial operations.

Governing Documents. The community's governing documents provide certain guidelines related to the association's financial activities. Financial statements are prepared per the accrual basis of accounting and prepared according to the fund reporting method. Using the accrual method ensures observance of limitations and restrictions on the use of financial resources that the governing documents require. The association board and staff also prefer to have an annual audit conducted because it gives the members a level of confidence that is not possible with a review or compilation. When it's all said and done, the board and the staff want their work scrutinized to the fullest extent.

Bank Statements. As per the association's *Financial Controls Manual*, the association's treasurer and controller's assistant reconcile Kiawah Island's bank statements monthly. This allows the association to regularly monitor its assets. The individuals responsible for reconciling the bank statements do not have check-signing authority. Authorized signatories on all bank accounts are the board treasurer, the general manager, the controller, and the assistant general manager. Regular checking transactions require two of the aforementioned representatives' signatures. Access to the association's reserves accounts requires the board president's and treasurer's signatures.

Financial Statements. Association financial statements are produced monthly to keep the board up to speed on operations. The financial statements are discussed every six weeks at a board meeting. Board meeting minutes are posted on the association's Web site for membership review. Financial statements (and annual financial audits) are always available at the association office for members' review and the financial audit is provided once per year as part of the annual meeting packet materials.

Write-offs. Further, the association has a set process by which "write-offs" (delinquencies) are approved—the controller approves accounts with a balance of less than $100,

*Source: http://www.cairf.org/research/bpfinancial.pdf. Accessed: 1/14/06 Used by permission.

350

the manager approves accounts with a balance of more than $100 but less than $500, the treasurer approves accounts with a balance of more than $500 but less than $1,000, and the board must vote and approve write-offs for accounts with a balance of more than $1,000.

Budgeting. Kiawah Island's board and staff also work to develop and follow a comprehensive budget each fiscal year. Budget items are allocated to the month during which expenses occur. For example, the pool contractor provides a specific annual schedule for the coming year listing the services and personnel he is providing each month and their cost. These monthly allocations are included into the annual budget because it makes sense to match expenses with income. For example, during the months that the pool contractor is providing services, the pool is open and income is being generated.

Unbudgeted expenditures more than $2,000 must have prior board approval. Approval may be obtained either at regularly scheduled board meetings, or by mail vote, when necessary.

Unanimous approval is needed for a mail vote to pass. Also, the Finance Advisory Committee is informed of such expenditures and makes their recommendations to the board prior to the meeting or mail vote.

To facilitate association operations when unbudgeted expenses of a serious nature arise, the budget may contain a line item for contingencies, not to exceed the limit approved by the board. The guidelines for the use of these funds are: (1) an unanticipated emergency (e.g., hurricane, flood, fire, etc.), (2) the replacement or repair of equipment that either fails or is destroyed unexpectedly and is considered by the general manager to be critical to the efficient operation of the association, or (3) for the protection of association property from imminent damage. The reason for this line item is that time required to obtain board approval for unbudgeted expenditures may, under certain conditions, cause significant unnecessary expense to the association, or that approval may be unattainable due to the unavailability of board members, and so on. The use of this line item, within the guidelines above, is to be in the Operating Committee's discretion only. When expenditures are made, the general manager is to seek board ratification immediately, of both the expenditure and his or her justification for the use of the contingency funds versus the regular process for advance approval of nonbudgeted expenditures more than $2,000. Once approved by the board, the expense will be moved to the correct line item and/or department. The board has the authority to suspend use of the contingency line item at any time, by written notification to the general manager.

Competitive Bids. The general manager, at the direction of the board, is the contracting agent for the association. The general manager will sign all bilateral contracts. The general manager may delegate purchasing authority and the ability to sign purchase orders to various department heads. However, the general manager may not delegate authority to sign general insurance or employee benefit contracts. Where feasible, all contracts and purchase orders will be in the association's standard format appropriate to the type of purchase. The general manager reserves the right to have the contract reviewed by legal counsel and/or insurance representatives. Whenever a form of contract or purchase order other than the association's standard is used, appropriate review will be exercised. The general manager reserves the right to require that the standard format be used. All contracts valued annually at $25,000 or more require competitive bidding. Competition for contracts less than $25,000 is not precluded and is recommended when time and cost for obtaining quotes is reasonable. Staff is expected to perform due diligence in obtaining bids, when required. Contracts with fewer than three responses must contain a certification from the requesting manager that all available responsible bidders were sought and suitable follow-up performed to get as many bids as possible, with explanations of unusual circumstances. The board must approve any sole-source award in advance. Similarly, any contract to be awarded to other than the lowest bidder must have prior approval by either the board or, for reserve projects, the Major Repair & Replacement Committee.

Any contract in excess of $25,000 must either be approved in the annual budget or have specific prior board approval, except in the case of emergency or contingency purchases. Additional board approval is required in cases where conditions change, before or after the contract is let, which significantly affect the scope or cost of the contract (more than 20%). No service contract may be automatically renewed for more than 12 months without additional approval sought from the board. There will be no contracts between the association and one of the association's employees, board members, committee members, or their respective relatives, regardless of dollar value.

Long-Range Fiscal Planning. The board directs the Finance Advisory Committee to develop a five-year fiscal plan, which includes disaster, insurance, and facilities acquisition components. The committee receives information about the capital projects proposed for the future from the Long-Range Planning Committee. In their disaster planning, the committee considers financial disasters (for example, they determine what happens if revenues become reduced). Draft plans are presented to the full membership at open forums and via mailings for comments before the board approves them.

EVALUATING SOCIAL ENTERPRISES

In this appendix, we present a diagnostic tool to assist in evaluating social enterprises (some of which may be referred to as "earned income ventures") from a liquidity perspective. We start with a brief argument for considering liquidity, follow with a numerical example, and then show how the graphical Financial Return & Financial Coverage Matrix (FRFCM) may be used in decision-making.[1]

If the ALT (Approximate Liquidity Target) Theory is approximately correct,[2] and/or liquidity is of paramount importance (say, because the nonprofit is capital constrained and engaging in moderate or extreme capital rationing), then calculated Social Return on Investment (SROI, as presented by REDF and others) might be supplemented with or replaced by a form of Social Return on Financial Coverage Ratio (SROFCR). Regardless, the framework that follows should prove useful to nonprofits considering for-profit business ventures.

Hypothetical Organization XYZ has four possible business ventures to consider: A, B, C, and D. Which one(s) should it favor, and which ones avoid? As input into this, consider the table of relevant data for the ventures (Exhibit 9B.1).

These data plot as the bubble graph in Exhibit 9B.2, which is labeled the Financial Return & Financial Coverage Matrix (FRFCM).

FRAMEWORK INTERPRETATION AND IMPLEMENTATION

The FRFCM Framework is diagnostic, not prescriptive. In general, managers should invest in projects to the right of the vertical axis, with further right and larger bubble size denoting more desirability. The vertical axis (at the origin) separates projects consuming more than (to the left) or less than (to the right) "organization available funds." Projects to the left are major liquidity drains, while the further to the right a project plots, the more it adds to the organization's liquidity. Large bubbles represent projects with large (projected) social returns. Management and the board may well decide to go out and get funding for "large bubble" projects that plot left of vertical axis. Otherwise, the fact that these projects are to the left, and the further they are to the left, provides indication of need to delay the project until additional funding is in place.

In both the table and the graph, Project A is a significant liquidity drain but a large social return project. B drains less liquidity, but again would put the organization's liquidity into a negative, illiquid posture. C and D would not exhaust current liquidity, and B provides significant social returns. D is most easily funded from the current liquidity position, but provides lesser social returns. The officers and directors are faced

Bubble Graph Data

Social Return, Financial Return, and Liquidity Analysis for New Nonprofit Business Ventures

Project	Social Return (5 year Projected)	Initial Investment*	Target Liquid Funds**	Financial Coverage Ratio: ABS(TLF/II)-1	Financial Return Present Value	Memo: NPV
A	300,000	$(100,000)	$35,000	−0.65	$30,000	$(70,000)
B	75,000	$(50,000)	$35,000	−0.30	$25,000	$(25,000)
C	45,000	$(25,000)	$35,000	0.40	$25,000	$ —
D	5,000	$(5,000)	$35,000	6.00	$10,000	$5,000

* Initial Investment probably best defined as all financial outlays to get venture up and and running, including working capital outlays, less restricted funds designated (and restricted) for the venture and monies known with certainty to be forthcoming for the project within the next 6–12 months.

**Target Liquid Funds = Unrestricted Cash & Cash Equivs.
  + Unrestricted ST Investments
  + (Total ST Borrowing Capacity − Used ST Borrowing)

EXHIBIT 9B.1   BUBBLE GRAPH DATA

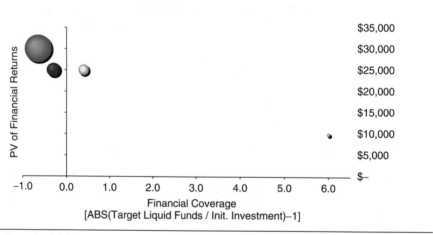

Bubble Size = Social Return

EXHIBIT 9B.2   FINANCIAL RETURN AND FINANCIAL COVERAGE MATRIX

with finding funding for A and/or B if they wish to achieve the projects' significant social benefits. It appears that C might be a more logical choice than B, given the fact that it drains the liquidity position less and yet provides almost equivalent social returns. At best, these are difficult decisions, and nonprofits often lack the managerial abilities as well as the financial resources to properly harness the business potential of these ventures.[3]

CAVEATS

There are several important reasons that this framework should be challenging for managers to implement:

1. Estimation error is inherent in the initial investment, present value of future returns, and social return estimations.

2. Incoming funds specific to the project may be sufficient to allow for investment in a certain project—if known this may be subtracted from Initial Investment to arrive at (modified) Net Initial Investment.

3. Near-term deficits or other planned capital or financial outlays may dictate turning down even those projects that appear feasible.

4. There may be restricted funds for project(s) that must be used to reduce initial investment or override diagnosis.

5. No obvious accept/reject criteria are presented; merely guidance to board and officers.

6. No clear ranking criteria are provided from either table or graph, especially in light of the varying NPV prospects (see the rightmost memo column).

7. This shows projects' effect on the organization's insolvency risk, but there are other risk types and dimensions.

8. Managers should really supplement this analysis with payback period statistics.

New research currently being conducted should shed more light on the strains placed on organizations that are launching social enterprise ventures.

Notes

1. This framework is part of a larger paper that was presented in 2000 to two nonprofit conferences. References are as follows: John Zietlow, "Social Enterprise Financial and Nonfinancial Evaluation," paper presented to the *29th Annual ARNOVA Conference* (New Orleans, LA: November 16, 2000); and John T. Zietlow, "Social Enterprise Financial and Nonfinancial Evaluation," presentation to the Alliance for Nonprofit Management (Cleveland, OH: April 21, 2001).

2. See Chapter 2 for our reasoning on why this approximate liquidity target should serve as the primary financial objective of noncommercial nonprofits.

3. For more on the difficulties involved in these projects, see John T. Zietlow, "Social Entrepreneurship: Managerial, Finance and Marketing Aspects," 2001 special issue of *Journal of Nonprofit & Public Sector Marketing*, 9 (1), pp. 19–44.

CHAPTER **10**

MANAGING YOUR
ORGANIZATION'S LIABILITIES

10.1 MANAGING THE BALANCE SHEET   357

  (a) Balance Sheet Management: Benefits and Steps   358
  (b) Determining Your Organization's Debt Capacity   361

10.2 PAYABLES   362

10.3 SHORT-TERM BORROWING   363

10.4 STRATEGIC FINANCING PLAN   365

  (a) Borrower's Strategic Financial Objectives   365
  (b) Borrowing Requirements   366

10.5 STEPS TO SUCCESSFUL BORROWING   366

  (a) Understanding Debt   367
  (b) Loan Approval Process   368
  (c) Alternative Sources of Short-Term Funds   370

10.6 MATCHING FINANCIAL SOURCES TO STRATEGIC OBJECTIVES   371

10.7 PREPARING THE FINANCING PROPOSAL   372

  (a) Term Sheet   372
  (b) Plan Overview   372
  (c) Presentation Contents   372

10.8 MAKING THE PRESENTATION   373

  (a) Importance of Questions   373
  (b) Answering Objections   373
  (c) Personalizing the Presentation   374

10.9 OTHER FACTORS IN BORROWING/LENDING DECISIONS   374

  (a) Borrowing from the Bank   374
  (b) Trends in Short-term Lending   377

10.10 MUNICIPAL AND TAXABLE BONDS   378

  (a) Municipal Bonds   378
  (b) Taxable Bonds   382
  (c) What Qualifies My Organization to Issue Bonds?   383
  (d) What If My Organization Is Not Perceived as Creditworthy?   384

10.11 LEASING AND NONTRADITIONAL FINANCING SOURCES   384

  (a) The Leasing Process   384
  (b) Leasing versus Borrowing   385

10.12 DEVELOPING A DEBT AND HEDGING POLICY   385

10.13 LIABILITY MANAGEMENT IN PRACTICE   387

10.14 CONCLUSION   389

The nonprofit landscape is littered with failed organizations that presumed on their financial futures by taking on too much debt. Denver aquarium Ocean Journey overestimated its annual visitors and had to declare bankruptcy within two years of opening because it was unable to make payments on its $57 million of debt.[1] The Allegheny Health, Education, and Research Foundation (AHERF) filed bankruptcy with $1.3 billion in debt and 65,000 creditors—primarily due to too-rapid expansion, unfulfilled merger operating-result projections, and an overload of debt that it accumulated: Debt mush-roomed from $67 million to $1.2 billion over a 12-years. The liquidity challenges we identified in Chapter 2 for nonprofits came to the fore: AHERF tried to grow via acqui-sition to become a statewide provider, had no ability to tap equity financing (as would a for-profit), and purchased hospitals with negligible operating cash flow.[2] Other orga-nizations, such as the American Red Cross and the $1 billion line of credit it tapped for $340 million in 2005, borrow because cash outflows temporarily exceed cash inflows or their ability to mobilize those inflows to the locations where cash outflows are occurring.

Properly used, debt financing may provide an important piece of the financial flexi-bility that organizations require, as unused borrowing capacity is one component of the target liquidity level. This chapter provides guidance for an organization that chooses to borrow with short-term loans, long-term municipal bonds, or mortgage loans. The starting point is a consideration of the balance sheet, as your organization establishes its capital structure. We also profile the lender's view on a borrower's creditworthiness. Furthermore, we mention sources of funds that your organization may tap other than through arranged borrowing. Recall from the Lilly study that two out of three of the organizations surveyed never do short-term borrowing, and only one in eight organiza-tions is a perennial short-term borrower.[3] Yet all organizations benefit from a knowledge or borrowing alternatives and the borrowing process: Many of these same faith-based organizations have mortgage loans. Finally, in this chapter we discuss different liability, or borrowed fund, accounts.

10.1 MANAGING THE BALANCE SHEET

Your financing decisions, including whether to borrow and how much to do, require a context. That context is the *target capital structure*, or how much of various financing sources your organization shall employ to finance its assets. You should have your phi-losophy and strategy stated in a *debt and hedging policy*. That requires another look at the balance sheet, or statement of financial position (SFP).

Every dollar of assets on the balance sheet must be financed with either a dollar of debt (borrowed money) or equity (net assets). As we noted in Chapter 9, you should project assets, which represent a funding need, out to at least three to five years in the future. As you project your statement of activity (SA), you will determine your additional equity capital: To the degree your revenues exceed expenses, you will earn a surplus (change in net assets) that will provide "equity capital" to self-fund your assets. As a nonprofit may not issue stock, you are limited to this net revenue source of equity capital. *Any other asset growth will have to be financed by liabilities, or debt. Correspondingly, the upside to using debt is that your organization may grow more rapidly, providing more services, if it chooses to use debt financing.*

The main downside to using debt financing is the additional risk to your organization's stability. *Financial risk* is the possibility that your organization will not be able to meet its fixed, financing-related obligations. We saw examples of this in our chapter-opening vignettes. One cannot "lay off" interest or principal payments as one lays off workers or cuts back on other discretionary expenses. Arranged borrowing, whether a bank credit line or bonds issued to investors, represents a contractual agreement that must be taken very seriously. Your organization and its stakeholders stand to lose if you are not prudent in your use of debt.

(a) BALANCE SHEET MANAGEMENT: BENEFITS AND STEPS.   What constitutes a well-managed balance sheet? According to Wareham and Majka, a well-managed balance sheet:

- Supports the organization's strategic plan within an appropriate credit context
- Provides the most flexibility, given market expectations and legal considerations
- Reflects the optimal capital framework, given the organization's needs, capabilities, and risk profile
- Provides the lowest overall cost for the risk of the asset and liability portfolios
- Allows for future financing needs[4]

Balance sheet management requires a six-step approach to qualify as proficient financial management. These steps are:

1. Analyze your cash levels and debt capacity—no surprise here. We have emphasized that the achieving and maintaining your target liquidity level is your number-one financial objective.
2. Assess your capital needs.
3. Match capital needs with capital sources.
4. Consider alternative capital sources.
5. Mitigate risks.
6. Monitor the balance sheet on an ongoing basis.[5]

Let's look at each of these steps briefly.

Step 1, analyzing your cash levels and debt capacity, involves determining days' cash on hand from all unrestricted sources (cash plus short-term investments plus unrestricted long-term investments, divided by [(total expenses − depreciation expense)/365], the current ratio, the ability to cover debt service (both interest payments and principal repayments), and days' sales outstanding (if your organization has any credit sales). You may wish to refer to Chapter 7 (including the appendixes) for a review on the relevant measures. Debt capacity may be assessed as the ratio of your operating cash flow to the maximum annual debt service (the highest level of payments that your financing source could charge on your financing), the ratio of debt to total capital (arranged debt plus all net assets), or the balance sheet ratio of cash to debt. Days cash on hand and the ability to cover debt service stand out as the primary indicators that predict the organization's borrowing ability.

Step 2, assessing capital needs, includes internal analysis, external analysis, and your capital budget. Your long-range financial plan should have already provided you with a financial snapshot of future years' needs, so we will not elaborate on this step here. The key is to maintain strategic priorities in your financial plans.

Step 3, matching capital needs with capital sources, includes consideration of multiple factors, which are listed in Exhibit 10.1. Primary attention should be given to cost of capital and to covenants. The mainstream approach to cost of capital must be modified to fit nonprofits, as the cost of equity capital is not easily estimated.

In Chapter 9 we showed how to calculate net present value (NPV) and return on invested capital (ROIC). The discount rate for NPV, and the comparison rate (sometimes called the benchmark, or hurdle rate) for ROIC, is the weighted average cost of capital. Put more simply, on capital projects that generate revenues or reduce costs, we make

*Criteria Related to Capital Source *	Criteria Related to Capital Project
• Cost of capital • Covenants • Rate of return required • Wishes of philanthropic donors • All-in borrowing rate • Costs of issuance of the debt • Structure of the financing documents and underlying security requirements • Maintenance and incurrence covenants • Principal amortization • Interest-rate risk • Average useful life versus average maturity • Disclosure requirements • Prepayment penalties and unwind provisions • Accounting treatment	• Criticality of the project to the organization's core mission • Expended life of technology or equipment • Need to partner with key stakeholders (e.g., physicians) **Criteria Related to Organization** • Tax status or other tax implications • Debt capacity • Timing of the funding need • Tax-status implications of the use of proceeds • Credit position • Control issues (how much control must your organization give up?) • Potential for investment-grade rating • Potential to obtain credit enhancement

Source: *Financing the Future Report* Copyright Healthcare Financial Management Association. Used by permission.

EXHIBIT 10.1   CHECKLIST OF CRITERIA FOR EVALUATING APPROPRIATE CAPITAL SOURCES

the go/no-go decision based on comparing the financial return with the financing costs of the funding required for the investment. To calculate the cost of capital, we take the proportion of financing from a given source and multiply it by its cost, then sum these products. Let's say that your organization has no "permanent" short-term debt (it uses its credit line only occasionally for emergency needs), has issued bonds yielding 6 percent, and has its long-term cash reserves invested at 8 percent. We look at your organization's condensed balance sheet and see:

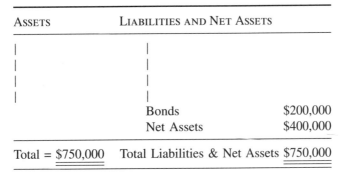

The formula for calculating the weighted average cost of capital (WACC) is:

$$WACC = \text{Cost of Net Assets} \times (\text{Net Assets/Total Capital})$$
$$+ \text{Cost of Debt} \times (\text{Debt/Total Capital})$$

Be careful to include in "Total Capital" only your arranged permanent debt financing, including any permanent short-term and medium-term funding (i.e., a seven-year term loan). Here your organization has $600,000 of total capital ($200,000 in bonds plus $400,000 in net assets, or equity). For the cost of net assets, ideally you should be capturing the riskiness of your assets. Since asset risk is almost impossible to estimate precisely for most nonprofits, we recommend using a proxy measure called the "opportunity cost of investment." Technically, this is the rate of return you could earn on long-term investments of similar risk to your assets. Based on the variability of operating cash flows experienced by most nonprofits, we know that the *business risk* of nonprofits is high, and the required return on net assets (equity) should be correspondingly high.

Since the exact amount of risk of your assets is hard to pin down, simply use the long-term investment return you could earn if you invested those funds in a well-diversified stock mutual fund or in your endowment fund (if you have one). For most organizations, using long-term stock returns would imply an opportunity cost of investment of around 13 or 14 percent.[6] We will use 14 percent for your organization's achievable long-term investment return. Someone may object: "But our equity represents surpluses earned on operations over the years, much of which was based on fundraising, and we expensed all the costs of that fundraising in the past." Nevertheless, those funds could be deployed in an alternate use to those to which they are being invested (on the asset side of your balance sheet at present), and so you are giving up the investment return that could be earned on those funds.

Substituting your numbers in the formula, we compute your cost of capital (WACC):

$$\text{WACC} = \text{Cost of Net Assets} \times (\text{Net Assets/Total Capital})$$

$$+ \text{Cost of Debt} \times (\text{Debt/Total Capital})$$

$$\text{WACC} = 14\% \times [(\$400,000/(\$400,000 + \$200,000)]$$

$$+ 6\% \times [(\$200,000)/(\$400,000 + \$200,000)]$$

Expressing the cost percentages in decimal form:

$$\text{WACC} = 0.14 \times [0.6667] + 0.06 \times [0.3333]$$

$$\text{WACC} = 0.093338 + 0.019998$$

$$\text{WACC} = 0.113336, \text{ or } 11.33\%$$

In general, your goal is to *minimize the weighted average cost of capital*. The chief constraint here is to maintain an assured pipeline of financing, which on occasion means you may include one or more long-term sources of funds that cause you to pay more than you would for the minimum-cost mix of long-term capital. One more time, we are made aware that the principal financial objective is not to maximize stockholder value or minimize expenses (including interest expense) in order to maximize profits, but rather to achieve and maintain a target liquidity level. Some healthcare or educational organizations, which could adopt a for-profit status, may view their objectives with an eye toward profitability—and value cost minimization more highly.

Another issue to be careful about is the imposition of covenants when borrowing from a financial institution or when issuing bonds. These normally restrict your organization in some fashion, and may have tough remedies in the event you are not in compliance with one or more of the covenants. A key point to be aware of: In some cases covenants can be negotiated out of loan contracts or bond indentures. *Maintenance covenants* indicate the financial ratio values or other financial requirements your organization must maintain as long the debt is outstanding. For example, your organization may need to maintain a certain level of days' cash on hand (creditworthy hospitals typically have eight months or more of unrestricted cash on hand) and have a debt service coverage ratio of at least 1.1 times to be viewed as very creditworthy. *Incurrence covenants* indicate what events would be viewed as negatively impacting existing debtholders, and therefore your organization is pledged not to initiate. Examples are issuance of additional debt, merging with another organizations, or selling specific assets.

Step 4, considering alternative capital sources, addresses the fact that borrowing may not be your first or best funding source. Consider operating cash flows, fundraising, and leasing as alternatives to bank loans or bond issues. The capital investment size, life expectancy (you may be better off leasing equipment that will become obsolete quickly), time-sensitivity, relation to your mission, and expected return all have a bearing on how you might best finance the investment. *The effect of the capital source selected on both your cash position (or target liquidity level) and debt burden is also important.* A real estate investment trust may buy one or more of your buildings and then lease space back to your organization, enabling your organization to monetize some of its fixed assets and build cash and liquidity. We will return to the topic of alternatives to borrowing in a later section of this chapter.

Step 5, mitigating risks, might include the use of interest rate swaps and other derivatives, as interest rate spikes threaten your organization's surplus and cash position. Newly issued bonds may include interest rate swaps, and if you have existing debt, you may use a swap or perhaps an option to enter a swap (swaption) as well. We return to this topic in Chapter 14.

Finally, step 6 indicates that setting debt levels and the mix of short-term versus long-term debt are not one-time decisions: You must monitor the balance sheet on an ongoing basis. Here you review changes in asset amounts, current liabilities, long-term liabilities, and net assets. Calculation and review of key financial ratios are essential, along with a look at how these changed year over year. "Get behind the numbers" by interpreting the reasons for those changes. Consider opportunities that may arise, including:

- Have interest rates dropped enough to warrant a look at possibly refinancing?
- Should you change the mix of variable-rate and fixed-rate debt, possibly through a transaction in the swap market?
- Should you obtain a realized cash gain by reversing a swap?
- Have our financials changed enough to discuss a possible rating upgrade with credit rating agencies (Moodys, Standard & Poor's, Fitch, Dominion, and A.M. Best)?[7]
- Can we match up asset life spans to liability life spans?[8]

(b) DETERMINING YOUR ORGANIZATION'S DEBT CAPACITY. One of the key considerations in your capital structure decision-making is your organization's *debt capacity*. One way to assess this is to "back into" that capacity via calculation of relevant financial ratios. Wareham and Majka, of Kaufman, Hall and Associates, suggest a weighted approach to doing this for healthcare organizations that makes sense for many commercial or partly commercial organizations, as noted in Exhibit 10.2.[9] For donative nonprofits, scale the "indicated capacity" numbers down, because lenders and investors will be reluctant to finance to these levels in cases where the revenues of the organization come from

Approaches to Calculating Debt Capacity			
Ratio	Key Target	Indicated Capacity (*dollars in millions*)	Weighting
Debt service coverage Excess of revenue over expenses + Interest + Depreciation + Amortization/MADS	3.0x	62.3	45%
Debt cash flow Long-term debt + Short-term debt/Exces of revenue over expenses + Depreciation + Amortization	4.0x	60.3	15%
Cash to debt Cash and marketable securities + Board-designated funds/Long-term debt + Short-term debt	100%	38.3	15%
Debt service to revenue MADS/Total operating revenue	4.0%	49.1	15%
Debt to capitalization Long-term debt (lesscurrent portion)/Long-term debt (less current portion) + Unrestricted net assets	50%	68.0	10%
Weighted capacity			57.0

MADS is maximum annual debt service.
Note: Certain ratio definitions vary a bit by rating agency.
Source: Kaufman, Hall & Associates, Inc. Used with permission.

Source: Healthcare Financial Management Association, Financing the Future II: Report 2: Strategies for Effective Capital Structure Managment (Westchester, IL: Author, 2005). Used by permission.

EXHIBIT 10.2   CALCULATING YOUR DEBT CAPACITY

dues, contributions, endowment income, or grants, as opposed to product or service sales. This is due to the fact that the former do not make good sources of collateral, or security, on loans or bonds. The example organization has a debt capacity of $57.0 million, as shown on the bottom right of the exhibit.

As a final note on balance sheet management, not all of your organization's risks and vulnerabilities are captured on the balance sheet. Potential liabilities arise from many sources. Consequently, we will address risk management in Chapter 14.

We now turn to the specific forms of debt financing that your organization may procure. A liability that gets little attention but that can provide an organization much-needed and interest-free financing is discussed first—accounts payable.

10.2 PAYABLES

Think of the accounts payable function as a source of interest-free financing from suppliers. True, the cost of this credit extension is built into the price of the supplies you are buying. Correspondingly, the seller expects you to take advantage of the credit period offered. Common terms are "net 30," meaning the full amount of the invoice is due and payable 30 days after the date of the invoice. The Lilly study revealed that a minority of nonprofits still think it is commendable if they "pay the invoice the day it hits our desk." Such a policy is simply an unwise use of scarce cash resources. Pay on time, but not early. For many businesses, accounts payable are the single largest source of financing used.

It is unethical to "stretch payables" to wring more financing out of one's suppliers. While stretching payables may be the single most unethical practice in corporate America, it is unethical both because one has agreed to pay invoices at the stated terms when beginning to buy from the supplier, and because the buyer is in effect borrowing more from its suppliers without their knowledge or approval. Each dollar of extra interest income put in one person's pocket is taken out of another's pocket—the supplier's. If you foresee problems paying invoices on time, contact your supplier, explain the situation, and ask the supplier for additional time—making sure to communicate your willingness to pay and your proposal for how and when you will pay.

Some credit terms are stated like this: "2/10, net 30." This means a 2 percent cash discount is being offered if the bill is paid within 10 days of the invoice date, or the full amount of the invoice may be paid in 30 days. Should you take the cash discount, paying $98 per $100 invoice amount in 10 days? Almost invariably, the answer is "yes." You are giving up a 37 percent rate of return by foregoing the cash discount. This is demonstrated in the following formula:

Cost of forgone discount

$$= \frac{\text{Cash discount percent}}{(100 - \text{cash discount percent})} \times \frac{365}{(\text{normal credit period} - \text{cash discount period})}$$

This formula is used to estimate the cost of a foregone discount (the rate of return you could have had if the cash discount was taken) with 2/10, net 30 terms:[10]

$$\text{Cost of forgone discount} = \frac{2}{(100-2)} \times \frac{365}{(30-10)} = \frac{2}{98} \times \frac{365}{20}$$
$$= 0.3724 \text{ or } 37.24 \text{ percent}$$

Surprisingly, many of the nonprofits surveyed in the Lilly study indicated they either chose to or had to forgo cash discounts some or most of the time. Such a policy is unwise—you would be better off using some of you short-term credit line, if necessary, to have the funds take the discount. The preference for borrowing to take the discount applies as long as the annual interest rate of the credit line is less than the cost of the forgone discount—37.24 percent in our example.

10.3 SHORT-TERM BORROWING

A nonprofit might borrow money for eight reasons:

1. Borrowing is much faster than grants or fundraising for bringing money into the organization, with funds made available within days or a few weeks.
2. Borrowing can stabilize the organization's cash flow and compensate for temporary revenue shortfalls. For example, borrowed funds can be used to meet payroll when in a temporary cash crunch.
3. Borrowing can prevent costly delays in starting new projects. This "bridge financing" is an important role for borrowing. Government agencies at the state and local level issue bond anticipation notes for this purpose.

4. Borrowing can increase earned income by speeding up the start of a revenue-generating project. Getting income-producing ventures off the ground may necessitate start-up financing or financing to fund the expansion of the new venture.

5. Borrowing can help consolidate bills. The idea here is to enable the organization to take cash discounts or maintain good supplier relationships (by enabling your organization to pay on time).

6. Borrowing can initiate or build on long-term relationships with financial institutions. Individuals know the value of an established credit history, and the same holds true for a nonprofit organization.

7. Borrowing can help improve the organization's financial management. Financial institutions require financial reports with a fair amount of detail and the calculation of key financial ratios. Organizations that previously managed without key financial data will be pressed to improve their financial and accountability structures.

8. Borrowing can help the organization achieve independence. By replacing restrictive donations or grants/contracts, the organization may be freed to pursue the mission it is called to accomplish. The flip side is that your organization may be limited via restrictive loan covenants placed on you by the financial institution. Limiting the borrowing and keeping the loan payments current will enable your organization to avoid becoming the "servant to the lender."[11]

Furthermore, there is a cost to raising funds through donations and grants. Let's say that $100 is raised for every $10 spent. That amounts to a 10 percent interest rate if $10 is taken as "interest" and $100 as principal. The main difference, of course, is that the donation funding stream must be renewed every year, while the borrowed funds are there until "maturity"—which is when the organization must make the principal repayment on the borrowed funds. Our point is that there is a cost of funds, regardless of how you acquire them.

Planning for short-term borrowing must take place within the context of the organization's overall strategic planning process (see Chapter 3) and long-range financial plan (see Chapter 9). Otherwise, borrowings may cost more than they should or funds will be borrowed on the wrong terms, or both.

Financial managers have two different ways with which to plan and manage an organization's debt and capital structure: (1) the *at-whatever-price theory*, and (2) the *strategic planning theory*. The at-whatever-price theory is related to the traditional supply-and-demand concept and is based on the belief that any financial manager can raise enough capital to do business if there is sufficient pressure.

Under the at-whatever-price theory, capital is like any other commodity: The greater the need, the higher the cost. Unfortunately, this theory suggests that the most advantageous time for an organization to borrow money is when it does not need to borrow money, and the most advantageous time being when borrowing is least expensive. In some cases, such blind financing can be attractive. It can be less expensive and less restrictive than financing under more pressing circumstances, for instance, when the organization has an acquisition target in mind, has committed to a major construction project, or needs to purchase a major piece of equipment. Bankers are then aware of the urgency of the need to obtain money and may be inclined to dictate stiffer terms.

The more advantageous financial approach is to make capital and debt management crucial parts of the organization's strategic planning process. In fact, capital and debt management should be accorded as important a place in strategic planning as revenue projections, cost containment programs, community marketing programs, and expansion plans. If capital and debt management is part of an organization's strategic planning process, its long-range goals and objectives can be considered under all types of financing options.

10.4 STRATEGIC FINANCING PLAN

The basis for your strategic financing plan for financing are your organization's strategic plan, discussed in Chapter 2, and its long-range financial plan, which we discussed in Chapter 9. A *strategic financing plan* should be a specific statement of an organization's financing goals. A debt manager must become a team member when it is time to establish a plan for the organization's capital and debt strategy. By assisting in this aspect of the strategic plan in advance, a financial manager can ensure that the organization obtains financing on the most favorable terms.

Most important, when setting a strategic financing plan, the organization must ensure that the plan dictates financing requirements; financing requirements should not determine the plan. The plan must include considerations of the organization's present assets and debt, internal funding sources, and management's expansion goals. Other pertinent factors to consider regarding the organization are:

- Mission or charter
- Financial and operational goals
- Market and competitive analyses
- The target liquidity level
- Strategies for achieving goals and objectives

No strategic financing plan can answer every question. There is always uncertainty about future business conditions, government regulations, information technology and other technological advances, and new service delivery techniques. A good plan, however, will include various scenarios, thus adding a degree of flexibility.

The nonprofit organization must develop a strategic financing plan to ensure its long-term fiscal health. The absence of identifiable shareholders does not relieve the financial manager from operating the organization as a business and strategically planning its fiscal health. A nonprofit organization exists to serve members of the public, who are its very real, although anonymous, shareholders. Failure to maintain fiscal health over the long term is the death knell of all organizations, public or private.

(a) BORROWER'S STRATEGIC FINANCIAL OBJECTIVES.   Answers to these questions will begin the process of identifying the institution's strategic financial objectives:

- How much risk is management willing to take for various financing alternatives?
- How much interest can the institution afford?
- Does the institution intend to provide collateral to the lender, such as assets or stock, which the lender could take possession of in the event the loan is not fully repaid?
- Can another party provide a guarantee to secure a loan?
- What type of covenants and restrictions is management willing to allow?

- How much control does management want to retain?

- What limitations in other agreements must the institution consider when pledging assets?

By answering these questions, a financial manager can help to clarify the organization's current financial status and to determine the direction in which management is moving or wants to move the organization. The answers also help specify financing sources and keep short-term strategy consistent with long-term capital management objectives.

(b) BORROWING REQUIREMENTS.   A strategic financing plan should evaluate short-term borrowing requirements. Lean periods never can be fully anticipated, so an institution always requires a contingency plan that may include short-term borrowing to tide it over until cash flow resumes. Before a plan can be developed, however, the financial manager must monitor and understand the elements of the institution's cash flow. Cash flow should be forecasted and monitored on monthly, weekly, and daily bases.[12] When studying cash flow, these factors should be considered:

- Seasonality of revenues

- Collection periods and timeliness of disbursements

- Regulatory changes and economic trends

- Contingency plans

Seasonality of revenues can have a tremendous impact on a nonprofit organization's short-term borrowing requirements. By looking at historic seasonal revenue patterns, a financial manager can obtain part of the picture needed to plan borrowing strategy. In other words, the financial manager must monitor and measure the lag time between the provision of services and the collection of revenues (whether from donations, grants, or fees charged) as well as predict the amount to be collected. Fewer receivables and more payables may dictate that the institution borrow money to see it through the lean months. By analyzing the institution's cash flow, the financial manager can anticipate this situation and plan accordingly.

10.5 STEPS TO SUCCESSFUL BORROWING

Management will be ready to approach potential financing sources after determining strategic objectives and developing a cash flow forecast that indicates the amount of money needed, when it must be borrowed, and when it can be repaid. Before any financial source is approached, however, financial managers must understand:

- Debt and what borrowing involves for the organization

- The loan approval process

- The various short-term borrowing alternatives

- The suitability of financing sources versus strategic objectives

- The preparation and presentation of a loan request

(a) UNDERSTANDING DEBT. Debt is a way of life for most consumers and business organizations. It is interesting to note that borrowing and investing are two sides of the same coin. "Capital" can be defined as the resources that an organization needs to attain a financial objective. There are two broad categories of capital: equity and debt. Equity is money belonging to the organization, and debt is money belonging to another person or organization. Because borrowed funds carry the borrower's obligation to repay the debt and lenders furnish money for the sole purpose of earning more money, the only differences between debt and equity appear to rest with the person who provides the capital and the return that person seeks. Our focus, since we are dealing with nonprofits, is debt. Our references to the characteristics of equity are to provide a basis for comparison.

(i) Risk-Reward Trade-Offs. Although similarities between debt and equity capital exist, the returns that accrue on each type of funding are very different. Debt capital, in the form of financing received from a lender, generally is priced in terms of an interest rate. Equity capital is "priced" in terms of appreciation of a organization's stock or assets. For example, small business entrepreneurs often are willing to receive little monetary return in the short run in order to develop a business idea. A nonprofit founder or donor contributing capital requires an in-kind return, namely service provision in line with the organization's mission. A lender financing the entrepreneur's dream, however, sees the opportunity quite differently. As a financing source for a risky venture, the lender will expect a large return to compensate for the risk.

An important element in the pricing of debt and equity is the relationship between risk and reward: The greater the risk, the greater the reward. Whether that reward is garnered in terms of equity or in terms of debt depends on the perspective of the person providing the funds. The lender or bond investor is willing to risk the possible loss of money in return for monetary rewards. The "junk," or high-yield, bond market that developed during the 1980s illustrates the lender's perspective. An organization that wants to issue long-term bonds but that does not have an investment-grade rating (the top four creditworthiness rating categories, AAA, AA, A, and BBB in Standard and Poor's framework, are considered investment grade) must issue noninvestment-grade bonds and pay a higher return to attract the needed funds than would an investment-grade company. When managing debt, a financial manager must assess the level of risk that the firm presents to a financing source, the resulting availability of financing, and the cost that the financing will carry.

(ii) Leverage. Leverage is defined as the use of another person's or organization's financial resources. The more leverage (the greater the proportion of debt to equity) that an organization has—the greater the risk to the organization and to the lender that the organization will be vulnerable to the impact of external factors. So think of equity, or net assets, as a cushion for the lender or bond investor. The effects of external factors, such as business conditions and interest rates, are magnified by leverage, sometimes positively and sometimes negatively.

The amount of leverage that a nonprofit organization can take on without risking future loss of control to the institution's lenders varies. For example, in the nursing home and home healthcare industries, markets must be served; lenders can be instrumental in forcing changes where existing management demonstrates lack of ability. Where the market already is well served, lenders are usually inclined to limit their losses by simply closing down an inefficient or ineffective business. Financial managers can get a good idea of where they stand in the eyes of a lender familiar with the nonprofit industry by studying the financial statements of other nonprofit organizations in similar service arenas. Doing this will also assist financial managers in determining the financial alternatives available.

(b) LOAN APPROVAL PROCESS.   It is essential that financial managers understand what lenders and bankers consider important in making decisions to provide financing. The decision to lend capital may be an emotional one based on the personalities of the lender and the borrowing organization's officers. Before the financial manager attempts to make a presentation to a lender, he or she should have some idea of the type of personality who will be sitting across the table. Although the stereotype of the banker-lender is not a totally accurate gauge, it does point out some common traits that lenders share. Lenders tend to be conservative, cautious, and pessimistic. They will look at what is wrong with a borrowing proposal and appear to exclude what is right.

(i) Basic Preparation for a Loan Presentation.   In order to be successful in obtaining financing, a financial manager must distinguish the institution's presentation from all others that lenders evaluate. The financial manager should also try to discern what the lender already emotionally believes about the deal and attempt to reinforce a positive belief and reverse a negative one. To be effective, a financial manager should be aware that lenders, too, think in stereotypes about nonprofit organizations that seek financing. They perceive nonprofit officers who make financial presentations as generally unprepared, hopelessly optimistic, and out of touch with economic reality. When presenting a loan proposal, therefore, the successful financial manager should demonstrate better preparation, greater knowledge about the organization and its financial prospects, and better capability of repayment than any other customer who approaches the lender.

The financial manager can assess the level of preparedness to make a loan proposal by addressing these questions:

- Why would a nonprofit organization borrow money?
- What does a lender want to know immediately?
- How does a lender evaluate a loan proposal?
- How does a borrower generate funds to repay a loan?
- Under what reasonable circumstances would a lender agree to refinance a loan?

None of these questions is particularly easy, but the right answers may very well predict the success of a loan proposal.

(ii) Reasons for Borrowing.   The reasons why a person or organization does something are important. Knowing the reasons and, more important, explaining them quickly are crucial when a financial manager must persuade a lender that the nonprofit organization deserves a loan. The three essential reasons for borrowing are to:

1. Buy an asset
2. Pay an expense
3. Make an acquisition

Knowing those reasons, however, is not sufficient. Financial managers also must know how different lenders view these reasons. For instance, leasing firms financing equipment purchases have no interest in funding other investments. Banks are more interested in providing short-term working capital financing for seasonal needs and modest longer-term financing for equipment and construction.

(iii) Immediate Concerns of Lenders. The immediate concerns of a lender are important because they generally dictate the terms and conditions of the loan. These concerns include:

- How much money do you need to borrow?
- How long do you need to keep the money?
- What do you need the money for?
- How do you plan to repay both the principal and the interest?
- What contingency plans do you have in case your intended source of repayment does not work?

The most important of these questions, of course, are the last two, the repayment method and the contingency plan. Above all, a financial manager must be able to show a lender how the loan will be paid back, in scenarios of both expected conditions and unexpectedly negative circumstances.

(iv) Evaluating the Application. All lending decisions are based on the same classic set of factors known as the "5 C's of credit":

1. *Character* of management. This measures the willingness to pay.
2. *Capital* available to the organization. This typically is measured as the amount of net assets on the balance sheet.
3. *Capacity* to earn cash flow to repay the loan.
4. *Conditions* of the market. This includes the economy, the borrower's industry, the local marketplace.
5. *Collateral* that the borrower has available to pledge. For short-term loans, this is typically accounts receivable or inventories, but for many nonprofits, the only receivables that might be acceptable would be those related to grants or contracts.

Of these factors, the two more critical are the character of management, which may account for as much as 80 percent of a lender's evaluation, and cash flow. If one of the other factors is inadequate, a borrower can usually obtain the loan, although the source of financing, the approach to obtaining it, and its interest rate may be altered. The borrower will not be able to raise external capital, however, if there are deficiencies in either the character of management or the organization's cash flow.

(v) How Lenders Are Repaid. There are four ways to repay lenders:

1. Use net revenues and cash flow.
2. Borrow more money.
3. Find another lender.
4. Sell existing assets.

Borrowing more to repay a loan is often acceptable, but it can be an expensive proposition. Selling assets also can be acceptable, especially as part of a contingency plan, but the best way to repay a loan is to generate cash flow. *Consequently, a financial manager is wise to keep borrowing plans confined to the capacity of the organization to generate sufficient cash flow to repay the loan within a reasonable period.* Lenders much prefer this method of repayment, even when they tell you they insist on having collateral to back up their loans. They would much rather not have to think about seizing and selling that collateral, especially given the public relations problems that action can cause the lender when foreclosing on a charitable institution. Furthermore, the collateral—such as a church building—may be a "limited use" asset that has questionable market value due to there being few potential buyers.

(vi) Refinancing.   Barring a decision to restructure a borrower's total debt, perhaps to save on interest expense due to declining interest rates, a borrower seeks to refinance loans for either of two reasons: The original plan did not work, or the borrower did not use the money for the intended purpose. No lender is sympathetic to a borrower who did not use the money for the purpose stated in the loan proposal. Most lenders, however, understand that not all business plans work as intended. The fact is that most business plans do not work as originally intended, but they do work after they have been modified. Lenders understand that planning is a dynamic process and that flexibility is part of it. Therefore, business plans that do not work are generally considered valid reasons for lending more capital.

(c) ALTERNATIVE SOURCES OF SHORT-TERM FUNDS.   Before a nonprofit organization commits itself to borrowing money, it should look within. Often there are internal sources of funding that are not immediately apparent. Indeed, one of the objectives of making debt and capital management part of the institution's strategic plan is to identify such internal sources of funds before management seeks funding from outside. Five primary internal financing sources, along with methods to use them, are listed next.

1.   Aggressive working capital management (see Chapter 11):

   ○   Improve collection practices.

   ○   Extend terms of payables.[13]

   ○   Reduce idle cash.

   ○   Sell nonproductive assets.

2.   Existing operations:

   ○   Increase service fees.

   ○   Charge for services previously provided free.

   ○   Increase marketing effort for donations and grants (this takes time).

   ○   Reduce operating costs.

   ○   Sell fixed assets unrelated to core mission.[14]

   ○   Sell and lease back ("monetize") fixed assets related to core mission.

3.   Short-term investments:

   ○   Liquidate securities (see Chapter 12; if balances were part of target liquidity level, quickly replenish those after funding need has been met).

4.   Overfunded pension plans:

   ○   Seek to recapture assets in the plans for the institution's use.

5. Change in business structure:

   ○ Seek strategic alliance partnerships and joint ventures with other service providers (see Chapter 9).

These internal alternatives will not meet the needs of all organizations. The financial manager is then faced with a long list of creative financing alternatives. Consider, for instance, these financing possibilities for a nursing home or home healthcare agency. It could:

- Obtain a bank loan, either secured by assets (or in a truly desperate situation, we have seen board of directors' personal guarantees as security) or unsecured.
- Sell accounts receivable without recourse. (The nonprofit does not have to stand behind sold accounts that prove to be uncollectible.)
- Sell accounts receivable with recourse.
- Securitize accounts receivable for offering in public or private markets.

The differences among these short-term financing alternatives lie in the source rather than the particular use of the funds, and they are based on the criteria that a lender considers when making a loan decision. There are three basic criteria:

1. How much debt capital must be raised?
2. How long a term does the borrower need to repay the loan?
3. What return will the lender receive for the loan?

10.6 MATCHING FINANCIAL SOURCES TO STRATEGIC OBJECTIVES

It is difficult to match the best capital source to the strategic objectives of a nonprofit organization; few financial alternatives provide perfect matches. When attempting to match financial sources to strategic objectives, however, financial managers should:

- List the strategic objectives in the order of their apparent levels of priority.
- Summarize in writing the alternative choices.
- Seek advice from consultants or others who are involved in matching strategic planning and financial sources.
- Consider the decision carefully and preferably without pressure of time.

The first two items listed force the financial manager to focus on the organization's critical issues, because they involve ranking objectives. By reducing these issues to a one-page summary, the financial manager can identify the major financing alternatives. Doing this requires that the major advantages and disadvantages of each alternative be considered. It can be helpful to develop a scoring system to rate financial alternatives, although such a system is only as good as the idea behind it.

The time criterion is also particularly important. Making a final decision a day or a week after completing the list of alternatives is generally a good idea. This provides the financial manager time to reflect on the institution's strategic objectives and whether the alternative choices meet them. All alternatives should be thoroughly evaluated before a decision is made. Yet delay in the name of perfection can be counterproductive. A financial manager can delay a deal so long that interest rates rise before a choice is made. Financial markets also lose interest when they believe that management is only shopping around and is not serious about a deal. It is good to generate competition among financing sources, but not to the point that the borrower is paralyzed and unable to meet its objectives in the most effective manner.

10.7 PREPARING THE FINANCING PROPOSAL

After the financial manager has determined what type of financial source is best to meet the institution's particular short-term capital needs, it is time to obtain the financing. The basic tool for this task is the financing proposal package. The financial manager uses this document to present the institution's "story" as well as to anticipate and answer all questions posed by the lender. Of utmost importance in telling that story are the five criteria essential to all lenders, beginning with the character of organization management (see Section 10.5, "Steps to Successful Borrowing").

(a) TERM SHEET. One of the most important parts of the proposal is called the "term sheet." In this part of the plan, the financial manager must answer the five basic questions a lender will ask: how much, how long, what for, repayment plan, and contingent repayment plan.

(b) PLAN OVERVIEW. A financing proposal must contain a brief overview of the plan. Bankers and other lenders tend to make decisions quickly. Review committees, for instance, generally rely on a subordinate's summary and recommendation when evaluating loan requests. A review committee may spend only two or three minutes looking at what took weeks, even months, for a financial manager to assemble. As a result, when a business plan is turned into a proposal, it must include an "executive summary." This should be the most sparkling part of the package.

The overview must describe the essential nature of the organization's service offerings, list its major services, and characterize its management people. The overview focuses on facts, but the facts should be presented in such a way that a potential investor—that is, after all, what a lender is—gets a positive emotional feeling about the institution.

(c) PRESENTATION CONTENTS. The overview can be supplemented with marketing brochures, testimonials, and perhaps even a video presentation to enhance the written word. A full set of financial statements for three years is essential. The financial statements will be used to evaluate the risk of the proposed loan and determine the terms and conditions of any financing deal. The statements should be supplemented with explanations wherever appropriate. For example, the statements of some healthcare providers contain quirks that may confuse a lender unless they are explained. When dealing with a lender who is basically unfamiliar with the healthcare field, some explanation of reimbursement methods and the handling of unreimbursed charges is desirable so the lender can understand the inevitable write-offs of receivables. This explanation should extend to both the balance sheet and the statement of activities.

Nonprofit business plans also need to cover the basics of an organization's operations: Delivery of service, marketing, and accounting/finance. The plan should show how the desired financing will enhance these areas. However, the projections should be realistic. Lenders often believe that a borrower is hopelessly optimistic, and aggressive revenue projections will make them even more skeptical. In fact, it is always better for management's position if actual operating results turn out to be higher than anticipated by the projections, rather than using forecast figures that are too rosy. If management really does believe that revenues will grow by 200 percent, however, then substantiating information should be included in the plan along with documentation showing why the projections are realistic. Detail is crucial in a business plan. Any error in calculations, for instance, can threaten a plan's credibility; it gives the impression of sloppy management.

10.8 MAKING THE PRESENTATION

Even more important than a detailed business plan is the ability to communicate it with confidence and forcefulness to potential lenders. Financial managers may not think of themselves as salespersons, but that is exactly what they are when they represent the institution that requires financing. They must sell the entire organization, its operations and service delivery processes, plans, and creditworthiness. Having the would-be borrower ask questions during the presentation is an excellent technique as it focuses the presentation on the needs of the audience, the potential lender. A pointed presentation is important, because it shows that the organization has thought out its financing needs. This distinguishes it from other organizations competing for the same scarce financing dollars.

(a) **IMPORTANCE OF QUESTIONS.**   Questions can be the most effective tool for the financial manager in preparing and making the presentation. They provide valuable information and allow the financial manager to focus the presentation. Close scrutiny is avoided until the financial manager has all the necessary information to test assumptions regarding the audience, confirm suspicions, and figure out what the lender considers important, before making the actual request for financing. Consequently, the financial manager is better able to handle objections. It is surprising how good questions will keep the mood relaxed and the conversation flowing.

Financial managers should not feel inadequate when they ask about the lending and loan approval process. Each lender does things a little differently. A financial manager should also ask for a copy of the financial analysis the lender performed on the institution. The analysis can provide valuable information the next time financing must be sought. Asking questions about the process will also show that the borrower is more sophisticated and thus a better credit risk.

(b) **ANSWERING OBJECTIONS.**   No matter how controlled and tightly organized the presentation may be, objections will arise and the financial manager will have to answer the lender's questions. Further questions by the borrower can be excellent answers to lender questions. For instance, if the lender's major objection focuses on collateral, the financial manager might ask, "Isn't it the case in bankruptcy that legal fees cause liabilities to increase while the value of collateral generally decreases?" The financial manager might further ask, "Doesn't the organization's real value lie in its ability to generate cash flow rather than its present holdings of assets?" And "In a bad loan situation, does the amount of collateral really make much of a difference?" Almost any objection can be handled by turning it around with a simple question. By understanding the motive of the lender in making an objection, the financial manager can gauge what response will be most appropriate.

The importance of questions does not end with the presentation and objections. Questions are even more important when a loan has been turned down; they may even be able to salvage a rejection or make it easier to obtain financing from the same source the next time around. Potential questions should be designed to discover why the proposal was declined, where such financing could be obtained, what would make this financing more attractive, and how the lender who turned down the proposal would respond to inquiries from other lenders. As with the other questions, this information can provide feedback that will help in the next presentation.

(c) PERSONALIZING THE PRESENTATION.   Finally, anything that will personalize the presentation will usually work to a borrower's benefit. It is also helpful for the financial manager to invite a representative of the potential lender to tour the nonprofit institution's facilities before the presentation. This will get the lender more emotionally involved with the institution and more concerned about its future success. It also provides a more personal and relaxed atmosphere to make initial contact with a lender. The key to obtaining a loan is to connect emotionally with the lender, to persuade the lender that the institution's success is the lender's success as well.

10.9 OTHER FACTORS IN BORROWING/LENDING DECISIONS

Borrowing and lending decisions would be easy if the loan criteria just listed were as straightforward as they sound. A financial manager would then choose the alternative that raises the most capital at the least cost over the longest term. Unfortunately, however, one alternative generally raises the most funds, while another has the longest term, and yet a third costs the least. The lender's decisions also would be more mechanical if each element to be considered were based merely on its own merits. Intangible factors, however, often complicate borrowing and lending decisions. These factors include a number of questions involved in loan evaluation:

- Is the transaction flexible enough to be structured to meet the institution's financial needs?
- Does the borrower have confidence that the lender will be able to complete the transaction?
- Can the deal be documented and negotiated within the borrower's time frame?
- How complex is the legal documentation?
- Can the borrower afford the front-end fees associated with the transaction?
- Will the borrower be able to cancel the deal if circumstances dictate, and how much it will cost to do so?
- What requirements does the investor have for credit support?

(a) BORROWING FROM THE BANK.   Nonprofits borrow short term for seasonal working capital, to cover abrupt changes in payment patterns or unexpected expenses, and when net revenue is not adequate to support continued operations. Banks traditionally have provided most of the short-term and medium-term loans for nonprofits.

About half of short-term bank loans are unsecured (usually in the form of a line of credit), and the others are secured (where collateral is required to ensure an adequate secondary source of repayment). Like small businesses, nonprofits have found bank lending officers more favorable when a long-standing relationship is in place, as the bank's comfort level with the character of the borrower and likely sources of repayment will be higher.

We survey bank credit and credit-related services by noting the major domestic and international services offered, and we conclude the short-term lending discussion by talking about some lending trends.

(i) Domestic Short-Term Bank Loans. Bank lending alternatives are best described in terms of their maturities, or how long they allow borrowers to use the money. The shortest-term lending generally takes the form of a *line of credit*, which allows the organization to borrow up to a prearranged dollar amount during the one-year term. Credit lines may be established on an uncommitted or committed basis, and they sometimes have the added feature of overdraft protection.

An *uncommitted line of credit* is technically not binding on the bank, although it is almost always honored.[15] Uncommitted lines are usually renewable annually if both parties are agreeable. These informal arrangements are appealing to organizations that only rarely need to draw down the credit line, maintain a consistently strong financial position, and like the fact that uncommitted credit lines do not require a fee to be paid on unused balances. The only charges are interest on amounts borrowed. Banks like the flexibility offered by such arrangements, which free them from providing funds in the event of deterioration by the borrower or due to capital restrictions being imposed on the bank by federal regulators.

A *committed line of credit* is a formal, written agreement contractually binding the bank to provide the funds when requested. Committed lines usually involve commitment fees of up to 1 percent of unused balances. Whether uncommitted or committed, an overdraft credit line has the added feature of being automatically drawn down whenever the organization writes a check for which it does not have sufficient funds. The treasurer is thereby delegating to the bank the need to carefully monitor disbursement account balances and to fund it when necessary.

A noteworthy trend regarding credit lines is the rapid growth of the *standby letter of credit*, which guarantees that the bank will make funds available if the organization cannot or does not wish to meet a major financial obligation, such as a very large purchase.

The second type of bank financing is intermediate term. The two major forms of this are revolving credit agreements and term loans. A *revolving credit agreement*, or "revolver," allows the borrower to continually borrow and repay amounts up to an agreed-upon limit. The agreement is annually renewable at a variable interest rate during an interim period of anywhere from one to five years. At the end of the interim period, the agreement generally is converted to a term loan for a period of years. The key advantage to the borrower is assured credit availability for the life of the agreement, regardless of overall economic conditions and credit availability. Like on a committed credit line, the bank will charge a commitment fee on unused amounts of revolvers, along with interest on drawn-down amounts. Revolving credit agreements are usually unsecured.

A *term loan* is simply a loan made with an initial maturity of more than one year. Maturities for bank-originated term loans range from over 1 year to 10 years. Like revolving credit agreements, they involve an extensive written loan agreement and an in-depth "due diligence" analysis of the organization's management and financial position. Term loans are generally repaid in equal monthly or quarterly payments and may be fixed or variable rate. Nonprofit organizations use term loans to replace other loans or to finance ongoing investments in working capital, equipment, and machinery. The main advantage is that they provide a stable source of funds.

Some secured bank loans are a form of *asset-based lending*. Like any collateralized lending, such lending has a claim on an asset or group of assets, ordinarily receivables or inventory that could be easily sold if the borrower defaults on the loan. The difference is that while most conventional lending relies on the cash flows from the overall business for repayment, asset-based loans are offered based on anticipated cash flows arising from the sale or conversion of a specific asset or group of assets, such as inventories. These loans are especially attractive to small, growing organizations that may only qualify for this form of borrowing and whose management is willing to pay the higher interest rate necessary to compensate the bank for continuous monitoring of the asset serving as collateral.

One final borrowing-related service that many banks offer is a *swap*. In its simplest form, an organization engaging in a swap exchanges a fixed interest rate obligation for one that has a variable, or floating, interest rate. Nonprofit organizations that qualify for a lower variable rate spread (the amount of extra interest the organization must pay over and above the bank's cost of funds is lower on variable rate loans than on fixed rate loans, or perhaps the bank does not wish to make a fixed rate loan) might enter into a variable to fixed rate swap to eliminate the risk of rising interest rates and the resulting higher monthly payments. Banks usually serve as the opposite side on the swap, called the *counterparty*, but they may later find another counterparty that wants to make the opposite exchange.

(ii) International Short-Term Bank Loans.

The nonprofit organization operating in multiple countries must consider a more complex set of bank lending services because operating abroad introduces the treasurer to different economic and banking regulations, the uncertainty about how exchange rates will change in the future, and new customs and cultures. U.S.-headquartered banks provide a valuable service simply by introducing the treasurer to foreign banking officers and to the different payment systems that will be encountered. In addition, three major lending services are offered internationally:

1. Documentary credit

2. Asset-based lending

3. Traditional forms of bank lending

Banks doing business abroad, whether United States or foreign banks, offer various forms of *documentary credit*, including sight and time drafts, bankers' acceptances, and letters of credit. The *sight draft* is a formal, written agreement whereby an importer (drawee) contracts to pay a certain amount on demand ("at sight") to the exporter. The bank is not extending credit but simply helping in the payment process by receiving the draft and presenting it to the drawee. A *time draft* does involve a credit element, because the payment obligation agreed to by the drawee is designated as due at a specified future date. A *bankers' acceptance* is a time draft drawn on the buyer, whose bank agrees to pay (accepts) the amount if the buyer does not. In essence, the bank's creditworthiness is exchanged for the buyer's, and there is an active secondary market where these acceptances are traded. The bank charges the buyer a fee for this service. Related to this, a *short-term acceptance facility* allows the selling firm to initiate drafts (bills of exchange) against the buyer's bank instead of against the buyer, which can be discounted at the bank.[16] This facilitates foreign trade, but in the United States and United Kingdom it also is used to finance working capital needed to conduct domestic trade. A *commercial letter of credit* is a guarantee of payment by an importer, made by its bank, which becomes binding when the shipping and other documents related to the goods sold are presented to the bank.[17] Exporters appreciate the bank guarantees involved in acceptances and letters of credit due to the lack of information about foreign customers, as well as the shifting of the complexities and costs that might be involved in collecting on unpaid accounts. Note that most letters of credit used in international business are unconditional, differing from the standby letters of credit we discussed earlier.

Banks increasingly are getting involved in international asset-based lending. As with domestic asset-based lending, lending is done mainly by banks and commercial finance, companies, with the collateral and source of the cash flows counted on for debt service usually being inventories or accounts receivable. Asset-based lending has been utilized in the United States for some time, and with the growing unification of European economies, most observers anticipate asset-based lending to expand rapidly in Europe. Banks based in the United States hope to capture a large share of the European secured lending volume.

There also are several traditional forms of bank lending abroad. Nonprofit organizations are offered *overdraft services* that are renegotiable each year, may be secured, and are generally based on some percent above the bank's base rate. For example, a strong organization might be charged 1 percent above the base rate, which is often the London Interbank Offered Rate, or LIBOR. Whether the bank uses LIBOR or not, the base rate is reflective of that bank's cost of funds. Organizations are prohibited by law from over-drafting demand deposit accounts in the United States, although banks have permitted intraday ("daylight") overdrafting (debits to a checking account when it is known that offsetting credits will come later that day).

Another standard lending service seen abroad is an *advised line*, which is very similar to a credit line in the United States. This involves unsecured lending of up to one year in maturity, available on short notice to the borrower. The rate is somewhat less than would be the case for overdraft services, but is still calculated from the base rate.

The foreign parallel to the term loan is called a *committed facility*. The bank charges a fee to compensate it for agreeing to lend upon request for a period of five to seven years. Loan terms and conditions, including whether the funds made available will be in the home currency or some other currency, and the formula for calculating the interest rate, are described in a written agreement.

Our discussion of international bank services up to this point fits the major industrial economies of the world but not developing countries. Recent survey evidence suggests that most undeveloped countries do not yet have connections to the major global cable and payment settlement mechanisms, making it almost impossible for nonprofit organizations operating in those countries to tap international financial lending sources for domestic borrowing.

(b) TRENDS IN SHORT-TERM LENDING.   More and more banks are going after smaller businesses and nonprofit organizations as part of their client base. For example, Wells Fargo offers small businesses a credit card that acts as a committed line of credit.[18] As a general rule, your chances of getting a short-term loan are higher if you approach a smaller bank in your local market.

Banks' reliance on asset-based lending, term loans, and revolving credit agreements (especially to smaller businesses) has grown largely because of the lack of competition from the commercial paper and loan participation markets. The extent of nonbank penetration into lending is illustrated by the fact that total debt held outside the banking industry is at least equal to that held by banks. Finally, globalization is occurring in lending services.

10.10 MUNICIPAL AND TAXABLE BONDS

(a) **MUNICIPAL BONDS.**   Before looking at the current market environment for municipal bonds, let's retrace a key development in the "muni" marketplace. In the fall of 1987, many large municipal bond underwriting firms either curtailed or completely eliminated their activities in the municipal bond market. Salomon Brothers (now part of Smith Barney, which in turn is part of Citigroup), Kidder Peabody (now subsumed in UBS PaineWebber), L. F. Rothschild (now defunct), and E. F. Hutton (now also a part of Smith Barney) were among these firms. The turmoil occurred as a result of two specific changes in the municipal bond market during the preceding two years:

1. Fewer municipal bonds could be issued due to recent tax law changes.[19] Therefore, municipal bond firms had much less "product" to sell and the reduced volume made dealing in municipal bonds less profitable. Tax law changes included:

    o The loss of "arbitrage" profit opportunities

    o A limit of 2 percent on the cost of issuance related to initiating new bond issues

2. The desire by most securities dealers to leave the municipal bond area. In addition to carrying an inventory of bonds that they sell to investors, most securities trade or speculate in bonds for their own profit. Many dealers had misjudged the market and consequently suffered substantial losses from their speculative trading.

Since 1987, trends in default rates contain both good news and bad news for nonprofit issuers and their investors, as this recent report indicates:

> Cumulative default rates were found to be lower for bonds issued after 1986. Fitch attributed this to the Tax Reform Act of 1986 (which restricted the issuance of tax-exempt debt, particularly poor performing industrial development bonds), better disclosure, better financial management practices by issuers, greater scrutiny by different stakeholders, and improved economic conditions, including lower interest rates, which lowered the cost of borrowing.

> Default rates, however, varied significantly across municipal sub-sectors, even though the overall rate was low compared to many fixed-income sectors. The study found that the 16 to 23 year cumulative default rates for tax-backed and traditional revenue bonds were less than 0.25 percent. Industrial revenue bonds had a cumulative default rate of 14.62 percent, multi-family housing 5.72 percent, and non-hospital related healthcare 17.03 percent. These three sectors accounted for 8 percent of all bonds issued but 56 percent of defaults. Education and general-purpose sector bonds accounted for 46 percent of issuance but only 13 percent of defaults.

> Another new finding was that defaulted municipal bonds have a fairly high recovery rate of 68.33 percent based on the number of defaults. Recovery can be made in a couple of ways. The borrower may get out of the default situation by making full debt service payments or collateral securing the bonds may be liquidated. Most issuers, particularly providers of essential services such as water and sewer, resume paying debt service. These types of securities are backed by physical assets that are public property. Thus they are never pledged to bondholders. In such cases, bondholders maintain a lien on revenues, which often enables full recovery. Industrial development bonds and multifamily housing bonds, the two sectors with the highest default rates, are often backed by collateral leading to higher than average recovery rates.

The 1999 Fitch study of municipal debt defaults was followed by a revision of its rating criteria for many sectors of public finance. The study concluded that management practices were more important for predicting credit performance than had been thought in the past. The three most important management practices identified that led to stronger credit and lower defaults were:

- Superior disclosure
- Maintaining rainy day funds or operating reserves
- Implementing debt affordability reviews and policies[20]

These changes were rather substantial and obvious, but there have been other, more subtle effects on the municipal bond market. This brief section of the chapter focuses primarily on the impact of the just-mentioned changes on nonprofits that borrow in the debt markets through the issuance of municipal bonds.

(i) Selection of an Underwriting Firm. Because of the limited choice available, a nonprofit organization must be particularly careful in its selection of a capable and experienced underwriting firm. The nonprofit financial manager must first determine that the underwriting firm plans to continue in the municipal bond business for at least a sufficient period of time to market the bond issue. A firm that knows its bond operations will be terminating soon is simply interested in getting the issue sold as quickly as possible without the attention necessary to present it in the market in a proper and competitive fashion, and make a market (buy and sell the bonds) in the bond issue until it becomes seasoned.

If the bond issue is a floating rate, put-option bond (investors can cash out by "putting" the bond back to the issuer) and the investor has the right to redeem it for the return of principal on a one-day or one-week notice, what is known as a "remarketing agent" is required. This agent provides the vital function of accepting bonds tendered, or put, by investors and immediately finding other investors to purchase the bonds. A continuing underwriting responsibility exists to accommodate both investors and the borrower, whose interest it is to see that the issue continually remains in the hands of investors. The remarketing responsibility is usually assumed quickly and efficiently by other institutions.

Although most issues, once sold, do not trade actively in the secondary market, it is important to the nonprofit organization that its bonds receive reasonable secondary market activity, particularly if it expects to sell bond issues in the future. The institution does not want to lose potential investors because they had purchased its previous bonds and had been unable to sell them due to a weak or, worse yet, "no-bid" situation.

After a municipal bond issue has been sold, securities dealers frequently buy the bonds from investors who sell them before maturity to sell them to investors who are looking for secondary (or already-issued) bonds. It is important to maintain a relatively stable market price for the bond issue after its initial sale to the public. Therefore, the underwriting firm or group of firms that brought the issue to the public market should continue to participate actively in buying and selling the bonds in the secondary or resale market.

(ii) Preparation of Bond Documents. After selecting a bond underwriter and other professionals necessary to complete the financing task, including bond counsel, the actual indenture or disclosure statement is one of several documents that must be prepared. Of particular importance is the segment of the borrowing indenture that lists the instruments

considered acceptable for investment of the bond issue proceeds prior to their disbursement or ultimate use. In the case of rated nursing home and educational facility debt, the credit rating agencies, such as Moody's Investors Service and Standard & Poor's, have their own rating criteria that include specific information about the instruments in which bond proceeds may be invested. However, very often the bond counsel for the underwriters uses a file form for the compilation of indenture clauses, including one listing acceptable investments. This file is often outdated and inappropriate for the listing of acceptable investment instruments.

It is very important for the nonprofit financial manager to submit to the underwriter a list of investments that the nonprofit institution considers safe and appropriate. The list should be broad enough in scope to meet the bond's indenture requirements. Typical instruments that can be listed are U.S. Treasury securities, government agency securities, certificates of deposit and banker's acceptances issued by major creditworthy banks, commercial paper, and other corporate obligations rated in one of the top rating categories by the nationally recognized credit rating agencies. If others involved in the borrowing process disagree with this list, they should make it known, so that the list can be negotiated to one that is acceptable to all parties. However, the financial manager, after researching the appropriate investments to be included, should initiate a list of acceptable investments and not wait until the indenture is essentially complete before submitting it to the underwriter.

Another area of concern with respect to the process of investing bond proceeds is the specific approach of actually implementing these investments within the approved list of instruments included in the indenture. In considering the question of investing the proceeds from a bond issue pending their final disbursement, it is important to recognize the arbitrage provisions of the tax code. Briefly stated, these provisions will not allow the borrowing institution to benefit from any profit received on the investment of funds from a bond issue. Specifically, if the interest earned on the funds from a bond issue exceeds the cost of the interest on the money borrowed by the bond issue, that excess must be returned to the federal government. At the time of this writing, the Bond Market Association provides this information regarding tax code arbitrage provisions:

> Arbitrage regulations under the U.S. tax code limit the rate of return issuers of tax-exempt bonds can earn on the proceeds of tax-exempt bonds. Issuers—particularly those using bonds to finance construction—need to keep bond proceeds in an escrow account. The earnings on these escrow accounts must be disclosed to the IRS in a filing to determine whether the issuer must rebate any "arbitrage" to the government.[21]

Certain arbitrage rebate restrictions are waived if the amount of the bond issue proceeds is substantially spent down within two years for construction project bond issues (state and local governments and qualified 501(c)(3) organizations). Again, the intent of the provisions is to discourage entities from borrowing at a low interest cost through the sale of municipal bonds and investing the proceeds at a higher return, if the primary goal is to capture a profit from the privilege of being able to use municipal bonds as a borrowing vehicle.[22]

Most municipal bond issues are subject to the arbitrage provisions of the tax code. In this context, arbitrage refers to borrowing at a relatively low interest rate and then investing the proceeds in a higher-rate investment security. It is obvious that an issuing organization will not benefit from any interest earned that is in excess of interest cost unless interest rates fall sharply during the five-year period during which the yield is averaged. This situation certainly will not provide an incentive to earn maximum interest on the proceeds of the bond issue until such time as the funds are finally disbursed. Therefore, it is important that under no circumstances should aggressive investment techniques be used or higher risks taken simply to earn additional interest income. It takes a substantial amount of additional interest income to equal principal lost through unwise investment of bond proceeds.

These limitations on earned interest are referred to as "permitted yield." Although they provide no incentive to earn yield in excess of interest cost, there are other situations that must be considered. The institution may find itself in a low-interest-rate environment and need to be a competitive investor simply to earn the level of return to equal the cost of money borrowed. In this situation, it is extremely important that investment yields be taken seriously to minimize the interest cost incurred on municipal bond borrowing.

Whatever interest conditions prevail at the time the municipal bond issue is brought to market, it is important to be a prudent and efficient investor. There are many alternatives available for the investment of proceeds from the bond issue. In examining these alternatives, the financial manager should be aware of the institution's needs, not only with respect to arbitrage provisions but also as to internal management capabilities, proper compliance with indenture investment limitations, and sound overall financial practices.

(iii) Municipal Bond Issuers and Purposes. Increasingly, private colleges and schools, nonprofit associations, and even some religious organizations are issuing taxable municipals or tax-exempt municipal bonds. Federal Reserve statistics document over $2 trillion in municipal bonds outstanding, issued by over 60,000 entities. However, the percentage of nonprofits having tax-exempt bonds outstanding is small—only about 1 percent of arts organizations are presenting using this financing source.[23] An estimate of the amount of church bonds issued annually is $1 billion, as compared with total church financing of $20 billion to $40 billion annually.[24]

A category of municipals, called "501(c)(3) bonds," are issued by governmental units on behalf of private nonprofits, such as colleges and private schools, hospitals and other healthcare organizations, and museums. These "pass-through" or "conduit" bonds keep the responsibility for interest and principal payments with the nonprofit issuer rather than the government issuer. When tax exempt, the interest paid to investors is exempt from federal income taxation and may also be tax exempt for state or local income tax purposes if the investor lives in the issuer's state. Most municipals, or munis, as they are called, are tax exempt. Because of the tax-exempt feature, the yields on munis are lower than those on comparably rated (equally risky) taxable securities. Much of the issuance goes to pay for building refurbishment or new construction to keep the institution competitive from a physical facilities standpoint. Many college issuers would rather leave investment funds in their endowments, gaining interest and building larger principal amounts, instead of spending these monies on buildings. Nonhospital nonprofit institutions formerly faced a limit of $150 million in tax-exempt securities they may issue (although proposals for eliminating this limit have been made recently), but 1997 legislation largely released the limit on new bond issues. According to the National Association of Bond Lawyers:

> Present law. The Taxpayer Relief Act of 1997 provided for the partial repeal of the $150 million limitation on qualified 501(c)(3) bonds used to finance facilities besides hospitals for Section 501(c)(3) nonprofit organizations. Vestiges of the $150 million continue to apply to qualified 501(c)(3) bonds in a number of circumstances, including: (i) outstanding bonds issued before August 5, 1997 for capital expenditures; (ii) certain refundings of those bonds; and (iii) nonhospital bonds 5 percent of the net proceeds of which were used for working capital expenditures.

Example. If bonds were issued in 1996 to construct a Section 501(c)(3) university building, those bonds were, and continue to be, subject to the $150 million limitation. Also, certain bonds now issued to refund those bonds are subject to the limitation. If $50 million of bonds are now issued to finance a Section 501(c)(3) university classroom building and more than $2.5 million (5 percent of $50 million) of proceeds are used for working capital, then those bonds are also subject to the $150 million limitation.[25]

Some securities are short-term notes, but these are quite often issued by municipalities awaiting funds forthcoming from taxes or the sale of a bond issue.

Let's illustrate how your organization can use tax-exempt bonds. In a three-year period, four private nonprofit organizations issued tax-exempt bonds in central Indiana. Here are some features of those bonds:

- Pleasant Run Children's Home issued bonds "induced" by the city of Indianapolis—meaning that they were issued in the name of Indianapolis but were not a direct obligation of the city. These bonds were 7-day variable rate bonds, or "low floaters" as they are called, and paid between 3.75 percent and 4.25 percent during their first year in the market. The bonds were used to raise funds for facilities. The organization's foundation guaranteed payment on the bonds, and the issue was backed by a letter of credit from Fifth Third Bank of Central Indiana. For a fee of just over 1 percent of the amount of the issue, the bank stands ready to make interest payments or principal repayment if the issuer cannot.

- Archdiocese of Indianapolis issued $48 million in bonds to finance facilities and construction of private schools and cemeteries. The archdiocese did not need a letter of credit and took 18 months to close the deal from start to finish. This issue was the first of its kind in the United States.

- Lutheran Child & Family Services issued bonds to finance a treatment facility for children, also structured as a seven-day low floater, with a letter of credit backing the issue.

- Goodwill Industries issued bonds to pay for construction costs for new thrift stores, instead of getting a 10- or 15-year commercial mortgage on each new store that it opened. The $8.5 million issue refinanced existing mortgages and funded several new retail stores. Again, this issue was backed by a bank letter of credit.

To get these issues induced by the municipality, discussions and presentations were held with the mayor's office and appropriate city offices.

(b) TAXABLE BONDS.   Many bonds issued by nonprofit organizations are not tax exempt in that the bond investor must pay income tax on the interest received. Church bonds, bonds issued to pay for private schools, and nursing home bonds illustrate the taxable bonds issued by nonprofits. The flexibility of the investment banker structuring the borrowing allows these to be used for bridge financing, working capital loans, or construction. Sometimes the state or city in which the nonprofit operates can lend its tax-exempt status to allow what would normally be a fully taxable bond to be issued as a tax-exempt bond, as noted earlier.

(i) How Can My Organization Use Taxable Bonds?   Let's illustrate the use of taxable bonds. BC Ziegler and Company (Milwaukee, WI),[26] is an investment banker that assists

many healthcare, retirement, educational, and religious organizations that may not be able to issue tax-exempt bonds.

Ziegler arranges the public sale and distribution of first mortgage bonds, which are secured by a mortgage on the property. These bonds are certificates of indebtedness issued by churches, private schools, and other nonprofit organizations to provide funds for acquisition of property, building expansion, and debt retirement.

For example, Ziegler served as underwriter for the Lookout Mountain Community Church in the Denver metro area when it built a new 41,000-square-foot sanctuary and educational building.[27] The cost for the new facility, including construction, site development, furnishings, architect, and miscellaneous soft costs, was forecasted to be almost $10 million. The church used a combination of a capital fundraising campaign and a taxable bond issue of $7.85 million to finance the new building complex. The church could prepay bond principal when the old building was sold and was given the flexibility of paying down principal from future capital fundraising campaigns without prepayment penalties or restrictions. The church also had minimal loan covenants, giving it more freedom to later add capital improvements.

Many of the organizations issuing bonds through Ziegler do so because financing from banks was not available or not available at acceptable terms (interest rate, down payment, or maturity). For churches, many of the bond investors are members or friends of the borrowing organization. The bond issue is normally structured so that some of the bonds mature each six months, with the final set maturing in 15 years. The bonds are taxable, meaning that investors will have to pay tax at the ordinary income tax rate on interest received. Bonds are usually sold in a minimum amount of $5,000 and then in incremental amounts in $1,000 denominations, or in a minimum amount of $2,000 for IRAs. Most of the bonds are not rated by one of the credit rating agencies, because of their size: Most church-bond issue amounts range from $1 million to $5 million, with around $25 million being a maximum amount. However, nationwide, the default rate on church bonds is only about $1/2$ of 1 percent, as compared to a corporate bond default rate of 3 to 5 percent.[28]

(ii) Can I Also Get Short-Term Financing through Taxable Bonds? Although banks are the primary lenders for short-term funding needs, if a need is construction related you might use an underwriting organization to help you raise the funds via a bond issue. Let's say you need some money up front to build part of a project. You might do a 36-month revenue bond if your long-term financial track record shows you are reliable in paying your bills on a timely basis. In evaluating your suitability for issuing such bonds, the investment banker will look at:

- Purpose—what you want the money for
- Timing—how soon you need the money
- Insufficiency of other sources—why you need bond financing

(c) WHAT QUALIFIES MY ORGANIZATION TO ISSUE BONDS? Investment bankers will look for these facts on mortgage bonds:

- Borrowing amount not to exceed 3.5 times annual gross revenues
- Projected cash flows showing enough excess cash inflow to make interest payments and principal repayment (or a realignment of cash uses to free up necessary cash flows)

- The total amount financed not to exceed 70 or 75 percent of the property's appraised value

Credit checks will also be performed on the borrower's chief administrators, and the investment banker will look for evidence that the organization will stand behind the bonds, even if the administrators depart.

Organizations that have defaulted on their bonds are characterized as lacking in understanding about what they are getting in to and/or resolve about debt repayment.

Interest payments cannot be "laid off" like employees when times get tough. Furthermore, the organization will lose the property if it does not make debt payments. Out of this understanding, and based on members' integrity, should come the resolve to stay current on debt repayment.

(d) WHAT IF MY ORGANIZATION IS NOT PERCEIVED AS CREDITWORTHY?   When your organization does not have the creditworthiness to receive a high credit rating, what can you do to still issue a bond? Consider credit enhancement, including bond insurance, a bank letter or credit, or a third-party guarantee:

> Credit Enhancement *is the use of the credit of an entity other than the issuer to provide additional security in a bond. The term is usually used in the context of bond insurance, bank letters of credit, state school guarantees and credit programs of federal and state governments and federal agencies but also may apply more broadly to the use of any form of guaranty secondary source of payment or similar additional credit-improving instruments.*

> Bond Insurance *is a guaranty by a bond insurer of the payment of principal and interest on municipal bonds as they become due should the issuer fail to make required payments. Bond insurance typically is acquired in conjunction with a new issue of municipal securities, although insurance also is available for outstanding bonds traded in the secondary market.*

> Letter of Credit *a commitment, usually made by a commercial bank, to honor demands for payment of a debt upon compliance with conditions and/or the occurrence of certain events specified under the terms of the commitment. In municipal financings, bank letters of credit are sometimes used as additional sources of security with the bank issuing the letter of credit committing to in the event the issuer is unable to do so.*[29]

The majority of municipals are credit-enhanced, and most of that enhancement comes through bond insurance; about half of all new munis are insured. We see many nonprofits, however, using bank letters of credit to provide enhancement. Be open to many avenues for a guarantee. For example, a church may be able to get a guarantee from the state or national denominational headquarters.

10.11 LEASING AND NONTRADITIONAL FINANCING SOURCES

A broad definition of leasing is the use of equipment for money.

(a) THE LEASING PROCESS.   The process you would follow to get equipment or vehicle lease financing from a lease finance company includes these seven steps:

1. Fill out a lease application and mail or fax it to the lease financing company (lessor).
2. Within 24 hours, the lessor will accept or deny the application.

3. Lease documents are prepared (assuming your application was accepted).

4. Documents are then properly executed by your organization (lessee), and equipment or vehicle is acquired.

5. You return the documents, along with the equipment or vehicle invoice, to lessor.

6. You are contacted by lessor via phone to provide verbal acceptance (which authenticates the mailed documents).

7. Lessor pays vendor within 24 hours.

(b) LEASING VERSUS BORROWING.   There are several advantages to using lease financing, several of which result from the fact that you are not buying the equipment or vehicles as you would under a loan arrangement:

- You may get longer-term and, therefore, lower monthly cost financing due to the two- to five-year lease terms (or seven years on certain equipment), possibly longer than what a bank would allow.

- You may get almost 100 percent financing, as opposed to 20 percent down or a compensating balance requirement when using bank financing.

- When squeezed for liquidity, you will appreciate having both your cash and your machines or vehicles for use, as opposed to outright purchase of the items.

- Capital project restrictions on outright purchases (whether using cash or bank borrowing), perhaps due to delays in getting a capital campaign off the ground, will not impede critical purchases that can be made with lease financing.

- It protects your organization against owning computers or other equipment that rapidly become obsolete.

- You may gain flexibility, both on the lease terms and on what your options are at the end of the lease: Renewal, purchase, or return of equipment.

These advantages come at a cost, as you well know if you have considered a personal lease on a car purchase. And, unless you are using the leased items in a for-profit subsidiary, you will not get the tax advantage that motivates some businesses to lease: Lease expense is tax-deductible, and if the lease period is shorter than the depreciation schedule that would apply to a purchase, the lease can lower your tax bill. However, a lease may fit your organization's need to finance copiers, computers, computer software, construction equipment, or an entire office. And as is true of so many other business transactions, you can now apply for an equipment lease right from your computer.[30] Finally, more healthcare organizations are now selling some of their facilities, perhaps to a real estate investment trust, and then leasing them back. This "monetizes" the asset, reducing the balance sheet investment that the organization must make while enabling continued utilization of the facility.

10.12 DEVELOPING A DEBT AND HEDGING POLICY

A *debt and hedging policy* should include some of these items, according to PriceWaterhouseCoopers:[31]

- Short-term debt objectives and approaches

  o   4-week and 12-month rolling cash forecasts regularly completed and reviewed

- o Liquidity availability at a suitable cost ensured
- o Borrowed funds availability adequate for liquidity requirements assured
- o Alternate sources of funding maintained in order to enhance financial flexibility
- o Costs of short-term borrowing minimized while adequacy ensured
- o Excess cash balances automatically used to pay down credit lines because of the lower interest yield on cash balances relative to the interest rate charged on the credit line
- • Short-term debt instrument authorizations for some or all of the following:
  - o Commercial paper, bank credit line, revolving credit facility, bank loan syndication or participation, uncommitted credit line, reverse repurchase agreements, intercompany loans
- • Long-term debt objectives and approach
  - o Consistent supply assured at reasonable cost and terms
  - o Present value of the debt portfolio minimized
  - o Flexible financing of unanticipated future needs assured
  - o Reasonable debt covenants negotiated
  - o Insolvency and debt default risks minimized
  - o Maintaining a target debt-to-net assets ratio
- • Long-term debt instrument authorizations (which and how much)
- • Who is responsible for debt management (centralized or decentralized)
- • Short- and long-term debt management strategies
  - o Use of foreign debt sources
  - o Importance of cash forecasts
  - o Maintaining a good credit rating with credit reporting agencies
  - o Relatively more short-term borrowing when interest rate outlook is uncertain
  - o Match maturity of debt to life span of asset being financed
- • Interest rate risk management
  - o Interest rate risk profile or appetite
  - o Creation of a risk committee
  - o Objectives and approach
    - ▷ Fixed-to-floating rate balance
    - ▷ Interest expense minimization
    - ▷ Change in net asset threshold amount to be protected against
    - ▷ Hedging of interest rate risk through swaps, and so on
    - ▷ Developing balance sheet flexibility

- ○ Hedge program guidelines

  - ▷ Active management of risk based on proximity (current quarter and fiscal year more important) and materiality (effect on change in net assets and on organization's growth rate)
  - ▷ Feasibility and desirability of actively managing the exposures

- ○ Responsibility for interest rate risk management
- ○ Instruments authorized for interest rate hedging
- ○ Interest rate risk management strategies to be followed

  - ▷ Refinance risk
  - ▷ Short-term exposures versus long-term exposures
  - ▷ Overlap with debt management strategies

- ○ Interest rate risk management operating controls

  - ▷ Identify operational risks
  - ▷ Protect against operational risks
  - ▷ Who is authorized to execute strategies and trade
  - ▷ What authority is delegated and to whom
  - ▷ Segregation of duties
  - ▷ Approved counterparties
  - ▷ Dealing limits and how this is to be monitored
  - ▷ Process to manage exceptions
  - ▷ How performance will be measured and evaluated

- ○ Use of benchmarks

  - ▷ How will market risk be measured and analyzed
  - ▷ Management reporting
  - ▷ Accounting and disclosure
  - ▷ Business continuity planning and plan for disaster recovering

Rules of thumb are sometimes used in implementing hedging strategies. For example, a number of larger healthcare systems include in their policies stipulation regarding when they will exit an interest hedge (as when interest rates fluctuate a certain amount).[32] You may also wish to disclose why your organization uses hedges in the financial section of your stakeholder annual report.

10.13 LIABILITY MANAGEMENT IN PRACTICE

In addition to the statistics we have included in this chapter from the Lilly study and other data, we note two studies that shed light on actual nonprofit use of debt. We will also provide a recent statistic on mortgage and notes payable debt reported by nonprofits on their Form 990s.

The first study, conducted by Tuckman and Chang, documented the use of debt by 6,800 tax-filing charities in 1986.[33] They find that the majority (71 percent) of nonprofits had at least some debt (other than deferred revenue, which they excluded) and that the percentage increases with asset size (from a low of 64 percent for relatively small nonprofits (less than $500,000 in assets) to 93 percent for those having over $1.5 million in assets. However, for those organizations having debt, the median debt level is low, at $11,200; the median leverage ratio (debt to net assets) is 27 percent. The use of debt was very sector-specific: Large percentages of housing/shelter and healthcare organizations had debt, and almost no science and technology research, recreation/leisure/sports/athletics, public safety, philanthropy and voluntarism, and animal-related organizations had any debt. The median amount of debt in religion-related/spiritual development organizations was also very low, at $2,400, as you would expect given the Lilly findings referenced at the chapter's outset. Interestingly, at least one-half of the organizations across every nonprofit sector studied had zero or very low levels of debt. It appears that those nonprofits that borrow hold the lion's share of the debt: Nonprofits with at least $3 million of debt constituted only 8 percent of all organizations having debt, but held over 91 percent of the total debt in this sample. Tuckman and Chang did not specify in what form this debt was held, possibly because of data limitations. We return to this important issue below when we present our review of the most recent Form 990 data.

The second study, easily the most interesting and useful study done since the Tuckman and Chang study, is taken from 1991 to 1994 Form 990 data, and conducted by Woods Bowman.[34] Bowman uses large nonprofits, those with at least $10 million in assets, to study two competing corporate finance explanations for debt usage: the pecking order hypothesis and the static trade-off hypothesis. The pecking order hypothesis suggests that nonprofits finance assets first with net revenues, then asset conversion (including selling off short-term investments), then with additional debt. The static trade-off hypothesis proposes that the various costs of issuing debt, including transactions costs and higher likelihood of financial distress and bankruptcy, be considered by the financial manager in determining what source of financing to use. Bowman finds limited support for the static trade-off hypothesis. However, in his full-scale model, the effect of liquid asset holdings on the proportion of assets financed by debt is negative, which is at odds with the idea that lower bankruptcy and financial distress costs coincide with a relatively greater use of debt. We believe the pecking order explanation is more realistic for noncommercial nonprofits, in that we see a great degree of self-financing of large capital investments, and this requires a gradual buildup of cash and short- to medium-term investments that may not ever coincide with increased debt usage. Again, the target liquidity objective appears to best explain nonprofit financial behavior in our opinion.

Because the two studies are now over a decade old, we took an updated look at the data. Our own survey of the data uses the Core Data File available at the NCCS Data Web (http://nccsdataweb.urban.org/NCCS/Public/index.php). For the fiscal year 2000, of 22,031 nonprofit organizations reporting year-end totals on the Form 990, 18,382 report $0 of mortgages and other notes payable debt (this is reported on Line 64b of the Form 990). That constitutes 83.4 percent of the reporting nonprofit organizations in this set of data. So only 16.6 percent of the nonprofits indicated any amount of mortgage and other notes payable debt. The average amount of mortgage and other notes payable, for those having some of this type of debt, was $1.2 million. Furthermore, 0.9 percent, or less than 1 percent, of the 22,031 organizations had any tax-exempt bonds at the end of FY 2000. Apparently, the organizations that did have liabilities had them in the form of accounts payable (see section 10.2), grants payable, or "other liabilities." The percentage of nonprofits with arranged external debt is extremely small, based on this recent data. Form 990 data is thought to be fairly reliable with respect to asset and liability amounts, unlike the amounts that may be reported for various expense categories. Our findings indicate, once again, that nonprofits place great weight on yearly net revenues and buildup in target liquidity to self-fund major asset purchases.

10.14 CONCLUSION

Borrowers come in all shapes and sizes, and the astute lender must seek a way to differentiate between good loans and potentially unsuccessful loans. The financial manager must assist the lender in discerning the differences between the good loan represented by the financial manager's organization and all others.

The process begins with the preparation of a strategic financing plan that is part of the institution's overall strategic business plan. Then the financial manager must garner all the relevant facts and information that the lender will require, anticipate the lender's questions, and assemble a presentation to the lender. The presentation is a combination of written information and oral discussion, often including an onsite tour of the nonprofit's facilities. To be successful in the borrowing process, the financial manager must ensure that the selected lender matches the intended use of the funds and the duration of the loan. Banks, leasing companies, and insurance companies all have different objectives. The financial manager must recognize these differences and position itself toward the lender's interests.

Proficient financial managers with significant funding needs investigate bond financing as well as bank or insurance lease financing companies. They will also ensure that the organization pays its bills on time and makes interest payments and principal repayments as required. Because the worst time to contact a lender is when you finally really need them, they plan liquidity and capital project needs well in advance.

Notes

1. Eric Minton, "Staying in the Swim: Why Aquariums Succeed or Fail," *Planning* (June 2003): 14–19. Ocean Journey's long-range financial plan was based on 1.3 million visitors for each of the first three years, but after the first year's 1.4 million visitors attendance dropped in year 2 to 742,000 visitors. We emphasized in Chapter 9 doing scenario and what-if analysis for just this type of situation, and debt service (interest payments and principal repayments) should not require optimistic projections to be realized.
2. Lawton R. Burns and James Joo-Jin Kim, "Lessons from the Allegheny Bankruptcy," *LDI Issue Brief 5* (February 2000).
3. See Lilly study results in Appendix 1A.
4. Quoted from Theresa L. Wareham and Andrew J. Majka, *Best Practice Financing* (Northfield, IL: Kaufman Hall, 2003).
5. HFMA, "Competency 2: Managing the Balance Sheet," *Financing the Future Report 5: How Are Hospitals Financing the Future? Core Competencies in Capital Planning* (Westchester, IL: Healthcare Financial Management Association, 2004). This section is based closely on the HFMA framework, which applies most closely to hospitals. Capital structure concepts have been developed more in the hospital sector than any other nonprofit sector, with the possible exception of colleges and universities.
6. An index fund, without any fees, would be a good measure here. Many (possibly most) nonprofits have operating risk at least as high as an average company, and we would argue that the donative organizations or healthcare organizations in highly competitive markets experience more risk (see Chapter 2 on the financial risk of donative organizations). An

endowment fund that includes alternative investments (see Chapter 12), such as Harvard's, might provide a more accurate picture of returns mirroring the risk of a typical nonprofit than would the more conservatively managed endowment funds commonly observed in the nonprofit sector. Our approach mirrors "Method 2" in HFMA, "Competency 2: Managing the Balance Sheet."

7.   For more on credit reporting agencies, including the list of those nationally recognized by the U.S. Securities and Exchange Commission (SEC), see www.sec.gov/answers/nrsro.htm.

8.   Id.

9.   Wareham and Majka, *Best Practice Financing.*

10. The effective cost formula ignores compounding, and so slightly misstates the true cost of not taking a cash discount. See Thomas W. Oliver, Paul Kim, Antonio Que, and Chin W. Yang, "The Calculation of the Effective Annual Cash Discount Rate Revisited," *American Business Review* 18 (June 2000): 50–53.

11. Adapted from Edward Skloot, *Smart Borrowing: A Nonprofit's Guide to Working with Banks* (New York: New York Community Trust, n.d.), 3–4.

12. See Chapter 8 for more on cash forecasting.

13. This may be by negotiating with the supplier, or it may simply mean only paying invoices early when there is a cash discount offered.

14. Wood Bowman points out that businesses, and possibly nonprofits, often have a "pecking order" of long-term financing that consists of using net revenues first, then "asset conversion," or selling off assets prior to issuing external debt or (for businesses) equity. See Woods Bowman, "The Uniqueness of Nonprofit Finance and the Decision to Borrow," *Nonprofit Management & Leadership* 12 (Spring 2002): 293–311.

15. The banks give themselves the flexibility to deny some borrowers credit if many requests are received at the same time. Thus, total credit lines for a given bank exceed its ability to finance them simultaneously. Furthermore, material changes in the potential borrower's financial condition might result in the bank's denial of credit for an uncommitted line, although this also is rare.

16. When drawn against the buyer, these drafts are called bills of exchange, but when a bank sets up an acceptance facility, the seller draws against the bank, and the resulting instrument is called an acceptance credit. The bank will pay the seller the discounted value of the acceptance's face value, with the amount of the discount based on prevailing money market rates.

17. The same transaction often has both a commercial letter of credit and banker's acceptance involved: The letter of credit may be sent to the exporter's bank, which in turn draws up a time draft and shipment documents, and sends those back to the importer's bank. If the importer's bank accepts the draft, guaranteeing the payment of the draft at the due date, a banker's acceptance is created.

18. Approximately 35 to 40 percent of small businesses get some form of bank credit assistance. As nonprofits are generally the same size as small businesses but are disqualified from receiving SBA loans, it is likely that a smaller percentage is offered credit lines by banks. Primary bank lenders for nonprofits include Evangelical Christian Credit Union (Brea, CA) and Bank of the West. We profile other banks with strong nonprofit interest and product focus in Chapter 11.

19. This information is not to be construed in any way as providing legal advice. Readers should verify current laws with their tax or bond counsel.

20. Good Jobs First, "Public Bonds," June 2004. Available at: www.publicbonds.org/public_fin/default.htm. Accessed: 2/4/06.

21. Statement of the Bond Market Association before the House Ways and Means Committee, October 2004. Available online at: http://waysandmeans.house.gov/hearings.asp?formmode =view&id=2458. Accessed: 2/4/06. This information is not to be construed in any way as providing legal advice. Readers should verify current laws with their tax or bond counsel.

22. This information is not to be construed in any way as providing legal advice. Readers should verify current laws with their tax or bond counsel.

23. Author's tabulation based on data provided publicly by the National Center for Charitable Statistics at http://nccsdataweb.urban.org/. Accessed: 2/3/2006.

24. "A Fund with the Almighty on Its Side," *Dallas Morning News,* November 26, 2005. Reprinted online at:www.investing-news.com/artman/publish/printer_1496.shtml. Accessed: 1/14/2006.

25. National Association of Bond Lawyers, letter to the House Ways and Means Committee, Subcommittee on Select Revenue Measures, October 8, 2004. Available online at: http://waysandmeans.house.gov/hearings.asp?formmode=view&id=2464. Accessed: 2/4/06. This information is not to be construed in any way as providing legal advice. Readers should verify current laws with their tax or bond counsel.

26. BC Ziegler and Company, founded in 1902, underwrites bonds for "churches, schools, synagogues, temples, hospitals, healthcare institutions, CCRCs (continuing care retirement communities), assisted living centers, retirement communities and senior living providers," and is "a recognized leader in providing financing to nonprofit organizations.... In recent years, we have financed in excess of $1.5 billion annually for our nonprofit clients." Available online at: www.zieglerloan.com. Accessed: 2/1/2006.

27. Information available online at:www.zieglerloan.com/display/DocMgmtDisplayFile.aspx? fileid=10 587. Accessed: 2/4/06.

28. "A Fund with the Almighty on Its Side."

29. The Bond Market Association, *Municipal Bond Credit Report*, January 2006. Available online at:www.bondmarkets.com/assets/files/MunicipalCreditReport05Q3.pdf. Accessed: 2/4/06. This information is not to be construed in any way as providing legal advice. Readers should verify current laws with their tax or bond counsel.

30. As best we can determine, the first leasing company to offer "lease by Internet application" was First Credit Corporation. Their Web address at the time of this writing was: www. firstcredit.com/.

31. Fred Cohen and Timothy T. Hesler, "Debt and Interest Rate Risk Management Policy Guidelines," *AFP Manual of Treasury Policies* (Bethesda, MD: Association for Financial Professionals, 2001).

32. HFMA, "Competency 2: Managing the Balance Sheet."

33. Howard P. Tuckman and Cyril F. Chang, "How Well Is Debt Managed by Nonprofits?" *Nonprofit Management & Leadership* 3 (Summer 1993): 347–361.

34. Bowman, "The Uniqueness of Nonprofit Finance and the Decision to Borrow."

CHAPTER 11

CASH MANAGEMENT AND BANKING RELATIONS

11.1 INTRODUCTION

The U.S. cash management environment is one in which check usage and the cost of information technology are on the decline and interest rates and the use of electronic payments are on the upswing. Add in the phenomenal opportunities to harness the Internet

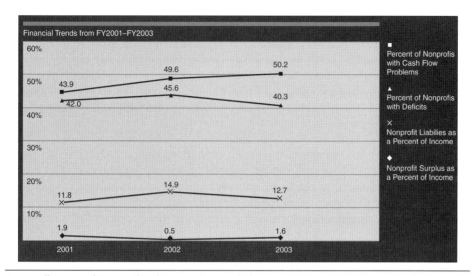

Source: Illinois Facilities Fund and Donors Forum of Chicago, "Getting It Right: How Illinois Nonprofits Manage for Success," 2004. Located online at: http://www.donorsforum.org/forms-pdf/GettingItright.pdf. Accessed: 3/4/2006. Used by permission.

EXHIBIT 11.1   NONPROFITS EXPERIENCING CASH FLOW PROBLEMS

for banking and other finance tasks, and you have a recipe for remarkable improvements in nonprofit cash management. And improvements are needed to help prevent financial crisis for many nonprofits: The 2001 to 2003 survey of Illinois-based nonprofits finds that only about one-third of nonprofits see themselves as financially healthy and not presently financial vulnerable; the other two-thirds were either seeing themselves as financially vulnerable for the future or experiencing chronic financial problems.[1] The survey also documents that fully one-half experienced cash-flow problems in 2003 (as shown in Exhibit 11.1), with the primary reasons being delays in government payments, normal business cycles, unmet fundraising goals, or a prior year deficit.

Fundraising is central to many nonprofit organizations. For most outside of education and healthcare, the treasury function primarily revolves around collecting, handling and managing cash gifts. For others, managing liquidity to support borrowing and investing decisions is also vital to ensure funding for the nonprofit's varied activities. For yet others, trying to bridge the gap until government grants or contracts get disbursed and received is the primary challenge. Having funder monies restricted to programs further intensifies the cash flow difficulties of many nonprofits.[2] Today it has become increasingly important for these functions to be carried out efficiently to maximize resources and control costs. Treasury responsibilities have evolved from paper-based, manual processes to highly automated and sophisticated systems that interface seamlessly with banks, service providers, and other internal operating units.

Cash management is a subset of treasury management, and it involves the collection, mobilization and disbursement of cash within a business enterprise. Moving funds and managing the information related to the funds' flows and balances are fundamental to good cash management. With a strong understanding of the banking system and the products and services offered by banks, the cash manager can achieve effective mobilization of funds, prudent investing of these funds, and cost-effectiveness in services used.

Depending on its size and scope of activities, a nonprofit's financial structure may range from simple to highly sophisticated. In any case, a system needs to be designed to monitor the cash flow timeline that links revenue/cash receipts and purchasing/cash disbursements. For some, transactions can be more complex when cash flows cover large payrolls, sizable inventories, vehicle fleets, and other supplies for an organization like the Red Cross or a major healthcare facility with heavy financing and working capital needs.

A comprehensive understanding of an organization's operational processes is basic to structuring a sound cash management program. Identifying and quantifying the activities, interfaces, and resources that make up the collective cash flow can lead to a better assessment of service requirements for banks and other financial service providers. Significant advances in technology have impacted the delivery of cash management services and offered numerous opportunities for managing deposits, funds concentration, disbursements, and information and control. As new applications have emerged, automated and electronic processing capabilities have replaced paper-based information and inquiry systems. Cash managers now use the Internet and/or computerized workstations (which are actually just specialized software packages) to execute transactions and gather information ranging from bank balances to investment transactions and other financial activities. Processes that required manual intervention are now routinely handled by innovative electronic collection, concentration, and disbursement applications. Cash management activities are being carried out better, faster, and cheaper. With increased productivity through automation and "smart systems," there are many opportunities for cash managers to add value and enhance service support to other parts of the organization. With nonprofits expected to do more with less, reengineering and outsourcing possibilities should be considered alongside traditional approaches. A good example here is establishing a temporary lockbox service with a bank or third-party provider to handle the annual fund donation flow.

The primary goal of this section is to identify the trends and opportunities that nonprofits should consider to enhance treasury functions relating to cash management. Collection and disbursement mechanics that have benefited from technological advances will be highlighted, along with regulatory and banking developments. Identifying electronic systems for accelerating the collection of remittances and controlling disbursements to ensure timely and orderly outflows will be explored. Last, the strategy for identifying, selecting, and working with the right bank or financial service provider will be addressed. What is the bank's breadth of product, systems, and service levels? How committed is the bank to maintaining and improving its product and service offerings? How important is this account to the bank? What is the bank's financial strength? With the right financial service provider(s) as partner(s) and the appropriate technology to support operations, many benefits and opportunities can be maximized.

11.2 WHAT IS CASH MANAGEMENT?

Cash management encompasses a number of activities within these primary functions:

- Cash collection
- Cash concentration
- Cash disbursements

- Investment of surplus cash, if any

- Financing or borrowing

- Forecasting "cash flows"

- Managing bank relations

The fiduciary responsibility of nonprofits must be balanced in the way business is conducted. Financial risks should be recognized and appropriate measures taken to safeguard assets. In designing and structuring a good cash management program, distinguishing day-to-day functions from strategic objectives is important. At the same time, focusing on efficiency must take into account control and flexibility in managing cash, based on a strong understanding of organizational cash flows (see Exhibit 11.2).

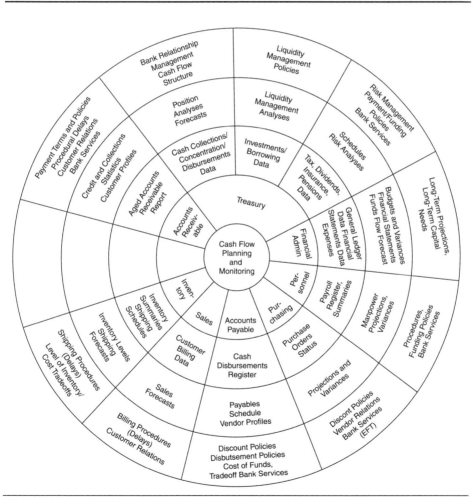

Source: Aviva Rice, "Improving Cash Flow Control Throughout the Corporation." © 1997 by the Association for Financial Professionals, all rights reserved. Used with permission of the Association for Financial Professionals.

EXHIBIT 11.2   COMPREHENSIVE CASH FLOW MANAGEMENT

(a) BANKING ENVIRONMENT.   Commercial banks serve as depositories for cash and also act as paying and receiving agents for checks and other fund transfers.

Banks have been a traditional source of financing for short- and medium-term needs, providers of investment services, fiduciary/trust services, and global custody.

A number of financial institutions now have dedicated nonprofit departments or groups, and their specialization may be a significant advantage for your organization. Illustrating, the Evangelical Christian Credit Union (Brea, CA) and the Bank of the West specialize in making loans to nonprofits. SunTrust, Mellon Financial, JP MorganChase, Fifth Third, KeyBank, and others have nonprofit departments (recognize that sometimes the names are not indicative of this focus: SunTrust calls its group "I & G," for "Institutional & Governmental," in its Atlanta and Nashville offices). Perhaps the most creative and unique initiative is Fifth Third's "Community Belief Banking" office in Columbus, Ohio. This program offers a well-designed bundle of services to the faith-based organization and its membership. These services include depository services for both the organization and its individual members, working capital loans not collateralized by inventory or receivables, payroll services, direct payments by which member checking accounts are electronically debited so members can give without writing a check and can honor pledge obligations over a number of months in a convenient manner, trust and other investment services, and free financial seminars for members.

Building a good relationship and partnership with the right bank offers many advantages. A growing nonprofit organization will benefit from the right association and could leverage such a relationship to integrate services such as cash management, trust, capital markets, and credit. With few exceptions, a full-service commercial bank can offer a range of cash management services that will meet all the requirements of a nonprofit institution. Some smaller banks, sometimes dubbed "community banks," value nonprofits more, may offer a special mix of services, and often have better pricing. In certain situations, "unbundling" services and seeking out multibank relationships may be appropriate where services are required in different geographic regions of the country or even overseas. International banking is offered by many major banks, and specialized needs for foreign exchange, letters of credit, and other international transactions are easily met. Pricing, quality of service, support, and technology are factors that must be considered in deciding on a single or multibank setup. Nowadays, technology for cash concentration can link multiple accounts in different banking relationships without slowing cash transfers or incurring added expense. What value-added benefits can be realized in a single or multibank relationship is a question that needs to be explored.

SERVICES PROVIDED BY TREASURY MANAGEMENT BANKS	
Account Reconciliation	Information Reporting
Automated Clearing House (ACH) Services	Retail Lockbox
Check Clearing	Sweep Accounts
Controlled Disbursement	Treasury Management Software
Demand Deposit Accounts	Wire Transfers
Electronic Data Interchange (EDI)	Zero Balance Account

(b) PURCHASING BANK SERVICES.   When purchasing bank services, a formalized approach will help ensure that important decision factors are not overlooked in the evaluation and purchase of cash management services. In certain situations, an informal or partial request for a product or service may be conducted. However, there are potential disadvantages to such a process that can be eliminated through the use of two suggested critical steps: A request for information (RFI) and a request for proposal (RFP). As we prepare to consider the RFI and RFP, consider the steps involved in changing banks, including implementation, profiled in Exhibit 11.3.

The RFI is part of a structured information-gathering effort to identify potential vendors and their product offerings. Through trade directories, publications, and referrals,[3] this informal process can provide data on banks and vendors that will include such information as experience, technological capabilities, and creditworthiness. This process could potentially eliminate the need for an RFP when there is clearly one superior vendor or when specific service requirements can only be met by one or two vendors. While not optimal, this approach provides a basis for a more informed decision than one based solely on previous relationships and price. At least once every few years, an RFI is helpful in comparing capabilities outside of an existing relationship and staying current with changes in the industry.

An RFP is the next step to take when soliciting bids for several cash services and a comprehensive search is warranted. The process can be fairly involved and time consuming. Key to an RFP would be a statement of the nonprofit's objective in soliciting the proposal. This would include:

- A description of the service sought
- The preferred location
- The volume of transactions by service (measure costs under various activity volumes)

Exhibit 11.4 provides an outline of a sample RFP for lockbox processing. In addition, specific service requirements should also be addressed:

- Any special features or customization required
- Level of support service expected (who, hours, level of authority)
- Problem-resolution procedures
- Automation capabilities
- Mechanisms for funds transfer
- Availability of information (cutoff times, cost)
- Level of quality expected
- Pricing information; pro forma account analysis
- Questions relating to product-specific issues and buyer requirements for special transaction requirements
- Deadline for response
- References (do a thorough check)
- Contact person

Spelling out both general and specific qualifications and requirements will provide a more objective approach and meaningful comparison of service levels. When the best vendor is identified, the next step is to secure a commitment in writing and document the details and fees involved. This should also include deviations from the RFP, specific computations, price commitment, change notification periods, cost of uncollected funds, overdrafts, and daylight overdraft provisions. Use of a matrix that scores the responses from banks or vendors is recommended.

Changing your Cash Management Bank

Why?
There are many reasons why a corporate should want to change its bank, including:

1. *Change of policy by the bank* Occasionally, banks pull out of certain countries or decide to focus on another aspect of banking. (It probably also means that they weren't very good at transaction banking.)
2. *Reduction in the bank credit rating* Most corporates set minimum bank credit ratings for their banks, and if their transaction bank slips below that rating, a change of bank should be considered.
3. *Lending requirements* Lending facilities offered by a particular bank may depend on moving transaction banking to them.
4. *Dissatisfaction* This is one of the main reasons for changing banks, and the contrast to 1–3 is that it is discretionary. If this is the case, the corporate must recognise that the process is often difficult and the benefits can sometimes be hard to achieve, so that it should only be considered if the dissatisfaction with the existing bank is extreme!

The Tender Process
When selecting a new bank, it is normal to go through a formal tender process. For that, the corporate needs to be clear about its objectives and requirements:

1. These **objectives** may include:

   - Reducing banking costs
   - Reducing liquidity requirements—squeezing unnecessary liquidity out of the system
   - Providing a good transaction banking service

2. **Analyse the requirements**

   - It is important to understand how divisions, subsidiaries or departments—both in centralized and decentralized companies, use all of the accounts. This needs to be clear before preparing the Request for a Proposal (RFP).

3. **Identify the potential new banks**

   - Contact them beforehand to explain your objectives and to warn them that a tender document is being sent to them, so that it will go to the correct person, who will treat it with sufficient importance, and in a timely manner.
   - Will the existing transaction bankers be included?

4. **Information**

   - Give as much information to the prospective banks as possible, including a description of the corporate's needs, transaction volumes and values.
   - Describe clearly the corporate's objectives.

5. **Set a realistic timetable for the process**

   - At least 1 month for the initial response
   - The estimated time for consideration of the proposals, to reach a shortlist, proposed dates for presentations, the decision, and implementation (don't be over-optimistic).

Exhibit 11.3   Reasons for Changing Banks and How to Proceed

6. Specify what the response should include

- Description of the service the bank is able to provide, including support and Service Level Agreement.
- Details of the pricing they are offering
- Technical details of their electronic banking system
- Lending and overdraft facilities available (and interest rates)
- Money market and other treasury lines which might be available
- How they would handle implementation of the transfer of the business
- Names of similarly sized customers, for reference

Meeting The Short-Listed Banks

To enable a good comparison of the short-listed banks, it is important to compare them under similar conditions, including:

- A strict timetable and agenda
- Specifying the areas which are important to the corporate, such as pricing, systems, and service

It is sometimes revealing to compare who they send to give presentations such as existing or prospective account managers, their level of seniority and experience and whether they bring their implementation team.

Implementation

Once the decision has been reached, implementation needs to be managed very carefully, involving the operational personnel who will be handling the process.

The process includes:

1. Meeting with the successful bank to plan the implementation. This covers:

- A realistic timetable
- Regular progress reporting
- Documentary requirements
- Agreeing on a training schedule for any new software being provided

2. Meeting with the outgoing bank to agree a hand-over procedure

It needs to be emphasized that implementation can be a major exercise. In addition to the actions to be taken by the bank, the company will need to consider the various issues, including changing payment instructions for existing customers if they credit your bank accounts electronically, and changing internal systems which have been set up to interface with the existing bank.

Do not underestimate the potential for things to go wrong and to take longer than expected, as the sales teams from the new bank do have a tendency to promise more than their bank can deliver.

Finally

When the new system has been in place for 3 or 6 months, a review needs to be conducted to check that the anticipated savings and benefits are being achieved and that the new systems are working as the bank had promised, and to identify actions to be taken if that is not the case.

Source: Brian Welch, "Changing Your Cash Management Bank," *Global Treasury News* (June 23, 2000). Located online at: http://www.gtnews.com/cash/home.html. Accessed: 3/4/06. Used by permission.

EXHIBIT 11.3 REASONS FOR CHANGING BANKS AND HOW TO PROCEED (*continued*)

GENERAL QUALIFICATIONS

1. Monthly volume in total and for the three largest customers
2. General work flow description
3. Equipment used in processing
4. Problem-resolution procedures
5. Bank/vendor output records for receivable/payables accounting
6. Methods and timing of data transmission
7. Mechanisms for funds transfer
8. Timing of balance report on daily activity, etc.

PRODUCT-SPECIFIC ISSUES

1. Flow of mail through bidder's postal facility
2. Zip code arrangements (unique, zip + 4, other)
3. Schedule of daily and weekend post office collections
4. Delivery site and resulting delay of mail distribution within bidder's premises
5. Staffing and experience of lockbox operation
6. Maximum daily volumes that can be processed for same-day ledger credit
7. Timing/security for transmission of lockbox data, including remittance media
8. Error rate in lockbox processing, etc.

BUYER'S PROCESSING REQUIREMENTS

1. Specific volume projections, now and in three years, at peak and average
2. Geographic distribution of customers
3. Processing exceptions as to payee, check date, nonmatching dollar amounts, missing check signature, and foreign items
4. Handling of customer correspondence
5. Anticipated data-capture requirements from scanline or from remittance documents
6. Procedures for charging nonsufficient funds items
7. Delivery procedures for remittance advices, deposit slips, and other materials
8. Data transmission baud rates, timing and security, etc.

SUPPLEMENTAL INFORMATION

1. Product brochures
2. Sample contract or agreement of service
3. Phoenix-Hecht Postal Survey data on mail and availability times
4. Sample output from bank or vendor processing
5. Customer references
6. Complete product pricing schedule
7. Chart of service area organization
8. Implementation checklist, etc.

Source: From James S. Sagner and Larry A. Marks, "A Formalized Approach to Purchasing Cash Management Services," Sagner/Marks, Inc., *Journal of Cash Management* 13, No. 6.

EXHIBIT 11.4   SAMPLE RFP: LOCKBOX PROCESSING

In putting together an RFP, questions can be organized from the general to the specific. Exhibit 11.5 contains examples of methods that may be used.

For assistance in preparing RFPs for banking services, the Association for Financial Professionals (AFP) and the Bank Administration Institute have developed a publication to help in selecting cash management banks. *Standardized RFPs for Global*

LIST 1 Organizing Questions by Functional or Organizational Areas

1. Accounting

   - Reconciliation
   - Reporting

2. Cash management

   - Balance reporting
   - Funds transfer: wire transfers, ACH

3. Control

   - Security
   - Audit trail

LIST 2 Organizing Questions by Product Line, Including Current and Future Needs

1. Controlled disbursement

   - Current needs
   - Future needs

2. Lockbox

   - Current needs
   - Future needs

3. Funds transfer

   - Current needs
   - Future needs

Source: From James S. Sagner and Larry A. Marks, "A Formalized Approach to Purchasing Cash Management Services," Sagner/Marks, Inc., *Journal of Cash Management*, 13, No. 6.

EXHIBIT 11.5 RFP QUESTIONS

Treasury Services, published by the Association for Financial Professionals, provides a comprehensive list of questions on all aspects of bank services. Detailed RFPs are available for these cash management services:

- Automated Clearing House (ACH) services such as direct payments
- Controlled disbursement, account reconciliation, and positive pay
- Depository services
- Electronic data interchange (EDI) services
- Information reporting
- Wholesale lockbox, including electronic lockbox and network services
- Wire transfer

Steps should be taken to build and strengthen the relationship once a vendor is selected and a contract signed. Keeping the account officer well informed of activities, changing requirements, operational processes, policies, and future plans is fundamental. Giving honest feedback also ensures a productive partnership. In the long run, negotiations are made easier, and the account officer becomes very knowledgeable about the nonprofit's operations. The account officer's input can be a resource in identifying opportunities for improvement. Developing a consultative partnership can be useful in analyzing treasury functions and getting valuable suggestions for process improvement. An annual review between banker and client completes the process toward constructive relationship building.

What can the cash manager and banker do to get the most from a bank relationship? What are each other's expectations, objectives? Are they attainable and reasonable? Building a relationship requires a real investment of time for all parties involved. Strategies for relationship building are premised largely on trust, open communications, honest feedback, and team building. Setting realistic objectives is fundamental and provides the framework for implementing agreed-on procedures and service requirements. When a client calls a banker only when a problem arises, the relationship stands on shaky ground. Regular meetings and follow-ups ensure open communication. With the rise in bank mergers, takeovers, and consolidations, managing a relationship has become increasingly challenging. The consistency in quality, service, and price that a client seeks in a bank tends to be disrupted as bank cultures change and personnel turnover creates dislocations. When a strong relationship has been cultivated, problems and uncertainties will be more manageable and less stressful to handle. A win-win situation is a likely by-product of a healthy relationship.

(c) MANAGING BANK SERVICE CHARGES.   What does it cost to do business with your bank? How are balances determined? What are the reserve requirements? What is the basis for calculating the earnings credit rate? Are all the services needed? How should the services be paid: by fees, balances, or a combination of both? Answers to these questions can be gathered from an account analysis statement, which presents a clear picture of bank services and account status. This monthly statement contains two separate sections on balance and service information. It is critical to understand the account analysis statement and its terms and components to verify the accuracy and level of charges. Understanding the services used and relating this usage to the pattern of collections and disbursements could lead to potential cost savings. When multiple banks are used, comparisons using spreadsheets would be necessary on a monthly basis.[4] Basic to the analysis are:

- Cutoff, preparation, and timing of analysis statement by bank
- Bank service charges organized by type of service: depository, remittance banking, reporting, disbursement, lending

The balance section should be reviewed in terms of where the information comes from, the type of activity and the service charge associated with each activity. Reconciliation helps ensure accurate and timely assessment of balances. How best to compensate the bank can also be answered when investment alternatives offer higher rates of return than the earnings credit rate (ECR; sometimes called an earnings credit allowance) banks allow against collected balances. In such a scenario, paying by fees may be more advantageous when one can invest collected balances and earn a higher interest income.

Computation of the ECR may be tied to a market rate, such as the 90-day treasury bill rate, or a managed rate determined by the bank based on factors, such as cost of funds and competitive pressures. The formula for calculating an ECR must consider the impact of the reserve requirement on bank charges. Until recently, deposit insurance was also charged; when added together, both costs drastically lowered balance levels. In considering payment by fees or balances, compensation to banks must be analyzed and negotiated to understand which arrangement is cost effective. A clear agreement must be in place to identify the method and timing of compensation, especially if a method other than monthly settlement is preferable. Banks prefer monthly settlement, but when balances are used for compensation, quarterly, semiannual, or annual settlements may be appropriate to maximize use of excess balances that occur within the settlement cycle. Carrying forward excess balances must be negotiated, and the time period should be stated. Whenever settlement occurs, deficiencies should be billed and may be debited directly from the checking account.

Auditing and reviewing the account analysis statement could spot price changes and potentially identify cost-cutting opportunities. Working together with the bank relationship manager, a review may suggest ways to cut bank costs that are more directly tied to how the cash management system operates. Examples would include:

- *Payment alternatives*. Paying by ACH is cheaper than Fedwire transfers, and using PC-initiated wire transfers is cheaper than phone-initiated transfers.
- *Account maintenance*. Combine or eliminate checking accounts, since $25 to $50 can be charged each month per account.
- *Checks deposited*. Consider encoding or sorting checks or doing remote deposit capture.
- *Stop payments*. Use an automated system.
- *Account reconciliation*. Use a paid-only (partial) reconciliation service instead of a full account reconciliation program.

Refer to Exhibit 11.6 for definitions of terms used in an account analysis statement and Exhibit 11.7 for a description of the components of the account analysis statement.

11.3 COLLECTION SYSTEMS: MANAGING AND ACCELERATING RECEIPT OF FUNDS

Electronic collection, technically called direct payment if the amount is taken out of one's account on an ongoing and preauthorized basis without a card being used, is slowly replacing checks as the payment of choice. Although donations are still collected largely from checks mailed by donors, electronic payment options are gaining acceptance. This acceptance has been influenced by factors such as an increase in comfort with electronic products, personal convenience, and an increased sense of security about the medium. Cash substitutes in the form of debit and prepaid cards, direct payments through the ACH, and ACH debits are growing. The ACH is basically a computerized network for processing electronic debits and credits between banks for its customers through the Federal Reserve System. A dedicated Web site is now available for nonprofits considering the advantages of direct payment (electronic collection of donations using the ACH system): www.directpayment.org/dpnp1.html. Appendix 11A provides a Nonprofit Organization Guide to Direct Payment. Recent surveys indicate that almost one-half of U.S. households use direct payment, and 84 percent of users are very satisfied with it.[5]

Credit card and debit card payments are also used increasingly but may cost more than checks or ACH payments, depending on the transaction size. Electronic transmittal of credit card and debit card transactions offers cost advantages over paper-based processing with the potential for a reduced discount rate (charge by "merchant bank") and direct

Average ledger balance	The sum of the daily, end-of-day gross balances on deposit divided by the number of days in the period
Average float	The sum of the daily amount of deposited items that were in the process of collection divided by the number of days in the period
Average collected balance	The sum of the daily ledger balances less "uncollected" balances (float) divided by the number of days in the period
Reserve requirement	The amount that a bank is required to leave on deposit with the Federal Reserve; currently, 10 percent of checking balances
FDIC	Federal Deposit Insurance Corporation—assesses bank's premiums to federally insure deposits
ECR	The rate established by a bank, adjusted for the reserve requirement—applied to collected balances to derive the fee equivalent of balances maintained
Earnings allowance	The amount available to support services—calculated by multiplying the ECR times collected balances
Service description	Description of the services used
Unit price	The bank pricing for each transaction; unit price may or may not be the bank's standard price
Volume	The number of transactions for each service
Service charge	The results of the calculation of unit price times volume
Collected balance required	The balances needed to compensate a bank for services rendered

EXHIBIT 11.6   DEFINITION OF TERMS USED IN AN ACCOUNT ANALYSIS STATEMENT

Customer information	General customer information such as name and address, account title and number, period covered, and bank contact
Current/historical balance and compensation information	Section containing current and historical ledger, collected and uncollected balances and any adjustments for the period, and current and historical excess/deficit balance positions. The current and subsequent months ECRs displayed, along with the earnings allowance and total monthly service charge and, in many instances, the multiplier (collected balance required to support $1 of fees)
Adjustment detail	Any adjustment for a prior period is included in this section, which indicates description, transaction date, date of adjustment, amount, and the number of days included in the adjustment
Summary of accounts	This section shows all of the accounts included in the account analysis statement, along with selected summary information (e.g., average balances, float, total service charge)
Service description and cost information	This section is usually grouped into categories, and shows services used, monthly volume, unit and total price, and collected balance equivalents that require close scrutiny and can often result in cost savings.

EXHIBIT 11.7   COMPONENTS OF THE ACCOUNT ANALYSIS STATEMENT

credit to the organization's bank account. Upon transmission, notification is immediately provided on any discrepancy in account information by a payor or disallowed transaction (e.g., credit limit exceeded). As the volume of credit card and debit card payments increases, an annual review should be conducted. Keeping track of card amounts and activity will be helpful in negotiating a lower discount rate since merchant banks base their pricing on average ticket size and volume.

When agreements are in place to collect pledges using an ACH or other electronic payments, the cash forecast is significantly improved. Money becomes available at the agreed-on monthly or quarterly interval. Within 48 hours from initiation of an ACH debit, funds will be credited to the organization's checking account or swept to its concentration account. Credit card transactions can be collected within one to three days. The percentage of collections handled through check substitutes is still low but is gaining acceptance. The experience of nonprofits that have used ACH debits (also called automatic bill payment, automatic debit, electronic bill payment, or direct debit) suggests that a pilot test and survey must first be conducted to gauge the willingness of donors to participate in such a program. One foundation has been using ACH debits for quarterly payment of its annual fund pledge payments. Specifying a cutoff amount that will be cost effective to handle is also recommended, and it is advisable to start with a focus group or payment type. The process saves staff time, postage costs, and other expenses associated with issuing pledge reminders and invoices. One large ministry organization determined that the average cost of donation processing if made by ACH debit was 22 cents, if made by check was 80 cents, and if made by credit card was $1.42.[6] A broader research study, profiling mostly businesses, found an average 11.5 cent processing savings per payment processed when comparing direct payment to check payment.[7]

An ACH credit is a payment choice for more and more corporations that have matching gift programs for their employees. The ABC Educational Foundation signed up for a pharmaceutical company's matching gift program and now receives a direct payment to its bank checking account. Like any other automated transaction, the payment is clearly identified and shows up in the bank balance report. For beneficiary distributions to planned giving donors, the foundation makes monthly or quarterly payments by ACH. This replaced check payments that required more staff time to process. A donor's financial institution or bank does not charge for ACH remittances, unlike a wire transfer which could cost $10 to receive. The only drawback encountered with ACH payments occurs when a donor designates a nonbank account to receive the deposit. For example, a deposit to a brokerage money market account cannot be accommodated with the limited message field that shows further credit instruction. The transfer may end up in a suspense account or the brokerage firm's depository account, and a trace would be needed to ensure further credit to the beneficiary account.

Check collections can also be accelerated through pre-encoding the amount in the magnetic ink character recognition line or "presorting" by drawee bank locally, by city or region. Using these two options, depositors can avail themselves of preferential pricing and better availability from their banks. Costs for check processing are also decreasing as a result of regulatory edicts and improved processing capabilities. The Federal Reserve's Same Day Settlement (SDS) initiative permits a collecting bank to present items to any paying bank directly, without establishing a relationship with that bank or paying presentment fees. SDS has spurred more efficient clearing mechanisms by eliminating intermediary check "clearers" and ultimately decrease clearing float and costs.

Electronic check presentment and check truncation, growing rapidly due to Check 21 provision for an "image replacement document" to be electronically transmitted and be considered the legal equivalent to a paper check when presented to the bank on which the original check was drawn, promise to revolutionize check collection by clearing checks and identifying return items using data transmissions rather than moving paper checks. Consultants' projections show that banks' usage of check image exchange (check truncation and electronic transmission of the ensuing electronic transaction) is growing at exponential rates and may surpass 60 percent of all transit (interdistrict checks) checks by as early as 2007.[8] Combined with image processing, information on returned checks and access to gift data can be gathered sooner and at less cost.

(a) LOCKBOX PROCESSING. The lockbox system was developed to accelerate check collection and expedite deposit of accounts receivable. The concept began 60 years ago with the recommendation to use a post office box (lockbox) to collect large-dollar remittances. A corporation, through an authorization letter to the postmaster, permits a designated bank to extract mail from the corporation's box around the clock. With frequent pickups throughout the day, a bank can process remittances faster compared to directing mail to company premises. The objective is to minimize mail and processing time so that checks are converted into available funds more rapidly.

Many nonprofits today use lockbox services to process gift checks, membership dues, and other receivables associated with marketing and merchandising activities. You may opt to have the lockbox service opened for only part of the year, when your inflow of mailed checks is highest. In addition to banks, other service providers now offer lockbox processing. Current generations of lockbox services employs automated production interfaces, including bar code technology to receive and sort the mail; automation to encode, endorse, and photocopy checks; high-speed capture of payor bank routing information; and Internet access to confirm balance and receivables information.

If outsourcing collection processing makes sense, a lockbox service should be evaluated. In selecting a vendor, these factors must be considered:

- Types of plans offered
- Vendor's operational capability
- Automation
- Professional staff (years experience, turnover)
- Quality-control checkpoints (low error rates)
- Number of pickup times per day (but make sure this translates into a better availability schedule and/or later cutoff times)
- Availability schedule (when do deposits become available for investing, paying down loans, or for funding disbursements?)
- Support and problem-resolution responsiveness
- Cutoff times (how late can you get the checks and still have them count for ledger credit?) and weekend processing
- Pricing
- Reporting capabilities
- Interface with accounts receivable system or an integrated accounting software system
- Disaster and continuity provisions

In using a lockbox service, the cash manager should coordinate with other departments' specifications relating to invoices and other remittance material. These specifications may include image-ready invoice redesign, proper ink colors, background print elimination, proper specifications for window envelopes, use of bar coding, and strategic location of key pieces of information (donor identification numbers, mail zip codes, return address). The cash management account officer of the bank or vendor should be consulted for assistance in designing the remittance document to providing more efficient processing and data capture in an electronic format. Reporting can also be streamlined so that the appropriate service plan can be identified and the pertinent information can be captured. Otherwise, the cost can be high.

Advances in imaging technology may replace costly printouts for lockbox remittance information that take longer to produce and deliver. Image technology can capture details on invoice data, donor name, address, or dollar amount, and eliminate the need for stapling the invoice, envelope, and check photocopy. Information can be captured electronically and the image transmitted over the Internet. Data can be sorted and users can store large volumes of data. Backup storage media include optical disk, CD-ROM, tape, or magnetic storage. Paper documents are replaced by images warehoused in a relational database management system. The database is accessible from multiple locations, possibly via an intranet or over the Internet, and can automatically route information to various points within an organization. A development officer inquiring about a donor's gift can access a file containing the image of the check and the solicitation document. Both can be transmitted through e-mail or accessed through a network database. Where marketing is involved, inventory tracking is also enhanced and payment information is readily accessible.

Outsourcing through a lockbox service has its advantages and is an option that merits comparison against internal processing. The cash manager must evaluate the cost and staffing associated with internal processing, notably peak-period demands as well as the break-even receivable size. In cases where check or receivables processing is close to full capacity, this limits the internal processing facility's flexibility in bringing in trained personnel at peak periods, and outsourcing may be worth considering.

(b) CHECKLIST OF COLLECTIONS-RELATED SERVICES AND ACTIVITIES.   This list of collections-related services and activities holds the promise for nonprofits, based on our experience and our conversations with banking professionals:

Get the checks out of the inbox! Too many nonprofits allow time to elapse from the point when donors or clients mail the checks and those checks are deposited and become spendable funds at the bank. If you cannot or do not prefer to improve your processes on your own, enlist the help of another organization or a financial institution. Christian Children's Fund (CCF), an international relief and development agency located in Richmond, Virginia, is a superb example of this. Treasurer Bill Hopkins located a nonbank company that had worked to expedite check collections in-house and had excess capacity. Now CCF authorizes the processing company to pick up checks received at CCF's post office boxes, pre-encode the checks with the dollar amounts and image those checks, and make the check deposits at CCF's bank. For the checks CCF receives its offices, CCF scans and images them and delivers the check deposits to its bank daily. CCF is now discussing with its bank the possibility of providing the bank images of checks handled by its processor as well as those processed in-house, instead of the physical checks, in order to save costs and gain better availability.

Use lockbox services. Many other large nonprofits tap bank or other third-party lockbox services in which donors' checks are received at a dedicated post office box, which is emptied by processor couriers 15 to 20 times a day and then taken to a specialized check processing operations center for automated document and check processing. Organizations get possible reductions in mail float and assured reductions in processing float and availability float in return for the monthly fee the processor charges. SunTrust and some other banks offer a service for organizations that only have high check deposit volumes twice a year during fundraising campaigns, allowing a minimal maintenance lockbox fee to be assessed during the months in which the service is not being used. Your organization may also elect to use a lockbox service during its capital campaign.

Use check truncation and check conversion. Check truncation (related both to Check 21 legislation implemented in October 2004, and to bank-to-bank bilateral image exchange) and check conversion (point-of-sale conversion of a check to an electronic debit, being used by some healthcare organizations, and lockbox "ARC" conversions of mailed checks to electronic debits) are cutting the processing delay as well as the availability delay in having spendable funds. The effects on your funds' availability of Check 21, which allows check images to be transmitted and then replaced with image prints called "substitute checks," may not be as dramatic or immediate as you hear in the press, however, according to two experts: Carolyn King, vice-president of treasury management, Fifth Third Bank (Columbus, OH), and Wayne Kissinger, group vice-president, Central Region, SunTrust Bank (Atlanta). Also, once new truncation and conversion procedures are implemented and reducing check float, will banks pass all the float gains on to their clients? Maybe not immediately, as they try to recoup some of the infrastructure investments they have made to implement the new clearing processes.

Learn about image capture. Here you feed checks into a scanner-like device attached to your PC and convert them to images, which you then transmit as an electronic deposit to your bank from the location and at the time you choose. "Electronic depositing augments the migration toward paperless banking, using remote capture technology to process images as opposed to the actual paper checks," explains Georgette Cipolla, vice president of product development and product management at Fifth Third Bank. "Whether our customers receive checks by mail, in a drop box, or over the counter, they can deposit them from the security of their own office, significantly reducing the time, effort, and resources expended on remittance processing." You may also be able to deposit items later in the day—Wells Fargo allows customers to electronically deposit as late as 7:00 P.M. Pacific time.

Consider pre-encoding deposits before transporting them to the bank. This process, in which you imprint the dollar amount of the checks on them in magnetic ink, makes sense for organizations having at least 4,000 or 5,000 checks in their monthly deposits, according to William Michels, assistant vice president of global treasury management sales for KeyBank (Cleveland, OH). This gets the organization reduced fees or better availability.

Utilize banks' deposit reconciliation services. Here special deposit tickets cause your deposits from various branches in a geographic region to get deposited into one account (discussed in more depth later in the chapter). This gives you automatic funds concentration and location-by-location accounting. Furthermore, check out zero balance accounts (ZBAs), which allow your deposits in various locations to get transferred via bookkeeping entries to a master account at the same bank that same day without individual transfer fees. You may avoid transfer fees as well as multiple investment sweep fees (discussed later) by using ZBAs.

11.4 DISBURSEMENTS

Just as speeding collections is a recognized cash management tool, so too is the control of disbursements. Disbursements in the form of checks and drafts typically include all payments a nonprofit makes in the course of doing business. These may include payroll, vendor payments, grants, and distributions, to name a few.

(a) DESIGNING THE DISBURSEMENT SYSTEM. A well-planned disbursements system includes well-defined, systematic, and accurate procedures for authorizing, generating, and accounting for payments. Whether a system is paper-based, as with the use of checks, or electronic wire transfers and ACH, the cash manager's task is to orchestrate all the elements of checks, bank services, and the check-clearing process to monitor and control the outflow of funds. A sound disbursement system will help maximize the working capital funds available and enhance overall liquidity.

The disbursement function is handled primarily through bank checking accounts. In the past, delaying payments has been a technique employed to maximize disbursement float—the amount of time that elapses from the moment a check is released to the moment a check is charged to the issuer's account. This disbursement float consists of the sum of mail float, processing float, and clearing float. Managing float is less relevant in a low-interest-rate environment. Furthermore, with electronic payment mechanisms and image exchange of transit checks, float is being largely eliminated from the U.S. payments system.

(b) FRAUD AND INTERNAL CONTROL IN DISBURSEMENTS. Effective check disbursement practices are important for all organizations since many rely on checks as a payment mechanism. The treasury professional will be well served to have check disbursement controls in place to avoid fraud and potential losses. These recommendations for internal control should be built into treasury operations:

- Implement stringent disbursement approval, release, and stop-pay procedures. Ensure that only authorized personnel are performing these functions and that all procedures are documented and kept up-to-date.

- Secure check stock and facsimile signature plates. Remove check stock from printing equipment and store in a locked location when not in use.

- Maintain current signature card and bank agreement files. Update authorized signatories for all organizational and bank network changes. Notify bank of approved signatories on a periodic basis to ensure accuracy of records. Conduct periodic reviews to verify that currently used bank services and all applicable laws are reflected in bank agreements.

- Segregate the disbursement and account reconciliation duties of staff.

- Perform timely checking account reconciliations, preferably before the next month-end.

- Implement stringent voided check procedures. Punch out the signature on the voided check and promptly void the check in the accounts payable system.

- Consider using bank or internal automated account reconciliation, and almost all organizations should use a bank's positive pay services (discussed in more depth later).

- Stay on top of fraud issues related to remote capture of donors' or customers' checks.[9]

- Conduct periodic treasury/internal audit review.

11.5 STRUCTURING A FUNDS MANAGEMENT SYSTEM

The use of a general bank account or a set of accounts for deposits and disbursements is a decision that varies from one nonprofit to another. The choice is largely dictated by the type, size, and complexity of transactions associated with the nonprofit organization's activities. A well-designed bank account configuration is needed to maximize flow of funds, enhance earnings, improve efficiency, and facilitate better control of financial resources.

Cash concentration and *controlled disbursement accounts* are two cash management structures that separate the collection and disbursement of funds. If multiple locations deposit funds, cash concentration can be accomplished electronically through the ACH through the Fed's ACH system. A cash concentration service will transfer funds from any financial institution in the country to a designated bank where the concentration is centralized. Transfers can be prepared at specified cutoff times each day, and funds will be available in one business day. This service offers a number of benefits: It eliminates idle funds in local depository accounts, speeds up identification of available cash, provides the potential for increased earnings on investments or reduced interest costs on debt as a result of funds centralization, enhances control over funds, facilitates quick decision making through timely receipt of deposit information, and provides data for monitoring deposits and balances.

Controlled disbursement eliminates guesswork from daily funding requirements on checks presented for payment. Through a controlled disbursement account, checks are paid through one or more disbursement accounts. Information on checks presented for payment is reported daily, and automatic transfers are made from a checking account to cover the day's disbursement activity. This service can reduce overdrafts and the use of credit lines. With computerized reporting, accurate data collection is possible and clerical workload can be reduced through automatic funding and reporting.

Another cash management tool for disbursement and concentration is an automated *zero balance account*. The process links any number of disbursement or depository accounts. At the end of business each day, all balances over designated cash levels are transferred to a concentration account. Conversely, all balances below the designated level are automatically covered by transfers from a concentration account. Funds transfers from and to a single concentration account are handled automatically, and balances in disbursement and depository accounts can be set at a target amount or at zero. By eliminating idle balances in accounts and centralizing cash, better control will reduce overdrafts and increase efficiency in managing cash.

11.6 MONITORING BANK BALANCES AND TRANSACTIONS

Accurate and timely information on cash balances is essential to managing liquidity and making critical financial decisions about the use of funds. Today information on bank transactions, deposits, payments, return items, and other activities are readily accessible through a wide variety of mechanisms. These range from manual reporting by voice operator and touchtone devices to Internet access to balance data. Account reconciliation services help your organization "balance its checkbook."

(a) BALANCE REPORTING AND TRANSACTION INITIATION. *Bank-balance reporting* is a product that conveniently provides the cash manager access to bank account activity and information. Using a computer, dial-ups or web browser access to a bank's portal can be automatically programmed to gather balance information from as many banks as required or manually initiated. Balance reports include current ledger and collected balances, deposits subject to one- and two-day availability, error adjustments and resolutions, balance history, and average balance over previous time periods. Details of debits and credits, lockbox transactions, borrowing and investments, concentration reports, and other transactions can also be downloaded.

In addition to information retrieval, initiation of transactions such as wire transfers and ACH payments is now possible using cash management software and over the Internet. Services can be customized and expanded as needs change. Security features include passwords and multiple levels of identification codes, along with some new handheld devices. The use of cash management and information systems offers many benefits in terms of monitoring and controlling account activity, locating cash surpluses or shortages for more productive use of funds, enhancing cash forecasting, allowing stop payments, and reducing clerical time and expense in tracking cash positions. Investment activity and foreign exchange reporting can also be downloaded using bank information systems.

Automated information systems are widely available and competitively priced. They offer convenience and efficiency in cash management, and nonprofits are well served to use them. Information gathering is significantly enhanced, and the demand for timely information by management and trustees can be satisfied.

(b) ACCOUNT RECONCILIATION. Timely and accurate reconciliation of check payments is now effectively handled through account reconciliation services. Many banks offer a full or partial *account reconciliation service* to provide accounting on the status of checks issued. This can include paid, outstanding, exception, stopped, voided, or canceled items. Use of the service helps to balance an account faster, improves audit control, and provides protection against unauthorized, altered, and stopped checks. This service is most advantageous when a significant number of checks is written each month. It can simplify bookkeeping procedures and reduce staff time in balancing accounts.

Deposit reconciliation is another application suited to nonprofits with multiple locations depositing into a single account. The service segregates deposits by location and lists nonreporting relations. Through special serial-number groupings, daily reporting, and comprehensive monthly reports, the service facilitates auditing and enhances control over local depository activity. At the same time, the convenience and economy of a single depository account can be retained.

An invaluable service now offered by banks is *positive pay*. This option provides daily access for authenticating check payment by comparing checks issued to checks paid. A bank provides a daily list of nonmatching checks paid, and the exception is submitted to the organization. Instruction for payment or return of checks on the list can be given to ensure payment of legitimate checks only. This service is another tool for controlling fraud and is accessible online with the bank.

Overdrafts are likely to occur without a reliable cash forecasting and balance reporting system. Timely information on the status of disbursing accounts will enable a cash manager to move funds and avoid overdrafts. Monitoring funds availability is also important to minimize ledger overdrafts. When overdrafts occur, there are costs incurred aside from the interest expense charge or one-time fee that is assessed. Opportunity costs arise in terms of income lost from forgone investments, costs associated with transferring funds, and costs of delayed payments on bills (lost discounts, ill will, and other related costs). For a nonprofit institution making distributions to planned giving donors, donor relation issues are very sensitive, and accuracy is critical. Arrangements for overdraft protection or a line of credit would be advisable.

Aside from normal overdrafts, *daylight overdrafts* occur when funds are not sufficient to cover a transfer although the negative balance is covered by the end of the day. With Federal Reserve policy discouraging daylight overdrafts, banks pass charges to their customers. To avoid daylight overdrafts, accounts should be monitored intraday. Fedwire payment outflows can be timed to correspond with the availability of Fed funds from incoming transactions. Another technique is to match the method of payment with the source of covering funds. For example, wires and ACH payments settle differently, and it would be costly to rely on ACH deposits that may not be available to cover the amount of outbound wires.

11.7 CASH FORECASTING

The cash management practice we see as the most ripe for improvement in the nonprofit world is cash forecasting. An organization is hindered in numerous ways when not having an updated forecast of forthcoming cash inflows, outflows, and the resulting cash position. Three results we observe often are:

1. Spending cash that would have been held had one foreseen that a seasonal "dry period" was ahead

2. Holding minimal cash reserves due to ignorance regarding the cash drain attending program growth

3. Holding large cash reserves and giving up interest yield because too large a portion of the organization's funds are held in overnight investments or a demand deposit account

Treasury Strategies finds that companies that forecast cash positions and also base their investment maturity selection on the forecast earn an additional 31 basis points in yield per year (about 3/10 of 1 percent).[10] We expect nonprofits would earn this same additional yield.

Cash forecasting is a valuable treasury tool. It begins with a definition of objectives for the forecast and a realistic assessment of the structure and activities of an organization. Forecasting allows management to evaluate changing conditions and formulate appropriate financial strategies. As a planning tool, cash forecasts (also called cash budgets) have to be monitored and updated to reflect both short- and long-term variables. (See Chapter 8 for more on cash budgeting.)

Depending on a nonprofit's funding and operational needs, cash forecasts can determine optimal borrowing and investment strategies. Many nonprofits rely on gift contributions for funding, and their timing is difficult to project. Accordingly, gathering information from internal sources is more predictable, particularly with the expense side of the equation. Common sources of receipt data are a nonprofit's sales (or program) units and accounts receivable departments. Disbursement data would come from those responsible for purchasing and accounts payable, as well as the human resource area for payroll and benefits data.

(a) CASH SCHEDULING.   For some organizations, a monthly cash forecast does not give enough detail, and *cash scheduling* may be a more relevant technique in determining the organization's short-term cash position (one day to six weeks). The process begins with a forecast of deposits to plan the timing and amount of funds for cash concentration. Simultaneously, estimates are made on when checks will be presented. When concentration and disbursement accounts are used, cash scheduling will help the cash manager to mobilize funds without giving up the opportunity costs associated with excess and idle balances. Ideally, balances can be maintained at target levels in the appropriate concentration or disbursement account.

(b) DATA ELEMENTS FOR CASH FLOW ESTIMATES.   Receipt and disbursement items vary among nonprofits but mirror treasury transactions in a typical corporate environment. In a broad sense, projecting collections and payables is necessary to determine the timing of each cash flow component, although there may be little control over certain inflows associated with fundraising. Trends and patterns over certain time periods can provide a good basis for arranging financing alternatives during slow months or investing surplus cash longer without risking penalty for early termination of an investment position. Statistical methods of analysis and qualitative techniques may be used in combination to arrive at a reasonable cash forecast.

Estimating the amount and timing of various receipts and disbursements can be time consuming. However, with coordination from various units that have an input to the process, a reasonable forecast can bridge gaps and improve financial planning. Management and marketing/public relations issues must be considered along with payment policies on early-payment discounts and costs that may be unnecessarily incurred due to overdrafts.

Receipts	Disbursements
Lockbox collections	Vendor (supplier) payments
Deposits	Payroll, benefits
Loans/credit lines	Programmatic expenses
Pledge payments	Grants and allocations
Debt proceeds	Debt repayments and interest expense
Maturing investments	Insurance payments
Income from investments	Distributions for planned gifts
Endowment fund distributions	
Stock gift proceeds	

11.8 SHORT-TERM BORROWING

External financing is an alternative source of funds when no surplus cash is available to meet working capital shortfalls. To account for both short- and long-term financing needs, it is necessary to have a complete picture of the sources and uses of funds, linked to both operational and strategic plans of the organization. Major capital and program expenditures would require a different type of financing, and, typically, loans have to be collateralized.

For liquidity purposes, a bank credit line may be sufficient to fill temporary or seasonal financing needs. This credit line is generally an unsecured loan made on the basis of the borrower's financial strength. Borrowing against a line of credit is usually in the form of specific notes for set maturities, such as overnight, 7 days, 14 days, or 60 days. The cost to borrow varies and is usually negotiated or reconfirmed annually. Most credit lines carry a variable interest rate based on an agreed base rate. Depending on the perceived risk and the negotiating position of the organization, the interest rate may include a specified spread over the base rate. Interest payments are frequently made monthly or at the maturity of the loan.

Banks usually require compensation for offering a credit line in the form of balances and/or fees. The interest rate on a loan may be negotiated depending on the level of balances held at the bank. Likewise, other activities in the relationship and the overall profitability of the nonprofit's account will affect pricing.

In addition to a bank line of credit, deferring payment on disbursements can be a temporary source of liquidity applying to vendors and other suppliers. However, deferred payments should not be pursued without taking into account the cost of missed discounts in the terms of sale or a penalty fee for late payment. Implicit costs associated with loss of goodwill and damaged credit rating should not be overlooked. In certain situations, internal financing may also be an option. For example, borrowing against an endowment portfolio may be possible on an arm's-length basis. For such transactions, careful attention must be given to the terms and conditions of the loan to avoid any potential conflict of interest. For more on financing, see our extended presentation in Chapter 10.

11.9 SHORT-TERM INVESTING

Chapter 12 discusses strategies and instruments for short-term investing. This section addresses some basic considerations. When surplus cash is available, it can be managed to meet liquidity needs or invested. The first step is to determine whether funds are cash reserves solely for operating purpose or available over a longer time frame. Understanding this would enable the cash manager to develop an appropriate strategy to maximize earnings and satisfy liquidity requirements.

With funds managed in a fiduciary capacity, the cash manager's foremost investment objective is safety of principal. Many investment instruments are available, and it is important to understand the market and the types of securities that are bought and sold. Whatever the reason for short-term investing, specific policies and guidelines should be defined prior to making any investment. Investment policies and guidelines should state investment objectives, define tolerance for risk, address liquidity factors, identify the level of return or yield acceptable for different instruments, and identify personnel roles and responsibilities regarding the implementation and monitoring of an investment program. Poor investment judgment, assumption of imprudent risks, assignment of responsibilities to unqualified personnel, and fraud can lead to opportunity costs and loss of principal.

From a cash management perspective, these suggestions are offered:

- Provide copies of investment guidelines to your banker, money manager, or broker with whom you will trade; this will be a good basis for developing appropriate investment strategies and identifying suitable financial instruments.

- Arrange for safekeeping of securities; this offers added security and control and facilitates the audit of securities held. If safekeeping is maintained with the relationship bank, include cost of service in bank account analysis.

- In the absence of a custody or safekeeping account, document instructions for transfer of funds and designate specific accounts for payment of trade proceeds.

- Institute proper operational procedures and controls for investment activities.

- Provide a list of authorized personnel and their specimen signatures.

- Review all portfolio holdings for compliance with credit quality ratings.

- Determine the value of portfolio holding and marked-to-market securities.

- Assimilate investment activities into funds-flow forecasts to manage liquidity.

In addition to these general recommendations, we have these specific recommendations. Consider this question: What can the organization do once it has the cash in position to invest (assuming it has paid down short-term borrowings)?

First, what are you still doing with a "free checking" account? You can do better, unless your financial institution is providing you with an abnormally high earnings credit rate that is applied to your average balance to offset service fees. Like consumers, nonprofits are eligible for Negotiable Order of Withdrawal (NOW) accounts that pay interest. The interest rate paid on these accounts may be negligible, however, and must be compared to the fees charged by the bank for its banking services. As the organization becomes larger and begins to consistently hold five-digit balances in the account, it is time to be manually moving some of that to savings or money market accounts. For organizations with $60,000 or more in liquid funds, consider automatic sweep accounts, in which monies above a set dollar amount are automatically "swept out" of the account at the close of business and into an interest-earning investment; these funds are then returned to the account the next day to cover disbursements. (We present more information on sweep accounts in the next section.)

For larger organizations having the time to manage excess funds, Mellon Global Cash Management has a Web-based investment tool called Liquidity Management Service (LMS). This appeals to organizations wishing to invest money actively in a menu of options including Mellon mutual funds as well as other investments available from a broker-dealer. The investor does not have to have a bank account at Mellon and can purchase money funds and securities online through LMS, which already has $5 billion in assets.

(a) BANK SWEEP ACCOUNTS/INVESTMENT SERVICES.   One way to handle short-term investing is through *sweep accounts*. It is natural for banks, the location where your surplus funds build up, to offer fee-based investment services. Banks offer their own securities as well as serve as brokers for other institutions' securities. The bank offers investors its own instruments, or those of its parent holding company, as a means of purchasing funds that the bank can loan out or invest. In addition to offering investment securities, many banks offer corporate agency services to safeguard the company's investments, manage trusts and pensions, and handle record keeping related to bonds your organization has issued.

Popular investments your organization can buy through a bank include repurchase agreements (often as part of a sweep agreement), commercial paper, certificates of deposit, and treasury bills. We will discuss only repurchase agreements and sweep accounts here.

A repurchase agreement, or "repo" as it is often called, involves the bank selling the investor a portfolio of securities, then agreeing to buy the securities back (repurchase) at an agreed-on future date. The securities act as collateral for the investor, to protect against the possibility that the bank will default on the repurchase. The difference between the selling price and the repurchase price constitutes the interest.

Quite often, banks will set up a sweep arrangement to automate the repurchase decision-making process, sparing the treasurer daily investment evaluations. All balances above those necessary to compensate the bank for services or to fund disbursements are swept nightly into repos. The bank may also impose a $1,000 minimum sweep amount to eliminate small-dollar transfers. Transfers are accomplished by a set of bookkeeping entries at the bank. Excess balances are invested for one business day, with the principal amount credited to the checking account the following day. An investment report is produced daily, indicating the amount of the daily investment, the interest rate, the amount of interest earned, and what investment security stands behind (is collateralizing) the investment. As an added advantage of such arrangements, some banks will not charge the company for an overdraft if the sum of the available balance and the repurchased amounts is sufficient to cover presentments, choosing instead to cover the checks with the bank's funds.

You may wonder what interest rate you can receive on such a short-term investment. Exhibit 11.8 shows the rate structures that existed at one point in time for two large midwestern banks. Bank A calculates its interest rate in this way:

- Up to $1 million, Fed funds rate minus 1.3 percent
- From $1 million to $5 million, Fed funds rate minus 1 percent
- Over $5 million, Fed funds rate minus 0.6 percent

The message is clear: If you still have a (NOW) account, you are better off transferring your money into an overnight investment because the yield pickup is significant. Finally, you will be charged a monthly fee plus a daily transfer fee for the sweep account, and the automated sweep-account fee is slightly higher than a manually operated sweep. These fees must be weighed against the increased interest revenue to determine if your organization would profit from establishing a sweep account.

As an example of a sweep account and two choices that you may have in establishing one, consider KeyBank's product offering (see Exhibit 11.9). The sweep account interest rate was between 5.5 and 6.0 percent in 2000, but the interest rate dropped to 3.3 percent in late 2001 and further as the Fed cut interest rates. Rates again climbed in 2005 and 2006 as the Fed raised interest rates. Key's sweep accounts include a monthly fee and a fee if the organization either falls below the minimum balance or exceeds the

	Bank A	Bank B
Amount Invested	Annualized Interest Rate* (%)	Annualized Interest Rate (%)
$0–$999,999	4.00	4.85
$1–$2M	4.25	4.90
$2–$5M	4.25	4.95
$ 5–$10M	4.45	5.05
$10M +	4.45	5.15

*Bank A does not have a minimum transfer amount, and calculates yield using a formula based on the amount invested each day.

EXHIBIT 11.8   EXAMPLES OF INTEREST EARNED ON REPOS

KeyBank offers two sweep accounts:

- **Business Total Access** sweeps anything over $10,000 daily into any of seven Victory funds, KeyBank's proprietary mutual funds. Nonprofits or sole proprietors have the option to sweep into FDIC-insured products, as well. The fee: $11.50 a month or $125 annually. The fall-below fee is $10.75 a month.

- **Business Investment Account** is a zero-balance account where all incoming funds are put to work. ZBA accounts are tailored to upper-end small businesses ($7 million-plus) seeking the greater returns of a cash management service. This account fee is $125 a month.

Source: http://www.bankrate.com/.

Exhibit 11.9   Two Types of Sweep Accounts

maximum number of monthly free sweep transactions. In 2003 many nonprofits turned off their sweep accounts, as the fees exceeded potential interest yield from the accounts.[11] Notice in the first sweep account that nonprofits have the advantage of getting monies swept into either mutual funds or FDIC-insured accounts.

The economics of sweep accounts change as interest rates move up or down. Both Carolyn King (Fifth Third Bank) and Wayne Kissinger (SunTrust Bank) note that a number of their clients' sweep accounts that were inactive are being turned back on now that short-term interest rates have risen above 2 percent and continue to rise. The economics are straightforward: Let's say the organization is receiving a negligible interest rate on its checking account and would pay $150 per month to have the sweep service in place. If it can normally sweep $60,000 out on an overnight basis, with interest rates of 3 percent, it is exactly covering that $150 monthly cost ($150 × 12 = $1,800 per year; $1,800 = $60,000 × 0.03); either higher balances or higher sweep investment account interest rates provide an interest income for the organization and make it profitable to use the sweep account.

(b) INSTITUTIONAL MONEY MARKET FUNDS.   Many sweeps will move your money into an institutional money market mutual fund. Or you may choose to invest in a money fund via a separate investment decision, done manually. To know whether your yield is competitive on a money fund, compare it to iMoneyNet's published yields. For example, in early 2006, the leading institutional money funds were yielding over 4.5 percent, with a weighted-average maturity (WAM) of investments in their portfolios of between 15 and 52 days (see Exhibit 11.10). The longer the WAM, the more the yield will lag further upward movements in short-term interest rates (an advantage if rates are moving lower, but a disadvantage as rates move higher).

Treasury Strategies survey research indicates that the vehicle into which sweep monies is moved is approximately equally divided between money market mutual funds, direct investments (repos or commercial paper), and offshore instruments.[12]

If you have operations abroad, the availability of bank-provided overnight investing varies considerably. In many cases, you will want to invest foreign cash flows abroad in order to minimize the need to convert to dollars and back to foreign currency for later needs, which incurs charges for you in transactions costs as well as the risk you bear of the exchange rate changing.

Prime Institutional MMFs data as of February 28, 2006

Fund Name	7-Day Yield (%)	WAM	Assets ($mils)	Minimum Investment
State Street Instit Liquid Reserves (877) 521–4083	4.57%	31	$2,452.0	$25,000,000
Credit Suisse Instit MMF/Prime/Cl A (800) 222–8977	4.53%	36	$755.4	$1,000,000
Frank Russell MMF/Cl S (800) 787–7354	4.52%	47	$3,447.7	-
BGI Instit MMF/Instit I (877) 244–1544	4.51%	38	$3,877.0	$10,000,000
Morgan Stanley Instit Liq/MMP/Instit (888) 378–1630	4.51%	37	$3,594.6	$10,000,000
AIM STIT STIC Prime/Instit (800) 659–1005	4.49%	15	$5,915.1	$10,000,000
Amer Beacon MM Select Fund (800) 231–4252	4.49%	30	$7,299.8	$25,000,000
Columbia Prime Reserves/Capital (800) 353–0828	4.49%	43	$2,779.7	$5,000,000
Morgan Stanley Instit Liq/Prime/Inst (888) 378–1630	4.48%	34	$18,077.0	$10,000,000
Putnam Prime MMF/Cl I (800) 225–1581	4.48%	52	$339.3	$10,000,000
Reserve Primary Fund Cl 8 (888) 851–7237	4.48%	45	$13,284.8	$50,000,000
Vanguard Prime MMF/Instit (800) 662–7447	4.48%	37	$5,314.3	$5,000,000

Note: Rankings include only funds with $100 million or more and exclude restricted funds.

E-mail iMoneyNet: info@imoneynet.com

Source: http://www.imoneynet.com/. Used by permission..

EXHIBIT 11.10   LARGE INSTITUTIONAL MONEY MARKET FUNDS

11.10 BENCHMARKING TREASURY FUNCTIONS

Benchmarking is a process through which an organization compares its internal performance to external standards of excellence. For example, short-term investment performance results are compared by one organization to the Merrill Lynch institutional money fund yield as well as to LIBOR (the London InterBank Offered Rate, which is the rate at which large banks lend and borrow U.S. dollars in the London market). The objective of benchmarking is to achieve and sustain optimum performance through continual process improvement. Unless an effort is made to clearly understand the non-profit's mission, operations, staffing, and services provided as well as its customers and other stakeholders, improvement will be slow.

(a) LARGER ORGANIZATIONS.   Total quality management (TQM) is a process that has been applied to treasury functions. Many times it is simply called continuous improvement. The four steps involved include: (1) Creating a vision and mission statement; (2) understanding suppliers, customers, and the "big picture"; (3) encouraging cross-functional collaboration; and (4) focusing problem solving on removing root causes in order to produce significant gains. Involving the bank relationship manager and other vendors in assessments will provide valuable feedback to internal staff. Strengths and weaknesses are addressed for various types of processes. The TQM process also relies on quantitative measures and statistical data gathering to evaluate results and monitor process improvement. Through regular reviews/audits, fine-tuning can be pursued and changes can be instituted in an organized manner. Nonprofits must approach their business in the same way as for-profit corporations. In so doing, they will be more proactive than reactive, and, ultimately, better efficiency will result in cost savings.

The account analysis statement is a useful source of information for evaluating the quality and cost of various bank services. Transaction volumes can be plotted and analyzed to gauge patterns in lockbox collections, wire transfers, and return items, to name a few examples. Benchmarking can be valuable and should encompass a broad range of activities to provide a meaningful basis for improvement.

(b) SMALLER ORGANIZATIONS.   We have developed a checklist for the many nonprofits that are smaller (i.e., $2.5 million in annual revenues or less) so that you can compare your practices and policies to what might be considered "best practices" (see Exhibit 11.11).

11.11 UPGRADING THE CALIBER OF TREASURY PROFESSIONALS

Cash managers of nonprofits must stay abreast of regulatory, service, and product changes. Many major cities have regional treasury associations that provide extensive educational opportunities for practitioners. These typically have as part of their organizational name either "Treasury Management Association" or "Financial Professionals." Participation in treasury conferences, such as the Association for Financial Professionals (AFP; see www.afponline.org),[13] or other forums on electronic payments (the annual AFP Payments Forum, as well as the National Automated Clearing House Association's (NACHA's) annual payments conference or the five-day Payments Institute; see www.nacha.org) will provide tremendous exposure to current and emerging technologies and information. Industry publications, bank newsletters, and technical books are additional sources of information.

Likewise, network with peers and corporate treasury professionals to accelerate learning opportunities and implement changes that can be applied in your treasury department. An enlightened treasury professional is an asset to every nonprofit, and management must invest in staff advancement opportunities.

Cross-training of staff should be supported to ensure continuity in operations. Ongoing training is recommended with backup personnel assigned to critical treasury functions. As advances in technology lead to changes in how tasks are performed, it is advisable to document procedures. A manual should be maintained and updated to reflect any organizational, bank, and system changes that may occur in procedures for initiating wire transfers and ACH transactions. Documentation pertaining to banking resolutions, authorized signatories, and investment guidelines should also be included. Centralized record keeping will ensure continuity and minimize disruptions in operations.

This checklist outline, while applicable to nonprofits of all sizes, especially fits the environment in which smaller nonprofit organizations operate.

I. Cash Management: General Guidelines and Best Practices
   A. Organizational Issues
      1. Policies in place for cash management, who is authorized to do what (with dollar limits), short-term investments, and long-term investments.
      2. Board has one or more persons with financial expertise and has a functioning and effective finance committee and audit committee
      3. CFO/Treasurer has financial education, training, a heart for the mission, ability to say no persuasively, and (ideally) nonprofit experience
      4. Organization taps service provider expertise
         (a) Bank or Credit Union
         (b) Auditor
         (c) Information System Provider
      5. Organization uses volunteers and college interns effectively
      6. Organization taps the power of Microsoft Excel™ for financial reports and modeling
   B. Cash Management
      1. Brings cash in quickly and accurately
         (a) Donations and dues: collects electronically if possible
         (b) Loans and advances: doesn't allow delays in related payments
         (c) Service fees and sales revenue: is assertive, does not allow buyers to "stretch payables"
         (d) Uses bank/third-party and/or internal treasury information services as an ally to verify inflow amounts and timing
      2. Mobilizes cash: pooling, employing, protecting, amassing, monitoring funds
         (a) Pools funds: does not allow small balances to remain in multiple accounts
         (b) Employs funds: puts "funds awaiting investment" to work
         (c) Protects funds: watches for and guards against foreign exchange risk and interest rate risk
         (d) Amasses funds (some controversy here):
             i. Faith-based organizations do not excuse lack of planning, but exercise collective faith proactively (build now) rather than reactively (scramble once in crisis) to assemble needed cash reserves[a]
             ii. 3–6 months of expenses in operating reserves for emergencies, rainy-day fund, missed forecasts, unforeseen opportunities
             iii. As much as 1–2 years of expenses in pre-funding account for planned needs such as loan repayments, capital expenditures, program expansion, earned income venture launch, etc; this is driven by inability to issue stock and/or inability or unwillingness to use various forms of debt financing
         (e) Monitors funds using bank/third-party and/or internal treasury information services as an ally to help control fund balances
      3. Pay out cash slowly and cautiously
         (a) Uses separate disbursement account
         (b) Uses positive pay (provide check issue file to bank, bank contacts organization regarding any item discrepancies) or reverse positive pay (bank forwards file of presented items, awaits OK from organization)
         (c) Pays on terms, not before terms, unless receiving cash discount
         (d) Uses bank/third-party and/or internal treasury information services as an ally to verify outflow amounts and timing
         (e) Uses purchasing cards where appropriate
             i. Saving time and expense of purchase order processes
             ii. Possibly gaining quantity discounts or rebates for usage

EXHIBIT 11.11 CHECKLIST: CASH AND INVESTMENT MANAGEMENT BEST PRACTICES

---

4. Recognizes value of Internet-based bank and treasury information
   (a) Corporations report significant impact of Internet on treasury
       i. Finding better access for real-time treasury information
       ii. Finding wider access to bank data, including self-service bank account inquiry abilities, ability to work remotely, less need for treasury staff training, and ability to spend time on strategic issues
   (b) But also note that may have to shop and negotiate for these services
5. Forecasts cash position and cash needs
   (a) First converts operating budget to cash budget (a.k.a. cash forecast) or develops standalone cash budget (translate receivables, payables, depreciation amounts)
   (b) Starts with next year by months
   (c) Then develops forecast of next month by weeks
   (d) Then develops next week by days
   (e) Finally ends with setting daily cash position by midday, allowing better bank balance management and possibly authorizing sweep account for automated overnight investing

---

*a*The principle of saving relevant to many faith traditions is taught in the Old Testament (Proverbs 21:20): "There is treasure to be desired and oil in the dwelling of the wise; but a foolish man spendeth it up."

EXHIBIT 11.11 CHECKLIST: CASH AND INVESTMENT MANAGEMENT BEST PRACTICES (*continued*)

11.12 SECURITY AND RISK MANAGEMENT ISSUES

Nonprofit organizations have a fiduciary responsibility for the gifts and donations that constitute a large percentage of their revenues. Recent events associated with fraud, failed investments, rogue brokers, and other financial losses have created concerns beyond risks normally associated with financial instrument quality or creditworthiness. There are various types of financial risk, and a prudent risk management program is relevant not only for treasury functions, but also throughout the entire organization.

(a) TYPES OF FINANCIAL RISK. Here are the significant types of financial risk that may affect your organization:

- *Market risk.* Risk of change in market price of an underlying instrument, which may be due to adverse movements in currency exchange rates, interest rates, commodity and equity markets, as well as time value of money
- *Liquidity risk.* Risk associated with illiquidity which can adversely affect pricing of a security
- *Credit risk.* Risk of counterparty default on an obligation
- *Legal risk.* Loss exposure due to unenforceable contracts caused by documentation deficiencies
- *Funding risk.* Risk from internal cash flow deficiencies
- *Operational risk.* Risk of unexpected loss due to system malfunction, inaccurate accounting and record keeping, settlement failure, human errors, incorrect market valuation, and fraud

An effective risk management program begins with identifying and understanding risk. Top management must be knowledgeable about the types of risk that could potentially threaten financial and operational stability. Once identified, appropriate measures can be instituted and tolerance levels defined. The tolerance levels your management and board agrees can be assumed by your organization will have a bearing on the limits set for transactional volumes, the means of avoiding fraud, and the proper checks and balances to be instituted in operating setups. Protection against certain risks may translate into higher insurance premiums or added to the costs of doing business. Hedging strategies using derivatives are helpful in protecting investments or loans against adverse interest rate movement. However, the use of derivatives must be fully understood, and investment guidelines should clearly state which specific transactions are allowed or disallowed.

The most common financial risk for nonprofits may be related to market exposure and volatility for investment assets. Investment guidelines must be formulated to clearly define permitted transactions, credit quality, exposure limits, maturity or duration parameters, safekeeping, and trading authority. See Chapter 12 for more on these considerations.

(b) FRAUD.   Fraud is another type of risk that confronts many organizations, as we noted in our earlier discussion of internal control. Check fraud has led to mounting losses with illegal check schemes on the rise. The increase in check fraud is attributed primarily to the widespread availability of inexpensive desktop publishing software and laser printing equipment. Section 11.4 discusses in detail ways to counteract check fraud.

Natural disasters, fires, and other *forces majeure* have to be anticipated. Contingency plans for business resumption should be drawn, and recovery measures should be well communicated throughout the organization. Ongoing review and testing are imperative to cover changes in operations, personnel, and procedures. Offsite storage of critical documents, backup procedures for computer applications, emergency banking arrangements, and other key operations must be covered and priorities set. It is also worth looking at out-of-state banking alternatives and utilizing those accounts for emergencies. However, proper authorizations and procedures have to be spelled out. Nowadays, heavy reliance on electronic processing and initiation of transactions using computer terminals can lead to paralysis in the event of a power failure. Nonautomated alternatives should be explored particularly with funds transfer mechanisms (e.g., voice or phone transfers with callback procedures). Another measure includes documenting all account information, contact persons, telephone numbers, and other essential data in both hard copy and disk or other media. All should be housed in a separate but secure location. Redundant systems may save tremendous time and expense in the event of a disaster. Being without a contingency plan is risky, and adequate preparation is essential to every treasury operation.

Fraud is also possible with electronic payments. One concern is the fraud in telephone-initiated electronic payments, using the "TEL" format. Exhibit 11.12 profiles the issues from NACHA's perspective. If you are considering doing one-time pledge collections or other special one-time consumer receivables collections using telephone-initiated debits to individuals' bank accounts, you should be aware of the misuse and anticipate possible donor resistance to allowing these debits because of merchants' misuse.

11.13 TRENDS IN TREASURY MANAGEMENT

Nonprofit organizations are faced with increasing cost pressures and competition for donated funds. In such an environment, eliminating inefficiencies and maximizing cost savings have become imperative.

(a) REENGINEERING.   Total quality and reengineering processes are providing opportunities and solutions. Outsourcing is another option that has been gaining acceptance. It is best that treasury practitioners focus their resources on their core competencies

While the TEL application was developed to facilitate the use of automated payments for one-time consumer debit entries, intentional misuse of the application is resulting in an increasing number of unauthorized consumer debit entries. It has become apparent that some of these entries have been initiated as a result of deceptive and fraudulent telemarketing practices. Examples of the types of complaints that NACHA has received concerning misuse of TEL entries are described below:

- Merchants operating with fraudulent intent debit the consumer without having obtained the consumer's authorization for such a transaction.

- Merchants operating with fraudulent intent violate the rules by cold calling consumers with whom they have no existing relationship and subsequently debiting the consumer.

- Merchants operating within the boundaries of the TEL rules by using mail solicitations to instruct the consumer to initiate the telephone call to the merchant and subsequently attempting to sell their wares using deceptive marketing practices.

It has become obvious that there is a correlation between high return rates relating to unauthorized debits and originators that are violating the rules or that are engaged in fraudulent/deceptive marketing practices. These merchants are experiencing a volume of unauthorized returns in excess of the average for other unauthorized debit entries.

Source: http://www.nacha.org/, 2002_bulletins—2.doc. Accessed: 3/4/06. Used by permission.

EXHIBIT 11.12 TELEPHONE-INITIATED ELECTRONIC PAYMENTS FRAUD CONCERNS

and outsource tasks that can be handled effectively by external service providers. Notes Wayne Kissinger of SunTrust Bank: "For any bank product your organization is considering, ask yourself two questions: (1) Will this product make me more productive by taking activity and time commitment out of my back office and allowing me to focus on work that is more essential to my organization; and (2) Will this product give me valuable information, such as whether to honor a check that has been presented to my account that was not in my original check issue file?"

(b) AUTOMATION AND TECHNOLOGY. Technology is replacing many paper-based applications as it becomes more affordable and accessible. However, technology leads to the need for greater security, fraud control, and regulatory requirement. In implementing new processes driven by technological advances, nonprofits should not cut costs at the expense of flexibility and control.

Increased integration of business systems is another trend made possible by advances in technology. Functions such as accounting, accounts payable, accounts receivable, purchasing, and inventory can now be linked. Related financial services, such as cash management, securities, trust, and custody products, are available through computer interfaces and provide significant enhancement to information reporting. Fully integrated systems will serve as a cornerstone of the financial function of a nonprofit organization, providing control, decision support, and audit trails. Linking systems not only enhances productivity, but also minimizes input errors when rekeying information. Faster availability of financial information is helpful in analyzing and reengineering work flow.

As more of the treasury function becomes automated, the administrative costs savings mount. Exhibit 11.13 shows that the cost of the treasury function ranges from 0.02 percent to 0.42 percent of total revenues for businesses, with an average of 0.16 percent (16/100 of 1 percent). However, with automation, this average drops to 0.02 percent—a $14 million annual cost savings for a company with $10 billion in annual revenue.

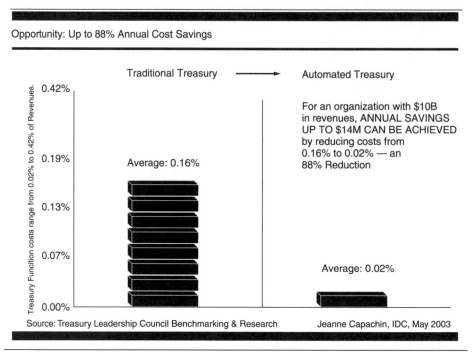

Opportunity: Up to 88% Annual Cost Savings

Source: www.trema.com/. Accessed: 3/3/2006. Used by permission.

EXHIBIT 11.13   SAVINGS REALIZABLE FROM TREASURY AUTOMATION

(c) TAPPING SERVICE PROVIDER EXPERTISE.   Partnerships with banks or service providers should be explored. Changes that can benefit treasury practices are oftentimes known in advance by bank officers. A good relationship can be a worthwhile investment.

(d) CASH MANAGEMENT IN PRACTICE.   In the appendix to Chapter 1 we noted the profile of cash management in the charitable nonprofit sector. In this brief overview, we note some newer evidence regarding cash and treasury management.

The good news is that, over the period from early 2003 to early 2005, one-fourth of all nonprofits indicated that they "added or strengthened asset or cash management procedures."[14] You may be surprised to find out why: The changes were in response to financial audits. We believe that most of these changes are internal control improvements, but the fact that any aspect of cash management is getting more attention is very positive.

The second trend regarding cash management in practice refers to what is happening on the banking front. According to the annual Ernst & Young "Cash Management Survey," low interest rates and declining paper-based payments are reducing cash management provider profitability. Lower profitability for electronic payments, and less importance attributed to convenient deposit locations, portends lower profits for cash management providers for the next several years.

A notable trend is increased sales of purchasing cards (also called procurement cards, or p-cards), which are reducing corporate check payments as well as related account reconciliation services. The number of active purchasing cards increased by 15 percent in 2004. These cards, which are dedicated purpose credit cards, greatly reduce costs (no more requisitions, purchase orders, postage, checks, check reconcilement for many small-dollar payments) and simplify reconcilement of payments. Another trend is the increased use of ARC (Account Receivable Conversion), which entails converting lockbox-received checks to ACH debits: This trend reduced the number of checks processed in the United States by 1 billion in 2004. Finally, almost every cash management bank now offers Internet-initiated transfers between accounts and Web-based balance and information reporting ability. Almost every cash management bank also offers initiation of ACH and wire transfers via the Internet. Larger banks are now offering handheld devices to maintain user access security, including smart cards, tokens, or SecurID®.[15]

The future holds more commoditization of cash management services, and the great leveler, the Internet, suggests that even the smallest nonprofits will be able to harness powerful banking services without paying significant fees.

Notes

1. Illinois Facilities Fund and Donors Forum of Chicago, "Getting It Right: How Illinois Non-profits Manage for Success.," 2004. Located online at: www.donorsforum.org/forms_pdf/GettingItRight.pdf. Accessed: 3/3/2006.

2. See Paul Brest, "Smart Money: General Operating Grants Can Be Strategic—for Nonprofits and Foundations," *Stanford Social Innovation Review* (Winter 2003): 44–53; and Nonprofit Finance Fund, "The Flap about General Operating Support: Risk Minus Cash Equals Crisis," 2004. Available online at: www.nonprofitfinancefund.org/docs/Risk_minus_Cash_Website.pdf. Accessed: 3/3/06.

3. Association for Financial Professionals Directory of Service Providers; this is now available online, searchable by service desired, at: www.afponline.org/pub/tsd/cgi/guide.cgi.

4. Powerful software is available to compare different banks' account analysis statements. The software, called BAWeb, may be reviewed at: www.weiland-wfg.com/ba_web.htm.

5. NACHA statistics, cited in PNC, "Direct Deposit/Direct Payment," located online at: www.treasury.pncbank.com/directpayment.html. Accessed: 3/3/2006.

6. Michael Becknell, "Why Electronic Giving Makes a Lot of Sense," *Church Executive* (June 2005): 20–21.

7. Research cited in PNC, "Direct Deposit/Direct Payment."

8. Celent, "The Future of Check Processing in the U.S.," October 27, 2004. The consulting firm Financial Insights made a similar prediction.

9. For more on this, see the BITS Financial Services Roundtable report, "Strategies for Mitigating Fraud Risks Associated with the Check Clearing in the 21st Century Act," available at the time of this writing at: www.bitsinfo.org/downloads/Misc/check21oct04.pdf.

10. Treasury Strategies, "2005 U.S. Corporate Liquidity Research Program Participants' Report" (Chicago: Author, 2005).

11. Treasury Strategies, "2005 Commercial Bank Sweep Research: Executive Summary" (Chicago: Author, 2005).

12. Id.

13. At the time of this writing, AFP holds a "nonprofit industry roundtable" breakfast or luncheon each year at its annual conference. It is attended by practitioners, bankers, and consultants.

14. Lester M. Salamon, "Communique No. 4 [Preliminary Results, April 4, 2005]: Nonprofit Financial Disclosure," Johns Hopkins University Center for Civil Society Studies Institute for Policy Studies Listening Post Project. Located online at: www.jhu.edu/listeningpost/news/pdf/comm04preliminary.pdf. Accessed: 3/3/06.

15. Ernst & Young, *22nd Annual Cash Management Survey: 2005 Executive Summary*. Available online at: www.ey.com/global/download.nsf/US/Cash_Management_Survey_2005/$file/2005CashManagementSurveyExecSummary.pdf. Accessed: 3/4/2006.

NONPROFIT ORGANIZATION GUIDE TO DIRECT PAYMENT*

IN THE DONOR RELATIONS GAME, YOU AND YOUR DONOR WIN WITH DIRECT PAYMENT

Excellent donor relations are good business. An easy way to sustain donor giving is to offer donors several payment alternatives for making their gifts. Win over your donors by adding direct payment to your menu of gift payment options.

WHAT IS DIRECT PAYMENT?

Direct payment is a method of electronically collecting regular financial gifts from your donors. With the help of your financial institution, you can collect donations through the Automated Clearing House (ACH), the same system used for the direct deposit of payroll. Donors who choose direct payment for regular financial gifts (monthly, quarterly, or annually) will authorize you to electronically debit their bank account on a regular basis for a predetermined amount. Direct payment provides you and your donors with an efficient electronic alternative to paper checks.

WINNING IS EASY WITH DIRECT PAYMENT

Whether you're collecting alumni association dues, annual subscription/membership renewals, or fund-raiser pledges, direct payment will help you by:

- *Increasing fulfillment rates.* With direct payment, pledge amounts and payment dates are set up in advance, and funds are collected automatically. You're assured that donor pledges will be received, as promised.
- *Improving donor retention.* Once your donors experience the ease of direct payment, they're more likely to continue giving. Collecting annual renewals is as simple as sending your donors a reminder.
- *Increasing pledge amounts.* Breaking up a single donation into smaller monthly or quarterly payments helps donors budget their gift dollars. Repeat donors tend to increase their donations with direct payment.

Source: Reprinted, with permission, from Federal Reserve Bank of St. Louis. For more information, visit their website at www.stls.Frb.org/epaymnts/nonprofit.htm.

- *Enhancing your image.* Direct payment shows your donors that you're donor-oriented and cost-conscious. You'll also be offering your donors a way to customize their payment method.

- *Improving your cash flow.* With direct payment, the timing of donations is more predictable and reliable. Your cash flow will be more manageable with stable donor gifts each month.

- *Lowering your costs.* Direct payment will reduce both the number of pledge reminders to be sent and low-dollar checks to be processed. By eliminating the manual, labor-intensive process of handling check payments, you can improve the cost effectiveness of your payment operations.

WIN OVER YOUR DONORS WITH DIRECT PAYMENT

In addition to providing you with many benefits, direct payment helps your donors by:

- *Saving time preparing payments.* All your donors need to do is enter the amount of their gift in their checkbook. No writing checks, addressing envelopes, or running to the mailbox. What could be more convenient?

- *Improving budgeting.* Donors who aren't able to give a large lump sum will appreciate the option of small, regular gifts. Budgeting for a smaller gift often allows donors to give a larger amount during the course of a year.

- *Saving money.* Your donors will eliminate postage costs and reduce checking account fees (if they're charged for each check) and check-printing costs.

- *Contributing more to your cause and less to your overhead.* As you are able to reduce your costs for collecting donations, your donors' gifts will go further to help achieve your organizations' goals.

- *Receiving fewer gift requests.* Once donors are set up with direct payment, there is no need to send them multiple gift requests throughout the year.

WHO'S WINNING WITH DIRECT PAYMENT?

Charitable organizations of all sizes are winning with direct payment. The following types of organizations and their donors enjoy the many benefits of direct payment:

- Public television
- Public radio
- Colleges and universities
- Religious organizations
- Cultural/arts organizations
- Humanitarian organizations

To learn more about how you and your donors can win with direct payment, call the National Automated Clearing House Association, toll-free, at 1-800-467-2329, extension 590, or the nearest Federal Reserve Bank. Become a champion with direct payment today!

A FEW NONPROFITS SUCCESSFULLY USING DIRECT PAYMENT:

For us, Direct Payment is a win-win service. The university benefits through higher donor retention and gifts, and lower processing costs, and donors benefit through increased convenience. A high percentage of donors who give automatically through direct payment continue giving year after year. And many of them increase their contributions each year.

—Jann Cutcher, Ohio State University

Some alumni who were giving $25 a year are now giving up to $100 a year because they're able to spread their donations out over the course of the year.

—Laura Scarlett, Massachusetts Institute of Technology

The ACH (direct payment) has been our saving grace in terms of cash flow and processing efficiency.

—Rafia Siddiqui, The Columbia Association

EasyGift (direct payment) means automatic money for us every month—guaranteed.

—Chris Prukop, WGBH Educational Foundation Public Radio and Television

DIRECT PAYMENT CASE STUDY*

DIRECT PAYMENT TESTIMONIAL: MICHELLE GLENN, KPBS PUBLIC TELEVISION, SAN DIEGO, CALIFORNIA

Michelle Glenn, Director of Membership for KPBS, San Diego's Public Broadcasting station, is very pleased with the results of Chexplan, the station's Direct Payment membership contribution program, which has been offered to members since 1996. "Direct Payment membership provides consistent support for our station," said Glenn. "Contributors who are on Chexplan give regularly and give more than they would if their contributions were not automatic. Making contributions automatically on monthly basis is easier and more affordable than writing one lump-sum check each year. Since they don't see the transactions, they don't miss the money as much."

KPBS has found that members on its Direct Payment plan also have more longevity than other members. More than half of KPBS members who are on Direct Payment have been contributing members for more than 10 years. The renewal rate for Direct Payment members is 91 percent.

In 2000, 26 percent of KPBS members were on some type of installment plan (cash, credit card, or Direct Payment). Of that 26 percent, 47 percent contributed by Direct Payment. Direct Payment members made an average annual contribution of $154 compared to the overall average member's annual contribution of $123. "Using Direct Payment to receive contributions saves KPBS money on a regular basis. With Direct Payment members, there is no need for us to mail out regular contribution requests or process checks. It is easier for us and easier for them."

*Source: http://www.directpayment.org/dpnp4.html, Accessed: 3/3/06. Used by permission.

CHAPTER 12

INVESTMENT POLICY AND GUIDELINES

12.1 INVESTMENT POLICY

A written document containing a statement of investment policy and a set of guidelines—a framework for achieving the investment goals—is absolutely essential for the success of both the short-term and long-term investing of an institution's funds. Individuals who function as fiduciaries to both the donors and the board have ultimate responsibility for investments for the nonprofit organization. The written investment policy and guidelines document forms the bridge of understanding between the board and the person(s) executing the investment program. In a very real sense, the policy and guidelines document, usually called an investment policy statement (IPS), is an agreement between the board and the investment manager and should describe the parameters of that agreement.

Although these terms are used differently among users, here are typical definitions used within the investment policy area discussed in this chapter.

- *Liquidity (new cash)*. Period of up to 180 days
- *Short term*. Period of up to 2 years
- *Intermediate term*. Period of 3 to 5 years
- *Long term*. Period of 5 years or longer
- *Endowment*. A fund invested to produce a steady flow of income, now and in the future

The investment objectives of an organization should be the first element(s) contained in a written investment policy. The importance of having a written investment policy in your organization cannot be overstated. The current trend toward engaging external professional money managers to provide investment management advice to the board, or its designee, makes this requirement more important than ever.

Without a well-defined investment policy, the *in-house* investment manager will make your organization's investments the way that he or she believes they should be made. In the absence of written policy, an *external* investment manager will probably make your investments in the same way he or she does for other clients. In order to ensure that investments are made to meet your organization's requirements, investment goals and objectives must be documented in a written investment policy; otherwise, the investment manager may make investment decisions that contravene your risk-return preferences.

To provide clarity and avoid confusion, it is recommended that the short-term investment policy of the institution be separate and distinct from the long-term investment policy. One reason is that short-term and long-term investment goals and instruments are clearly separate and distinct; however, intermediate goals and instruments can fall into either the short-term or long-term policy, depending on the organization. *In any case, the investment policy or policies must include a written statement of the investment objectives.* These objectives should be stated clearly and concisely and should set forth the order of priorities if there are multiple objectives.

In a short-term investment policy, investors typically have three objectives:

1. Preservation of principal
2. Maintenance of liquidity
3. Yield

It is important for your organization's policy to state these goals and place them in priority order. In a short-term portfolio, most nonprofit organizations' investment requirements would fall in this order: Preservation of principal and maintenance of liquidity often both take precedence over yield. Investment consultant and author William Donoghue coined the term "SLY" to denote safety first, then liquidity, then yield.

(a) SHORT-TERM INVESTMENT POLICY.   A typical investment policy statement for a short-term portfolio might read as follows:

> It shall be the policy of this organization to invest its temporary surplus cash in short-term and intermediate-term, fixed-income instruments to earn a market rate of interest without assuming undue risk to principal. The primary objectives of making such

investments shall be, in their order of importance, preservation of capital, maintenance of liquidity, and yield.

These two sentences clearly lay out the organization's objectives in priority order.

(b) LONG-TERM INVESTMENT POLICY.   After the short-term cash needs of the organization are met, the growing nonprofit organization will reach a level of maturity and financial condition where capital is available to invest for the long term. The next stage is to build operating reserves to buffer against large-scale revenue declines or expense increases, as noted in Chapter 2. Then many nonprofits will consult their strategic plan and long-range financial plan to determine how soon and to what degree they will self-fund expansions to programs and/or facilities. Eventually a nonprofit organization will likely have the assets to invest for longer periods in the form of endowment, which by its nature is invested for the long term to provide funds to support the intended programs in perpetuity. Typically, the larger a long-term endowment fund becomes, the more complex the investment decisions become.

A typical endowment investment policy is concerned with four areas:

1. Preservation of principal

2. Provision of a reliable source of funds for current and future use

3. A rate of return that maintains or enhances the purchasing power of the endowment over time (growth of principal)

4. Prudent levels of risk

Often the terms "long term" and "endowment" are used interchangeably. For purposes of ease in this chapter, we will use "endowment," which has the most stringent objectives in terms of protecting principal and providing an income stream in perpetuity.

Surplus assets (e.g., accumulated funds being held to fund the future construction of a building), which are *not* endowment, can be invested for the long term. Generally, funds of long-term investment pools and endowment pools follow the same investing parameters.

As with short-term investment policies, the long-term endowment policy must state the return objective in very clear terms. Since endowments are intended to exist in perpetuity, a typical return objective seeks to hedge against inflation. The goal is to maintain or enhance the purchasing power of the endowment to maintain the activities it supports. This objective should be stated in terms of the "real rate of return" defined as total return ("nominal return") less inflation. Real rate of return is more meaningful since inflation changes from period to period. A spending target stated in terms of fixed "nominal" return, rather than real return, can be misleading. Expressing the approximate relationship among nominal return, inflation, and real return[1] in a formula, we have:

$$\text{Nominal Return} = \text{Real Return} + \text{Inflation}$$

If one is forecasting future returns, the formula would be expressed slightly differently:

$$\text{Expected Nominal Return} = \text{Expected Real Return} + \text{Expected Inflation}$$

Illustrating, if an investor expects (or requires) a 2.5 percent real return for the upcoming year, and inflation is expected to be 3 percent for this period, she would be anticipating receiving 5.5 percent on her investment:

$$5.5\% = 2.5\% + 3.0\%$$

Notice that we have not addressed risk, or the additional yield she would require on her investment, known as a *risk premium*. Implicitly, then, we have either included risk premia in both the nominal return and real return, or we have profiled a risk-free security; U.S. treasury bills would fit this profile.

To be more precise, we may express our formula as including the expected *risk-free real return,* expected inflation rate, the risk premium, and the expected nominal return.

Expected Nominal Risk-free Return = Expected Risk-free Real Return

+ Expected Inflation

A risk premium is attached to the nominal risk-free return to get the expected nominal return:

Expected Nominal Return = Expected Nominal Risk-free Return + Risk Premium

This risk premium may consist of several types of risk. Chief among these risks is *credit risk,* also known as *default risk.* This compensates the investor, through higher return, for the possibility that the issuer will not make timely interest payments and/or principal repayments. *Liquidity risk* is posed by the possibility that the investor may not be able to quickly sell (liquidate) a security at fair market value. *Interest-rate risk* (sometimes termed *market risk*) refers to the fact that interest rate increases lead to price declines for fixed income securities, because the interest rate cannot be adjusted to be competitive with the new interest rate. This same risk leads to price increases when interest rates decline. Unfortunately, it is very difficult to predict when rates might rise or fall, leading investors to require a higher interest rate on longer-term securities.[2]

There are six essential elements of both a short-term and a long-term investment policy:

1. Who is responsible for the investing program?
2. Who does the investing?
3. How are assets to be allocated?
4. How is performance to be measured and reported?
5. What are the maximum risks to be assumed?
6. Who is responsible for the review and modification of the investment guidelines?

Exhibit 12.2, provided later in this chapter, serves as an additional checklist of essential elements.

12.2 INVESTMENT GUIDELINES

(a) WHO IS RESPONSIBLE FOR THE INVESTING PROGRAM? In a nonprofit organization, the board of directors is ultimately responsible for the investment program. The key principle to bear in mind here is the *prudent man rule.* Judge Samuel Putnam first articulated this principle in 1830: "Those with responsibility to invest money for others should act with prudence, discretion, intelligence, and regard for the safety of capital as well as income." In keeping with its fiduciary responsibility, the board sets policy, selects managers, oversees investment activities, reviews performance, and monitors compliance to guidelines.

In creating and managing an investing program, it is necessary for the board to place continuing responsibility and authority for the conduct of the program with a particular person or a specific committee. Actual investment management may be delegated to a particular person or external manager(s).

It is customary to establish an *investment committee* and to charge that committee with responsibility for managing all aspects of the investing program. The committee is normally made up of senior financial and administrative executives of the organization and may include representation from the board and other individuals with extensive financial or business expertise.

The investment committee normally drafts the policy and guidelines for board approval. However, the board may also delegate authority and responsibility for implementation to the investment committee.

Responsibilities of the investment committee include:

- Set policy determining how investments are to be managed.
- Make asset allocation decisions.
- Determine a spending policy.
- Select investment manager(s).
- Review the portfolio's performance.
- Provide reports to the board of trustees on investment results and operations.

The investment guidelines should clearly identify individuals responsible for managing the investing program and their respective levels of authority. The opening of accounts with brokers, dealers, and banks; the establishment of safekeeping accounts; arrangements for ongoing securities safekeeping; and authority to execute documents and agreements needed to implement the program may be delegated. The guidelines should also provide for the investment committee to select and employ independent investment advisors, if deemed advisable.

(b) WHO DOES THE INVESTING?   The guidelines should clearly delegate operating authority and responsibility to the financial officers who will actually execute transactions, if an external investment manager is not contracted. Commonly, such authority for entering into agreements is granted to the financial manager, or chief financial officer (CFO), the treasurer or controller, and the assistant treasurer or assistant controller. For example, it may provide for the CFO to act together with either the treasurer or assistant treasurer, but neither of the latter two individuals may operate alone.

It is essential, however, for one qualified individual to be available at all times to execute investment transactions. That authority should be strictly and clearly delegated within the limitations defined in the investing guidelines. Typically, such authority is granted to the CFO, who, in turn, may redelegate the authority to subordinates within the treasury function. It is usually required, through copies of corporate resolutions, to notify banks and securities dealers in writing of the scope of authority granted to each authorized person.

(c) HOW ARE ASSETS TO BE ALLOCATED?   Asset allocation (also known as *strategic asset allocation*) is one of the primary responsibilities of the investment committee. How an organization allocates its assets mainly determines its return: One widely quoted study found that 90 percent of the ups and downs in a pension fund's returns over time could be linked to the normal policy weights for the various asset classes (e.g., 60 percent stocks, 40 percent bonds). Another study found that after accounting for timing, security selection, management fees, and expenses, the typical balanced mutual fund and pension fund were not adding value relative to what their policy benchmarks were earning.[3]

Asset allocation has two major components: selection of assets in which to invest and assignment of those assets to investment managers with delegated responsibility for them.

Asset allocation is the division of an organization's total assets (e.g., cash, stocks, bonds, real estate) among the best mix of investments in ideal proportions. Asset allocation includes estimating expected returns on investment, risks, and price movements among the various asset classes. It is the most successful investment technique available to investment portfolio managers today.

Asset allocation can be active or passive. *Active allocation* allows a money manager to shift monies from one asset class to another within prescribed limits. For example, if it is determined that the optimum strategy to obtain the best investment performance results entails this mix of assets—35 percent bonds, 45 percent stocks, 10 percent cash, and 10 percent other—an active allocator could adjust (on a daily basis, if necessary) the mix of assets owned in these and the other categories to try to achieve maximum performance. This reallocation would be done as the outlook for the performance of the asset classes changed.

A *passive allocator*, however, would typically invest the portfolio in a mix of assets (cash, bonds, equities, other) and rebalance the portfolio once a year. Exhibit 12.1 shows an example of one organization's asset allocation target for a long-term endowment portfolio.

(i) Investment Instruments. The investing guidelines must describe the instruments in which the company will invest. The guidelines should further state that unless specifically permitted under the guidelines, all other investment instruments are prohibited. (A good

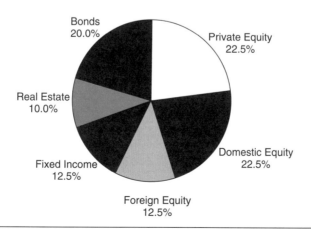

EXHIBIT 12.1 EXAMPLE OF ASSET ALLOCATION

reason to require an annual review of the guidelines is because new instruments may be introduced in which the organization is prohibited from investing. The guidelines should be modified to permit such new instruments, if and when warranted.)

Appendices 12.E and 12.F present a brief summary description that should be provided to those who must approve the policy of the most common investment instruments. This listing will be useful in creating or revising investment guidelines. The allocation of dollars between these various instruments is called *asset allocation* or *strategic asset allocation*. Short-term and long-term policies usually call for the inclusion of some element of fixed income instruments in the investment portfolio. Short-term investment portfolios do not include equities due to the risk of price changes—a violation of the "safety-first" notion. Investing guidelines typically permit several kinds of investment instruments.

(ii) Fixed Income Instruments.   Fixed income instruments include:

- U.S. treasury securities
- U.S. government agency obligations
- Municipal securities
- Bank obligations
- Certificates of deposit (CDs)
- Fixed time deposits
- Banker's acceptances (BAs)
- Commercial paper
- Loan participations
- Corporate notes and bonds
- Repurchase agreements involving permitted securities, usually treasuries and agencies
- Money market mutual funds

(iii) Equity Instruments.   The list of equity instruments includes:

- Common stocks
- Convertible securities
- Preferred stocks
- Index funds
- Exchange-traded funds (ETFs)
- Warrants
- Rights (corporate action)
- Rule 144a stock
- American depositary receipts (ADRs)

(iv) Alternative Investments.   Alternatives to fixed income and equity instruments are:

- Private investments
- Hedge funds
- Event-driven investment instruments
- Market-neutral instruments

(v) Socially Responsible Investing. In short-term and long-term investment programs, investable funds offer an organization certain choices and considerations, including using funds to achieve nonfinancial goals. One specific nonfinancial consideration is to lend support to a social cause through the types of investments that are made or not made. The number of socially responsible mutual funds has exploded in the United States.

Causes to consider. When making investment decisions, many investors avoid providing indirect support to the alcohol or tobacco industries because of their link to many diseases. Defense companies are avoided by some investors. Also, most socially conscious investment programs for years have refused to invest in companies that conduct business with various oppressive governments. Many organizations believe that doing business in such countries provides support for the economic strength and authority of the nation's government. A good example is the decisions in 2005 and 2006 by the Harvard University endowment and the Yale University endowment to discontinue investments in large oil companies that were aligned with or supportive of the oppressive Sudanese government, which was at that time linked with genocide—over 180,000 deaths due to militia raids and ensuing diseases linked to food or water—as well as the displacement of 2 million people. "The time-honored principles that Yale observes as an ethical institutional investor have guided us to take this strong action," stated the president of Yale, Richard Levin.[4]

Other social concerns often prompt institutional investors to use their dollars in promoting a better international society. They exclude companies that pollute the environment or disregard the ecology of areas where they do business.

Developing a socially responsible investing policy. When an organization has identified the social issues its investment program should or should not support, a method for efficiently implementing an investment policy is needed. If funds will be managed by an external advisor, the investing organization should provide specific instructions. Similarly, if funds will be internally managed, an organization's financial staff should be given a written investment policy reflecting management's views on social issues.

These actions should be included when developing an investment policy with socially conscious objectives:

- Develop a comprehensive set of investment guidelines with a statement of social objectives.

- Provide direction on types of investments to be excluded from the investment program.

- Review investment and social goals of the investment policy and adopt guidelines to validate their accuracy and timeliness on an annual basis.

Taking these steps will help to maintain a socially responsible investing program and to adjust the direction of investment activities as circumstances warrant.

For organizations that internally manage their investments, information will be needed on which investments to avoid. A list should be compiled of corporations that act in a manner contrary to the organization's socially responsible investment objectives. After a list is established, investment staff members should be instructed not to purchase obligations issued by particular organizations. Internally maintaining a socially responsible investing (SRI) program also may require additional time to complete investments, including record-keeping responsibilities.

Before deciding on an investment program that includes socially responsible objectives, an organization's managers should remember that a degree of yield or return on investment may be sacrificed by such a program. From 2000 to 2005, for example, SRI fell behind the market as a whole: As measured by the SRI index called the Domini 400 Social Index, the exclusion of many petroleum and defense stocks hurt the SRI investor's performance relative to the Standard & Poor's 500 index. A Wharton business school professor estimated that SRI mutual fund investors were worse off by as much as 3 to 4 percent per year compared to mutual funds that were not limited in their investing.[5] However, this same source indicated that investing on one's own for the future would likely not involve this same compromise, as more and more companies are improving their ethics and practices and would therefore be candidates for the SRI investor.

The benefits and costs of a socially conscious investment policy must be weighed by an organization's managers—and its course must be set accordingly.

Once the asset allocation decision has been made, diversification strategies should be employed to further enhance the success potential for the long-term investment portfolio. The idea of spreading one's risk by not concentrating investments in one security, industry, geographical location, or asset class is the oldest known investment principle, finding its expression in the Old Testament of the Bible: "Give portions to seven, yes to eight, for you do not know what disaster may come upon the land" (Ecclesiastes 11:2, New International Version). Some strategies to be considered are diversification by:

- Investment type
- Manager style
- Type of issuer
- Industry sector
- Geography
- Time
- Foreign versus domestic
- Category

These and other techniques for diversifying the investment portfolio are discussed more fully in our guide *Cash and Investment Management for Nonprofit Organizations* (2007).

(d) HOW IS PERFORMANCE MEASURED AND REPORTED?

(i) Measurement. Measurement of investment performance is essential to the investment process. Furthermore, performance measurement criteria are key to the investment policy and guidelines of the institution.

Some elements of investment performance to be measured are:

- Overall results
- Return on investment
- Comparison to historical performance
- Comparison to performance by style
- Effectiveness of communication
- Cost of investing services

(ii) Reporting. Operating an investing program can create a nightmare of reports and paperwork. Therefore, it is essential for the investment committee, if not the board, to specify the type and frequency of reports needed. Otherwise, the financial manager who actually executes the transactions may feel compelled to furnish too much information to too many people.

A practical approach is to establish tiers of reports, as in a pyramid. Proceeding upward in an organization, the volume of reported data gets smaller. The financial manager who executes the transactions maintains the bottom tier and must be responsible for total detail concerning these transactions. The financial manager also must be responsible for ensuring that appropriate information is fed to the accounting department to record the transactions properly in the company's books and records.

For the financial manager's own use, it is generally necessary to have a daily or weekly report of securities held and the instruments listed in maturity date order, with the earliest maturity listed first. The manager may also need to have the same information sorted: (1) by issuer, to ensure that there is no undue concentration of funds invested in any one issuer; (2) by type of issuer, such as bank holding company, industrial company, finance company, domestic issuer, and foreign issuer by country; and (3) by safekeeping agent or other location where the securities are held in custody. The investment manager needs all this information in order to conduct the day-to-day investing operations.

The level of detail that the financial manager needs is not necessary for his or her immediate superior, other senior management, and members of the investment committee. Thus, the investment committee and the board should specify the level of detail and the frequency of reports they require. Typically, these reports contain a listing of all securities held, including maturity dates and yields, as well as a weighted average yield of the entire portfolio. The reports are often produced on a monthly basis and may be accompanied by a schedule of transactions conducted since the last report.

By using computers, database management software, and spreadsheets, much of the report data can be handled easily and sorted by different fields to produce the desired results. Computerized programs are also available to handle short-term investment portfolio reporting. If an outside investment manager is used, the reports they provide should be adequate for your internal reporting needs.

(e) WHAT LEVEL OF RISK IS TO BE ASSUMED? Investment guidelines should include a statement about the safeguards required by the investment program of your institution. Risk avoidance techniques should be explained.

(i) Limitations on Maturity. Because the short-term investment portfolio has primary objectives of preservation of capital and maintenance of liquidity, the investing guidelines should contain a statement that limits the maturity of the portfolio to avoid interest-rate risk. The limitations can relate to both the weighted average maturity of the entire portfolio and maximum limitations on maturity of any one instrument. For example, the guidelines might restrict the maturity of any one instrument to "not more than five years from the date of purchase," and the weighted average maturity of the entire portfolio may be no more than three years.

Two dimensions of maturity limitation working together can prevent the occurrence of several interesting, but potentially detrimental, activities. For example, if the guidelines address only the weighted average maturity of the portfolio, the financial manager may use a "barbell" strategy. In such a strategy, one-half of the portfolio is invested in very short-term instruments, such as 30- and 60-day maturities, and the other half in relatively long-term instruments maturing in 8 to 10 years. Mathematically, the weighted average maturity of the portfolio could be within the 3-year limitation. Clearly, however, the actual deployment of funds does not meet the safety of principal and liquidity goals that management had set due to the inclusion of longer-term securities.

However, simply limiting the length of maturity of any one instrument may be inadequate. If the guidelines restrict the maturity of any one instrument to two years, for example, the financial manager may feel at liberty to invest virtually all of the portfolio in instruments maturing in about two years. This, too, could work in opposition to the stated objectives of preservation of capital and maintenance of liquidity.

(ii) Currency Denomination.   The institution's investing guidelines should clearly stipulate that securities must be denominated in U.S. dollars or in currencies other than U.S. dollars, if permitted. This denomination reporting choice is an important distinction because investments in securities denominated in foreign currencies introduce a new element of foreign exchange risk. Unless an organization understands and accepts that risk, the guidelines should stipulate that all investments be denominated in U.S. dollars. Recalling that our goal with short-term portfolios is "safety first," investments would normally be dollar-denominated. For endowments, however, international investing is a prudent way of reducing risk for a given level of return, or increasing return, for a given level of risk.

Consider the home-country return that an investor earns, assuming a particular foreign-country return and a specific change in exchange rates. Our next formula shows us this relationship:

$$(1 + \text{Home Country Return}) = (1 + \text{Foreign Country Return})$$
$$\times \ (\text{Current Exchange Rate/Initial Exchange Rate})$$

For the U.S. investor, the exchange rate should be expressed as $/unit of foreign currency. For example, let's say our investor earned 7 percent by investing for one year in German medium-term notes. He is expecting his interest proceeds soon, as his investment has just matured. He goes online (http://finance.yahoo.com/currency) and determines that the year-end exchange rate expressed as $/€ to be $1.19/€1, and the exchange rate one year earlier (when he invested) to be $1.31/€1. What would his return be when converted back into dollars? Put the foreign country return into decimal form (7 percent ⇒ 0.07), and then plug the numbers into the formula:

$$(1 + \text{Home Country Return}) = (1 + 0.07)(\$1.19/\$1.31)$$
$$(1 + \text{Home Country Return}) = (1.07)(0.90476)$$
$$(1 + \text{Home Country Return}) = (0.9681)$$

Subtracting 1 from both sides yields the home country return:

$$\text{Home Country Return} = -0.0319 \ \text{or} \ -\underline{3.19\%}$$

For this year, the depreciation of the euro relative to the dollar (the exchange rate depreciation from €1 buying $1.31 to €1 buying $1.19) decreased the 7 percent euro-based return to −3.19 percent in dollar terms. The reverse effect is also possible: The euro could appreciate, leaving the U.S. investor with more than his foreign earnings of 7 percent.

The moral of the story here, though, is that the U.S. investor would have been much better off leaving his money invested in lower-yielding U.S. securities, thereby taking less risk. It would be very unusual for a short-term IPS to permit unhedged foreign investments, and many will proscribe non-U.S. dollar investments.

In the event that the IPS permits some foreign exchange risk, which makes sense only for long-term portfolios, it is important for the amount of the investment, including principal and total interest due at maturity, to be partly or totally hedged with a foreign exchange forward or futures contract. Even though the security is denominated in a foreign currency, this will help ensure that the ultimate proceeds will be converted into a known quantity of U.S. dollars at maturity. For most institutions, the institution's guidelines should specifically require that all investments be made in U.S. dollars or be fully hedged into U.S. dollars if made in foreign currencies.

Investments in foreign instruments can be done on a hedged or unhedged basis, both of which have risk/cost implications. We return to the subject of hedging in Chapter 14.

(f) REVIEW AND MODIFICATION OF THE INVESTMENT GUIDELINES: WHO IS RESPONSIBLE FOR WHAT? Even the best-designed investing guidelines must be periodically reviewed and modified to accommodate changes in the organization's own situation and in conditions prevailing in the securities markets. The guidelines themselves should contain provision for their review and modification.

The investment committee should have the responsibility of initiating additional reviews and modifications and perhaps delegating the responsibility to the CFO for making recommendations for modification as conditions warrant. Many organizations require an annual review of the guidelines. The investment committee also often delegates authority to the CFO, who may, in turn, redelegate it to the vice president (VP) of finance to make the current investing program more restrictive than defined by the guidelines. For example, the guidelines may permit investment of funds in a particular area, such as obligations of foreign banks. It may come to the attention of that VP that the economy of a particular country has suddenly weakened. The VP may choose to restrict investment in obligations of banks domiciled in that country as a temporary measure (see Appendix 12A).

12.3 CHECKLIST OF ELEMENTS FOR LONG-TERM ENDOWMENT INVESTMENT POLICY AND GUIDELINES

Does your long-term endowment policy include clear, concise statements? (See Exhibit 12.2.)

12.4 INVESTMENT POLICY SUMMARY

A written investing policy and set of investing guidelines are essential elements in both the successful short-term (liquidity) and long-term (endowment) investing program of a nonprofit institution. The document is a contract between the board of directors or trustees and the financial manager. The policy statement describes the parameters within which the financial manager shall perform the tasks of investment management. The guidelines can be simple or complex, they can be restrictive or liberal, and they can cover a liquidity portfolio or dedicated proceeds of a bond issue or endowment fund within a single document or multiple documents.

Element	Location in Appendix 12D (Sample of Investment Policy for Long-Term Endowment Pool)	√ Done
• Purpose of the endowment	Opening paragraph	
• Responsibilities assignment	Opening paragraph	
• Investment objectives	I	
• Reference to endowment spending policy	I, Paragraph 2	
• Asset allocation	II	
○ Minimums, targets, maximums		
○ Fixed income vs. equities		
• Guidelines for selection of fixed-income securities	III	
○ Diversification	III.A	
○ Quality	III.B	
○ Duration	III.C	
• Guidelines for selection of equities	IV	
○ Diversification of manager	IV.A	
• Performance	V	
• Permissible and nonpermissible assets	VI	
• Selection of investment managers	VII	
• Responsibilities of the investment manager	VIII	

EXHIBIT 12.2   CHECKLIST OF ELEMENTS FOR LONG-TERM ENDOWMENT INVESTMENT POLICY AND GUIDELINES

A well-structured investment policy and guidelines document clearly places authority and responsibility for management of the investing program and enables modifications to the guidelines within reasonable bounds. The guidelines further set forth the requirements for reporting the investment activities and portfolio condition, and they clearly describe the types of securities that are acceptable for investment. They also address the operational issues of executing and verifying transactions and of holding the investment instruments in safekeeping for maintenance of appropriate security.

The financial manager should never invest in an instrument that he or she does not understand. It is essential for the financial manager to understand the risk/reward relationship and be comfortable with the level of risk assumed when making investment decisions for the nonprofit organization.

Notes

1. A more exact relationship is: Nominal Return $= (1 + \text{Real Return})(1 + \text{Inflation Rate}) - 1$, with all rates and returns expressed in decimal form.
2. Technically, it is not maturity that dictates interest rate risk, but the duration and convexity of the security. Duration is a measure of a security's interest rate sensitivity. If duration is 2, for example, a 1 percent increase in interest rates will cause a 2 percent price decline,

approximately. For more on this, see Chapters 12 and 20 of Frank K. Reilly and Edgar A. Norton, *Investments*, 7th ed. (Mason, OH: Thomson South-Western, 2006).

3. On ups and downs in the same investment fund, consult these two studies: Gary P. Brinson, L. Randolph Hood, and Gilbert L. Beebower, "Determinants of Portfolio Performance," *Financial Analysts Journal* 42 (July-August 1986): 39–46; and Gary P. Brinson, Brian D. Singer, and Gilbert L. Beebower, "Determinants of Portfolio Performance II: An Update," *Financial Analysts Journal* 47 (May-June 1991): 40–48. On performance of balanced mutual funds and pension funds relative to policy returns, consult Roger G. Ibbotson and Paul D. Kaplan, "Does Asset Allocation Policy Explain 40, 90, or 100 Percent of Performance?" *Financial Analysts Journal* 56 (January-February 2000): 26–33.

4. AP, "Yale Divests Of Companies Tied to Sudan," *New York Sun*, February 17, 2006. Available online: www.nysun.com/article/27814. Accessed: 2/21/06.

5. Christopher Charles Geczy, Robert F. Stambaugh, and David Levin, "Investing in Socially Responsible Mutual Funds" (October 2005). Available at SSRN: http://ssrn.com/abstract=416380 or DOI: 10.2139/ssrn.416380.

SAMPLE OF SHORT-TERM INVESTMENT POLICY AND GUIDELINES

This example may be best suited for a large organization and may be compared and used in the development of organizational policies.

INVESTMENT COMMITTEE

Within the spectrum of activities of this organization, it is necessary to provide a framework for the regular and continuous management of investment funds. Because there is currently no formal Investment Committee, the Directors will assume this responsibility.

INVESTMENT POLICY

The policy shall be to invest excess cash in short-term and intermediate-term fixed-income instruments, earning a market rate of interest without assuming undue risk to principal. The primary objectives of such investments in order of importance shall be preservation of capital, maintenance of liquidity, and yield.

INVESTMENT RESPONSIBILITY

Investments are the responsibility of the Vice President of Finance. This responsibility includes the authority to select an investment advisor, open three accounts with brokers, establish safekeeping accounts or other arrangements for the custody of securities, and execute such documents as necessary.

Those authorized to execute transactions include: (1) Vice President of Finance, (2) Director of Accounting, and (3) cash manager. The Vice President of Finance shall ensure that one qualified individual is always available to execute the organization's investments.

REPORTING

The Treasurer shall be responsible for reporting the status of investments to the Directors on a quarterly basis. Those reports should include a complete listing of securities held, verified (audited) by parties either inside or outside this organization who have no connection with the investment activities.

INVESTMENTS

(a) OBLIGATIONS OF THE U.S. GOVERNMENT OR ITS AGENCIES.   Specifically, these refer to the U.S. Treasury, Federal Home Loan Bank, Federal Home Loan Mortgage Corporation, Federal National Mortgage Association, Federal Farm Credit Bank, Student Loan Marketing Association, and Government National Mortgage Association. Note: When-issued items must be paid for *before* they may be sold.

(b) BANKS—DOMESTIC.   The organization may invest in negotiable CDs (including Eurodollar denominated deposits), Eurodollar time deposits (with branches domiciled in Cayman, Nassau, or London), and BAs of the 50 largest U.S. banks ranked by deposit size. Thrift institutions whose parent has long-term debt rated A by Moody's or Standard & Poor's are acceptable. Exceptions may be local banks or thrift institutions that have lent the corporation money or that would be appropriate to use for some other reason. (These banks and institutions should be listed, along with the maximum dollar amount of exposure allowable for each.)

(c) BANKS—FOREIGN.   The organization may invest in negotiable CDs (including Eurodollar denominated deposits), Eurodollar time deposits (with branches domiciled in Cayman, Nassau, or London), and bankers' acceptances (BAs) of the 50 largest foreign banks ranked by deposit size. However, the issuing institution's parent must have a Moody's or Standard & Poor's rating of at least A.

Limitations

1.   The organization's aggregate investments with foreign entities shall not exceed 50 percent of total investments.

2.   No more than 10 percent of total investments shall be exposed to any one foreign country's obligations, or $X million per country, whichever is greater.

(d) COMMERCIAL PAPER.   All commercial paper must be prime quality by both Standard & Poor's and Moody's standards (i.e., A-1 by Standard & Poor's, P-1 by Moody's, and F-1 by Fitch).

(e) CORPORATE NOTES AND BONDS.   Instruments of this type are acceptable if rated at least A by both Moody's and Standard & Poor's credit rating services.

(f) MUNICIPALS.   Municipal or tax-exempt instruments (suitable only if your organization pays federal income tax). Only tax-exempt notes with a Moody's Investment MIG 1/VMIG 1 rating, or bonds that are rated by both Moody's Investor Service, Inc., and Standard & Poor's as A, may be purchased. Not more than 15 percent of the total issue size should be purchased, and issues of at least $20 million in total size must be selected.

(g) REPURCHASE AGREEMENTS.   Repurchase agreements (repos) are acceptable, using any of the securities listed above, as long as such instruments are negotiable/marketable and do not exceed other limitations as to exposure per issuer. The firm with whom the repo is executed must be a credit-acceptable bank or a primary dealer (reporting to the Federal Reserve). Collateral must equal 102 percent of the dollars invested, and the collateral must be delivered to the organization's safekeeping bank and priced to market weekly (to ensure correct collateral value coverage) if the repo has longer than a seven-day maturity.

(h) MONEY MARKET FUNDS.   Acceptable funds are those whose asset size place them among the 30 largest according to the Morningstar Report and that are rated Aaa by Moody's Investor Service or rated AAAm by Standard & Poor's Corporation.

(i) SAFEKEEPING ACCOUNTS.   Securities purchased should be delivered against or held in a custodian safekeeping account at the organization's safekeeping bank. An exception shall be: (1) repos made with approved (see above) banks or dealers for one week or less, and (2) Eurodollar time deposits, for which no instruments are created. This safekeeping account will be audited quarterly by an entity that is not related to the investment function of this organization and the results of that audit shall be provided to the Vice President of Finance.

(j) DENOMINATION.   All investments shall be in U. S. dollars.

(k) DIVERSIFICATION OF INVESTMENTS.   In no case shall more than 15 percent of the total portfolio be invested in obligations of any particular issuer except the U.S. Treasury.

MATURITY LIMITATIONS

Overall, maximum weighted average maturity shall be three years. However, on "put" instruments, which may be redeemed (or put) at par, the put date shall be the maturity date.

REVIEW AND/OR MODIFICATION

The Vice President of Finance shall be responsible for reviewing and modifying investment guidelines as conditions warrant, subject to approval by the Directors at least on an annual basis. However, the Vice President of Finance may at any time further restrict the items approved for purchase when appropriate.

Source: Alan Seidner.

ABC FOUNDATION UNENDOWED SHORT-TERM INVESTMENT POOL POLICY

This example might be more easily adaptable to small- or medium-sized organizations.

GENERAL POLICY

The basic objective of the Unendowed Investment Pool is to maximize returns consistent with safety of principal, liquidity, and cash flow requirements. The maximum maturity shall be five years except for mortgage notes related to ABC Foundation property transactions, the XYZ Department Loan Program, and mortgage-backed securities with an average life not to exceed five years. The portfolio shall be invested at no less than 20 percent for under one year. The Vice President–Finance is responsible for arranging the actual investments pursuant to this policy. All investment activity shall be under the general jurisdiction of the Investment Committee.

AUTHORIZED INVESTMENTS

The following categories of investments shall be authorized as indicated:

A. Commercial Paper—rated A-1 (Standard & Poor's), P-1 (Moody's), and F-1 (Fitch).

B. Bankers Acceptances—any bank rated A or better by Standard & Poor's or Moody's.

C. Eurodollars—an amount not to exceed 10 percent in banks or subsidiaries of banks rated in the top two investment-grade categories by a bank rating service. (No Eurodollars shall be purchased with a term greater than one year.)

D. Certificates of Deposits—not to exceed 10 percent in any bank whose parent rated A or better by Standard & Poor's or Moody's. (For banks not rated, investments shall be limited to amounts within FDIC's insurance limit.)

E. U.S. Treasury Bills, Notes, and Bonds—no limitation on amount invested.

F. U.S. Government Agencies—no limitation on amount invested.

G.   Repurchase Agreements—there shall be no limitation on the amount invested, provided the vehicle is collateralized by U.S. government securities.

H.   Corporate Bonds and Medium Term Notes—rated investment grade BBB/Baa by Standard & Poor's Corporation or Moody's Investor Services.

I.   Master Participation Notes—notes of issuer shall be rated A1/P1/F1 for its commercial paper or BBB/Baa or better for its long-term debt.

J.   Mortgage-backed Pass Through Securities—rated AAA and an average life not to exceed five years.

K.   Floating Rate Securities—debt of issuers with maturities not to exceed five years, provided interest rates reset at least every 90 days to reflect changing market conditions.

L.   Bargain Sale Investments—not to exceed $500,000 per individual transaction, as authorized by the Planned Gifts Committee unless approved by the Board of Directors.

M.   Mortgage Notes—related to ABC Foundation property transactions and second trust-deed program for the Athletic Department and Coaches Loans.

N.   Mutual Funds—domestic or global funds invested in a portfolio of high quality debt securities. (Funds must have a reasonable performance record and net asset value in excess of $100 million.)

O.   Equity Securities—limited to investment grade, high yielding equities. (When such equities are in a managed portfolio, a proven hedging strategy must be in place to significantly reduce exposure to principal erosion caused by changing market conditions.)

P.   Other Investments—between meetings of the Investment Committee, if deemed advisable, other investments not specifically authorized by this policy may be made if approved by both the Vice President–Finance and Investment Committee Chairman. (Any such action shall be taken to the Investment Committee at its next meeting for approval.)

INVESTMENT PROCEDURES

Selection of the appropriate investment from among the approved alternatives shall be determined by relative availability and maturities required. All other things being equal, the investment providing the highest return will be preferred.

DIVERSIFICATION

Securities purchased shall be diversified in terms of industry concentration as well as type of investment instrument.

QUALITY RATINGS

Quality rating is defined in terms of the underlying credit of an issuer in a particular transaction. For maturities over one year, the minimum acceptable rating is BBB or Baa based on Standard & Poor's and Moody's ratings. For short-term securities, the equivalent commercial paper rating of A-1/P-1/F-1 is the minimum acceptable rating. If a security has a Letter of Credit (LOC)/guarantee supporting it, then the issuer is the entity providing the LOC/guarantee.

The quality rating guidelines to be used shall be the ratings as of the date of purchase of the security. If a rating change occurs that disqualifies a security that is already held in the Pool, the security must be reviewed for determination of possible sale.

Ratings on securities purchased shall be, as indicated in this policy or in its absence, an equivalent rating as appropriate in keeping with ABC Foundation guidelines on quality.

MARKETABILITY

Securities purchased should be readily marketable and should meet the quality guidelines of this policy.

SAFEKEEPING

Securities purchased shall be held in the ABC Foundation safekeeping account at its principal banks except for Repurchase Agreements and Branch Certificates of Deposit, which shall be held by the branch bank.

SHORT-TERM INVESTMENT POLICY
FOR HIJ FOUNDATION

This example of a short-term investment policy is concise and includes all the necessary components that may be used for any size organization.

The undersigned hereby certify that the following investment policy was duly adopted and approved by the act of a majority of the Directors of the Foundation present at a meeting of the Board of Directors held on the 14th day of March, 2XXX, at which a quorum was present.

RESOLVED, that the purpose of this policy is to define the criteria to be followed by the HIJ Foundation for investment of surplus cash. All investments are to be made in conformance with the following criteria listed in the order of importance.

1. Safety of principal
2. Liquidity
3. Yield

Surplus funds, in excess of short-term future needs, may be invested in the following:

a. Short-term CDs, U.S. or Eurodollar time deposits, or BAs having maturities not exceeding six months with any commercial bank having a combined capital and surplus of not less than $500 million, not to exceed 10 percent in any bank rated *A* by Standard & Poor's Corporation and Moody's Investor Service, Inc.

b. Commercial paper of U.S. industrial issuers maturing no more than 270 days from the date of acquisition thereof and, at the time of acquisition, having a rating of A-1 (or better) by Standard & Poor's Corporation, P-1 by Moody's Investor Service, Inc., or F-1 by Fitch.

c. Repurchase agreements entered into with investment banks having shareholders' equity of at least $500 million; such repurchase agreements to be collateralized at least 100 percent by negotiable securities of a type described in (d) below.

d. U.S. Treasury bills, notes, and bonds and other marketable direct obligations insured or unconditionally guaranteed by the United States of America or issued by any sponsored agency thereof and having a remaining maturity of five years or less.

e. U.S. corporate bonds and medium-term notes having a remaining maturity of five years or less and rated A or better by Standard & Poor's Corporation and Moody's Investor Services, Inc., with diversification in terms of industry concentration.

f. Any mutual fund with a net asset value in excess of $100 million that invests solely in U.S. treasury bills, notes, and bonds (or agencies backed by the U.S. government) and such securities have a remaining life of 13 months or less and the fund maintains a net asset value of $1.00 per share.

The adoption and approval of the foregoing resolution constitutes the act of the Board of Directors of the HIJ Foundation pursuant to Article II, Section 5, of the Restated By-laws of the HIJ Foundation.

SAMPLE OF INVESTMENT POLICY STATEMENT FOR THE ABC FOUNDATION'S LONG-TERM ENDOWMENT POOL

The purpose of the ABC Foundation's endowment is to support the educational mission of the ABC University by providing a reliable source of funds for current and future use. Investment of the endowment is the responsibility of the Investment Committee (Committee). The Committee establishes investment objectives, defines policies, sets asset allocation, selects managers, and monitors the implementation and performance of the Foundation's investment program. The Committee is supported by the office of the Vice President–Finance, which analyzes investment policies and management strategies, makes recommendations to the Investment Committee, and supervises day-to-day operations and investment activities.

STATEMENT OF INVESTMENT OBJECTIVES

The endowment will seek to maximize long-term total returns consistent with prudent levels of risk. Investment returns are expected to preserve or enhance the real value of the endowment to provide adequate funds to sufficiently support designated University activities. The endowment's portfolio is expected to generate a total annualized rate of return, net of fees, 5 percent greater than the rate of inflation over a rolling 5-year period.

The Foundation's spending policy governs the rate at which funds are released to fund-holders for their current spending. The Foundation's spending policy will be based on a target rate set as a percentage of market value. This rate will be reviewed annually by the Investment Committee. The spending target rate is 5 percent for Fiscal Year 1995–1996.

ASSET ALLOCATION

To ensure real returns sufficient to meet the investment objectives, the endowment portfolio will be invested with the following target allocations in either domestic or global securities:

	Minimum	Target	Maximum
	(%)	(%)	(%)
Fixed-Income	30	35	40
Equities	60	65	70

The Investment Committee may appoint equity and fixed-income managers, or select pooled investments, when appropriate. It is the overall objective to be 100 percent invested in equities and fixed income. If at any time the equity manager determines it is prudent to be invested at less than 80 percent, the Committee shall be notified. Equity managers may invest cash positions in marketable, fixed-income securities with maturities not to exceed one year. Quality rating should be prime or investment grade, as rated by Standard & Poor's, Moody's, Fitch, and Dominion for commercial paper, and a comparable rating on bank CDs. The managers are expected to reasonably diversify holdings consistent with prudent levels of risk.

At the discretion of the Committee, the endowment portfolio will be rebalanced annually to target allocations as opportunities permit.

GUIDELINES FOR THE SELECTION OF FIXED-INCOME SECURITIES

(a) DIVERSIFICATION.   Except for the U.S. government, its agencies or instrumentalities, no more than 5 percent of the fixed-income portfolio at cost, or 8 percent at market value, shall be invested in any one single guarantor, issuer, or pool of assets. In addition, managers are expected to exercise prudence in diversifying by sector or industry.

(b) QUALITY.   All bonds must be rated investment grade (BBB/Baa or better) by at least one of the following rating services: Standard & Poor's or Moody's, except that bonds not receiving a rating may be purchased under the following circumstances:

- The issue is guaranteed by the U.S. government, its agencies, or instrumentalities.
- Other comparable debt of the issuer is rated investment grade by Standard & Poor's or Moody's.

The average quality rating of the total fixed-income portfolio must be AA or better. Securities downgraded in credit-quality rating subsequent to purchase, resulting in the violation of the policy guidelines, may be held at the manager's discretion. This is subject to immediate notification to the Investment Committee of such a change in rating.

(c) DURATION.   At the time of purchase, the average duration of the bond pool should be no longer than the average duration of the current Merrill Lynch 3–5 Year Treasury Index plus one year.

GUIDELINES FOR SELECTION OF EQUITIES: DIVERSIFICATION FOR EACH MANAGER

No more than 5 percent at cost, and 10 percent at market value, shall be invested in any one company. In addition, managers are expected to exercise prudence in diversifying by sector or industry.

PERFORMANCE

Performance of the endowment and its component asset classes will be measured against benchmark returns of comparable portfolios as follows:

Total Endowment	SEI Balanced Median Plan, Trust Universe Comparison Service Median Fund, Merrill Lynch Balanced Universe
Domestic Equities	S&P 500 Index, Russell 2000 Index, Dow Jones Wilshire 5000 Total Market Index, Russell/Mellon Trust Universes Endowment—Equity
Global Equities	MSCI World Index, Dow Jones STOXX Global 1800 Index, S&P/Citigroup Global Equity Index: Broad Market Index, Russell Global Equity Index
Fixed-Income	Lehman Universal U.S. Bond Index, Lehman Brothers 1–5 Year Treasury Index, Merrill Lynch Government/Corporate 1–5 Year Index, Russell/Mellon Trust Universes Endowment—Fixed Income, Fixed Income Manager Universe

At least annually, the Investment Committee will conduct performance evaluations at the total endowment, asset class, and individual manager levels. At the total endowment level, the Committee will analyze results relative to the objectives, the real rate of return, and composite indices. Further, investment results will be reviewed relative to the effects of policy decisions and the impact of deviations from policy allocations.

On the asset class and individual manager levels, results will be evaluated relative to benchmarks assigned to investment managers or pooled investments selected. These benchmarks are a vital element in the evaluation of individual and aggregate manager performance within each asset class.

The Committee may utilize the services of performance measurement consultants to evaluate investment results, examine performance attribution relative to target asset classes, and other functions as it deems necessary.

PERMISSIBLE AND NONPERMISSIBLE ASSETS

All assets selected for the endowment must have a readily ascertainable market value and must be readily marketable. The following types of assets are permitted:

Equities	Fixed-Income
Common stocks	U.S. Treasury and agency obligations
Convertible securities	Mortgage-backed securities of U.S. government
Preferred stocks	Money-market funds
Warrants	Short-term investment fund accounts
Rights (corporate action)	Certificates of deposit
Rule 144a stock*	Bankers acceptances
American Depositary Receipts (ADRs)	Commercial paper
American Depositary	Repurchase agreements
Receipts (ADRs)	Asset-backed securities/collateralized bond obligations
Corporate securities	gations
Collateralized mortgage obligations	
ABC Shared Appreciation Mortgage Program	
First trust deeds of gift properties	
Index funds and Exchange-Traded Funds (ETFs)	

*This exception assumes the endowment continues to meet requirements specified under SEC Rule 144A. If the endowment does not meet those requirements, it is also expressly prohibited from trading in Rule 144A securities.

Within the mortgage-backed securities and collateralized mortgage obligations sector, investments in CMO tranches with reasonably predictable average lives *are* permitted, provided at time of purchase the security does not exceed the average duration of the current Merrill Lynch 3–5 Treasury Index plus one year. Interest-only and principal-only (PO) securities—or other derivatives based on them—are prohibited, as are securities with very limited liquidity.

Emerging market investments are permitted within the global equity manager's portfolio, subject to a maximum of 10 percent. Likewise, currency hedging as a defensive strategy is permitted in the global portfolio.

The following types of assets or transactions are expressly prohibited without prior written approval from the Investment Committee:

Equities	Fixed-Income
Commodities	Unregistered securities, except Rule 144A securities
Margin purchases	Tax-exempt securities
Short selling	Any asset not specifically permitted
Put and call options	
Direct oil and gas participations	
Direct investments in real estate	

SELECTION OF INVESTMENT MANAGERS

The Investment Committee may choose to select and appoint managers for a specific investment style or strategy, provided that the overall objectives of the endowment are satisfied.

RESPONSIBILITIES OF THE INVESTMENT MANAGER

(a) ADHERENCE TO STATEMENT OF INVESTMENT OBJECTIVES AND POLICY GUIDELINES

1. The manager is expected to observe the specific limitations, guidelines, and philosophies stated herein or as expressed in any written amendments or instructions.

2. The manager's acceptance of the responsibility of managing these funds will constitute a ratification of this statement, affirming his or her belief that it is realistically capable of achieving the endowment's investment objectives within the guidelines and limitations stated herein.

(b) DISCRETIONARY AUTHORITY.   The Manager will be responsible for making all investment decisions for all assets placed under his or her management and will be held accountable for achieving the investment objectives stated herein. Such "discretion" includes decisions to buy, hold, and sell securities (including cash and equivalents) in amounts and proportions that are reflective of the manager's current investment strategy and that are compatible with the endowment's investment guidelines.

DEFINITIONS OF FIXED-INCOME INSTRUMENTS

U.S. TREASURY SECURITIES

The U.S. Treasury finances federal deficits by issuing debt instruments called Treasury bills, notes, and bonds. The credit standing of each is the same, and the sole difference is the length of maturity. Treasury bills are issued for periods of one year or less, notes are issued to mature from more than one year but less than 10 years, and bonds are issued to mature from more than 10 years up to 30 years. Because of the credit quality of U.S. Treasury securities, investors from all over the world with all forms of investment needs are attracted to these instruments. As a result, the market for these securities enjoys a depth that provides for substantial liquidity.

U.S. GOVERNMENT AGENCY OBLIGATIONS

Various agencies of the U.S. government issue debt securities to finance various types of public operations. The agencies that issue the most popular securities, and probably issue the largest volume of government agency securities, are the Government National Mortgage Association (GNMA, commonly referred to as Ginnie Mae), Federal National Mortgage Association (FNMA, commonly known as Fannie Mae), Federal Home Loan Mortgage Corporation (FHLMC, commonly known as Freddie Mac), Federal Farm Credit Banks (FFCB), and Student Loan Marketing Association (called Sallie Mae).

With the exception of the Farm Credit Banks and Sallie Mae, debt instruments issued by the agencies are often in the form of certificates of participation in the ownership of pools of mortgage loans. While the certificates of participation themselves are not obligations of the U.S. government, the underlying mortgages owned by the pools usually are guaranteed by an agency of the government, such as the Federal Housing Administration (FHA) or the Veterans Administration (VA) in the case of Ginnie Mae.

Both FNMA and FFCB are privately owned organizations that perform specific functions in the public interest. They have strong ties to the federal government; however, there is only implied federal responsibility for the financial health of the institutions and protection of investors in the debt instruments issued by these institutions.

When an investor is considering a certificate of participation or a debt obligation of a federal agency, the investor should make a diligent investigation into the adequacy of the instrument for its purposes. In some cases, the cash flow emanating from certificates of participation is very good; the certificates provide current income and repayment of principal to the investor. At the same time, however, accounting considerations are complicated because of the combination of both principal and interest in the cash stream. Moreover, before making the investment, the investor in certificates of participation should understand the nature and long maturity of the mortgages or other debt contained in the investment pool.

For example, a GNMA pool of FHA mortgages may have an average maturity of 17 years, but in a period of declining interest rates, many of these loans in the pool may be prepaid by their respective homeowners/obligors as they refinance their home mortgages at lower interest rates. As a result, the investor in the GNMA pool will realize a more rapid return of capital and a smaller total income figure than had been anticipated. This situation may not fit into the investor's plans for providing cash flow over a budgeted period, or the heavier than anticipated stream of cash flow may cause the investor problems in reinvesting the excess funds.

MUNICIPAL SECURITIES

These are instruments issued by various nonfederal government political entities, such as states, counties, water districts, etc. They provide, in most cases, tax-exempt income to investors who pay taxes. However, increasingly, they are appropriate for investors who have no tax liability. Municipal securities come in a variety of types and maturities, often providing a yield advantage over government securities or corporate instruments of similar credit ratings.

BANK OBLIGATIONS

Bank obligations are evidenced either in the form of deposits in the bank or instruments that have been guaranteed or endorsed by a bank *and* offered in the secondary (resale) markets, such as banker's acceptances.

There are two basic forms of interest-bearing bank deposits: (1) negotiable time certificates of deposit, known as certificates of deposit (CDs) and (2) fixed-time deposits.

CERTIFICATES OF DEPOSIT   CDs maturing in a year or less are payable to the "bearer" and therefore, if properly held by a New York custodian, are liquid in the hands of the holder, if the CD is issued for at least $1 million. Many banks and investment dealers establish markets in CDs of the leading banks of the world and offer to buy and sell CDs for their own account. This is known as the secondary market. An investor can purchase a CD from one of these banks or dealers in the secondary market. Alternatively, an investor may initiate the bank deposit directly, in which case the CD is known as a primary certificate of deposit. If the investor chooses to sell the primary CD prior to maturity to recoup its cash funds early, it may sell it in the secondary market to another bank or dealer. A bank is not permitted to repurchase its own CDs; this would be tantamount to early redemption of the deposit and subject to penalties. It is critical to note that a secondary market exists only for CDs issued by better-known banks and savings and loan institutions. Also, the instrument itself must be in correct negotiable form and available for prompt delivery in New York. A CD issued by a bank located offshore—usually London, Cayman Islands, Nassau—is called a Eurodollar CD.

FIXED-TIME DEPOSITS   Fixed-time deposits are similar to negotiable CDs except that a bearer certificate is not issued. Fixed-time deposits often are issued domestically for amounts a bank wishes to accept. However, amounts of $1 million and more are usually required in London branches of major banks located in London, Nassau, the Bahamas, and the Cayman Islands. These are called Eurodollar time deposits since they are placed in offshore branches. Because these deposits are not represented by negotiable certificates, they are not liquid. Therefore, they often carry a higher yield to the investor than CDs.

BANKER'S ACCEPTANCES   A banker's acceptance (BA) is a draft drawn by a bank customer against the bank; the instrument is then "accepted" by the bank for the purpose of extending financing to the customer. The bank's acceptance of the draft means that the bank plans to sell the instrument in the secondary market, and it also indicates the bank's unconditional willingness to pay the instrument at maturity. A BA often originates as the result of a merchandise transaction (often in international trade) when an importer requires financing.

As an investment instrument, a BA of a particular bank carries higher credit quality than the same bank's CD, because it is not only a direct obligation of the bank, like a CD, but is also an obligation of an importer and usually collateralized by the merchandise itself. However, BAs are not deposits and do not carry the $100,000 insurance coverage of the Federal Deposit Insurance Corporation. Often BAs can be purchased at a few basis points' higher yield than a CD from the same issuing bank, because many investors are not as familiar with BAs as they are with CDs.

ASSET-BACKED SECURITIES

These are securities where some type of collateral, or pool of assets, serves as the basis for the creditworthiness of the security. Earlier in this section were referenced Government National Mortgage Association securities whose underlying collateral was a "pool" of mortgages. Also, many other nongovernmental securities are issued with collateral such as auto loans or credit-card loan receivables.

COMMERCIAL PAPER

Commercial paper traditionally has been an unsecured promissory note issued by a corporation. The issuer may be an industrial corporation, the holding company parent of a bank, or a finance company that is often a captive finance company owned by an industrial corporation. Commercial paper is issued to mature for periods ranging from one to 270 days. Corporate obligations issued for longer than 270 days must be registered with the Securities and Exchange Commission; therefore, companies needing short-term financing typically restrict the maturities of this debt to 270 days or less. Commercial paper is available to the investor through many major banks that issue the bank's holding company commercial paper or act as an agent for other issuers, and through investment bankers and dealers who may underwrite the commercial paper for their clients. A growing percentage of the commercial paper issued today is now secured, or asset-backed commercial paper.

LOAN PARTICIPATIONS

A loan participation as an investment medium is attractive to an investor because it presents an opportunity to invest in a corporate obligation that is similar to commercial paper but normally carries a somewhat higher yield. Banks have invested in loan participations of other banks for decades as a means of diversifying loan portfolios. However, the use of loan participations as an investment medium for corporations was a new development during the late 1980s.

The loan participation investment medium begins when a bank makes a loan to a corporation using standardized loan documentation. After the loan has been made, the bank seeks investors to buy "participations" in the loan. The investor in the loan participation has the obligation to investigate the credit of the obligor, since the bank selling the participation offers no guarantee or endorsement, implied or otherwise. Many companies that are obligors of these loans are rated by the commercial paper rating agencies, such as Standard & Poor's and Moody's Investors Service. In some cases, the entire short-term debt of the issuer is rated, while in other cases only the commercial paper of the company is rated. However, if the short-term debt or commercial paper is unrated and an investor must rely on his or her own credit analysis, the investor must use extreme caution due to the difficulty in ascertaining the credit soundness of the investment. Loan participations may have maturities ranging from one day to several months. Occasionally, the investor may be able to obtain a loan participation to suit his or her precise maturity requirements, particularly when large amounts (in excess of $1 million) are available for investment.

The investor should be aware that a loan participation is not a negotiable instrument and, therefore, is not a liquid investment. It does not constitute good collateral for the investor who needs to pledge part or all of his or her investment portfolio to secure certain obligations. A loan participation, however, may be a good investment from the standpoint of yield, subject to appropriate credit investigation by the investor.

CORPORATE NOTES AND BONDS

Corporate debt instruments with maturities longer than 270 days are considered notes if they mature within 10 years from their original issue date. The instruments are considered bonds if they mature more than 10 years from the original issue date. Notes with maturities up to approximately three to five years can play an important role in portfolios where the objective is to increase yield over what is available from strictly short-term portfolios, and where nearly perfect liquidity is not necessarily required. Because they have a longer maturity than money market instruments, corporate notes are subject to greater market risk due to changes in interest rates. However, because the maturities may be only three to five years, the instruments are not subject to swings in market values as much as bonds.

Corporate bonds are often included in investment portfolios in which the time horizon is much longer than liquidity portfolios. Bonds are seldom included in liquidity portfolios unless they will mature in one year or less.

REPURCHASE AGREEMENTS

A repurchase agreement is an investment transaction between an investor and a bank or securities dealer, in which the bank or dealer agrees to sell a particular instrument to the investor and simultaneously agrees to repurchase that instrument at a certain date in the future. The repurchase price is designed to give the investor a yield equivalent to a rate of interest that both parties negotiate at the time the transaction is initiated.

On its face, a repurchase agreement transaction, commonly referred to as a "repo," appears to place full and complete ownership of the underlying securities in the hands of the investor. However, a number of incidents of default by dealers occurred during the 1980s, resulting in court rulings that brought the fundamental nature of repos into question. Those rulings implied very strongly that a repo was not, in fact, a purchase with a simultaneous agreement to repurchase the underlying securities, but rather a loan made by the investor to the dealer secured by the pledge of the underlying instruments as collateral to the loan. This viewpoint was bolstered by the fact that in the repo business, the underlying instruments always have been called "collateral." Investors who were previously authorized to invest in instruments subject to repurchase were now faced with making secured loans to banks and brokers.

Because repos traditionally have been a fundamental investment medium used by institutions to invest temporarily surplus funds overnight and for periods of approximately one week, the court rulings seriously undermined the viability of the repo for this important purpose. It was not until Congress adopted the Government Securities Act of 1986 (as supplemented by regulations issued by the Treasury Department early in 1988) that the investment community regained its confidence in the repo as an investment medium. That act, however, addressed only part of the issue. It laid out very clearly the rights, duties, and obligations of the dealer in a repurchase agreement as long as the dealer is not a bank. However, it left hanging in the wind the relationship of the dealer if the dealer is a bank. This void continues to exist.

In order to fill the void, the investor should enter into an underlying written agreement with the dealer or bank as the counterparty to the transaction. The agreement should spell out very clearly the rights, duties, and obligations of each of the parties, particularly in the event of the default of one of them. The agreement should also state clearly that the transaction is intended to be a purchase/repurchase transaction and explicitly is not a loan by the investor to the dealer or bank. The agreement should further provide that in the event of the default of the dealer, the investor has the right to take possession of the collateral, if the investor does not already have such possession, and to dispose of that collateral in order to recover its investment.

The Public Securities Association, an organization of securities dealers, prepared a model agreement in 1986 that many banks and securities dealers have adopted and which they require their repo customers to execute. This model agreement appears to have been drafted in an even-handed manner and supports the interests of both counterparties in the repurchase transaction. Therefore, if the bank or securities dealer does not offer such an agreement, the investor should ask for the agreement from the bank or dealer.

Because of past history involving the collapse of some investment houses that were heavily involved in repos, an investor should be forewarned that the real risk in entering into a repo is the risk of failure of the counterparty (i.e., either a dealer or a bank) to perform under the agreement. Before the spate of failures during the 1980s, the investor typically looked only to the collateral for safety of principal. The investor, however, should recognize that the success of the transaction actually depends on the viability and willingness of the dealer or bank to repurchase the securities at maturity of the transaction. Accordingly, the investor must be diligent to investigate the credit standing of the counterparty to the transaction.

As an additional protection, the investor should specify to the dealer or bank those securities that are acceptable as underlying collateral. Investing guidelines should specify that such underlying collateral may consist of only investment instruments permitted by the guidelines. Moreover, the guidelines should require that in a repo transaction, the value of the underlying collateral should exceed the amount of the investment transaction by some small increment, usually stated in terms of 102 percent of the amount of the transaction. This should be monitored by the investor on a regular basis to keep current on the market value of securities used as collateral. One final point to be considered is whether the collateral is set aside for the investor and does actually exist.

MONEY-MARKET MUTUAL FUNDS

A money-market mutual fund is itself a portfolio of money market instruments. It provides a reasonable vehicle for investing modest sums where the amount may be too small to manage an effective investing program. For example, in managing amounts of less than $3 million, an investor is hard-pressed to meet the objectives of preservation of capital, maintenance of liquidity, and yield because money-market instruments normally trade in $1 million pieces. The portfolio loses some diversification because of the large size required. If diversification is necessary, it forces the size of any one investment to be less than $1 million, and the company will sacrifice liquidity.

One solution to this dilemma is to invest in a money-market mutual fund where the amounts invested may range from a minimum of perhaps $1,000 (in a retail oriented money-market fund) to many millions of dollars. Various kinds of money-market mutual funds exist. The more popular funds cater to consumers and businesses with modest amounts available, and others serve institutional investors with large amounts of investable funds. Generally, both categories of funds operate similarly, with the institutional funds requiring larger minimum investments and often taking smaller management fees.

The mutual fund affords the investor the opportunity to meet its investment objectives of safety of principal, maintenance of liquidity, and yield provided that the investor carefully selects the particular fund. Fund selection should be based on a thorough review of the prospectus, with particular attention paid to the investment objectives of the fund, the experience and investment record of the fund's management, and the quality and liquidity of the investment instruments that the fund maintains in its portfolio.

The investor should inquire about redemption privileges and requirements of the fund and the fund's "pain threshold" for withdrawals. Most money-market mutual funds allow withdrawal virtually on demand either by check (which is actually a draft drawn against the fund) or by electronic funds transfer to the investor's bank account. Electronic funds transfer may be either a wire transfer for value the same day as the withdrawal, or it may be an automated clearinghouse transfer with settlement the following day. The pain threshold refers to the size of withdrawal that the fund can tolerate without incurring its own liquidity problems. For some of the very large money-market mutual funds, an immediate withdrawal of $50 million can be tolerated with little pain because of the fund's size. On the other hand, a small fund of less than $500 million may have a problem meeting a withdrawal request for $5 million. The size factor should be seriously considered when selecting a money-market mutual fund.

DEFINITIONS OF EQUITY INSTRUMENTS

American Depositary Receipts American brokers function as intermediaries in the purchase and sale of foreign issues by acting as a conduit for shares that are listed on international exchanges. A broker retains shares in a pool, which are represented by salable depositary receipts (ADRs).

Common Stock A security that represents an ownership interest in a corporation.

Convertible Securities Bonds, debentures, or preferred shares of stock that may be exchanged by the owner for common stock or another security of the issuing firm. These issues are particularly useful in new ventures when the founders are seeking capital and include several types of both convertible equity and convertible bond issues.

Index Funds A mutual fund whose portfolio matches that of a broad-based index such as Standard & Poor's Index and whose performance, therefore, mirrors the market as a whole.

Preferred Stock A class of stock with a claim on the company's earnings before payment may be made on the common stock that is usually entitled to priority over common stock if the company liquidates it; its investors is usually entitled to dividends at a specific rate when declared by the Board of Directors and before payment of a dividend on the common stock and depending on the terms of the issue.

Rights (Corporate Action) Rights offerings entitle owners of common stock to purchase shares of new stock issuance at a price somewhat below the current market price; usually the right has a duration of 90 days following the issuance of new common stock.

Rule 144a Stock A pool of common shares that has been authorized by a corporation's Board of Directors that is usually not entirely disbursed or marketed for sale, but is held in an internal pool known as treasury stock. A certain number of shares from this pool is often set aside for internal distribution, and hence is never registered with the Securities and Exchange Commission. Prior to registration, these Rule 144 shares are not used in calculations of a company's worth such as P/E ratios or book value.

Warrants A certificate giving the holder the right to purchase a fixed number of common stock securities at a stipulated price within a specified time limit or perpetually. Warrants are created by a corporation to facilitate the sale of debt or preferred stock.

GLOSSARY

AMERICAN DEPOSITARY RECEIPTS (ADRS)

American brokers function as intermediaries in the purchase and sale of foreign issues by acting as a conduit for shares that are listed on international exchanges. A broker retains shares in a pool, which are represented by salable depositary receipts (ADRs).

ASSET-BACKED SECURITIES (ABSS)

Mostly AAA-rated securities secured by consumer credit card receivables. These issues are credit-enhanced by overcollateralization, letters of credit, and subordination of portions of cash flow to cushion against any losses is the underlying receivables.

COLLATERALIZED MORTGAGE OBLIGATIONS (CMOS)

A multiclass bond backed by a pool of mortgage pass-through securities or mortgage loans.

COMMON STOCK

Represents equity ownership in a corporation, though the right to residual claims on corporate assets is subordinated to the rights of debt holders, in the event of liquidation. Further rights guaranteed by common stock ownership can generate entitlements that have intrinsic marketable value. These include *rights offerings,* or *preemptive rights,* which entitle the holder to purchase shares of a new stock issuance at a price somewhat below the current market price; usually the right has a duration of 90 days following the issuance of new common stock. *Warrants* provide the holder the right to purchase a fixed number of shares of common stock at a predetermined price during a specific period, though some warrants are perpetual. Warrants are created by a corporation to facilitate the sale of debt or preferred stock.

CONVERTIBLE DEBT INSTRUMENTS

These securities act like convertible equity issues, but have fundamental pricing differences. Usually, the conversion on bonds is expressed as a conversion price rather than as a ratio, as is the case with convertible equity issues.

CONVERTIBLE PREFERRED EQUITY ISSUES

The convertible preferred equity issue can be exchanged, at the shareholder's option and at any prespecified ratio or at a preestablished conversion price, for shares of a company's common stock. The conversion ratio is the par or stated value of the preferred stock divided by the purchase price; conversions of equity issues usually occur at a conversion ratio as opposed to a particular price.

CONVERTIBLE SECURITIES

Debt instruments and equity securities that are convertible into forms of common stock. These issues are particularly useful in new ventures when the founders are seeking capital, and include several types of both convertible equity and convertible bond issues.

INDEX FUND

Mutual fund whose portfolio matches that of a broad-based index such as Standard & Poor's Index and whose performance, therefore, mirrors the market as a whole.

INVESTMENT KATINESS

Various ratings services publish analyses on the array of investment instruments currently available on the markets. Among the most widely known fixed-income ratings services are Moody's and Standard & Poor's (S&P). Their investment ratings are as follows:

Company	High Quality	Quality	Below Investment Grade	Very Poor Quality
S&P	AAA–AA	A–BBB	BB–B	CCC–D
Moody's	Aaa–Aa	A–Baa	Ba–B	Caa–C

PREFERRED EQUITY REDEMPTION CUMULATIVE STOCK (PERCS)

A type of convertible preferred stock first brought to the market in 1991, PERCs automatically convert to common stock at the termination of a three-year period, unless called prior to that by the issuer. A cap is set on the conversion value, generally at about 30 percent above the common stock price at the time the preferred stock is issued. If at the end of the three-year period the stock is trading at or below the common stock price, holders receive one share of common stock for each PERC share. PERCs are marketable, although as with all equity securities, a market is never guaranteed.

PREFERRED STOCK

An equity issue that has fixed-income characteristics; preferred shares have a fixed dividend, which is stated as a percentage of par value. These shares usually do not have preemptive rights or voting rights, though they are senior to common shares in terms of liquidation claims.

REAL ESTATE MORTGAGE INVESTMENT CONDUITS (REMICS)

Various mortgage tranches, or classes of bonds, are offered (e.g., planned amortization class, inverse floaters, sequential pay, etc).

RULE 144 STOCK

A pool of common shares that has been authorized by a corporation's Board of Directors is usually not entirely disbursed or marketed for sale, but is held in an internal pool known as treasury stock. A certain number of shares from this pool is often set aside for internal distribution, and hence is never registered with the Securities and Exchange Commission. Prior to registration, these Rule 144 shares are not used in calculations of a company's worth such as P/E ratios or book value.

CHAPTER 13

INFORMATION TECHNOLOGY AND KNOWLEDGE MANAGEMENT

13.1 INTRODUCTION

Andy Bryant, chief financial officer (CFO) of Intel, leads Intel's human resources, information technology (IT), and procurement, and is heavily involved in strategic decision making. He sees this expansive role as the trend for the future in businesses. For many nonprofit CFOs, such a multifaceted role is normal, not exceptional. Bryant believes that Intel's IT is better managed now that it is under finance, and he also thinks the finance office acts more appropriately toward the IT staff due to having the reporting relationship.[1]

Information technology has been the buzzword for the past two decades. The rush to automate and implement new technologies and better harness data for improved performance and greater effectiveness has yet to slow down. Technology has been seen as the solution to increase productivity, reduce errors, keep up with the increasing demands for more and more information, and improve performance. Information technology is "concerned with all aspects of managing and processing information,"[2] and may be defined as "the use of hardware, software, services, and supporting infrastructure to manage and deliver information using voice, data, and video."[3] Consider how the state of North Dakota frames IT and the budget implications for its agencies (see Exhibit 13.1).

The top priorities at the end of the first decade in the new millennium, for corporate IT directors, are largely about service levels, implementing project initiatives, automation of business processes, maintaining adequate security and data protection, aligning IT with corporate strategy and getting better operational data, meeting regulatory compliance requirements (largely Sarbanes-Oxley), finding qualified staff, and launching or expanding e-business efforts.[4] Other than a lower ranking for regulatory impetus and a higher ranking for staff recruitment, most nonprofits would largely mirror these priorities.

Finance staff is in a key role in regard to IT spending, both because IT spending is largely made at management's discretion and because of the large financial impact of IT expenditures. Notes Michael Blake, a financial officer at nonprofit healthcare services firm Kaiser Permanente, "Finance has to play both an oversight and a consultative role, and play them both well... finance has to be discerning about budget decisions or risk thwarting strategic growth [such as ordering an across-the-board reduction in IT expenses]."[5] About three in ten corporate CFOs believe the IT area should report to the finance area, about six in ten believe IT should not report to finance but that they should work closely together, and the remainder are evenly split on having them collaborate only on matters of spending or work entirely independent of each other.[6] Finance staff should push for adequate technology to assist it in its critical role as risk management captain—with proper data, overall risk exposure to all the different risks the organization faces may be assessed, monitored, and managed.[7] (See Chapter 14 for coverage of risk management and Appendix 14A for coverage of derivatives.)

To properly evaluate the need for technology tools and how to implement them, it is necessary to explore what each can offer and attempt to forecast the future capabilities, direction, and growth of each industry. These tools improve and expand rapidly. They are out of date the moment the purchase order is issued; however, finding some stability in this arena is both possible and necessary before their introduction into the workplace.

Recent surveys in the state of Iowa indicate that most nonprofits are "small and struggling" and that one of their chief challenges is "keeping up with technology."[8]

When many people hear the term "information technology, " the computer is the first tool that comes to mind; however, technology tools have been with us in the workplace since the first abacus was introduced to accounting. The migration to advanced technology tools—personal computers (PCs), networks, banking and purchasing over the Internet, electronic payments and donation collections, e-mail, voice mail, fax, and so forth—has been thought to alter radically how we work, when actually it has simply improved on what is familiar by repackaging these tasks and work flow to be smarter, faster, and more efficient.

Information Technology Includes:

- All computers with a human interface
- All computer peripherals that will not operate unless connected to a computer or network
- All voice, video, and data networks and the equipment, staff, and purchased services necessary to operate them
- All salary and benefits for staff whose job description specifically includes technology functions (i.e., network services, applications development, systems administration)
- All technology services provided by vendors or contractors
- Operating costs associated with providing information technology
- All costs associated with developing, purchasing, licensing, or maintaining software

Agencies may wish to include other costs at their discretion. For example, an agency may wish to include digital cameras in their IT budget even though they can be operated standalone. Data entry personnel may be included if they are considered part of the technology staff. Costs that are excluded above may be included if they are an integral part of a computer application or would be difficult to break out because the costs are included with other information technology costs.

Examples of Information Technology:

- Telephone and radio equipment and switches used for voice communications
- Traditional computer applications that include data storage and programs to input, process, and output the data
- Software and support for office automation systems such as word processing and spreadsheets, as well as the computer to run them
- Users' PCs and software
- Server hardware and software used to support applications such as electronic mail/groupware, file and print services, database, application/web servers, storage systems, and other hosting services
- Data, voice, and video networks and all associated communications equipment and software
- Peripherals directly connected to computer information systems used to collect or transmit audio, video, or graphic information, such as scanners and digitizers
- Voice response systems that interact with a computer database or application
- The state radio communications network
- Computers and network systems used by teachers, trainers, and students for educational purposes
- "Open/integrated" computer systems that monitor or automate mechanical or chemical processes and also store information used by computer applications for analysis and decision-making, such as the Metasys building management system
- All operating costs, equipment, and staff time associated with supporting the technology infrastructure of the agency, possibly including items excluded above, such as video equipment used for technology training that is included in the information systems cost center for the agency.

Source: http://www.nd.gov/.

EXHIBIT 13.1 INFORMATION TECHNOLOGY EXPLANATION AND EXAMPLES

13.2 HOW MUCH TECHNOLOGY AND WHICH TO CHOOSE?

IT tools can dramatically improve performance if they are used appropriately and wisely. They can also be used inappropriately and damage a smooth-running operation. For example, many companies are opting for the use of electronic receptionists, offering their customers a series of questions to direct their calls. This technology can be very useful in the right environment, such as a highly technical customer base; however, if the customer base is nontechnical (more service based) or if the service is not highly dependable, the selection of this technology may damage customer or client relations.

The same is also true with the use of computers, either PCs or midrange ones. There should be a good, sound reason to automate a task or process, not just a desire to jump on the *technology bandwagon.* To analyze your organization's need for technology, use the checklist in Exhibit 13.2.

(a) WHAT TYPES OF TECHNOLOGY TOOLS SHOULD I CONSIDER?   Before deciding on a specific platform (e.g., PCs or Macs), six questions should be answered:

1. *What software is available for this system that the business will require?* Traditionally, Macs have been used in businesses that produce graphics (e.g., advertising,

---

To determine whether a task or process could benefit from automation, use the following checklist:

Why Do I Want To Automate This Process?

1. *To handle a redundant process (The same task is repeated over and over.)* Any task that is repeated could greatly benefit from automation. Computers are good at doing that same thing repeatedly.

2. *To share or manipulate information* If there is a need to share information across departments, divisions, or work groups, or a need to have the same information manipulated for different audiences, then maintaining it in a computer is the best way to accomplish the task.

3. *To enable staff to do more work* This is a common reason for the decision to automate. It, in itself, is not a valid reason for automation, nor will automating for this reason yield the desired results. This is the most common erroneous justification for automation. There must be something specific about the task or process that could be streamlined, simplified, or improved on with the use of an automated technology. This reason is sound only if it is followed by a qualifier, such as, "To enable staff to do more work ... by automating the routine tasks they perform, thus reducing their workload."

4. *To reduce errors* There can be a great reduction in errors with the use of technology if the systems, processes, and rules can be built; however, if the system design is as freeform as the manual process, those same errors will be introduced into the automated process. In addition, since the automated process will be new, more errors will be made as staff members are learning to use the technology.

5. *To produce multiple outputs (e.g., reports, cards, badges, graphs, charts, form letters)* This is one of the best reasons for automation (where the same information is used for different reasons). If done well, automating this type of process can dramatically reduce errors and workload, and increase productivity.

EXHIBIT 13.2 TECHNOLOGY CHECKLIST

marketing) and PCs have been used for number crunching (e.g., accounting, forecasting). While the differences between the two platforms are diminishing rapidly, the majority of accounting applications, for example, are available only for the PC, and some design packages are available only on Macs.

2. *Who will need to access the information?* Will a network need to be established linking the computers? If so, there may be a need to standardize around a certain type of architecture and possibly compromise on the financial management needs with that of the rest of the business. If not, a diversity of platforms will not hinder or interfere with your specific needs in the financial management arena. It is also possible to establish two different networks—one for the administrative/business needs of the organization and one for the creative aspects.

3. *Are there sufficient resources (financial and staff) to implement a new technology?* It is easy to budget the costs of the equipment, but the less obvious costs of down time, training, installation, maintenance, new supplies, and other factors are not as easy to predict, manage, or forecast.

4. *What does the research of others in a similar industry suggest?* With noncompeting organizations, it is often possible to develop strategic alliances to share expertise and reduce development costs and the risks associated with the implementation of new technologies. Also, Gifts in Kind International (www.giftsinkind.org) has been a valuable source of inexpensive software for nonprofits. At the time of this writing, Lotus Smartsuite (including word processing, database, financial spreadsheet, presentation graphics, and personal information management programs) was available to nonreligious, nonpolitical 501(c)(3) organizations for a $25 administrative charge (www.giftsinkind.org/pdf/lotusw.pdf).

5. *Is there a suitable software product available on the market, or will a customized product be required to meet the need?* Operating system and equipment advancements occur almost annually. If a nonstandard software or hardware is selected, these systems will become obsolete (nonupgradable) almost immediately. Most organizations learned this lesson too late and are faced with the task of reintroducing automation. To avoid this obsolescence, an off-the-shelf package, moderately customized to meet the organization's needs, should be selected. Selecting the appropriate software package should be done carefully and after checking with staff at organizations similar to your own.

6. *Have the findings and decisions been reviewed carefully?* All decisions, assumptions, and recommendations should be discussed with peers. If possible, a consultant with expertise in this specific area should be contracted to review the plans.

All but the very smallest organizations will also require a computer network to allow data and possibly software sharing. If yours is one of the many one-person nonprofit organizations, you should consider the need for a network as you begin to make plans for onsite volunteers and additional staff. The key items to consider in designing and purchasing your network are:

• Know what you need and what you don't need—get input from staff.

• Consider new functionalities that are available, such as remote access via the Internet to your network (for telecommuters and staff as they travel).

- Determine responsibilities for various aspects of the new equipment and software (and consider whether having extra features available for in-house use is cost-effective).

- Obtain multiple bids.

- Get referrals from trusted sources, possibly utilizing a freelance technology expert to help with your decision making.[9]

(b) ARE THEY REQUIRED?   If a task or process can be effectively performed manually, technology tools may not be required; however, the ability to converse with other businesses or individuals may require automation or the introduction of technologies. The fax, for example, is a technology that became a standard for almost all organizations, even though at first the need to receive a fax may have greatly outweighed the need to send a fax.

If there is a need to communicate and share information with other organizations, businesses, government agencies, bureaus, or the like, technologies should be introduced that will enable compliance with these demands. Implementation strategies should include the immediate need(s) as well as long-term strategies for applying new technology in other areas of the organization.

(c) DO I NEED THEM?   In a nonprofit business, technology may not be required for all applications. In the financial arena, however, the capabilities provided by new technologies will dramatically improve the quality of work or at least streamline or simplify the process. The migration from "counting beans" to "analyzing trends and forecasting needs" is the major thrust of automating the process of financial management.

The major focus of financial management is the ability to: review financial information to make decisions; forecast needs, especially cash requirements and the resulting cash position; evaluate performance; and assess progress. The quality of financial management is based on the integrity of the information reviewed and evaluated. The manual process of accounting has provided a level of accuracy and quality that for many years was acceptable. The introduction of technology and the automation of the process provide a higher quality of data than can be provided by a manual accounting process. The removal of as much human error as possible from the process is the single most important reason to automate. While it is still necessary to have a human enter the information into a system, review what is entered, and to reconcile the information against other documents, the simple enhancement of the computer over the 10-key adding machine can dramatically reduce errors and speed up the process.

(d) WHAT WILL THEY DO FOR ME?   Many financial-type software programs on the market resemble easy-to-use checkbooks. While some organization's financial management needs may be much more sophisticated, one of these programs can provide all that is needed to automate the financial operation of many businesses. These software programs, if set up properly, will enable individuals to enter information in a format and style that is easy to understand and use. The ability to produce reports and retrieve information from these systems is quite remarkable. With most of these off-the-shelf programs, a balance sheet can be produced as swiftly and easily as a transaction record.

(e) WHAT WILL THEY NOT DO FOR ME?   Technology cannot solve the organization's problems that are caused by human resources conflicts, poor organizational structure, or complex or ineffective policies or procedures. In fact, the introduction of technology will bring these problems to the surface and, in many cases, magnify their impacts on the organization. It is not uncommon, when technology implementations are under way, for the technology to be blamed for crippling the organization, when in fact the organization was already crippled by these other factors.

It is important to remember that technology tools automate a predefined task or process. Technology does not define the process. If there are existing problems with the processes, there will be problems in the automation of the process.

(f) CAN I AFFORD THEM?   For software purchase and licenses alone, surveyed nonprofits spend $26,000 on average per year, with about one in eight nonprofits spending over $100,000 annually (see Exhibit 13.3). Were there more awareness of appropriate software tools, no doubt many nonprofits would spend even more. The same survey finds that:

> Only 58% agreed with the statement "We have in general the right set of software tools to allow us to do our jobs." Only 49% agreed with the statement "Our tech team is aware of most of the software tools that are likely to be helpful to us."[10]

As you might gather from the previous statistics, software and hardware technologies can be expensive. The initial costs of the equipment and software are only the beginning of the expenditure requirements. With any decision to purchase, there must be a justification for the expenditure. Exhibit 13.4 illustrates one method of determining if there is a justification for the introduction of a new technology.

Exhibit 13.4 assumes the cost of a typical PC configuration at $3,500. At Line 2 of the data in the bottom panel, a 10 percent increase in productivity (or elimination of an extra position at that percentage) recovers the costs of the typical configuration in the first year. Each subsequent year, a savings of $3,500 can be achieved.

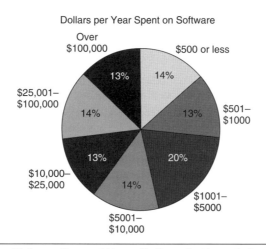

Dollars per Year Spent on Software

Source: Laura S. Quinn, "Software Costs and Usage: Findings of a Nonprofit Sector Survey" (September 2005). Located online at: http://www.idealware.org/. Used by permission.

EXHIBIT 13.3   NONPROFIT SPENDING ON SOFTWARE PURCHASES AND LICENSES

One-Time costs	$1,250
Typical PC configuration	
Software	750
Printer	250
Other	250
Total	2,500
Annual costs (recurring)	500
Training	
Supplies	300
Maintenance	200
Total	1,000
	$3,500

Average Annual Staff Salary	Productivity Increases (% of Position Eliminated)	Annual Net Savings
$35,000	5%	$1,750
$35,000	10%	$3,500
$35,000	15%	$5,250
$35,000	20%	$7,000
$35,000	25%	$8,750
$35,000	30%	$10,500
$35,000	35%	$12,250

Exhibit 13.4   Determination of Expenditure Need

The chart ends at 35 percent. However, if one staff person or the need to hire an additional staff member can be eliminated, the costs of the technology are assuredly justifiable.

(g) WHAT CHANGES WILL THEY INTRODUCE TO MY ORGANIZATION?   All change is dramatic to an organization. Managing the change is the only way to assure that the introduction of new technologies will provide a desired and positive outcome. Accepting that all change is challenging, the introduction of technology has its own set of change issues and concerns. Many of these issues and concerns are unfounded and are based on myths about technology, but they still need to be addressed and discussed.

Assimilating the new technology will not be automatic. Depending on the level of change, new work flows, diagrams, work rules, policies, and procedures will need to be reviewed and, in most cases, revised or rewritten. Putting a computer on someone's desk will not automatically provide increases in productivity. In most cases, the transition process will yield a decrease in productivity until the training and assimilation process is complete. All support systems and processes need to be reviewed, and your staff members need to be retrained.

(i) Example 1: Slow Integration.   In one organization, the use of the computer was widely accepted, and staff learned quickly how to enter the information into the system. Reports were produced, data appeared to be of higher quality, and the staff should have had more

time for analysis; however, the support structure for the system had not been redesigned. Staff members were still maintaining all of the paper documents in cross-filed indexes and logs, as they always had. They had learned to provide others with the information they needed but had not yet learned how to use the information themselves, nor did they believe it was their place to make major changes in the way they maintained their records.

(ii) Example 2: Flawed Integration.   In another organization, a request was made of one staff member to provide historical information about spending on an item type. The staff member went immediately to her paper files rather than the computer. When questioned about it later, she stated that the individual wanted a specific item rather than information on one of the categories of expenditures. When reminded that this person bought only that item, so that item matched up one-to-one to a single category, she realized she could have retrieved the information from the computer system.

In many other implementation situations, the biggest problem is the dramatic cultural change regarding what is valued in the organization. Rules and regulations that had taken decades to learn and memorize were suddenly programmed into the system. Individuals who had spent so much time learning these rules were suddenly no more qualified or valued than the newest person in the organization. So, in addition to new work flows, ways of positively rewarding and recognizing tenure need to be established in the organization.

Another challenge to the introduction of technology is fear: fear of a machine, fear of losing one's job, fear of not being able to use the technology. The greatest pacifier is open communication.

To introduce technology into an organization:

- Determine what impacts the new technology will have on the organization.
- Develop a strategy for communicating the plan and the change to the staff within the organization.
- (Also refer to Appendix 13B.)

  The strategy should include:
- Why and how the need for technology was determined
- Management's commitment to the change
- How the technology will be introduced, who will be affected, what it will do
- How training will be handled
- The timeline (schedule) for the implementation
- The support systems that will be available
- How future communication about this change will be administered
- How this technology will be applied within the organization, what manual process or previous technology it will replace, what policies or procedures will be altered, and so forth

13.3 KNOWLEDGE MANAGEMENT AND INFORMATION TECHNOLOGY

(a) HOW CRITICAL IS DATA?   "Bad data, bad decisions." Many nonprofits make poor decisions because they do not have the information available, do not know how to process or analyze the information, or do not have the time to carefully consider the decision alternatives and the information related to each of those alternatives. Furthermore, the Lilly study documented that the use of IT (particularly PC technology) was closely correlated with the proficiency of the organization's overall financial management effectiveness. Using the information processing power of the basic financial spreadsheet, in particular, is essential to your organization's financial decision making. Facing complex environments and scarce resources, nonprofits must manage the knowledge resource effectively and efficiently.[11]

(b) KNOWLEDGE MANAGEMENT.   Many nonprofits use knowledge intensively—a prime example is philanthropic foundations. Identifying cutting-edge grantees or grant ideas, evaluating grant proposals, processing grant progress reports, and publishing policy reports are all knowledge-based activities. However, if these organizations do not invest in the proper systems, people, and organizational infrastructure, they will be hampered in their efforts. One foundation, the Casey Foundation, went to the extent of having a team classify everything the foundation had ever learned from the studies it had funded, so this knowledge could be accessed quickly and efficiently.[12]

One of the most exciting prospects for your organization is to begin to teach (or enable the learning of) your employees and volunteers, as well as your board, the linkages between your organizations's activities and its hoped-for outcomes. Researcher Natalie Buckminster[13] argues that this activity-outcome instruction is a tremendous way to promote organization learning; we concur.

(i) Is Yours a Learning Organization?   Peter Senge, probably the leading world expert on organizational learning, defines a learning organization as one in which "people continually expand their capacity to create the results they truly desire, where new and expansive patterns of thinking are nurtured, where collective aspiration is set free, and where people are continually learning to see the whole together."[14] How are your staff members' capacities being expanded? Do those with innovative ideas, or who challenge the conventional wisdom, get their ideas dismissed abruptly or shot down by the leaders? Do leaders help team members "see the big picture"? In particular, effective businesses have a "value culture," in which all employees are guided toward the likely effects of their activities and decisions on the company's stock price, or value. In nonprofits, the effect of activities and decisions on mission attainment is key, but so too is the likely effect on the liquidity position of the organization. Constant training, normally done informally in "teachable moments," helps your employees see the connection of their tasks to cash inflow and outflow timing, amount, and risk. Working to model the type of culture you wish to create is essential, as noted by Gard Meserve, chief information officer (CIO) of Clarkson University.[15]

(ii) Steps Toward Building a Learning Culture.   Senge identified five disciplines that must be harnessed for your organization to become a learning organization:

1. Systems thinking (Look at your organization as a whole, including how it fits into its environment, and recognize all of its parts work together and not independently.)

2. Personal mastery (There is no way your organization can be a learning organization if individuals are not learning individuals.)

3. Mental models (Understand or picture how the world works in some specific arena.)

4. Development of a shared vision (How will the world be different if our organization succeeds in achieving its mission?)

5. Team learning (Team members must learn to exchange ideas, which necessitates suspending assumptions and regarding others as colleagues, and stimulating this dialogue often requires a facilitator to help the process.)[16]

(iii) Managing Intellectual Capital. The more knowledge-based your organization (think educational institution), the more important it is to recruit, select, retain, and tap into your human resources. Beyond that, shepherding great ideas and processes, learning from successes as well as failures, learning from others in similar organizations, protecting unique ideas from theft or piracy, and maintaining a usable "knowledge database" are all key features to effective management of intellectual capital.[17]

13.4 INFORMATION TECHNOLOGY IN TODAY'S NONPROFITS

(a) ELECTRONIC COMMERCE. Electronic commerce, or e-commerce, is the electronic exchange of information and/or payment flows. It could be between organizations or involve individuals. Some label this process as "e-business," not e-commerce.[18]

(i) Doing Business Electronically. There are many functions that your organization may carry out electronically. Doing business electronically offers the possibility of doing things faster, with less human involvement, and more accurately. We shall expand on specific processes and functions a bit later.

(ii) Your Organization's Web Site. A key component of your IT is your organization's Web site. Potential board members, employees, volunteers, clients, and donors all gather information and build an image of your organization from your Web site. This is also a perfect spot to post annual reports and annual financial statements. Fundraising potential is high too; we return to this topic in a later section.

(b) SPREADSHEETS AND BEYOND FOR DATA AND DECISIONS.

(i) Spreadsheets. Flexible, easy to use, and yet prone to error—this is the way most users view spreadsheets. Almost all businesses and nonprofits find some use for spreadsheets, including their function as a basic database.

(ii) Data Warehouse. A data warehouse is "a collection of data gathered and organized so that it can easily be analyzed, extracted, synthesized, and otherwise used for purposes of further understanding the data."[19] This warehouse is created by indexing transactions data and setting up a table of contents, chapters, and then paragraphs. Make it available to others in your organization, with password protection, and place it on your network.[20]

(iii) Bank/Financial Service Provider Online Services. We most often think of bank portals or other Web sites when we consider online services. These are extremely useful for looking up account balances, seeing if items have cleared, finding out if electronic transactions were executed, and viewing the front and back of images of checks that were presented to see if there might be fraudulent activity. However, larger organizations are now moving to the next generation of services, consistent with the outsourcing issue we covered earlier. For example, consider the possibility of outsourcing your disbursements. "EDI" refers to electronic data interchange, which involves "the electronic transfer of information or data between trading partners and to communications between the company and its bank."[21]

An example of a bank's comprehensive disbursements system is presented in Exhibit 13.5. You may wish to refer to Chapter 11 for greater detail on automated clearinghouses (ACH), wire, and check payment media.

According to the most recent Ernst & Young "Cash Management Survey" available, almost all large banks and many midsize banks now offer Internet-based transfers between accounts, balance and information reporting, and ACH and wire transfer initiations. About four-fifths of these banks also allow organizations to view images of paid items (usually in connection with the bank's "positive pay" service, which triggers exception authorizations whenever checks presented differ from the issued-items database held by the organization) and lockbox items (typically both the checks and the remittance document). The organization's deposit item images are available via the Internet at close to half of the major banks.[22]

(iv) Application Service Provider.   Rather than purchase software, why not "rent" software that is hosted on the vendor's Web site? This is the idea behind application service provider offerings. For example, SunGard offers its AvantGard application service provider (ASP), which is oriented to businesses with between $250 million and $1 billion in sales. Selkirk Financial Technologies, Inc., has a Web-based service (Treasury Anywhere) that it sells through banks.[23] We believe that in the near future these platforms will migrate to smaller businesses and to small-to-midsize nonprofits.

EDI Comprehensive Disbursements

How Mellon Rem*EDI*® Comprehensive Disbursements Works

Company   Trading Partner

1. Your company delivers a single standards-based file containing payment and remittance information for all your payment types.

2. Mellon Rem *EDI* converts your payment instruction file into the required format for all payment applications, including automated clearing house (ACH), check and wire transfer.

3. Your trading partner is paid and remittance detail is forwarded to your trading partner according to your instructions.

Source: Mellon Bank. Located online at http://www.mellon.com/.

EXHIBIT 13.5   OUTSOURCED DISBURSEMENTS

(v) Treasury Workstation.   For larger organizations, there is treasury workstation (TWS) software. Most large businesses use TWS software to assist in the treasury function. JP Morgan offers a PC-based system called Insight that may work for midsize or smaller organizations. It enables the user to get detail on changes to cash positions and initiate multibank, multicurrency operations. Add-on modules include an interface to the general ledger, a foreign exchange trading module, and an investment and debt management module.[24]

(vi) Enterprise Resource Planning System.   Here is a good definition of enterprise resource planning (ERP) systems: "ERP systems are comprised of software programs which tie together all of an enterprise's various functions—such as finance, manufacturing, sales and human resources."[25] These systems are expensive, so they should be considered by larger nonprofit organizations.[26] As noted earlier, there is a trend toward hosted ERP systems, following the ASP model of software delivery.[27]

(c) DEDICATED SOFTWARE.   Consider single-purpose software as another option in your IT toolbox. We will briefly discuss five forms of this: dashboards, fundraising, purchasing/e-billing/e-payment, budgeting and planning, and human resource management.

(i) Dashboards.   A dashboard is a single interface that gives your management access to "key performance indicators," which are action-oriented measures that help monitor and trigger corrective actions.[28] Your balanced scorecard may have a number of metrics that are monitored via your dashboard, for example. Dashboard design includes these steps, according to Daryl Orts, Vice-President of Advanced Solutions for software provider Noetix Corporation:

- Refine the user interface and control flow.
- Confirm the data sources for each data element.
- Determine how to "persist" data when historical trending information desired but unavailable from the transaction database.
- Define the queries needed to retrieve each data element.
- Determine drill paths.[29]

(ii) Fundraising Software.   Software from vendors such as Blackbaud (Raiser's Edge) are popular applications in the nonprofit world. What excites most nonprofits, though, is the potential to raise funds via their Web site. Consider these survey statistics:

- A majority (58 percent) of donor participants reported they use the Internet to search for information, volunteer, donate, and sign petitions for causes or organizations they want to support.
- Three out of four [donor] respondents take some additional action—on-line or off-line—after visiting a charity-oriented Web site. Some 60 percent stated that had they not visited the charity site, they either definitely would not have taken further action or were unsure that they would have taken additional action.
- The nonprofits use the Internet to provide information on their missions, goals, issues, achievements, financial data, and to gather support by encouraging Web site visitors to become members, donate, volunteer, sign a petition, or buy a product.[30]

(iii) Purchasing, E-Billing, and E-Payment Software.   In the business sector, when companies embrace Internet applications, they experience a reduction in total financial transaction costs drop as much as 40 percent compared to average firms.[31] Even more impressive, companies that move from paper to electronics in payables areas, including supplier invoicing to vendor payments, experience costs reductions of up to 90 percent, according to Hackett Group research. Comparing top-quartile cost to bottom-quartile cost companies, and factoring in their sizes, this constitutes a $590,000 savings per $1 billion in sales.[32]

(iv) Budgeting and Planning Software.   As we discussed in Chapter 8, planning and forecasting software (sometimes called business performance management software) is touted by some as offering a significant analytical advantage. This software is offered by vendors such as Hyperion (www.hyperion.com; see the higher education profile at www.hyperion.com/solutions/industry_solutions/higher_ed/). Other than financial spreadsheets, basic budgeting and planning systems are the only finance-specific software technologies used by businesses, according to a survey of 168 finance executives.[33]

(v) Human Resource Management Software.   The very first ERP software applications were focused in the area of human resource planning and management. Oracle (which acquired PeopleSoft in 2005) and SAP are two of the largest vendors in this marketplace of about 30 vendors. At a minimum, consider having a human resource information system (HRIS) to keep track of your workforce. Many organizations now provide all of their benefits information and forms online.

13.5 WHAT SHOULD I KNOW/DO BEFORE INVESTING IN TECHNOLOGY TOOLS?

With the introduction of any new technology, there will be changes and unexpected delays and costs; plan for them. If no other method of allowing for hidden expenditures is possible, an extra line item should be added to the budget of "Unforeseen Expenditures" as a percentage of the total budget.

If a vendor or a contractor promises to deliver a product by a certain date, penalties or rewards for meeting or missing the deadline should be included in the contract.

In addition:

- Budget time for planning the implementation.

- Recognize that not all staff members will agree with the decisions, and some will try to stop or sabotage the implementation, either directly or indirectly.

- Accept that some staff members may not be able to deal with the changes and may leave on their own, or they may need to be removed from the organization or retrained for other positions.

- Seek advice from colleagues and peers from other organizations. Pay careful attention to their experiences, and assume that any problems or obstacles they faced will occur in your organization, no matter how well the implementation plans and strategies are carried out.

- Realize that mistakes will be made along the way.

	No. of Employees
1998	15
1999	30
2000	45
2001	47
2002	49
2003	55
2004	89
2005	92
2006	92
2007	97
Average:	*61*

EXHIBIT 13.6   GROWTH ANALYSIS

(a) PLANNING FOR GROWTH.   The biggest challenge of any new venture is predicting future needs. With technology, this predicting activity can be especially critical. Many technologies are sold in blocks, accommodating a specific number of users, telephones, connections, and the like. While it is never wise to overpurchase, it is also imprudent to replace existing equipment unnecessarily or too quickly.

Predicting future growth does not have to be as unscientific as reading a crystal ball; however, an accurate prediction of future needs should not be expected. Projections should be conservative, either in terms of growth or investment. The best measurements begin with an analysis of historical growth, plus or minus contributing factors.

Exhibit 13.6 lists the total number of employees for a given organization over the last ten years, with an average of sixty-one employees. Predicting that the organization will have an average of sixty-one employees per year would be a misinterpretation of the data. Examining the data more closely shows that a greater pattern of growth occurred during the first five years, with a steady but slower growth in the second five years.

Microsoft Excel™ has a handy built-in formula for calculating the compound annual growth rate (CAGR) of a data series. This function, RATE, uses this format for our entire ten years of observations (nine years of growth):

$$=RATE(9, 0, -15, 97, 0, 10)$$

The first item is the number of years of growth, which is nine in our example. The second number is the payment per period, which is 0 in our example. (For a loan payment, enter the payment per period). The third number is the starting value, or "present value" in the series, which is $15 in our case. (You must put a negative sign in front of it.) The fourth number, 97, is the ending value, or future value. The following 0 indicates that the employee number are at the end of the respective periods. The 10 is a starting guess for the percent growth rate—if you don't have any idea, 10 is a good number to use. Excel™ gives us a result of 23.05 percent for the entire period. However, just as your visual examination of the data suggested, when we use only the first 5 years or only the last 5 years (each of which spans four years of growth) in the growth calculation, we get very different growth rates:

1998–2002	**34.44%**
2003–2007	**15.24%**

Clearly, a new trend better characterizes later years, and to the extent "nothing significant has changed" for the future, we would want to extend the data at a 15.24 percent rate of growth, not a 23.05 percent rate of growth. Watch for pattern or trend changes in your organization's revenues and costs, and capture these when doing your projections.

(b) OUTSOURCING?   Outsourcing of IT comes in various forms. You may outsource your entire IT department, outsource software by using hosted software on a vendor's computer system, or merely outsource certain functions such as payroll processing (many organizations do the latter through ADP or Paychex). It is always a consideration in any IT-related decision that you make.[34]

13.6 SOFTWARE: DESIGN INTERNALLY OR PURCHASE?

Many software companies are now working with clients to lease/finance software. Leasing costs more but is often worth it in the longer term. A typical approach in many organizations who need to purchase computer technology (hardware and software) is to engage in a lengthy process of identifying needs, shopping vendors, and so forth. After identifying the needs, they prepare a request for proposal including all the specifications they want and need.

A shortcut many take is to network with other similar organizations and approach a vendor to design a system that works for everyone. The vendor maintains the right to sell the product to similar organizations. The end result is that the development costs are spread among a greater number of users.

As discussed earlier, during the 1980s, organizations generally designed their own software. The latest trend is to purchase existing software and tweak it to meet unique needs. In most cases, at least three major vendors, in any given area, provide software for a specific task or process. It is easier, cheaper, and safer to purchase one of these products than to design a new one. In addition, these vendors will also provide (generally free of charge) hardware specifications for the application.

Changing technology requires the technology manager to constantly review what the organization's systems do and do not do, and to modify needs based on current procedures and task flows.

13.7 DISCLOSURE, THE LAW, AND SECURITY

There are many laws regarding the disclosure of information. A public institution's financial records may be public record; however, in many instances a portion of the data does not need to be disclosed, and in some cases, disclosure of certain pieces of information is illegal. It is imperative that a thorough investigation of the laws and policies pertaining to the types of data maintained be reviewed (see Chapter 15 for additional resources on maintaining data).

(a) A COMPANY DATA POLICY.   Establishing a policy regarding the use of company data will also provide a mechanism for training staff about the security requirements of the data.

Exhibit 13.7 provides a sample policy that pertains to maintaining sensitive and/or confidential information. Exhibit 13.8 provides a sample communication policy checklist, which guides you in setting policy governing the increasingly sensitive area of electronic

You as volunteers and staff are involved extensively in fund-raising, governmental relations, and public communications programs. You are acting as agents of <Organization Name> and have been chosen for your abilities to be representatives of <Organization Name>.

In this capacity, you are often provided with personal information on individuals (e.g., name, address, telephone number, employer). This information is maintained on the <System Name> database and its auxiliary systems. We consider the information on these databases protected information that should be handled with appropriate care. Use of this information should be guided by the following policies:

Under the 1977 Information Practices Act, <Organization Name> is able to retain personal information on individuals upon informing them of their rights, that our use of the information will be limited to the furtherance of the <Organization>'s business, and that the information will not be disseminated to others except as required by law. It is proper for <Organization Name> to share with our volunteers and staff a certain degree of personal information on individuals to enable them to carry out their respective assignments. However, we have an obligation both to the volunteers, staff, and individuals on whom we retain information to inform them that this is: (1) personal and confidential information which we are allowed to retain under the Information Practices Act; (2) only to be used to carry out the <Organization>'s work; and (3) not for dissemination to third parties.

It is our policy not to release address and telephone information for any records to a third party either over the phone or in person. When asked to verify a individuals involvement with <Organization Name>, you can transfer the request to the <individual/department>.

Information in the form of lists, labels, computer tapes, diskettes, CDs or DVDs, USB flash media, downloads, and reports is available only to authorized <Organization> representatives in support of approved activities and authorized <Organization> business. It is the responsibility of the unit requesting information to maintain the confidentiality of that information.

EXHIBIT 13.7   GUIDELINES FOR USING PERSONAL INFORMATION ON INDIVIDUALS

communications, especially e-mail. While written for associations, it generalizes nicely to all nonprofits.

(b) SECURITY ISSUES AND TRENDS.   It is hard to overemphasize the importance of security for your IT area. Not only is the number of security breaches growing rapidly, but also the loss of productivity and time involved in correcting problems is a serious issue. Spyware, instant messenger and peer-to-peer (P2P) threats, as much as 60–80 percent of incoming e-mail being spam or having viruses attached, and "phishing" attacks (e.g., phony bank inquiries that attempt to get employees to divulge sensitive personal or organizational information) are some of the trends organizations grapple with.[35] Losses per company of security breaches are estimated by the companies at about $204,000. A large-scale survey finds that the top three causes of loss are (1) viruses, (2) unauthorized access, and (3) theft of proprietary data.[36] To try to combat these attempts, businesses spend about 1 to 5 percent of their IT budgets for security expenditures, according to the Computer Security Institute. One of the biggest issues, in our judgment, is the ultimate effect of the privacy and data security concerns of individual donors on their online giving.

One issue requires special attention for healthcare organizations: Electronic records management. Sarbanes-Oxley legislation and the Health Insurance Portability and Accountability Act (HIPAA) both stipulate fines and/or prison sentences for the mishandling of certain kinds of records.[37] HIPAA also requires that healthcare organizations maintain customer information for six years. E-security and retention are consequently vitally important for healthcare organizations.

13.8 NEEDS ASSESSMENT AND ANALYSIS

Before deciding on the type of technology, needs and requirements must be determined. The tool the experts use for seeking out this information is a *needs assessment.* There are as many ways to conduct a needs assessment as there are technologies from which to choose. After completion of the assessment, an analysis of the information is performed to evaluate the results. The steps involved in conducting a needs assessment are shown in Exhibit 13.9.

(a) ASSESS.   In the first portion of the process, after determining what information is needed and choosing a method for gathering the information, the assessment is conducted. The broader the sampling (meaning, the greater the number of people contacted for the assessment), the more accurate the results. Methods of assessment include the following four data collection techniques:

1. *One-on-one interview.* The most effective method of gathering information is using an interview technique. The most important steps with this technique are to develop a preestablished list of questions and to conduct the interview without judgment. The art of interviewing for a needs assessment is not dissimilar to playing poker: wearing a poker face, never letting on what information the interviewer hopes to prove or disprove.

2. *Telephone interview.* This method can be very successful, especially if the questions asked are of a personal nature. The lack of face-to-face contact with individuals may make it easier to ask personal questions. However, it also precludes the interviewer from reading facial clues or gestures that are very valuable in changing the interview's tone to probe further on a particular question.

3. *Meeting.* A meeting can be a very effective forum for gathering information for an assessment, although it can be extremely challenging and taxing for the facilitator. Often a round-table discussion will develop as attendees hear how other people answer the questions. This method is also useful in that it immediately identifies where there is consensus and where there will be conflict.

4. *Questionnaire.* The least effective of the four methods, this is the most commonly used because it efficiently allows a broader audience to be contacted. The ability to survey a larger group can often outweigh the benefits of the time-consuming task of one-on-one interviews.

(b) ANALYZE.   In this portion of the process, the information collected is evaluated, tabulated, and summarized. You may use a weighting table to give greater emphasis to certain questions in the needs assessment, and you may use return-on-investment analysis to evaluate some investment proposals.

(i) *Weighting Table Analysis.*   Weighting the questions for relevance and applicability to a specific respondent can be very important. For example, if an assessment was conducted with order takers, the response of a person who takes many orders each day

WHAT TO INCLUDE
Appropriate Use

☐ Explain the extent of personal use allowed (if any).

☐ If your association has a unionized workforce, make sure that any personal use restrictions do not infringe upon protected, concerted, activities.

☐ Identify types of messages, browsing, and other content that are prohibited.

Mointoring

☐ State whether, and on what terms, monitoring will occur (periodic, random, content-flagged, or reasonable suspicion, and so on).

☐ State that information on the system is not private and passwords and codes do not guarantee privacy.

Confidentiality

☐ Prohibit electronic transmission of confidential information and trade secrets or define the terms under which such transmission can occur.

Control and Ownership

☐ State that the association is the sole *owner of all systems and all materials* created, received, transmitted, and stored on those systems.

☐ Advise that the association has copies of all passwords and codes and has access to information on its systems at all times.

Association Representation

☐ State that electronic communications are tantamount to written documents and require observation of appropriate business etiquette.

☐ Remind the sender that an electronic transmission can be forwarded, printed, and otherwise distributed with the sender's (and the associations's) name intact, but without their knowledge.

Discipline

☐ Warn that violations will result, in disciplinary action, up to and including termination.

WHAT EMPLOYERS SHOULD DO
Take Appropriate Precautions

☐ Provide advance notice of the policy's implementation (at least two full weeks prior to the policy's *effective date*).

☐ Obtain a signed acknowledgement from every system user, an express consent to monitoring.

☐ Investigate and install any necessary blocking, screening, or monitoring software.

Publicize and Distribute

☐ Publicize and distribute the policy at its enactment and periodically there after (at least annually).

☐ Consider adding to the log-in of each user a banner providing notice of possible monitoring.

Be Wary

☐ Review and update the policy frequently, especially as laws change.

☐ Train management on how to properly administer the policy, and assure monitoring is occurring in accordance with the terms of the policy.

Source: Victoria L. Donati and Jennifer A. Hardgrove, ''The Importance of Being E-Conscious,'' *Association Management* (June 2002): 59–63. Used by permission.

EXHIBIT 13.8 SAMPLE COMMUNICATIONS POLICY CHECKLIST

or whose only responsibility is to take orders, as opposed to someone who took fewer orders, would have greater relevance. This person's opinions would be more valuable than another's.

When using the weighting table (Exhibit 13.10), answers given by someone who took 1 to 10 orders per day would count one time, whereas the answers of someone who took 51 to 60 orders per day would be counted six times (as if six people had taken the survey).

Another set of criteria is to weight the answers based on the relevancy of the question itself. Some questions may be much more critical than others. A similar weighting method should be used for each question.

Exhibit 13.9   Needs Assessment Flowchart

Finally, there may be questions that need to be evaluated against another question, or a combination of questions. For example, if one was asked, "How proficient are you with Microsoft Windows: Excellent, Good, Fair, or Novice?" the question should be balanced with a series of questions specific to Microsoft Windows (e.g., asking specific questions of skills or tasks the person could perform in the program, such as saving a file, opening a file, cutting and pasting). If an individual stated that he or she had excellent skills with Microsoft Windows but answered "no" to the question "Can you open a file in Microsoft Windows?" one could logically assume that the person inaccurately answered the question about proficiency.

(ii) Return on Investment or Benefit-Cost Analysis.   To illustrate return on investment (ROI) analysis, or benefit-cost analysis, consider an investment in a treasury management system. There are six treasury information management "value drivers":[38]

1. Information availability
2. Information accuracy
3. Information timeliness
4. Information system cost
5. Automation of information generation, transmission, analysis, and decision making
6. "Electronification" of information and payment systems

If someone in the organization proposes an investment in IT, automation, or moving to electronic data or payment transmission, evaluate this proposal using one or more of the value drivers. Then compare the value added by one or more of these items to the overall costs of the proposal to see if it should be implemented.

More formally, you can calculate ROI, net present value (NPV), or internal rate of return (IRR) on IT projects (see Chapter 9 for more on these calculations). A survey found that evaluating computer security software and services is done with ROI (38 percent of respondents), NPV (18 percent), or IRR (19 percent). However, many respondents also

No. of Orders Taken per Day	Weight Factor
1–10	1
11–20	2
21–30	3
31–40	4
41–50	5
51–60	6

Exhibit 13.10   Weighting Table to Determine Relevancy of Answers

note that IT security is a "must-do" item that is implemented regardless of immediate financial impact.[39]

(c) CRITIQUE.   After analyzing the information, it should be determined whether there are results that may be in conflict. In this step, an evaluation of the results is made to verify whether they are as expected or completely off the scale as compared to the original assumptions. Do not assume that the original assumptions were incorrect; but also, do not assume that the results of the survey are correct. Following up with a few respondents may determine that they misunderstood the question or had other reasons (sometimes personal or political) for answering in the manner they did. As a general rule, obscure or irregular results may be disregarded. At a minimum, obscure survey answers should be investigated vigorously. It is possible that the person being surveyed misunderstood the question, but that should never be assumed. It is more likely that there is something unique about the individual's work or assignments that caused the obscure answer. It is just these types of issues that the needs assessment attempts to flesh out. If possible, contact the individuals who provided the answers for a follow-up assessment to gather more information to clarify the issue.

(d) DECIDE.   The last step is to make a decision by reviewing the information collected, so an educated nonbiased decision can be made.

(e) IMPLEMENT: GETTING PEOPLE TO USE THE NEW TOOL.   It does not matter how wisely the information was evaluated, how successfully the purchase contract was negotiated, or how accurately the needs of the organization were determined, if the staff cannot be motivated to use the tool. If it is not used, the implementation and the tool is a failure. Before making the final decision to purchase or implement, the purpose of the new tool and the willingness or ability of the staff to use it need to be reevaluated.

There can be hundreds of reasons why staff in an organization will refuse to use a new tool. Each person may have his or her own specific reasons; however, in general, the reasons a new tool is not used fall into one of the categories described in Exhibit 13.11.

13.9 POLICIES AND PRACTICES IN KNOWLEDGE MANAGEMENT AND INFORMATION TECHNOLOGY

The Indiana University study of Indiana-based nonprofits documents these technology-related opinions and practices:

- More than one-half of the organizations see effective use of IT is at least a minor challenge, and 15 percent label it as a major challenge (26 percent say it is not a challenge, and 18 percent say it doesn't apply, presumably because they have no IT, according to the study authors).

- The highest percentage reporting that effective IT use is a major challenge is found in the healthcare sector (28 percent), followed by religion field (20 percent) and then the arts/culture/humanities field (19 percent).

- Interestingly, larger nonprofits were more likely to say that effective IT use posed a major challenge.[40]

Reason	Description	Solution
"I don't know how to use it."	The biggest reason why people will not use a new tool is the most obvious one: They just don't know how to use it.	Provide training in the new tool or system.
"I went to the training, but I still don't know how to use it."	After training is conducted, it is likely that staff will not immediately begin using the system, unless a schedule or an assimilation plan for each individual or group has been created. So often in organizations, staff learn to ignore change as a way of making it go away.	Develop an implementation strategy that includes post-training follow-up. Monitor the progress of each individual or group, setting goals or milestones that need to be achieved by a specific time. Establish rewards (or punishments, if necessary) to encourage meeting these targets
"Training was bad."	A common complaint about any new system or tool not being used is that the training was ineffective. While it may be considered as a viable reason, it is more likely that there are other causes or reasons besides the training the individual received.	Evaluate the effectiveness of the training as part of the training process. Avoid the use of "smile sheets" (measurement tools that evaluate only how some liked or felt about the training) as opposed to good measurements that evaluate what they knew before they attended training and what they knew immediately after training.
		Another important factor in the training program is the relevance to the person's job. If the training examples used are too vague or general, the individual will not be able to assimilate the information. The closer the examples are to the real-life situations or tasks the individual will perform, the more likely the individual will be able to remember (assimilate) the information.
"I forgot what I learned."	Individuals may report that they found the training useful, but it was so long ago that they forgot what they learned.	It is possible that the training was ineffective and the step above should be employed in this example as well. More likely the reason will be that the training occurred too early, before the tool was available. Training should occur no earlier than one month before the tool is available. It is best if the tool is in place before the training is received.

EXHIBIT 13.11   REASONS/SOLUTIONS FOR REFUSAL TO USE A NEW IT TOOL

| "This isn't as good as the old way." | Looking at information or performing a task in a new way may cause some individuals to judge the process as ineffective. This comment should be interpreted not as a judgment but as a request for clarity about why things needed to change. | Make sure that staff have the prerequisite knowledge to successfully use the new tool or complete the training course. If a new computer system is being introduced, and staff have never used a computer before, basic computer training must be provided *before* beginning training on a specific application or system.

This prerequisite training does not need to be time consuming or detailed, but provide a basic level of understanding from which the individual can build his or her knowledge of the new tool. |

EXHIBIT 13.11   REASONS/SOLUTIONS FOR REFUSAL TO USE A NEW IT TOOL (*continued*)

If you would like to learn more about technology deployment in nonprofits, a great resource is N-TEN (the Nonprofit Technology Enterprise Network; www.nten.org). It hosts an annual nonprofit technology conference and also has an e-mail newsletter, a listserv, and informal interest groups that meet in 19 cities in the United States.

Notes

1. Anne Hamersky, "On the Record: Intel's Andy Bryant," *CFO* 21 (November 2005): 48–50.
2. "Information Technology," www.webopedia.com/TERM/I/IT.html. Accessed: 3/18/06.
3. North Dakota Information Technology Department, "Definition of Information Technology," www.nd.gov/itd/planning/definition.html. Accessed: 3/18/06.
4. Bob Violino, "'06 IT Directions," *CFO* 22 (January 2006): 68–72.
5. Id.
6. Id.
7. Russ Banham, "Time to Fatten Up," *Treasury & Risk Management* 15 (October 2005): 26–32.
8. Report of the Governor's Task Force, "The Role of Charitable Nonprofit Organizations in Iowa" (2005), and a 2000 survey done at the University of Iowa. Located online at: http://nonprofit.law.uiowa.edu/updates/GovTaskForce/Report.pdf. Accessed: 3/8/2006.
9. Rebecca Walker, "Designing a Network for You," *Association Management* (December 2002): 72.
10. Laura S. Quinn, "Software Costs and Usage: Findings of a Nonprofit Sector Survey" (September 2005). Located online at: http://www.idealware.org/IW_software_survey_report.pdf. Accessed: 3/11/06.
11. For more on the role of knowledge management in enabling nonprofits to succeed in difficult environments, including an exploratory survey of Italian nonprofits, see Emanuele Lettieri, Francesca Borga, and Alberto Savoldelli, "Knowledge Management in Non-Profit Organizations," *Journal of Knowledge Management* 8 (December 2004): 16–30.
12. Maria M. Capozzi, Stephanie M. Lowell, and Les Silverman, "Knowledge Management Comes to Philanthropy," *McKinsey Quarterly: The Online Journal of McKinsey & Co.* Located online at: www.mckinseyquarterly.com. Accessed: 3/8/2006.

13. Natalie Buckminster, "Associations Between Outcome Measurement, Accountability, and Learning for Non-Profit Organizations," *International Journal of Public Sector Management* 12 (April 1999): 186–197.

14. Peter M. Senge, *The Fifth Discipline. The Art and Practice of the Learning Organization* (London: RandomHouse, 1990): 3.

15. John Burton, "The Changing Face of IT Executives," *University Business* 8 (June 2005): 58–62.

16. For more on learning organizations, see www.solonline.org/.

17. For more on the topics of knowledge management and intellectual capital, see various issues of *Journal of Knowledge Management* and *Journal of Intellectual Capital* (information on both available at www.emeraldinsight.com).

18. A formal definition of e-business might include these items: "(1) E-business involves company-to-company trading activity and data exchange; (2) E-business activity often involves many line items per order, each with specific delivery confirmation dates, quantities, delivery points, and shipping methods; (3) E-business uses an interface that may provide user-selected information type/content/scope and associated interaction tools, reflecting the system's greater scale, scope, and depth of functionality; (4) E-business uses PO numbers, releases against blanket POs, and involves invoicing and payment methods; (5) E-business includes transactions using any or all EDI (electronic data interchange) protocols, Web-based screens, thin-client networks, browser screens presenting system displays and interaction, faxing, and automatic interception of electronic servicing by customer response teams; (6) E-business offers internal employee services, such as self-service access to personnel records, travel and expense reporting, and nonproduction procurement." Dave Monroe, Plant-Wide Research Group, quoted in Janet Gould, "What's the Difference Between E-Commerce and E-Business? And Why Should You Care?" *SCS Magazine* (November 1999). Located online at: www.scs-mag.com/reader/1999_11/what1199/what1199.htm. Accessed: 3/24/06.

19. Denise Shephard, "Balancing Act: How to Become Your Organization's Finance and Technology Hero," *Fiscal Fitness* (April 2005). Located online at: www.blackbaud.com/files/Newsletters/FiscalFitness/2005/FiscalFitnessApril2005.htm. Accessed: 4/15/2005.

20. Id.

21. Terry S. Maness and John T. Zietlow, *Short-Term Financial Management: Text and Cases*, 3rd ed. (Cincinnati: South-Western, 2005): Chapter 19.

22. Ernst & Young LLP, "22nd Annual Cash Management Survey: 2005 Executive Summary." Available online at: www.ey.com/global/download.nsf/US/Cash_Management_Survey_2005/$file/2005CashManagementSurveyExecSummary.pdf. Accessed: 3/24/06.

23. John Lebate, "Is There Life Without Excel?" *Treasury & Risk Management* 14 (February 2004): 20–24. Also see John A. Bielic, "Emerging Trends in Technology: The Application Service Provider Model in Higher Education," *University Business* (May 2005): 21.

24. Lebate, "Is There Life Without Excel?"

25. WSReview.com (formerly EDI World Magazine). Located at www.wsreview.com/resources/glossary/default.cfm?KeywordID=E. Accessed: 1/31/04.

26. A good primer on the basics of ERP systems is available at the time of this writing at: www.microsoft.com/dynamics/product/erp_primer.mspx.

27. John Edwards, "Pay-Per-View ERP: Is On-Demand Transaction Software Ready for Prime Time?" *CFO* 22 (February 2006): 64–68.

28. Daryl Orts, "Dashboard Development and Deployment: A Methodology for Success," *Supplement to KMWorld* (January 2006): S14.

29. Quoted from id., "

30. Quoted from Suzanne E. Coffman, "Nonprofits and Individuals Meet in Cyberspace". Located online at: www.guidestar.org. (2003) © Philanthropic Research, Inc. The donor surveys were conducted by Network for Good and are based on 10,000 respondents, and the organizational survey was conducted jointly by GuideStar and Network for Good, and is based on replies from approximately 1,000 respondents.

31. Jeffrey S. Rosengard, "Transforming Finance into a Competitive Weapon," *Financial Executive* 16 (July/August 2000): 51–52.

32. Treasury & Risk Management Express e-mail listserv. "Looking for Savings? Try Getting Out of the Paper Business When it Comes to Accounts Payable." November 17, 2003.

33. Don Durfee, "Cost and Integration Problems Remain the Top Barriers to Implementing New Finance Technologies," *CFO* (June 15, 2004). Available online at www.cfo.com. Accessed: 11/23/2005.

34. For a discussion of some of the forms of IT outsourcing, including local area networks, wide area networks Internet access, Internet services such as e-mail and websites, hardware and software, and user services (help desk, support, and training), see Michelle Murrain and Douglas Cohen, "Infrastructure Outsourcing for Nonprofit Organizations," (February 6, 2003). Available online at: www.lahsa.org/pdfs/Current/Infrastructure%20Outsourcing%20for %20Nonprofit%20Org.pdf. Accessed: 3/24/2006.

35. Chris Thatcher, "Top Security Trends for 2006," www.csoonline.com, January 2006. Also see Donna Howell, "Stealthy Threats Dominate Online Security Today," *Investors Business Daily* (March 8, 2006): A5; and John McPartlin, "Hackers Find Backers," *CFO* 22 (January 2006): 75–77.

36. McPartlin, "Hackers Find Backers.,"

37. Yasmin Ghahremani, "An Ounce of Retention," *CFO IT* (September 15, 2005). Available online at: www.cfo.com/article.cfm/4390992. Accessed: 11/23/05.

38. Terry S. Maness and John T. Zietlow, Short-Term Financial Management: Text and Cases, 3rd edition (Cincinnati: South-Western, 2005): Chapter 19.

39. McPartlin, "Hackers Find Backers."

40. Kirsten A. Gronbjerg and Richard M. Clerkin, *Indiana Nonprofits: Managing Financial and Human Resources* (Bloomington, IN: Indiana University School of Public and Environmental Affairs, August 2004).

GLOSSARY OF BASIC TECHNICAL TERMS

All disciplines have a vocabulary spoken by the experts. In the technology arena, the explosion of terms and acronyms, *tech speak,* leaves many feeling that it is a language they can never understand.

ACCOUNTING

Accounting programs perform all the routine and complicated tasks of accounting. Many programs are sold in modules, such as General Ledger, Accounts Payable, Accounts Receivable, and Payroll, while others for home or small business are available as a complete package. Most businesses, when performing their accounting functions manually, had to choose single-entry accounting as their method of recording transactions. With the use of computers, double-entry accounting is the standard.

CLIENT/SERVER

Client/Server technology has made it possible to replace or enhance mainframes or midrange computers in a way that peer-to-peer or traditional server-based networks have not. While the increase in PC capabilities has been enormous, the size and requirements of data-processing needs of many businesses cannot be handled on a PC and still require the speed and magnitude of a mainframe or midrange computer to store and process their central data. Mainframe technologies have not been as user friendly as PC technologies, so a bridge between the two, client/server, has enabled the two technologies to merge.

COMMUNICATION TECHNOLOGIES

Technologies enhancing or replacing the capabilities of the phone line have continued, with VOIP technology allowing long-distance calls over the Internet. These technologies have literally revolutionized the way in which we communicate and have completely changed the dynamic of time and distance. Technology allows voice mail to be autodirected to your e-mail account as a sound file to be listened to at your convenience.

DATABASE

Databases are collections of information in a structured format. Phone books, Rolodex cards, member lists, and date books are examples of databases used everyday. The computer handles databases exceptionally well.

DESKTOP PUBLISHING

Desktop publishing programs automate the manual task of paste-up. What was once performed with typesetting machines, photographs, razor blades, glue, and tape is now performed electronically with desktop publishing software.

E-MAIL

Electronic-mail (*e-mail*) replaces or enhances myriad business communications. First and foremost, electronic mail is used to write and distribute letters or notes. It is also used to deliver phone messages; schedule meetings; and send files, pictures, sounds clips, and so forth to co-workers across the desk or across the globe in seconds.

FAX

Paper facsimiles (*faxes*) provide a method of sending a copy of a document to another location. In combination with electronic mail, the fax has in many cases replaced the need for telex or wires in the workplace.

GRAPHICS

Graphics programs replace the paintbrush, pen, chalk, and easel of the art world. In addition, other graphics packages allow the manipulation of photographs, pictures, and any other graphic media.

HARDWARE

Hardware is the term used to describe any tangible piece of computer equipment, meaning it can be touched or felt. Printers, computers, diskettes, computer boards, chips, and monitors are all examples of computer hardware.

INTERNET

The *Internet* is a series of connected computers. The Internet began as a way of connecting government, research institutions, and colleges and universities, but has exploded into the new communication medium. Banking and other financial transactions continue to migrate to the "Net." By searching the Net, using a search engine such as Google, one can find and retrieve information on just about any topic around the globe. A Web site presence on the net, usually in the form of what is called a "home page," is becoming a standard for all businesses. Donations may be received through various payment media from your website's visitors.

MIDRANGE COMPUTERS

Midrange computers, formerly called minicomputers, are medium-sized computers or servers, typically used to host an organization's network.

NETWORK

Network is the term used to describe computers that are connected to one another. A network can be as small as two computers connected by a single wire, or as large as a major network linking thousands of machines through a variety of technologies, including wire, telephone, and cellular or satellite.

OLE

OLE is the acronym for Object Linking and Embedding, meaning an object from one software application (such as a spreadsheet) is embedded (copied) into another application (such as a memo in a word processing application). Optionally, linking is when the applications are instructed to keep track of the status of each of the documents and to automatically (or with warnings) update the embedded object when the source object is modified or changed. More simply, a spreadsheet can be produced and included (embedded) in a memo or report. If the spreadsheet is changed, it will automatically be updated in the memo (linking).

OPERATING SYSTEM (OS)

The *operating system (OS)* constitutes the basic instructions a computer uses to communicate with the user and how it stores, retrieves, and structures data. Software programs use these common instructions for a variety of functions including how data are stored on disk, how documents are printed, and how files are viewed. MS Windows XP, MacIntosh, and UNIX are all examples of standard operating systems. It is important to know that certain hardware systems and software programs may be available for a limited number of operating systems.

PC

Personal computer (PC) is the term used to describe any desktop or laptop computer; however, for many, the term PC is used to describe the IBM/AT technology. Conversely, the term "Mac" is used to describe the Macintosh technology from Apple. Both Macs and PCs are personal computers, but the term PC generally applies to the IBM/AT platform.

PEER-TO-PEER

Peer-to-peer is a type of network that connects a series of computers in a continuous chain, rather than a central network server. Each computer can perform its own singular function or can be accessed by others on the chain.

SERVER

Server networks use one or more computers, as the center of the network, similar to the center of a wheel with each of the connected computers as the spokes. All the other computers are connected to it, allowing communication back and forth from the server. Each computer connected to the server can perform singularly, but access to other computers connected to the server is not possible.

SOFTWARE

Software is the term used to describe programming instructions to a computer. Any set of instructions that cause the computer to carry out a set of instructions or commands is software; however, most commonly, software is used to describe major sets of programs, such as word processing and database.

VOICE MAIL

Voice mail has provided a personal receptionist for its users. Rather than talking with a person to leave a message, voice mail enables callers to record a message, similar to phone answering machines.

WORD PROCESSING

Word processing programs allow the manipulation and storage of text for the production of any printed media. There is a wide diversity of products on the market, ranging from simple to complex. The word processing programs on the market today, costing about $230 (or about one-half of that for an upgrade), are more powerful than the dedicated word processing machines sold in the late 1970s and 1980s costing over $100,000.

FRAMEWORK FOR AN IMPLEMENTATION STRATEGY

The following information should be contained in a communication/implementation strategy provided to all employees affected by a new system or process:

    I. How did we get here?

        a. What is the time line?

        b. What are the current conditions?

        c. What has historically occurred?

   II. What were we looking for?

        a. Is this a new way of doing business?

        b. Is this a new venture?

        c. Was this caused by growth?

        d. What is the strategy?

  III. Who was involved?

        a. Was this a partnership among units or unit involved (departments)?

        b. Who were the individuals?

        c. Who is affected?

  IV. What did they do?

        a. Did they conduct a series of interviews?

        b. Did they hold meetings and discussions?

        c. What were the results?

        d. What conclusions were drawn?

    V. What were the guidelines?

        a. How did they select appropriate technology?

        b. Which requirements were targeted?

        c. How will infrastructure be built?

        d. Will implementation teams be created?

VI. What are we going to have when we're done?

    a. What will the system do?

    b. What will it provide?

    c. What will it replace?

    d. How long will it last?

VII. How are we going to do it?

    a. How will it be introduced?

    b. What support will be available?

    c. What training will be available?

    d. How will individual needs and requirements be dealt with?

VIII. When will the system be available?

    a. What will the system do for me?

    b. What will I see?

    c. What can I view?

    d. What can I produce?

IX. What is it?

    a. What will it look like?

    b. How will it perform?

    c. How will I use it?

X. Who will use it?

    a. In the long term?

    b. In the short term?

XI. What is my role and responsibility?

XII. How do I protect the information?

XIII. What support will be available?

    a. User guides

    b. Reference materials

    c. Glossaries

    d. On-line help

    e. Labs to practice using the system

    f. One-on-one follow-up

    g. Support assistance

        ▷ Help desk

        ▷ Training classes

        ▷ Refresher sessions

        ▷ One-on-one support on-call

APPENDIX **13C**

CASE STUDY: USING TECHNOLOGY TO IMPROVE CASH AND TREASURY MANAGEMENT*

THE SAN DIEGO ZOO'S CFO BROUGHT THE RIGORS OF CASH FLOW FORECASTING

What's that elephant doing in my cash flow forecast? For Paula Brock, it's a pretty typical query. As CFO for the Zoological Society of San Diego, which operates the renowned San Diego Zoo, Wild Animal Park, and Center for Conservation and Research on Endangered Species (CRES), she deals with problems when constructing her cash flow forecast that it's safe to say few other finance chiefs need confront. Last year, some of Brock's most sizable unexpected expenses came in the form of not one but 11 African elephants that had to be transported safely and quickly from Swaziland, Africa, to the United States—four to Florida and the rest to California. Now, those are shipping and handling costs that could make a serious dent in any CFO's working capital projections.

THE CULTURAL REVOLUTION

But Brock didn't panic. As the former manager of a $3 billion mortgage portfolio at ITT Capital, she learned forecasting in the rigorous shop run by CEO Harold Geneen. Precise forecasting meant professional survival at ITT, where managers were rewarded on their ability to accurately forecast their results no matter how events played out and punished when they failed. "He built a culture of demanding taskmasters," Brock recalls. "In eventful times, managers were expected to manage through unplanned calamities and take advantage of opportunities that arose to optimize results, then reissue new, accurate forecasts reflecting those changes." So it's not surprising that three years ago, when the Zoological Society recruited Brock, she introduced her own brand of forecasting to an organization that had never really done any before. "Forecasting has made a cultural change in how we operate," she observes. "We have about 145 departments, so we're a large, complex organization. We've been able to automate the forecasting process by

*Richard Gamble, "The Wild Life of Working Capital Management," *Treasury & Risk Management* (November 2004). Available online at: www.treasuryandrisk.com/issues/2004/treasury_management/340-1.html. Accessed: 11/23/05. © Copyright 2005 Treasury & Risk Management. Used by Permission.

495

designing templates that are tailored to the way each unit or department operates," she explains. "We were able to accomplish all of this in significantly less than a year."

Every 28 days—13 times a year—each department or unit has to revise its forecast and send the updated template to the finance staff. Finance then aggressively reconciles forecasts against actual performance each period and asks questions when a significant gap occurs, she explains. When facing the prospect of transportation costs for 11 elephants, the unit responsible for acquiring the animals simply reflected the change of events in their template and rolled it up into the consolidated forecast spreadsheet that Brock's team maintains. The Excel™-based templates are generated by Timeline Inc. software using a data warehouse. Department figures are populated from the data warehouse into each template, Brock explains. Using the template, each department manager adjusts his or her forecast. Then, the numbers are submitted directly to the data warehouse through Timeline's writeback process, she notes. Reports can then be run, pulling the data from the data warehouse. The current forecasting goes through the end of each year. The plan for 2005 includes converting forecasting into a 13-period rolling forecast, she says.

With practice and corrections has come success. "It's not a perfect process and never will be," Brock concedes, "but we've made it a priority and become pretty good at it. With good forecasts, we can time the maturity of our short-term investments and, more importantly, we can use our credit line efficiently and draw the right amount for the right period of time. It's critical to minimizing our borrowing costs."

For many treasury staffs, a working capital forecast that goes out beyond a week or so worth of cash needs is the metaphoric elephant at the cocktail party—the large presence that cannot be ignored but that somehow doesn't fit into the graceful elegance of an otherwise automated system. Theoretically, long-range forecasting should be a success story, given that the computing power is available to most treasuries through workstations and ERP systems and access to greater and greater amounts of relevant data is possible. Yet, treasuries generally are dissatisfied with their forecasting capabilities and are even reluctant to talk about them. "Companies are pushing to make their longer-term forecasts better. A lot of them have developed some forecasting tools, but there's still a lot of room for improvement," reports consultant Mike Gallanis, a Chicago-based principal at Treasury Strategies Inc. "It's a high priority, but more companies are deficient at this point than are proficient at forecasting."

One reason is that there are no real plug-and-play solutions, Gallanis says, because the factors that affect each business's liquidity forecast (e.g., elephant transport) will be unique. "For some elements of cash flow, regression analysis is very effective. For others, a time series works best. It takes testing and trial and error to find the methodologies that work best with each company's pattern of cash inflows and outflows," he says.

Gallanis and Treasury Strategies work with companies to build customized forecasting models, but he admits it takes effort and time and may prove too expensive for some treasuries. Typically, a company that builds a forecasting model maintains it as a separate application (not part of an ERP system or treasury workstation) and feeds data into it from other systems. But it doesn't need to be that high-powered to produce meaningful results. Certainly, that has been Brock's experience working with cash flow elements that are more manageable than those for most companies.

When forecasting the Zoological Society's revenue of about $160 million a year, for instance, there are a limited number of revenue streams to take into account: $5 million from a decades-old tax on San Diego property owners; another $4 million from grant money; $24 million from fundraising campaigns; and the remainder from memberships, admissions, and sales of auxiliary items like food and Zoo merchandise, Brock explains. While San Diego is a powerful tourist magnet and the Zoo enjoys a world-class reputation, revenue is not always a straight, upward-sloping line. "Ticket sales depend on people getting here," Brock says. That takes disposable income, so recessions will usually dampen ticket sales. Even more disruptive are disasters like 9/11 and the destructive forest fires that ravaged the San Diego area last year. For instance, the Zoo was forced by security authorities to shut down and evacuate for less than a day shortly after 9/11, for the second time in its 88-year history, she recalls. That was clearly an expense not anticipated in the forecast. "But because of our process, we were able to make the appropriate adjustments necessary to our operations in a timely manner so that we were able to land on our feet," Brock observes. To assure liquidity, the Zoo keeps a credit facility with Bank of America and draws on that line as needed to cover cash shortfalls. Having a viable forecast is "essential" to making efficient use of the bank credit, Brock says. As a result she has been able to significantly reduce borrowings over the last year.

There's plenty of pressure, coming from the CEO, CFO, and the analysts and shareholders who question them, to forecast liquidity further out with greater accuracy, reports Lisa Rossi, head of U.S. liquidity management services for Deutsche Bank Global Treasury Services. And companies are trying to leverage the technology available from banks and from ERP and treasury workstation vendors to help them do this, but progress generally has been mixed, she explains. Companies that have formalized, consistent processes like electronic invoice presentment and payment generally fare best. And of course the job is easier for some companies than others. Companies that get most of their revenue under contracts, for example, can better forecast incoming cash, Rossi adds.

Longer-term working capital forecasts need a data pull that spans and penetrates the organization. "You need clear, timely input from the parts of your organization that interact with your customers and suppliers so you get a sense of what's happening out in the supply chain," Gallanis says.

ALMOST IN REACH

The simplest way is to parse out the forecasting duties and make each unit or department continually revise its forecast, then let the piecemeal forecasts roll up into a consolidated corporate forecast. But that strategy relies on coordinating lots of pieces, and it can be labor-intensive at the unit level. Treasury doesn't control the process unless senior management mandates participation, and treasury doesn't control the quality except through after-the-fact reconciliations and pressure on units to improve faulty forecasts.

The vision is tempting: forecasting software that mines all the relevant data in a company's ERP system, capturing contract data, purchase orders as soon as they are created, and future receivables as soon as orders are entered. Then it taps external databases to pull in future prices of key commodities. If it ships by truck and its contracts allow carriers to pass on fuel price increases, it factors in oil price projections. If it relies on parts made from aluminum and its contract with its key supplier expires in the next six months, it factors in probable price increases for inventory after that point. And so it goes up and down the supply chain: Elements must be identified that affect cash intake and outflow; historic correlations must be found; and then all of these must be built into the forecasting model. So far, reality falls short of the vision, and no one is confident enough to forecast when that is likely to change.

CHAPTER 14

MANAGING RISK, LEGAL ISSUES, AND HUMAN RESOURCES

14.1 WHAT IS RISK MANAGEMENT?

Effective risk management is the process of evaluating and guarding against potential losses to the organization. The chief financial officer (CFO) of a nonprofit organization should be very concerned about risk management issues because they directly affect the use of financial and other resources. Effective risk management can save significant resources, which ultimately translates into money. In the corporate world, treasury staff is being given greater responsibility in the area of risk management, and a newer approach to risk management is being taken: enterprise risk management.[1] This involves "identifying, assessing, quantifying, and mitigating the broad range of strategic, operational, financial and other risks confronting the [organization]."[2] Put another way, this approach to risk management brings financial risks (price risk, interest rate risk, foreign exchange risk) together with nonfinancial risks (business risk, insurance, operating risk, contingency planning) in one framework for one group within the organization to oversee. The possible downside to a too-narrow view of risk is identified by consultant Stephen Baird of Treasury Strategies, Inc.:

> While risk compliance is a process of identifying, tracking and mitigating risk... strategic risk management is a process of applying a high-level analytical framework to understand the composition of a company's risk. The former is a tactical approach that misses the connections between risks, addresses risks individually and overlooks some risks entirely. The end result of a successful execution of the latter can be determining the most value-added strategies for accepting, transferring or mitigating risks for an entire enterprise. "Treasurers are better equipped than anyone in the organization to develop and apply these frameworks...."[3]

We concur with this view. The Committee Of Sponsoring Organizations of the Tread-way Commission (COSO) recommended ERM framework (Enterprise Risk Management—Integrated Framework), while not mandatory for any business or nonprofit organization, provides new impetus to take a broader view of risk and to integrate it into the strategic management process.[4] Treasury Strategies survey data indicates that the most common arrangement for corporate enterprise risk management reporting responsibility is to have it housed in the treasury function.

Risk management has two major components:

1. Loss prevention
2. Loss control (reduction of loss)

Most nonprofit leaders and managers fail to understand that risk management involves matters of risk associated with their assets. An asset is "the entire property of a person, association, corporation, or estate applicable or subject to the payment of debts."[5] In financial terms, assets are things owned by the organization and reported on the organization's balance sheet. In more general terms, assets are resources or anything that provides value to the organization, whether tangible or intangible. The major types of assets include:

-   People (employees, members, volunteers, independent contractors, board members)
-   Property and equipment (monies, property, equipment, technology, trade secrets, goodwill)

When viewing assets in this way, initiatives such as an employee retention program—to retain key employees—become a vital piece to the organization's overall

- Leadership sets the tone and demonstrates their compliance.
- Leaders stay informed and demonstrate their interest and concern for this area.
- Education and training convey policies and procedures as well as organizational attitudes toward the safeguarding of assets.
- Risks are known.
- Risks are prioritized.
- A Safety Officer is appointed.
- Counselors, consultants, and practitioners (private, public, or pastoral) are consulted and used when necessary.

Exhibit 14.1 Checklist for Setting up a Risk Management Program

risk management program. Risks include many areas, including property, income, liability, people, reputation and mission, volunteers, governance and fiduciary considerations, client relationships, and collaborations.

Exhibit 14.1 presents a checklist for setting up a risk management program.

In order to be effective, risk management must be proactive. Proactive steps include:

- Acknowledge the critical importance of risk management at the highest level.
- Define risk management roles and responsibilities.
- Delegate or assign risk management responsibilities and accountabilities.
- Incorporate a regular inspection where losses could occur.
- Review the organization's risk management program in detail regularly.
- Communicate that risk management issues must be considered when evaluating the cost of doing business, including the review of existing and new programs.

For more on this, see Herman, Head, Jackson, and Fogarty.[6]

The CFO has one additional responsibility:

- Communicate illiquidity risk, the primary financial risk, regularly, accurately, and in terms that staff can understand.

This ongoing focus on illiquidity risk meshes well with "post-loss goals" of risk management, which include survival, growth, stability of operations, and required financial results.[7]

The advantages of proactive, enterprise-wide risk management are profiled in Exhibit 14.2.

Motivation to do the hard work of risk management comes from the five "whys" of risk management, as identified by Herman, Head, Jackson, and Fogarty:

1. *Asset stewardship*. Your organization gains from a stewardship focus a stronger position from which to avert erosion of core assets (property, income, liquid assets, goodwill, human resources).

√ *Aligning risk appetite and strategy*—Management considers the entity's risk appetite in evaluating strategic alternatives, setting related objectives, and developing mechanisms to manage related risks.

√ *Enhancing risk response decisions*—Enterprise risk management provides the rigor to identify and select among alternative risk responses: risk avoidance, reduction, sharing, and acceptance.

√ *Reducing operational surprises and losses*—Entities gain enhanced capability to identify potential events and establish responses, reducing surprises and associated costs or losses.

√ *Identifying and managing multiple and cross-enterprise risks*—Every enterprise faces myriad risks affecting different parts of the organization, and enterprise risk management facilitates effective response to the interrelated impacts, and integrated responses to multiple risks.

√ *Seizing opportunities*—By considering a full range of potential events, management is positioned to identify and proactively realize opportunities.

√ *Improving deployment of capital*—Obtaining robust risk information allows management to effectively assess overall capital needs and enhance capital allocation.

Source: Committee of Sponsoring Organizations of the Treadway Commission (COSO), *Enterprise Risk Management—Integrated Framework Executive Summary* (September 2004).

EXHIBIT 14.2 ADVANTAGES OF PROACTIVE ENTERPRISE RISK MANAGEMENT

2. *Achieving public accountability.* Every facet of nonprofit management is enhanced when the organization earns a reputation of trust and fidelity as well as prudence in its risk management.

3. *Attracting stakeholders.* If an organization is seen as careless or uncaring, it loses support from volunteers, staff, donors and other funders, and the community.

4. *Freeing up resources for mission.* Accidental or intentional losses are costly, often more so than preventive measures, and absorb valuable staff time.

5. *Staying true to mission.* Any time harm results from a nonprofit's operations or activities, the fallout is detrimental to staff or volunteer focus on mission as well as to the mission-accomplishment image of the organization.[8]

(a) WHO IS RESPONSIBLE FOR MANAGING RISK IN THE NONPROFIT ORGANIZATION?

The board of trustees is responsible for setting policy and assigning responsibility for risk management functions in the nonprofit organization. In the event of a loss and subsequent legal exposure resulting from this loss, it is likely that the board could be held accountable for losses if appropriate policies and procedures do not exist. Risk management issues are broad and pertain to paid staff and volunteers as well as to the general public who may be involved with the organization. Risk management is part of the cost of doing business and should not be ignored by the board of trustees.

(i) Board Duties. As responsible leaders, board members:

- Know the rules in the organization, including by-laws, policies, and procedures
- Understand the risk management process
- See that organizational policies are communicated and implemented

- Stay informed about issues such as law (and the aspects of Sarbanes-Oxley that apply to nonprofits; see Chapter 5), litigation, compliance, ethics, and disclosure

We note particularly the whistleblower provisions of Sarbanes-Oxley. Many allegations against nonprofits, mostly related to excessive compensation, self-dealing, and ineffective governance, have come from whistleblower disclosures.[9] This fact suggests that your organization, at a minimum, should adopt a whistleblower policy and protection program with these five action points: (1) provide employees multiple avenues to report concerns; (2) establish an ombudsman program; (3) most important, adopt a policy prohibiting retaliation; (4) train managers and supervisors; and (5) take disciplinary action against those who engage in retaliation.[10]

(ii) Leadership Sets the Tone. Control cues are the written and unwritten messages sent to an organization by its leadership, management, and staff on what is expected of the entire workforce to safeguard its resources. These messages continually communicate by word and action that the workforce is responsible and accountable for protecting and preserving the organization's assets so that they are available to carry out its mission.

(b) COMMUNICATE RISK MANAGEMENT POLICY. In order to be meaningful and effective, risk management policies must be communicated to all who have a reasonable need to know or a role to play in adherence to the policy. Traditionally a policy and procedures manual is developed and distributed to accomplish this task. The manual must be kept updated to maintain its relevance and effectiveness. However, a policy and procedures manual is not the only way to effectively communicate policies, roles and responsibilities, and expectations. Any method of communicating that works effectively for the organization is acceptable.

14.2 IDENTIFYING RISK

Your organization's people and property invite and cause risks in several distinct areas. Exhibit 14.3 summarizes some major areas of risk with specific examples.

14.3 PRIMARY FINANCIAL RISK: ILLIQUIDITY

We have emphasized throughout this book that managing your organization's liquidity is paramount in your financial management. Further evidence of the effects of your organization's primary financial risk, a situation called "illiquidity"—that of not having enough liquidity—is provided by the 2005 NYC Nonprofit Executive Outlook Survey (see Exhibit 14.4). Quoting the study's authors, Jack Krauskopf and Gregg Van Ryzin: "More than 60 percent of the [surveyed] agencies have had to close programs, and nearly as many have laid off staff. Overwhelmingly, these reductions are due to financial stress, rather than to strategic choices they have made."[11] Poor cash flow management and underfunded agencies are more characteristic of the nonprofit sector than many recognize.

By regularly communicating the need for a liquidity target, degree of achievement of the target, and how achievement or maintenance of that target strengthens the organization, the CFO or board treasurer enables a greater degree of understanding and buy-in for

Major Area of Risk	Examples
Legal records	Articles of incorporation
	Bylaws
	Meeting minutes
	List of members
Officer's and director's liability	Theft (assets, ideas, credibility)
	Compliance
	Conflict of interest
	Duty of care
	Duty of loyalty
Members of the nonprofit organization	Loss
Employees	Theft
	Lawsuits
	Safety
	Productivity losses
Volunteers	Exposure
	Space
Personnel and payroll	Employee benefits
	Sexual harassment
	Background checks
Financial management	Liquidity level
	Budget
	Cash handling
	Bonding
	Confidentiality of records
	Loan management
	Net assets
Investment management	Risk
	Image with constituents
Child care	Injury
Counseling	Liability insurance
Insurance	Rates
	Ranking
Fire protection	Insurance
	Fire alarms
	Disaster preparedness
	Emergency procedures
Injury prevention	Unenforced policy
Vehicles	Accident
	Theft
	Inappropriate or personal use
Copyrights and publications	Theft
	Inadequate protection
Programs and activities	Productivity losses
	Reputation
Miscellaneous	Disasters (any kind)
	Ethics

EXHIBIT 14.3 MAJOR AREAS OF RISK

this objective. Furthermore, nonprofits are beginning to use derivatives to better manage interest expense and the risk of higher interest expense as well as price risk and foreign currency risk. See Appendix 14A for a derivatives checklist, and Exhibit 14B for a case study on how to handle foreign currency risk without the use of derivatives.

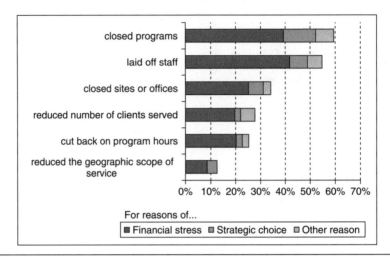

Note: The question asked was "In the past few years has your organization..."
Source: Jack Krauskopf and Gregg Van Ryzin, *New York City Nonprofit Executive Outlook Survey* (New York: Baruch College, School of Public Affairs Nonprofit Group and Survey Research Unit: Spring 2005). Used by permission.

EXHIBIT 14.4 FINANCIAL PROBLEMS AND EFFECTS ON MISSION ACHIEVEMENT

14.4 LEGAL ENVIRONMENT

(a) SARBANES-OXLEY IN THE NONPROFIT SECTOR.   Elsewhere, we have noted that Sarbanes-Oxley legislation has brought new impetus to governance and control issues. We simply note there that 97 percent of surveyed nonprofits believe corporate governance reforms have impacted their organizations already and that many of these organizations are already implementing such reforms in advance of possible federal or state extensions of such reforms to the nonprofit sector.[12]

(b) ETHICAL CONSIDERATIONS.   At a minimum, your organization should have a code of ethics that is known by appropriate parties, emphasized by the executive director/chief executive director (ED/CEO) and the board, and enforced by top management and the board. A model that some organizations have used is the Financial Executives' Institute Code of Ethics, shown in Exhibit 14.5.

(c) RELEVANT AGENCY AND REGULATORY RULES.   One item sometimes overlooked by nonprofits is the relevant federal, state, and local regulatory or agency requirement for a particular process. An example: If you are doing business with the federal government, be aware of the raft of regulations related to cash management.[13]

14.5 SAFEGUARDING PEOPLE

A nonprofit organization's most valuable asset is the people who contribute resources (service and monies) in support of its mission. The staff and volunteers in your organization perform these needed activities and tasks, and both groups use and develop resources.

FEI Code of Ethics

FEI's mission includes significant efforts to promote ethical conduct in the practice of financial management throughout the world. Senior financial officers hold an important and elevated role in corporate governance. While members of the management team, they are uniquely capable and empowered to ensure that all stakeholders' interests are appropriately balanced, protected and preserved. This Code provides principles to which members are expected to adhere and advocate. They embody rules regarding individual and peer responsibilities, as well as responsibilities to employers, the public, and other stakeholders. Violations of FEI's Code of Ethics may subject the member to censure, suspension or expulsion under procedural rules adopted by FEI's Board of Directors.

All members of FEI will:

1. Act with honesty and integrity, avoiding actual or apparent conflicts of interest in personal and professional relationships.
2. Provide constituents with information that is accurate, complete, objective, relevant, timely and understandable.
3. Comply with applicable rules and regulations of federal, state, provincial, and local governments, and other appropriate private and public regulatory agencies.
4. Act in good faith, responsibly, with due care, competence and diligence, without misrepresenting material facts or allowing one's independent judgment to be subordinated.
5. Respect the confidentiality of information acquired in the course of one's work except when authorized or otherwise legally obligated to disclose. Confidential information acquired in the course of one's work will not be used for personal advantage.
6. Share knowledge and maintain skills important and relevant to constituents' needs.
7. Proactively promote ethical behavior as a responsible partner among peers, in the work environment and the community.
8. Achieve responsible use of and control over all assets and resources employed or entrusted.
9. Report known or suspected violations of this Code in accordance with the FEI Rules of Procedure.
10. Be accountable for adhering to this Code.

EXHIBIT 14.5 FEI CODE OF ETHICS

First and foremost, you must provide a safe working environment for your staff and volunteers, regardless of whether work is performed onsite, at your organization's offices, in the field, in a donor's home, or in the staff or volunteer's residence or place of business. While you cannot completely safeguard your staff and volunteers outside your organization's place of business, you may be at risk if you are aware of a potential hazard and do not take action to protect the individual from harm.

(a) TOOLS FOR EFFECTIVE HUMAN RESOURCE MANAGEMENT. The dominant trend in liability for nonprofit organizations is related to employment practices liability.[14] Job descriptions, background checks, and notification that bonding is required for finance-related positions are all helpful in reducing the potential for litigation and unfavorable judgments.

(i) Job Descriptions. Job descriptions include the tasks, duties, and responsibilities of a job, along with the minimum education, experience and skills necessary for the job. They also include the job title, location, whether exempt or nonexempt (for Fair Labor Standards Act classification purposes, with overtime pay implications), position summary, and working conditions (including hazards). Be prepared to defend any education, experience, abilities, and skill requirements you have included.

(ii) Background Checks.   More and more organizations are conducting background checks for employees and even volunteers. One form of background check is a criminal history record check. Not only are criminal checks being done as a screening device for positions having significant direct contact with children or clients who might be considered vulnerable[15] (often checked by a third party, with prior consent by the potential employee or volunteer), but for financial positions a credit record check is often conducted as well. Applicants should have an opportunity to challenge the accuracy of information you receive, in that errors may occur in criminal history records and credit histories. Also, do not misuse or negligently handle (e.g., be careful to not accidentally disclose negative items) any information you receive, as you and/or your organization could then be susceptible to civil or criminal penalties.

(iii) Bonding.   Bonding is a precaution that a nonprofit organization should consider in its corporate stewardship. Bonding buys insurance on those handling money for the organization and ensures its constituency that the finances are being handled properly.

Some nonprofit organizations are reluctant to bond money handlers, in the belief that it questions the integrity of the people involved. Unfortunately, irregularities in the handling of money in nonprofits occur often enough that this potential cannot be ignored. Whether or not the money handlers are bonded, the organization should safeguard its money and money handlers by engaging an auditor to conduct an annual audit. There is a wide variety of bonding patterns. In some instances the individual is bonded; in others the position is bonded, so that a change in personnel does not affect coverage. Group bonds cover everyone who handles the money.

Costs of bonding vary widely, depending on the number of individuals involved and the amount of money handled. The insurance carrier for the organization is the best source to begin the process of determining how to meet its bonding needs. In our estimation, the cost is very reasonable relative to the protection such as policy provides. In some nonprofit arenas, specialized providers offer tailored policies at attractive rates.

(b) PHYSICAL AND EMOTIONAL SAFETY.

- Your facilities (electrical, plumbing, fire sprinklers, etc.) should comply with standard codes for your region. Adherence to Americans with Disabilities Act (ADA) regulations regarding handicap access are vitally important.

- Doorways and fire exits should be kept clear and accessible.

- If crime (e.g., assault or theft) is prevalent in your locale, doors should be locked after hours, and individuals should be escorted to parking structures or accompanied to their transportation sites.

- Emergency service numbers, such as 911 stickers, should be placed on telephones.

- Basic safety procedures, such as what to do in an emergency, should be included in your staff and volunteer orientation materials.

- If staff or volunteers use vehicles to conduct work (other than traveling to and from their work site), you need to ensure that they have a good driving record, have up-to-date insurance coverage, and understand their responsibilities with respect to chauffeuring others in their own or company vehicles.

- If staff or volunteers need to move heavy items, such as furniture, inventory, or stock, these individuals need to be provided with safe-lifting instructions, lift belts, and proper tools, such as ladders and hand trucks.

With regard to emotional safety:

- Employee workplace guidelines specific to sexual harassment should be distributed to all individuals and supervisors, and managers should receive training on how to recognize a potential harassment situation and what steps or actions to take if it does occur. Employees should sign documents indicating what training was received and when it was received. (The latter documents are vital in any case in which the organization is sued in determining whether it is liable.)

- Staff and volunteers should be instructed on how and to whom to report a potentially harmful situation if a supervisor or manager creates unnecessary stress for their subordinates.

- When considering expansion, growth, or organizational changes of any kind, the risk, stress, or burden on the staff and volunteers should be appropriately evaluated as one of the costs of the change.

(c) PROTECTING THE ORGANIZATION FROM LAWSUITS AND GRIEVANCES. The most obvious way to prevent lawsuits and employee grievances is to comply with all laws, regulations, and policies that affect your region and organization. In addition to protecting the organization from lawsuits and grievances, you need to ensure that your staff and volunteers are protected. Going beyond the letter of the law to ensure ethical behavior is only wise.

(d) DEALING WITH DIFFICULT OR PROBLEM EMPLOYEES. Regardless of how careful the organization may be in the selection process for hiring new employees ("hire hard, manage easy" is a good approach for recruitment and selection), eventually it may be faced with terminating a problem employee who does not perform up to standard. To avoid financial risk to the organization, these actions should be taken:

- Each employee has an up-to-date and accurate job description detailing his or her work assignments and responsibilities.

- Periodic evaluations should be performed, using only the tasks and assignments on the job description as criteria for evaluating employee performance.

- Once a problem employee is identified, the supervisor must document in writing all conversations, meetings, job complaints, assignments, errors, omissions, or violations of policy; discuss them with the employee and have the employee sign them; and maintain copies of these documents in the employee's personnel file.

- The first step to termination is a counseling session to notify the employee that his or her performance is not satisfactory. Reasonable steps to provide additional assistance or training, areas to improve, and other specific information should be discussed with the employee, and a written document detailing the discussion—signed by the employee—should be given to him or her, with a copy maintained in the personnel file. If termination appears to be imminent, a time period (or deadline) within which the employee's performance must be up to standard should be predetermined and discussed with him or her. Interim sessions to monitor progress, or lack of progress, should be conducted and documented.

- The decision on whether to terminate or ask the employee to resign should be evaluated carefully. Very often problem employees are willing to resign if offered an attractive severance package. The costs of the severance package should be evaluated and compared against the potential risk of lawsuit or grievance, as well as the increase in unemployment insurance if the employee is terminated. Often tensions become high when an employee needs to be separated from the organization. The decision to fire someone may seem warranted but may not be the most appropriate action for the organization. In many cases, there will be less of a financial burden and risk to the organization if the employee is willing to resign as opposed to being terminated.

- Employees can be terminated (fired) only for cause. Separating an employee for lack of work, lack of funds, or change in mission or responsibilities is not considered "termination for cause." This is generally referred to as a "layoff" and will have a financial impact in the form of workers' compensation increases. When a layoff is performed, the only criteria that may be used are seniority, job title or description, employee skills, and how critical the person's job or responsibilities are to the organization. Performance or specific salary level cannot be used as the reason for selecting one employee over another for layoff. If an employee is laid off out of order of seniority, it is critical that you document legitimate and legal reasons for performing a layoff in this manner.

(e) GROUNDS FOR IMMEDIATE TERMINATION.   There are instances where it is necessary to remove an employee immediately. Labor relations laws vary from state to state, and a lawyer specializing in human resources issues should be consulted regarding the legality of the termination before any decision is finalized. Generally, the following are grounds for immediate termination when the employee places the organization, its staff, or its volunteers at substantial risk:

- Theft or fraud
- Threatening or lewd behavior (sexual harassment) in the workplace
- Lying about use of sick leave
- Racial, ethnic, gender, age, or religious discrimination
- Using illegal drugs or other illegal substances in the workplace
- Bringing weapons and other dangerous or hazardous items into the workplace

Even with the severity of the examples just listed and the assumption that "everyone should know they cannot do this stuff at work," it is important to document in your personnel policies those behaviors or actions that will warrant immediate termination. It is essential that all new employees receive training on what constitutes sexual harassment and sign a document indicating that they have received this training. Employees in supervisory and recruitment or selection roles should also receive training on ADA-related issues.

Many companies place employees on "investigatory leave" (leave without pay) if allegations of any of the listed activities are suspected. This benefits the organization by removing the employee from the workplace immediately and providing it with time to investigate and confirm the allegations prior to the completion of the actual separation. If it is determined later that the employee was falsely accused, back wages can be paid and the employee can be restored to his or her position. Again, policies and procedures for placing employees on investigatory leave should be documented in the organization's personnel policies, with copies provided to all employees when hired.

(f) COMPENSATION. The intangible rewards of working in a nonprofit environment enable organizations to hire qualified individuals who are dedicated to the mission of the organization at wages below the industry or local average for the region. Taking advantage of this situation can greatly aid the organization in keeping its employee compensation rates down; however, there may be hidden costs in using this practice recklessly or assuming that employees will work indefinitely for low wages. These costs include:

- Eventually, even the most dedicated employee will succumb to offers for better wages. High employee turnover reduces productivity and creates an unstable image in the eyes of donors and a general sense of unease and instability with other staff and volunteers.

- Ineffective or unqualified staff or volunteers use resources. Often one highly qualified individual can perform the task of several underqualified staff and lower the overall cost to the organization. In addition, productive staff and volunteers may lose morale if unproductive staff and volunteers are allowed to remain with the organization.

- A low-paid development staff or director may be less effective at raising money than a higher-paid individual. The net effect to the organization will be a decrease in overall resources: "Penny wise and pound foolish."

- Specifically in the financial arena, a highly qualified individual may be able to forecast and manipulate resources in a way that greatly benefits the organization and protects it from loss, while a lesser-qualified individual may be careless and less savvy in managing resources. We note that reliance for financial management on someone with training only in accounting leaves important treasury management and risk management issues undermanaged.

- You may wish to consider pay for performance, a practice that is spreading to many nonprofit organizations. This merit-based pay is seen as more fair by productive employees, who are discouraged when seeing less productive employees get the same pay or pay raise as they get.

(g) PERSONAL USE OF ORGANIZATIONAL RESOURCES. Unless there are specific policies and active monitoring of resource use in your organization, a substantial loss can result in the personal use of resources by volunteers or staff in the following ways:

- Phone
- Fax
- Photocopying equipment
- Typewriters
- Computers (much time theft due to browsing the Internet)
- Office supplies (paper, pens, etc.)

While all of us at one time or another have accidentally placed a pen or pencil belonging to another in our purse or pocket, this practice is theft if done consciously. If your organization has a policy prohibiting its resources from being used for personal use, then staff and volunteers need to be reprimanded when minor infractions, such as those listed, occur. Many organizations adopt a policy that allows staff and volunteers to use organizational resources as long as it does not become excessive (e.g., using the phone to call home, the copier to copy an occasional legal document, the fax machine to send an important document). The difficulty of this type of policy is the definition of *excessive* may vary for each individual. One employee who lives close to his or her work site and calls home during breaks may not incur a significant cost in long distance charges to the organization; however, another employee who lives much farther away and does the same may result, over time, in a significant cost to the organization. It is important for limits to be established that do not discriminate from one employee to the next. If a policy places a $5 maximum on personal telephone calls per month as opposed to a time limit for personal use, it may be interpreted as unfairly penalizing one employee. *It is important to remember that the organization is not required to allow any of its resources to be used for personal use.*

(h) CONFLICT OF INTEREST. A conflict of interest may exist when a decision is made that may personally benefit a board member, an employee, or a volunteer. For example, a staff member may have a spouse who works for a travel agency. Using that particular travel agency may be viewed by potential donors or auditors as unfair. However, if the travel agent agreed to reduce travel expenses by 5 percent, the decision to use this particular vendor might be the most financially advantageous to the organization.

A potential conflict of interest does not mean that the organization cannot do business with friends or family of its staff or volunteers. It is critical in these circumstances to have full disclosure of the connection to this particular individual and to have someone other than the individual who may benefit make the final determination.

Development of and compliance with a carefully drafted conflict-of-interest policy will lessen the financial risk to the organization as well as reduce the appearance of impropriety with respect to donors. Refer to Chapter 5 regarding such a policy.

(i) GETTING THE MOST "BANG FOR YOUR BUCK." If the organization is not utilizing a resource to its fullest potential or purpose, the organization is actually wasting it. If staff or volunteers have special skills and abilities that are not being utilized, if they are not mentored properly to work to their fullest potential, or if they are not trained or given sufficient flexibility to perform their tasks or responsibilities, your organization is wasting resources. In addition, if staff or volunteers are performing unsatisfactorily, they are consuming resources. Your organization should also consider the human resource management function itself: Should some or all of it be outsourced? Benefits administration, payroll administration, and selection/recruitment are commonly outsourced by organizations of many sizes.[16]

(j) STAFF AND VOLUNTEERS—WHAT MOTIVATES THEM? Three qualities of all productive staff and volunteers are listed in Exhibit 14.6. We would add, in the commitment section, that a spiritual commitment is typically seen in employees and volunteers in faith-based organizations.

- Commitment
  - To their work
  - To their constituents
  - To their customers
  - To their community
  - To themselves

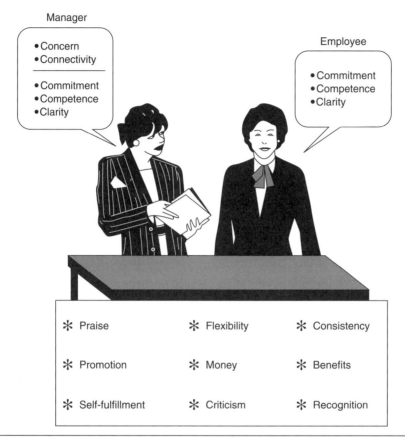

Exhibit 14.6   Motivation Factors

- Competence
    - In their work
    - In their relationships with other staff and volunteers
    - In dealing with donors
- Clarity
    - About their roles and responsibilities
    - About the purpose of the organization and its mission

As discussed earlier, salaries paid to employees in nonprofit organizations are often below for-profit levels. This means that individuals accept positions with nonprofits because there are motivating factors beyond income. One expert, David Mason, calls nonprofits "values-expressive organizations," and economist Estelle James has documented that workers take below-market wages to dedicate themselves to cause-related nonprofits. This commitment to the organization should be recognized and, wherever possible, acknowledged and rewarded in nonfinancial ways. Exhibit 14.7 demonstrates that pay issues are the single most significant problem faced by most New York City

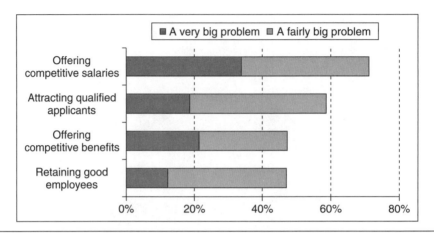

Source: Jack Krauskopf and Gregg Van Ryzin, *New York City Nonprofit Executive Outlook Survey* (New York: Baruch College, School of Public Affairs Nonprofit Group and Survey Research Unit: Spring 2005). Used by permission.

Exhibit 14.7   Major Human Resources Issues Faced by NYC Nonprofits

nonprofits. Respondents were asked: "How much of a problem if at all are the following human resource issues for your organization?"

On the negative side, it is also reasonable to assume that some individuals will gravitate toward positions with nonprofits that pay lower wages because they believe the workload and expectations will be lower, commensurate with the pay scales. Thus, an individual's commitment to the organization should be evaluated on a case-by-case basis. It should never be assumed that a willingness to work for lower pay constitutes a high degree of commitment to the organization.

Paying someone below-market wages does not necessarily mean that you will have substandard employees. If wages were the only motivating factor in a person's decision to accept or remain in a position, individuals would change jobs much more frequently, as offers for higher pay were offered. In each position, a staff or volunteer also evaluates the intangible rewards:

- Sense of community: relationships with coworkers and friends
- The mission and goals of the organization
- Logistical factors (e.g., proximity from home to workplace)
- Educational or learning opportunities
- Working hours
- Access to other individuals and community (e.g., a museum attracting aspiring artists or a library attracting aspiring writers)
- Feeling of pride and receipt of praise and attention for their efforts
- Flex-time
- Telecommuting

Beyond the intangible rewards, individuals also evaluate the tangible rewards that nonprofits can offer:

- Benefits (vacation, sick leave, health insurance)
- Discounts or "freebies" (e.g., educational discounts; mentoring opportunities; ability to attend performances, screenings, or presentations at little or no cost)

It is important to remember that each individual has his or her own set of motivators for doing good work:

- Praise
- Recognition
- Promotion of a valued cause or belief system
- Flexibility
- Autonomy
- Criticism
- Consistency
- Personal growth
- Benefits
- Money
- Safety
- Proximity to home or family/children

(k) WHAT QUALITIES SHOULD LEADERSHIP POSSESS? Supervisors, managers, and board members must have the qualities, motivators, and skills of all staff and volunteers, as well as concern and connectivity.

(i) Concern. Managers and board members should show concern for the staff and volunteers, donors and community, the integrity of the workplace, and the success and failure of the organization.

(ii) Connectivity. To the infrastructure of the community (global and local), both non-technological and technological, it is the responsibility of leadership to:

- Set vision
- Establish goals and priorities, including financial objectives
- Motivate and mentor staff, volunteers, donors, and community
- Establish a personality/culture for the workplace
- Foster integrity
- Demonstrate support for ethical standards, rules, laws, fiduciary responsibility, and compliance

14.6 DIRECTORS' AND OFFICERS' LIABILITY

A major concern of nonprofit boards is the unprecedented liability exposure faced by their directors and officers. A significant rise in the number of liability suits and in insurance costs has made it increasingly difficult for officers and directors to protect themselves. This situation affects the quality of governance and leadership that nonprofit organizations can attract.[17]

(a) METHODS BY WHICH BOARDS CAN PROTECT THEMSELVES.   These are the main risk areas boards face:

- Not exercising due diligence when recruiting/selecting board members
- Not enforcing term limits (if they exist)
- Not properly recording board actions/decisions in the board minutes
- Not giving comprehensive new board member orientations
- Not requiring or enforcing board member performance expectations (e.g., attending a specific number of meetings over a particular period of time)
- Not providing board members with the requisite data and background information for informed decisions[18]

It is critical for the nonprofit organization to review its liability coverage for directors and officers and make the required adjustments, if the organization is underprotected. One caution: Insurance companies have very specialized directors and officers ("D&O") policies, so check them carefully to see that they include (1) a requirement to advance defense costs, (2) a broad definition of who is insured (including in the organization itself along with any natural person who "was, is or becomes a director, trustee, officer, employee, committee member, or volunteer" in the organization), and (3) broad coverage of employment practices liability.[19] Along with obtaining and acting on the liability insurance information, a board can take other actions to protect itself and limit its liability and risk. They include:

- Ensure board minutes are complete and accurate.
- Engage paid legal counsel.
- Expand management information.
- Review organizational policies.
- Formulate conflict-of-interest policy.
- Add and/or recruit new board members to include specific expertise.
- Form new board committees.
- Bring in outside experts.
- Strengthen the finance committee.
- Strengthen legal expertise.
- Strengthen insurance expertise.
- Strengthen audit and accounting expertise.[20]

(b) CONFLICTS OF INTEREST.   Consider various professionals who may hold membership on your board. A banker who tries to steer the organization's lending to his or her organization, a lawyer who insists that his or her law firm do all the organization's legal work, an insurance agent getting all of the organization's insurance business without any other agency getting to bid, and similar situations all comprise potential conflicts of interest. It is essential to have arm's-length transactions, to have a carefully spelled-out conflict-of-interest policy, and to make sure that any apparent conflicts of interest are approved by the full board with adequate disclosure regarding the precautions taken and reasoning behind the decisions made.

(c) **EXECUTIVE PAY.** Excessive compensation is another hot-button issue to be wary about in your organization. Make sure you find out comparable pay for your ED/CEO in like organizations, and include these data in your board discussions and minutes.

(d) **DUTIES OF CARE, LOYALTY, AND OBEDIENCE.** The three duties that a board should always exercise are care (conducting organizational affairs with competence), loyalty (putting organizational interests above selfish interests), and obedience (adherence to the organization's mission and values in decision making). Prudence, careful decision making, gathering and using facts and data, and paying attention to the organization's financial situation are ways in which these duties are exercised.

14.7 SAFEGUARDING YOUR FINANCIAL AND PHYSICAL ASSETS

(a) **INSURANCE.** Insurance does not mitigate all risk management issues in your organization. Some of the reasons are:

- Insurance does not cover every risk.
- Coverage may be limited.
- Claims today may raise premiums tomorrow.
- Claims may be rejected if negligence is discovered by the insurance company.

In recent years, insurance premiums have made insurance less affordable for many nonprofits. The New York City Nonprofit Executive survey quoted earlier finds that some of the biggest cost increases incurred by nonprofits are in the area of insurance, as noted in Exhibit 14.8.

Risks to an organization can be reduced, but they cannot be eliminated. Fires, floods, thefts, property damage, and earthquakes will occur despite the best efforts of your organization in the area of risk management.

Know what the insurance choices are and why the organization has made them. Exhibit 14.9 presents a checklist of factors to consider when choosing insurance.

In general, you should know the limitations and exclusions of policies and perform periodic reviews of coverage to verify that they are up-to-date for claims and losses in your region.

Trends for nonprofit liability insurance include: higher limits purchased by some nonprofits ($2 million or more), and coverage for:

- Punitive damages
- Defense expenses beyond policy limits
- Independent contractor claims
- Third party or leased employee claims

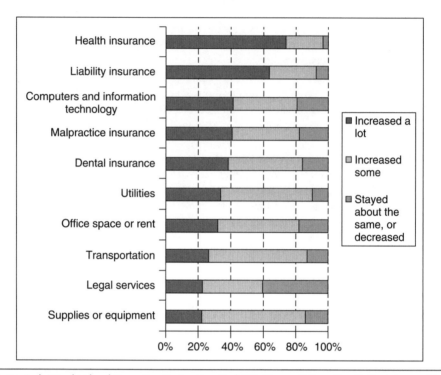

Source: Jack Krauskopf and Gregg Van Ryzin, *New York City Nonprofit Executive Outlook Survey* (New York: Baruch College, School of Public Affairs Nonprofit Group and Survey Research Unit: Spring 2005). Used by permission.

Exhibit 14.8   Five-Year Price Changes Experienced by NYC Nonprofits

- Fiduciary duties
- Employee Retirement Income Security Act of 1974 (ERISA) compliance-related claims
- Excess benefits claims[21]

Also, consider pooled insurance groups, such as the Alliance of Nonprofits for Insurance Risk Retention Group (ANI-RRG), which operates in several states.

(b) RISK RETENTION VERSUS RISK TRANSFER.   *Risk retention* means just what it says: Your organization either pays a certain portion of each loss or for specific types of losses. This may be done with "funded loss reserves," which are established based on likelihood of future losses. *Risk transfer* involves either having insurers bear some of the financial results from losses or having other parties absorb losses (as in hold-harmless agreements and indemnification agreements).[22] Your organization must determine to what degree it can retain losses and how it will finance those losses, or transfer the risks it faces. Even if you transfer risk to an insurer, will you purchase as much insurance as you can afford, or merely have catastrophic exposures and losses covered by the policy?

What does the policy cover?
☐ Property or liability risks
☐ Risks from all causes
☐ Named perils such as earthquake, flood, lightning

What are you covered for?
☐ Theft by employees and/or others
☐ Legal negligence
☐ Personal injury
☐ Sexual misconduct
☐ Negligence of member, employee, or any other person associated with the organization
☐ Medical bills
☐ Volunteer activities
☐ Vehicular-related activities
☐ Auto insurance
☐ Workers' compensation insurance
☐ Inventory

What do you know about your policy?
☐ Are there exclusions?
☐ How much coverage do you carry and based on what? Are these amounts up-to-date?
☐ Is actual cost or replacement cost covered?
☐ Is replacement cost at 100 percent vs. other percentages?
☐ How is depreciation handled?
☐ Are the contents or inventory of buildings accurate and up-to-date?
☐ Are rare or other especially valuable items covered, such as art or other precious objects?
☐ Is your policy contingent upon construction codes in your area? If so, do you comply and have proof of compliance?
☐ Do you have a physical inventory, pictures, and other documentation that could be used as proof of loss?

EXHIBIT 14.9   CHECKLIST OF FACTORS TO CONSIDER WHEN CHOOSING INSURANCE

(c) INTERNAL CONTROLS.   Occupational fraud strikes nonprofits in significant ways: In 2004, 12.2 percent of frauds occurred in the nonprofit sector, with a median loss of $100,000 to the nonprofits (up from $40,000 in 2002).[23] Almost one-half of the nonprofit cases were billing schemes, which may be largely prevented or caught more quickly by having the proper internal controls. In the broadest sense, internal controls include a large number of systems and business practices combined that, when observed, protect the assets of the organization and thereby reduce the risks associated with loss of resources.

Six important elements of an internal control system are:

1. Setting the tone through leadership (control cues).

2. Communicating the policy.

3. Segregating the duties.

4. Keeping records.

5. Preparing and monitoring budgets.

6. Reporting to all stakeholders.

Taken together, these policies outline the acceptable boundaries for fiscal decisions, govern the way resources are allocated, provide information for evaluation, and define the processes to be used in carrying out the organization's mission.

(d) FUNDRAISING.

(i) Charitable Solicitations. Be careful not to take undue risk when raising money from donors. The Nonprofit Risk Management Center notes five risks:

1. Aggravating a donor by violating his or her privacy.
2. Accepting a donation from an individual or organization you don't want associated with your charity, or returning/refusing a donation for the same reason.
3. Projecting donations during extreme fluctuations in the economy or stock market.
4. Valuing and handling bequests inappropriately.
5. Not conducting due diligence on donated property and valuing the benefits and costs of such donations.[24]

Also, be aware of each state's charitable solicitations law, as well as all federal regulations.

(ii) Philosophy and Practice. Before delving into the philosophy and practice of fundraising, we note that in general, there are two types of funding:

1. *Unrestricted funds.* Those that may be used at the discretion of the board (or a particular individual within the organization). Unrestricted funds are commonly received as a result of an annual campaign or other general fundraising effort. It is critical for a nonprofit to have a portion of its funding in unrestricted funds. This gives the board the flexibility to direct funds and efforts toward the greatest need.
2. *Restricted funds.* Those that must be used for a specific purpose or project. Much of restricted funds are received through government contracts or grants, but restricted funds may also be received from nongovernmental sources.

It is not uncommon for many funding types to fall somewhere between these two definitions.

The key managerial requirement is to ensure that all restrictions are honored, whether time (such as "may not be used until" a certain year) or purpose restrictions.

There are also ethical aspects to fundraising, as we noted in our Chapter 5 presentation on ethics. A fundraising philosophy or policy is helpful.[25]

(e) HOW TO BEGIN THE FINANCIAL ASSESSMENT PROCESS. Your organization should have an annual financial audit, or at least a compilation or review (see Chapters 5 and 6). An organization with no history of having an external review of its financial records may want to begin with a compilation and move to a review and audit in the future. If the organization is unable to afford the costs associated with an external review of the entire financial program, it has the option to engage the external examination on important specific parts of the financial statement or program. Examples of specific external examinations to be considered, if a full examination is not possible, are:

• Review policies and procedures manual for completeness, accuracy, and availability.

- Perform a proof of cash on one, some, or all of the bank accounts of the organization.
- Scan canceled checks and debit entries accompanying the bank statement for any unusual payees or endorsements.
- Confirm contributions made by donors.
- Confirm loan balances with lenders.
- Confirm all payments made during a specific period with some or all vendors.
- Compare annual operating budget to operating expenses, and analyze variances.
- Inquire as to how transactions are processed (e.g., deposits made, bills approved and paid) to ensure proper system of internal controls and detect errors.
- Perform a financial or management review of a specific program.
- Perform an examination to determine the accuracy of inventory.
- Check for control of petty cash funds.
- Check savings accounts for amounts, interest, and conditions.
- Check to determine if designated (restricted) funds are used only for the purpose contributed.
- Investigate checks or other debit entries outstanding for more than 30 days.
- Review all bank account reconciliations for timeliness and accuracy.
- Examine payroll records to ensure compliance with government regulations related to payroll, payroll taxes, income taxes, and so on.
- Account for all checks used and all debit entries made to the account.
- If purchasing cards or travel/entertainment cards are issued, review statements promptly and isolate and resolve questionable entries.
- Ensure spending limits are not violated on debit or credit cards.

(i) Due Diligence—Compliance with Policies, Procedures, and Guidelines. Documenting your policies and procedures is the first step in managing your risks and establishing a willingness to follow proper business practices. The next step is to verify that, at all times, policies and procedures are being followed.

During an audit of your financial statements, the benchmark used (beyond that of acceptable business practices) is the organization's own policies. Failure to comply with existing organizational rules can cause the most harm.

In the event of a lawsuit or a dispute, the organization's proof of compliance and an opinion by the courts are arbitrators of whether the company showed due diligence with respect to laws, guidelines, regulations, policies, and procedures. To verify that adherence to these documents, a periodic internal review of procedures should be conducted, and the resulting reports or documentation should be presented for review to the board of trustees.

(ii) Solutions: To Reduce Risk and Stay Out of Court.
- Education
  - New resources
- Training
- Adequate insurance coverage

- Loss-prevention programming

    ○ Videos (including Web-based clips)

    ○ Books

    ○ Consultants

- Conflict resolution

- Training

- Arbitration

(iii) Disaster Preparedness and Business Continuity Planning.   Is the organization prepared in the event of a disaster? Business continuity planning helps an organization to "develop and document the policies, procedures, activities and protocols necessary to resume essential business operations immediately following a business interruption, no matter the cause."[26] A good example of such planning is the ability of a charitable foundation that had an office in the World Trade Center to restart operations following the terrorist attacks in 2001.[27] Regardless of whether the organization has liability coverage for such disasters, important documents, records, and other properties need to be protected. While an insurance company may pay for the cost of computers and other office equipment lost in a fire, it cannot restore the data or other vital informational assets lost during the disaster. Liability insurance will not provide the protection from loss of trade secrets, data, contacts, or other business information used by the organization on a day-to-day basis.

To be disaster prepared, your organization needs to determine which items or information are needed to continue to be a viable operation after the disaster. These items should be replicated, copied, vaulted, or whatever action is necessary to assure that they will be

Data	In addition to routine periodic backups of computer data to prevent loss from normal occurrences, such as computer shutdowns or power surges, additional copies should be made for off-site backups and/or fire-resistant vault storage.
Records, files	Duplicate copies of all important records should be kept in fire-resistant vaults either on the premises and/or in another location.
Staff and volunteers	During fire, flood, earthquake, or other disasters that place your workplace at risk, your staff and volunteers should be protected through emergency exit plans and hurricane/tornado/earthquake kits (water, food, etc.).
	During an actual emergency, the ability to account for all persons on your premises will be vital to assisting emergency workers with locating and rescuing individuals. Team captains or safety officers should be appointed and given responsibility for communicating with emergency workers and assisting them in locating these individuals at the work site.
Physical inventory	A physical inventory (pictures, lists, bills of lading) that would be used to prove loss in an insurance claim should be duplicated and stored off-site as well as in fire- and flood-protection vaults on the premises.
Contact information	During and after a disaster, the ability to contact staff and volunteers should be maintained by assigning specific individuals this responsibility and by maintaining copies of employee and volunteer contact information in their homes and vehicles, so all staff and volunteers can be contacted and/or accounted for after a disaster.

EXHIBIT 14.10   BASIC DISASTER PREPAREDNESS

available after a disaster. The manner in which these items and information are protected depends greatly on the type of disaster. The region may have specific types of natural disasters that are not common in other areas. For example, earthquakes are prevalent in the western United States. The after-effects of earthquakes may include fire as well as access difficulties to the original premises. Offsite backups of items and information are necessary in earthquake regions. In the midwestern United States, floods, fire, and tornadoes are more threatening disasters. Storm shelters and fire- and flood-resistant vault storage are necessary to protect items in these regions (see Exhibit 14.10). Other causes of operation disruption are riots, police action, computer virus or worm infestation (see Chapter 13), workplace violence, fire, loss of electrical power, corruption of financial or donor databases, loss of critical funding stream (hence the need for the liquidity reserve), bomb threat, and loss of key staff or executive team members.[28] Put yourself in the shoes of staff, clients, and donors: How would they view your organization if it was closed for several weeks, and they had no way of contacting you or others at the organization?

Your insurance company can be a valuable ally in disaster preparedness. Most insurance companies can provide general guidelines for dealing with and preparing for emergencies in your region.

14.8 RISK MANAGEMENT AND HUMAN RESOURCE MANAGEMENT PRACTICES

We cite some statistics from two Iowa studies to fill out the nonprofit human resource and risk management environment and practices. We learn from these studies about the relatively small staff size of many nonprofits, and the nature of organizations' primary human resource management challenges. In one study, it was determined that most nonprofits have six or fewer employees. In another survey, "employee turnover" and "volunteer recruitment" were the two human resource-related challenges that were cited by a large number of Iowa nonprofits.[29]

Finally, based on its research, the Nonprofit Risk Management Center suggests that an effective risk management plan follows these six best practices:

1. Reflects a wide range of views and perspectives in an organization

2. Expresses the nonprofit's belief in and support of risk management

3. States that personnel at all levels of the organization play a vital role in protecting the nonprofit's mission, reputation, and assets

4. Incorporates the existing risk management policies of the organization

5. Reflects the nonprofit's goals and aspirations for its risk management efforts

6. Focuses on priority risks and considers secondary risks[30]

Notes

1. Findings of the 2005 Treasury Strategies survey of 375 U.S. corporate treasurers, as summarized in *Corporate Treasury Research Program Results* (2005). Available online at: www. treasurystrategies.com/resources/research/05TSICorpTreasuryResearch.pdf. Accessed: 3/10/06.

2. Russ Banham, "Time to Fatten Up," *Treasury & Risk Management* (October 2005): 26–32.

3. Quoted in Ann Lubart, "Enterprise Risk Management," *Treasury & Risk Management* (March 2005): 32–35.

4. At the time of this writing, an excellent executive summary of the COSO ERM framework was available at: www.roberthalfmr.com/html/downloads/COSO_ERM_IntgFrame.pdf. Accessed: 3/10/06.

5. Merriam-Webster Online Dictionary, www.m-w.com. Accessed 3/10/06. Another, expanded definition of asset is: "Any item of economic value owned by an individual or corporation, especially that which could be converted to cash. Examples are cash, securities, accounts receivable, inventory, office equipment, real estate, a car, and other property. On a balance sheet, assets are equal to the sum of liabilities, common stock, preferred stock, and retained earnings. From an accounting perspective, assets are divided into the following categories: current assets (cash and other liquid items), long-term assets (real estate, plant, equipment), prepaid and deferred assets (expenditures for future costs such as insurance, rent, interest), and intangible assets (trademarks, patents, copyrights, goodwill)." www.investorwords.com. Accessed: 3/10/06.

6. Melanie L. Herman, George L. Head, Peggy M. Jackson, and Toni E. Fogarty, *Managing Risk in Nonprofit Organizations: A Comprehensive Guide* (Hoboken, NJ: John Wiley & Sons, 2004): 14–33.

7. Id., 253.

8. Id., 4–6.

9. Jason M. Zuckerman, "Whistleblower Protections in the Nonprofit Sector," *Community Risk Management & Insurance* 14 (September/October 2005): 2–3.

10. Id.

11. Jack Krauskopf and Gregg Van Ryzin, New York City Nonprofit Executive Outlook Survey (New York: Baruch College, School of Public Affairs Nonprofit Group and Survey Research Unit, Spring 2005).

12. Paul D. Broude and Richard L. Prebil, "The Impact of Sarbanes-Oxley on Private & Nonprofit Companies," Foley & Lardner LLP 2005 National Directors Institute, Chicago, IL, March 10, 2005.

13. See Appendix D: Regulations. Available online at the time of this writing at: www.fms.treas. gov/eft/regulations/CASHMGMTAppendixD.pdf.

14. Eric Schall, "Liability Trends for Nonprofit Organizations," *Community Risk Management & Insurance* (Fall 2000). Available online at: http://nonprofitrisk.org/nwsltr/archive/ trendb09002000-p.htm.

15. Nonprofit Risk Management Center, "Checking Criminal Histories: Considerations Before You Begin," *Community Risk Management & Insurance* (Summer 1998). Available online at: http://nonprofitrisk.org/nwsltr/archive/employment05001998-p.htm.

16. For an excellent perspective on human resources outsourcing for colleges and universities, see Carol Patton, "The Grass Isn't Always Greener," *University Business* 9 (March 2006): 29–30.

17. See Steven Gladstone and Daniel J. Standish, "Survey of Recent Legal Developments: Coverage Issues Under Directors and Officers Liability Policies" (February 2000). At the time of this writing, this survey was available online at: www.wrf.com/docs/publications/7852.pdf.

18. Herman et al., *Managing Risk in Nonprofit Organizations*: 170.

19. Pamela Davis, "Professional Liability and Governance Exposures: A Closer Look," *Community Risk Management & Insurance* (Fall 1997). Available online at: http://nonprofitrisk.org/ nwsltr/archive/insurance09101997-p.htm.

20. KMPG Peat Marwick, "Directors' and Officers' Liability: A Crisis in the Making," Peat, Marwick, Mitchell & Co., 1987.

21. Schall, "Liability Trends for Nonprofit Organizations."

22. For more on risk retention and risk transfer, see Herman et al., *Managing Risk in Nonprofit Organizations*: 254–258.

23. Association of Certified Fraud Examiners, *2004 Report to the Nation on Occupational Fraud and Abuse*. Cited in Andrea McNeal and Jeffrey Michelman, "CPAs' Role in Fighting Fraud in Nonprofit Organizations," *The CPA Journal* (January 2006): 60–63.

24. Nonprofit Risk Management Center, *No Strings Attached: Untangling the Risks of Fundraising & Collaboration* (Washington, D.C.: Author, 1999).

25. For more on this, see Whitney T. Kuniholm, "A Biblical Foundation for Fund Raising," *Boardwise,* no. 6 (March/April 1997); and Rebekah Burch Basinger and Thomas H. Jeavons, "Aiming for the Heart: Fundraising as Ministry," Giving, Ecumenical Stewardship Center, 2001.

26. Peggy M. Jackson, "Keeping Your Organization Viable for the Future," *Community Risk Management & Insurance* (Winter 2002). Located online at: http://nonprofitrisk.org/nwsltr/archive/crisis11132002-w.htm. Accessed: 3/10/06.

27. Id.

28. Id.

29. Both statistics from Report of the Governor's Task Force, "The Role of Charitable Nonprofit Organizations in Iowa" (2005). The challenges mentioned were from a 2000 survey done at the University of Iowa. Located online at: http://nonprofit.law.uiowa.edu/updates/GovTaskForce/Report.pdf. Accessed 3/8/2006.

30. Quoted from Nonprofit Risk Management Center, *Community Risk Management & Insurance* 14 (September/October 2005): 1, 7.

DERIVATIVES CHECKLIST

A derivative is an investment or other financial instrument whose value is dependent on, or derived from, another asset. More formally, "A derivative is a risk-shifting agreement, the value of which is derived from the value of an underlying asset. The underlying asset could be a physical commodity, an interest rate, a company's stock, a stock index, a currency, or virtually any other tradable instrument upon which two parties can agree" (International Swaps and Derivatives Association). For example, a stock option is the right to purchase (or sell) a specific company's stock, and the value (price) of the option is linked to the price of the company's stock.

Major types of derivatives are options, forwards, futures, and swaps. Although only a modest number of nonprofits outside the healthcare sector have used derivatives as part of their financial management processes—mostly swaps to lower or reduce the variability of interest expense—a number of endowments and foundations have lost money in investment derivatives such as collateralized mortgage obligations (CMOs). The infamous 1994 debacle that bankrupted Orange County, CA, also related to derivatives-based investment instruments.

In this appendix a checklist of evaluation factors is provided to guide your organization regarding the use of derivatives.

WHY DERIVATIVES?

The use of derivatives can actually reduce the riskiness of an organization's cash flows, although the main cases that get into the newspaper are those in which a speculative position was taken (mostly bets on the direction of interest rates) and the value of the underlying asset resulted in a large loss to the derivative user. When an organization uses derivatives to reduce risk, it is said to be *hedging*. Organizations such as Orange County (CA) were not using derivatives to reduce risk, but to take on additional risks.

Formally, hedging is defined as protecting an existing business position by counter-balancing the position with an exactly offsetting position. The existing business position may be a foreign exchange exposure, meaning the organization's cash flows will be less if a specific currency depreciates or appreciates vis-à-vis the dollar. Or, it may be interest rate risk, meaning the organization's cash flows will be less if interest rates increase or decrease.

Illustrating, one Colorado-based charity had to lay off 20 percent of its headquarters staff because short-term interest rates declined, reducing the cash flow from its investment reserves that it had been depending on for covering this overhead expense.

Two possible hedging positions your organization may wish to consider are the use of interest rate futures or forward contracts and exchange rate futures or forward contracts. A forward contract is "an agreement reached at one point in time calling for the delivery of some commodity at a specified later date at a price established at the time of contracting," whereas a futures contract is "a forward contract traded on an organized exchange with contract terms clearly specified by the rules of the exchange."[1]

The futures of most value to your organization are financial futures, which are based upon underlying financial instruments. *Foreign currency futures* allow for delivery of a specified amount of foreign currency, at an agreed-upon future date, in return for a specified payment of U.S. dollars. The underlying financial instrument for an *interest rate future* is a debt instrument such as a Treasury bill or Treasury bond. Correspondingly, the contract is fulfilled by delivering the specified amount of T-bills or T-bonds. With *stock index futures,* there is no delivery of underlying assets at the contract's expiration, but rather a cash payment linked to the change in the underlying stock index (such as the Standard & Poor's 500 index).

FORWARDS VERSUS FUTURES

Although very similar, forwards differ from futures in three main ways:

1. *Advantage*:   They may be customized as to dollar amount and maturity.
2. *Disadvantage*:   They are not traded on exchanges, and finding a trading partner wishing to take the exact opposite position to that you wish to hedge may be very difficult.
3. *Disadvantage*:   They are difficult to reverse, meaning that if your organization wishes to end its hedge before the agreed-upon date, it may be costly or impossible to reach agreement with the trading partner.

Based on these considerations, your organization may be more or less inclined to use forward versus future contracts.

GUIDELINES FOR DERIVATIVES USE: A CHECKLIST

The following are some of the considerations to be addressed to guide the use of derivatives:[2]

1. Determine at the highest level of policy and decision making the scope of its involvement in derivatives activities and policies to be applied.
2. Value derivatives at market, at least for risk management purposes.
3. Quantify its market risk under adverse market conditions against limits, perform stress simulations, and forecast cash investing and funding needs.
4. Assess the credit risk arising from derivatives activities based on frequent measures of current and potential exposure against credit limits.
5. Reduce credit risk by broadening the use of multiproduct master agreements with closeout netting provisions, and by working with other participants to ensure legal enforceability of derivatives transactions within and across jurisdictions.
6. Establish market and credit risk management functions with clear authority, independent of the dealing function.

7.   Voluntarily adopt accounting and disclosure practices for international harmonization and greater transparency, pending the arrival of international standards.

8.   Have clearly defined policies dealing with interest rate risk and foreign exchange risk, including:

   ○   Clear policy objectives

   ○   Board approval of the policy

   ○   Specified reporting requirements, such as nature and frequency of reports to the board

   ○   Defined exposure definitions

   ○   Limits to exposure

   ○   Specified authority for who may make trades, including annual letters to the banks identifying these individuals

   ○   Segregation of duties, so that traders do not handle the accounting or funds transfers

   ○   Credit limits on counterparties (those with whom the derivatives contracts are made)

9.   Before entering into derivatives usage, the organization should have an organization risk management plan meeting three criteria:

   a.   Does it demonstrate to top management that the use of derivatives can produce a reduction in the variability (volatility) of the organization's financial results (as evidenced through the Statement of Activity, Statement of Cash Flows, and/or Statement of Financial Position)?

   b.   Does it include quantitative measures of both the forecast profitability (financial advantage of using the derivative) and risk associated (what is the possible loss to the organization of using the derivative, if any) with derivatives-enhanced activities?

   c.   Are the actual results of derivatives activities identifiable and verifiable by accounting (and internal auditors, if the organization has them) independently of input from the trader? Systems or guidelines should be in place to prevent the trader from making his position look better than it really is.

Regarding the second and third criteria, an example would be a "synthetic refunding" in which a nonprofit which is unable to refinance debt instead uses a "forward swap" along with a new issue of floating-rate "current-period refunding bonds" that in combination results in a fixed-rate refunding at current lower interest rates.[3]

A few final comments will provide some added guidance. First, not only should the direct user ("trader") of the derivatives be knowledgeable and competent, but your board and senior management should have some background in derivatives. Including in-house accounting, audit, and legal personnel in your organization's derivatives training is essential. Additionally, make sure that the most suitable instrument is used. Many times there are multiple instruments for a particular situation: forward and futures contracts, options, and another derivative known as swaps may be eligible. The swap (exchange of cash flows linked to the movement of interest rates, for example; see Exhibit 14A.1 below) has counterparty risk (risk of non-performance, perhaps due to financial difficulties, of the opposite party) that is nonexistent with futures or options. These types of considerations

Terms:
Fixed rate payer: Alfa Organization
Fixed rate: 5 percent, semiannual
Floating rate payer: Strong Financial Corp
Floating rate: 3-month USD Libor
Notional amount: US$ 100 million
Maturity: 5 years

A fixed-for-floating interest rate swap is often referred to as a "plain vanilla" swap because it is the most commonly encountered structure

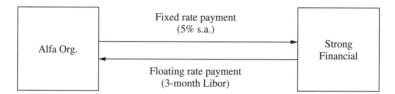

• Alfa Org. agrees to pay 5.0% of $100 million on a semiannual basis to Strong Financial for the next five years
  – That is, Alfa will pay 2.5% of $100 million, or $2.5 million, twice a year
• Strong Financial agrees to pay 3-month Libor (as a percent of the notional amount) on a quarterly basis to Alfa Org. for the next five years
  – That is, Strong will pay the 3-month Libor rate, divided by four and multiplied by the notional amount, four times per year
    • Example: If 3-month Libor is 2.4% on a reset date, Strong will be obligated to pay 2.4%/4 = 0.6% of the notional amount, or $600,000.
  – Typically, the first floating rate payment is determined on the trade date
• In practice, the above fractions used to determine payment obligations could differ according to the actual number of days in a period
  – Example: If there are 91 days in the relevant quarter and market convention is to used a 360-day year, the floating rate payment obligation in the above example will be (91/360) × 2.4% × $100,000,000 = $606,666.67.

Adapted and used by permission. Copyright ® 2004 International Swaps and Derivatives Association, Inc.
EXHIBIT 14A.1   INTEREST RATE SWAP EXAMPLE

are important in determining suitability. Finally, get more than one opinion. If one bank tells you their approach is foolproof, check with another bank. Shopping around for a better deal is sometimes also prudent, all other things equal.

Bear in mind that few people understand how these derivatives operate, and many of the models upon which the expected performance of these derivatives were based failed in practice to anticipate real-world market performance. Caution is advisable in the use of any derivative, and your organization will likely limit its use to hedging known risks.

One survey of practices found that 8% of New Jersey's nonprofit healthcare providers used interest rate derivatives—primarily interest rate swaps and caps—to limit their interest rate volatility and interest rate expense. They were able to generate an additional 1–2% of their operating cash flows through use of these risk management instruments, indicating a prudent and successful use of derivatives.[4]

Notes

1.   Robert W. Kolb, *Financial Derivatives,* 2nd edition (Cambridge, MA: Blackwell Publishers, Inc., 1996), 2. We strongly recommend study of Kolb's book for those needing more information on derivatives.

2.   The first seven guidelines are quoted from The Group of Thirty (G30) Global Derivatives Study Group, *Derivatives: Practices and Principles* (1993). The eighth is from Greenwich Treasury Advisors, and found in Jeffrey Wallace, "Controlling Derivatives Activities," *TMA Journal,* September/October 1994. The final listing is from James Kurt Dew and Neil Murphy, "Managing the Use of Derivatives," *TMA Journal,* March/April 1997, 57.
3.   For the specifics of this and how the financial results may be documented at the beginning of the swap agreement, see Eric Jordahl and Kevin T. Pantan, "Synthetic Refunding: A Financial Tool for a Lower Interest-Rate Environment," *Healthcare Financial Management* (May 2003): 102–104.
4.   Louis J. Stewart and Vincent Owhoso, "Derivative Financial Instruments and Nonprofit Health Care Providers," *Journal of Health Care Finance* 31 (Winter 2004): 38–52.

CASE STUDY OF ASSOCIATION'S FOREIGN EXCHANGE RISK MANAGEMENT

GLOBAL EXCHANGE

FINANCE

The Ins and Outs of Operating in Euros

When the International Society for Pharmaceutical Engineering, Tampa, first entered the European market in the early 1990s, we made a concerted effort to appear international rather than American. One of the key features of this policy was to allow members to pay dues and other fees in their own currency. The result was bank accounts in eight currencies, a horrendously complicated billing system, and useless accounting software. The next stage was to accept membership dues only in the currency of the country where our European office is located and conference fees only in the currency of the host country. We were able to simplify the issue even further with the advent of the euro, which allowed us to deal with only one currency—even though we still do events in Switzerland and the United Kingdom (both of which still use their own currencies).

The pros and cons

Without question, going with the euro has its benefits. Most obvious, it looks European and is user-friendly for our European members. It also eliminates or reduces wire charges for Europeans, thereby making our dues less expensive for them. Finally, by operating in euros, we can pay for services without having to worry about the exchange rate on the day we pay the bills.

Operating in euros is not without challenges, however. European banks are expensive and not easy to deal with. We are currently enjoying the best success we have had because we have someone in our association management company in Europe reconciling our account almost daily. While it's a nice problem to have, we end up with a number of payments (dues, registration fees, publication payments, and so on) for which we have no idea who should receive credit, since Europeans wire payments into banks without a lot of backup information.

The conversion choice

One issue that the euro does not eliminate is how to figure currency gains and losses into dues setting and product and service pricing. One option is to set a value that changes regularly—anywhere from daily to weekly to annually—which allows you to reduce your losses from currency fluctuations. We take this route for publications, changing their value annually because they are all printed in and shipped from the United States. On the downside, when you choose this option, dues and prices are constantly increasing or decreasing for European members. (For us, it's been mainly an increase the past few years.)

The other option is to set values that change infrequently. We use this approach with our dues, adjusting them only when we increase our U.S. dues. Euros that we receive from members partially fund operations in Europe; this somewhat levels the effect of currency fluctuations—although we still end up with a sizeable balance of euros that need to be converted because we pay for some of the European membership services in dollars rather than euros. While adjusting U.S. and European dues simultaneously gives equal treatment to all members, the natural downside is that we have had to accept the fact that in terms of U.S. dollars, some of our members are paying below market rate.

Submitted by Susan Humphreys Klein, executive vice president and chief financial officer, International Society for Pharmaceutical Engineering, Tampa. E-mail: SKlein@ispe.org.

April 2002

CHAPTER 15

EVALUATING YOUR POLICIES AND PROGRESS

15.1 INTRODUCTION

We have presented a variety of information in this book to assist the nonprofit financial manager in being more effective in his or her position. Much of the information presented has been tangible: Steps, actions, knowledge—facts that a financial manager can apply to produce positive results in an organization.

Some might say that the annual balance sheet, statement of activities, or statement of cash flows is the "final exam" for the effectiveness of the financial manager. While any of these or annual shareholder returns may be valid and appropriate measurement instruments in a for-profit organization, none is the end-all in a nonprofit organization. As we have emphasized throughout, liquidity target management and cash flow management are the primary *financial* metrics. You would not want to assess the overall *program* effectiveness or efficiency with these *financial* metrics. Program evaluation, while a critically important task, is beyond the scope of this book[1].

The overarching measure of success for a nonprofit organization is how well it is able to deliver on its mission. The reviews do not come primarily from the financial statements, but from a combination of elements, most important from the vantage point of the nonprofit's customers and constituents.

In the simplest terms, if your organization was able to deliver on its goals and objectives for the year—perhaps as guided by the strategic plan (Chapter 3) and/or your organization's balanced scorecard (also in Chapter 3) and end the year flush and achieving the liquidity target, a basic level of success has been achieved. The next step is to evaluate how the actions taken this year will affect your organization's ability to perform in subsequent years.

Throughout this book we have presented and examined:

- How to manage your day-to-day operations
- How to achieve short- and long-term financial objectives
- How to establish policies and procedures to streamline the organization
- The unique requirements of the nonprofit's funding sources
- How technology can be best applied in the organization
- How to effect and manage positive external relationships
- Ways to limit liabilities and protect and increase resources

To evaluate the effectiveness of the financial manager in a nonprofit organization, we need to evaluate two vastly different categories:

1. Tangible results

    ○ Target liquidity
    ○ Adequate funding
    ○ Expense control
    ○ Revenue balance
    ○ Fund balances
    ○ Interest income
    ○ Resources inventory
    ○ Assets and so on

2. Intangible results

    ○ Risk taking
    ○ Working environment
    ○ Flexibility/adaptability
    ○ Ethics/integrity

To evaluate the tangible results, an audit of the financial well-being of the organization can be performed by reviewing the financial reports (Chapter 6) and calculating appropriate ratios (Chapter 7). In this chapter, we present a checklist of financial health to supplement those indicators.

As the manager of the financial resources, you have taken every care in monitoring the day-to-day activities of your organization. The previous chapters of this book have provided information to assist you in doing your job effectively and measuring that success. How do you know if you have done a good job? How do you know if your organization is doing well? Here we present a method for evaluating the less tangible skills and characteristics that a financial manager brings to a nonprofit organization. Then we profile some guidelines for assessing policies in the critical areas of governance and accountability, fundraising, risk management, investments, human resource management,

15.2 EVALUATION

Effective, proficient financial management requires that you are in a constant state of review, remaining fluid in your procedures and priorities and making changes and corrections where needed. These questions may be used to begin evaluating your own performance as well as the performance of the organization.

- Were your decisions appropriate?
- Have you communicated effectively with others in the organization?
- Are the staff and volunteers performing optimally?
- Your organization may have met payroll and paid expenses, but what is the financial health of your organization in relation to accomplishing its mission and goals?

15.3 EVALUATING YOUR DECISIONS AND ETHICS

"Hindsight is 20/20" is a phrase we are all familiar with in evaluating anything that we have done in the past. Certainly there will be new information available that would have had a bearing on a decision you have made. Those considerations are not necessary in evaluating the effectiveness of your decisions. You cannot foresee all external shocks or dramatic changes, but you can factor in recurring changes in market activity and seasonal changes, and prepare for potential disasters.

Determining whether you made the *right* decision requires an understanding of what *right* is. Often, we confuse the term as meaning either "yes, the decision was correct" or "no, it was wrong," but there is a range of correctness and appropriateness in almost every decision (see Exhibit 15.1). A *risk* continuum might characterize your decision. For example, you could be wrong either because you did not take enough risk (left anchor) or took too much risk (right anchor). Or a *frequency* continuum may best fit your decision context. We see some organizations that do too few direct-mail appeals per year, others that do too many direct-mail appeals. "Degree of cost coverage" when setting dues, contract fees, prices, or premiums, serves as a third example of range or appropriateness. Illustrating, did your organization agree to a lower total cost amount for certain items in order to win a foundation grant?

Within the range of correctness, you can self-evaluate your decisions using these criteria:

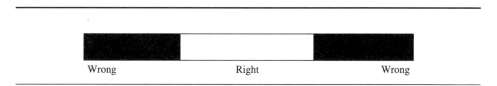

| Wrong | Right | Wrong |

Exhibit 15.1 Decision Correctness Scale

- Did the decision stand the test of time?
- Would you make the same decision today?
- What factors, if any, would you have weighted more heavily now than you did then?
- Would you have sought the advice of the same individuals?
- Were reference materials, literature, or any other information available that you did not review but would review now?
- Were there signals, clues, indicators, reports, or advice that you ignored or would have considered more heavily?

We provide additional guidance for your decision-making self-evaluation in Exhibit 15.2

Evaluating your ethics, and the influence of your ethics on the organization, is more difficult. Your conscience is a guide, but not always a trustworthy one—we all have blind spots, and are capable of being self-deceived. Consider these "everyday lies" identified by Erline Belton, the CEO of the Lyceum Group in Boston:

1. Exaggerating or underplaying the truth
2. Shading the truth—possibly to protect one's self, team, or teammate, or to support one's point
3. Beating around the bush or throwing up a smoke screen—usually a delay tactic, possibly by withholding an opinion or not telling a person where they really stand with you, or you don't say no directly even though that is what you mean
4. Pretending certainty or expertise—which sets your colleagues up for later surprises later when things don't pan out as expected
5. Not letting others know your true position—especially when there is controversy or ambiguity
6. Consciously withholding relevant information—typically as a power play, and as a form of manipulation of those who should get the information
7. Perceptions of powerlessness—when teams have strong leaders people may feel they do not have a legitimate voice, and may withhold valuable information
8. Perceptions of invulnerability—when successes come easily or consistently, carelessness and information distortion may also come
9. Misplaced loyalty or dysfunctional rescuing—especially when there are long-standing relationships
10. Failing to give due credit—and so engaging in self-promotion
11. Deluding yourself, or self-deception—probably the most common source of everyday lies[2]

The importance of ethics, especially integrity, in the finance function cannot be overemphasized; in fact, a 2004 *CFO* magazine survey disclosed that the number-one personal attribute business chief financial officers (CFOs) look for in hiring entry-level finance recruits is ethics—above communications skills, computer skills, interpersonal skills, or decision-making ability.

One instrument that you may use to self-evaluate your ethics is the "Moral Capabilities Inventory." The four key aspects that are scored are integrity, responsibility, compassion, and forgiveness. After self-scoring your ethics using this set of questions, you may consult with others who know you well to see if they agree with your self-appraisal.

The charts and questions that follow allow you to evaluate your decision-making abilities. Before beginning the evaluation, reflect over your decisions of the last several months. Determine which five decisions you plan to evaluate:

1. _____
2. _____
3. _____
4. _____
5. _____

For each of the questions below (A–E), consider each of the five decisions you just listed and determine which score most accurately applies in that specific case.

As you answer all the questions below, *do not* consider new information that was not available at the time you made the decision, unless it was information which you either neglected to consider or chose to ignore.

A.   Would you come to the same conclusion today and make the same decision?

Decision	Yes, without reservation Score = 5	Yes, but with minor modification Score = 4	Yes, but with reservation Score = 3	Probably not Score = 2	Definitely, no Score = 1	Score
1						
2						
3						
4						
5						
Total:						

B.   With each decision made, there are generally facts and information that conflict. At the time You evaluated those inconsistencies and ruled out specific information. Would you rule out the same information today?

Decision	Yes, without reservation Score = 5	Yes, but with minor modification Score = 4	Yes, but with reservation Score = 3	Probably not Score = 2	Definitely, no Score = 1	Score
1						
2						
3						
4						
5						
Total:						

C.   You sought the advice of others and considered their advice or opinion when making your decision. This information may have been gathered over time and not specifically at the time you made the decision. You either rejected this individual's advice or used their opinion as a major justification for the decision. Would you come to the same conclusions today?

Exhibit 15.2   Decision-Making Evaluation

Decision	Yes, without reservation Score = 5	Yes, but with minor modification Score = 4	Yes, but with reservation Score = 3	Probably not Score = 2	Definitely, no Score = 1	Score
1						
2						
3						
4						
5						
Total:						

D. You may have reviewed reports, evaluated literature, or done other types of research when you made your decision. Would you use that same information today as a justification for your decision or weight it as heavily?

Decision	Yes, without reservation Score = 5	Yes, but with minor modification Score = 4	Yes, but with reservation Score = 3	Probably not Score = 2	Definitely, no Score = 1	Score
1						
2						
3						
4						
5						
Total:						

E. Decisions often have long-term consequences for your organization. A decision that was appropriate in the short term may become detrimental in the long term. When making decisions, you need to consider both the short- and long-term impacts. Considering how this decision has impacted your organization in both the short and long term, would you make the same decision today?

Decision	Yes, without reservation Score = 5	Yes, but with minor modification Score = 4	Yes, but with reservation Score = 3	Probably not Score = 2	Definitely, no Score = 1	Score
1						
2						
3						
4						
5						
Total:						

Totaling your score:
Copy the scores from each of the above questions into the table below; then, total your score for each question and for each decision:

Decision	Question A	Question B	Question C	Question D	Question E	Total Score	Average (Total/5)
1							
2							
3							
4							
5							
Total:							

Exhibit 15.2 Decision-Making Evaluation (*Continued*)

Reviewing your scores:
For each question and for each decision, there is a maximum total score of 25 and a lowest possible score of 5.

- A score of 25 indicates that you have exceptional decision-making abilities.
- A score of 20–25 indicates that your decision-making skills are very good.
- A score of 15–20 indicates that your decision-making skills are fair but could use some improvement.
- A score of 10–15 indicates that your decision-making skills are in need of improvement.
- A score of 5–10 indicates that your decision-making skills were poor in this particular set of instances.

General indicators:

- If there is a significant difference between the totals in the score column for each decision, it may indicate that you are inconsistent in the effectiveness of your decision making. It may also indicate that you are sometimes forced to make decisions without having the time to appropriately consider or weigh the information to make an effective decision.
- For each of the questions, if there is a low or high score in a particular area, consider what was unique in that instance that caused you to make an inappropriate decision; conversely, in areas where you made a good decision, consider what was unique about that particular situation.

For the future:
When making decisions in the future, you can refer to the following checklist before making your final decision:

- ❏ I have weighed conflicting information, based on my experience and the integrity of the information in the past, and have chosen to ignore specific information for legitimate and appropriate reasons. Or, I have chosen to weight heavily specific pieces of information.
- ❏ I have considered the opinions of others and, based on my experience of the soundness of their advice, I am either ignoring their advice or factoring it highly in making this decision.
- ❏ I have reviewed all materials that may impact this decision. I have either chosen to follow the advice gleaned from these materials or, based on my experiences in the past, chosen to disregard this advice.
- ❏ I have considered both the short-term and long-term impacts of this decision after carefully weighing the risks and benefits.
- ❏ I have taken the time to carefully consider all the information available to me and am not making this decision in haste without properly evaluating the appropriateness or legitimacy of this decision.

EXHIBIT 15.2 DECISION-MAKING EVALUATION (*Continued*)

This inventory and the scoring grid interpretations are included in Appendix 15A. Two cautions as you use it:

1. It can easily be "gamed" by someone wanting to get a good score. Do not use it for evaluating others or for comparing scores among people.

2. Take seriously the aspect of getting a reality check from others, probably from those outside your organization, to see whether their perceptions mesh with the scored results.

For more on managing ethics and devising ethics policies, refer to Chapter 4.

15.4 EVALUATING YOUR COMMUNICATIONS

Communicating the problems, goals, status, and issues to your management team and staff is one of your main responsibilities. As discussed earlier, we make decisions based on the information available to us. The leaders in your organization base their decisions on the financial information you are providing to them. As one of the individuals responsible for financial management, you have special skills and abilities that allow you to understand the intricate details and nuances of the finances in your organization; others do not. One of your major responsibilities is communicating to others in a manner that matches their ability to understand the financial implications of their decisions (Exhibit 15.3).

If others in your organization are continually making decisions that have a detrimental financial impact to the organization, these questions should be considered:

- Are your recommendations being ignored? If so, why?
- Is there a thorough understanding of the information you are providing?
- Are your reports, memos, and correspondence easy to understand?
- When presenting your information at meetings or answering questions are you using lay terms or financial jargon?
- When you are presenting your opinion, are you thoroughly explaining your reasons or the facts that you considered when making that decision?
- Does your communication strategy or style need to improve?
- When you speak to individuals or groups, is their body language open and interested?
- Are you respectful and thoughtful in considering differing points of view?

It is helpful not only to diagnose your past communication style and effectiveness, but to also plan your future communication. When interacting and communicating in the future, you can refer to this checklist:

- ❐ I am sensitive to the unique needs of each individual, including their diversity.
- ❐ I consider the skill level of the individuals in this exchange and am speaking or writing in a manner that matches their ability to comprehend.
- ❐ I consider the ranking or position of each individual and provide the appropriate level of summary or detail.
- ❐ I present an image and a style that allow others to comfortably question my opinions.
- ❐ I demonstrate a willingness to be wrong, am open to suggestions and differing points of view, and am certain that my motives are appropriate and in the best interest of the organization and my constituents.

15.5 EVALUATING YOUR MENTORING AND SUPERVISORY SKILLS

As a leader in your organization, one of your responsibilities is to supervise staff, volunteers, functions, areas, or tasks. One of the ways you can evaluate your own performance is to evaluate the successes of those reporting to you and the areas for which you have responsibility.

Before beginning the evaluation, reflect on your communications over the last several months. These will include meetings, correspondence or memos, e-mail, instant messenger, and impromptu and telephone conversations.

Choose five instances to evaluate that provide a general sampling of your communications over the last several months:

1. _____
2. _____
3. _____
4. _____
5. _____

An effective communication interchange requires that the individuals involved have a willingness to communicate effectively, openly, and honestly. There may be individuals who do not meet these criteria. At any particular time, there also may be other factors that make a meaningful exchange difficult (such as if the person you are speaking to is ill or under considerable personal or work stress at that time). Unless you were insensitive to an individual's specific problems or situation, do not factor these situations in your answers.

A.   Were you respectful and thoughtful in your communication?

Interchange	Yes, without reservation Score = 5	Yes, but with minor modification Score = 4	Yes, but with reservation Score = 3	Probably not Score = 2	Definitely, no Score = 1	Score
1						
2						
3						
4						
5						
Total:						

B.   How an individual ranks in your organization may determine the amount of detail or summary you provide. Often, upper management does not require communications with elaborate details, while staff performing clerical-type duties may require specific details. One of the major skills in communication is providing enough information, without miring an individual with unnecessary details. In each interaction, finding the balance between detail and summary is your main challenge. Did you provide the appropriate level of detail or summary in this exchange?

Interchange	Yes, without reservation Score = 5	Yes, but with minor modification Score = 4	Yes, but with reservation Score = 3	Probably not Score = 2	Definitely, no Score = 1	Score
1						
2						
3						
4						
5						
Total:						

Exhibit 15.3   Evaluating Your Communication Skills

C.   In order for others to accept and consider your opinions, you need to provide them with your reasoning or logic for coming to a specific conclusion. This requires that you provide information that illustrates how you came to a particular conclusion or assumption. In this exchange, did you provide information that allowed the individual to understand your opinion and point of view?

Interchange	Yes, without reservation Score = 5	Yes, but with minor modification Score = 4	Yes, but with reservation Score = 3	Probably not Score = 2	Definitely, no Score = 1	Score
1						
2						
3						
4						
5						
Total:						

D.   Your special skills and abilities in the financial arena allow you to understand terminology specific to the discipline. Others may not have this same level of understanding. In order to have an effective communication, you need to use the appropriate level of technical and lay terms to present your information. The use of technical terms and jargon with an individual who does not understand them would lead to an ineffective exchange. In this engagement, did you use the appropriate level of terminology?

Interchange	Yes, without reservation Score = 5	Yes, but with minor modification Score = 4	Yes, but with reservation Score = 3	Probably not Score = 2	Definitely, no Score = 1	Score
1						
2						
3						
4						
5						
Total:						

E.   Often, individuals are giving us cues as to whether they understand the information presented. There may be obvious cues, such as the individual stating that he or she doesn't understand. There may be less obvious cues, such as the same or similar question being asked repeatedly or closed body language. In this engagement, were you factoring in these cues as a measure of the effectiveness of your exchange and making adjustments in your presentation based on these cues?

Interchange	Yes, without reservation Score = 5	Yes, but with minor modification Score = 4	Yes, but with reservation Score = 3	Probably not Score = 2	Definitely, no Score = 1	Score
1						
2						
3						
4						
5						
Total:						

EXHIBIT 15.3   EVALUATING YOUR COMMUNICATION SKILLS (*Continued*)

Totaling your score:

Copy the scores from each of the above questions into the table below, then total your score for each question and for each interchange:

Interchange	Question A	Question B	Question C	Question D	Question E	Total Score	Average (= Total/5)
1							
2							
3							
4							
5							
Total:							

Reviewing your scores:

For each question and for each interchange, there is a maximum total score of 25 and a lowest possible score of 5.

- A score of 25 indicates that you have exceptional communication skills.

- A score of 20–25 indicates that your communication skills are very good.

- A score of 15–20 indicates that your communication skills are fair but could use some improvement.

- A score of 10–15 indicates that your communication skills or style is in need of improvement.

- A score of 5–10 indicates that your communication skills are poor or your style of communication is ineffective.

General indicators:

- If there is a significant difference between the totals in the score column for each interchange, it may indicate that you are inconsistent in your communications or your style is not always appropriate or effective. There may be other factors that caused this particular exchange to be effective or ineffective, such as information that was not available at the time of the interchange or political issues within your organization that prevent a meaningful exchange.

- For each of the questions, if there is a low or high score in a particular area, consider what was unique in that instance that made that particular exchange effective or ineffective.

EXHIBIT 15.3   EVALUATING YOUR COMMUNICATION SKILLS (*Continued*)

When evaluating the performance of other individuals, there are two main factors to consider and evaluate:

1. *Your skills*. This area includes your skills in effectively managing, supervising, and mentoring this individual.

2. *Their skills*. This area refers to the individual's capabilities, skills, willingness to perform and learn, and dedication to the jobs, personal growth, and integrity.

Managing staff and coordinating volunteers require a set of skills unique to these particular disciplines. Some may have exceptional skills in financial management and analysis but may lack the skills necessary to effectively supervise and motivate individuals who report to them. Individuals also may be performing well despite being ineffectively managed. Some people may also have exceptional expertise in a particular subject matter but are ineffective in sharing that information and training other staff and volunteers.

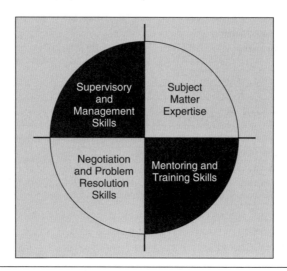

EXHIBIT 15.4   EFFECTIVE LEADERSHIP

Exhibit 15.4 highlights the skill set needed to be an effective leader, supervisor, or manager. These skills include:

- *Supervisory and management.* These are traditional skills that we often think are the only skills in managing and supervising others. These skills include the ability to monitor the activity of others, keep proper records of attendance and performance, write and conduct performance appraisals, counsel staff, and so forth. Clear instructions motivate.

- *Subject matter expertise.* A supervisor needs to have a level of competency regarding the tasks or functions that his or her staff members perform in order to accurately evaluate their performance. It is not necessary for a supervisor to possess the same or superior skills as all his or her staff, but he or she must have a general understanding, sufficient to comprehend and communicate effectively with them.

- *Negotiation and problem resolution.* Regardless of how efficiently an organization may function, there will be situations where competent staff and volunteers will have conflicting opinions, goals, or plans. A supervisor will be responsible for resolving these conflicts in a manner that leaves all parties feeling validated and needed.

- *Mentoring and training.* Above and beyond supervising an individual, a manager accepts responsibility for the personal growth of the individuals in his or her area. Whether the organization has formalized programs for career succession planning or training or not, it is the manager's responsibility to foster excellence in his or her staff and assist them with advancement, either within the same managerial area or within the organization.

15.6 TESTING YOUR SUPERVISORY AND MANAGERIAL SKILLS

If you do not have supervisory responsibility for staff or volunteers, skip this portion (Exhibit 15.5) of the evaluation. If you supervise fewer than five individuals, limit your evaluation to that number. You may also choose to list a staff member or volunteer who is no longer with the organization.

15.7 EVALUATING THE STRATEGIC NATURE OF YOUR ROLE

Proficient financial management requires the CFO and other top financial roles—including the board treasurer—to be strategic in focus. But how does one assess that? Craig Jeffery, Senior Vice-President and Practice Leader for Wachovia Treasury and Financial Consulting has developed a framework that provides an excellent guide.[3]

Given that "strategic" means something "highly important to the intended objective," a strategic financial manager is one whose objectives clearly support the organization's overarching objectives. The financial manager is not merely sought out "after the fact" to procure financing, set up a bank account, or conduct a financial transaction, but is consulted as key decisions are being formulated and made. Consider how well you meet these six criteria:

1. *Do you take a partner perspective?* "Think like a partner, not a vendor." Go beyond just meeting liquidity needs to relating with key operating personnel on an ongoing basis.

2. *Are you developing a successful track record?* If you are seen as relevant and effective in the areas over which you wield control or influence, your purview of the order-to-cash or grant/donation-to-cash cycle will cause others to tap your expertise. Your credibility is built on your previous successes and contributions.

3. *Do you use your whole mind?* Assist others in their decision making by helping them simplify complex problems. Synthesize facts, data, and analysis into action-able and sound recommendations. Helping others see the influence of multiple and complex factors on the organization as a whole is very valuable. Leverage your intellectual curiosity to gain a better understand of the "financial model" of the organization (specifically, how and why it derives the financial results it does), then translate to others. For example, Home Depot is dedicated to transforming its finance function away from a tasking organization and toward a thinking orga-nization. Your biggest impediment to doing this will be the time pressures arising from operating activities and an understaffed finance function.

4. *Are you stretching your skill set?* Gaining leadership and broader operational acumen will give you a better shot at gaining a seat at the table when big financial and nonfinancial decisions are being made.

5. *Are you making your partners successful?* Do you engage in teamwork with other top-level decision makers in your organization. You must make no excuse for a failure to communicate with others at your level before you or they bring resource allocation proposals to the ED/CEO (executive director/chief executive officer) or the board.

6. *Are you relevant, translating or devising metrics where possible?* Your insights must be placed at a level at which others can understand, and appropriate metrics need to be in place. For example, Dell has a "golden triangle" of liquidity,

Select five staff members or volunteers you supervise.

1. _____
2. _____
3. _____
4. _____
5. _____

There may be situations, hopefully rare, when you will be responsible for supervising an individual who may be suffering from severe psychological problems or have an alcohol- or substance-abuse problem, causing a significant impact on his or her ability to function. These individuals may pose a physical threat to the staff and volunteers in your organization. The unique set of skills required to handle this are not typically thought of as a management requirement. Outside experts may need to be called upon (psychologist or psychiatrist, police officer, crisis specialist) to either handle the situation directly or give you guidance in handling the situation. If you are experiencing a situation with this severity, the following questions will not apply.

A.   Have you maintained proper records of your staff or volunteers' attendance, performance, and job descriptions?

Staff or Volunteer	Yes, without reservation Score = 5	Yes, but with minor modification Score = 4	Yes, but with reservation Score = 3	Probably not Score = 2	Definitely, no Score = 1	Score
1						
2						
3						
4						
5						
Total:						

B.   Do you possess sufficient knowledge or familiarity with the responsibilities of a staff member or volunteer to determine accurately if he or she is performing the job optimally?

Staff or Volunteer	Yes, without reservation Score = 5	Yes, but with minor modification Score = 4	Yes, but with reservation Score = 3	Probably not Score = 2	Definitely, no Score = 1	Score
1						
2						
3						
4						
5						
Total:						

C.   When in meetings or conversations with more than one individual, are all individuals given equal participation in the exchange and are each individual's opinions, problems, and issues given equal consideration?

Exhibit 15.5   Testing Supervisory/Managerial Skills

Staff or Volunteer	Yes, without reservation Score = 5	Yes, but with minor modification Score = 4	Yes, but with reservation Score = 3	Probably not Score = 2	Definitely, no Score = 1	Score
1						
2						
3						
4						
5						
Total:						

D. Assuming that an individual possesses the skills necessary to assimilate new or more challenging responsibilities, has your training (either formal or informal) been effective?

Staff or Volunteer	Yes, without reservation Score = 5	Yes, but with minor modification Score = 4	Yes, but with reservation Score = 3	Probably not Score = 2	Definitely, no Score = 1	Score
1						
2						
3						
4						
5						
Total:						

E. At some point you may become ill, go on vacation, or leave your organization. Is there an individual or group of individuals who has/have sufficient understanding of your job to assume responsibility for it, if you were to be unable to perform your duties?

Staff or Volunteer	Yes, without reservation Score = 5	Yes, but with minor modification Score = 4	Yes, but with reservation Score = 3	Probably not Score = 2	Definitely, no Score = 1	Score
1						
2						
3						
4						
5						
Total:						

Totaling your score:
Copy the scores from each of the above questions into the table below, then total your score for each question and for each staff or volunteer:

Staff or Volunteer	Question A	Question B	Question C	Question D	Question E	Total Score	Average (Total/5)*
1							
2							
3							
4							
5							
Total:							

Exhibit 15.5 Testing Supervisory/Managerial Skills (*Continued*)

Average**

*If you are evaluating less than five staff members or volunteers, divide your total by the total number of staff members or volunteers listed.
**Calculate this row only if you used less than five staff members or volunteers for your evaluation.

Reviewing your scores:
In this summary section, it is possible that some of your totals will not correspond to the total scores listed in the scoring grid below, as you may have evaluated interchanges with fewer than five staff members or volunteers. You can still do the evaluations by using average scores: Base your evaluation on each question by viewing the *average* of that column's total (shown on the last row) to determine your results. For example, divide that column's total score by three if you had only three staff members or volunteers.

For each question (if you had five staff members or volunteers) there is a maximum *total* score of 25 and a lowest possible score of 5.

- A score of 25 (column average = 5) indicates that you have exceptional supervisory and managerial skills.

- A score of 20–25 (column average = 4) indicates that your supervisory and managerial skills are very good.

- A score of 15–20 (column average = 3) indicates that your supervisory and managerial skills are fair but could use some improvement.

- A score of 10–15 (column average = 2) indicates that your supervisory and managerial skills are in need of improvement.

- A score of 5–10 (column average = 1) indicates that your supervisory and managerial skills are poor.

General indicators:

- If there is a significant difference between the totals in the score column for each staff member or volunteer, it may indicate that you are inconsistent in your supervisory and managerial delivery. There may be other factors, such as inconsistencies in staff responsibilities, personal attitudes, political issues, or other unique situations that may cause this fluctuation.

- For each of the questions, if there is a low or high score in a particular area, consider what in that instance made that particular supervisory and managerial situation unique.

For the future:
When managing and supervising your staff and volunteers, you can refer to the following checklist:

☐ All the job cards or descriptions of my staff and volunteers are accurate and up to date.

☐ All my staff and volunteers have received a copy of their job descriptions and have received a performance appraisal, where applicable.

☐ When faced with a conflicting situation or plan, I have considered the opinions of all staff and volunteers when determining which situation or plan to approve.

☐ I have trained or am in the process of training an individual or group of individuals to perform my job in the event I am unable to perform it temporarily or if I decide to leave the organization.

☐ I have carefully documented issues, meetings, and conflicts, and have taken a proactive approach to assuring that the staff and volunteers under my responsibility are performing optimally. I have taken the necessary actions to remove staff or volunteers who are not performing effectively.

EXHIBIT 15.5   TESTING SUPERVISORY/MANAGERIAL SKILLS (*Continued*)

profitability, and growth. Your organization may have a "golden triangle" of liquidity (including cash flow), cost coverage, and accountability. Then translate this for your employees so they can see the importance of each metric and how their activities may have an impact on the metric.

Home Depot's translation of its sales objective is that sales would increase $1.2 billion if each customer added just one $1 item to his or her shopping cart.

The primary revenue sources your organization relies on should be known and understood by all employees. The same is true for the major cost elements. When important things change, communicate clearly the change and the strategic reasoning spurring the change. Finally, translate the views of outsiders so that insiders may understand. For example, guide your employees toward an understanding of the greater emphasis on accountability and outcome measures coming from granters, government contracts, and donors.

15.8 EVALUATING THE FINANCIAL HEALTH OF YOUR ORGANIZATION

The previous evaluations have measured the quality of your specific skills. In this section, you will assess the financial health of your organization to evaluate how effectively you are performing.

(a) **IMPORTANCE AND DEFINITION OF FINANCIAL HEALTH.**   Financial health is critical for mission achievement. Consider this finding from a 2005 Washington State nonprofit survey: In spite of the fact that fundraising either was stable or improved for most of the surveyed nonprofits, almost one in three organizations had to reduce services in order to meet financial challenges over the most recent two years. Two in five human services organizations had to cut services due to financial shortfalls.[4] We emphasize again the critical importance of targeting, achieving, and maintaining an appropriate level of liquidity (see Chapter 2). Growing organizations and those with an aging physical plant will need to allocate strategic reserves in addition to the six months of expenses they hold in operating reserves.

Defining "financial health" can be somewhat difficult. You may have sufficient resources to cover your payroll and pay your outstanding invoices, but:

- Have you used your resources wisely?
- Have you made purchasing or other financial decisions that may have negative short-term impacts but wise long-term implications?
- Has the debt service—loan/bond interest payments and principal repayments as well as lease payments—stressed your organization or limited its financial flexibility for the future?
- Has your conservatism in financial matters limited your organization's ability to accomplish its mission and goals?
- Did you take unnecessary risks that may have put your organization at risk?
- Did you fail to take limited risks that might have positioned your organization better for the future or made it better able to accomplish its mission and goals?
- Has your organization limited its administrative and programmatic abilities and achievements by underinvesting in organizational infrastructure (fundraising, accounting and finance function, information technology, human resources, buildings and equipment)?

- Has your organization been positioned for growth or replacement of major assets for the next five years? Ten years? Will the organization's target liquidity be intact at both of those points in time?

(b) CRITERIA FOR MEASURING YOUR FINANCIAL HEALTH.

- Your bank may determine that financial health means that you have money in the bank and have managed your cash flow between your checking and other short-term or long-term interest-bearing investment accounts.
- Your creditors may determine that you are financially healthy if you pay your invoices on time.
- Your contributors may determine you are financially healthy:

  o If you have the lowest possible overhead[5]

  o If you accomplished or achieved your mission and goals

  o If your expenditures were appropriate and legitimate

- Your board of directors may determine that you are financially healthy if you have positioned the organization well, balancing the needs of all your constituents, and assisted the organization in successfully meeting its mission and goals.

To determine whether your organization is financially healthy, you must consider all the factors just mentioned. The evaluation detailed in Exhibit 15.6 will assist you in evaluating your organization's financial health.

15.9 EVALUATING YOUR FINANCIAL POLICIES IN FIVE KEY AREAS

We have addressed financial policies in some detail in Chapter 5 and with greater specificity in the various chapters in which we discussed risk management, investments, cash management, and other vital topics. In this chapter on evaluation, we offer some checklists and references for guidance on evaluating your policies and practices in five critically important areas: governance and accountability, investments, fundraising, risk management, and human resources.

(a) GOVERNANCE AND ACCOUNTABILITY.   Although some nonprofits have adopted a head-in-the-sand perspective on the corporate sector Sarbanes-Oxley legislation and the future implications of expanded calls for better governance and accountability, proactive nonprofits are already adopting better internal controls, governance mechanisms, and accountability structures. Notably, bond rating agencies that rate nonprofit debt (Fitch Ratings, Standard & Poor's, and Moodys) are issuing statements and/or revising their credit ratings criteria for healthcare institutions. Fitch Ratings notes three aspects that it deems most relevant to nonprofits, which are items for your organization to consider regardless of whether yours is a healthcare organization or about to request a bond rating:

1. Appropriate relationships with outside auditors, particularly regarding rotation of audit teams and limits on nonaudit services

A.   Did you make any financial or purchasing decisions that had short-term benefits but long-term negative impacts to your organization?

Yes	Probably, yes	Maybe	Probably not	Definitely, no
Score = 1	Score = 2	Score = 3	Score = 4	Score = 5

B.   At any time in the evaluating period did you incur expenses (such as bank penalties or fines, short-term loan charges) that could have been avoided if expenditures and investments would have been more appropriately delayed or handled differently?

Yes, often	Yes, occasionally	Seldom	Almost never	Never
Score = 1	Score = 2	Score = 3	Score = 4	Score = 5

C.   Did you take unnecessary risks?

Yes, often	Yes, occasionally	Seldom	Almost never	Never
Score = 1	Score = 2	Score = 3	Score = 4	Score = 5

D.   Did you take appropriate and well-calculated risks?

Never	Almost never	Seldom	Yes, occasionally	Yes, often
Score = 1	Score = 2	Score = 3	Score = 4	Score = 5

E.   Is your overhead or percentage of expenditure on overhead versus programmatic expenses consistent with other similar organizations?

Below average	Slightly below average	Near or matching	Above average	Exceeding average
Score = 1	Score = 2	Score = 3	Score = 4	Score = 5

F.   At any point during the evaluation period did you restrict the use of resources that could have been used more appropriately to accomplish the organization's mission and goals?

Yes	Probably, yes	Maybe	Probably not	Definitely, no
Score = 1	Score = 2	Score = 3	Score = 4	Score = 5

G.   At any point during the evaluation period did your actions put the organization at unnecessary risk or were you unable to meet expenses?

Yes	Probably, yes	Maybe	Probably not	Definitely, no
Score = 1	Score = 2	Score = 3	Score = 4	Score = 5

H.   At any point during the evaluation period did you allow an inappropriate or illegitimate expenditure or transaction without taking necessary action to stop or rectify it?

Yes	Probably, yes	Maybe	Probably not	Definitely, no
Score = 1	Score = 2	Score = 3	Score = 4	Score = 5

I.   During your evaluation period, did you ever fail to pay your invoices on time or take advantage of net discounts and rebates?

Yes	Probably, yes	Maybe	Probably not	Definitely, no
Score = 1	Score = 2	Score = 3	Score = 4	Score = 5

EXHIBIT 15.6   FINANCIAL HEALTH EVALUATION

J.   At any time, did you suffer an increase in loan rates or other negative impacts due to a bad credit rating?

Yes	Probably, yes	Maybe	Probably not	Definitely, no
Score = 1	Score = 2	Score = 3	Score = 4	Score = 5

Transfer your Scores and total below:

A. _____
B. _____
C. _____
D. _____
E. _____
F. _____
G. _____
H. _____
I. _____
J. _____

Total: _____

Reviewing your Scores:

- A score of 45–50 indicates that your organization tests well and your organization could be considered financially healthy.

- A score of 35–45 indicates that your organization tests well and, while improvement may be needed in specific areas, is relatively healthy.

- A score of 25–35 indicates that your organization did not fare well in this test and there may be cause for concern or changes in managing your organization's financial resources.

- A score of 15–25 indicates that your organization's health may be at significant risk and major changes are indicated.

- A score of 5–15 indicates that your organization is not healthy, and serious changes and a re-examination of priorities need to occur immediately.

EXHIBIT 15.6   FINANCIAL HEALTH EVALUATION (*Continued*)

2.   Better internal processes, including audit committee charters and documentable financial expertise for audit committee members, certification of financial statements (CEO and CFO both sign off on for-profit statements now), code of ethics adoption, and bonus forfeiture when financial statements are restated

3.   Internal control adequacy assessment (including whistleblower and compliance procedures)[6]

Fitch Ratings intends to query board members regarding these issues when doing ratings evaluations to assess healthcare organization creditworthiness preparatory to issuing tax-exempt debt.[7]

(b) INVESTMENTS.   The six key questions to ask on an ongoing basis regarding your organization's investments are:

1.   (Assuming the organization has an endowment): Is the endowment spending policy being followed, and it is appropriate?

2. Are investment policy statement (IPS) prescriptions being followed? If overly inflexible or outdated, is the IPS being updated and revised, with ensuing board oversight and approval to be recorded in the board's minutes?

3. Is return sufficient relative to the risk being borne on investments?

4. Is "safety first" the guiding principle for all short-term investments?

5. Are appropriate performance measurement benchmarks for short-term cash reserves being tabulated and used for comparison purposes? The Association for Financial Professionals (www.afponline.org) makes two short-term benchmarks available to its members for monthly returns.

6. Are appropriate performance benchmarks being tabulated and used for comparison purposes for long-term investments (endowments, pooled investments, annuities, donated securities, pensions, trusts)?

Careful oversight of outside investment managers is also important. Few nonprofits have board members or staff with sufficient training, expertise, and time to manage properly investments portfolios. More nonprofits are shifting portfolio allocations toward socially responsible investing (SRI). If your organization is not doing so, reasons for not doing so should be known by all top managers and the board of directors. For more on SRI, consult www.socialinvest.org/. For SRI benchmark data, consult www.kld.com/. Trade associations are excellent sources of comparative investment return and risk data. If you serve in an educational institution, you will want to access the National Association of College and University Business Officers (NACUBO's) educational organization endowment benchmark data: Navigate to www.nacubo.org and then select the "Research" tab. You may also wish to contact Commonfund—which is itself a nonprofit organization that invests funds for nonprofits in the healthcare, educational, and foundation fields—for its annual "Commonfund Benchmarks Study" covering each of these organizational types.

For more training on endowment investing, consider attending the Commonfund's five-day "Endowment Institute. It is billed as "a rigorous and intensive educational program developed by Commonfund Institute and designed exclusively for trustees and investment officers who wish to enhance their contributions to the nonprofit institutions they serve." The annual conference of the AFP also has broad coverage of many financial topics and now includes a breakfast "nonprofit industry roundtable" at each annual conference (www.afponline.org).

(c) FUNDRAISING. In working with the fundraising function, be cautious to ensure the organization thinks through the effect of being opportunistic and reactive to new funding streams; otherwise the organization's ability to sustain itself may be jeopardized.[8]

Evaluating your fundraising figures is a three-part process, as noted by Mary Beth McIntyre, Vice President of Relationship Management, Target Analysis Group:

1. Drive relevance into your annual analysis by carefully determining at the outset how to segment (group) your donors; make sure to discuss your needs for usable information in detail with any outside source assisting you with your review of your fundraising file.

2. Derive and comprehend clear metrics and use them on an intrayear basis—as you get the quarterly measures in and study them, use them to reshape remaining-year strategies.

3. Use your benchmark data (Giving USA, Target Analysis Group National Index, Paradyz Matera Performance Watch, Campbell Rinker and Industry publication studies) to get a context for understanding, to gain perspective, and to prioritize goals and inform management.[9]

If you can locate a peer benchmarking group, tap into its expertise. An excellent online source for fundraising statistics, including some benchmark data, is the AFP's Research and Statistics site: www.afpnet.org/research_and_statistics/fundraising_research. For example, the site includes research from the Creative Direct Response Group (Crofton, MD) that indicates best practices for direct mail appeals include: (1) 8 to 12 appeals per year for minimizing the cost of funds raised, or more frequent mailings if you wish to maximize the amount of funds raised; (2) most nonadvocacy charities do better using premiums for at least some of their appeals, including a higher return on investment; (3) the best experiences in gaining deferred-giving donors is based on age and frequency of giving to your charity, with simple bequests being the most frequent form of deferred or planned gift.[10]

Finally, try to assist your ED/CEO in addressing his or her concerns with fundraising. These concerns were identified by a 2006 CompassPoint Nonprofit Services and Meyer Foundation survey of CEOs/EDs:

1. *Boards of directors.* The key area in which boards might improve was fundraising (70 percent of respondents listed this), particularly in improving their own efforts and then assisting the executive and the organization.

2. *Institutional funders.* Grantmakers are seen as making the ED/CEO's job more difficult. The biggest improvements that could be made would be more general operating support (restricted funding not as helpful) and more multiyear grants.[11]

3. *Desire to gain more knowledge and skill in fundraising and financial management.* Many EDs/CEOs perceive in themselves a lack of understanding of fundraising or financial management and would like to gain a great understanding in these areas. As financial educator, you have a wonderful opportunity to help fill at least one of these knowledge gaps.

(d) RISK MANAGEMENT. A key issue in risk management is the use of internal versus external performance measures.[12] Benchmarking enables you to make internal comparisons and to match your performance up to similar organizations. If you use a new risk management product, you may then compare your performance to the internal baseline you have in your database. Internal data also serve as a basis for comparison when you do new training programs. External benchmarks match your organization to peers, so you can see how you are doing on a relative basis. You should maintain data on how frequent and how severe (costly) your claims are, as a starting point. Higher frequency rates usually point to the need for more emphasis on loss prevention, such as identifying location of incidence and the need for protective equipment or safety training. Claims analysis includes a look at the relative amount of medical expense, legal expense, and claim payout duration. The next step is to identify key cost drivers. Benchmark data then help to see what cost drivers lay behind your severity rates.

(e) HUMAN RESOURCES. A major concern in the area of human resources is executive burnout and turnover. With CompassPoint survey data from almost 2,000 executives indicating that as many as 70 percent of EDs/CEOs are planning on leaving their present positions within five years (but most of them staying in the nonprofit sector), succession planning is a vital concern. Furthermore, salary compensation and employee benefits are huge concerns. Salary data is readily available (navigate to www.idealist.org/career/salarysurvey.html), and there is a growing database of benefits data as well.

The buzzword in the for-profit sector today is "human capital metrics." Companies are trying to link people measures to key performance indicators (KPIs), in the spirit of the balanced scorecard approach to performance management (see Chapter 3). Achieving this linkage requires a close working arrangement between human resources (HR) and finance, which should be easier for the typical nonprofit organization since HR is often housed in the finance area. Companies are attempting to focus more on top performers within their employees and also spend more of their HR time and budget on high-return-on-investment activities.[13] Incentives, hiring, and training practices in the organization can then be modified based on the numerical measures being tabulated. The Conference Board survey of 104 HR executives at midsize and large businesses indicates that 12 percent of companies now tie people measures to strategic targets or KPIs, but another 84 percent of these companies intend on increasing their use of people measures for these purposes.[14] As people-intensive as service-oriented nonprofits are, this application holds great promise for the future. Care must be exercised in overburdening an already stretched workforce, however. Working smarter, not harder, should be the intended target. Benchmarks may be set for human resource expense (HR department costs), total investment in human capital (total HR expenses plus non-HR staff salaries and benefits), HR expenses by function (e.g., compensation costs as a percentage of operating expenses), HR expenses by process/programming (e.g., operations and maintenance costs as a percentage of total HR), and miscellaneous HR costs (e.g., turnover costs per employee leaving, absenteeism cost as a percentage of average wage rate, health care cost per employee).[15]

15.10 EVALUATING QUALITY AND OUTCOMES

Quality is notoriously difficult to evaluate in service organizations. Yet you are probably aware of some educational and healthcare provides that are applying "Six Sigma" process evaluation to their organization's processes and services. Determining what root problems are "critical to quality" for an organization's outputs is the key part of those applications. The concern here is "how well a business process, product, or service is meeting the requirements of the marketplace,"[16] and Six Sigma refers to 3.4 defects per 1 million customer requirements. If quality is an issue for your organization, Six Sigma thinking is worthy of your consideration. The metrics should naturally follow your application efforts.

Getting the organization's radar on outcome measures and measuring effectiveness or mission achievement is more difficult. Paul Light, in his study of several hundred high-performing nonprofits, finds they share one thing in common—and it's an item of great relevance to the CFO: These nonprofits achieved their standing by "strengthening their organizational capacity to withstand the uncertainty ahead... [they] have become robust."[17] Light identifies four pillars of robust nonprofit groups: (1) alertness to what lies ahead (reflect on the "environmental scanning" we profiled in Chapter 3); (2) agility, which entails "recruiting, training, retaining, and (if necessary) redeploying a talented, flexible work force"; (3) adaptability; and (4) alignment of all the organization's operations toward the mission. The latter is dependent on strategic planning and "tough conversations about mission."[18] But we single out Light's insights on adaptability, which mesh most closely with our observations over several decades:

> ... high performers... manage to build reasonable reserve funds in spite of objections from donors and frequently challenge the assumptions that underpin their missions by asking themselves why they exist, whom they serve, and how they will know when they have succeeded.[19]

Will your organization swim against the tide of default practice in the nonprofit sector and insist on having a reasonable target liquidity level along with a long-range financial planning framework in place, tied to your organization's strategic plan? The mental model paradigm shift this entails is a sea change but worthy of all of your efforts to achieve it. It likely entails having to explain to donors and even board members why it is valuable to have a board-designated endowment with cash reserve set-asides for various purposes. Furthermore, as a primary internal consultant, you may continue to present in discussions and meetings the "why," "how," and "success metric" issues. You can be vigilant to ensure that metrics being used are actually helpful in steering your organization toward mission accomplishment. One danger to be aware of: An organization may fall into a "measures orientation" rather than being oriented toward activities that are most relevant and facilitating of mission achievement.[20] According to Susan Eagan, executive director of the Mandel Center for Nonprofit Organizations at Case Western Reserve University, an organization is effective "when it consistently achieves its mission, or perhaps put another way, when an organization makes increasing and measurable progress on the issues it was established to address."[21] Eagan notes that this requires a *culture of performance*, which you may assist in promoting by the reports you help to devise and require as part of the reporting cycle in your organization:

> A culture of performance includes continuous learning within the organization, ongoing evaluations of programs and projects, being mindful of what works and what doesn't, and a commitment to innovation—a willingness to try new services and products.[22]

15.11 USING EXTERNAL CONSULTANTS AND DATA SOURCES

A full discussion of whether and how to use external consultants is beyond our scope, but we note that outside of fundraising, audits, strategic planning, basic board training, and perhaps IT or ED/CEO search services, nonprofits make little use of consultants. One unscientific survey found the median expenditure on consultants and contractors to be $25,000 in 2004.[23] The good news is, you may be able to get foundation or government grants to pay for fundraising, planning, staff/board training/development, outcomes evaluation, graphic design/copywriting, or IT services.[24]

If you decide to do your own in-house "self-audit," you may wish to review these seven areas (some of which overlap with topics already covered), gaining feedback from your board of directors, staff, volunteers, major donors, and clients:

1. Relationship/connectedness
2. Mission/goals/feedback
3. Current project assessment
4. Effectiveness/efficiency/sustainability

5. Leadership

6. Volunteer management

7. Donor direction of gifts[25]

This list, from consultant Chuck Maclean, is one that you may wish to rotate through—do one or two each year, based on the time and resources you have to devote to the self-review.

As with other major purchases, talk with peer organizations about their experiences with consultants to see who might be available and what experiences they (or someone they know) have had with the potential consultant. While you may not be able to quantify benefits before the fact, quite often the insights gained from an objective outsider are indispensable. "Where no counsel is, the people fall: But in the multitude of counsellors there is safety," as the wise proverb has it.

15.12 CONCLUSION

None of these evaluations should be taken out of context or used as a justification or reason for making significant changes in your organization. It is important to use these evaluations as one of many tools for measuring your performance as well as that of your organization. There may be unique factors in these evaluations that cause your scores to be inaccurately high or low. Performing this evaluation quarterly or semiannually and averaging your results after a year or two may also provide a better picture of your performance. Performing this evaluation on an ongoing basis ensures that you are as effective as you can be for the organization you serve.

Regarding your organization, we started this book arguing for financial management proficiency. We end it pleading for organizational effectiveness. The role you can play in tying these two ideals together? You can be the strategic financial manager or treasurer, the internal business consultant and team player that your organization needs. We close with an aspiration and a promise from Proverbs in the Bible: "Do you see a man diligent and skillful in his business? He will stand before kings; he will not stand before obscure men."

Notes

1. For more on program evaluation, see Joseph S. Wholey, Harry P. Hatry, and Kathryn E. Newcomer, eds., *Handbook of Practical Program Evaluation,* 2nd ed. (San Francisco: Jossey-Bass, 2004); and a brief checklist of key elements at www.eval.org/EvaluationDocuments/progeval.html.

2. Erline Belton, "Truth or Consequences: The Organizational Importance of Honesty," *Non-profit Quarterly* 11 (Summer 2004). Available online at: http://www.nonprofitquarterly.org/section/524.html.

3. Craig A. Jeffery, "Six Essentials for the Strategic Treasurer," *Financial Executive* 20 (June 2004): 32–34.

4. The Collins Group, *2005 Washington State Nonprofit Resources Survey: Executive Summary.* Located online at: www.collinsgroup.com/pdfs/05-WA_nfpResourcesExecSum.pdf. Accessed: 4/1/06.

5. The interest on the part of donors or charity watchdog agencies in keeping overhead cost or fundraising cost ratios down is often dysfunctional: The Nonprofit Overhead Cost Project, conducted jointly by the Center on Philanthropy at Indiana University and the

Center on Nonprofits and Philanthropy at the Urban Institute, noted that "no organization in our study was an extravagant spender on fundraising or administration. Yet contrary to the popular idea that spending less in these areas is a virtue, our cases suggest that nonprofits that spend too little on infrastructure have more limited effectiveness than those that spend more reasonably." Mark A. Hager, Thomas Pollak, Kennard Wing, and Patrick M. Rooney, "Getting What We Paid For: Low Overhead Limits Nonprofit Effectiveness," *Nonprofit Overhead Cost Project: Brief No. 3* (August 2004) Available online at: http://nccsdataweb.urban.org/kbfiles/311/brief%203.pdf. Also, see Clara Miller, "The Looking-Glass World of Nonprofit Money: Managing in For-Profits' Shadow Universe," *Nonprofit Quarterly* 12 (Spring 2005):.

6. Andrew J. Demetriou, "Nonprofit Governance Reform: Rating Agencies Join the Fray," *Corporate Compliance & Regulatory Newsletter* 3 (January 2006). Available online at: http://www.abanet.org/health/esource/vol2no7/demetriou.html.

7. Id.

8. This is the view of Susan Eagan, executive director of the Mandel Center for Nonprofit Organizations at Case Western Reserve University (Cleveland, OH). See her insightful interview with The Foundation Center at http://fdncenter.org/cleveland/cl_interview_eagan3.html. Accessed: 3/30/2006.

9. "Benchmarking... Understanding How All Data Works Together," *NPT Instant Fundraising* e-mail newsletter, January 5, 2006, 1.

10. Association for Fundraising Professionals, "Best Practices in Direct Mail Fundraising," September 19, 2005. Available online at: www.afpnet.org. Accessed: 4/1/06.

11. Jeanne Bell, Richard Moyers, and Timothy Wolfred, "Daring to Lead 2006: A National Study of Nonprofit Executive Leadership," CompassPoint Nonprofit Services and the Meyer Foundation, 2006. Available online at:www.compasspoint.org/assets/194_daringtolead06final.pdf. Accessed: 4/1/06.

12. This section is based on Catherine D. Bennett, "Benchmarking for Improved Decision-Making Capabilities in Today's Public Sector," *PERI Benchmarking Series* (Fairfax, VA, Public Entity Risk Institute, July 2004). Available online at: http://www.riskinstitute.org/NR/rdonlyres/E8DE521B-E19B-4033-BC72-0837A0E9C645/0/BenchmarkSeriesBenchmarking forImproved.pdf.

13. Craig Schneider, "The New Human-Capital Metrics," *CFO* 22 (February 2006): 22–24, 26–27.

14. Id.

15. These are taken from a more complete listing included in Jack Phillips, *Investing in Your Company's Human Capital* (New York: AMACOM Books, 2003). Cited online at:www.workforce.com/. Accessed: 7/19/2005.

16. Dick Smith and Jerry Blakeslee, "The New Strategic Six Sigma," *TD* (September 2002): 45–52.

17. Paul C. Light, "What It Takes to Make Charities Effective," *Chronicle of Philanthropy* 17 (September 1, 2005): 45-46. Also see Paul C. Light, "The Spiral of Sustainable Excellence," *Nonprofit Quarterly* 11 (Winter 2004): 56–64..

18. Light, 2004.

19. Light, 2004.

20. This is the view of Susan Eagan.

21. Interview of Susan Eagan by The Foundation Center (Cleveland, OH), located online at http://fdncenter.org/cleveland/cl_interview_eagan.html. Accessed: 4/1/06.

22. Id.

23. Based on a convenience sample of 91 responses, published in "Survey Results-How Do Nonprofits Use Consultants and Contractors?" *Not-for-Profit eNews,* April 8, 2005. Received via e-mail on April 8, 2005. Accessed: 5/25/2005.

24. Id.

25. Charles B. Maclean, "To Self-Audit... Or Not?" (2002). Located online at: www.philanthropynow.com/pn/self_audit_or_not.htm. Accessed: 12/21/2005.

MORAL COMPETENCY INVENTORY (MCI)

- Please choose one rating in response to each statement by circling the number that corresponds to your rating.
- You will get the most value from this assessment if you respond honestly. It may be tempting to give yourself a high rating because the statement sounds positive, but please do your best to rate yourself accurately in terms of how you really behave.

1. I can clearly state the principles, values, and beliefs that guide my actions.

   1 = Never
   2 = Infrequently
   3 = Sometimes
   4 = In most situations
   5 = In all situations

2. I tell the truth unless there is an overriding moral reason to withhold it.

   1 = Never
   2 = Infrequently
   3 = Sometimes
   4 = In most situations
   5 = In all situations

3. I will generally confront someone if I see him or her doing something that isn't right.

   1 = Never
   2 = Infrequently
   3 = Sometimes
   4 = In most situations
   5 = In all situations

4. When I agree to do something, I always follow through.

   1 = Never
   2 = Infrequently
   3 = Sometimes

4 = In most situations
5 = In all situations

5. When I make a decision that turns out to be a mistake, I admit it.

1 = Never
2 = Infrequently
3 = Sometimes
4 = In most situations
5 = In all situations

6. I own up to my own mistakes and failures.

1 = Never
2 = Infrequently
3 = Sometimes
4 = In most situations
5 = In all situations

7. My colleagues would say that I go out of my way to help them.

1 = Never
2 = Infrequently
3 = Sometimes
4 = In most situations
5 = In all situations

8. My first response when I meet new people is to be genuinely interested in them.

1 = Never
2 = Infrequently
3 = Sometimes
4 = In most situations
5 = In all situations

9. I appreciate the positive aspects of my past mistakes, realizing that they were valuable lessons on my way to success.

1 = Never
2 = Infrequently
3 = Sometimes
4 = In most situations
5 = In all situations

10. I am able to "forgive and forget," even when someone has made a serious mistake.

1 = Never
2 = Infrequently
3 = Sometimes
4 = In most situations
5 = In all situations

11. When faced with an important decision, I consciously assess whether the decision I wish to make is aligned with my most deeply held principles, values, and beliefs.

    1 = Never
    2 = Infrequently
    3 = Sometimes
    4 = In most situations
    5 = In all situations

12. My friends know they can depend on me to be truthful to them.

    1 = Never
    2 = Infrequently
    3 = Sometimes
    4 = In most situations
    5 = In all situations

13. If I believe that my boss is doing something that isn't right, I will challenge him or her.

    1 = Never
    2 = Infrequently
    3 = Sometimes
    4 = In most situations
    5 = In all situations

14. My friends and co-workers know they can depend on me to keep my word.

    1 = Never
    2 = Infrequently
    3 = Sometimes
    4 = In most situations
    5 = In all situations

15. When I make a mistake, I take responsibility for correcting the situation.

    1 = Never
    2 = Infrequently
    3 = Sometimes
    4 = In most situations
    5 = In all situations

16. I am willing to accept the consequences of my mistakes.

    1 = Never
    2 = Infrequently
    3 = Sometimes
    4 = In most situations
    5 = In all situations

17. My leadership approach is to lead by serving others.

    1 = Never
    2 = Infrequently

3 = Sometimes
4 = In most situations
5 = In all situations

18. I truly care about the people I work with as people—not just as the "human capital" needed to produce results.

1 = Never
2 = Infrequently
3 = Sometimes
4 = In most situations
5 = In all situations

19. I resist the urge to dwell on my mistakes.

1 = Never
2 = Infrequently
3 = Sometimes
4 = In most situations
5 = In all situations

20. When I forgive someone, I find that it benefits me as much as it does them.

1 = Never
2 = Infrequently
3 = Sometimes
4 = In most situations
5 = In all situations

21. My friends would say that my behavior is very consistent with my beliefs and values.

1 = Never
2 = Infrequently
3 = Sometimes
4 = In most situations
5 = In all situations

22. My co-workers think of me as an honest person.

1 = Never
2 = Infrequently
3 = Sometimes
4 = In most situations
5 = In all situations

23. If I knew my company was engaging in unethical or illegal behavior, I would report it, even if it could have an adverse effect on my career.

1 = Never
2 = Infrequently
3 = Sometimes
4 = In most situations
5 = In all situations

24.   When a situation may prevent me from keeping a promise, I consult with those involved to renegotiate the agreement.

    1 = Never
    2 = Infrequently
    3 = Sometimes
    4 = In most situations
    5 = In all situations

25.   My co-workers would say that I take ownership of my decisions.

    1 = Never
    2 = Infrequently
    3 = Sometimes
    4 = In most situations
    5 = In all situations

26.   I use my mistakes as an opportunity to improve my performance.

    1 = Never
    2 = Infrequently
    3 = Sometimes
    4 = In most situations
    5 = In all situations

27.   I pay attention to the development needs of my co-workers.

    1 = Never
    2 = Infrequently
    3 = Sometimes
    4 = In most situations
    5 = In all situations

28.   My co-workers would say that I am a compassionate person.

    1 = Never
    2 = Infrequently
    3 = Sometimes
    4 = In most situations
    5 = In all situations

29.   My co-workers would say that I have a realistic attitude about my mistakes and failures.

    1 = Never
    2 = Infrequently
    3 = Sometimes
    4 = In most situations
    5 = In all situations

30.   I accept that other people will make mistakes.

    1 = Never
    2 = Infrequently
    3 = Sometimes

4 = In most situations
5 = In all situations

31. My co-workers would say that my behavior is very consistent with my beliefs and values.

1 = Never
2 = Infrequently
3 = Sometimes
4 = In most situations
5 = In all situations

32. I am able to deliver negative feedback in a respectful way.

1 = Never
2 = Infrequently
3 = Sometimes
4 = In most situations
5 = In all situations

33. My co-workers would say that I am the kind of person who stands up for my convictions.

1 = Never
2 = Infrequently
3 = Sometimes
4 = In most situations
5 = In all situations

34. When someone asks me to keep a confidence, I do so.

1 = Never
2 = Infrequently
3 = Sometimes
4 = In most situations
5 = In all situations

35. When things go wrong, I do not blame others or circumstances.

1 = Never
2 = Infrequently
3 = Sometimes
4 = In most situations
5 = In all situations

36. I discuss my mistakes with co-workers to encourage tolerance for risk.

1 = Never
2 = Infrequently
3 = Sometimes
4 = In most situations
5 = In all situations

37. I spend a significant amount of my time providing resources and removing obstacles for my co-workers.

> 1 = Never
> 2 = Infrequently
> 3 = Sometimes
> 4 = In most situations
> 5 = In all situations

38. Because I care about my co-workers, I actively support their efforts to accomplish important personal goals.

> 1 = Never
> 2 = Infrequently
> 3 = Sometimes
> 4 = In most situations
> 5 = In all situations

39. Even when I have made a serious mistake in my life, I am able to forgive myself and move ahead.

> 1 = Never
> 2 = Infrequently
> 3 = Sometimes
> 4 = In most situations
> 5 = In all situations

40. Even when people make mistakes, I continue to trust them.

> 1 = Never
> 2 = Infrequently
> 3 = Sometimes
> 4 = In most situations
> 5 = In all situations

SCORING THE MCI

If you are using the paper version of the MCI that appears in this book, you now need to use the following scoring sheet to produce your survey results:

1. Transfer your ratings for each item to the scoring sheet. Your item 1 rating should be placed next to the number "1" in column A. Your rating for item 2 should be placed next to "2" in column B, and so on. Continue until you have transferred your ratings for all 40 items.

2. Add each column and place the total in the box indicated.

3. Add columns A through J and place the total in the box indicated. Columns A through J are subscores for each of the 10 moral competencies discussed in Chapters 5–7 of the book *Moral Intelligence Enhancing Business Performance and Leadership Success* by Doug Lennick and Fred Kiel (Upper Saddle River, NJ: Wharton School Publishing, 2005).

4. Divide the total from columns A–J (step 3a) by 2 and place in the box indicated. This is your total MC (Moral Competency) score. The maximum MCI score is 100.

5. Using the Moral Competencies Worksheet below the scoring sheet, transfer your scores for each column—A through J—to the corresponding list of competencies that are listed after each corresponding letter.

MCI Scoring Sheet

Item	A	Item	B	Item	C	Item	D	Item	E	Item	F	Item	G	Item	H	Item	I	Item	J	3a. Add columns (A–J)
1		2		3		4		5		6		7		8		9		10		
11		12		13		14		15		16		17		18		19		20		
21		22		23		24		25		26		27		28		29		30		
31		32		33		34		35		36		37		38		39		40		
Add Col A →		Add Col B →		Add Col C →		Add Col D →		Add Col E →		Add Col F →		Add Col G →		Add Col H →		Add Col I →		Add Col J →		4a. Divide by 2 →

MCI Score

MORAL COMPETENCIES WORKSHEET

_____ A. Acting consistently with principles, values and, beliefs

_____ B. Telling the truth

_____ C. Standing up for what is right

_____ D. Keeping promises

_____ E. Taking responsibility for personal choices

_____ F. Admitting mistakes and failures

_____ G. Embracing responsibility for serving others

_____ H. Actively caring about others

_____ I. Ability to let go of one's own mistakes

_____ J. Ability to let go of others' mistakes

WHAT YOUR TOTAL MCI SCORE MEANS

Your total score is a measure of alignment. If your score is high, it is highly likely that you typically act in ways that are consistent with your beliefs and goals. If your score is low, it is likely that your typical behavior is out of synch with what you believe and what you want for yourself. The table below shows the distribution of MCI scores from very low to very high.

Total MCI Score (Alignment Score)

Score	Ranking
90–100	Very High
80–89	High
60–79	Moderate
40–59	Low
20–39	Very Low

INTERPRETING YOUR MCI SCORES

There are quite a few different ways to look at your MCI scores. No single interpretation is correct, and no test is the last word on your capabilities. We recommend that you reflect on each of these aspects of your MCI scores to see whether they trigger the self-awareness that is so crucial to ongoing moral development. We think you will find your results to be interesting and illuminating. If aspects of the MCI interpretation are confusing or don't make sense to you, we trust that in the final analysis, you know yourself better than any paper-and-pencil assessment. That said—here are some ways to interpret you scores.

- The maximum possible score is 100. A score of 100 would mean that you answered every item on the MCI with a "5" and would indicate that you believe you are completely competent in all 10 moral competencies assessed by the inventory. Because no human being is perfect, a perfect score on the MCI might mean that you have some difficulty acknowledging areas of weakness.

- The minimum score is 20. Most people have some degree of moral competency; therefore, low and very low scores may reflect excess self-criticism rather than genuine moral incompetence. In our experience, scores below 60 are extremely rare, most likely because corporate leaders do not succeed without some degree of moral competency.

- MCI scores fall most frequently in the moderate range (between 60 and 79).

- Your total MCI score is simply a snapshot of your overall moral competence. If you take the MCI every year or so, your total score can help you see whether your overall level of moral competence is increasing.

HIGHEST AND LOWEST COMPETENCY SCORES

- Most people who complete the MCI have one or two moral competency scores that stand out as higher or lower than the bulk of the scores. When you completed the MCI worksheet, you identified your highest and lowest scores in each competency area. Take a look at them now.

- Do your highest scores fit your understanding of your own strengths? If so, these are the competencies that you know how to use to maintain alignment and promote high performance. Are there any high scores that surprised you? If so, they may represent areas of strength that you had not been aware of and are competencies that can further help you to achieve your goals.

- Do your lowest scores fit your understanding of where your weaknesses lie? If so, you have an opportunity to develop your competencies if you decide that improvement in those competencies is important to you. Are there any low scores that surprised you? If so, they may represent blind spots that are keeping you from reaching your goals.

INDIVIDUAL ITEM SCORES

- Go back to the scoring sheet and look for very high and very low scores. If you have a few scores of "5," those items may be areas of particular strength that you should recognize, appreciate, and use. If you have a majority of "5s" you may be extremely morally competent across the board, but you also may have overrepresented your strengths. People with very high scores across the board may need to solicit feedback from others to confirm the accuracy of their scores.
- If you have some scores that are "2" or "1," what weaknesses do those items represent? Given that most people who take the MCI have very few item scores below "3," low item scores usually represent wonderful opportunities for removing obstacles to high performance.
- Take a look at the item scores for your highest and lowest competencies. Was your lowest competency score a result of midrange scores for each of the four related items, or was your competency score low because of one very low item score? If so, you might find that paying attention to that single aspect of the competency could greatly boost your competence in that area.

REALITY TESTING

How much do you trust your self-assessment of your moral competencies? Most of us have some degree of difficulty seeing ourselves as other see us. As a reality test, we recommend that you share your MCI scores with one or two trusted friends or colleagues. Here are some questions you can ask them:

- How well do my strengths as reported on the MCI reflect your perception of my strengths?
- How well do my weaknesses as reported on the MCI reflect your perception of my strengths?
- Are there other moral competencies that you see as my strengths?
- Are there other moral competencies that you see as weaknesses?
- On a scale of 1 to 10, how would you rate me on integrity?
- On a scale of 1 to 10, how would you rate me on responsibility?
- On a scale of 1 to 10, how would you rate me on how well I show compassion?
- On a scale of 1 to 10, how would you rate me on my capacity for forgiveness?

DO YOUR SCORES MATTER?

- All the competencies included in the MCI are important, and all act synergistically. But realistically, we are all human and need to concentrate on developing the competencies that will have the most impact on us and our organizations.

- You already have decided whether your scores accurately reflect your areas of moral strength and weakness. At a deeper level, how well do your scores represent competency areas that are important to you? After all, you can be good or bad at things that you don't care about. So, we encourage you to think about the extent to which the competencies identified are consistent with your moral compass and your goals that you explored in Chapter 3. Completing the Alignment Worksheet helps you to decide how much effort to put into developing specific emotional and moral competencies. In the first column, you see the list of competencies.

- In the second column, record your relative scores (e.g., was it your highest, lowest, or midrange score for each scale?).

- In the third column, rate each competency in terms of its importance to your personal guidance system. For example, is "admitting mistakes and failures" high, medium, or low in its importance to your principles, values, and beliefs?

- In the fourth column, rate each competency in terms of its importance to accomplishing your goals. For example, is "actively caring about others" high, medium, or low in its importance to your ability to accomplish your goals?

NOW WHAT?

By completing the alignment worksheet, you have prioritized competencies in terms of their importance to you. You have identified:

- Areas of strength and weakness that are important for alignment

- Areas of strength and weakness that are less important for alignment

- Competency areas that are neither strengths nor weaknesses that are important for alignment. Your scores for a competency may be midrange, but because it is a highly important competency for maintaining alignment with your guidance system or to accomplish your goals, it is worth your effort to enhance that competency to the fullest

Source: Appendixes B and C from *Moral Intelligence Enhancing Business Performance and Leadership Success* by Doug Lennick and Fred Kiel (Upper Saddle River, NJ: Wharton School Publishing, 2005). Used by permission.

INDEX

M